A Section 1983 Civil Rights Anthology

ANDERSON'S
Law School Publications

ADMINISTRATIVE LAW: CASES AND MATERIALS
by Daniel J. Gifford

APPELLATE ADVOCACY: PRINCIPLES AND PRACTICE
Cases and Materials
by Ursula Bentele and Eve Cary

CASES AND PROBLEMS IN CRIMINAL LAW
by Myron Moskovitz

COMMERCIAL TRANSACTIONS: PROBLEMS AND MATERIALS
Vol. 1: Secured Transactions Under the Uniform Commercial Code
Vol. 2: Sales Under the Uniform Commercial Code and the Convention on International Sale of Goods
Vol. 3: Negotiable Instruments Under the Uniform Commercial Code
by Louis F. Del Duca, Egon Guttman and Alphonse M. Squillante

A CONSTITUTIONAL LAW ANTHOLOGY
by Michael J. Glennon

CONTRACTS
Contemporary Cases, Comments, and Problems
by Michael L. Closen, Richard M. Perlmutter and Jeffrey D. Wittenberg

A CONTRACTS ANTHOLOGY
by Peter Linzer

A CRIMINAL LAW ANTHOLOGY
by Arnold H. Loewy

CRIMINAL LAW: CASES AND MATERIALS
by Arnold H. Loewy

EFFECTIVE INTERVIEWING
by Fred. E. Jandt

ENDING IT: DISPUTE RESOLUTION IN AMERICA
Descriptions, Examples, Cases and Questions
by Susan M. Leeson and Bryan M. Johnston

ENVIRONMENTAL LAW
Vol. 1: Environmental Decisionmaking and NEPA
Vol. 2: Water Pollution
Vol. 3: Air Pollution
Vol. 4: Hazardous Wastes
by Jackson B. Battle, Mark Squillace and Maxine Lipeles

FEDERAL INCOME TAXATION OF PARTNERSHIPS AND OTHER PASS-THRU ENTITIES
by Howard E. Abrams

FEDERAL RULES OF EVIDENCE
Rules, Legislative History, Commentary and Authority
by Glen Weissenberger

INTERNATIONAL HUMAN RIGHTS: LAW, POLICY AND PROCESS
Problems and Materials
by Frank Newman and David Weissbrodt

INTRODUCTION TO THE STUDY OF LAW: CASES AND MATERIALS
by John Makdisi

JUSTICE AND THE LEGAL SYSTEM
A Coursebook
by Anthony D'Amato and Arthur J. Jacobson

THE LAW OF DEFAMATION, PRIVACY, PUBLICITY AND "MORAL RIGHTS"
Cases and Materials on Protection of Personality Interests
by Sheldon W. Halpern

THE LAW OF MODERN PAYMENT SYSTEMS AND NOTES
by Fred H. Miller and Alvin C. Harrell

Continued

LEGAL RESEARCH, WRITING AND ADVOCACY, SECOND EDITION
by Welsey Gilmer, Jr.

PATIENTS, PSYCHIATRISTS AND LAWYERS
Law and the Mental Health System
by Raymond L. Spring, Roy B. Lacoursiere, M.D., and Glen Weissenberger

PROBLEMS AND SIMULATIONS IN EVIDENCE
by Thomas F. Guernsey

A PROPERTY ANTHOLOGY
by Richard H. Chused

THE REGULATION OF BANKING
Cases and Materials on Depository Institutions and Their Regulators
by Michael P. Malloy

A SECTION 1983 CIVIL RIGHTS ANTHOLOGY
by Sheldon H. Nahmod

SPORTS LAW: CASES AND MATERIALS
by Raymond L. Yasser, James R. McCurdy and C. Peter Goplerud

A TORTS ANTHOLOGY
by Lawrence C. Levine, Julie A. Davies and Edward J. Kionka

TRIAL PRACTICE
Text by Lawrence A. Dubin and Thomas F. Guernsey
Problems and Case Files with *Video* Presentation
by Edward R. Stein and Lawrence A. Dubin

A Section 1983 Civil Rights Anthology

Edited with Comments by

Sheldon H. Nahmod

Anderson Publishing Co.

A SECTION 1983 CIVIL RIGHTS ANTHOLOGY

Contents

Preface

42 U.S.C. sec. 1983 is probably the most important federal civil rights statute. Enacted in 1871 but dormant until 1961, section 1983 has emerged as a source of a great deal of federal (and state) litigation involving damages claims grounded on Fourteenth Amendment violations. The Supreme Court has paid it considerable attention as well: hardly a term of the Court goes by without a half-dozen or more section 1983-related decisions.

Section 1983 is controversial for many reasons. It implicates Fourteenth Amendment interpretation because of its close relationship with that amendment; it raises difficult federalism issues because section 1983 defendants are ordinarily state and local government officials and local governments themselves; it forces us to consider the proper balance between compensating for constitutional deprivations and overdeterring government officials in the performance of their duties; and it generates questions about the efficient use of federal and state judicial resources.

This Section 1983 Civil Rights Anthology, organized on the basis of section 1983's statutory language, collects important articles dealing with section 1983. It is intended as a supplement to the casebooks used in many civil rights, federal courts and constitutional torts courses. But it can also be used to supplement non-casebook materials developed personally by teachers of these courses.

This Anthology does not purport to set out the complicated doctrine of section 1983; users may consult my section 1983 treatise[1] and other treatises for this purpose. Rather, the articles I have included here are deeply theoretical articles that raise fundamental questions about section 1983 interpretation, policy and federalism. These questions will not go away, regardless of changes in doctrine and Supreme Court personnel.

For the most part I edited each article with a light hand, and preferred longer excerpts over shorter ones, so that the scope of an author's position is fully explicated. I deleted all footnotes (including case citations) so as not to interfere with the flow of argument.

I welcome your comments and suggestions.

Sheldon H. Nahmod
Distinguished Professor of Law
Chicago-Kent College of Law
Illinois Institute of Technology
565 W. Adams Street
Chicago, Illinois 60661
312-906-5000

---

[1] S. Nahmod, Civil Rights and Civil Liberties Litigation: The Law of Section *1983 (3d Ed. 1991).*

Every person who, under color of any statute, ordinance, regulation, custom or usage, of any State or Territory or the District of Columbia, subjects, or causes to be subjected, any citizen of the United States or other person within the jurisdiction thereof to the deprivation of any rights, privileges, or immunities secured by the Constitution and laws, shall be liable to the party injured in an action at law, suit in equity, or other proper proceeding for redress.

Part I

Interpreting Section 1983: Its History and Purposes

42 U.S.C. sec. 1983 was enacted in 1871 by the 42nd Congress pursuant to section 5 of the Fourteenth Amendment for the purpose of enforcing the provisions of that amendment. While its language is very broad, section 1983 was effectively dormant for ninety years because of the Supreme Court's narrow readings of the state action doctrine and the privileges or immunities clause. Another factor was the Court's reluctance to incorporate the provisions of the Bill of Rights.

All of this changed dramatically in 1961 when the Supreme Court decided the seminal case of *Monroe v. Pape*, 365 U.S. 167 (1961), prominent in the following four articles. Professor Shapo's article, written soon after *Monroe*, was apparently the first to use the term "constitutional tort." In it, he discusses extensively the legislative and judicial history of section 1983. He maintains that the proper standard of section 1983 liability should be "outrageous conduct" going beyond the garden variety tort action.

My article focuses on the application of *Monroe*'s "background of tort liability" dictum to the problem of interpreting section 1983. I discuss the relevance of tort concepts to that problem and suggest that they may be useful by analogy. However, I caution that "courts in 1983 cases must be careful not to let tort law alone determine 1983 liability; for not only possibly different purposes, but different interests as well are usually at stake."

Professor Zagran's article focuses on section 1983's "under color of" law language. Revisiting *Monroe*, he argues for a major change in the current interpretation of section 1983: in his view, the challenged conduct must have been authorized by state law or custom. He contends that this is the original understanding of "under color of" law.

Justice Blackmun, too, interprets the legislative and judicial history of section 1983, but from a very different perspective: his position as a justice of the Supreme Court of the United States. He asserts that the current Court has improperly cut back on the scope of section 1983. Justice Blackmun considers section 1983 to be both a "symbol" and a "working mechanism for all of us to protect the constitutional liberties we treasure."

Marshall S. Shapo, *Constitutional Tort:* Monroe v. Pape, *and the Frontiers Beyond,* 60 Northwestern University Law Review 277 (1965)

***

I

THE EVOLUTION OF A STATUTE: THE FIRST NINETY YEARS

A. *The Legislative History*

The statute which we are considering poses an instructive development from the standpoint of statutory "intent" and "meaning." Provocative questions present themselves as to this statute's intended breadth, the nature of the situation in which it was rooted, and the vision of its framers as to the uses it might serve. It is unquestionable, however, that this statute was born of an outrageous situation—and that within that context the contending legislative forces thought it a vehicle of considerable scope. Section 1983 in its present form, which is substantially unchanged from its passage in 1871, reads:

> Every person who, under color of any statute, ordinance, regulation, custom, or usage, of any State or Territory, subjects, or causes to be subjected, any citizen of the United States or other person within the jurisdiction thereof to the deprivation of any rights, privileges or immunities secured by the Constitution and laws, shall be liable to the party injured in an action at law, suit in equity, or other proper proceeding for redress.

What was generally considered the key provision of the bill of which this section was a part created criminal and civil penalties for conspiracies to do enumerated acts in violation of the federal constitutional rights of citizens.

The proposed statute was lengthily debated against the sanguinary background of Reconstruction in the wake of the postwar constitutional amendments. A controlling concern of the proponents was reflected in their repeated citation of stories concerning the depredations of the Ku Klux Klan. Congressman Cobb of North Carolina, for instance, spoke of the "social and political disability" imposed on Negroes and white Republicans by "violence and lawlessness." Congressman Coburn of Indiana emphasized that it was not "the commission of isolated outrages" that caused the concern, but rather "crimes perpetrated by concert and agreement, by men in large numbers acting with a common purpose for the injury of a certain class of citizens entertaining certain political principles." Senator Pool of North Carolina said the actions of the Klan impressed "the public mind with the conviction that the communities in which they occur are wanting in that moral tone and sentiment which distinguish well-regulated society from a condition of general demoralization and violence." In short, the legislators who proposed this bill were concerned about a widespread outbreak of violence, principally fostered by an organization of marauders.

It is important to note that in their eyes this situation was exacerbated by the relative inaction of state and local governments. A reading of the entire debates compels the conclusion that the statute was aimed at a situation which bordered on anarchy. Thus we find Representative Garfield of Ohio, the future President, noting that the problem was not unequal laws, "but that even where the laws are just and equal on their face, yet, by a systematic maladministration of them, or a neglect or refusal to enforce their provisions, a portion of the people are denied equal protection. . . ." Senator Pool noted that no member of the Klan "ever has feared any punishment for a crime committed in pursuance of the orders of the Klan." And Senator Osborn maintained that "The state courts, mainly under the influence of this [Klan] oath, are utterly powerless":

> What shall we do to maintain order and to punish the guilty in a community where a large proportion of the people are bound together by oaths and obligations, having pass-words, signs of recognition, and whose well-defined and clearly-proven object is to gain political control by intimidation and murder, solemnly obligated to clear the guilty or condemn the innocent,

> according as the one may be a brother in crime and the other a political opponent?

The debates thus lay bare the background of the bill: Outlaws whipping, robbing and murdering with the tacit complicity (if not the active conspiracy) of those responsible for the enforcement of local police regulations. The recurrent use of the word "outrages" throughout the debates bespeaks the fact that strong medicine was contemplated for what was thought to be a ravaging disease. The strength of that medicine may be inferred from the apparent belief of Congressman Dawes that the bill would fully incorporate the Bill of Rights—a thesis the modern implications of which will be touched upon later.

The plenitude of power which it was thought the bill bestowed is perhaps best deduced from the outcries of its opponents. By their complaints, they, in effect, conceded the breadth of the legislation. Several of these declarations are perhaps the most telling arguments favoring the broad kind of interpretation made in *Monroe*. Senator Thurman spoke to this point with his statement that the deprivation of constitutional right "may be of the slightest conceivable character, the damages . . . may be . . . merely nominal damages; and yet . . . this section . . . in effect may transfer the hearing of all such causes into the Federal courts." In more general language, Congressman Kerr of Indiana spoke of a "covert attempt to transfer a large portion of jurisdiction from the State tribunals, to which of right it belongs, to those of the United States." Congressman Hawley recognized explicitly the potential of the bill as a vehicle for suit against even judges and "ministerial officers." It should be noted, however, that Senator Trumbull of Illinois, one of the supporters of the legislation, declared that he did not

> suppose there is a single person on this floor who would be in favor of Congress passing a law punishing larceny, assault and battery, and all sorts of crime in the different States of the Union, and taking control of all the contracts made between individuals, because that would be destructive at once of the State governments.

The broad reach of the bill was confirmed by the view of a relatively disinterested observer, Carl Schurz of Missouri, who had investigated the situation in the South at President Johnson's behest just after the war ended, but who generally opposed the bill. His opposition was founded on what he called its "encroachment of the national authority upon the legislative sphere of local self-government." His objective remarks were premised on the idea that the disorders in the South were simply a natural historical phenomenon: "[O]ne of those second fermentations which almost uniformly follow great civil convulsions."

To summarize, the debates supply a certain amount of foundation for both broad and narrow constructions of the statute with reference to isolated violations of personal and property rights today. It is obvious from the words spoken on both sides that the framers contemplated a bill of great scope. They wished to expand federal jurisdiction significantly as to offenses which generally had been considered "local" ones. On the other hand, it is necessary to view this proposal for expansion against what seems an inextricable part of its background—the presence of vigilante committees in a large section of the nation, defying laws, perhaps even acting effectively as the law, and piling senseless brutality on lawless outrage. In stressing the reach of the legislation, therefore, it is well that we remember the anarchy and the outrageous crimes which compelled its passage—as well as the Act's roots in the racial problems which prompted the passage of the fourteenth amendment.

B. *The Judicial History to 1945*

The post-Reconstruction judicial history of the civil-damage section of the Ku Klux Act is relatively skimpy up to 1939. Unsurprisingly, there was no objection to using the section to redress violations of the voting rights of Negroes. As early as 1915, the Supreme Court affirmed judgments for Negro plaintiffs against Maryland election officials who denied them the right to vote pursuant to a state statute with a grandfather clause. The constitutional basis for the action under the forerunner of section 1983 was the fifteenth amendment.

Twelve years later, the Court reversed a dismissal of a damage action brought against election judges who followed a Texas statute in refusing to permit the Negro plaintiffs to vote in a Democratic primary. Mr. Justice Holmes, writing for a unanimous court, found it "unnecessary to consider the Fifteenth Amendment, because it seems to us hard to imagine a more direct and obvious infringement of the Fourteenth Amendment." He declared that the fourteenth amendment, "while it applies to all, was passed, as we know, with a special intent to protect the blacks from discrimination against them."

After another interval of a dozen years, the Court upheld the right of Negroes to sue for damages sustained because they were deprived of the right to vote under an Oklahoma statute. This legislation, purporting to reform a grandfather clause, gave them only a 12-day period in which to register. The constitutional basis this time was the fifteenth amendment. To the fact that the cases of primary significance in this pre-1939 period dealt with the voting rights of Negroes should be added the notation that all these cases were "color of laws" cases, *i.e.*, they each involved official action taken pursuant to an unconstitutional state statute.

The prevailing view of the reach of section 1983 developed significantly in the six years following 1939. On one front, the foundation was laid for the expansion into areas other than that of its previously predominant application to cases involving the political rights of Negroes. On another, judicial decision placed a gloss of far-reaching significance upon the interpretation of the "under color of" phrase in a similar criminal statute. These developments took place in mottled fashion, through a series of divided Supreme Court opinions.

First came *Hague v. CIO.* In this decision, which called forth five separate opinions, the Court affirmed an injunction restraining various Jersey City officials from interfering with the right of the plaintiffs to discuss the National Labor Relations Act. One element of the case was standard: The action of the officials was taken pursuant to local ordinances which prohibited public meetings unless a permit were issued by the director of public safety. The bill charged that the ordinances were unconstitutional or were being enforced in an unconstitutional way, and the decision focused on the validity of the ordinances. Justice Roberts, joined by Justice Black, wrote the principal opinion, declaring the ordinance void and thus enjoining enforcement of it. This opinion saw the right to discuss federal legislation as a national privilege or immunity, secured by the fourteenth amendment. Justices Stone and Reed concurred on grounds of due process, refusing to accept the privileges and immunities theory. Chief Justice Hughes concurred separately, accepting the ground that the right to discuss the legislation was a national "privilege," but agreeing with Justice Stone in his view that the record did not adequately support jurisdiction on that ground. However, despite the diverse approaches the Court had opened the way for a broad application of the statute in matters lying outside the racial discrimination area.

The gateway for the next significant development opened with a criminal case, *United States v. Classic.* An indictment was brought under the predecessors of the present sections 241 and 242 of Title 18, United States Code. These sections respectively make it a crime to conspire to deprive a person of his constitutional rights, and to "willfully" subject a person to the deprivation of those rights while the defendant is acting "under color of" law. It was alleged that the defendants had willfully altered and falsely counted ballots in a Louisiana primary. The Supreme Court reversed a dismissal, finding that the right to vote in primaries which involved a "necessary step" in the choice of candidates for elections was a right under article I, section 2 of the Constitution. Commenting on the "under color of" phrase of section 242, the Court's opinion lit the fuse under the premise, previously taken for granted, that the phrase required action taken pursuant to a state statute:

> Misuse of power, possessed by virtue of state law and made possible only because the wrongdoer is clothed with the authority of state law, is action taken 'under color of' state law.

The next link in this complex chain came with a case in which the Court refused to find that a plaintiff had stated a cause of action under the predecessor of section 1983, when he alleged that the defendants had not certified him as a Republican nominee for state representative, as he said they were required to do by state law. The Court rejected the plaintiff's fourteenth amendment contentions *seriatim.* It concluded that the right he sought pertained solely to state citizenship and therefore was not a national "privilege or immunity," that a right to state political office was not "a right . . . secured by the due process clause," and that as to equal protection, the law required a showing of "purposeful discrimination between persons or classes of persons." Significantly, however, the Court implicitly accepted the propositions that the statute applied to actions by state officials in *violation* of state law and embraced a wide range of fourteenth amendment rights not necessarily pertaining to the racial discrimination-voting rights. As to the former point, Mr. Justice Frankfurter raised in his concurrence the crucial contention that he could not "grasp the principle on which the State can here be said to deny the plaintiff the equal protection of the laws of the State when the foundation of his claim is that the Board had disobeyed the authentic command of the State."

The blockbuster in this series was *Screws v. United States*, decided in 1945. This case involved the conviction under the predecessor of section 242 of a Georgia sheriff for a frightful, fatal beating which he gave a young Negro after they arrived at the courthouse subsequent to an arrest. A four-man plurality voted to reverse for a new trial because the trial judge had not defined with sufficient precision the statutory word "willfully"—a word which does not appear in section 1983, the civil counterpart.

The pith of the plurality opinion went to the question of whether this beating with fists and a two-pound blackjack for a period of up to half an hour was administered "under color of" law. Mr. Justice Douglas said,

> They were officers of the law who made the arrest. By their own admissions they assaulted Hall in order to protect themselves and to keep their prisoner from escaping. It was their duty under Georgia law to make the arrest effective. Hence, their conduct comes within the statute.

From this somewhat loose reasoning he proceeded to the rather more precise formulation that this was not a case "where an officer not authorized to act nevertheless takes action," but that instead

> Here the state officers were authorized to make an arrest and to take such steps as were necessary to make the arrest effective. They acted without authority only in the sense that they used excessive force in making the arrest effective. *It is clear that under "color" of law means under "pretense" of law.* Thus acts of officers in the ambit of their personal pursuits are plainly excluded.

The basic foundation for *Monroe* was thus laid.

Justice Roberts, joined by Justices Frankfurter and Jackson, voted for outright reversal: "Instead of leaving this misdeed to vindication by Georgia law, the United States deflected Georgia's responsibility by instituting a federal prosecution." The dissent was founded, basically, on the distinction it took between an interpretation which insists that the offensive conduct be "under color of" specific state laws—and which in effect thus demands a more classic state action concept—and the majority's construction of the statute to mean "under pretense of" law. The basic thrust of Justice Roberts' opinion was toward the potential mischief which the majority view might cause in destroying the federal-state balance in the criminal law field.

In any event, *Screws* clearly joined the issue which had come to dominate this area of the law. By the narrowest of margins, it appeared to settle that in the criminal sphere, "under color of" meant "under pretense of." Further, it confirmed the evolving extension of the "under color" statutes to cases which involved issues different from the racial-political area to which the bulk of the litigation had been restricted since 1939. It was these developments which supplied the background for the pushing and hauling which marked the litigation in the lower federal courts for the next sixteen years, as plaintiffs' attorneys sought to extend the rationale of *Screws* to a variety of civil actions.

C. *From* Screws *to* Monroe

Monroe constituted a dramatic move by the highest tribunal to expand the *Screws* principle into the civil area, but the lower federal courts had rather fully presaged this result during the intervening period. We may conveniently categorize the cases of this era by discussing first those which have to do with police functions and other allegations of direct physical coercion and confinement, and then the cases which concern other kinds of complaints, including those economic in nature.

1. *Previews of* Monroe: *Police Brutality and Other Kinds of Official Action Directed Against the Person*

The first case of consequence after *Screws* was one of the most amazing decided from that day to this, for its gigantic embrace reached even beyond *Monroe*. In *Picking v. Pennsylvania R.R.*, an "inept," 154-paragraph complaint was brought against several defendants in connection with the arrest in Pennsylvania and extradition to New York of the plaintiff and her husband. The court's holding that a cause of action was stated as to Pennsylvania police officers might have been conceded to fall within the *Screws* rationale as extended to the civil side. But it then proceeded to pin potential liability on a Pennsylvania justice of the peace, the governor of the state, and perhaps even the Pennsylvania Railroad!

As to the justice of the peace, the court declared that Congress by passing the statute had sub judice "abrogated" the absolute privilege of judicial officers. In this connection, it explicitly cited *Screws*—although that case involved no judge as defendant—to emphasize that this civil statute should be construed "in pari materia" with the criminal statute used in that case. With respect to the governor, it once more rejected immunity arguments, saying among other things that "if a state statute purports to confer immunity upon an official of the state who has violated the Third Civil Rights Act by depriving an individual of a federal right, the state has invaded the liberties of the individual which are protected by the Fourteenth Amendment." As to the railroad, the court noted that it was alleged that the railroad had participated "materially and physically" in the alleged conspiracy. The court said it could not conclude that there was no cause of action because the railroad had not utilized the various procedural devices available to force the plaintiffs to clarify the case.

The court noted specifically that the complaint had alleged that the arrests were made in violation of the Uniform Criminal Extradition Law, which obtained in Pennsylvania. However, as to the argument that the "under color of" phrase of the civil statute should be restrictively interpreted, the court explicitly adopted Mr. Justice Douglas' rationale in *Screws* that the phrase included actions taken under "pretense" of law.

After this, several federal courts threw open their doors to allegations of police brutality, virtually all of them explicitly accepting the "color"-"pretense" equation of *Screws*, and most of them citing *Picking* as well. One early district court case granted an injunction restraining the further detention of the plaintiff without a warrant, as well as further questioning without his consent. Another much-noted decision by the same circuit which had decided *Picking* held that a claim was stated by a racially integrated group of plaintiffs who had been thrown out of an amusement park by the defendant chief of police. The court rejected the proffered defense that the chief's action had actually been in defiance of the New Jersey public accommodations law, quoting *Picking* to the effect that *Screws* had given "virile meaning" to the "under color" phrase.

Several other cases upheld complaints for damages in ordinary police brutality situations without racial overtones. A representative decision involved allegations that the plaintiff had been subjected to an arrest and search without a warrant, that he had been treated brutally, interrogated without being given the right to contact counsel or friends, and denied the right to go before a magistrate for 155 hours. It is hard to determine from this case and several others like it whether they focus on a single tortious element as the operative offense, or whether they treat the complaint as a unified gestalt.

In any event, it will be noted that so firmly had the transfer from *Screws* become accepted that in at least one case during this period, the court apparently took for granted the application of the civil damage statute to allegations of police brutality. In another decision, the court quotes a defendant's memorandum as accepting this application of the civil remedy.

Also worth mention at this point is a district court decision in a police brutality case which added a slight air of mystery to the proceedings. The court in this case refused to enjoin the use and compel the return of the property taken by state and city law enforcement agents in an allegedly illegal search and seizure. It did take jurisdiction under the jurisdictional statute for the predecessor of section 1983, but it denied the injunction because of the rule, since discarded, that the use of unlawfully seized property in state criminal trials does not violate the fourteenth amendment. However, it did say in a cryptic dictum that the "plaintiff's allegations might be held to state a claim for damages." The thrust of this dictum seemed to include within the scope of the civil damage action a police violation of constitutional rights involving no hint of physical coercion.

Two other cases involving *non*-police coercion exercised on the body of the plaintiff provide an illuminating comparison. In one, the Ninth Circuit held that a plaintiff had stated an actionable claim on his allegations that he had been confined in a state hospital for the mentally ill under an alleged conspiracy. The defendants against whom the claim was held to lie included two county health officers, alleged to have taken the plaintiff to the hospital in contravention of a court order. Another was a private doctor—linked with the health officers under the "under color of" phrasing because of the conspiracy allegation. The court's historical analysis of the statute included the declaration that until the *Classic* case its application had been limited to "class legislation or acts discriminatory toward negroes." But, determining the scope of the legislation from the later cases, it saw as the touchstone "purposeful discrimination" between persons or classes of persons.

The First Circuit expressed a contrary view on a young plaintiff's claim that his rights were violated by his transfer to a state farm from a school for the feeble-minded, where he was a voluntary inmate, on the ground that he was a defective delinquent. The discussion centered on the alleged liability of the superintendents of the state farm and of the reformatory to which the plaintiff later was transferred. The court spoke through Judge Magruder, whose careful opinions in this case and another set the tone during this period for the advocates of a stricter construction of the statute. The basis of his thinking was the historical context in which the statute was passed—"in the turbulent days of Reconstruction." It was against this background that he adduced as a rule of construction that statutes should be confined, "within reason, to those situations which might possibly have had the approval of the Congress if it had specifically adverted to the particular cases, bearing in mind the basic purposes which gave rise to the legislation in the first place." Applying this rule, he found that this was a situation "far removed from those which were no doubt predominantly in the minds of the members of Congress in 1871." The policy basis for the decision lay in Judge Magruder's conception of the federal balance; he foresaw an "appalling inflammation of delicate federal-state relationships" should an extended interpretation be accepted.

2. *Breaking New Ground: Herein, of Issues Involving the Pocketbook*

While several cases applied the *Screws* rational to cases involving physical deprivation—and while damage actions continued without impediment in voting discrimination cases—the decade and one-half after *Screws* saw several attempts, some successful, to extend the application of the statute to alleged injuries primarily economic in nature.

In one of the most remarkable cases, Judge Learned Hand opened to plaintiffs a greatly broadened avenue for relief. The plaintiff in *Burt v. City of New York* claimed that his applications for permits which would permit him to do his work as an architect were being denied because he had been singled out for oppression. Judge Hand's opinion reversed a dismissal, noting that the plaintiff had alleged the purposeful discrimination which a pre-*Screws* landmark case had stressed, and emphasizing that *Screws* itself had "laid to rest" doubts on the proposition that "the act of a state officer is the act of the state, if done under the pretended justification of a statute." He noted that "the difficulty of proving such cases . . . is great," but said that it appeared that public officers would have to defend any such actions "in which the plaintiff, however irresponsible, is willing to make the necessary allegations."

The next year, the Sixth Circuit granted a cause of action under the statute on allegations that the plaintiff's liquor license had been revoked intentionally and discriminatorily, for political reasons. Without any ruminations on the scope of the statute, the court held that an equal protection claim had been stated. Thus, even before 1950, some courts had built the Ku Klux statute into a weapon for damages to redress economic wrongs committed by officers acting arbitrarily.

A First Circuit decision in 1953, which involved a three-way split on a three-judge panel, supplied a classic illustration of the building tensions in this area. The court held that a claim was stated by a complaint of school teachers who contended that their contract rights had been violated by defendant city officials, who prevented appropriation of enough municipal funds to pay the plaintiffs' salaries in full. Judge Hartigan, writing the principal opinion, said simply that the court's jurisdiction was properly invoked by the plaintiffs' allegations of a conspiracy to deprive them of their constitutional contractual rights "by employing state law to abrogate" those rights. Judge Woodbury dissented, emphasizing that the complaint lacked "any well pleaded allegations of unworthy purpose on the part of the individual defendants."

Chief Judge Magruder, writing in a slightly more liberal vein than that which characterized his next opinion in this area, agreed that the dismissal below should be reversed. His analysis of the statute recognized its breadth, literally applied: it would create, a federal tort, upon proof that the defendants did in fact cause a deprivation of constitutional rights while acting under color of law. For this bald standard, he found a practical qualification—that the statute "merely expresses a prima facie liability, leaving the courts to work out, from case to case, the defenses by way of official privilege which might be appropriate to the particular case." He then formulated what he thought a "roughly accurate" test: that officers not having complete immunity "would have a qualified privilege, giving them a defense against civil liability, for harms caused by acts done by them in good faith in the performance of their official duty as they understood it." To prove their case, the plaintiffs must show that the defendants must have "realized that they were subjecting plaintiffs to harm by an unconstitutional impairment of the obligation of their contracts with the City."

Yet having concurred on the basis of this formulation, Judge Magruder spoke concernedly of fundamental issues of federalism. Noting that there was "ample procedure under state law by which plaintiffs' substantive rights . . . may be vindicated," he said that he could not "escape the feeling that this case does not belong in the federal courts."

A similar point of view pervaded a district court decision during the same period, rejecting a resourceful attorney's contention that his client had been deprived of his freedom of worship. The body of the plaintiff's brother had been taken from the hospital where he died, for medical school use. The plaintiff sued university and medical school officials, doctors and a funeral director, contending that they had prevented her from performing religious services and sacraments at her brother's deathbed. The district judge, dismissing, expressed his forebodings that to apply the statute to this kind of situation would open the federal courts to "all that vast array of controversies which characteristically have been raised in State and other tribunals," simply on the basis of allegations naming the fourteenth amendment or the contracts clause:

> It is unthinkable that any court, mindful of the Federal nature of our system, of the great wisdom displayed by local State tribunals, and

> of the risks of vesting in single District Judges in the Federal Court the vast Constitutional area now sought to be embraced within that jurisdiction, would for a moment accept the contentions of jurisdictional nature now urged upon this tribunal by this plaintiff.

Such cases raised in the fifties the great issues that lay behind the problem of the sixties. The statute in question was born of the Civil War, and of the powerful federal interest in protecting those in its wake who were helpless to protect their very lives. Now, the changing of times had produced new applicants for the protection of the old words. The criers of alarms said that in areas of the law which had been generally considered the province of the states, "constitutional rights" could not be bruited about in federal courts *in vacuo*; they must be enforced in the context of a delicately balanced federalism.

II

Monroe v. Pape

The fundamental issue of governmental structure lay at the root of the judicial quarrel which the plaintiff's story of terror in the night provoked in *Monroe v. Pape*. The essential allegations already have been discussed.

Mr. Justice Douglas' majority opinion in *Monroe* was focused on the unreasonable search and seizure allegation, which he immediately characterized as stating a fourteenth amendment claim under the statute. Justice Douglas then proceeded to the crucial question of whether the phrase "under color of" included the brutal actions alleged. As to the contention that the phrase referred only to action taken pursuant to state law, he relied on *Classic* and more particularly on *Screws*—in both of which that argument was discussed and the statute construed to include actions taken contrary to law. He noticed the use of the phrase in the civil rights legislation of the fifties and sixties, saying that in none of the hearings had the previous construction of the phrase been challenged. Analyzing the legislative history, he stressed that although the statute had been directed to the South at the time, its language was general and was "as applicable to Illinois as it is to the States whose names were mentioned over and over again in the debates."

Then, in a sentence of great breadth, Justice Douglas interpreted the statute as affording

> a federal right in federal courts because, by reason of prejudice, passion, neglect, intolerance or otherwise, state laws might not be enforced and the claims of citizens to the enjoyment of rights, privileges and immunities guaranteed by the Fourteenth Amendment might be denied by the state agencies.

He dealt specifically with the contention that the traditional remedy for this kind of act was found in state law. This, he said, is "no answer": "The federal remedy is supplementary to the state remedy." On the other hand, he found in the legislative history a clear intent to omit municipalities from liability under the statute, and thus dismissed the complaint as to the city.

This argument and Mr. Justice Harlan's concurring "doubt" that § 1983 was limited to state-authorized unconstitutional acts, drew a characteristically complete answer from Mr. Justice Frankfurter. He argued that "under color of" meant pursuant to state authority—an interpretation which merged into the general argument that the majority's holding altered an important division of authority within the federal system. *Classic* and *Screws* themselves, he declared, had made a "revolutionary turnabout" "without acknowledgment or indication of awareness" of the sharp turn the Court had taken.

The issue which he posed for reexamination was basic to the federal structure—"the relation of the Nation to the States in the critically important sphere of municipal law administration." His analysis of the facts in *Monroe* emphasized the difference between the misconduct of individual municipal police officers, subject to the effective oversight of state administrative and judicial authorities," and a situation in which the states allowed the existence of the lawless conditions fostered by the Klan. He raised the specter that the decision would put the federal courts in "the business of making 'general law.'" He noted that private litigants could not be expected to show restraint in selecting the federal remedy—the restraint of the Justice Department in criminal prosecutions having been urged in favor of the broadened interpretation adopted in *Screws*.

Probing what one cannot doubt is the major underlying motive for the majority's extension of the statutory language, Justice Frankfurter recognized that it was "obvious" that the misconduct of individual police officers demanded "more effective modes of redress." But he saw the solution as best coming from the legislature, because of "both the insistence of the needs and the delicacy of the issues." However, the issue had been settled by a solid majority, and the events of the next four years have broadened the battleground considerably and quickened the need for a new synthesis.

* * *

Constitutional Limitations and Constitutional Torts: A Search for Justice, A Need For Standards

The judicial history of section 1983 presents a dramatic picture of jurisprudence in flux. As a lesson in the development of statutory interpretation alone, it is worth study. Moreover, the explosive issues it has raised and the conceptual confusion it has caused in the last few years demand an attempt at synthesis and a proposal for solution.

As we have seen, the events which gave rise to the statute were the outrageous violations of physical integrity, set against a background of the virtual breakdown of law and order. It is difficult to judge any statute's "meaning" from the half-spoken premises and the conflicting interests which lie behind it. But it is reasonable to say that when the framers of this statute spoke of persons acting "under color of" law, they meant marauders who represented the only effective power in lawless countrysides. Viewed with this historical coloration, the meaning of the statute differs qualitatively from the monochromes presented on both sides in recent disputes about it—both the contention that the statute referred only to persons acting directly under state "authority," and the argument that it referred only to persons acting under "pretense" of law.

The pre-World War II judicial history of the statute revealed primarily a concern with Negro rights, chiefly those dealing with suffrage. This is easily referable to the statutory history, because the pre-1940 period presented a situation in which the effective power of the state—including the power of the dominant political party—was flagrantly violating rights which theoretically had been assured by the Union victory in the Civil War.

Developments of the last quarter century, however, have projected the statute into new areas. The bulk of the recent cases has dealt with the area of intentional torts by policemen and prison officials. No pervasive breakdown of legal systems characterizes the background for these cases, and the actions that give rise to them are not necessarily born of racial prejudice, although that may play a part in some of them. This group of decisions is joined with a small but spicy pot pourri of cases based on deprivations of rights usually economic in nature, but often involving other rights, such as those of the first amendment.

It is as if the courts had rung down a curtain on the historical "legislative intent" of the statute, and had determined to take the bare broad language for all it is worth. A curtain analogy is apt, for the development took place with striking suddenness. In a real sense, it began and took almost final shape in the *Screws* case, and the essential development took no longer than six years. The *Monroe* case was in that sense a rather simple analogical extension.

Behind this development and others like it lie what some critics see as serious structural weaknesses in judicial craftsmanship and in the synthesis of precedents. However, it does not seem a gross oversimplification to say that underlying is a judicial impatience in the search for individual justice, for *effective* remedies to salve individual injustices. It is thus, as the subject area becomes quickened with a principle—however ill-defined—that precedential distinctions fade, and the judiciary makes itself a veritable conscious instrument of historical development. This deeply felt sense of "justice" may be seen at work in the reapportionment cases; in the minute review of records in state criminal matters; and in the widening application of various provisions of the Bill of Rights through the fourteenth amendment.

It is the area last mentioned which coincides vitally with many of the questions raised by *Monroe* and its progeny. The crucial question is what interests, when violated, give rise to claims under section 1983. That question, in turn, stimulates the query: what does the statute mean when it refers to "rights, privileges and immunities secured by the Constitution." In discussing the scope of the statute in terms of rights, we may note two major problems at the outset. The first is "the double-shorthand problem." If it is argued that the fourteenth amendment works a kind of shorthand incorporation of the first eight amendments, this is only the first step; for, the apparent thrust of recent decisions is that this statute serves in turn as a shorthand for all rights protected by the fourteenth amendment. The second problem, already touched upon, grows out of the first. It arises from the fact that the first eight amendments historically have been adapted to protect criminal defendants and convicts against arbitrary governmental action. Even given the broad language of the statute, it seems questionable that a breach of this constitutional shield must in all cases call forth the response of this statutory sword.

We may turn now to an analysis of the clauses upon which the recent decisions rely. The keystone in practically all cases is the fourteenth amendment. It appears that most of the cases which invoke fourteenth amendment clauses *simpliciter* are those which concern economic rights and allied areas. Fourteenth amendment due process standing alone, as well as equal protection and in one case the privileges and immunities clause serve as foundations for plaintiffs' claims. The fourteenth amendment alone occasionally has been utilized with respect to an arrest without probable cause and there also has been a double-barreled use in police cases of a privacy concept drawn from the fourteenth alone as well as the fourth. The bulk of the issues arising from the application of the fourteenth alone, however, concern situations involving no use of violence and generally no physical deprivation.

The incorporation cases are more numerous, and are usually although not invariably in the police area. It may be said, generally speaking, that the post-*Monroe* decisions have included at least a suggestion of a claim under each separate clause of the Bill of Rights excluding, however, what might be classified as the clauses concerned with judicial mechanics, where the use of the immunity defense would be automatic. As to the first amendment, there are cases held to state claims on freedom of speech, freedom of press and right of assembly theories, as well as freedom of religion. The fourth amendment prohibition against unreasonable searches and seizures has been a popular vehicle for section 1983 claims, including those based on privacy theories. Even the sixth amendment guarantee of a speedy trial by an impartial jury is argued, sometimes successfully, in a variety of ways. Finally, there is authority that section 1983 is a double shorthand for the prohibition against cruel and unusual punishments.

It thus appears that what is developing is a kind of "constitutional tort." It is not quite a private tort, yet contains tort elements; it is not "constitutional law," but employs a constitutional test. Because of this interesting amalgam, serious questions arise about the measurement of the substantive right. It may well be argued that given the broad language of *Monroe* construing the already broad language of the statute, every policeman's tort and every denial of a license by a state or local board will give rise to an action under section 1983. The question may be turned around by asking whether it would violate the tenth amendment if Congress passed *Monroe* and its police-tort descendants as a statute. A cogent argument could be made that the punishment of police offenses clearly is reserved to the states. However, the recent interpretation of the statute evades that argument. By defining the fourteenth amendment to include various provisions of the first eight, the Supreme Court has made violations of these provisions a "deprivation of . . . rights . . . secured by the Constitution"! Even though it be conceded, for example, that fourteenth amendment due process *simpliciter* demands qualitatively more offensive conduct than fourteenth amendment "incorporation," the language of the statute pushes into the Bill of Rights, thereby invoking a more liberal standard. That this kind of standard is in fact being applied by the courts becomes obvious from the nature of the claims which succeed—and also of the defenses which proved successful. The only successful defenses, by and large, have not been directed to the quality of the act, but rather to the "pretense" of the defendant to authority—the "color of" law question—and to the nature of the defendant's work or his identity, as in various kinds of immunity cases.

The explosive potential of *Monroe* adds to a growing catalogue of issues concerning the role of the states in the federal system. The basic question in this case is whether absent specific legislation, the federal government should be projected into what basically is local tort law, under a statutory vehicle passed in response to torts which generated a widespread national concern. Not even the admission by the author of the dissent in *Monroe* that police violations of civil rights are widespread will wash away that issue. It is obvious that the statute as originally conceived is still usable in situations which rival for general lawlessness and outrageous conduct those which gave rise to its enactment. Recent events in Alabama and Mississippi make clear that the melancholy story of 1871 is repeated every day in 1965. But even here, the practical usefulness of the statute is limited because, as the ex-head of the Civil Rights Division of the Justice Department has said with reference to a proposal for more federal action on the criminal side, "The truth of this matter is that there is no acceptable Federal solution to this law enforcement problem." Yet the real problem arises when the courts extend the statute to situations not involving a virtual breakdown of law. These cases, dealing with factual situations ranging from gambling to inflammatory town meetings, underline the idea that the federal judiciary should tread warily in utilizing a civil damage remedy against local law enforcement officers, where much that is vital to the case grows uniquely from the local situation.

Just how explosive the expanded interpretation of the statute is may be seen from the fact that the yearly number of private actions under civil rights statutes increased by more than half in the two years after *Monroe*—and fourteen-fold in the eighteen years following *Screws*. The pressure will undoubtedly increase. Plaintiffs' attorneys will utilize not only the recent holdings, but will no doubt seek to extend the frontiers of the statute, as they look to recent dicta and reserved questions as well as to pre-*Monroe* rejections. Perhaps, for example, there is room under the new view of the statute for a section 1983 damage action for deprivation of counsel in certain situations, or for the destruction of a garage business by regulatory ordinances—or for many other complaints previously rejected.

The judicial development of a kind of federal quasi-common law of police torts, and perhaps economic torts as well, may not in itself be condemned out of hand. Nor may a legislative history followed by seventy years of acceptance of a narrow interpretation based in that history change the impact of a *fait accompli.* The shibboleths of the healthiest imaginable federalism and complaints about denigration of local responsibility by federal intrusion will not gloss a substantial number of instances in which local responsibility fails. Also unpersuasive is the argument that it is futile to use a civil damage action to achieve *in terrorem* a change in a situation calling for broad legislative reform—if indeed that will prove a solution. But these fears must count for something, when taken with the fundamental problem which underlies the whole phenomenon. That problem may be characterized as the development of a variety of federal common law without a correspondingly compelling federal interest. The structural weakness of this development is evident from the fact that it is based on the attempted transfer of rules historically designed or practically interpreted as serving defensive purposes to the formulation of a direct civil remedy. From these conceptual and political problems arises the need for an analytical standard to which concrete cases may be referred.

Two short-range escape hatches may be dismissed quickly. The first of these solutions would be to declare the range of the statute concomitant with the reach of local tort law. That is obviously unsatisfactory, for to raise every police tort and every denial of a license to the level of a federal "constitutional tort" seems out of keeping with any conception of a viable federal scheme. A second solution would call for incorporation into the statute of the present state of federal constitutional law relative to fourteenth amendment "incorporation." As suggested before, this seems an over-facile extension of defensive safeguards as standards for civil damage actions. Further, it raises acute definitional problems, aggravated by the flux which now seizes this area of the law.

The ideal judicial solution must be one with enough substance to supply a standard of flexibility to cover a broad range of interests. It should call upon decided case law—preferably case law which has wrestled directly with the problem. Ideally, the standard should bear an umbilical relation to the statute. These requirements are best met by the simple demand that *the defendant's conduct be outrageous.* Harking to the legislative history, this standard would call for a brutality or arbitrariness which goes beyond the garden variety state tort action. In many of the post-*Monroe* decisions under section 1983, this standard finds support in declaration that actionable conduct should be "reprehensible," or "callous and shocking," that "trivial" violations will not suffice, and even that in some cases "'bad' motive may . . . become critical." Although this test heavily blends questions of fact into questions of law, it should prove, in the long run, to be a most workable one.

The effects of this kind of standard should be substantial. As to the police area, the statute should operate only in cases involving extraordinarily offensive conduct—which surely was the case in *Monroe.* The issue, laden as it is with problems of federalism, seems to call for a new analogue to the "concept of ordered liberty." A recent case in the federal district court for Northern Illinois will illustrate that the outrageousness standard is administrable in concrete situations. In this case, the trial judge dismissed a complaint founded on the theory that the plaintiff's person had been searched unreasonably. This theory already had served the plaintiff as a shield, for it had been the basis of a reversal by the Illinois Supreme Court of his state conviction on a narcotics charge. However, the federal court emphasized that what is "unreasonable" for fourteenth-fourth amendment defensive purposes is not necessarily unreasonable for the purpose of a civil rights complaint.

In the cases which do not focus on physical coercion, the courts may apply a supplementary test, also closely related to the statutory history. This standard would require that the plaintiff's complaint allege facts showing that a theoretical system of local law had become so corrupt as to be virtually nonexistent. An illustration of the kind of case which this test might rationalize would be a complaint that although an application had met all requirements, a liquor license had been denied arbitrarily because a system of ward courtesy prevailed in the issuance of licenses. Arguably, to uphold this complaint allows the federal courts to act on matters which essentially involve local political questions. But this kind of standard, combined with an "outrageousness" test, should help to strike a true balance, for it will allow the federal courts to act only in situations in which local officials are operating in a legal vacuum. For example, a newspaper publisher's complaint that he is being denied school facilities for a banquet and access to an employment service would surely be eliminated on the pleadings.

Furthermore, the statute should also be given play to operate in cases involving first amendment rights, which traditionally have received zealous judicial protection. Such an interpretation would satisfy the original promulgation of the "concept of ordered liberty," as well as rationalize some post-*Monroe* per curiams by the Supreme Court.

In brief, the tests which we describe would preserve the pith of the statute, the thrust of *Monroe* and the dignity of a "constitutional tort" justifying the exercise of federal judicial power.

Sheldon H. Nahmod, *Section 1983 and the "Background" of Tort Liability,* 50 Indiana Law Journal 5 (1974)

A group of Chicago police officers assisted in the development of new constitutional doctrines one morning in 1958, when they allegedly entered the home of one James Monroe without warning and forced the occupants to stand naked in the living room while the entire house was ransacked. Mr. Monroe was arrested and later released without charges being preferred against him. He later brought suit against the officers and the City of Chicago under 42 U.S.C. § 1983 for the deprivation of "rights, privileges, or immunities secured by the Constitution . . . ." *Monroe v. Pape* eventually reached the Supreme Court, where eight justices held that the alleged misuse of authority could support a 1983 action against the police officers (though not against the City of Chicago) for denial of fourth amendment protection against unreasonable searches and seizures. Because the fourth amendment had earlier been held by the Court to be applicable to the states through the fourteenth amendment and since section 1983 was enacted pursuant to authority granted Congress by the fourteenth amendment, the Court reasoned that the alleged fourth amendment violation by defendants was actionable under section 1983. The Court also held that specific intent to deprive a person of a federal right was unnecessary to state a 1983 claim.

It is the Court's reason for its holding on this latter issue that primarily concerns us here. Justice Douglas, in a statement whose impact has been considerable, asserted: "Section 1979 [now 1983] should be read against the background of tort liability that makes a man responsible for the natural consequences of his actions." If tort concepts are applied to the alleged facts in *Monroe*, the defendants probably committed intentional torts such as assault, battery, false imprisonment, intentional infliction of mental distress, and invasion of privacy. Justice Douglas seemed to imply that the common law of intentional tort—*i.e.,* liability even absent specific intent to interfere with a common law interest so long as the result of the conduct is intended—should apply by analogy to section 1983.

In *Monroe*, defendants' alleged intentional conduct was such as to be a cause in fact of plaintiffs' confinement and search which, because conducted without probable cause, amounted to a deprivation of plaintiffs' fourteenth amendment rights. Inasmuch as the plaintiffs' fourteenth amendment interests and their common law interests such as freedom from confinement, from offensive bodily contact and the apprehension thereof, from mental distress, and from invasion of privacy seemed to coincide, *Monroe* was a relatively easy case in which to apply tort concepts.

However, one wonders how far to apply the "background of tort liability" in a 1983 context. Some federal courts interpret this dictum literally, thus making tort concepts determinative of 1983 liability. Yet it is, after all, a federal statute that is involved, one which refers in relevant part to constitutional rights, privileges, and immunities. This article will therefore explore the relevance of tort concepts in a 1983 context, including the issues of duty, proximate cause, negligence, strict liability, and defenses.

The Scope of Section 1983

In *Monroe*, Justice Douglas suggested three purposes of section 1983: to "override certain kinds of state laws," to provide "a remedy where state law [is] inadequate," and "to provide a federal remedy where the state remedy, though adequate in theory, [is] not available in practice." This approach, based on inadequacy of state law, was apparently expanded later in the opinion: "The federal remedy is supplementary to the state remedy, and the latter need not be first sought and refused before the federal one is invoked." As a result of such language, and because of the apparent breadth of the language of section 1983, there has been considerable dispute over its scope.

While such debate is thoughtful, reflecting as it does a legitimate concern with the federal-state relationship, for practical purposes it has been mooted. *Monroe* clearly adopted the supplementary remedy approach and did not use a balancing test in order to determine whether a constitutional right had been violated so as to be actionable under section 1983. Additionally, it has been pointed out that "[s]evere deprivations can result from civilized conduct" as well as from outrageous conduct. A sheriff's honest mistake resulting in erroneous continued imprisonment of an inmate, for example, and the failure of a court clerk to accept for filing a prisoner's petition for post-conviction relief, while "civilized," have nevertheless been held actionable under section 1983.

The broad scope of section 1983 is reflected in two lines of cases. The first involves sections of the Bill of Rights previously thought to serve only as a shield against governmental action. These cases reflect a double incorporation approach, in which certain sections of the Bill of Rights are made applicable to the states through the fourteenth amendment; violations of those sections are then made actionable by section 1983. The second line of cases involves deprivations of rights secured by the fourteenth amendment "directly," not through incorporation of a specific article of the Bill of Rights. Both indicate that it is constitutional interpretation which is involved in 1983 cases, and that section 1983's broad language is being taken at face value.

Inasmuch as constitutional or federal statutory issues are necessarily implicated by section 1983, that section should properly be interpreted as creating a cause of action for damages which is national in scope, uniform in application, and hence not dependent upon local tort law. When Justice Douglas spoke of the "background of tort liability," he may have been suggesting the development of a specialized federal common law of tort in 1983 cases. Because tort law and section 1983 might serve different purposes and protect different interests, this federal common law should be developed with a view to effectuating the purposes of section 1983.

Until recently one could confidently stand with Professor Seavey, who viewed the tort action essentially, though not exclusively, as a means "to compensate for harm." In contrast, commentators have lately argued that the dominant function of tort law, including negligence theory, "is to generate rules of liability that if followed will bring about, at least approximately, the efficient—the cost-justified—level of accidents and safety." There are, however, practical problems with such an approach, including the assumption of perfect foresight by the parties involved, and the necessity of an after the fact assessment of relative costs of accident and avoidance by the trier of fact. One therefore ought to be careful about broad generalizations respecting the functions of tort law. Perhaps the most that can be said for present purposes is that different functions may be served at the same time. While compensation should no longer be considered the essential function of tort law, perhaps it nevertheless remains an important one.

So far as appears from the legislative history, with its references to the reluctance of the South's legal systems to provide remedies for unpopular plaintiffs, compensation is similarly a function of section 1983. Compensation would appear to be an especially significant function of section 1983 when there is no adequate state remedy. The Supreme Court, however, emphasized in *Monroe* that even where the plaintiff has adequate recourse against a state official under state law, the 1983 remedy is still available, indicating that compensation is not currently thought to be the major function of section 1983. Rather, because constitutional interests are at stake, deterrence, as furthered by the private enforcement of fourteenth amendment guarantees, might be more important under section 1983 that it is under tort law. This is not to say either that compensation and deterrence are mutually exclusive categories, or that this general sense of section 1983's functions, gathered from its legislative history, can be any more than a rough guide for approaching 1983 cases. Nevertheless, it is important to be sensitive to the possible differences in function of tort law and 1983 liability.

That the purposes of section 1983 are not necessarily consistent with those of tort law appears by analogy from the Supreme Court's more recent decision in *Bivens v. Six Unknown Named Agents of the Federal Bureau of Narcotics*, where the Court held that the fourth amendment may give rise to a cause of action for damages for its violation by federal officers. This decision may have been prompted in part by the Court's sense that the exclusionary rule alone does not operate effectively to deter police misconduct. If so, a fourth amendment tort action or a 1983 action could serve the necessary deterrent function. This is especially true where the plaintiff, for theoretical or practical reasons, has no effective state cause of action against the defendant. Moreover, even if the 1983 action is supplementary to an existing and adequate state remedy, it might still help deter unconstitutional conduct because it provides access to a federal forum which might not only possess greater expertise and sympathy with respect to constitutional rights than a state forum, but also might not have the state forum's "inherent potential for bias." Significantly, because of the aforementioned differences in purpose of section 1983 and general tort law, the application of tort doctrine in a 1983 context may lead to a result inconsistent with federal policy. This danger is emphasized by the Court in *Bivens* in its response to the defendants' argument that the fourth amendment only limits federal defenses to a state law claim and may not be the source of an independent claim:

> The interest protected by state laws regulating trespass and the invasion of privacy, and those protected by the Fourth Amendment's guarantee against unreasonable searches and seizures may be inconsistent or even hostile.

Unfortunately, many 1983 cases apply tort law as if with blinders respecting the federal policy involved, seemingly making tort law determinative of 1983 liability. It is clearly unfair to blame Justice Douglas' dictum for this, but it is apparent that many courts have seized upon the "background of tort liability" catch phrase with little consideration given to the background of 1983 liability.

The Prima Facie 1983 Cause of Action

Duty and Standard of Conduct

In the usual tort case involving either intentional or negligent conduct, the issues of duty and standard of conduct are characterized as questions of law. Section 1983, in contrast, is silent on the question of the basis of liability, *i.e.*, whether liability must be based on intentional or negligent conduct, or even conduct without fault. However, section 1983 does indicate what must be caused by a defendant's conduct: "the deprivation of any rights, privileges, or immunities secured by the Constitution . . . ." And because it is constitutional interpretation that is taking place when section 1983 is involved, the constitutional standard of conduct is a question for the court, not the factfinder, although whether it has been departed from is for the factfinder (assuming reasonable men can differ) just as it is in ordinary tort cases. Similarly, whether defendant in a 1983 case is under a duty to conform to the constitutional standard of conduct is a question for the court and is also answered by reference to constitutional interpretation.

Consequently, in every section 1983 case a constitutional duty and standard of conduct must be identified and constitutional policy considered. This was apparently *not* done in an influential Fifth Circuit decision which, although a "false imprisonment" case, has occasionally been improperly cited for the proposition that negligence may serve as the basis of liability under section 1983. In *Whirl v. Kern*, defendant sheriff had not been apprised of the dismissal of charges against plaintiff, who was in custody; and as a result plaintiff "languished in jail for almost nine months after all charges against him were dismissed." Upon a jury finding that plaintiff's detention was not the result of negligence, judgment was entered for defendant on the 1983 claim.

The Court of Appeals for the Fifth Circuit reversed, stating:

> While not easily characterized, the case at bar seems to us closest to the situation where the jailor keeps a prisoner beyond the lawful term of his sentence. In such circumstances, as in the one before us, ignorance of the law is no excuse.

The court thus indicated that absence of notice of unlawful confinement is irrelevant to the existence of the tort of false imprisonment and hence to the 1983 claim. Alternatively, the court resorted to the fiction of constructive notice of the termination of charges against plaintiff.

In its discussion, the court assumed that the elements of the 1983 claim before it exactly tracked the elements of the common law tort of false imprisonment. Only in a footnote did the court mention that the defendant did not "contest the fact that [plaintiff] was deprived of liberty and due process as guaranteed by the fourteenth amendment." But even assuming a fourteenth amendment violation, why should defendant's reasonable mistake be actionable under section 1983? There is a hint of an answer respecting the prima facie 1983 claim in the court's discussion of whether good faith should be a defense in the case before it. In responding in the negative, the court reasoned that "as a matter of federal policy such a defense should not be available to a jailor in circumstances like those before us." A failure of communication, the court said, should be the responsibility of the jailor, not the prisoner. The court emphasized the relative leisure available to a jailor in the performance of his duties, as compared with a policeman making an arrest.

While the court does not elaborate upon this "federal policy," it seems, at least implicitly, to have weighed the interests involved in arriving at its conclusion. Such interests include not only the abilities of the respective parties to avoid the unjustified imprisonment of the plaintiff but also the latter's interest in not being imprisoned, an interest seemingly based upon the fourteenth amendment. Apparently *Whirl* stands for the proposition that a person acting under color of law who confines another against his will may be liable under section 1983 even though the confinement is based upon a reasonable good faith mistake. Put another way, the person has a fourteenth amendment duty not to confine another illegally.

While this is consistent with tort law, which imposes liability for false imprisonment even for a reasonable mistake as to the identity of plaintiff or the existence of a privilege to detain, tort law in this regard might go further than section 1983 should. Compensating an injured plaintiff for false imprisonment might be appropriate even where a defendant had acted reasonably. In contrast, because section 1983 was enacted in part to assure state compliance with the fourteenth amendment, a relevant question for 1983 liability in this kind of situation should be whether such liability furthers adherence to the commands of the fourteenth amendment. Perhaps the court thought that imposing liability upon sheriffs would indeed encourage them and their employers to institute procedures which would prevent such errors. On the other hand, the court in *Whirl* might simply have adopted the compensation approach to section 1983. This could explain why it shifted the loss to the defendant despite the fact that he apparently had to bear it alone. In either case the Fifth Circuit should explicitly have dealt with such considerations.

Negligence as a Basis of 1983 Liability

From the perspective of tort law, *Whirl* is in reality a false imprisonment case involving intentional conduct, that is, the confinement of the plaintiff. There are, however, a few cases which have expressly upheld a 1983 action based on negligent conduct. In *McCray v. Maryland*, petitioner alleged that the Clerk of the Baltimore City Court had negligently impeded the filing of his petition for state post-conviction relief. The district court dismissed the complaint because there was no allegation of a violation of a federally protected right. The Fourth Circuit Court of Appeals reversed, holding that plaintiff's constitutionally based right of access to the courts had been violated, and that his complaint therefore stated a negligence claim cognizable under section 1983. It first cited three recent decisions for the proposition that "a section 1983 action may be based on negligence when it leads to a deprivation of rights." The court then proceeded to characterize the injury to plaintiff as a denial of a constitutional right of access to the courts based apparently on the fourteenth amendment *simpliciter*. But the court nowhere explains how it reasoned from the existence of a violation of plaintiff's constitutional right of access to a determination that the alleged negligence could serve as the basis for the plaintiff's 1983 claim for damages.

Negligence involves the departure from a standard of conduct arrived at by weighing factors such as the gravity of harm, the probability that harm will occur, and the cost of avoiding the risk-creating conduct. But these factors are not relevant when the standard of conduct is derived from a statute; here the legislature's standard is often binding, and departure from it constitutes (for want of a better term) negligence per se. Even though such statutes are often more specific in defining the conduct regulated than is section 1983 on its face, where the duty is derived from the Constitution its breach might also be the equivalent of negligence per se. Moreover, if this breach may not be excused, then it becomes the equivalent of strict liability. Indeed, it seems proper to characterize *Whirl*, discussed earlier, as a case in which the fourteenth amendment functions to impose on the defendant a duty to release, the breach of which renders him *absolutely liable*. From a tort perspective, this duty might be analogized to statutory duties whose breach may not be excused because the person adversely affected is not in a position to protect himself. In contrast to *Whirl*, the court in *McCray* speaks of negligence, thus implying that if the defendant is ultimately found to have acted reasonably, hence non-negligently, he will not be liable.

Even if it is found that a defendant in a *McCray*-type case has acted reasonably, there still would seem to be a fourteenth amendment violation for which injunctive relief would be available. This is comparable to various constitutionally based exclusionary rules in criminal contexts which operate as a general matter irrespective of the reasonableness of the conduct of the police officer. Thus, in *McCray*, the reasonableness of the defendant's conduct seems relevant only with respect to liability for damages and not the existence of a fourteenth amendment violation. Hence it is important to ask what the function of reasonableness should be. If an essential goal of section 1983 is the effective enforcement of fourteenth amendment rights, then a fourteenth amendment duty approach seems preferable to a negligence approach. The plaintiff should not have to prove that defendant's conduct was unreasonable to state a 1983 cause of action. In addition, the purpose of compensating for injuries to constitutional interests seems promoted if plaintiff does not have this burden. Under this approach, moreover, the articulation of the constitutional standard of conduct properly becomes a question for the court; the jury would consider only the issues of breach, causation and damages. Finally, removing the inquiry into reasonableness from the prima facie 1983 claim clarifies the constitutional issues which may be involved, and is consistent with the language of section 1983 itself.

***

Proximate Cause

Notions of negligence and intentional conduct tend to obscure the threshold concern in 1983 cases. That concern should be whether a constitutional duty derived from the fourteenth amendment has been breached. The tort concept of proximate cause similarly obscures the difficult 1983 policy question of the extent of liability where there has been a clear infringement of constitutional rights. Even where section 1983 is found to impose the equivalent of absolute liability for breach of a fourteenth amendment duty as in *Whirl*, the question of the extent of the defendant's responsibility is still present; and, therefore, the equivalent of a proximate cause inquiry may still be required. The point, however, is that this inquiry should not be governed by tort concepts.

The Seventh Circuit's opinion in *Duncan v. Nelson* is an example of the misuse of the tort concept of causation in a 1983 context. Plaintiff, after being held in solitary confinement for 18 days on another charge, was interrogated by defendants for over 20 consecutive hours. Finally, he confessed to murder. This confession was admitted into evidence, and plaintiff was sentenced to 30 years imprisonment. After he had served eight years, the Illinois Supreme Court held that the confession should have been excluded and remanded the case for a new trial. Plaintiff was acquitted at the second trial, and brought a 1983 action against defendant police officers, seeking damages for his interrogation, conviction and incarceration.

The district court dismissed the complaint because "the act of the trial judge in admitting the confession was a superseding, intervening cause for which the defendants cannot be held liable." The Seventh Circuit conceded that at first blush, a foreseeability test for proximate cause would seem to extend to the plaintiff's incarceration. The court nevertheless stated that the defendants were

> presumed to have known the then existing law concerning involuntary confession . . . . Therefore . . . the defendants knew or should have known that their actions in extracting this confession from the plaintiff would render it involuntary and hence inadmissible.

Hence the court characterized as untenable the conclusion that the defendants would foresee that the trial judge would erroneously admit the unlawful confession.

As further support for its decision affirming the district court as to plaintiff's conviction and incarceration (but reversing as to his interrogation) the Seventh Circuit argued that, with respect to cause in fact, there was no compelling inference that the confession "was the sole or even material basis for [plaintiff's] initial conviction." The court also noted that sentencing is a complex decision involving many factors and "it does not follow that the particular sentence imposed upon the plaintiff was a proximate result of that conviction."

Had the court directly approached this case as one involving policy under section 1983 and not tort principles alone, it would have confronted the question of whether imposing liability on the defendants for the conviction and incarceration is consistent with the purposes of section 1983. Instead, the court used a *negligence* concept of superseding cause which even from a tort perspective should not necessarily be used to limit defendant's liability in an *intentional* conduct context such as *Duncan*. Furthermore, the concept of proximate cause in tort law involves policy considerations respecting accountability for harm caused which might be different from those considerations respecting accountability under section 1983. For example, as mentioned earlier, one function of liability under section 1983 might be deterrence. In *Duncan*, holding defendants liable would arguably further the goal of preventing police officers from abusing their authority in order to obtain a conviction.

In short, it aids analysis, and is more consistent with the fourteenth amendment enforcement purpose of section 1983 as well as that section's language, to suggest that it is the nature and scope of the particular fourteenth amendment duty, and not traditional tort concepts, which determine whether a defendant is liable and the extent of his liability.

Eric H. Zagrans, *"Under Color Of"* What *Law: A Reconstructed Model of Section 1983 Liability,* 71 Virginia Law Review 499 (1985)

***

II. Towards a Redefinition of "Under Color of" Law

The *Monroe* decision and its construction of section 1983 must be scraped away like a layer of old paint before the statute and its key phrase, "under color of" law, can be viewed clearly and in their original condition. With the biases of the *Monroe* decision aside, it is possible to take a fresh look at the origins of section 1983 and to arrive at the correct definition of its key phrase.

A. The Transformation of Section 1983: The Monroe *Doctrine Revisited*

Monroe v. Pape induced little immediate critical response from legal scholars. Although numerous student notes were written in the year following the opinion, they were uniformly brief and most praised the decision as a step forward in the protection of civil rights. The first major articles on *Monroe* did not appear until 1965 and 1969. The proliferation of section 1983 litigation had already begun by that time, and the scholars proposed ways to limit application of the statute. Nevertheless, even these scholars accepted *Monroe* largely without critical analysis.

In the more than two decades since the decision, however, whatever merit the expansionist doctrine of *Monroe* may have originally possessed has dissipated in the confusion that now plagues the federal courts dealing with section 1983. The opinion deserves a hard look also for its glaring deficiencies of scholarship. After examining the principal justifications and legal reasoning offered by the majority in *Monroe,* I will evaluate the Court's use, or rather misuse, of the legislative history of section 1 of the Civil Rights Act of 1871 as the keystone of its interpretation of section 1983. Finally, I will explore and criticize the Court's reliance on *United States v. Classic* as its primary authority for the proper construction of section 1983.

1. The Reasoning of the Majority

The central issue in *Monroe* was whether thirteen Chicago police officers, who had broken into the Monroes' home "in the early morning, routed them from bed, made them stand naked in the living room, and ransacked every room" without a search warrant, had acted "under color of the statutes, ordinances, regulations, customs, or usages" of the State of Illinois. In holding that the acts were under color of state law, the Court relied extensively upon its interpretation of the congressional intent behind the express language of section 1983.

Justice Douglas, writing for the majority, asserted that "[t]here are threads of many thoughts running through the debates," and indeed there are. The debaters spoke of many ills that they wished to cure, and the Ku Klux Act, as the Civil Rights Act of 1871 is also known, fashioned several different remedies to treat various different aspects of the Klan problem. The Court's tendency in *Monroe,* and ultimately its error, was to attempt to demonstrate the expansive scope of section 1 of the Act by weaving all of these threads into its fabric and then stretching that fabric to cover problems meant to be corrected by other sections of the Act.

The *Monroe* opinion found three aims in section 1 of the Act. The first aim was straightforward and ineluctable; the Court stated that section 1 was intended to "override certain kinds of state laws." As will be demonstrated in Part II.B, this aim was in fact the only purpose of section 1.

The statute's second aim, as discerned by the Court, was to provide "a remedy where state law was inadequate." This statement is arguably true insofar as it means that a plaintiff was to be allowed a federal forum in which to sue state officers when the state would not provide one. Nonetheless, Justice Douglas' description of this second aim was misleadingly broad. The language could embrace federal suits against private wrongdoers (Klan members, for instance) if there is no adequate state remedy. Yet the enactors never spoke of section 1 in relation to

---

the Klan, and the Court itself said that the section "was not a remedy against . . . [the Klan] or its members."

The Court's reference to the legislative history does not clarify this second aim. Quoting Senator Sherman's complaint about the dearth of state convictions of whites for crimes against blacks that had resulted from state laws against blacks' testimony, the Court implied that section 1 would alleviate that situation by authorizing federal *criminal* prosecutions of whites for their offenses against blacks. But section 1 could not reach this problem because it authorizes only *civil* actions.

In fact, Senator Sherman's statement is the first of several quotations that the Court takes flatly out of context. The Senator spoke not of section 1 nor of any other provision of the Ku Klux Act; that bill had been introduced in the House only two days earlier and was not to come before the Senate for another week. Senator Sherman was describing a resolution instructing the Senate Judiciary Committee to report a bill of its own to deal with the Klan. The Senator pointed out that the myriad offenses committed by whites against blacks in Kentucky had resulted in only two convictions, both in federal court under existing federal statutes. Section 2 of the Act, not section 1, was designed to deal with Sherman's concern. Thus, it is unclear what Justice Douglas meant by this "second aim" or why Senator Sherman's statement would support it.

The third aim of section 1, according to the Court, was "to provide a federal remedy where the state remedy, although adequate in theory, was not available in practice." The opinion broadens this proposition each time it is discussed. Six pages later Justice Douglas rephrased it; the statute was meant, in part, "to afford a federal right in federal courts because, by reason of prejudice, passion, neglect, intolerance or otherwise, state laws *might* not be enforced." Finally, Justice Douglas decided that the state's fault was no longer a precondition to relief, and the proposition evolved into this much-quoted statement: "It is no answer that the State has a law which if enforced would give relief. The federal remedy is supplementary to the state remedy, and the latter need not be first sought and refused before the federal one is invoked." Thus, in the space of nine pages, Justice Douglas artfully transformed this third aim from the not unthinkable idea that section 1 would allow a federal forum when and because the state customarily would not enforce its own laws, to the broad implication that section 1 could provide a remedy even if the state were ready and willing to provide its own. This final version of the third aim is cut from whole cloth. It does not logically follow from the original formulation of the proposition, and as will be shown, the Court supplies no direct support from the legislative record for it or even for its predecessor versions.

The Court's third aim for section 1 presents an even greater analytic difficulty when used to justify the liability of the police officers in *Monroe.* The Court asserts that, under the third aim, section 1 was to impose liability upon state officers who "were *unable* or *unwilling* to enforce a state law" against Klan members. Thus, liability was to be imposed on third parties removed from the deed itself. In *Monroe,* by contrast, liability was imposed on officers who themselves violated state law. These two applications of section 1 are distinct, and the first does not necessarily support the second.

Perhaps Justice Douglas intended to describe a *fourth* aim for section 1, one that would apply to state officials who abuse their power, whether or not the state itself stands ready to prosecute them. Whatever policy arguments may now favor such an aim, they were not adopted by the Forty-second Congress. This "fourth aim" neither follows from Justice Douglas' argument for the original third aim nor is supported by the legislative record that he surveyed. Whether Justice Douglas relied on any fourth aim or merely on his final version of the third aim, drawing the holding of *Monroe* from either premise was a neat bit of judicial legerdemain.

2. *The Support of the Legislative History*

Justice Douglas masked this illusion by presenting numerous quotations from the 1871 debates on the Ku Klux Act to support his assertion that acts of state officials outside their authority are under color of state law. Unfortunately, these quotations offer no such support; each is either taken out of context or contradicted by other comments of the same speaker.

To support the conclusion that section 1983 grants a remedy for deprivations caused "by an official's abuse of his position," Justice Douglas began by quoting Representative Arthur, who asserted in opposition to the Act that "[i]t overrides the reserved powers of the states." This statement does not support any particular construction of section 1. Representative Arthur opposed federal protection of constitutional rights, believing that such protection was best provided by the states. Federal jurisdiction, which he called the "despotic circle of central power," should extend only to claims arising on federally controlled land. Thus, in Arthur's view *any* federal cause of action would improperly override state powers.

The Court stated next that "the failure of certain States to enforce the laws with an equal hand . . . furnished the powerful momentum behind [the Act]." This assessment is true; the failure of state protection was the chief justification advanced by the bill's proponents for the use of federal power. But this general problem does not necessarily define the scope of section 1. In fact, the two Congressmen quoted by the Court to support this proposition were speaking of other elements of the bill. Representative Beatty spoke in favor of section 3. Representative Lowe's remarks do not demonstrate a view that the failure to enforce a state law is an action under color of law. To justify the parts of the Act that provided direct federal protection against the Klan, many supporters, including Lowe, argued that the equal protection clause of the fourteenth amendment should be expanded beyond the mere prohibition of discrimination to a requirement that protective enforcement replace state inaction. Accordingly, Representative Lowe distinguished between discriminatory acts done under color of law and the equally unconstitutional denial of equal protection caused by state inaction. Lowe asserted that a state without unconstitutional laws may nonetheless violate the fourteenth amendment if it "permits the rights of citizens to be systematically trampled upon *without color of law.*" Thus, a failure to enforce a state law, according to Lowe, is not an action under color of law even though it violates the fourteenth amendment and triggers other provisions of the Act.

The Court next announced that section 1 sought to deter Klan activities by providing "not a remedy against it or its members but against those who representing a State in some capacity were unable or unwilling to enforce a state law." To support this conclusion, the Court first quoted Senator Osborne's criticisms of state court proceedings. These remarks, however, are not on point. Osborne believed that the presence of Klan members on state juries, not the failure of state officers, put "the preservation of life and property . . . beyond the power of the State government." The statement quoted by the Court advocated not section 1 but rather an amendment to retain a law that imposed a jury oath preventing Klan conspirators from serving on federal juries.

The Court then asserted that the states' failure to enforce their laws must have been Congress' main concern, because Congress had "no quarrel with the state laws on the books." The Court quoted Representatives Porter, Burchard, and Hoar and Senator Pratt to back this view. Their comments do not support the Court's position. Representative Porter was concerned not with the lack of enforcement of state laws but with the laws themselves. Porter explained that, because the Democratic Party was in power in Virginia, the Klan was unnecessary and inactive in that state; the oppression of blacks and of white Republicans in Virginia was accomplished through the legislature and the judiciary. In fact, Porter complained that the bill "does not reach . . . , and is not intended to reach," this type of oppression. Porter's view of section 1 is aberrant; by any construction, including that given by the Court in *Monroe,* section 1 at least reaches acts done by the state.

Representative Burchard spoke in support of section 2 of the bill, not section 1. Like Representative Lowe, he sought to justify the use of federal power in section 2 because he believed that state inaction on behalf of blacks was a denial of equal protection. He felt no need to justify section 1 in this way; in fact, he saw no objection to it at all, and therefore, could not have seen it as extending to state nonenforcement.

Representative Hoar never referred to section 1. Like Representative Lowe, he spoke on the reach of the equal protection clause. Although his view of section 1 cannot be accurately determined, it is clear that he did not believe section 1 reached random unauthorized acts like those in *Monroe* because he thought that federal power should be exercised only in the face of *pervasive* state inaction.

Senator Pratt criticized the denial of equal protection to Union sympathizers. He was not speaking of section 1, however. In fact, he believed that "[t]he State officers . . . who refuse to do their duty are beyond our reach." His proposed solution, similar to section 2 of the Act, was to create a federal crime, not a civil remedy. "We cannot touch any State official for malfeasance, or misfeasance, or non-feasance; but we can say to all . . . the States, '. . . We will describe and punish as crimes against the United States that class of offenses . . . which you fail to punish.'"

In a final effort to bolster its construction of section 1, the Court referred to complaints by three of the bill's opponents about the "breadth" of the remedy it provided. The comments of Representatives Kerr and Voorhees quoted in support of this proposition are aberrant and contradict other statements they made during the debates. Their true views are discussed in Part II.B of this article. Senator Thurman's comment is off point and lends no aid to a construction of "under color of" law. His complaint was that section 1 had no minimum jurisdictional amount.

Little needs to be said about the Court's discussion of section 2 of the Ku Klux Act. As Justice

Douglas pointed out, the evolution of that section is "utterly irrelevant to the problem before us, *viz.*, the meaning of 'under color of' law." Unfortunately, the Court did not heed its own admonition, for it immediately proceeded to relate the scope of section 1 both to the "extension of federal power" accomplished by the whole bill and to Representative Hoar's quoted justification for such power. The Court persisted in inferring that, because the whole Act supplied a remedy when a state official refuses to act, section 1 must necessarily reach just as far. As Part II.B will show, section 1 is simply not that broad.

Section 1 was of little concern to most of the enacting legislators. It had not the breadth of the other sections of the bill, nor was it designed to reach the equal protection problem. In the Court's tortured attempt to stretch the legislative history of section 1983 to fit the Procrustean bed it built upon the facts in *Monroe*, the Court distorted the statute and left its opinion much weaker than if the Court had left the Congressional Globe unopened.

3. *The Court's Reliance on* United States v. Classic

Justice Douglas did not rest his construction of "under color of" law upon the legislative history alone. He also relied on *United States v. Classic*, which had construed the identical phrase as it appeared in section 2 of the Civil Rights Act of 1866, now codified in amended form at 18 U.S.C. § 242, the criminal analogue to and model for section 1983. In *Classic* the commissioners of elections for a New Orleans precinct had been indicted for altering ballots cast in a congressional primary. The Court held that the alterations violated the constitutional rights of the voters and then considered whether the commissioners had also violated section 242. The Court concluded that "'under color of' state law" includes the "[m]isuse of power, possessed by virtue of state law and made possible only because the wrongdoer is clothed with the authority of state law." In other words, because the laws that created the commissioners' positions had given them the ability or the power, although not the authority, to alter the ballots, the commissioners had acted under color of those laws.

Classic thus directly supported *Monroe;* in both cases the defendants had violated state law yet were held to have acted under color of state law. But *Classic* has analytical weaknesses that attenuate its support for *Monroe.* Although the Court stated in *Monroe* that *Classic*'s construction of "under color of" law was "formulated after mature consideration," the *Classic* opinion in fact made no use of the legislative history of section 242. Instead, the Court relied exclusively on constitutional interpretations dating back to 1879.

Reliance on these cases was misplaced. Justice Stone's majority opinion in *Classic* first cited *Ex parte Virginia.* In a sweeping interpretation of what the fourteenth amendment "must mean," the Court in *Virginia* had defined state action as any act "by virtue of public position under a State government, . . . [done] in the name and for the State, [by one] clothed with the State's power." The *Classic* Court erred in adapting this definition to the section 242 context for two reasons. First, reading the *Virginia* language as encompassing acts done contrary to public authority goes well beyond the facts of that case. *Virginia* concerned a state judge who had discriminated against blacks in the selection of jurors. State law gave the judge the discretion to select those persons whom he shall think "well qualified to serve as jurors." Thus, although the judge misused the authority granted him under state law, he nonetheless acted *within* that authority and did not violate the state law that gave him power. Any language from *Virginia* that was extended in *Classic* beyond this original context should be considered mere dictum.

Second, *Virginia* defined "state action" for purposes of the fourteenth amendment, not acts committed "'under color of' law" for purposes of a statute passed two years before that amendment was ratified. Whatever the proper scope of the fourteenth amendment, it does not follow that Congress intended the scope of section 242 to be exactly coextensive with it. At a minimum, *Classic* should not have presumed such a conclusion without an inquiry into the legislative history of section 242.

Classic also cited *Home Telephone & Telegraph Co. v. City of Los Angeles* to support its construction of "under color of" law. As authority for *Classic,* however, *Home Telephone* suffers from the same weaknesses as *Virginia.* First, *Home Telephone* did not deal squarely with the issue of actions taken contrary to the authority granted to the actor. The case involved an investor-owned telephone utility that had claimed that a municipal ordinance fixing telephone rates in Los Angeles was confiscatory and thus unconstitutional. Because state law apparently gave the city discretionary authority to enact rate-fixing ordinances, the city may have misused its authority but did not violate it. This fact distinguishes the case from *Classic,* where the commissioners had been given no discretion in counting the ballots, and the alterations they made clearly violated state law. Second, as in *Virginia,* the Court in

Home Telephone had interpreted the reach of the fourteenth amendment, not the meaning of the statutory phrase "under color of" law.

The only other case cited by the Court in *Classic* was *Hague v. C.I.O.,* also not on point. The deprivation complained of in *Hague* was the disruption of the meetings of a communist organization, an interference allowed by a municipal ordinance. Because the wrongful acts were authorized, *Hague* gives no support to the conclusion that unauthorized acts may be under color of state law.

The weaknesses of *Classic* were compounded when the decision was used in *Monroe* to construe a different statute. The Court tried to fend off anticipated challenges to the authority of *Classic* with a quotation from *Screws v. United States,* a section 242 case that had also followed *Classic:*

> The *Classic* case was not the product of hasty action or inadvertence. . . . We are not dealing with constitutional interpretations which throughout the history of the Court have wisely remained flexible and subject to frequent reexamination. The meaning which the *Classic* case gave to the phrase "under color of any law" involved only a construction of the statute.

The Court in *Monroe* further defended its reliance on *Classic* by noting that Congress had not criticized the interpretation despite several opportunities to do so. The Court reasoned that "[i]f the results of our construction of 'under color of' law were as horrendous as now claimed . . . surely the voice of the opposition would have been heard in those Committee reports." Even assuming that congressional silence signified acceptance of the Court's construction of section 242, such silence does not mean that Congress intended to endorse the same construction for section 1983, especially given the absence of prosecutorial discretion under section 1983 to screen out the less egregious violations of state law.

In *Monroe* the Court assumed that "'under color of' law" was intended to have the same meaning in section 1983 as in section 242. This premise is true, as Part II.B will show. But the premise also leads to the conclusion that if one case is incorrect, so is the other. The Court's misconstruction of section 1983 flows in a direct chain of inferences from *Virginia*'s broad language concerning the fourteenth amendment, through *Classic*'s use of *Virginia*'s constitutional interpretation for statutory purposes in disregard of legislative history, to *Monroe*'s reliance on *Classic* as a bridge between the nearly identical statutes. But *Classic* is the weak link that makes the chain fail. If the Court in *Classic* had followed the legislative intent to limit section 242 to authorized actions, the Court in *Monroe* would have been guided to the analogous result for section 1983.

The majority opinion in *Monroe* utterly fails to support the conclusions it reaches. The last section of the opinion, which deals with municipal liability, has already been overruled. The rest of the opinion is equally misconceived and deserving of reevaluation. To understand the correct scope and purpose of section 1983 it is necessary to put *Monroe* aside and go back to "square one"—the legislative record.

B. Square One: The Legislative History

The legislative history relevant to section 1983 begins not in 1871, when the section was enacted, but five years earlier. Section 2 of the Civil Rights Act of 1866 served as the textual model for section 1 of the 1871 Act. Although the two statutes provide different remedies, they use the phrase "under color of" law identically. A careful examination of the legislative history of both acts clearly reveals the meaning of that phrase and the purposes of the two statutes.

1. The 1866 Act

The Civil Rights Act of 1866 was the precursor for both section 1983 and the first section of the fourteenth amendment, which was passed by Congress in 1866 and was ratified by the states in 1868. The bill, entitled "An act to protect all persons in the United States in their civil rights, and furnish the means of their vindication," became law on April 9, 1866.

The Thirty-ninth Congress was concerned with the appearance in the southern states of the "Black Codes"—laws passed after the abolition of slavery that so discriminated against the freed blacks as to render "illusory" the liberty newly conferred by the thirteenth amendment. Pursuant to section 2 of that amendment, Congress could attack the Black Codes in two ways. It could enact legislation to supersede and to annul such state laws, or it could prevent their enforcement by punishing persons who acted pursuant to them. Congress enacted section 1 of the 1866 Act to accomplish the first aim, annulling discriminatory state laws, and section 2 to accomplish the second, deterring their enforcement. More specifically, section 1 declared the freed blacks to be United States citizens entitled to the same contract and property rights as whites. Foreshadowing section 1 of the fourteenth amendment, section 1 of the 1866 Act also declared all citizens to be entitled to equal protection and to be subject to equal punishment under the laws of the states. Section 2 provided criminal sanctions against any person who, acting under color of any law, deprived another of the rights protected by section 1 or subjected him to different punishments on account of race.

The language of these two sections manifests the congressional scheme. Section 1 secures certain rights, "any law, statute, ordinance, regulation, or custom, [of a state] to the contrary notwithstanding." Section 2 punishes the deprivation of these rights under color of "any law, statute, ordinance, regulation, or custom" of a state. One cannot mistake the identity of purpose revealed by the identity of language. The debates on the 1866 Act leave little doubt that section 2 was intended solely to deter the enforcement of laws that abridge section 1 rights. Section 2 received scant attention in the first round of Senate debates. The principal focus of the pre-veto Senate debates was section 1; the principal question was who, besides the freed blacks, would be declared citizens of the United States. Nevertheless, the few references to section 2 unambiguously emphasize that only acts done pursuant to discriminatory state laws were actionable. Senator Trumbull of Illinois, chairman of the committee that reported the bill, described the purpose of section 2 in his introductory remarks:

> When it comes to be understood in all parts of the United States that any person who shall deprive another of any right or subject him to any punishment in consequence of his color or race will expose himself to fine and imprisonment, I think such acts will soon cease.

The only comments in the Senate debates concerning the reach of section 2 came from dissenters, all of whom objected to imposing liability on persons who had followed state law. Senator Cowan of Pennsylvania, for example, feared that the act would make criminal any state judge's conviction of a black under a discriminatory state law, despite the judge's honest belief in the law's propriety. Senator Davis of Kentucky foresaw the same fate for judges and juries who convicted blacks under laws prohibiting interracial marriages. The potential conviction of judges, a common theme in both houses, is not germane to the issue of whether "under color of" law extends beyond state-authorized acts. The opposing senators did not express concern that persons who had not acted pursuant to state law would be liable.

The House, by contrast, discussed the meaning of "under color of" law at the outset of the debates. The introductory address of Representative Wilson of Iowa, the House manager of the bill and the chairman of the Judiciary Committee, was interrupted by Representative Loan of Missouri, who saw the phrase as a limiting device and wondered why the act did not also cover persons acting in purely private capacities:

> Mr. Loan. . . . I desire to ask the chairman who reported this bill, why the committee limit [sic] the provisions of the second section to those who act under color of law. Why not let them apply to the whole community where the acts are committed?
>
> Mr. Wilson. . . . That grows out of the fact that there is discrimination in reference to civil rights *under the local laws of the States.* Therefore we provide that the persons who *under the color of these local laws* should do these things shall be liable to this punishment.
>
> Mr. Loan. What penalty is imposed upon others than officers who inflict these wrongs on the citizen?
>
> Mr. Wilson. . . . We are not making a general criminal code for the States.

This colloquy leaves little doubt as to the meaning of section 2. Whatever other discrimination might have existed in the community as a whole, section 2 was intended only to reach discrimination accomplished pursuant to discriminatory state laws. Most of the bill's opponents in the House, like their colleagues in the Senate, objected to the imposition of liability on officials who were merely doing their duty. For example, Representative Kerr of Indiana, who later would be much more vocal in opposition to the 1871 Act, described the operation of the bill, which he apparently felt was *a priori* objectionable:

> Under the laws of Indiana no person except white male inhabitants can be allowed to engage in the business of retailing spirituous liquors. But a negro procures the requisite petition and applies to a county board for a license to retail liquors. It is refused. Now, this discrimination is based both upon color and race. And the county board, by refusing the license, violates the second section of this act, and thereby commit [sic] a misdemeanor . . . .

This example is the archetypal application of section 2 as originally conceived—the section was to reach the state official who enforced a discriminatory state law.

The speech of Representative Shellabarger of Ohio in favor of the bill near the end of the House debates solidified this interpretation of "under color of" law. Speaking on the need for section 2, Shellabarger, who would later introduce the 1871 Act in the House, said:

> If the States may abridge or destroy rights of citizenship which the United States confers and is bound to secure, . . . then the United States is no nation. Then South Carolina may do, with utter impunity, a violence to an

> American citizen which all the armies and navies and treasures of the Republic must be exhausted in order to prevent at the hands of a foreign State. It must be noted here that the violations of the citizens' rights, which are reached and punished by this bill, are those which are inflicted under "color of law" . . . . The bill does not reach mere private wrongs, but only those done under color of State authority; and that authority must be extended on account of the race or color. It is meant, therefore, not to usurp the powers of the States to punish offenses generally against the rights of citizens in the several States, but its whole force is expended in defeating an attempt, *under State laws,* to deprive races and the members thereof as such of the rights enumerated in this act. This is the whole of it.

Two aspects of Shellabarger's remarks deserve special mention. First, his reference to actions performed by South Carolina illustrates that the bill's overall purpose was to reach the state, not the state official. Second, Shellabarger stated that the complainant must be a victim of state authority. It is insufficient that the act deprives someone of federally protected rights; the authority behind the act must likewise be aimed at the derogation of such rights.

President Johnson vetoed the bill, stating that he doubted Congress' power to exert direct control over state laws. His construction of section 2 was identical to that of the bill's proponents:

> This section seems to be designed to apply to some existing or future law of a State or Territory which may conflict with the provisions of the bill now under consideration. It provides for counteracting such forbidden legislation by imposing fine and imprisonment upon the legislators who may pass such conflicting laws, or upon the officers or agents who shall put, or attempt to put, them into execution. It means an official offense, *not a common crime committed against law* upon the persons or property of the black race.

The President's interpretation reinforces the conclusion that the Act was aimed at improper state laws and that section 2, in particular, was targeted to those who enforce them. The section does not reach conduct that violates state law.

During the post-veto debate in the Senate, the bill's proponents addressed the President's assertion that it unduly interfered with state autonomy. Senator Stewart of Nevada reasoned that, because Georgia had no discriminatory laws, a person could not commit a crime under section 2 in that state:

> He must do it under the color of a law. If there is no law or custom in existence in a State authorizing it, it will be impossible for him to do it under color of any law. This section is simply to remove the disabilities existing by laws tending to reduce the negro to a system of peonage. It strikes at that; nothing else.

Senator Trumbull also tried to show that federal intrusion was limited:

> These words "under color of law" were inserted as words of limitation . . . . If an offense is committed against a colored person simply because he is colored, in a State where the law affords him the same protection as if he were white, this act neither has nor was intended to have anything to do with his case, because he has adequate remedies in the State courts; but if he is discriminated against under color of state laws because he is colored, then it becomes necessary to interfere for his protection.

Thus, if no state laws authorized discrimination, no criminal liability exists under section 2 of the Act.

The House overrode the President's veto without debate, although Representative Lawrence of Ohio gave a speech on the bill before the vote. Lawrence's argument in support of Congress' authority to enact the legislation shows that section 2 was intended to reach only acts committed under state authority: "The whole question of the power of Congress to enact this bill is resolved into this: when the Constitution recognizes and secures rights which are denied by State laws, may Congress declare it a crime to execute or enforce unconstitutional laws, to deprive a citizen of a constitutional right?"

In light of this legislative record, it does not appear that section 242 was intended to reach the state official who defies state law, even if such conduct also violates the fourteenth amendment. The phrase "under color of" law in section 242 clearly describes only authorized acts. Section 1983 can reach no further, unless the debates over the 1871 Act show that Congress attached a different meaning to the term in 1871.

2. *The 1871 Act*

Section 1983 was one of six sections enacted as the Ku Klux Act of 1871. The bill was drafted by a special joint committee, formed in response to President Grant's call for legislation to deal with the Klan.

The bill was prompted by tales of lawlessness in the southern states caused by a large, organized, and as yet unvanquished Ku Klux Klan. Sections 2 through 6 of the 1871 Act shored up state authority to deal with the problem. Section 2 imposed federal criminal and civil liability upon persons who conspired to hinder state and federal officers in the performance of their duties or otherwise to obstruct justice or to deprive others of equal protection of the laws. This section gave the federal government a means of prosecuting Klan members who had been escaping justice in the state courts. Section 3 authorized the President to employ the militia to put down widespread insurrection by the Klan. Section 4 further allowed the President to suspend the writ of habeas corpus if warranted by the scope of the insurrection. Section 5 prohibited persons whom the court believed to be Klan members from serving on juries in cases arising under the Act. Section 6 provided that damages be paid to a victim of Klan violence by any person who was aware of the proposed violence and, having the power to do so, had refused to prevent it.

By contrast, section 1 did not reach the Klan at all, if "under color of" law means "under authority of" state law as in the 1866 Act. The section is actually an interloper in the Ku Klux Act. Indeed, the enacting Congress seemed to view section 1 as an amendment of or addition to the 1866 Act, and not as an integral part of the solution to the Klan problem that the rest of the 1871 Act provided. This point is of great significance to the proper construction of section 1, because it implies that many of Congress' reasons for enacting the 1871 Act, particularly the states' failure to provide equal protection, are irrelevant to section 1.

Debate on the bill was extensive. Over one hundred members of both houses presented speeches, most of them opposing passage. Only twenty-eight speakers, less than one-third of those addressing the Act, mentioned section 1. Of those, about half opposed the section; four who opposed the bill in general nonetheless approved of section 1.

a. The House Debates.

Section 1 was conceived as the civil correlative to the criminal provision of the 1866 Act. Representative Shellabarger, who as the head of the Judiciary Committee introduced the bill in the House, gave a straightforward description of the history and scope of section 1 in his introductory remarks:

> The model for [the first section] will be found in the second section of the act of April 9, 1866, known as "the civil rights act." . . .
>
> . . . .
>
> The section being in its terms carefully confined to giving a civil action for such wrongs against citizenship as are done under color of State laws which abridge these rights, it goes directly to the enforcement of that provision which says the State shall not make or enforce any law which shall abridge any privileges or franchises of citizens.

Other speakers noted the correlation between section 1 of the 1871 Act and section 2 of the 1866 Act. Representative Coburn of Indiana, a supporter of the bill, stated that "[t]he measure under consideration gives a civil remedy parallel to the penal provision based upon the first section of the civil rights act. If this penal section is valid, and no one dares controvert it, the civil remedy is legal and unquestionable." Congressman McHenry of Kentucky, who opposed section 1 because he doubted that Congress had the power to enforce the fourteenth amendment directly, stated simply that "[t]he first section of the bill is intended as an amendment of the civil rights act. . . ."

Although these comments support adopting the 1866 construction of "under color of" law, five years had elapsed and two constitutional amendments had been adopted since the 1866 bill. Nevertheless, these events apparently gave no new meaning to "under color of" law. For example, Representative Maynard of Tennessee noted: "It simply declares in substance that whoever interferes with the rights . . . granted . . . by the Constitution . . . , though it may be done under State law or State regulation, shall not be exempt from responsibility. . . ." Similarly, Representative Biggs of Delaware explained that "for the violation of the rights, privileges, and immunities of the citizen a civil remedy is to be had by proceedings in the Federal courts, State authorization in the premises to the contrary notwithstanding."

Representative (later President) Garfield of Ohio spoke briefly on section 1, although he gave greater attention to section 2 of the bill. Garfield called section 1 "a wise and salutary provision, and plainly within the power of Congress." Addressing section 2, he then asserted:

> But the chief complaint is not that the laws of the State are unequal, but that even where the laws are just and equal on their face, yet, by a systematic maladministration of them, or a neglect or refusal to enforce their provisions, a portion of the people are denied equal protection under them.

Garfield thus implied that section 1 applies to unequal laws, but that section 2 should take effect where equal protection is denied because equal laws are misapplied or not enforced.

Two speakers discussed section 1 of the 1871 Act in terms as limited as section 2 of the 1866 Act, although they did not refer to the earlier act. These speakers opposed the Ku Klux Act as a whole but believed that section 1, being limited to discriminatory legislation, would have little effect. Representative Sloss of Alabama said that the "object of this section is not very clear, as it is not pretended by its advocates on this floor that any State has passed any laws endangering the rights or privileges of the colored people." Representative Blair of Missouri gave the same reading to section 1. Unable to foresee the broad interpretation that future courts would give the provision, he also proved to be an innocent but false prophet:

> The first part of this section seems to contemplate that some State has or is about to legislate so as to abridge the rights conferred by the thirteenth, fourteenth, and fifteenth amendments upon the negroes. . . .
>
> . . . But as no State has or is likely to pass any such law as contemplated, that section is and will be inoperative, and hurt no one.

These remarks make clear that the targets of the 1871 civil provision were identical to those of the 1866 criminal statute—discriminatory state laws and acts done pursuant to them.

Opponents of section 1 also assumed that discriminatory state laws and the persons who act pursuant to them were the intended targets of the section. The common objection presented by these speakers was that a state officer who acts honestly in the enforcement of a state law should not be held liable just because that law is later found unconstitutional. In the words of Representative Whitthorne of Tennessee:

> [I]f a police officer of the city of Richmond or New York should find a drunken negro or white man upon the streets with loaded pistol flourishing it, &c., and by virtue of any ordinance, law, or usage, either of city or State, he takes it away, the officer may be sued, because the right to bear arms is secured by the Constitution, and such suit brought in distant and expensive tribunals.

The objections of two other opponents, Representatives Archer of Maryland and McHenry of Kentucky, show that section 1 applies only to authorized conduct. Archer stated that "it is difficult to say what the States may permit to be done with exemption from punishment, if, by any possibility, such State law could be construed to impair or infringe either the rights, privileges, or immunities of persons." Representative McHenry also saw section 1 reaching state laws and argued that Congress had no power to do so:

> It is for the States to enforce [section 1 of the fourteenth amendment] by abstaining from the enactment of such laws as conflict with it. . . . Because the state is forbidden to pass such laws it does not follow that Congress has the right to enforce this provision in the states.

For the most part, however, the opponents of section 1 were not concerned with the phrase "under color of" law. Rather, they focused on three main points. Some claimed that the provision usurped state court jurisdiction. Others felt that, although the bill was not improper, it was an unnecessary affront to local courts. Still others criticized section 1 as inefficient because of the added expense and trouble of suing in federal court. None of these complaints clarified the scope of the section.

Only three representatives made comments that may be construed as extending section 1 to cover acts done by officials in violation of state law. Representative Burchard of Illinois suggested that a claim of state authority would be sufficient, stating that section 1 affords "an injured party redress in the United States courts against any person violating his rights as a citizen under claim or color of State authority." Representative Voorhees used the idea as hyperbolic fuel in his denunciation of the bill:

> The first and second sections are designed to transfer all criminal jurisdiction from the courts of the States to the courts of the United States. This is to be done upon the assumption that the courts of the southern States fail and refuse to do their duty in the punishment of offenders against the law. . . . But I again deny your assumption. . . . I deny that the administration of justice in the South is a failure. . . .

Careless in his diatribe, Voorhees failed to distinguish between sections 1 and 2; section 1 did not, after all, provide for any of the criminal jurisdiction that he felt was wrongly being transferred to the federal courts. By his own admission, Voorhees had missed most of the eight days of debate that took place before the day that he spoke, and he may have misunderstood section 1. The third Representative to give a broad construction to section 1 was Kerr of Indiana, who noted that the offenses it would remedy "may be the common violations of the municipal law of [the] State." During the debates on the nearly identical section of the 1866 Act, however, Kerr had subscribed to a contrary view of the phrase "under color of" law. In his speech in opposition to the 1866 Act, he gave a half-dozen examples of persons who could be convicted under that statute. Each involved an official acting pursuant to state law.

The legislative history in the House is not unanimous—indeed, one would be astonished if it were. The clear weight of the evidence, however, supports the construction of "under color of" as meaning "by authority of" state law. The House view of section 1 may best be summarized by the statement of Congressman Wilson of Indiana:

> Suppose, now, that a State should pass a law authorizing slavery, or denying the right to vote to persons of color, . . . and suppose that, under color of such a State law, any person should deprive another of his liberty, or of his vote. . . . The State has no right to pass any such law. No one has any right to avail himself of any such law.
>
> . . . Now, I ask, what legislation could be more appropriate than to give to a person injured by another under color of such unconstitutional State laws a remedy by civil action?

b. The Senate Debates

The debate on section 1 of the 1871 Act took much the same form in the Senate as in the House. Senator Edmunds, who managed the bill in the Senate, remarked:

> The first section is one that I believe nobody objects to, as defining the rights secured by the Constitution of the United States when they are assailed by any State law or under color of any State law, and it is merely carrying out the principles of the civil rights bill, which have since become a part of the Constitution.

The senator thus also suggested that section 1 is merely a civil parallel to section 2 of the 1866 Act.

Senator Blair of Missouri, who opposed the bill, raised the familiar argument that section 1 was unnecessary because it was so limited: "[Discrimination] being forbidden by the Constitution of the United States, and all the judges, State and national, being sworn to support the Constitution . . . there could be no danger of the violation of the rights of citizens under color of the *laws* of the states."

Senator Thurman of Ohio spoke against section 1, as well as against the rest of the Act. Although he devoted more time to the section than any other speaker, most of his comments do not help to define the reach of the statute. He conceded that Congress could confer the jurisdiction granted in section 1, but he disapproved "of the centralizing tendency of transferring all mere private suits . . . from the State into the Federal courts." He objected that the provision was "a disparagement of the State courts" and opposed the "expense and inconvenience" that would result from conferring jurisdiction on the federal courts. The Senator also attacked section 1 as vague for not defining the rights it was to protect.

Senator Thurman's last objection reached the critical phrase; he feared that the "under color of" language could be used against state legislators and judges. These same objections had been put forth five years earlier against section 2 of the 1866 Act. The common objections show the similarity between the two provisions and underscore the Senator's construction of section 1 as limited to acts pursuant to discriminatory state laws.

Senator Sherman of Ohio, speaking late in the debates, gave the only Senate reading of section 1 that would allow it to reach beyond acts done pursuant to state laws to acts done without state authorization. Speaking of those who had fallen prey to the Ku Klux Klan, he said: "What remedy do you offer the victims and with what punishment do you threaten the guilty? First, the party injured may sue in the courts of the United States for money damages. Whom? Disguised outlaws. What is the use of suing them?" If the Senator was referring to section 1, he had a motive for trying to show its futility. Sherman had authored the Sherman Amendment, which would have granted redress to victims from counties where Klan outrages took place. At the time that Senator Sherman spoke, the amendment had just been dropped by a special committee convened to reconcile the House and Senate versions of the bill. In its place the committee added section 6, which made landowners liable for disturbances that they could have prevented but had allowed to occur. The Senator was probably making a last-ditch effort to resurrect his amendment by showing that, without it, the bill provided no adequate means of compensating victims of Klan violence.

The statements of Senator Frelinghuysen of New Jersey, a member of the drafting committee, summarize the dominant view in the Senate. He explained that because Congress "cannot reach" the legislatures that pass discriminatory laws, the victim must have recourse to the enforcers of those laws:

> As to the civil remedies, . . . when the courts of a State violate the provisions of the Constitution or the law of the United States there is now relief afforded by a review in the Federal courts. And since the fourteenth amendment forbids any State from making or enforcing any law abridging these privileges and immunities, as you can not reach the Legislatures, the injured party should have an original action in our Federal courts, so that by injunction or by the recovery of damages he could have relief against the party who under color of such law is guilty of infringing his rights. As to the civil remedy no one, I think, can object.

The foregoing discussion has attempted to catalogue every comment made about section 1 during the long debate on the bill. The variety of comments from the drafters gives a clear picture of the congressional intent behind section 1983. The picture becomes sharper when one recalls the debates on section 2 of the 1866 Act. Reading the whole of these debates, one cannot doubt that section 1983 was meant to create liability only for acts done with state authority. The enactors did not seek to punish the errant officer who misuses his power. Their purpose was to prevent the enforcement of discriminatory laws by making those who perform that task civilly liable to those whose rights are violated. To determine whether a plaintiff has a cause of action under section 1983, one must focus on the depriving act, not on the status of the actor. The focal inquiry is "under color of *what* law" was this deprivation accomplished, for the illegal law is the real target of the section. If such a law cannot be identified, if no state law has authorized the defendant's actions, there is no target for section 1983 liability and a claim for relief under the statute does not lie.

III. A Return to the Original Understanding

Having discerned the primary purpose of section 1983 and the intended meaning of the "under color of" language, the stage is set for an exploration of each of the various elements of a claim for relief under the statute and a reconstruction of the original understanding of its operation. The result is a consistent, comprehensive model of section 1983, free from the inconsistencies of its current jurisprudence. Section 1983 imposes liability upon

A. Every person who,
B. acting under color of
C. any statute, ordinance, regulation, custom, or usage of any state,
D. subjects, or causes to be subjected, another person to the deprivation
E. of any rights, privileges, or immunities secured by the Constitution and laws.

This part of the article will review the current treatment of these elements and present the correct interpretation of each as suggested by the original understanding. It will also explore two other issues relevant to the nature of a section 1983 claim for relief: the qualified good-faith immunity enjoyed by certain state officials and the problem of parallel state remedies.

A. *Every Person*

Three categories of "persons" are amenable to suit as defendants under section 1983: private persons (individuals and corporations), public officials, and local governmental entities (municipalities and counties). The current doctrines concerning the potential liability of each category of defendants have developed separately. Under the original understanding, however, all can be analyzed under a unified doctrine.

1. *Private Persons*

Section 1983 is not limited on its face to state officials, even though the debates focused almost entirely on their potential liability. In *Adickes v. S.H. Kress & Co.*, the Court held that private persons may be liable under section 1983, if there is sufficient nexus between the act of the private person and the state to satisfy the fourteenth amendment's state action requirement.

The analysis of the liability of private persons, however, should not focus solely on the state action doctrine as in *Adickes*. There may be few instances in which a private person can act under color of a state law—that is, with the authority of a law or custom—and state action may indeed have to be shown if the claimed deprivation involves a right protected by the fourteenth amendment, but the first element of section 1983 liability, whether the defendant is a "person" within the meaning of the statute, is satisfied regardless of the defendant's status.

2. *Public Officials*

Under current case law, any acts of a public official are automatically under color of a state law. Every state and local officer is a person acting under color of a state law simply by virtue of his public position; his section 1983 liability is identical to his fourteenth amendment liability. Under the proper analysis, however, his mere presence in office does not place his action under color of a state law. Instead, the official action must be authorized by a particular state law or custom. "Under color of" has a specific meaning, and the conduct of public officials must be considered separately from the offices they hold in light of that meaning.

The use of "state action" analysis to determine whether an official is a person acting under color of a state law creates an eleventh amendment problem. A suit against a state officer, if based on acts he committed in his "official capacity," logically should be considered a suit against the state and thus be barred by the eleventh amendment. The eleventh amendment difficulty is partially circumvented in state action analysis by use of the "individual capacity" concept announced in *Ex parte Young.* The Court held there that a state officer who violates federal law is "stripped of his official . . . character" by such an illegal act and becomes amenable to suit as an individual. Thus, even though the wrongful act of a state official is deemed to be state action for fourteenth amendment purposes, it is ironically deemed not to be state action for eleventh amendment purposes.

The need for the awkward *Young* fiction disappears when "state action" analysis is avoided and the officer and his act are properly considered under separate headings. Congress has the power under section 5 of the fourteenth amendment to abrogate the eleventh amendment immunity of the states. Thus, even if state officials normally enjoy eleventh amendment immunity, Congress, in passing section 1983 to enforce the fourteenth amendment, certainly intended to limit that immunity when state officials act under color of a state law to violate federally protected rights. Because the "official capacity" of the actor is not a primary concern under the original understanding, the *Young* fiction is functionally irrelevant. A public official is a "person" under section 1983. If the official uses a state law to deprive another of his protected rights, the official should be liable under section 1983, the eleventh amendment notwithstanding.

3. *Local Governmental Entities*

Monell v. Department of Social Services reversed *Monroe v. Pape* by holding that local governmental units were "persons" within the meaning of the statute and could be liable if the officer causing the deprivation of an individual's rights acted pursuant to official policy. The Court was careful to limit municipal liability under section 1983 by providing only for direct, and not for vicarious, liability. A municipality causes the deprivation, as required by section 1983, by its promulgation or adoption of a policy that prescribes the officer's conduct.

The local policy does not necessarily satisfy the requirement of action under color of a state law, however. After all, the proper target of section 1983 is the enabling state statute—one that might, for instance, have given the local unit too much discretion in forming local policy. Thus, the analysis does not end simply because the defendant is a local governmental entity with a policy behind the deprivation; state law must also have authorized the defendant's conduct.

B. *Acting Under Color of [a State Law]*

The requirement that deprivations of federal rights occur under color of a state law is the centerpiece of section 1983 and the primary prerequisite for its invocation. It is therefore disturbing that the Court's treatment of the phrase since 1961 has so blunted the phrase's original precision. Review of the current usage of the phrase shows that the Court has applied divergent constructions to it, some of which are tailored to the particular identity and status of the defendant and several of which are incompletely developed.

The concept of state action for the purposes of the fourteenth amendment is deeply engrained within the current understanding of the section 1983 phrase. This entanglement is the natural outcome of the Court's adoption in *Monroe* of the phrase's construction as announced in *United States v. Classic,* which was itself borrowed from the *Ex parte Virginia* construction of what the fourteenth amendment "must mean." The concepts have become so enmeshed that the Court's shorthand for the statutory phrase—"under color of law"—has been used in place of "state action" in cases outside of the section 1983 context. Consequently, whenever the defendant in a section 1983 suit is a state official, his conduct, which almost always constitutes state action, is likewise almost always held to be under color of a state law. This relationship holds true whether the conduct was authorized by or violated state law.

Although the cases are simple if the defendant is a state official, the Court has had more difficulty in applying the under color of a state law requirement to cases where the defendant is a private person. The seminal case in this regard is *Adickes v. S.H. Kress & Co.*; the most recent is *Lugar v. Edmondson Oil Co.* Together, these cases show the breadth of situations in which a private person can act under color of a state law—in both cases a mere finding of state action satisfied that requirement.

Adickes involved a store owner who refused service to the plaintiff, a white, because she was in the company of blacks. The plaintiff had two theories under which section 1983 would cover the behavior of the store owner, a private party. First, she alleged that the store owner had conspired with local police to discriminate. The Court agreed, holding that the state officials' participation in the conspiracy, unlawfully or not, satisfied the state action requirement, and that this same participation satisfied the under color of a state law requirement. The Court followed the "joint activity" rule announced in *United States v. Price,* which was a criminal prosecution under 18 U.S.C. § 242.

The plaintiff's second theory was that the private defendant, acting alone, had discriminated under color of "a custom of the community." After defining "custom," the Court concluded that state action is present in private discrimination when the State compels that discrimination. If the plaintiff could show that the defendant's "refusal to serve her was motivated by [a] state-enforced custom, she will have made out a claim under § 1983." Although the Court never discussed the under color of a state law requirement in the context of this second allegation, the clear implication is that an act motivated by a compelling state law or custom is performed under color of a state law.

In *Lugar v. Edmondson Oil Co.,* the Court attempted to clarify the relationship between the section 1983 requirement of action under color of state law and the fourteenth amendment requirement of state action. Writing for the Court, Justice White noted that, although the two requirements had often been treated as identical, they are "separate areas of inquiry." Nevertheless, the Court held that, at least in fourteenth amendment cases, if the challenged conduct constituted state action, "then that conduct was also action under color of state law." Consequently, the Court applied a state action test to the private defendant's use of a state prejudgment seizure statute that allegedly failed to provide due process. Because the seizure was authorized by statute and had to be performed by state officials, the Court found sufficient joint participation with state officials to make the private defendant a state actor. Therefore, the Court found state action and, *a fortiori,* action under color of law.

These two cases demonstrate the Court's belief that a private person acts under color of a state law whenever he "commits" state action. State action exists where state law compels the private individual's act, where the private individual joins in the authorized or unauthorized act of state officials, or where the private individual properly invokes a state-created procedure that requires the aid of state officials. Nevertheless, the Court has suggested that the reverse is not true, that state action is only a subset of the statutory requirement. The Court made this suggestion in a footnote in *Lugar* that referred to, but did not endorse, a statement made in *Adickes* that "under color of state law means nothing more than that the individual act 'with the knowledge of and pursuant to that statute.'" If this really is the definition of "under color of" a state law, it cannot be reconciled with the *Monroe* holding; officers who violate state law certainly do not act "with knowledge of and pursuant to that" law. One wonders whether the Court meant to provide two definitions: one tied to a state action concept, and one related to the actual words of the statute.

The relationship between state action and action under color of state law is even more confusing if the defendant is a municipality. *Monell* supplied the following construction of "under color," which apparently shows how the phrase applies to municipalities: Section 1983 "plainly imposes liability on a government that, *under color of some official policy,* 'causes' an employee to violate another's constitutional rights." Thus, it seems that municipalities act, according to *Monell,* under color of the laws and policies that they themselves promulgate.

This review of the current law reveals that the Court has been unable to focus on a comprehensive strategy for applying the phrase "under color of" state law. When the term is given a single appropriate definition, however, its application is much simpler.

Although nearly everything that a state official (or a municipality) does will constitute state action, not everything he (or it) does will satisfy the under color of law requirement. Only actions taken pursuant to state law or custom will meet this requirement. Similarly, not every action by a private person in conjunction with a state official, although state action, is under color of a state law. Only joint activities done pursuant to a state law or custom satisfy the section 1983 requirement. Thus, the Court was wrong in *Lugar* to satisfy the under color of requirement with a finding of state action. Conversely, private persons may act under color of or pursuant to state law without performing state action or having any nexus with the state. The Court in *Lugar* seemed to be reaching for this realization, but it has not yet dealt squarely with this issue.

1. *Individuals Acting Under Color of Law*

Section 1983 is most commonly applied to the intentional act of an individual line officer. The proper application of the "under color of" standard to the actions of such officers can be illustrated with five types of state laws. In each case, whether the deprivation caused by the officer was under color of a state law depends upon the character and content of the state law that initiates and informs the officer's conduct. These same principles apply equally to cases where the defendant is a private person.

a. Laws Requiring Unconstitutional Behavior

If the state law explicitly provides that the official *must* act in an unconstitutional fashion, any action taken by the official that results in the deprivation of constitutionally secured rights is under color of such state law. For example, a state law that requires officials to refuse licenses to Asian-American applicants, or to consider qualification criteria oriented to race or national origin in making licensing decisions, both requires the official to act unconstitutionally and renders the official's action under color of state law. Similarly, if a state law or municipal ordinance instructs police officers to conduct unreasonable body cavity searches of persons arrested for minor traffic violations, the officers' conduct is under color of such law.

b. Laws Allowing Unconstitutional Behavior

A similar conclusion would apply to a state law that explicitly allows a state officer to violate the Constitution or federal laws. If the state law provides that the official *may* refuse licenses to Asian-American applicants or *may* take race or national origin into account, or if the state law or municipal ordinance *allows* police officers to use excessive force in arresting suspects, then such conduct is under color of such laws.

c. Laws Granting Unlimited Power

If the state law grants unfettered discretion to an official, allowing him to use whatever decisionmaking criteria he wishes, the official's refusal of licenses to qualified Asian-American applicants is under color of such state law because the state has conferred the absolute discretion. Similarly, if the statute gives police officers unfettered discretion to decide how much force to use in making arrests, any exercise of force that violates arrestees' constitutional rights would constitute action under color of a state law.

d. Laws Requiring Constitutional Behavior

By contrast, if the state law provides guidelines for an official's actions that require adherence to the Constitution or laws of the United States, any conduct by the official that violates the Constitution or laws is not authorized by such state law—even if the state fails to provide an enforcement mechanism to deter or to remedy violations of the state law. A discriminatory application of a non-discriminatory law is not action under color of a state law. Because the actions of the thirteen Chicago police officers in *Monroe* violated state and local law prohibiting unreasonable searches, for example, the Court should have held that their conduct was not under color of a state law, even though it was committed under color of office or badge of authority. Similarly, if a state licensing law requires a state officer to license all qualified applicants, and if the qualification criteria prohibit consideration of race and national origin, the officer's failure to license qualified Asian-Americans is not authorized by law and is not under color of law.

The foregoing analysis raises the spectre of the undesirable result that the more severe the conduct, the more likely it is to escape section 1983 liability. When a police officer arrests someone, the less force he uses, the more likely it becomes that he is acting within the discretion conferred by state or local law, and therefore, the more likely that he will be sued under section 1983 in federal court because his conduct is under color of a state law. On the other hand, the worse the officer's conduct is—the more severe the beating—the greater the likelihood that he has violated state law or exceeded his authorized discretion, and therefore, the more likely that he cannot be sued in federal court because the act was not committed under color of a state law. This anomaly of "dark alley" forum shopping by police officers who may prefer to be sued in state rather than federal court will exist only so long as defense attorneys perceive that state courts will not vindicate federal rights as effectively as federal courts. State courts are institutionally as competent to adjudicate federal question claims as federal courts, and should be prepared to fashion effective relief when presented with egregious deprivations of federally protected rights.

e. Laws Silent Regarding the Challenged Conduct

Finally, if state law is silent on a subject, neither authorizing the deprivation nor prohibiting it, the unconstitutional actions of a line officer are ordinarily not under color of a state law. When state law fails to tell the officer how to act properly and when his superiors give him no direction, it may at first seem desirable to deem his conduct under color of law in order to grant the victim a remedy. Nonetheless, section 1983 does not "deal with the incidental evils which attend upon republican government," but with evils that have their source in unconstitutional laws. When the law is silent, that silence is not an evil at which section 1983 is aimed. The section responds to the enforcement of discriminatory laws, not to the failure to create and to enforce benign laws. More directly, the situation fails to satisfy the textual requirement—one cannot answer the question "under color of *what* law."

The state and its officials may not hide behind such silence, however. Section 1983 applies when the law makers' silence is part of a pattern of unconstitutional activity. Law makers should be deemed to have adopted the customs and usages that they have suffered to occur, and law users should be deemed to act under color of such customs or usages for section 1983 purposes.

2. Negligence

If the conduct must be authorized by law or custom to be actionable under section 1983, may negligent conduct ever be committed under color of a state law? Because the statute requires that the defendant act pursuant to a law or custom, a negligent deprivation will only be actionable if it results from systematic inadequacies in procedures or supervision that allow or contribute to the deprivation. In other words, negligence will be under color of a state law only if a statute, regulation, custom, or usage establishes inadequate procedural safeguards, or those that virtually ensure that a negligent deprivation will occur; forbids officials to act willfully or recklessly, but countenances negligent behavior; or confers complete discretion regarding whether to establish procedural safeguards or adequate supervision and if established, what they should be. On the other hand, if the deprivation of rights results from individual negligence that was not commanded or allowed by law, regulation, custom, or usage, the deprivation is not under color of a state law and no liability under section 1983 attaches. Absent a state law that mandates negligent conduct, the negligence of officers that deprives a person of his consitutional rights is not under color of a state law.

In *Parratt v. Taylor,* for example, had the deprivation of the prisoner's property resulted from systematic deficiencies in the handling of inmates' mail, the loss would have been under color of a state law. If a municipal building inspector driving a city-owned vehicle on his way to inspect a building runs a red light and strikes another car, he has acted within the scope of his municipal office to deprive someone of constitutionally protected interests. His action is not, however, under color of a state law, even if state law or municipal policy authorizes him to drive to his building inspections in city owned cars, unless such law or policy also allows him to drive negligently.

These last examples raise an additional question: must the defendant know or intend that he is acting under color of a state law? The primary purpose of section 1983 is deterrence. A state official cannot be deterred from enforcing an unconstitutional law if he does not know that he is enforcing it. Thus, if a state official knows that he is carrying out a state policy or custom, his deed is actionable under section 1983. If the official pleads ignorance of the procedures, the plaintiff would have to prove that the deed was done with knowledge of the procedure or custom.

3. Municipalities Acting Under Color of Law

The Forty-second Congress apparently believed that governmental units, as law "givers" or law "makers," could not be reached by federal power exercised pursuant to section 5 of the fourteenth amendment. Therefore, because Congress did not believe it could enact legislation to deter law makers from promulgating unconstitutional laws, it sought to deter those who enforce or wield state laws, *i.e.,* the "users" of illegal state laws, from using them to deprive others of federally secured rights. Municipalities, however, are both law makers and (state) law users. It is necessary, therefore, to ascertain whether a city can act under color of a state law in order to establish direct municipal liability under section 1983.

In *Monell v. Department of Social Services,* a municipal agency required each pregnant employee to take a leave of absence before it was medically necessary. If state law authorized the municipal policy, the city acted under color of such law in promulgating the policy. If the policy was not authorized by state law, the city did not act under color of a state law.

The facts of *Home Telephone & Telegraph Co. v. City of Los Angeles* offer a further example. California law apparently had given cities discretion to fix rates for public utilities, and Los Angeles was alleged to have enacted a confiscatory telephone rate ordinance in violation of both the state and federal constitutions. Although the state statute permitting the city to fix rates for utilities was unconstitutional only as applied by the city, the city's conduct should be deemed under color of the state law because that law allowed the city, without violating the statute, to act unconstitutionally. If, by contrast, the state statute had provided that cities within the state could not fix confiscatory rates, the ordinance passed by Los Angeles would not have been under color of a state law.

Suppose that an unconstitutional city ordinance were enacted prohibiting the peaceable assembly of three or more persons. To be liable directly under section 1983, the municipality must have passed the ordinance pursuant to a state grant of authority or discretion. If state law provides only that municipalities have general powers to ensure the health, safety, and welfare of their populace consistent with the federal and state constitutions, the city has not acted under color of such state law in enacting the unconstitutional ordinance. (The municipal officer who enforces the ordinance does act under color of the ordinance and would be amenable to suit under section 1983.) By contrast, if the state law provides that cities may act in any way that they deem advisable to protect the health, safety, and welfare of their people, the same municipal ordinance would have been enacted under color of that state law.

The practical result of the reinterpretation of direct municipal liability in accordance with the original understanding is that cities will rarely be directly liable. This result appears anomalous only to the analyst imposing the twentieth-century concern for remedies onto the structure of a nineteenth-century statute aimed at deterrence. The statute was intended to reach law users. Local governmental units, as law givers, were not generally contemplated as section 1983 defendants. Although modern jurisprudence requires a remedy for every wrong, section 1983 fulfills its intended purpose of deterring officials from carrying out unconstitutional laws and policies without imposing direct liability on municipal governments.

C. Any Statute, Ordinance, Regulation, Custom, or Usage of Any State

This element is given short shrift in the section 1983 case law, especially that concerning the liability of state officials. This is the logical result of equating under color of state law with state action; this element becomes mere surplusage. Ironically, under the original understanding, this phrase is the true heart of the statute. The laws that authorized the deprivations of federally protected rights were the special target of and the primary impetus for the legislation. Consequently, in stating a cause of action, the section 1983 plaintiff should be required not only to allege that the defendant acted under color of law in the sense described in the preceding section, but also to allege just what law authorized the deed.

Although the proper interpretation of this provision is fairly straightforward, the meaning of "custom or usage" is somewhat elusive. *Adickes v. S.H. Kress & Co.* was the first Supreme Court case to deal squarely with the definition of "custom." By a five-to-three majority, the Court held that "a 'custom, or usage, of [a] state' for purposes of § 1983 must have the force of law by virtue of persistent practices of state officials." Justices Douglas and Brennan would have applied a broader standard, requiring only that the custom reflect "a widespread and longstanding practice [among the people of a State] regarded as prescribing norms for conduct and supported by community sentiment or sanctions." They would read the words "of any State" as merely a geographical description of the community wherein the custom exists.

In 1871 Congress was all but silent on the separate meaning of the phrase "custom or usage"; only three Senators referred to the phrase. Senator Davis spoke of the practice of giving whites superior public accommodations and predicted failure for any federal efforts to undermine these customs, "to humiliate and degrade the white population . . . to the level of the negro race." By contrast, the two other senators appeared to support a construction similar to that adopted in *Adickes.* Senator Thurman, an opponent of section 1983, said in passing that the section referred to "either statute law or 'custom or usage' which has become common law." During the 1866 debates, Senator Trumbull referred to customs prevailing in a community, using as his example the practice of providing harsher punishments for blacks than for whites. Because such a practice would be perpetuated by state officials, probably pursuant to discretionary sentencing laws, it has the force of law. The fact that Congress frequently paraphrased the entire "under color of" list in terms of either "law" or "authority" is more enlightening.

The paraphrases and the explanations of Senators Thurman and Trumbull support the majority's position in *Adickes*: the custom must in some way be supported by state (in the political sense) authority, although the state need not actively enforce the custom. Thus, "custom" may include a practice of officers that, although not authorized by positive law, is nonetheless so pervasive and unchecked within the community that it has the force of law. By contrast, practices of which the state has no reason to be aware or those that the state is making a good faith effort to restrain cannot be said to be customs. Section 1983 is aimed at the state authority implied by acceptance of a widespread illegal activity. This view of "custom" supports Justice Frankfurter's observation in his *Monroe* dissent that the Chicago police might have been acting under color of law, on the grounds that a ten-hour detention on "open charges" was the normal practice among the Chicago police, regulations to the contrary notwithstanding.

The focus of a section 1983 suit should be the state law or custom that authorized the defendant's act. Although the defendant may have also violated some *other* state law, the suit should not be dismissed so long as there is an authorizing target law. For example, the city in *Home Telephone* acted under color of the state law allowing it to set utility rates, even though the city concurrently violated the state constitution. This "conflict of laws" is most likely to occur in the custom cases and in the cases in which the authorizing law is a grant of broad discretion.

The conflict of laws issue raises the additional question of whether section 1983 creates liability if the defendant's action is authorized only by the state constitution. The enumeration of state "laws" in the statute itself does not include constitutional provisions, and this omission from such a detailed list raises a presumption that Congress did not intend to include state constitutions. The legislative history provides no definitive answer. Nevertheless, supported by the statute's primary purpose, I would argue that state constitutional authority is often sufficient to satisfy the "under color of" requirement. First, many constitutional authority cases may be analyzed under the rubric of state-supported custom. Second, a defendant may properly be said to have acted under color of a state constitutional provision if that provision is self-executing and confers upon him a positive duty or responsibility.

D. *Subjects, or Causes to be Subjected, Another Person to the Deprivation*

Since *Monroe v. Pape,* section 1983 liability has been "read against the background of tort liability that makes a man responsible for the natural consequences of his actions." This premise affects two potential elements of the plaintiff's prima facie case: the defendant's state of mind and causation.

Prior to 1981, substantial commentary and case law debated whether negligent conduct would suffice to state a valid section 1983 claim. After twice avoiding the question, the Court held in *Parratt* that the prison officials' negligence in misplacing the prisoner's personal property was sufficient culpability under the section. Section 1983, the Court said, "affords a 'civil remedy' for deprivations of federally protected rights caused by persons acting under color of state law without any express requirement of a particular state of mind." The *Parratt* result is clearly correct; the language of section 1983 contains no explicit culpability standard. By contrast, the criminal counterpart to the section requires that the deprivation be accomplished "willfully."

State of mind is, nonetheless, an important factor in determining section 1983 liability. As has been shown, the defendant must have intended to act, or known he was acting, pursuant to the state law at issue, and he will be held liable for negligent conduct only when the negligence itself is authorized. Additionally, a particular state of mind may be required to make out a violation of the constitutional right involved. The Court held in *Parratt* that negligent conduct may violate the due process clause, but the eighth amendment, for example, protects against "cruel and unusual punishments inflicted" and implies by its terms that the punishment must be inflicted actively, not passively. Consequently, the Supreme Court has held that the "infliction of . . . unnecessary suffering" upon state prisoners by denying them medical care violates the eighth amendment only where such pain is inflicted through the "deliberate indifference" of prison officials to the serious medical needs of prisoners. In contrast, the fourth amendment establishes a right to be free from unreasonable searches and seizures, not just from intentionally unconstitutional searches and seizures.

The issue of causation is fairly straightforward with one interesting quirk. Generally the plaintiff can show that an individual defendant actually and proximately caused the deprivation. Where there is difficulty, as in some negligence situations, the issue can be resolved following normal tort principles in accordance with the rule from *Monroe.* When the defendant is a municipality, sued directly under section 1983, causation is less apparent. Such a defendant cannot subject a plaintiff to a deprivation in and of itself; it must act through others. Thus, the clause "or causes to be subjected" must be applied. The Court in *Monell* seized upon this clause to formulate its limitation on municipal liability. The Court held that in order to "cause" a deprivation the municipality must sanction the act of the individual through its official policy. If the individual is not executing official local policy, the local body cannot be said to have caused the act or the deprivation. Of course, the municipality's causal fault does not end the analysis. The city must also be shown to have acted under color of a state law itself.

E. *Of Any Right, Privilege, or Immunity Secured by the (i) Constitution or (ii) Laws of the United States*

Although the first four elements describe the type of conduct that section 1983 makes actionable, this final provision designates what section 1983 protects—the fundamental liberties secured by the Constitution and laws of the United States. There seems to be little justification for not construing this element as broadly as the Constitution allows. Indeed, when culpable conduct is properly limited to conduct authorized by the state, restriction of this element, for reasons of federalism, judicial economy, or the like, is unnecessary. The need for strong constitutional guarantees is manifest. Justice Frankfurter observed in the context of the fourth amendment, even as he advocated a narrower construction of section 1983 in *Monroe,* that "[m]odern totalitarianisms have been a stark reminder . . . that the kicked-in door is the symbol of a rule of fear and violence fatal to institutions founded on respect for the integrity of man."

The concept of state action will apply only to this element; it will have to be proven only if the underlying right enjoys fourteenth amendment protection. If the right flows from a federal statute or from a constitutional provision that does not have a state action requirement, such as the thirteenth amendment, a valid section 1983 claim exists even without a showing of state action.

F. *Judicially-Created Limitations on Section 1983 Liability*

1. *Qualified Good-Faith Immunity*

Certain state officials sued under section 1983 currently can claim an immunity if they neither knew nor reasonably should have known that their acts would deprive someone of a federally protected right. It is uncertain whether defendants need to prove the subjective component of the immunity, their lack of knowledge of the violation. With this question settled, the qualified immunity could be a valuable tool in section 1983 litigation under the original understanding.

The Court did not derive the good-faith immunity from the 1871 debates; it was an adaptation of common-law absolute immunities that existed for other state officials in 1871. Recognizing the importance of encouraging public servants to fulfill their duties without concern about personal liability for mistakes, the Court immunized only those officials who had no clear notice that they could be treading upon federal rights. This would include situations where a constitutional right has been newly developed by the Court, or where it is factually unclear that rights were violated.

The doctrine of qualified immunity for conduct in reasonable good faith could be used to fulfill the primary function of section 1983—to attack the improper state law—while protecting the innocent middleman who acted under color of law with no reason to know that the law was improper. A court could discharge both purposes by adjudicating the prima facie claim, holding that the state law or custom was indeed improper, and then upholding the affirmative defense exculpating the faultless defendant. With the impropriety of the state law settled, the deterrent function of section 1983 would be given full force because the knowledge that the law violates federal rights would be imputed to all future actors.

As a practical matter, however, this dual function may not be so neatly served. Because the immunity is likely to be easier to determine than the plaintiff's constitutional claim, the courts will prefer to dispose of the affirmative defense first, probably on summary judgment. If the Court has removed the subjective element from the immunity test, it has made early termination of the action easier by making the defense easier to prove. Because a ruling in favor of the defendant would be dispositive, the court would never reach the underlying claim. Indeed, this sequence appears to be what the Court hoped for in *Harlow v. Fitzgerald,* finding great value in the quick termination of "insubstantial lawsuits" against public officials. The courts will need to find a mechanism to put the states on notice that the challenged law or custom is improper and to prevent a second successful use of the immunity for an offense under the same law. Courts could rule, for instance, that prior claims against the state law preclude a subsequent good-faith belief in the law's validity.

The Court has speculated on the application of the good-faith immunity to private defendants. Seven Justices have concurred in opinions suggesting such an extension. With the original understanding's confirmation of the validity of suits against private actors, such an extension could serve the same purposes. Of course, the underlying interest of promoting the unrestrained execution of the duties of public office is not advanced by immunizing private defendants, but other, perhaps equally important interests, such as promoting reasonable faith in state laws, may be protected. In these cases, the extension of the immunity to private defendants may be warranted.

2. *Parallel State Court Remedies*

In 1961 Justice Douglas concluded that "[i]t is no answer that the State has a law which if enforced would give relief. The federal remedy [of section 1983] is supplementary to the state remedy, and the latter need not be first sought and refused before the federal one is invoked." Eighteen years later, Justice Rehnquist responded in his dissent in *City of Columbus v. Leonard:* "[T]he time may now be ripe for a reconsideration of the Court's conclusion in *Monroe* that 'the federal remedy is supplementary to the state remedy, and the latter need not be first sought and refused before the federal one is invoked.'"

The existence of a state remedy to redress the deprivations committed by the police was of great concern to the Court in *Monroe.* Justice Douglas used the "supplementary remedy" theory to justify the extension of section 1983 to acts by state officers that violate state law. As we have seen, however, none of the requisites for a section 1983 action involves consideration of the availability of a state remedy. The supplementary nature of a section 1983 action therefore lends nothing to our understanding of whether the statute reaches unauthorized conduct. Justice Harlan recognized this, if Justice Douglas did not, and tried to justify the majority's conclusion by arguing that Congress would not have intended to supplement state remedies for authorized conduct and not those for unauthorized conduct. Even this argument, however, is based on policy considerations and not on statutory construction.

The impetus to find that section 1983 reaches unauthorized conduct stems from a view of it solely as a remedial provision. If Congress' only concern were to give redress to the aggrieved individual, an adequate state remedy would undercut the need for a federal cause of action. Under a remedial theory, justifying the application of section 1983 to any case where the state provides a remedy becomes a major challenge—one that was unconvincingly met in *Monroe.*

The remedial focus also spawns limitations on section 1983 such as that suggested by Justice Rehnquist in *City of Columbus v. Leonard.* If held not to be supplementary, section 1983 might be altogether abolished; it would be difficult to conceive of any case in which the federal courts could exercise original jurisdiction under the statute. State courts have the jurisdiction to remedy deprivations of federal rights, unauthorized or not, that occur within their states or upon their states' citizens. Thus, state remedies are available. A plaintiff could only bring the federal claim if such remedies were wrongly refused or shown to be inadequate. This result would leave section 1983 a pale shadow of its original substance.

The original understanding answers this dilemma simply. The primary purpose of section 1983 is not solely remedial; it was enacted to deter the enforcement of improper state laws and customs. Providing a remedy against the user of such state laws was a means, not an end. Under this view, the state remedy is irrelevant; to say that the section supplements those remedies is only to state a truism, not a purpose. The only kind of state process that can fulfill the purpose of section 1983 and properly displace a section 1983 action is one that prevents the harm from occurring.

***

Harry A. Blackmun, *Section 1983 and Federal Protection of Individual Rights—Will the Statute Remain Alive or Fade Away?*, 60 New York University Law Review 1 (1985)

I

I suspect that even for those of us who are not lawyers the statute is not an unfamiliar one. It has become increasingly well known as the vehicle or, to put it less sympathetically, the "device" by which a citizen is able to challenge conduct by a state official that he claims has deprived or will deprive him of federal constitutional or statutory rights. Many of the Supreme Court's most significant constitutional decisions of the past generation, such as *Brown v. Board of Education* and the legislative reapportionment cases, were the product of suits brought under § 1983.

At the same time, the statute increasingly has become a source of controversy, a battleground on which is fought much of the continuing debate over the proper role of the federal courts in protecting individual rights. One brand of criticism has focused on the extent to which § 1983 cases are claimed to be overburdening the federal courts. Critics rehearse statistics as to the number of § 1983 actions filed each year, with emphasis on those filed by state prisoners challenging the terms or conditions of their confinement. There appears to be a growing belief that § 1983 actions are likely to be frivolous complaints by litigants who seek to use the statute to convert or bootstrap garden-variety state-law tort claims into federal cases.

A more far-reaching set of complaints concerns the perceived tension between § 1983 and traditional values of American federalism. With increasing frequency, § 1983 actions are condemned as being inconsistent with the thesis that federal courts not interfere with state affairs unless absolutely necessary. Particularly when the statute is used to challenge an action by an official not pursuant to a state policy, critics tend to view § 1983 as a misguided aberration, a left-over of the Supreme Court's allegedly activist period of two decades ago, when, in the view of some, responsible federalism concerns were thrown to the wind.

These perceptions have resulted in demands that § 1983 actions be restricted, both in their number and in their reach. Various proposals for "reform," short of repealing the statute, have been urged. These range from the imposition of an exhaustion requirement to the preclusion of damages awards, thus discouraging the initiation of § 1983 suits. Although many reform proposals have been directed at congressional action, others have been addressed to a judicial audience, with commentators arguing for more restrictive interpretations of § 1983 and its developed doctrinal basis. Perhaps not surprisingly, the latter criticisms have begun to find an echo in the judicial response to § 1983 actions. In particular, recent opinions of the Supreme Court appear to reflect a growing uneasiness with the heretofore pronounced breadth of the statute and, in my view, a tendency to strain otherwise sound doctrines in order to ease the perceived federalism tensions generated by § 1983 actions.

Controversy over the role of § 1983 has been going on for over a century, and it shows no sign of coming to an end. Because I believe it to be an important controversy, not only for lawyers and the courts but also for individual citizens, I think it is worth taking time to try to understand the role § 1983 plays in the protection of individual rights in this country and how this controversial statute came to play that role. I therefore shall pass on to you my thoughts on the current debates, particularly my concern that any restriction of what has become a major symbol of federal protection of basic rights not be made in irresponsible haste.

II

A

One must begin by going to the origins of the statute, for where § 1983 came from casts important light on how far it has come and on what it has become. Most of what I have to say in this recall of history is not at all new, but perhaps it is time to review and consider it seriously—and not unsympathetically—once again.

To appreciate fully the profound revolution in federalism of which § 1983 was a part, it is useful to remember just how limited a role federal law played in protecting individual rights against state governments before the War Between the States. For present purposes, three features of this "prehistory" of § 1983 are important. First, the Federal Constitution provides few substantive protections against oppressive state laws. Apart from § 10 of Article I, which forbids States from, among other things, passing any *ex post facto* law, bill of attainder, or law impairing the obligation of contracts, and apart from the developed application of the Bill of Rights to the States, the Constitution does not directly impose any barrier between the citizen and coercive state power. And even the protections guaranteed by the Bill of Rights, in their literal language, run against only the Federal Government. Second, federal law provided no affirmative remedy for the vindication of those constitutional rights that were specifically expressed and as to which state action was limited. To borrow a well-worn metaphor, the Constitution, as amended by the Bill of Rights, provided a shield rather than a sword. It is because of this that, in the first 70 years of the Republic, many of the Supreme Court's important constitutional decisions came in suits in which defendants sought, on constitutional grounds, to avoid liability, rather than in suits in which plaintiffs sought to obtain damages or injunctive relief for alleged constitutional violations. Third, federal courts had no general jurisdiction over federal claims, constitutional or otherwise. As a result, a litigant who wanted to challenge the constitutionality of state action was remitted to the state courts, unless the happenstance of diversity of citizenship allowed him to place his suit on the federal side. Almost without exception, the Supreme Court's most significant constitutional holdings in the years before the Civil War were reached in cases that came up through the state-court systems.

The War and Reconstruction transformed the legal relations between the Federal Government and the States in each of these three respects. The most obvious change is that which is visible on the face of the Constitution itself—the Thirteenth, Fourteenth, and Fifteenth Amendments, adopted in 1865, 1868, and 1870, respectively. The Thirteenth Amendment abolished slavery; the Fourteenth defined state and national citizenship and granted all persons constitutional rights enforceable against the States; and the Fifteenth prohibited States from denying citizens, on racial grounds, the right to vote. The specific goal of these Amendments was to dismantle the legal framework of slavery and to guarantee freed slaves the same political rights enjoyed by their former masters. The draftsmen of the Fourteenth Amendment, however, chose to speak in general terms that went far beyond the racial concerns of the moment—a decision whose significance, in retrospect, cannot be overstated.

This constitutional assault on the Old South was complemented by a series of statutes, the most significant of which were the several Civil Rights Acts passed between 1866 and 1875. The 1866 Act, which followed on the heels of the Thirteenth Amendment, was the statutory precursor to the Fourteenth Amendment. Section 1 of that Act granted citizenship to all persons born in the United States and provided that all citizens, without regard to color, were entitled to the equal benefit of the laws, including the rights to make and enforce contracts, sue, give evidence, and purchase and own property. Section 2 imposed criminal sanctions on any person who, "under color of any law," deprived any inhabitant of any State or Territory of rights recognized in § 1. Section 3 conferred jurisdiction on federal courts to hear all causes, civil and criminal, affecting persons who were denied or who could not enforce in state courts the rights secured by § 1.

Following the adoption of the Fourteenth Amendment in 1868, Congress reenacted the 1866 Act in the Enforcement Act of 1870, adding additional criminal penalties and specifically providing for jurisdiction in the federal courts over suits alleging racially inspired interference with the right to vote. In the following year came the 1871 Civil Rights Act, aimed specifically at the activities of the Ku Klux Klan. Section 1 of that Act, now § 1983, added civil remedies. It provided a civil remedy for deprivations, under color of state law, of any of the rights, privileges, and immunities secured by the Constitution. Sections 2 and 3 of the Act imposed civil and criminal penalties for conspiracies to deprive persons of constitutional rights. The Act was meant to reach the activity of a person who did not necessarily have the formal authorization of the state government involved, but for which the State either was unwilling or unable to provide a remedy. Finally, the 1875 Civil Rights Act outlawed racial discrimination in places of public accomodation and provided civil and criminal penalties for violation of its provisions.

During the same period, Congress in three significant ways enlarged federal-court jurisdiction. Between 1863 and 1866, Congress expanded removal jurisdiction by allowing removal of cases alleging state interference with civil rights, as well as all criminal and civil suits brought against federal officers for acts committed during the war under the authority of Congress or the President. In 1867, Congress passed a Habeas Corpus Act that for the first time gave federal courts authority to consider the judgments of jurisdictionally competent state courts. Finally, in 1875, Congress created general federal-question jurisdiction in civil actions.

Taken collectively, the Reconstruction Amendments, the Civil Rights Acts, and these new jurisdictional statutes, all emerging from the caldron of the War Between the States, marked a revolutionary shift in the relationship among individuals, the States, and the Federal Government. The Reconstruction Congresses vested individuals with three distinct kinds of protection against state governments, protections that were absent in the prewar structure: federal rights, federal remedies, and federal forums. It bears noting that § 1983 was only one arrow in this large federal quiver. The Supreme Court described the magnitude of the overall change in *Mitchum v. Foster:*

> This legislative history makes evident that Congress clearly conceived that it was altering the relationship between the States and the Nation with respect to the protection of federally created rights; it was concerned that state instrumentalities could not protect those rights; it realized that state officers might, in fact, be antipathetic to the vindication of those rights; and it believed that these failings extended to the state courts.
>
> * * *
>
> Section 1983 was thus a product of a vast transformation from the concepts of federalism that had prevailed in the late 18th century. . . . The very purpose of § 1983 was to interpose the federal courts between the States and the people, as guardians of the people's federal rights—to protect the people from unconstitu-

tional action under color of state law, "whether that action be executive, legislative, or judicial."

The significance of the reach of the Civil Rights Acts and their encroachment on state prerogatives was lost on no one. In debates over the 1866 Act, opponents of the bill described it as "one of the most dangerous that was ever introduced into the Senate of the United States," as proposing to "reform the whole civil and criminal code of every State government," as interfering with the duties of state officials, and as promising to result in a flood of petty cases removed to federal courts. Proponents, in their turn, conceded that its reach was substantial, but insisted that the unwillingness of the States to protect the freedmen or citizens of other States made the bill necessary.

The 1871 Act provoked similar outcries. Describing the bill as a whole, Representative Holman complained that "the jurisdiction of the Federal courts, hitherto confined to questions of national concern, is to invade the provinces of the State courts with new laws and systems of administration." Representative Eldridge found no apparent limit in the bill "beyond which the Federal Government may not go to the exclusion of the heretofore conceded jurisdiction of the States in the redress of the violation of the rights of person and property." Discussing § 1 of the Act, Representative Arthur described it in this way:

> It overrides the reserved powers of the States. It reaches out and draws within the despotic circle of central power all the domestic, internal, and local institutions and offices of the States, and then asserts over them an arbitrary and paramount control as of the rights, privileges, and immunities secured and protected, in a peculiar sense, by the United States in the citizens thereof. Having done this, having swallowed up the States and their institutions, tribunals, and functions, it leaves them the shadow of what they once were.

Section 2 of the Act, authorizing civil and criminal penalties for private conspiracies to deprive individuals of civil rights, was even more controversial. The Democrats saw the bill as an extension of federal authority over common crimes. In the words of Representative Arthur, the Act "absorbs the entire jurisdiction of the States over their local and domestic affairs: the first section as to civil rights and remedies, and the second as to wrongs and punishments."

B

Reconstruction thus established a new legal order that contemplated direct federal intervention in what had been considered to be state affairs, a system in which federal courts were to enforce newly created federal constitutional rights against state officials through civil remedies and criminal sanctions. The story of how this edifice crumbled during the succeeding half-century might be characterized by some as a somber one in American legal history. Even before the Civil Rights Acts found their places on the statute books, critics sharply questioned not only the Acts' expediency but their constitutionality. The crucial issue in this debate was the scope of the authority granted Congress by the Reconstruction Amendments, particularly the Fourteenth. The Radical Republicans, as they were called, defended the bills on the ground that the Fourteenth Amendment had altered the balance between the States and the National Government so that Congress for the first time had the authority to protect life, liberty, and property by legislating directly against offending activity. Moderate Republicans agreed that Congress had the authority, under the Fourteenth Amendment, to reach private action, although they disagreed with the Radicals over the actual scope of the bills. In the Democrats' view, however, the Fourteenth Amendment was simply a remedial measure—it stepped in to protect citizens directly only when the state government itself violated their civil rights.

Although the Radicals won the day in Congress and the Civil Rights Acts went into effect, the Supreme Court arrived at different conclusions about the scope of the authority granted Congress by the Fourteenth Amendment. In short order, the Court acted to declare numerous provisions of the Acts unconstitutional and to render others ineffectual by narrow construction. In 1873, in the *Slaughter-House Cases,* the Court construed the Privileges and Immunities Clause of the Fourteenth Amendment and concluded that the Amendment did not federalize any substantive rights that were not already incidents of national citizenship. The Court then reviewed a series of actions brought under the Civil Rights Acts and held in each that Congress' power under the Amendment was limited to addressing direct encroachment of civil rights by States. *United States v. Cruikshank* invalidated an indictment under the conspiracy section of the 1870 Act. A private conspiracy to violate constitutional rights, in the Court's view, lacked the state action required of legislation passed under the Fourteenth Amendment.

Similarly, in *United States v. Harris,* the Court found no constitutional basis for the criminal conspiracy section of the 1871 Act, because the section was aimed at private action. In the *Civil Rights Cases,* the Court invalidated the 1875 Act's prohibition of private racial discrimination in accommodations and public conveyances. The legislation could not be upheld under the Fourteenth Amendment, the Court ruled, because it was not aimed at state action. Nor could it be upheld under the Thirteenth, because even though that Amendment reached private action, denial of admission to a public place was not a badge or incident of slavery. Only the first Justice Harlan dissented. He would have found the statute supportable under the Thirteenth Amendment. More relevant to our purposes, his view of the necessary state action was less strict. The fact that most of the public accommodations at issue in the *Civil Rights Cases* were licensed by the States satisfied the requirement. He added the following prophetic conclusion:

> I may be permitted to say that if the recent amendments are so construed that Congress may not, in its own discretion, and independently of the action or non-action of the States, provide, by legislation of a direct character, for the security of rights created by the national Constitution; if it be adjudged that the obligation to protect the fundamental privileges and immunities granted by the Fourteenth Amendment to citizens residing in the several States, rests primarily, not on the nation, but on the States; if it be further adjudged that individuals and corporations, exercising public functions, or wielding power under public authority, may, without liability to direct primary legislation on the part of Congress, make the race of citizens the ground for denying them that equality of civil rights which the Constitution ordains as a principle of republican citizenship; then, not only the foundations upon which the national supremacy has always securely rested will be materially disturbed, but we shall enter upon an era of constitutional law, when the rights of freedom and American citizenship cannot receive from the nation that efficient protection which heretofore was unhesitatingly accorded to slavery and the rights of the master.

There is some debate about the extent to which the Supreme Court's 19th-century interpretations of the Fourteenth Amendment and the Civil Rights Acts really were inconsistent with then-prevailing notions of the proper relationship between the States and the Federal Government. The fact remains, nevertheless, that with a few quick thrusts, the Court cut the heart out of the Civil Rights Acts. Fundamental rights of citizenship were placed beyond the protection of the Fourteenth Amendment by the Court's narrow reading of that Amendment's Privileges and Immunities Clause. And the uncontrolled private abuses that had so concerned the majority in Congress apparently could not constitutionally be reached by the federal courts, since those private abuses did not constitute "state action." By the Court's decisions, major provisions of the Acts either were declared unconstitutional or were emasculated. Although the Court did not address § 1 of the 1871 Act and thus never held that the "color of state law" requirement of that section and of § 2 of the 1866 Act was limited to official state action, the tribunal's thinking and direction were clear. Those sections that were not struck down were largely forgotten.

There is another reason why the Civil Rights Acts slipped out of sight. The political climate changed and the harsh grip of the Radicals over the Southern States loosened. The Democrats made gradual gains in Congress. In 1875, in the last half of the second Grant administration, control of the House passed to them. By 1879 they controlled both the House and the Senate. In 1871, Congress repealed the requirement that former Confederate soldiers take an oath of allegiance to the Union and disavow their disloyal acts. In 1872, it restored full political rights to most of the former Confederates. Senator Lucius Q. C. Lamar of Mississippi, later an Associate Justice of the Supreme Court and the subject of a chapter in John F. Kennedy's 1956 book, *Profiles in Courage,* expressed the growing sentiment toward reconciliation. After the death of Republican Senator Charles Sumner of Massachusetts, Lamar in 1874 delivered in the House of Representatives a eulogy for Sumner that marked a significant change in attitude in both the North and the South toward the task at hand. According to Lamar, Summer,

> in life believed that all occasion for strife and distrust between the North and South had passed away . . . . Is not that the common sentiment, or if it is not ought it not to be, of the great mass of our people, North and South? . . . Shall we not, over the honored remains of . . . this earnest pleader for the exercise of human tenderness and charity, lay aside the concealments which serve only to perpetuate misunderstandings and distrust, and frankly confess that on both sides we most earnestly desire to be one . . .in feeling and in heart? . . .

* * *

> Would that the spirit of the illustrious dead whom we lament today could speak from the grave to both parties to this deplorable discord in tones which should reach each and every heart throughout this broad territory, "My countrymen, *know* one another, and you will *love* one another."

It indeed was time to rebuild and put old wounds behind. With the move toward reconciliation, however, the Nation lost the urgency of its zeal to protect the individual rights and freedoms for which the war in part had been fought. In the Revised Statutes of 1873, the Civil Rights Acts were divided and scattered. Federal prosecutions under the Acts declined precipitously. In 1873, 1,304 prosecutions were brought, 1,271 of which were in the South. By 1878, that figure dropped to 25. In 1877, Congress would have repealed much of the 1870 Enforcement Act, but President Hayes vetoed the measure. In 1894 and 1909, Congress repealed a number of the provisions of the Civil Rights Acts, including, in the former year, 39 sections of the Revised Statutes dealing with the right to vote.

Reconciliation grew into a nationwide amnesia about the events of the Civil War and Reconstruction. In 1876, President Hayes agreed to withdraw federal troops from the South. Almost immediately, Negroes were disenfranchised. In 1890, Mississippi passed a new suffrage law, imposing a $2 poll tax and exhaustive literacy requirements. In 1895, South Carolina did the same, adding to the list an imposing property requirement. Louisiana passed a similar statute, with a grandfather clause and prohibitive education and property requirements. By 1910, every Southern State had followed suit. The statutes served their purpose well. In 1896, 130,344 Negroes were registered in Louisiana. By 1900, only 5,320 remained on the books.

The first segregation laws were passed in 1892, requiring railroads to assign Negro passengers to separate cars. Jim Crow spread from passenger trains to streetcars, restaurants, washrooms, and residential communities. Lynch mobs reared their ugly heads. One author reports records of 3,000 lynchings from 1883 to 1903, with few if any reprisals against the participants.

Thus, as the 20th century dawned, the Nation's commitment to civil rights lay in remnants. It was our Dark Age of Civil Rights. For the first 40 years of this century, the only judicial relief available was in suits involving official action denying Negroes the right to vote. Whatever doubts there may have been about the intent of the Reconstruction Congresses, there was no denying Congress' purpose to ensure Negroes the right to vote. Even if there were any doubts about the reach of the Fourteenth Amendment, the Fifteenth stood as a certain basis for federal action to protect voting rights. In addition, the challenges almost always addressed only official state policy.

The significant cases are few and can be quickly recounted. In 1915, the Court relied on the Fifteenth Amendment to strike down "grandfather clauses" in the suffrage laws of Maryland and Oklahoma. In 1917, the Court struck down, as an infringement of property rights without due process of law, a racially restrictive city ordinance. In 1927, the Court granted injunctive relief under § 1983 and the Fourteenth Amendment against enforcement of a Texas statute which prevented Negroes from voting in Democratic primaries. Five years later, the Court granted a damages award against state officials who effectuated the same white primary, even though the State had shifted responsibility to an executive committee. Finally, in 1939, the Court granted damages under § 1983 and the Fifteenth Amendment against officials who had sought to avoid the earlier ruling against Oklahoma's grandfather clause by repealing the clause but giving Negroes only 12 days to register to vote after the repeal.

As one can see, from the 1890's to the 1940's, the Civil Rights Acts lay virtually dormant. Although they were called on occasionally to remedy the most blatant affronts to the Reconstruction Amendments, little thought was given to utilizing them to address other incidents of slavery.

Outside the courts, however, the Nation was not quiescent. Gradually and increasingly, public sentiment was growing against the continuing second-class status of Negroes. In the summer of 1905, a small group of Negroes met at Niagara Falls committed, as was stated a year later, to obtaining "every single right that belongs to a freeborn American, political, civil and social," and vowing that "until we get these rights we will never cease to protest and assail the ears of America." Shortly after that meeting, race riots in Springfield, Illinois served as the catalyst for a group of concerned white leaders who organized the first meeting of the National Association for the Advancement of Colored People.

The organization's first efforts were political. It fought for antilynching legislation. A bill was finally proposed in 1935, but did not pass. The NAACP sought President F. D. Roosevelt's help, but it is said the President could not afford to alienate the South and lose support for his New Deal legislation. By threatening a massive protest march on Washington, the organization did persuade Roosevelt to establish in 1941 a temporary Committee on Fair Employment Practices and to order that employers and unions "provide for the full and equitable participation of all workers in defense industries, without discrimination because of race, creed, color, or national origin." It also worked from World War I on to end segregation in the Armed Forces. President Truman finally agreed to this.

The NAACP also participated in and won some legal battles, even in the early years. It took part in *Guinn v. United States,* where the challenge to Oklahoma's "grandfather clause" amendment denying Negroes the right to vote was successful. It also participated in *Buchanan v. Warley,* where Louisville's racial zoning ordinance was struck down, and it persuaded the Court to overturn the death sentences of 12 Negroes convicted in a mob-dominated court.

Prior to 1939, the Association's legal work was done on an ad hoc basis by individual members of the organization and by volunteers. But a national legal committee was formed to advise the Association. Members included Clarence Darrow, Felix Frankfurter, Frank Murphy, Arthur Garfield Hays, and Morris L. Ernst. By 1939, however, the Association had determined to make a concerted legal effort to attack racial segregation in education, transportation, and housing. It established the NAACP Legal Defense and Education Fund, with Thurgood Marshall at its head.

The success of the Fund's subsequent efforts is well known. In 1948, it won its battle to have racially restrictive housing covenants declared unconstitutional. And in 1954, the Supreme Court, in *Brown,* finally rejected the "separate but equal" doctrine, and declared that racially segregated public schools deny the equal protection of the laws guaranteed by the Fourteenth Amendment. Beginning in 1939, however, the Fund was not alone in its efforts. In that year, the president appointed Frank Murphy Attorney General. Murphy set up the first Civil Rights Division in the Department of Justice. A year later, he succeeded Pierce Butler as an Associate Justice of the Supreme Court.

The work of the Civil Rights Division went on. In the early years, it focused primarily on police brutality and, despite the absence of federal antilynching legislation, on the prosecution of lynch mobs. In 1946, a series of lynchings prompted renewed efforts for an antilynching bill. William White, Secretary of the NAACP, sought the aid of President Truman. No bill was forthcoming, but Mr. Truman created the Presidential Committee on Civil Rights to study the growing racial problems. The Committee issued a report, entitled *To Secure These Rights,* on October 29, 1947. Among the recommendations of the Committee was a request that the Justice Department enter the fight against racially restrictive covenants. The week after the publication of the Committee's report, the Department decided to intervene as *amicus curiae* in *Shelley v. Kraemer.*

The report also assessed the weaknesses in the federal civil rights enforcement machinery. Prime among these was the lack of available tools with which to address the deprivations of which the Nation was becoming increasingly aware. That criticism soon became a familiar refrain. One author surveyed the statutory tools available and concluded:

> It is doubtful if much can be done by way of existing federal statutes to implement effectively the civil rights of individuals. There are some encouraging signs in the application of some of those statutes to the broad rights which have come to be protected against state action under the due process clause. But the greatest source of violations, the actions of private individuals, are beyond the power of present statutes to reach in any substantial degree.

The obstacles to the use of the Civil Rights Acts, in the view of the commentators, were two. First, the criminal provisions had limited value in view of the narrow construction the Court had given them during Reconstruction. And it was private action, uncontrolled by the States, that was the greatest source of violations. The civil provisions were subject to a similar narrow construction. In addition, a civil remedy was thought to be of limited value as a means of enforcing civil liberties. In a 1947 book about the Civil Rights Division, the author applauded its work, but insisted that existing statutory tools were inadequate for the Division to be effective. The criminal sanctions were too narrow and the civil sanctions, while they had been employed on a few occasions, could never be effective on a large scale. "The victim in a civil liberty case virtually is left to his own resources in invoking this sanction, and since the victim in such a case is usually a poor person, without standing or prestige in his own community, he often lacks the courage and financial ability to go to court in defense of his rights. Society cannot depend on this device to assure a thorough and continuing enforcement of legal controls."

Despite dire prophecies, the Civil Rights Division went to work with the tools it had and it is those efforts that paved the way for the rebirth of § 1983. Through the Division's efforts, the first crack in the armor the Court had built against effective use of the

Civil Rights Acts was made. Again, it appears that the weakest spot in that armor was in the area of voting rights. *United States v. Classic* was a 1941 case pursued by the Division to test whether the criminal provisions, now 18 U.S.C. §§ 241 and 242, authorized the Federal Government to prosecute state election officials accused of stealing and miscounting ballots in a state primary election. Section 51, originally § 6 of the 1870 Act, made it a crime for two or more persons to conspire to injure or intimidate any citizen in the free exercise or enjoyment of any right or privilege secured to him by the Constitution or laws of the United States. Section 52 made it a crime for anyone, under color of any law, willfully to subject any inhabitant of any State to the deprivation of any rights secured or protected by the Constitution or laws of the United States. The Court concluded that the right of the elector to have his ballot counted at the primary is protected by the Constitution. It also held that both § 51 and § 52 reached the challenged conduct. The aspect of that ruling that has had the most profound impact on the course of civil rights litigation is the Court's decision that the "under color of state law" requirement was satisfied even though the state officers were accused of committing acts clearly not authorized by state law.

The interpretation of "under color of state law" adopted in *Classic* was expanded beyond the protection of voting rights in the now well-known 1945 case of *Screws v. United States.* The background to the *Screws* case is worth recounting. Here is the first paragraph of the plurality opinion:

> This case involves a shocking and revolting episode in law enforcement. Petitioner Screws was sheriff of Baker County, Georgia. He enlisted the assistance of petitioner Jones, a policeman, and petitioner Kelley, a special deputy, in arresting Robert Hall, a citizen of the United States and of Georgia. The arrest was made late at night at Hall's home on a warrant charging Hall with theft of a tire. Hall, a young negro about thirty years of age, was handcuffed and taken by car to the court house. As Hall alighted from the car at the courthouse square, the three petitioners began beating him with their fists and with a solid-bar blackjack about eight inches long and weighing two pounds. They claimed Hall had reached for a gun and had used insulting language as he alighted from the car. But after Hall, still handcuffed, had been knocked to the ground they continued to beat him from fifteen to thirty minutes until he was unconscious. Hall was then dragged feet first through the courthouse yard into the jail and thrown upon the floor dying. An ambulance was called and Hall was removed to a hospital where he died within the hour and without regaining consciousness. There was evidence that Screws held a grudge against Hall and had threatened to "get" him.

The petitioners were convicted of violating § 52 of the Criminal Code. Before the Supreme Court they urged that whatever offense they had committed was one only against the State and that their action was not authorized by state law and therefore was not action "under color of state law." Justice Roberts, joined by Justices Frankfurter and Jackson, agreed. In their view, to construe § 52 to reach the conduct of the petitioners would be to attribute to Congress an intent it did not have, to make "overnight . . . a revolutionary change in the balance of the political relations between the National Government and the States." On the contrary, Congress intended "to leave undisturbed the power and the duty of the States to enforce their criminal law by restricting federal authority to the punishment only of those persons who violate federal rights under claim of State authority and not by exerting federal authority against offenders of State authority."

Relying on the Court's holding in *Classic* that "[m]isuse of power, possessed by virtue of state law and made possible only because the wrongdoer is clothed with the authority of state law, is action taken 'under color of' state law," the plurality of the Court disagreed. Justice Rutledge, in a separate opinion, noted that it did not appear that the State had taken any steps toward prosecution for violation of its law. One writer has pursued that point further. He examined the Justice Department's files in the case and found evidence that:

> the federal government made every effort to persuade the state of Georgia to prosecute the offenders. Georgia failed to take any action. The reason for Georgia's failure to prosecute the perpetrators of such an extremely brutal crime is not clear. Apparently, the state authorities were willing to see action taken, but the initiative in such an affair lay with local officers. The district solicitor general, whose duty it was to start criminal proceedings, is reported by the United States Attorney to have felt 'helpless in the matter.' 'He has no investigative facilities and has to rely upon the sheriff and policemen of the various counties of his circuit for investigation.' Such assistance in this case would have had to come from the accused persons themselves!

Classic and *Screws* signalled a general relaxation of the strict "state action" requirement that had shackled the Fourteenth Amendment and its enforcing Civil Rights Acts since Reconstruction. Shortly after *Classic,* the NAACP, in *Smith v. Allwright,* was successful in a § 1983 challenge to the Texas white primary. Relying on *Classic,* the Supreme Court held that although the State had delegated to a political party the responsibility for fixing qualifications for voting in a primary, the State endorsed and enforced the discrimination practiced by the party to decide who may vote. The action of the party therefore was taken under color of state law. Then, in *Shelley v. Kraemer,* the Court found sufficient state action in the willingness of the state courts to enforce private racially restrictive covenants.

Against this background, *Monroe v. Pape,* decided in 1961, should have come as no surprise. The issue in *Monroe* was whether 13 Chicago police officers charged with conducting an unconstitutional search and arrest could be liable under § 1983 even though their actions were not specifically authorized by state law. The complaint, as paraphrased by Justice Frankfurter in his opinion dissenting in part, alleged:

> that . . . thirteen Chicago police officers, led by Deputy Chief of Detectives Pape, broke through two doors of the Monroe apartment, woke the Monroe couple with flashlights, and forced them at gunpoint to leave their bed and stand naked in the center of the living room; that the officers roused the six Monroe children and herded them into the living room; that Detective Pape struck Mr. Monroe several times with his flashlight, calling him "nigger" and "black boy"; that another officer pushed Mrs. Monroe; that other officers hit and kicked several of the children and pushed them to the floor; that the police ransacked every room, throwing clothing from closets to the floor, dumping drawers, ripping mattress covers; that Mr. Monroe was then taken to the police station and detained on "open" charges for ten hours, during which time he was interrogated about a murder and exhibited in lineups; that he was not brought before a magistrate, although numerous magistrate's courts were accessible; that he was not advised of his procedural rights; that he was not permitted to call his family or an attorney; that he was subsequently released without criminal charges having been filed against him.

One commentator has noted the similarity between the complaint in *Monroe* and a story told by a South Carolina Negro, Joshua Wardlaw, and read into the record of the 42d Congress in 1871 while the Congress was debating the Ku Klux Klan Act. Wardlaw recounted:

> Pres. Blackwell kicked one of my little children that was in the bed. They took my brother-in-law's gun and broke it against a tree in the yard. They laid me down on the ground, after stripping me as naked as when I came into the world, and struck me five times with a strap before I got away from them. After escaping they fired four shots at me, but did not hit me. I was so frightened I laid out in the woods all night, naked as I was, and suffered from the exposure. Mr. Richardson afterward told me he was very sorry that I had escaped from them. My brother-in-law died from the beating he got that same night.

As in *Screws,* there was a strong voice in *Monroe* urging that the "color of state law" requirement should operate to confine the reach of the federal courts to official state conduct. Justice Frankfurter surveyed the legislative history and concluded that § 1 of the 1871 Act, unlike § 2, was not intended to extend beyond official state action. He then expressed sentiments remarkably similar to those of the opponents of the 1871 bill. In the Justice's view, to have § 1983 reach unauthorized acts of state officials would be to make "the extreme limits of federal constitutional power a law to regulate the quotidian business of every traffic policeman, every registrar of elections, every city inspector or investigator, every clerk in every municipal licensing bureau in this country."

Once again, however, a majority of the Court disagreed. The majority also surveyed the legislative history of the Act and concluded, as was done in *Classic* and in *Screws,* that the Reconstruction Congresses had intended to reach the kind of conduct complained of in *Monroe.* It found it "abundantly clear that one reason the legislation was passed was to afford a federal right in federal courts because, by reason of prejudice, passion, neglect, intolerance or otherwise, state laws might not be enforced and the claims of citizens to the enjoyment of rights, privileges, and immunities guaranteed by the Fourteenth Amendment might be denied by the state agencies." It emphasized that it was the activities of the Ku Klux Klan and the inability or unwillingness of the state governments to cope with those activities that prompted the Act. It noted that speaker after speaker had emphasized that the problem was not with state laws as written, but with the failure of the States to enforce those laws to protect Negroes and Union sympathizers. And opponents of the bill objected to the Act's "transfer [of] all criminal jurisdiction from the courts of the States to the courts of the United States . . . upon the assumption that the courts of the southern States fail and refuse to do their duty in the punishment of offenders against the law."

Monroe, although later overruled in part, is correctly credited as being a watershed in the development of § 1983. Between 1939 and 1961, the significant § 1983 cases, like those prior to 1939, were few. It is difficult to compile an accurate list. Often, there is no mention in the Court's opinions of the statutory basis for jurisdiction and remedial authority. An opinion might simply note that certain conduct is challenged as violative of the Constitution. I have not attempted to survey the significant § 1983 cases that did not reach the Supreme Court. I have looked back, however, into the complaints and records in a number of Supreme Court cases during this 22-year period before *Monroe.* The cases can almost be counted on one hand. They include a challenge to official state actions preventing the plaintiffs from assembling to discuss the National Labor Relations Act and to organize a union, the NAACP's successful challenge to the Texas white primary, and a First Amendment challenge to a state requirement that teachers file affidavits listing all the organizations to which they belong.

Probably the most significant pre-*Monroe* case was *Brown v. Board of Education.* Interestingly, in the Court's opinion there is no citation of either § 1983 or of the jurisdictional statute. Two of the *per curiam* opinions following *Brown,* with which the Court expanded *Brown* to beaches, buses, and other public accommodations, also were § 1983 cases.

After *Monroe,* however, the list expands. One now could claim surprise at the significance of the role that § 1983 played in civil liberties litigation in the last 20 years. It is also interesting to note that many of these cases probably could have been brought successfully before *Monroe*; *Monroe* simply focused attention on the availability of the § 1983 remedy.

In the context of racial equality, many of the major school desegregation cases were filed as § 1983 actions. In the First Amendment area, § 1983 was relied on for a challenge to state laws that required loyalty oaths, or prevented the wearing of armbands in protest of our policy in Vietnam. It was also used to restrain prosecutions under Louisiana's Subversive Activities and Communist Control Law. It was utilized by the NAACP to establish that organization's authority to advise Negroes of their legal rights. It was used to challenge bans on lawyer advertising and spending limitations on the public education activities of charities. Section 1983 has been the vehicle for establishing significant due process rights. The case establishing that a welfare recipient has a right to notice and a hearing before his benefits are terminated was a § 1983 case. Along the same line, § 1983 cases have confirmed the due process rights of recipients of utility service, of public employees, of employees entitled under state law to seek redress for unlawful discharge, and of debtors whose property is about to be seized by individuals or by the State. Section 1983 has been used to challenge mandatory maternity leave policies and state restrictions on social security benefits. This list includes challenges to state restrictions on the right to vote, from poll taxes and white primaries to unequal apportionment schemes. It includes a challenge of unequal age limitations for males and females on the sale of beer, and on limitations on the right to marry the person of one's choice. And it includes successful efforts by mental patients and by prisoners to achieve First Amendment freedoms, basic medical care, and due process rights while within institutional walls.

III

The current criticisms of § 1983 are a byproduct, of course, of the revival of the statute as a vehicle for vindicating constitutional rights against state officials. The least persuasive criticisms for me, or at any rate the least complete, are those that claim that § 1983 actions are burdening the federal courts. Since any such "burden" presumably is worth bearing when an action is meritorious, the criticisms must assume that the suits generally are without merit. But I am aware of no statistics demonstrating what percentage of § 1983 actions are bound to be meritless. Prisoners, especially those who proceed *pro se,* are popular candidates for the group likely to present consistently frivolous claims. But ever since *Jackson v. Bishop,* a case in which I take pride in having participated on the Court of Appeals, despite improvements in state prison systems, I am not prepared to exclude the possibility that a particular prisoner will be subject to a serious deprivation that warrants the attention of a federal court. In fact, I suspect that improvements in prison conditions of recent years are traceable in large part, and perhaps primarily, to actions under § 1983 challenging those conditions. In any event, it is not clear to me why screening out frivolous suits should be considered a problem peculiar to § 1983, rather than a part of a more general problem of federal litigation that must be addressed on its own terms. If critics are concerned by the sheer burden placed on the federal judiciary by § 1983 actions, they might do well to turn their attention, too, to other sources of federal litigation. My point is simply that if we want to nominate a particular group of cases for exclusion from the federal courthouse, we should look first at groups in which federal law is not sensitively at issue rather than at one in which fundamental constitutional rights are at stake.

The related concern that a § 1983 action may be used to bootstrap a state-law tort claim into a federal forum has been greatly undercut, in my view, by the combined effects of the Court's recent decisions in *Parratt v. Taylor*, *Hudson v. Palmer*, and *Pennhurst State School and Hospital v. Halderman*. Whatever else may be said about these decisions, they have made it difficult, if not impossible, for a plaintiff who has only a state-law tort claim against a state official to hale the official into federal court under the guise of a § 1983 action. The Supreme Court gives ample evidence of being able to devise protective measures for itself and other federal courts.

The criticisms on which I would like to focus particularly are those concerning the impact of § 1983 on federalism and federal-state comity. My first response is that the so-called federalism "problem" created by § 1983 is largely an illusory one. We tend to forget that § 1983 does not stand alone in the legal universe, but is part of a much broader set of legal protections for individual rights. Section 1983 is only a vehicle for substantive claims that have their base elsewhere. It is not an independent source of constitutional or statutory rights. Indeed, given the presence of *Bivens v. Six Unknown Fed. Narcotics Agents*, in which the Court implied a private right of action for damages against federal officials who violate the Constitution, it might well be that federal courts would feel obliged to assume the authority to remedy constitutional violations by state officials even without an imposed statutory remedy. Many complaints about § 1983's ostensible impact on federalism really are complaints about the breadth of the underlying constitutional rights—a separate issue that surely deserves to be debated on its own terms.

More importantly, the one-sided model of federal supervision of state officials that was put in place after the Civil War has given way, not especially by design, to a more balanced system of judicial protection of individual rights. The new balance of which I speak involves all three aspects of the post-Civil War revolution in federal power and individual liberty—that is, rights, remedies, and forums. As for rights, when the Supreme Court in 1954 brought about the "reverse incorporation" of the Equal Protection Clause into the Fifth Amendment in *Boiling v. Sharpe*, it ensured that all the fundamental constitutional rights of the Fourteenth Amendment bind the Federal Government as well as the States. Seventeen years later, in *Bivens,* the Court put together a working equivalent of § 1983 for constitutional claims against federal officials. Lastly, while the question has not been settled finally by the Supreme Court, the current weight of authority elsewhere is that state courts may assume jurisdiction over constitutional claims for injunctive relief or damages against federal officials. When these developments are looked at together, a surprising degree of symmetry emerges: individuals enjoy common constitutional rights against the Federal Government and the States; they may obtain injunctive relief and damages against both federal and state officials; and both state and federal courts may entertain constitutional suits and award constitutional remedies against any official, federal as well as state, who deprives or threatens to deprive an individual of his constitutional rights. Any perceived slight to state autonomy by reason of § 1983 actions looks much less compelling when viewed from this perspective than it does when § 1983 is viewed in isolation.

My second response to the criticisms concerning the impact of § 1983 on federalism is that to the extent the statute does create problems, those problems are political rather than judicial. It is not improper, of course, to take issue with the balance struck by the Reconstruction Congresses, nor is it improper to call for greater deference toward the States. We must recognize, however, that such arguments are better addressed to Congress than to the courts. It is not enough to argue before a court that a particular construction of § 1983 is inconsistent with "principles of federalism" of "federal-state comity." To do so is to put the cart before the horse, for the only principles of federalism and comity that justify restricting the scope of § 1983 are those found in the Constitution or § 1983 itself. We must avoid the temptation to let "federalism" become the Natural Law of the 1980's, a brooding omnipresence to which duly enacted statutes are made to pay homage. Indeed, there is more than a little irony in litigants' and commentators' asking the Supreme Court to restrict the scope of § 1983 in order to prevent unwarranted intrusions on the democratic processes of state governments. If § 1983 as presently construed does shift political authority from elected officials to unelected judges—and I do not concede that it does—the remedy, it seems to me, lies with the elected members of the Senate and House of Representatives and not with the unelected members of the Supreme Court.

It is in part for this reason that one might be troubled by the overtones of some of the Court's recent decisions in this area. The tenor of the times perhaps has changed, and the judicial pendulum, which swung from retrenchment in the years after Reconstruction to a renewal of federal responsibility for constitutional rights during the last two generations, may have begun to swing once more toward retrenchment. In certain instances, the Court appears inclined to cut back on § 1983 in any way it can, short of ignoring the language of the statute or existing rulings. The common theme of some of the recent decisions seems to me to be that § 1983 should be construed to minimize federal judicial intervention in state affairs whenever possible, regardless of the impact on the ability of federal courts to protect constitutional rights.

For example, the Court has limited damages awards available under § 1983 by expanding doctrines of immunity—an absolute Eleventh Amendment immunity for States, an absolute immunity from damages for judges and legislators, and a good-faith immunity for state and local officials that appears to require the plaintiff to demonstrate that the exact requirements of the constitutional right at issue had been spelled out by a federal court prior to the alleged violation. The Court's recent Eleventh Amendment ruling in *Pennhurst,* while not directly limiting relief available on a § 1983 claim, also whittles away at the § 1983 remedy, since a plaintiff with both state and federal claims against a state official no longer is able to seek relief for those claims in federal court.

Actions for damages have been limited in other ways as well. Although the Court thus far has declined to impose a requirement that § 1983 plaintiffs exhaust state remedies, the Court's holding in *Parratt v. Taylor* has the potential for doing just that. I joined the Court's opinion in *Parratt* and in the extension of *Parratt* last term in *Hudson v. Palmer,* but I am sensitive to the need to confine the *Parratt* rule lest it swallow the remedy it was designed only to limit. The Court in *Parratt* concluded that, where the claim was that a state prison official had negligently deprived the plaintiff of property, the availability of a state tort-claim procedure through which the plaintiff could be reimbursed for his loss satisfied the requirements of due process. As the six separate opinions in that case illustrate, there was little consensus as to why the plaintiff had not been denied due process. Justice Powell, for instance, concurred in the result because he saw no deprivation of life, liberty, or property in the negligent action of a state prison official. He expressed concern, however, over the implications of the Court's reliance on the availability of compensation under state law as sufficient due process for the deprivation of a substantive constitutional guarantee. I concurred on the understanding that the Court's opinion reached only negligent deprivations of property and that it would not apply to a case concerning deprivations of life or liberty.

Last Term, in *Hudson,* the Court extended the rule of *Parratt* to intentional deprivations of property. The holdings of *Parratt* and *Hudson* have been confined to unauthorized deprivations of property, and I would hope that they would continue to be so confined. In *Logan v. Zimmerman Brush Co.,* the Court did decline to rely on *Parratt* or to accept the availability of a state tort-claim procedure as sufficient to satisfy the constitutional demands of due process when a plaintiff had been deprived by the State of his interest in pursuing a state-created employment discrimination claim. Nevertheless, the reasoning of *Parratt* and *Hudson* could be used to deny a § 1983 action to anyone claiming a constitutional violation by an official unauthorized to act as he did, as long as the State provides a damages remedy after-the-fact.

Closely related to the issues surrounding *Parratt* and its progeny is a third way in which the Court has limited the damages remedy available under § 1983. Although *Parratt* and *Hudson* were careful not to say so, they suggest a reluctance on the part of the Court to find a constitutional violation in a state official's conduct if it is neither pursuant to an official state policy nor authorized by the State, unless and until the State declines to act to redress the injury. As I have indicated, the question of how far beyond official state action the Acts reach is a dispute at the heart of the federalism tensions inherent in the Civil Rights Acts. Thus, it is interesting to note that in two recent cases, the Court has addressed directly aspects of this fundamental issue. In both cases, the Court has given a narrow construction to the "color of state law" and "state action" requirements, reminiscent of the interpretations of similar issues in the last decades of the 19th century. In *Polk County v. Dodson,* the Court concluded that the official activities of a public defender, a fulltime state employee, were not "under color of state law." And, in *Carpenters and Joiners v. Scott,* the Court determined, despite the fact that § 2 of the Ku Klux Klan Act clearly reaches private conspiracies, that when the claimed deprivation was of First Amendment rights, state action was required in order for the plaintiffs to state a claim for relief under that section.

A similar litany can be recited of cases limiting the availability of injunctive relief. Although suits for injunctive relief are not so numerous and therefore in one respect not so troublesome as suits for damages, injunctive relief generally presents even greater federalism tensions than do suits for damages. Damages awards operate retrospectively, and often only against individual actors. Injunctive relief introduces an ongoing federal presence in the conduct of the affairs of a state or local government. To preserve the delicate balance, the Court had made clear that federal courts are not authorized to intervene in ongoing state judicial proceedings. But until recently, the Court had not extended the inviolate state realm beyond ongoing judicial proceedings.

In several cases, however, the Court now has expanded the prohibition against federal intrusion and refused to allow federal relief against alleged patterns of unconstitutional conduct. In *O'Shea v. Littleton* and *Rizzo v. Goode,* the Court concluded that plaintiffs could not obtain injunctive relief under § 1983 against alleged patterns of judicial and police mistreatment of minority citizens, because the threat of injury was not sufficiently real and immediate and because injunctive relief would constitute an unwarranted intrusion into an area that should be left to the discretion of state and local officials. Two Terms ago, relying on those cases, the Court, by a 5-4 vote, in *City of Los Angeles v. Lyons,* concluded that the petitioner lacked a sufficient stake in the outcome to bring a claim for injunctive relief against a police practice of using a chokehold where the arrested person presented no reasonable appearance of immediate use of deadly force. The basis for the Court's decision was that even though the petitioner had been subjected to the chokehold in the past when arrested for a traffic violation, there was no evidence that he would be arrested for such a violation in the future or that the officer who arrested him would use a chokehold. The Court went on to indicate that even if Article III were satisfied, the desired equitable relief would be unavailable, since "the need for a proper balance between state and federal authority counsels restraint in the issuance of injunctions against state officers engaged in the administration of the States' criminal laws." The dissenters, whom I joined, decried both aspects of the decision and asserted: "The Court's decision removes an entire class of constitutional violations from the equitable powers of a federal court. . . . The federal judicial power is now limited to levying a toll for such a systematic constitutional violation."

I do not mean to present a picture of uninterrupted retreat by the Court. In some contexts, the Court has held a firm line against procedural and substantive doctrines that would limit the role of § 1983. The Court has declined to read into the statute a requirement that a § 1983 litigant exhaust his state administrative remedies, or to accord immunity to a judicial officer against a § 1983 suit for injunctive relief, where there was no basis in the common law for such immunity. The Court also has been careful in addressing the question of what statute of limitations should be applied to a § 1983 action, deciding last Term that a 6-month state statute for an administrative proceeding was not the analogous statute for § 1983 because the purposes and policies behind the state administrative proceeding were inconsistent with § 1983's provision of an independent judicial remedy for a civil rights violation. Finally, the Court has been careful to maintain the independence of the remedy provided in § 1983 and the other Civil Rights Acts against implied repeal by other federal statutes, requiring that congressional intent to do so be clear.

Any desire for wholesale judicial retrenchment would be met by an additional obstacle—namely, the fact that the major questions of interpretation of § 1983 already have been settled. There is now little doubt that Congress was within its authority in authorizing remedies that reach private as well as state action. And the dispute over legislative intent has been resolved and the results accepted. For better or for worse, the Court agrees that Congress intended, in certain sections of the Civil Rights Acts, to reach private actions and, in § 1983, to reach unauthorized conduct of state officials. One of the sounder canons of judicial restraint is that once a court has spoken conclusively on a question of statutory interpretation, it should reconsider the question only when faced with compelling evidence that its initial answer was incorrect. Unless critics of the § 1983 precedents can produce the same kind of evidence that led the Court to reconsider the scope of municipal liability in *Monell,* the underlying principles of § 1983 liability should be secure.

IV

Despite these restraints on the impulse to restrict § 1983 through judicial revision, that impulse remains alive. In fact, both the impulse and the federalism concerns behind it will increase as state courts prove more willing to protect individual rights and less deserving of the mistrust that was the genesis of § 1983. For that reason, while it is not my purpose to review the various reform proposals that have been addressed to the Congress and the courts, I close by explaining why I am generally skeptical about proposals to limit the reach of § 1983.

In my view, any plan to restrict the scope of § 1983 comes with a heavy burden of justification—a burden that is both constitutional and historical. The constitutional burden is the need to demonstrate that the interests of federalism, comity, or judicial efficiency can be advanced without sacrificing protection for our constitutional rights. If increased state autonomy and reduced federal caseloads can be purchased only with the coin of more constitutional violations and fewer constitutional remedies, the price is high and is one I am not prepared to pay. Nor is it one, by the way, that critics of § 1983 usually attempt to justify.

The historical burden is the need to show, in light of the systematic disregard of civil rights by state governments and state courts that led to the original Civil Rights Acts, that constitutional claims can safely be committed to state courts, not only for the present but for the future. It is no reflection on the current good faith of state governments and state courts to observe that history is not a one-way street. While we all can work to prevent a return to the judicial indifference and paralysis of the past, none of us can guarantee that the day will not return when a litigant who cannot vindicate his constitutional rights in federal court will not be able to vindicate them at all. If that day should come, it will be far harder to reconstruct a statutory remedy that has been judicially interred or legislatively undone in the meantime than it would be to resort to a remedy that has been intact and working in the intervening years. In short, once we restrict the role of federal courts in protecting constitutional rights, we may find ourselves hard pressed to recover what has been given up.

In making this argument, I suppose that I am relying in part on the symbolic importance of § 1983. The symbolism that I have in mind, and the symbolism that § 1983 has come to possess for those whose rights depend on it, is not the symbolism the statute bore when it was enacted in 1871. Then § 1983 was part and parcel of the Radical Republican assault on the ashes of the Old South. Today, § 1983 properly stands for something different—for the commitment of our society to be governed by law and to protect the rights of those without power against oppression at the hands of the powerful. When the Fourteenth Amendment became part of the Constitution, it committed this Nation to an order in which all governments, state as well as federal, were bound to respect the fundamental rights of individuals. That commitment, too, is a part of "Our Federalism," no less than the values of state autonomy that the critics of § 1983 so passionately invoke. One might well ask, rhetorically, whether § 1983 could be enacted in today's political climate, or, indeed, whether we dare repeal it. What a vibrant and exciting old statute it is. As Edmond Cahn so aptly observed, "[F]reedom is not free." Whatever is the fate of § 1983 in the future, I do hope that it survives both as a symbol and as a working mechanism for all of us to protect the constitutional liberties we treasure.

Part II

"Every person": Theories of Local Government Liability

The availability of deep pocket defendants is obviously of practical significance for plaintiffs in general. It is often no less so for section 1983 plaintiffs. However, until the Supreme Court's 1978 decision in *Monell v. Department of Social Services*, 436 U.S. 658 (1978), local governments were not considered to be "persons" within the meaning of section 1983. *Monell* changed all that, rendering local governments potentially liable for compensatory damages for constitutional deprivations caused by their official policies or customs. The Court later ruled that local governments are not protected by qualified immunity from compensatory damages liability. However, they are absolutely immune from punitive damages liability. *See Owen v. City of Independence*, 445 U.S. 622 (1980) and *City of Newport v. Fact Concerts, Inc.*, 453 U.S. 247 (1981).

Local government liability raises deep theoretical issues which the next three articles address. Professor Whitman analyzes the language used in discussions of local government liability. She argues against using only terms borrowed from tort law because those terms developed in the context of individual wrongdoing. What is necessary, in her view, is a "vocabulary for resolving questions of institutional responsibility."

Professor Schuck criticizes the Court's decision in *Monell*, especially for its imposition of the official policy or custom requirement. He evaluates that requirement from the perspectives of private tort law and organization theory and concludes that it ought to be abandoned.

Professor Kritchevsky's article builds on the Court's official policy or custom requirement and its related causation component to contend that state of mind analysis should not be incorporated into section 1983 local government liability doctrine. She argues against such a fault-based model and in favor of a tort-causation model. Although the Supreme Court thereafter appears to have adopted a fault-based model in *City of Canton v. Harris*, 489 U.S. 378 (1989), a case involving local government liability for failure to train, Professor Kritchevsky's discussion remains valuable.

Christina B. Whitman, *Government Responsibility For Constitutional Torts,* 85 Michigan Law Review 226 (1986)

This essay is about the language used to decide when governments should be held responsible for constitutional torts. Debate about what is required of government officials, and what is required of government itself, is scarcely new. What is new, at least to American jurisprudence, is litigation against government units (rather than government officials) for constitutional injuries. The extension of liability to institutional defendants introduces special problems for the language of responsibility. In a suit against an individual official it is easy to describe the wrong as the consequence of individual behavior that is inconsistent with community norms; the language of common-law tort, which refers explicitly to those norms, has seemed to provide a useful starting point for evaluating that behavior. When the defendant is an institution, the language of tort provides no such ground because traditionally it has not been used to evaluate harms created by structures and contexts rather than by individuals. When discussions of institutional responsibility are couched only in terms borrowed from tort they are impoverished. The poverty of discussions cast in tort vocabulary can even be read to suggest that we simply have no norms for risk-creating behavior other than those applied to individuals.

* * *

I. The Language of Responsibility

The distortion begins in tort. The paradigm common-law case, the framework in which issues of tort liability have been discussed, sets an individual victim against an individual defendant who has done some specific, relatively discrete act that affirmatively caused harm. The question in torts, as in the common law generally, has been: "When must we limit the presumptively free conduct of an individual?" Legal standards are articulated as limitations on individuals. Liability is imposed when one individual goes too far and intrudes on the interests of another, presumably equally free, individual. Intrusive behavior is not flatly prohibited, as it is by criminal law. Assigning responsibility in tort is not, strictly speaking, dependent upon a conclusion that the defendant has gone too far by engaging in the harmful behavior; rather, it means that the defendant has gone too far if she fails to compensate those who have been injured by her conduct. The primary and most pressing questions in tort so defined do not address issues raised by more subtle or more diffusely caused harms, by affirmative obligations, or by claims that conduct should be prohibited and the resulting harm prevented.

It is certainly the case that not all tort litigants are individuals, but standards of behavior for groups and institutions have been derived without much modification from those devised for natural persons. There has been no separate language for harms caused by groups or institutions. The primary, and by now relatively comfortable, questions have been thought to be those raised by individual wrongs against other individuals. Individualism has been made into something more than an attractive ethical or political ideal. In litigation over harms, at least, it has been the method of analysis.

Tort law does not evaluate individuals as totally isolated units. To some extent, it has been sensitive to the contexts, organizational and otherwise, within which individuals act. Jurors are instructed that they are to evaluate the defendant's behavior by reference to what "the reasonably prudent person would do *in the circumstances*." This formulation has proved enduring precisely because it allows the consideration of behavior in context; people who sit on juries may bring to bear their own sense of the cultural and situational constraints on individual action. It may thus be acceptable, for example, to argue that an individual acted reasonably given the limited vision, information, or power created by his niche in a particular organization. Yet the focus of the inquiry is still on what is fair to expect of an individual in a given context, rather than on whether it is appropriate to require that the context be changed. The jury is asked to evaluate the particular, and relatively isolated, behavior of specified actors. The question, put that way, seems relatively straightforward. And many characteristics of tort litigation—the assumption that behavior can be fairly evaluated according to standards drawn from the jurors' own experiences; the rules about burden of proof, which fill in gaps in the narrative; and the abstract nature of the instructions to the jury—direct the attention of the court and the jury away from real difficulties in describing and understanding even individual behavior that causes discrete harm. Even less attention is paid to injuries that cannot be traced to particular behavior, but are attributable to institutions, or to communities or cultures within institutions—for the question is simply never put in that form.

In traditional tort law, the need to create standards uniquely addressed to organizational behavior has been avoided because questions of organizational responsibility have been assimilated into the doctrines of vicarious and strict liability. Under these doctrines, even when an institution is the defendant, the court focuses on the conduct of individual employees. Under vicarious liability, if the behavior of an employee is found wanting under the reasonably prudent person standard, the institution must pay. Institutional liability does not turn on a conclusion that the institution itself has been found to have caused harm; rather, the institution must pay because it employs a person who has caused harm. Doctrines of strict liability do hold institutions responsible without requiring evidence that an individual employee has done wrong. But here, too, liability is not based upon an analysis of the wrongfulness of the institution's conduct; it is justified, instead, as a mechanism for spreading the costs of injuries or for allocating costs to the enterprise in which the institution is engaged. Some forms of strict liability rest upon an inquiry into what the defendant has done in a way that seems to involve a moral evaluation of behavior; for example, strict products liability in torts requires a finding that the defendant has marketed a defective product. But the reference point for evaluation is still an individual decisionmaker, though often a hypothetical one. In cases seeking to impose strict liability for defective product design, for example, one way to put the question is to ask whether the design decisions that were made would have been made by a reasonably prudent designer.

These ways of avoiding direct evaluation of institutional conduct are not available in constitutional torts litigation. Vicarious liability of local governments for the torts of their employees has been emphatically rejected by the Supreme Court. Cost-allocation and cost-spreading rationales have been found to be inconsistent with the legislative history surrounding the enactment of section 1983, and both theories do seem out of place in constitutional litigation. Cost allocation is a way of encouraging appropriate reduction of accidents through the assignment of accident costs to those who can best decide whether the benefits flowing from an activity are worth the risks it runs. But cost allocation raises the possibility that an activity, if it is found to be too costly, will simply cease to take place. That is not an option for government, which cannot cease to exist. And, to treat constitutional wrongs as simply a cost of doing government business seems unpalatable. Both cost-allocation and cost-spreading rationales, if adopted, would suggest that constitutional injuries, like injuries redressed through more ordinary torts, may be incurred if the appropriate price is paid. Government without constitutional error, like a world without accidents, is impossible, but adopting a language for adjudication that focuses only on the decision of where to shift the costs of such error brings with it a measure of despair.

Since the devices that have deflected common-law tort doctrine from questions of institutional conduct have been eliminated in constitutional cases against government bodies, an opportunity has been created. The attention of the courts is necessarily directed toward the responsibility of the institution as distinct from that of the individual. It becomes possible to ask whether we have an adequate language for detecting and assessing injuries caused by organizations—for articulating what we expect from government as a system or structure, rather than what we expect from government officials as individuals.

What interests me is how difficult it has in fact been to talk about systemic or structural injuries, to ask (much less answer) these questions. Even though the Court has clearly posed the question as one of government responsibility independent of and distinct from vicarious responsibility for official acts, the Court's opinions, and the tests they articulate, still focus on the behavior of individual officials or postulate a hypothetical individual decisionmaker. I do not mean to suggest that the Court has been eager to hold individual officers liable. Quite the contrary. Individual officers are protected from personal liability by extensive immunities. These immunities are based on concerns that are unique to suits against individual defendants. Immunity doctrines reflect both the courts' lack of confidence in their own ability to evaluate and judge the behavior of persons in official positions who are subjected to conflicting, often extreme, pressures in their jobs, and a related sense that it may be both unfair and poor policy to burden individual human beings working under these conditions with the full weight of liability for often quite grievous harms. What we have, then, are many cases in which individuals as persons will not be held personally liable—the named defendants are the government as government and individual defendants sued only in their official capacity—but the discussion is still cast in terms of personal behavior and personal wrongdoing.

* * *

III. The Pull of the Individual Model

The effort to define the proper sphere for constitutional torts began with early efforts, not yet completely abandoned, to define a sufficiently egregious "state of mind" or "standard of care" to be applied to the individual officers named as defendants. Intent or deliberateness was often required. Once municipalities could be sued a similar approach took firmer root in cases against government defendants: those violations which are the government's "own," those for which it can appropriately be held to respond with damages or other relief, were defined as those that flow from choice or decision sufficiently deliberate to be called "official policy." This mode of analysis adopts tort concepts to evaluate questions that have not been posed in tort. It pushes the discussion into a search for a person whose mind or conduct can be evaluated in tort language and blinds courts to the ways in which harms can be caused by institutional structures and processes.

A. *Tort Analogies*

The *Rizzo* requirement of an "affirmative link" between the defendants' behavior and the plaintiff's injury, as applied to that case, seems to refer to common-law tort concepts of fault and causal connectedness, for tort provides the language that we use to attribute responsibility. It is this requirement of an "affirmative link" that "state of mind," "standard of care," and "official policy or custom" are meant to satisfy. To require the plaintiff to establish the defendant's "state of mind"—a particular intent, or attitude, or purpose—is to assume, quite literally, that the defendant will have a mind to evaluate. Presumably the mind is that of a designated official; there are obvious problems with finding where mind lies when the defendant is a government. When the requirement is put in terms of "standard of care" the problems are somewhat, but not entirely, different. At first glance it is not absurd to argue that section 1983 requires, even in actions against municipalities, something more than mere negligence, the violation of a more stringent standard of care than that applied in the routine common-law tort. Negligence is, first-year law students are taught, an "objective" standard, necessarily an evaluation of the defendant's conduct rather than of her mind. But negligent conduct may be said to be wrongful because of the attitude that it suggests, and in that sense an inquiry into the existence of negligence ultimately also refers to the evaluation of a mind. Whether analyzed as a moral or an economic injunction, negligence in tort is at root a variously elaborated requirement that the injurer take some care to anticipate the potential victim's interests and consider them sympathetically. It imposes, in a sense, a standard of empathy: We must weigh each other's interests as our own. It requires a reciprocity of concern. Another way of putting this, perhaps more congenial to economists, is that we must evaluate proposed conduct from a disinterested perspective, a perspective in which all merely personal choices are assumed to be of equal value. We are, it seems, still talking about a way of thinking. But, again, do institutions think?

Appropriately, the Supreme Court has never accepted a general requirement that something more than negligence be established in order to bring a claim under section 1983 against either municipal or individual defendants. The statute, as the Court has understood, provides a remedy for wrongs defined elsewhere; it does not establish substantive requirements of its own, other than that the violation of federal rights be "under color of" state or local law. But when the Court has looked elsewhere for the definition of those wrongs sought to be remedied in section 1983 litigation, it has often read specific constitutional provisions to include a "state of mind" requirement, to prohibit only government action taken with a specific, improper purpose or attitude. The eighth amendment, for example, has been interpreted to prohibit only actions that indicate "callous indifference" to the rights of others. And the equal protection clause has been read to require an "intent to discriminate." In these cases, the Court has not only required a showing of something more than negligent conduct, it has created a kind of "intentional tort" that is much more difficult to establish than any such tort at common law precisely because it requires evaluation of actual state of mind rather than of conduct as a clue to that mind.

One reason why it might have seemed plausible to ask whether something more than negligence must be proved in a constitutional case is that, to the extent that there are tort analogies to constitutional cases, they most often come from intentional torts. But even wrongs that can be described as trespass, assault and battery, false imprisonment, or defamation take on new urgency when the defendant is the government. When the government is the wrongdoer, ordinary injury is augmented by the abuse of government power, and the Constitution has appropriately been read to address these augmented injuries in their own terms, rather than by analogy to common-law torts.

When the Court requires the plaintiff to establish that the defendant had an intent to discriminate in an equal protection case, or finds dispositive an intent to penalize the exercise of speech in a first amendment case, it is looking for motive, for the purpose behind the act—an inquiry that is irrelevant to intentional tort at common law. The intent that triggers liability at common law represents a cruder attempt to detect those who harbor an improper attitude toward those around them. As in negligence, the improper attitude is assumed from the consequences. And those consequences need not support an inference of ill will or nefarious purpose; it is sufficient that they support an inference of intent to touch the person or property of another (or to move your body in a way that is "substantially certain" to result in such a touching). The constitutional requirement more deliberately and directly penalizes the defendant's attitude toward the plaintiff.

This emphasis on attitude and purpose, while it may be a troubling limitation in constitutional litigation generally, is nonsense in suits against defendants who are governments, for it focuses precisely on that element that exists in individuals but not in institutions—on mind. It is not that "mere negligence" should be enough to state a constitutional case, but that to ask about negligence, at least as a reflection of attitude or motive, is to pose the wrong question. When the defendant is an institution it has no human face. It is not surprising that the plaintiff may often see herself as an asserter of rights with no corresponding obligation in return. The root legal obligation cannot be defined in terms of empathy or mutual care. That cast of mind, implicit in many formulations of the negligence requirement, makes no sense when the defendant is necessarily not an individual, but an institution or its representative. There is no mind, and no possibility that she who sues as plaintiff could stand in the place of the defendant.

There is another way to read common-law negligence that makes no claim to evaluating mind. In this reading, negligent behavior is "at fault" and sufficient to trigger the responsibility to make an injured plaintiff whole because it is inefficient and wasteful of society's resources. As described by Judge Learned Hand in terms enshrined by Judge Richard Posner, tort liability sanctions negligence in order to provide incentives to engage in less wasteful behavior. It encourages actors to evaluate the risks and gains of various courses of conduct from the perspective of all those potentially at risk and to avoid those activities in which "the benefits in accident avoidance exceed the costs of prevention." There is some strain in applying this concept to individual behavior. If the standard upon which liability turns is not to be unduly harsh, there must be some fair expectation that potential defendants can and should act reasonably, that failure to do so is sufficiently aberrant to call forth heavy sanctions when another is injured. This expectation, applied to ordinary human conduct, may be unrealistic. We all act unreasonably much, perhaps most, of the time. By this I do not mean to say that rational behavior never occurs—I hope that it is not infrequent. My point is, rather, that the negligence standard is high and the failure to meet it is not always, or even typically, due to aberration or moral failure in any obvious or natural sense. Accidents are seldom simply the result of egregious carelessness or any other behavior that we can easily condemn as morally wrong. Physical incapacities, fatigue, inattention, preoccupation, and stress play a role. The rule of negligence sets a standard that none of us is capable of meeting much of the time. It is no answer to allow excuses for physical incapacity and other hindrances to rational behavior. Even if they could be the subject of proof, physical incapacities cannot be easily distinguished from those mental incapacities that affect the actor's ability to understand and conform to norms. And allowing excuses for mental incapacities of this sort calls the entire enterprise into question, for incapacity in this sense cannot in practice be neatly separated from the deliberate refusal to accept others' values. Our very ability to perceive and participate in the standards of the community in which we live varies from individual to individual in a manner inaccessible to evaluation by a court.

It might be argued that the negligence standards devised by tort law—even though they have been developed in response to questions about individual obligations and the propriety of specific, rather finite behavior—are particularly well-suited to evaluating the conduct of institutions once those standards are broken free from the concept of mind and only address behavior. Institutions, the argument would go, may be more able than individuals to make sophisticated analyses of the risks of courses of conduct. This is so because organizations, especially those organizations that engage in repetitive risky behavior, possess the resources to acquire large amounts of information over time and to hire employees with the training and expertise necessary to assess risk. To the extent that the negligence test is an effort to capture inefficient activities, it may seem to be most fairly applied to institutional actors, who are in the best position to perform the comparison of costs that the formula requires. Indeed, strict liability, if imposed to provide a practical assurance that an actor will fairly evaluate the interests of others before she acts, may be most appropriately applied to institutional actors for the same reason.

But even so formulated, negligence language, although it might make most sense when applied to institutions rather than to individuals, does not seem adequate to the task of charting institutional responsibility for injuries. The common-law negligence test as it has been applied, even in cases of institutional defendants, focuses on isolated decisions and isolated injuries. It overlooks issues that are unique to institutional behavior—for example, problems of massed power, of cumulative injury, and social planning. And, institutions are not immune from the problems of lack of information and incompetence that afflict individuals. The actors that compose institutions are individuals, and even in groups individuals may act in ways that reflect stupidity or inattention. In fact, institutional structures may create their own pressures toward "nonrational" or wasteful behavior. An employee may prefer inaction because that is least likely to get her into trouble. Her desire to please her superiors, impress her peers or put her subordinates in their place may lead her to rash and foolish, or simply evasive, behavior. Those in the position to set policy may find it easiest to overlook the misconduct of their subordinates. (Perhaps this is what happened in *Rizzo*.) The injury may be made much greater by the simultaneous or cumulative acts of several departments unaware of the steps being taken by each other, accidental injury may be the consequence of a series of decisions made by several employees, no one of whom perceived the whole and understood the risk being run. If institutions are to be held liable for these injuries it is because concepts of fairness in attribution of responsibility that have been developed for individuals are not applicable in imposing liability upon institutions. But the greater danger of our lack of language unique to institutional responsibility is that, by focusing only on one incident of decisionmaking or injury, injuries caused by institutional structures will not even be perceived.

B. *The Alternative*

The Supreme Court's response to these dilemmas . . . was not to move beyond casting the evaluation in terms of individual wrongdoing, but to look for an individual (or individuals) who could be analyzed in the government's stead because he could be said to act for the government. In addition, it was assumed without discussion that government acts as government only when it plays the role of decisionmaker, or legislature. So the inquiry took the form of a search for those persons, and those legislative bodies, who make decisions: government "policy or custom" was "made by [a local government's] lawmakers or by those whose edicts or acts may fairly be said to represent official policy." Much of the post-*Monell* litigation has revolved around the question of whether a particular official had sufficient status and authority to act as a decisionmaker for a municipality.

After *Monell* the Court was caught between its commitment to the rejection of government liability "for an injury inflicted solely by its employees or agents," and the only language it possessed for ascribing responsibility for injuries—tort language which describes wrongdoing and causation in terms that were devised for the actions of individuals. The Court had no language for describing how an institution or a government uniquely acts, so it looked to acts, such as passage of ordinances or regulations, or decisions by those with a very high level of authority, that, in essence, label themselves as institutional or governmental. There must, the Court seems to have decided, be some formal decision of this sort. To count every official's decisions as forming government "policy" would be tantamount to imposing *respondeat superior* liability. "Official policy or custom," defined as conscious choices made by high-level decisionmakers, seemed the only option between vicarious liability and no liability.

There are other alternatives. The Court in *Monell* implicitly referred to some of them in describing the extraordinary reach of the first conference substitute for the amendment proposed by Senator Sherman. That proposal

> imposed liability on the government defendant whether or not it has notice of the impending riot, whether or not the municipality was authorized to exercise a police power, whether or not it exerted all reasonable efforts to stop the riot, and whether or not the rioters were caught and punished.

Under a statute that, unlike the proposed amendment, accepted these limitations on municipal liability, a government could still be held liable for conduct that did not involve an official decision to act. That is, the municipal defendant could be held liable for those cases in which it had notice of an impending riot and possessed the power to stop it, yet reasonable preventative steps were not taken and the rioters escaped. Liability could be imposed in such a case—whatever the source of the failure, be it an official decision to turn a blind eye to the riot or simply excessive diffusion of responsibility—without encroaching on the concerns implicit in Congress' rejection of the Sherman amendment.

The Court's formulation ignores this option. It requires a decision. Caught by the language of tort, the Court apparently has concluded that liability based on, for example, cumulative inattention, or diffusion of responsibility, would be inconsistent with *Rizzo v. Goode*'s insistence on an "affirmative link" between individual victim and individual wrongdoer, the precursor of *Monell's* rejection of vicarious liability.

But the assumption that all categories of liability must be divided into either vicarious liability or affirmative decisions is not even supported by tort law as applied to individuals, and it is particularly strained and inappropriate in discussing the injurious effects of institutions. Even if individual liability for constitutional torts could be fairly limited to affirmative misbehavior, institutions occupy space in the world in a different way than individuals do, and the consequences, both beneficial and harmful, of their actions are created differently. The shape and the existence of institutional bodies are the result of choices that continue over time and that can be modified. This is simply not true in the same way of individuals. Institutions "think" differently, or, more accurately, they don't think at all, yet they create consequences. In evaluating individual liability, Anglo-American tort law has not as a general rule held defendants liable for omissions, for failures to act. This seems to have been what concerned the Court in *Rizzo*, and again in *Monell*. But institutions do something "affirmative" by simply existing, and, unlike individuals, they can change their form of existence or simply cease to exist.

One does not exhaust what an individual is and does by looking only to declared purposes and intent. That is even more true of organizations. I have suggested some of the problems above: Institutions cause consequences even through diffusion of responsibility. Or through common practices that are widespread but do not "have the force of law" and may even be flatly prohibited by "official" regulations. And there are structural disincentives to take action or to see problems, and, more affirmatively, communal mores or fellow feelings that lead those within an institution to rank the interests of each other higher than the interests of those outside. At the least, we cannot be as confident as the Court seems to be that the language of choice and intent and motive is adequate for evaluating the behavior of governments.

One danger of a narrowed inquiry into government responsibility is that it will prevent the Court from recognizing that consequences may be created over time, or that several branches of a government may work together to create a constitutional tort where no such tort would exist were the activity of only one branch considered. The Court has not been completely unwilling to evaluate the way in which an institution functions as a whole or over time. But the most obvious example of such thinking—the school desegregation cases following *Brown v. Board of Education*—reveals an entrenched unwillingness to follow such an approach to its conclusion. In the desegregation cases the Court, although requiring evidence of a deliberate discriminatory decision made by the board defendants, has evaluated each district's school board as an ongoing institution. A conclusion that the Constitution has been violated can be reached on the basis of acts of deliberate segregation committed by members whose service ended years before, and once such a conclusion has been reached it will support an order that remedial steps be taken by current board members who themselves have made no discriminatory decisions. But this step was relatively easy—the board could still be described, by analogy to an individual and like a legislature, as a single maker of formal decisions. Once a finding has been made that a board, albeit in an earlier incarnation, has unconstitutionally discriminated, the remedies for this discrimination have been broadly crafted to create a functioning desegregated system—a goal that necessarily requires a broad view of how the structure of schools within a district might best work to minimize the effects of past segregation. Aside from the remedial implications and the willingness to consider a school board as a single institution over time, rather than as a shifting group of individuals, these decisions break no very significant ground. In their refusal to reach *de facto* segregation the decisions retain the basic requirement that one individual, or a group of individuals, be shown to have made a decision motivated by an unconstitutional intent to discriminate on the basis of race. Even if the evaluation can extend back in time, the requirement that a particular state of mind be established in an identifiable individual or individuals remains. These cases are, from that perspective, quite consistent with the Court's insistence on reducing the question of institutional responsibility to one of individual wrongdoing. They represent no true alternative, but they suggest that movement away from the individual model is not impossible.

C. *Implications*

If it were to pursue seriously the matter of how an institution functions as a whole, the Court would have to ask questions that have no parallel in cases involving individual wrongdoing: Does the institution's structure encourage or discourage adherence to constitutional standards of behavior? Does the institutional arrangement conceal consequences or dilute responsibility in a way conducive to unconstitutional behavior? One of the consequences of this change in attention might be an expansion of what constitutes redressable harm. In the constitutional context, the harms in question are often something other than obvious physical injuries. The terms of the Constitution, read with an increased awareness of the ways in which governmental power is felt by citizens, draw our attention to nonphysical harms: emotional injuries, cumulative injuries inflicted by many small acts over time, and the more tenuous economic injuries, such as decreased opportunities for education or employment. Injuries of this sort may be attributed to institutional behavior only as courts become more sophisticated in tracing its effects; they may be easy to see only when courts stop searching for an identifiable individual decisionmaker.

Thinking about institutions as institutions breaks the model of reciprocal responsibility that is the basis of the common law. The language of common-law tort presumes that each litigant is potentially both plaintiff and defendant; the defendant is, at least theoretically, held only to those standards that could also be fairly applied to the plaintiff were their positions reversed. When the question of responsibility is not defined in terms of the reciprocal obligations of potentially equal individuals, it becomes possible for the plaintiff to ask that her interests be taken into account by the defendant to an even greater degree than has been required by the common law. She may also believe, and the judge may agree, that a government defendant can fairly be required to be more responsive to broad community values in a way that would be an inappropriate imposition on private or individual conduct, for the government is charged to reflect the goals of society as a whole rather than the narrower self-interest permitted private actors. At most, the redefinition of responsibility may take the form of a demand that the plaintiff be provided for, protected, maintained in a certain state of security and well-being. At the least, it leads to a demand for dignity—for fair consideration of one's concerns and interests, as at common law, but with specific and visible guarantees to assure the supplicant that the process is indeed fair; for freedom from stigma or improper categorization; for freedom to exercise certain rights, such as free speech or privacy. It goes too far to say that citizens are owed absolute protection from harm, or a minimum guarantee to the good life, from those who hold power, but there are injuries that may properly be the focus of litigation even though they cannot be analyzed by traditional tort doctrine.

If the court were to break free, in constitutional litigation (and perhaps in litigation against other sorts of institutions), from evaluating the defendant's acts as if they were the product of an individual mind, one consequence would be to bring to the fore the irrelevance of the categories of intent, negligence, and even strict liability derived from tort. Nor should that other indicia of "mind"—a formal decision—be required. The government, like other institutions, operates through structures that direct and dispose of power. These can injure grievously when deliberately used by individual human beings to do harm. And they can injure just as seriously through inertia, direction of energy to narrow goals, and oversight in the design of institutional structures. It is in this sense that focus on institutional structures may expand our sensitivity to previously disregarded harms. It may lead us to be more appreciative of the positions of some defendants as well. For example, when the defendant is in fact an individual, rather than an institution, an awareness of institutional structure, and of the incentive systems which that structure creates, may lead us to be more tolerant of the individual's oversight, lack of imagination, or failure to take care.

Even when the defendant is the government, or any institution of great power and complexity, it may not be fair to expect strict compliance with the obligation (whether embodied in tort law or in constitutional provisions) to consider the impact of one's activities on the interests of others. The scope of potential victims may include all of society, and the capacity of even a large and well-run institution to take all the relevant interests into account has limits. Damages as the price of failure may be too high. Yet, the price paid by the victim may also be severe and one for which it is indeed appropriate to hold the institution responsible. Moral evaluations of conduct, which are often used to justify the imposition of liability on individual defendants, need not be the sole basis of institutional obligation, particularly if the remedy is an injunction to take care rather than an order to pay damages. If this is what "responsibility" entails, it may have more to do with an assessment of the severity of the plaintiff's injury, and the conclusion that it may be avoided or reduced by the defendant, than with any evaluation of the "morality" of the defendant's acts. The point would be that there are certain *harms* that institutions should not inflict, or should pay for, or should make special efforts to minimize—rather than that a wrong decision has been made or wrongful conduct undertaken.

IV. The Alternative Applied

The very difficulty of formulating a vocabulary of responsibility that is not derived from tort suggests that the courts might be wise to avoid taking on the task of tracing the consequences of institutional structures and processes. Yet in some cases it has seemed most natural to think of the institution as a whole in attributing responsibility for harms. In these cases the Court's first instinct has been to frame the question in terms that break away from tort, and only as an afterthought has the language of tort exerted its pull. The cases do not engage in the full analysis of structure and context suggested above, but they do provide some indication that the Court's difficulties in articulating a theory of institutional responsibility are due to habits of language that can be overcome. One example can be found among the "official policy and custom" cases. The more imaginative efforts to think about these questions anew are found in cases involving due process claims, and it is from one of these efforts that the Court has retreated most dramatically.

A. *Institutional Wrongs:* Owen

Owen v. City of Independence indicates that, at least when there are explicit, decisive, and virtually contemporaneous actions by several top decisionmakers, the Court will recognize that several branches of the government, working together, can create a constitutional tort even though the action of any single branch is not by itself unconstitutional. *Owen* was an action brought against the city and several officials in their official capacity. The plaintiff was a former chief of police who had been publicly charged by the city council with abuse of his position and fired by the city manager on the following day. The case was complicated by evidence that the manager had made the decision to fire Owen before the council resolution and by the absence of any stated grounds for the termination other than a reference to a city charter provision that gave the manager sole authority to remove department heads. There was no indication that the city manager and the council had jointly planned the sequence of events. The court of appeals, applying *Monell*, held that the circumstances of the discharge had inflicted an injury to Owen's reputation that "was caused by the official conduct of the City's lawmakers . . . [and] amounted to official policy," depriving him of a protected liberty interest. There was no cross-petition by the city challenging this conclusion that Owen had been deprived of a "liberty" interest, so it was not properly before the Court. But Justice Brennan, writing for the majority, took the time in a footnote to state that "[w]e find no merit" in the city's contention that there was no deprivation of a protected interest. The problem was that no protected interest would have been impaired had the discharge occurred without any damage to plaintiff's reputation, and damage to reputation alone also does not implicate any constitutionally protected interest. In Owen's case, the manager performed the discharge, while the council issued the allegedly defamatory statements. Neither act, standing alone, amounted to a violation of the Constitution. Justice Brennan, however, saw no barrier to recovery: "[T]he city—through the unanimous resolution of the City Council—released to the public an allegedly false statement impugning petitioner's honesty and integrity. Petitioner was discharged the next day. . . . [T]he defamatory and stigmatizing charges certainly 'occur[red] in the course of the termination of employment.'" The Court, then, refused to divide the city of Independence into separate decisionmakers (the council and the manager) and require that one of these be found to have acted unconstitutionally. It emphasized, instead, the effect on the plaintiff of the city's actions, taken as a whole. It was enough that Owen had suffered an injury that would clearly implicate the Constitution had it been solely the result of either the manager's or the council's actions. Yet, the Court still thought it significant that both parts of the city government had issued overt and explicit announcements that decisions had been made. Both the manager's written notice discharging the plaintiff and the council's resolution fit easily with the language of purpose and decision devised in *Monell.* Under those circumstances the Court thought it fair to hold the city accountable. (It may also have been important that Owen could point to a subsequent decision that could be described as the unconstitutional act of a single actor: after the discharge, at a time when all were aware of the Council's actions, the city refused a demand from Owen for leave to appeal the discharge decision.)

However, in addressing the question upon which certiorari *had* been granted—a question of remedy, rather than of defining the wrong—Justice Brennan, writing for the Court, moved away from the analogy to individual responsibility that underlay *Rizzo* and *Monell.* Owen sought declaratory and injunctive relief, including a hearing, backpay, and attorney's fees, but during the course of litigation he reached the age of mandatory retirement, so his claim eventually reduced to a suit for damages in lieu of backpay. The question before the Supreme Court was whether the city could claim a qualified immunity of the sort available to an executive official in a damage action when he or she is said to have deprived someone of a constitutional right that was not clearly established at the time of the official's actions. In *Owen*, the court of appeals had held, a qualified immunity of this sort would relieve the city of liability, for the applicable constitutional rule requiring notice and an opportunity for a hearing had not been declared by the Supreme Court until ten weeks after the discharge of plaintiff Owen.

As in *Monell* this question of immunity was regarded as turning on the interpretation of section 1983: Had Congress, in enacting that statute, intended to preserve or create a qualified immunity for municipal corporations? The answer was no, the Court concluded, because by 1871, the year of the statute's passage, corporations, including municipalities, "were treated as natural persons for virtually all purposes of constitutional and statutory analysis." Justice Brennan found no relevant functional protections of the sort that had been found to immunize individuals sued for misconduct committed while in office. In this part of the opinion, the Court in *Owen*, as in *Monell*, built on a presumed statutory conflation of institutional into individual liability, but here, ironically, the ultimate effect is to expand municipal liability beyond that imposed upon individuals.

But Brennan departed from the *Monell* analogy between institutional and individual liability in his rejection of the argument that municipal immunity, even if not available at common law in 1871, must have been intended to have been incorporated into section 1983 because it is most compatible with the purposes of the statute. In this discussion, which focused on the consequences of imposing a damage remedy on a city, the Court accepted cost-allocation and loss-spreading arguments that had been implicitly rejected in *Monell* and other decisions that addressed the scope of municipal liability. Once the local government has been found to be "responsible" under the test imposed by *Monell*, the Court concluded, it is fair to impose damages in order to serve cost-allocation principles of deterrence and loss spreading. The justifications for such cost allocations are described with explicit reference to the possibility of controlling the more amorphous harms that can be caused by institutional structures. The threat of damage liability, Justice Brennan thought,

> may encourage those in a policymaking position to institute internal rules and programs designed to minimize the likelihood of unintentional infringements on constitutional rights. Such procedures are particularly beneficial in preventing those "systemic" injuries that result not so much from the conduct of any single individual, but from the interactive behavior of several government officials, each of whom may be acting in good faith.

Perhaps, the Justice added, the threat of liability would "increase the attentiveness with which officials at the higher levels of government supervise the conduct of their subordinates."

This seems quite unlike the caution inherent in the rationales of *Rizzo* and *Monell*, and indeed, these goals simply cannot be achieved given the Court's exclusion of most, perhaps all, systemic injuries from the sphere of "official policy." Yet the Court in *Owen* went even further: it concluded that it is fair to hold the government liable in damages simply as a matter of equitable loss spreading. The constitutional wrong becomes one of those "inevitable costs of government [which should be] borne by all the taxpayers [rather than] . . . those whose rights . . . have been violated." It may seem callous to talk about constitutional violations as an inevitable cost of government business. But Justice Brennan was talking about a constitutional development that, by hypothesis, "could not have been foreseen by municipal officials." It is also significant that this was litigation against the government as employer. It is easier to see the employment torts of government as simply the costs of government business. In most employment cases, in contrast to cases of, say, police or prison guard misconduct, the financial interest of the government is obvious and unremarkable, and the government seldom commits harms of that special level of seriousness that cannot be duplicated by private individuals. The Court was also, it is important to remember, careful to stress that rationales of deterrence and loss spreading would be heard only on the question of remedy. Loss spreading may have "joined fault as a factor in distributing the costs of official misconduct," but "the public will be forced to bear only the costs of injury inflicted by 'the execution of a government's policy or custom'" within the terms of *Monell*.

B. *Due Process:* Parratt *and* Logan

The Court has on other occasions found it easy, even natural, to evaluate the impact of an institutional structure as a whole on an injured individual. I shall describe two recent examples. One of them was overruled when the Court belatedly realized that it was slipping away from the individual wrongdoer model; the other is still sound law. Like *Owen*, they are both cases claiming a violation of due process: *Parratt v. Taylor* and *Logan v. Zimmerman Brush Co.*

In *Parratt* and *Logan*, even more than in *Owen*, it is not easy to say that there is an identifiable wrongdoer, or even an identifiable decision, and the Court does not point to either. *Parratt* was brought by a prisoner, Taylor, whose hobby kit, ordered through the mail, was lost at some point between its arrival at the prison and Taylor's release from segregation. Taylor sued the warden and the prison hobby manager, alleging that they had deprived him of his property without due process of law and seeking damages that reflected the (relatively minor) value of the lost kit.

Procedural due process cases like *Parratt* have frustrated the courts because they look, on their facts, so much like ordinary common-law torts, yet a constitutional claim is clearly being made. It was this sort of case that led some judges to conclude that negligent wrongdoing was not sufficient, absent proof of wrongful intent, to support a constitutional tort action. In *Parratt* the Supreme Court realized that requiring a showing of something more than negligence was the wrong answer to the wrong question, that neither section 1983 nor any general principle of constitutional law made degree of culpability relevant. The question whether something more than negligence might be required only seemed relevant because of the false analogy to common-law tort with its inquiry into individualized wrongdoing. To focus on the distinction between intentional and negligent acts was to lift common-law language inappropriately into a constitutional case.

Taylor could prove nothing more than negligence on the part of prison officials. Yet his claim that he had been deprived of his property without constitutionally required process was not implausible, for he had lost his property at the hands of people empowered by the state, and neither a prior hearing nor prior notice had been provided. The Court found, however, that Taylor had failed to state a constitutional claim—not because he could only allege negligence, but because postdeprivation remedies available through the state could provide due process. Obviously, this holding gave the prisoner less than he might have hoped; he had been seeking a postdeprivation remedy in the federal court. Yet the Court in *Parratt* still had done something remarkable. Its reasoning broke away from the common-law model—which defines the wrongdoer and the wronged narrowly—and evaluated whether a constitutional wrong had occurred by looking at the operation of the system as a whole. One branch of the state deprived Taylor of his hobby kit; another could provide the necessary hearing and, if appropriate, compensation.

Taylor might have expected a federal damage remedy because he was looking at his injury through the common-law model: he had been deprived of his property by the prison employees who lost the hobby kit, and he thought that he should have an action against them. Section 1983, if it were read to authorize an award of damages equivalent to the lost kit, could provide that action. Under that approach, however, the overlap between constitutional and common law would be too great. The Court adopted a broader perspective. It defined a wrong without a specifiable wrongdoer: any constitutional injury that might exist would be that inflicted by the state system as a whole where it failed to provide due process, and not by the individual employees who had allegedly lost the hobby kit. Under the circumstances, this analysis made considerable sense, for where the loss is not deliberate the actors responsible for the deprivation have made no decision of the sort that a prior hearing could inform. But the fact that a loss is not deliberate does not mean that no predeprivation steps are available to government actors. Where the risk of loss is foreseeable and sufficiently high, due process may be said to require that steps be taken to minimize that risk. Though the loss of the property in a situation like *Parratt* is not intended, the failure to provide these safeguards might itself be either deliberate or inadvertent, depending on whether the risk had been explicitly focused upon in the design of the institutional structure. The Court in *Parratt* did not address that question, perhaps because it assumed that "process" referred to the sort of safeguards, such as hearings, that might surround individuated decisions made in particular cases. It thought, therefore, only of what could be done for Taylor, and after-the-fact compensation seemed enough.

The Court did not say who could be sued if there were no postdeprivation procedures and their absence was found to violate the constitutional guarantees of due process. There was a suggestion that it might then be appropriate to sue the prison employees for the price of the lost property. That is, one way to redress a lack in the state remedial structure would be to provide an alternative damage remedy in federal court. This approach would not only raise the problem of overlap with tort described above, but would also provide, at best, a partial, temporary, solution. The prison employees who lost the kit were not in a position to remedy the constitutional lack of due process. They were unlikely to have either the power to create a postdeprivation remedy or the power to bring about changes in institutional processes that would minimize the risk of loss. Again, no single person or body in a *Parratt* situation is responsible for the harm. The injury is caused by the way in which the different parts of the system fit together. One arm of the state brings about the deprivation and another fails to provide the process required by law. An alternative remedy, one that would be more consistent with the theory of the case, would be to grant declaratory or injunctive relief against the state prison officials, requiring that adequate process be provided. This would avoid the unfairness of holding individual officials liable in federal court for a wrong attributable to the structure of the system. It would also respond to Justice Powell's concern, in his concurrence, that the real wrongdoers under the *Parratt* theory are the state or its lawmakers, both of whom are immune from damage liability.

Logan v. Zimmerman Brush Co. is also a due process case, though it stands on the border between procedure and substance. It was not an action brought under section 1983, but an appeal from a state supreme court decision in favor of a private employer in a case brought under the Illinois Fair Employment Practices Act. Appellant Logan had filed a charge of discrimination with the Illinois Fair Employment Practices Commission. Although the state statute required the commission to convene a factfinding conference within 120 days of the bringing of the charge, the conference on Logan's complaint was scheduled by the commission for five days *after* the expiration of the statutory period. The untimely scheduling of the conference was apparently inadvertent and, of course, completely beyond Logan's control. However, at the employer's petition the state supreme court held that this failure to comply with the statutory time limit deprived the commission of jurisdiction and extinguished Logan's claim.

The United States Supreme Court reversed, concluding that a state "may not finally destroy a property interest [here, Logan's right to use the commission procedures] without first giving the putative owner an opportunity to present his claim of entitlement." Again, it was only because of the combined effect of actions by several different arms of the state that a constitutional wrong had been done. The Court did not say that the commission had acted unconstitutionally in scheduling the factfinding conference beyond the 120-day period; in fact, the commission had denied the employer's request to dismiss Logan's complaint. What was unconstitutional was to give the commission's error the significance it was given by the Illinois Supreme Court, to make it the grounds for destroying Logan's claim. The United States Supreme Court found constitutional error by looking at the way in which the claim-processing system worked as a whole. It asked whether the state structure was consistent with constitutional requirements of fair procedure. The case stands at the border between substantive and procedural due process because the Court did not ask whether the decision to deprive Logan of his claim—a decision that can be said to have been made either by the state legislature in imposing the 120-day limit or by the state supreme court in enforcing that limit in this way—was made with fair procedures, but whether that decision could be reached at all.

In both *Parratt* and *Logan* the Court was properly sensitive to the design of a state system in its handling of citizen concerns, and to the possibility that structural design may create constitutional questions through either deliberate omissions or inadvertence. (It is possible, even probable, that the Illinois legislature in prescribing the 120-day limit never asked what sanctions would be imposed if the commission failed to act within that time period.) What the Court seemed to require of the system was not anything remarkable, but simply that fair weight be given to the interests of those whom the institution affects. This is a requirement that is reminiscent of the commands of common-law torts. But it takes special form when there is no single act or single actor. And, of course, when government conduct is at stake, the standards to be met are found in the particular requirements of the Constitution. When the defendant is no longer an individual like the plaintiff, nor private and thus presumably motivated by self-interest, greater claims may appropriately be made.

Although *Logan* and *Parratt* addressed the constitutional question whether due process had been complied with, rather than the statutory issue raised by suits against government defendants, the language used to attribute responsibility to government has influenced the discussion of these constitutional matters too. Both *Logan* and *Parratt* appropriately looked to the impact of the government's actions as a whole on the federal plaintiff, rather than engaging in a search for an individual or individuals whose culpability could be measured by standards familiar from tort. But the Court has not been able to maintain this direction without hesitation. When it found that applying *Parratt* would require it to address new questions in new ways, it retreated abruptly to the more familiar emphasis on state-of-mind and negligence-versus-intent borrowed from tort. The retreat came last Term in two prison cases, *Daniels v. Williams* and *Davidson v. Cannon*.

Neither action was a suit against a government entity defendant. Daniels, who had been a prisoner in a Richmond, Virginia, jail, sued a deputy who had negligently left newspapers and a pillow on a prison stairway. Daniels slipped on these materials, fell, suffered back and ankle injuries, and alleged in his section 1983 action that the state remedy for his injuries was inadequate. Davidson, while incarcerated in a New Jersey state prison, was attacked by another prisoner, who stabbed him with a fork about his face and body. Davidson's section 1983 action was brought against prison officials who had failed to respond to a note in which he reported a threat that preceded the attack and, at least implicitly, requested protection. New Jersey, by statute, provided that: "Neither a public entity nor a public employee is liable for . . . any injury caused by . . . a prisoner to any other prisoner." Both plaintiffs argued that the inadequacy of the state postdeprivation remedies violated due process under *Parratt*. The Supreme Court, in opinions by Justice Rehnquist, held that neither plaintiff had made out a constitutional case.

As in earlier opinions, Justice Rehnquist described the problem before the Court as "determining when tortious conduct by state officials rises to the level of a constitutional tort." He held that *Parratt* was in error insofar as it had concluded that an unintended loss caused by the negligent conduct of government officials could be a "deprivation" implicating the due process clause. If the plaintiff could prove no intent to deprive him of his property or to injure him physically, there was no "deprivation" of an interest and therefore no need to reach the question of what process was due. Once more, individual culpability—the ascertainment of a particular state of mind held by a government official or officials—was made an essential inquiry in establishing a constitutional claim. Justice Rehnquist's reasoning in *Daniels* was sparse at best. It consisted primarily of the announcement that the Court had been persuaded to adopt a concurrence written by Justice Powell in *Parratt*, along with brief quotations from that opinion and from Justice Stewart's concurrence in the same case. This is the heart of the *Daniels* opinion:

> Not only does the word "deprive" in the Due Process Clause connote more than a negligent act, but we should not "open the federal courts to lawsuits where there has been no affirmative abuse of power." [*Parratt*, 451 U.S.] at 548-549 [Powell, J., concurring in the result]; see also *id.*, at 545 . . . (Stewart J., concurring) ("To hold that this kind of loss is a deprivation of property within the meaning of the Fourteenth Amendment seems not only to trivialize, but grossly to distort the meaning and intent of the Constitution"). Upon reflection, we agree and overrule *Parratt* . . . .

The key to what rises to the level of a constitutional violation was described, appropriately enough, as the "affirmative abuse of power." The assumption in *Daniels*, however, was that power can be abused only through those particular acts that would also meet the requirements of the more egregious common-law torts. The claims made in *Daniels* and *Davidson*, Justice Rehnquist thought, would require that the Constitution "supplant traditional tort law in laying down rules of conduct to regulate liability for injuries that attend living together in society." The post-*Parratt* cases involving intentional acts by government officials were described as involving "quite different" claims. The distinction seems to be between negligence and intentional torts.

But neither Daniels nor Davidson had suffered ordinary injuries of the sort that private individuals inflict upon each other in the course of living together. As Justice Blackmun pointed out in his dissent, Davidson had been "stripped [by the state] of all means of self protection" and forced to live among very dangerous people. And, as *Parratt* accurately recognized, both Davidson and Daniels, unlike individuals injured by other individuals, had been deprived by the state of a remedy for compensation. Daniels' fall could have happened on any stairway—a point that eight Justices stress—but this stairway, unlike most others, was owned by an entity that could give itself special protection against suit. To provide that special protection may not be an abuse of power, but it is certainly an exercise of power that raises questions not reached by common-law tort.

The holding of *Daniels* and *Davidson* applies to all claims brought under the due process clause, for the requirements of that constitutional provision, be they substantive or procedural, apply only when the plaintiff has suffered a "deprivation." But the Court's emphasis on deliberateness and intent makes most sense as a narrow reading of those situations in which procedural safeguards are due. Read this way, *Daniels* and *Davidson* could be said implicitly to define procedural due process protections as necessary only when government "agents decide to 'deprive any person of life, liberty, or property,'" on the basis of facts that might be misperceived. If the only constitutionally required procedures are those designed to minimize factual error in government decisionmaking, it is plausible to insist on some showing that a decision has been made. The required procedures need not be adversarial. (They could, as was argued in *Baker v. McCollan*, consist of checking files to ascertain the true identity of a prisoner who protests that he is not the man wanted by the police.) And they could, perhaps, be provided after the fact. If a decision has been made and proper procedures have been followed, there should be no liability for error.

But *Daniels* and *Davidson* were not written as procedural due process cases. And, if the question of constitutional interpretation turns on the word "deprivation," rather than on what process is due, the quality of the loss to the plaintiff is at least as important as the wrongfulness of any official's conduct. If the cases were intended to address questions beyond the procedural safeguards necessary in the making of fact-based decisions, and the effect of government action on the plaintiff is to be weighed, it is not so easy to see why questions of abuse of power are not raised when the government fails to take steps to minimize inadvertent loss or provides itself with a unique immunity from suits for compensation. Government practices and institutional structures can create special and impermissible harms whether they are the result of deliberate decisions or inadvertence.

The Court dismissed the claims brought in *Daniels* and *Davidson* because the front-line officials—the deputy who left the pillow on the stairs and the correctional officials who failed to respond to Davidson's request for protection—had made no deliberate decision to injure the plaintiffs. But deliberate decisions were in fact at issue in both cases, for the basic challenge of each plaintiff was to the state's refusal to provide compensatory relief. A state's decision to invoke sovereign immunity raises a question that, even under the Court's analysis, should be asked: Is the decision to deny a remedy under the circumstances an "arbitrary exercise of the powers of government" or governmental power "used for purposes of oppression"? Justice Rehnquist overlooked these decisions—including the embodiment of New Jersey's choice in that most "official" of forms, a statute—because he saw these as tort cases between the individuals who had suffered loss and the government agents who had dealt with them directly.

To ask whether the invocation of sovereign immunity is an abuse of governmental power is not to answer that question in the affirmative. It is far from unreasonable, for instance, for government to provide protection for its agents, coupled with mechanisms for internal discipline and the possibility of compensation from public resources. Even a flat protection in certain cases, such as prisoner suits, may be found to be not unfair. Indeed, that was Justice Stevens' conclusion in *Davidson*, where he asked the question posed above and concluded that there was no violation of the Constitution.

If the Court could have preserved the analysis of *Parratt* and still defeated plaintiff's claim, why did it so forcefully back away from that case? The Justices may have feared that they were about to venture into an area where the temptation to ask too much of government would be very strong. But that temptation could have been addressed directly, as it was in Justice Stevens' concurrence. Instead, the Court's shift in direction seems to reflect the view, expressed most forcefully in *Rizzo v. Goode*, that constitutional litigation is not appropriately used to address questions of institutional structures and practices. In this view, constitutional litigation, by analogy to tort, redresses only those injuries caused by aberrant individual defendants who have violated social norms for personal behavior. Yet, from *Paul v. Davis*, in which Justice Rehnquist first expressed his concern that constitutional litigation not be "a font of tort law," through *Daniels* and *Davidson*, which are the most recent expression of that preoccupation, the Court has also sought to distinguish constitutional cases from tort. It has sought to do so by defining constitutional cases as falling into some particularly egregious subcategory of torts, rather than by taking the opportunity to develop a vocabulary, truly independent from tort, that could be used to discuss the special problems created by the massing of power in institutions. In due process cases, as in litigation involving municipal liability, the Court has assumed that those cases sufficiently serious to merit constitutional attention are the cases that parallel "the most serious" torts, where the plaintiff can point to a deliberate decision to act wrongfully. Yet, by the Court's own description, the special character of the

Constitution is that it directly addresses questions of structure and the abuse of power.

Focusing on structures and processes as mechanisms for the abuse of power may indeed lead the courts to questions that they have not faced before. Many of these questions will be difficult. But it will be even more difficult to maintain the fiction that all questions of responsibility for harm can be answered by reference to norms developed for individual behavior. The effort to maintain that fiction leads only to such futile doctrinal developments as the attempt to find a governmental "mind" or the refusal to recognize that a loss can be felt as keenly when it comes about through the negligent misuse of state power as when it comes about through intentional abuse. Legitimacy depends at least as much upon credibility as upon caution in asking new questions.

* * * * *

If a vocabulary for resolving questions of institutional responsibility were developed in constitutional litigation, it might, of course, prove useful in tort. Once we see how injuries can be caused by institutions in ways not analogous to harm caused by individuals, claims similar to those brought in litigation against the government might be raised against other powerful institutions. For example: The "due process" demand for access, for consideration, might as easily be made upon private but powerful institutions, and it could be vindicated, where appropriate, as a common-law tort. Or tort might address institutional practices that intensify the impact of racist or sexist biases. Tort law might focus more deliberately, not on actual or hypothetical individual behavior, but on whether practices or structures have contributed significantly to the creation of undesirable consequences.

A shift of focus beyond questions of individual wrongdoing is important. Our struggle with the consequences of racism and sexism has made us aware that injuries do not flow solely from the acts of evil or careless persons. And we have begun to be open to the possibility that characteristics attributed to women or minorities, as a class or as individuals, may be the consequence of social structures and expectations. Neither torts nor constitutional law can ensure individual fulfillment. Relief from abuse of power is important in furthering individual liberty, but so is a sense of responsibility for one's own life and the existence of groups that can be a source of strength and fellowship. The law cannot give us all jobs in a depressed economy. It does not help us to resist the temptations of flattery. It offers no relief from the casual cruelties of friends and strangers. But a law that addresses only the isolated behavior of individuals, whether private or official, sees only some of the ways in which power can be abused, and the abuse of power is a subject with which the law is properly concerned.

Peter H. Schuck, *Municipal Liability Under Section 1983: Some Lessons from Tort Law and Organization Theory,* 77 Georgetown Law Journal 1753 (1989)

* * *

I. Final Authority, Custom, and Causation

Under *Monell* a municipality may not be held liable under § 1983 simply because it employed the tortfeasor who was acting within the scope of his or her employment. Rather, it is only "when execution of a government's policy or custom, whether made by its lawmakers or by those whose edicts or acts may fairly be said to represent official policy, inflicts the injury that the government as an entity is responsible under Section 1983." Furthermore, one cannot establish the municipality's liability unless one can demonstrate that the enforcement of its policy—defined as "a course of action consciously chosen from various alternatives"—was the "moving force" behind the violation. In Part III, I consider the notions of "policy" and "final policymaking authority," suggesting that they are poor doctrinal touchstones because as understood by the courts they are conceptually muddled and bear little relation to the reality of bureaucratic decisionmaking. Here, however, I take the doctrinal categories seriously and show how they operate in § 1983 cases.

The existence of an official municipal policy can be shown in any of at least three ways. The most straightforward evidence is its formal embodiment in a policy statement, ordinance, or decision officially adopted by the municipality's governing body or top officials. In addition, a practice sufficiently persistent and widespread to constitute a governmental "custom" may be treated as tantamount to an official policy, even if it has not been formally adopted by the municipality's governing body. The most elusive and problematic determination to be made, however, is whether the behavior of certain officials constitutes "edicts or acts [which] may fairly be said to represent official policy."

The main difficulties in applying this doctrine arise in performing three analytical tasks: (1) identifying those officials whose decisions constitute official policy; (2) determining when a practice, which does not amount to an official policy, nevertheless establishes a governmental "custom" upon which liability can be premised; and (3) evaluating the causal relationship implied by the "moving force" requirement. Throughout this Article, I shall refer to these three tasks as the "final authority," "custom," and "causation" issues. In the following three sections of Part I, I shall summarize the state of the legal doctrines surrounding each of these issues. In particular, I shall show how each has been used to defeat § 1983 liability in situations in which, as Part II demonstrates, liability would routinely have been imposed upon a private organization even without resort to a respondeat superior theory.

Preliminarily, it must be emphasized that at a doctrinal and even at an analytical level, the final authority, custom, and causation issues are difficult to distinguish from one another and from a fourth issue: whether the municipality's level of fault extends beyond mere negligence, which no longer suffices to trigger § 1983 liability. Courts seem to use these issues quite interchangeably, and the courts' language often makes it impossible to know upon which of them their decisions are meant to turn. In that sense, the discussion that follows may seem to ascribe to the "official policy" doctrine an analytical clarity that is in fact absent from the cases.

A. THE "FINAL AUTHORITY" ISSUE

Only those officials who possess the requisite policymaking authority are capable of establishing "official policy" within the meaning of *Monell*. Subsequent cases have refined this proposition to limit the universe of such officials to those who possess "final authority to establish municipal policy with respect to the action ordered." Hierarchical position is not dispositive: municipal liability may be predicated upon the act of even a low-level subordinate who has been delegated final authority in a limited area, while a high-level official's order may not be actionable unless she possesses final policymaking authority as to the particular area in which she acted. But for an official with "final authority," even a single action may suffice to constitute municipal policy.

A search for one who possesses "final authority" often operates to immunize municipalities from liability for unconstitutional actions by police officers. Three cases will illustrate the genre. In one, the court ruled that even gross negligence by the defendant-town's chief of police in failing to train his officers in the use of weapons, as a statute required, would not support municipal liability for the wrongful shooting of the plaintiff. The town manager, who was responsible for hiring police officers and had some supervisory authority over the chief, was deemed the final policymaking authority in such matters. Only if he or "the town" knew (or should have known) of the chief's failure to train police officers properly and failed to rectify the situation could the town be held liable. In a second case, the court immunized a city whose police officers had set up a "vehicle safety check" outside a roller skating rink on "soul night" after having repeatedly harassed and threatened the owner because he actively solicited business from blacks. Although the court acknowledged that the police were given discretion to take appropriate action, it held that the final policymaker was the chief; only if he knew of the officers' activity and either failed to prevent it or affirmatively ordered them to set up the "safety check" for improper reasons might the city be held liable. In a third case, the court held that even an elected precinct constable lacked the authority required to hold the county employing him responsible for his misconduct.

B. THE "CUSTOM" ISSUE

Unless the action of officials with final policymaking authority is involved, municipal liability will be imposed only if a governmental "custom" caused the violation. A practice not formally authorized by law might be so permanent and well established as to constitute a custom that fairly represents official policy. A pattern or series of acts violative of constitutional rights in many cases raises an inference of municipal custom. However, a single, isolated incident of wrongdoing by a non-policymaker, even with official acquiescence, cannot establish a liability-creating custom.

Indeed, even a series or officially recognized pattern of similar incidents may not suffice to prove official "custom." The difficulty is exemplified by cases like *Hamilton v. Rodgers*, in which a municipality escaped liability for its fire department's toleration of racial harassment of minority employees despite the fact that perhaps a dozen such incidents had occurred in less than three years. Even more striking was a case in which a policeman severely injured the plaintiff by using a flashlight as a weapon. Although the police chief was aware that serious, sometimes fatal, injuries had resulted in other jurisdictions from the use of such flashlights as weapons and that his subordinates sometimes used them in that fashion, this did not amount to a "custom" upon which municipal liability could be predicated.

C. THE "CAUSATION" ISSUE

Municipal liability under § 1983 requires that the official policy be causally linked to—that it be a "moving force of"—the violation. Not surprisingly, the causal issue is most difficult when the plaintiff's claim is that the injury was caused by the municipality's failure to do something that it should have done.

Two cases serve to illustrate this point. In one, plaintiff, who had committed a traffic violation, was struck with a weapon by a police officer. The plaintiff contended that the village, by failing to comply with a state law requiring officers to complete a formal training program, had maintained an official policy of inadequate training. The court rejected this argument on the ground, *inter alia*, that the plaintiff had failed to show "that specific deficiencies in the training given police officers led the misbehaving officer to engage in the alleged misconduct." In the other case, even when the court assumed that the city's repeated condonation and reward of police brutality would constitute an unconstitutional official policy, it nonetheless dismissed for a lack of proof of causation. Although there was evidence that other city police officers had not been disciplined for civil rights violations, there was no evidence that the offenders in this case knew about the assumed condonation policy. "A causal link," the court held, "cannot be inferred from municipal inaction alone."

In general, however, the cases provide no guidance as to the nature of the causal nexus that the statute demands. An important reason for this judicial opacity appears to be that, as indicated earlier, the courts tend to subsume the causal issue within their discussion of other, cognate issues: whether a municipal policy or custom exists; whether it is unconstitutional, either itself or as implemented; and whether it constitutes more than mere negligence. As I discuss below, the courts in reality treat most causation issues in § 1983 cases as questions of substantive duty.

II. Private Tort Law Analogues

From the perspective of private tort law principles, perhaps the most striking feature of the Court's municipal liability doctrine under § 1983 is this: while relying upon some of private law's basic concepts and policy justifications, the Court uses them in ways that bear little resemblance to how they are applied in the private law settings from which they are derived. It is as if the Court ardently embraced a tort law model of § 1983 only to get cold feet once it realized just how expansive it has become. These differences profoundly affect individual litigants and the entire post-*Monell* structure of public law: if judges in § 1983 cases applied these concepts as judges in private tort law cases now routinely do, the outcomes would approximate those produced by a regime of respondeat superior, which *Monell* expressly proscribed.

The most important tort law concept that the Court has drawn upon to restrict governmental liability in § 1983 cases is causation. It has done so by according special prominence to the language in § 1983 that imposes liability upon "any person who . . . shall subject, or cause to be subjected" another to an actionable injury. Indeed, the Court in *Monell* went so far as to justify its rejection of respondeat superior liability wholly on the basis that this language "plainly" limits liability to "a government that, under color of some official policy, 'causes' an employee to violate another's constitutional rights."

Despite the Court's focus on this "causation requirement," it is fundamentally mistaken to think of the "official policy" test as an inquiry into the causal relationship between an agency and an injury. First, although the existence of an official policy authorizing or mandating injurious conduct would generally suffice to establish a causal link between the agency and the injury, it does not at all follow that only an official policy can do so. Second and related, § 1983 by its terms creates a remedy for injuries "under color of [law]." That language suggests a conception of the causal relationship between government actors and their victims that is far broader than past interpretations of either the "subject, or cause to be subjected" phrase (which by using the word "cause" leaves the meaning of causation unaffected) or the "official policy" phrase. Third, some causal nexus between agency and injury almost invariably exists as a factual matter, if only in the sense—a sense sufficient to support liability in private law cases quite apart from respondeat superior principles—that the agency employed and deployed the tortfeasor, providing the color of authority and other resources under which she acted and which were indispensable to the injury's occurrence.

The real question in most § 1983 cases in which the municipality's link to the injury is at issue, then, is not whether a causal nexus exists but how explicit, formal, or constraining that nexus must be before a court will regard the "official policy" test as satisfied. But this is not really a causal issue; it is preeminently an issue about legal duty—the term commonly used in private tort law. As elaborated in private tort cases, legal duty is essentially a question of social policy—a question of the set of persons to whom one ought to be liable when one's negligent or otherwise improper actions injure them. Today, the duty concept is applied so expansively in private tort law that the kind of comprehensive legal responsibility to injured third parties that respondeat superior provides is commonly and increasingly available without the need to invoke such vicarious liability theories.

The contemporary scope of the duty concept in private tort law can be vividly illustrated by examining four examples of ways in which it has recently been extended to impose broad, non-vicarious liability in factual situations that, except for the absence of a municipal defendant, resemble or are analogous to many typical § 1983 cases. These examples are: (1) the duty to control the conduct of others; (2) the duty of accountants; (3) the product manufacturer's duty to remote bystanders; and (4) the relatively new tort duties concerning entrustment, hiring, retention, supervision, and detention.

A. THE DUTY TO CONTROL THE CONDUCT OF OTHERS

In the much-discussed case of *Tarasoff v. Regents of the University of California*, the Supreme Court of California imposed an affirmative duty on the part of psychotherapists to protect third parties from risks of harm posed by people under the therapists' care. This duty, according to the Court, was one of "reasonable care" that would "vary with the facts of each case"; although it could often be discharged by a warning to the individual at risk, it might require other steps. Although some courts have narrowed the scope of the *Tarasoff* duty, most have actually expanded it. Thus, courts have adopted a broad view of victim identifiability; extended the duty to foreseeable bystanders or to all persons, known or unknown, who might foreseeably be endangered; refused to limit the duty to protect against risks of intentional, physical harm; protected third parties who suffer only property damage; and applied the duty in non-medical cases.

Indeed, this enlarged conception of the duty to protect third parties has now been embraced by the medical profession itself, at least for physicians whose patients are carrying the AIDS virus. Thus, in June 1988, the American Medical Association voted that, in certain situations, considerations of patient privacy and confidentiality must yield to a physician's obligation to warn the sexual partners of such patients.

B. THE DUTY OF ACCOUNTANTS

Until quite recently, an accountant owed no duty to third parties who were not in privity with her for economic loss suffered from reliance upon inaccurately prepared financial statements. This was the rule established by Judge Cardozo in the famous *Ultramares* case out of a concern over the prospect of "liability in an indeterminable amount for an indeterminable time to an indeterminable class," a concern that (stated somewhat less apocalyptically) is one of the asserted justifications for the "official policy" limitation on the § 1983 liability of municipalities. Today, the strong trend is to extend the accountant's duty far beyond the privity relationship. It now embraces not only all parties for whose benefit the information was prepared, which is the Restatement approach, but also all those who foreseeably may reasonably rely upon the information.

C. THE PRODUCT MANUFACTURER'S DUTY TO REMOTE BYSTANDERS

A manufacturer's duty to market reasonably safe products runs to purchasers and users of the product and also, in many jurisdictions, to members of a purchaser's or user's household. Today, that duty is increasingly being extended to protect any individual who happens to be within the area of contemplated or normally intended use and who foreseeably may be endangered by a defective product. A product seller's duty also protects bystanders against the emotional harm that results from witnessing a product-related accident. These duties cannot always be discharged by providing a warning to the immediate purchaser.

D. ENTRUSTMENT, HIRING, RETENTION, SUPERVISION AND DETENTION

Perhaps the closest private law analogues to cases in which *Monell*'s "official policy" requirement operates to impose municipal liability are those involving the relatively new torts of negligent entrustment, negligent hiring and retention, negligent supervision of parolees, and negligent failure to detain drunk drivers. Often, these private tort cases are ones in which the courts are quite clearly circumventing various state law limitations on vicarious liability theories such as respondeat superior.

In recent years, courts have extended liability to parents and other people who permit minors or other imprudent individuals to have a "dangerous instrumentality," like a weapon or automobile, that causes an injury to a third party, or who leave such objects in places where minors are likely to find and use them. The negligent hiring analogy is even more on point, for it imposes liability upon employers even when respondeat superior would not apply because, for example, the employee's action was outside the scope of employment. In private tort law, employers are now liable for actions of employees when the employer should have known that the employee posed an unreasonable risk of harm to third parties. Employers are also liable for harm that results from retaining an unfit employee who foreseeably endangers others, rather than retraining, reassigning, or discharging that employee.

In a wide variety of situations, then, private tort law routinely provides damage remedies against individuals or enterprises that, through the agency of individuals whom they employ or for whom they bear some other responsibility, cause harm to third parties. The private law theories of recovery upon which these remedies turn do not depend upon respondeat superior or other types of vicarious liability. Yet these theories are wholly consistent with, and often closely analogous to, the kinds of relationships and responsibilities that local governments have toward their citizens. Even more significant than the absence in private law of any doctrine analogous to the "official policy" limitation is the fact that public tort law has largely managed to do without one. Neither state or local officials' liability under § 1983, nor the liability of the United States under the Federal Tort Claims Act (FTCA), is subject to such a limitation.

The Supreme Court's recent decision in *Sheridan v. United States* suggests just how far public tort law has come in this regard. In *Sheridan*, individuals sued the United States under the FTCA for injuries sustained when an intoxicated off-duty naval medical aide employed at the Bethesda Naval Hospital fired several rifle shots into their automobile on a public street near the hospital. Earlier that evening, three servicemen had encountered the drunken aide but fled when they saw the rifle. The government defended on the ground that the claims were barred because they were claims "arising out of" an assault or battery, which along with other specified intentional torts are expressly excluded from the government's waiver of immunity under the Act. The government also emphasized that the assailant was off-duty and not acting within the scope of federal employment at the time of the incident. The Court nonetheless permitted plaintiffs' claims to proceed to trial. It did so because plaintiffs, in addition to alleging the intentional tort, had alleged that the government negligently breached "good Samaritan" duties voluntarily undertaken through regulations and other means designed to prevent the possession of firearms on the base, especially by inebriated individuals, and to keep such individuals from injuring themselves or others.

The Court's approach in *Sheridan* seems highly relevant to my private tort law-based critique of the "official policy" limitation under § 1983. The Court reasoned that the fact that governmental liability on a respondeat superior theory was barred by a special statutory exception did not preclude governmental liability derived from another, independent, common law-based theory of responsibility. When applied to the judicially created bar against respondeat superior liability under § 1983, this reasoning has special force. It suggests that the *Monell* "official policy" preclusion of liability need not defeat liability based upon other theories grounded in independent common law principles. This is especially compelling when, as in § 1983 cases, no statutory preclusion exists and when the alternative liability theories emphasize quite different factors: the nature of the municipality's relationship to the risk rather than the tortfeasor's employment status.

Thus if courts wish to hold municipalities responsible for certain types of official misconduct for which private defendants must now routinely answer in analogous circumstances, § 1983 doctrine raises no insuperable impediment (*Monell* itself aside, of course). Several theories of responsibility that do not require courts to impose vicarious liability under respondeat superior principles are readily available in the private tort case law. The real question, then, is whether such expanded municipal responsibility is desirable as a policy matter. This question is addressed in Part IV. Before reaching that question, however, I wish to show that the concepts comprising the "official policy" test bear little relation to the decisionmaking process in most public service bureaucracies.

III. Bureaucratic Policymaking

In its insistent flight from respondeat superior, the "official policy" doctrine necessitates a search in each case for municipal officials who possess something called "final policymaking authority," for only their actions can subject a municipality to § 1983 liability. This requirement, as the Court recently acknowledged, has bred persistent conflicts among the lower courts and sharp divisions among the Justices themselves.

Sometimes, of course, the Court's test may possess perfectly adequate resolving power. There are indeed cases in which the locus of formal authority and the sources of policy influence can be traced to a particular public official or entity. *Monell* was such a case; it involved a formal board of education rule that was applied as written and was unconstitutional on its face. But that is not the kind of case that has reached the courts in the post-*Monell* era.

More typical of the genre—especially in view of the pronounced ambiguities of the "final policymaking authority" test—is *Praprotnik*. In contrast to *Monell*, *Praprotnik* presented a number of threshold questions. The Court first had to identify the specific policy area implicated by the challenged action. Only by so identifying such a policy area was it be [sic] possible to move to the second question: whether any policy relevant to that area even *existed*. If so, then a third question had to be answered: was "final authority" concerning that policy area exercised by the officials who made the allegedly invalid decisions? If it was, then (and only then) the court could proceed to the merits of the § 1983 claim.

These are difficult questions. The first is conceptual and taxonomic; its answer depends entirely upon how one chooses to think about the various functions of government and to classify particular actions. The second also is conceptual; to answer it, one must define "policy." This is a notoriously elusive and controversial idea, especially when applied to the kinds of unusual, uncoordinated actions of individual government officials that arise in cases like *Tuttle*, *Pembaur*, or *Praprotnik*. But the question is empirical as well, requiring an assessment of information about how officials have actually behaved in the past. The third question, likewise, is both conceptual (what is "*final* policymaking authority'?) and empirical (did a particular official exercise that authority?).

How is a judge to answer these questions in the more typical, post-*Monell* kind of case like *Praprotnik*? The *Praprotnik* plurality's effort to provide "useful guidance" in fact furnished precious little. After reiterating the principle (established in an earlier case) that the requisite policymaking authority for municipal liability under § 1983 was "the authority to make *final* policy," the plurality went on to find the Civil Service Commission to be the final personnel policymaker wholly on the basis of city charter language stating that its decisions were final (subject to judicial review). To the objection that (as the court of appeals had found) the commission accorded great deference to some lower-level personnel actions and failed to review others at all, the plurality responded that acquiescence in a subordinate's discretionary decisions is not a delegation of policymaking authority because it "is equally consistent with a presumption that the subordinates are faithfully attempting to comply with the policies that are supposed to guide them."

This response is inadequate for at least two reasons. First, it is analytically irrelevant. While the quoted language describes one possible way to characterize this acquiescence, it also recognizes the existence of at least one other possibility (i.e., that the acquiescence constitutes a *de facto* delegation or abdication of effective policymaking authority to subordinates). Indeed, a third possibility is that *both* of these are true: the superior may essentially (but informally) delegate or abdicate her authority to subordinates on the assumption that they will comply, but her assumption may turn out to be false without her having learned of her error (until the claim is filed). The plurality in *Praprotnik* provides no reason to prefer any particular version of how policymaking authority is allocated. In fact, as we shall see, organizational analysis suggests that the second or third possibilities may be at least as common as the first in the kinds of public agencies that give rise to most § 1983 cases.

The plurality's response fails for a second reason: it is decidedly formalistic in an area in which the dangers of formalism are especially great. Formalism, of course, may appear to be a considerable virtue to a court seeking a manageable doctrinal test for deciding hard cases. After all, the fluid, fragmented, informal, organizationally diverse, and politically competitive processes of municipal policy formation are complex; their relationships are intertwined and difficult to grasp. For a judge to locate policymaking authority by simply reading an agency's organic statute is an attractive tactic precisely because the reality of local government policymaking is so messy and elusive. In some subset of cases, moreover, that tactic will produce the correct result.

On the other hand, confining judicial attention to the formal definitions and allocations of legal authority exacts a very heavy price. By fastening upon the mere possibility of administrative review of decisions without regard to its probability or character, the plurality in *Praprotnik* exposes itself to the concurring Justices' accusation that "even the hollowest promise of review is sufficient to divest all city officials save the mayor and governing legislative body of final policymaking authority." The more fundamental defect, however, goes to the basic purpose of § 1983's municipal liability doctrine. In the many cases in which official policy is not (as it is in *Monell*) embodied in a straightforward, published rule promulgated by a highly visible political organ such as a city council, so crabbed an inquiry is unlikely to identify those situations in which the government should properly be held responsible for constitutional injuries to citizens.

But a doctrinal test like that of Justice Brennan's concurring opinion in *Praprotnik* is also objectionable, albeit on altogether different grounds. In essence, Justice Brennan would invite juries to determine the actual, rather than the formal, distribution of policy influence in the relevant community. While more realistic in principle, as a practical matter such a test would be impossible to administer. It would require litigants to expend great time and expense to assemble an enormous amount of political information, much of it from "experts," to resolve what is, or at least ought to be, a peripheral issue. Subjective, partisan judgments by jurors (and the judges that charge them) would be difficult to control. And in the end, outcomes would be wildly unpredictable and haphazard; as the "community power" studies indicate, even (or especially) political scientists are unable to agree upon the character and significance of this kind of information. The answer to the question "Who governs?" in a particular urban community seems to vary across policy areas; indeed, even within a policy area "Who governs" may vary from issue to issue.

What political scientists and other students of behavior in public agencies *would* agree upon, I think, is that a legal doctrine whose application depends upon a court or jury being able to identify something called "policy" and someone called a "final policymaking authority" is fundamentally misguided. Studies of organizational behavior and public administration strongly suggest that these categories utterly misconceive how public bureaucracies and the policymaking process actually function. Thus, even if one could ignore the defects of the "official policy" doctrine that I have already discussed in this Part—that is, even if the doctrine's cornerstone did not consist of often meaningless legal forms, ill-defined and highly controversial concepts, and empirical data that are neither practically obtainable nor readily comprehensible—the weakness of its behavioral foundations would still undermine its integrity.

Studies of organizations in general and public bureaucracies in particular reveal two major incongruities between the Court's "official policy" doctrine and the actual behavior of officials in agencies. Both incongruities relate to the nature of the policymaking process. The first involves the question of what is meant by the term "policy." The second involves the questions of where and by whom policy is made.

It is a remarkable—and revealing—fact that the "official policy" doctrine, as elaborated by the courts, contains no clear definition or even widespread consensus concerning what constitutes a "policy." Indeed, the Court has been, and continues to be, sharply divided by precisely this question, although it is usually formulated in ways that distract attention from the core definitional issue. For example, much disagreement has occurred over whether and under what circumstances an "isolated" act or decision may amount to a policy, the type and level of official whose actions or pronouncements may create a policy, the magnitude of the wrongdoing required to prove the existence of a policy, and whether a policy that is not unconstitutional in itself but only as implemented can ever form the basis of municipal liability.

The closest the Court has come to a definition appears in *Pembaur*. A "policy," we learn there, need not be a fixed plan for the future; indeed, a wholly isolated, present-oriented, situation-specific decision may be a "policy" so long as it is made by "authorized decisionmakers." One can identify these decisionmakers, we are told, because they are the officials "who establish governmental policy." A more indiscriminate, question-begging definition of policy can scarcely be imagined.

We need not analyze bureaucratic behavior to see that this definition of policy is virtually useless as a tool for deciding specific cases. But bureaucratic analyses do help to underscore an important gap between the premises of the "official policy" doctrine and the way in which agencies actually behave. That doctrine takes no account of the fact that efforts to implement a policy almost invariably transform it. It is not simply that policy goals are seldom completely realized when they confront institutional complexity, instrumental detail, and revised information. The more important point, convincingly established in numerous empirical studies, is that this encounter actually creates new and different goals, often supplanting or at least fundamentally altering the original ones.

If "policy" is an inherently inchoate, ill-defined, and controversial conception, and if any particular policy is constantly changing as it seeks implementation, one can readily see why a judicial doctrine whose application requires courts to identify a discrete, static "official policy" would be highly vulnerable and unstable. But the doctrine's weakness flows from more than its reductionistic, distorted view of the *nature of policy*. It also reflects a misunderstanding of the *locus of policymaking*.

In formulating the doctrine, the Court has implicitly employed a conventional pyramidal model of the policymaking process in public bureaucracies. According to this model, formal legal authority to make policy on the agency's behalf is located at the top of the agency pyramid. That authority is deployed by officials at or near the top to develop policies and to issue to the officials located further down toward the base those implementing directives that will conform their behavior to the agreed-upon policies. As an idealized, schematic view of the bureaucratic policy process—indeed, as a rough working description of a certain kind of agency—it is accurate enough. But it bears only a superficial resemblance to the type of public agency at which § 1983 claims are typically directed.

That kind of agency has been aptly described by political scientist Michael Lipsky as "street-level bureaucracy." Such agencies—which include the police and other law enforcement operations, public schools, public welfare, public health, and associated "casework" bureaucracies—possess certain characteristic features. These agencies principally provide services directly to members of the public and perform this function largely through low-level (but often professionally trained) personnel who interact with the public "on the street." These personnel, although subject to many operating rules, effectively function with broad autonomy and discretion, often work under conditions of physical and emotional stress and danger, and frequently must make rapid decisions with a high risk of error.

Although the formal policymaking processes of these "street-level" agencies may conform to the pyramidal model described above, those processes are constrained by, and sometimes subordinated to, informal ones that operate in ways that are not merely different but often diametrically opposed. In particular, the behavior of low-level officials in street-level agencies is significantly shaped by their operating routines, situation-specific social and emotional needs, peer subculture norms and ideologies, and the dynamics and economy of their daily interactions with the public. To a considerable extent, then, their behavior is determined from the bottom up rather than from the top down.

Such agencies do influence officials' behavior through their formal decision processes. But the crucial point for present purposes is this: *low-level, bottom-up processes also shape officials' behavior, and these more informal influences make "policy" in almost every important sense of that word.* Indeed, published studies of agency behavior justify an even stronger assertion—that "[i]n a significant sense . . . street-level bureaucrats *are the policymakers* in their respective work arenas."

This conclusion carries disturbing implications for the "official policy" doctrine. That doctrine, after all, has precipitated a quest not only for a discrete, static, readily definable norm (the "policy") but also for an easily identifiable, high-level progenitor of the norm (the "final policymaking authority"). In many cases, however, entities of that kind turn out not to exist in the real world—at least not in the form or in the hierarchical location that the doctrine demands. The result is that municipal liability under § 1983 is attributed or denied without any systematic connection to the statutory purpose of deterring local government violations of federal law.

IV. The Search for Municipality Responsibility

The "official policy" doctrine, then, encourages courts to ask the wrong questions and to derive the wrong conclusions. By seeking the wrong thing and searching for it in the wrong places, the doctrine displaces what should instead be the focus of inquiry under § 1983: whether the municipality properly bears responsibility for the injury.

To formulate the issue as one of "responsibility," of course, risks begging the essential question of what behavior or relationships suffice to establish it. Current doctrine seeks to avoid circularity by assuming that the requisite responsibility can only flow either from a formal policy authorized by a high-level official or from a well-established but informal custom or usage. In fact, however, most of local government's "outputs," including those that potentially violate § 1983, are best described as falling somewhere in between these two categories. These are activities—most commonly police practices and personnel actions in § 1983 litigation—for which the municipality is "responsible" in three non-question-begging senses: legal, moral, and functional. If these three inquiries were to become the analytical foci of the municipal liability issue, as I urge, the "official policy" test could be abandoned.

First, local government's nexus to the violation will typically be close enough—quite apart from a respondeat superior theory—to satisfy both the cause-in-fact and proximate cause criteria, as those concepts are understood in private tort law. The "under color of [law]" language of § 1983 strengthens this nexus. Having authorized (perhaps mandated), supervised, trained, equipped, and paid the individual who causes injury, the municipality has placed her in a position in which the violation is possible, perhaps (on some facts) even probable. It has (to use a traditional private law metaphor) launched the instrumentality of harm, a traditional basis of legal responsibility.

Second, local government is essentially a monopolist provider of many (perhaps most) of the public services that occasion § 1983 violations. As such, it takes on special moral obligations to perform them in socially beneficial ways. This is especially true of services, such as law enforcement and welfare, for which most citizens cannot afford the private market substitutes that may in principle be available. Citizens' lack of alternatives, and their resulting dependence upon government for these services, heightens the municipality's moral responsibility to act in ways that protect rather than injure them.

Third, the policy justifications for imposing liability upon risk-creating enterprises apply at least as strongly to risks created by local governments in violation of § 1983 as they do to those created by private firms in violation of tort law. Obviously, deterrence of misconduct by local officials could only be strengthened by providing a remedy against errant municipalities, and such a remedy would not create any risk of over-deterrence beyond the risk that Congress accepted in adopting § 1983. That statute, after all, has always promised the remedy; it is only a court-made doctrine, and a relatively recent one at that, which has withheld it. Compensation and loss-spreading would also be advanced by municipal liability; the pool of municipal taxpayers is large and insurance could enlarge the tax pool even further. Since adjudication is already the established mode of resolving § 1983 claims and damage awards are common in cases against non-municipality defendants, an issue of institutional competence and legitimacy simply would not arise. Finally, there is no reason to believe that system efficiency would be threatened by permitting claims against municipalities; the indeterminacy of the existing "official policy" limitation is surely a source of wasteful litigation, while the additional claims that might be filed can hardly be counted as an unwelcome cost if they are meritorious.

Several other objections to imposing municipal liability under § 1983 on the basis of private tort law principles of organizational responsibility (short of respondeat superior vicarious liability) must be considered. First, it might be argued that this approach would run afoul of the Court's determination not to allow § 1983 to supplant or federalize state tort law. The Court's concern in this regard may have been a realistic one when *Parratt v. Taylor*, which held that an official's mere negligence might amount to a constitutional deprivation triggering § 1983 liability, was the law. That decision raised several spectres that surely haunted the Court: exposure of hard-pressed local governments to massive damages liability; federal jury second-guessing of the judgments of local officials on the basis of nothing more determinate than a "reasonableness" standard; legal uncertainty concerning when state law provides an "adequate remedy" for the deprivation within the meaning of *Parratt*; and the diversion of a large number of state law tort actions—many of them (as in *Parratt* itself) for trifling amounts of money—into the federal courts where, among other advantages, attorneys' fee awards would be available to plaintiffs. But by overruling that part of *Parratt* and holding instead that plaintiffs must prove more than mere negligence in order to impose § 1983 liability, the Court has now reduced those concerns.

Even if some of these federalism concerns persist, however, the overriding question that remains is whether the "official policy" requirement is a sound way to address them. The foregoing analysis strongly suggests that it is not. By artificially separating organizational responsibility and liability, the requirement contradicts well-established private law principles that increasingly seek their convergence. By grounding itself in false assumptions about the decisionmaking process in public service bureaucracies, the Court confounds its own doctrinal categories. And by immunizing injurious wrongdoing, the Court tends to defeat strong social policies favoring deterrence, compensation, loss distribution, administrative efficiency, and moral equivalence in punishment.

A second, somewhat related objection is concerned with the strong federal interest in a uniform, consistent interpretation of § 1983. This objection emphasizes that § 1983 claims are wholly creatures of federal statutes and (at least as to substantive law questions) must be decided according to federal law principles rather than turn upon the vagaries of state tort law. This objection, however, confuses two very different kinds of constraints on the federal courts. It is, of course, true that a federal court is neither limited nor bound by state law doctrines in § 1983 cases, and that uniform interpretations of the statute among different federal courts is an important desideratum. But this does not mean, however, that federal courts may not or do not look to the kinds of common law concepts of duty and causation described in Part II when they decide, as a matter of federal law, whether a violation has occurred, and if so, who is responsible for it. Nothing in the statute or the case law even remotely suggests such a limitation on the permissible sources of judicial guidance. Indeed, it would be strange if courts seeking to define and apply the § 1983 analogues of familiar state law concepts like duty, intention, and causation (however denominated) did not consult the vast store of state law materials relevant to those issues. In fact, of course, courts in § 1983 cases do this all the time. Finally, it is doubtful that any lack of uniformity caused by looking to private tort law concepts for guidance would match the extraordinary unpredictability of the "official policy" test.

A third objection goes to the wisdom of the private law principles themselves. It argues that these principles, by extending liability too far, have produced undesirable policy effects, including large price increases due to high insurance premiums, the complete withdrawal of certain valuable products and services, and regressive distributional impacts. Rather than view these principles as an appropriate model for federal law, the argument goes, the federal courts should reject them by retaining the "official policy" requirement.

Expanded liability, of course, does raise serious policy concerns, even if, as I am urging here, what is expanded is not the underlying substantive liability but merely the class of defendants who may be held responsible for it. At most, however, these concerns suggest that courts should proceed with caution in defining the precise parameters of municipal liability for officially-caused harms under § 1983. Upon careful reflection, some of the private law principles may seem to advance § 1983's purposes while others may not. But it would be foolish for courts to allow generalized concerns about the effects of expanded liability to justify a categorical refusal even to consider familiar private law conceptions of responsibility. Courts should take a more discriminating approach than is possible when they are bound by the crude prophylactic device of the "official policy" requirement.

A final, related objection emphasizes the need to limit the potential liability of municipal wrongdoers. Spokesmen for state and local government often make arguments along these lines. They maintain that the nature of these bureaucracies, especially the difficulty of controlling behavior of low-level officials, makes violations inevitable. They further point out that local governments, as "deep pocket" defendants, would attract many spurious or marginal claims, and they predict that large damage judgments, which are now often uninsurable, would threaten the maintenance of vital public services, jeopardizing the safety and welfare of numerous innocent citizens in order to benefit a handful of individuals. And they insist that political controls are a more effective mechanism for holding officials accountable than are costly, protracted lawsuits, which may discourage vigorous decisionmaking by officials.

I have succeeded in demonstrating, I think, that these arguments against reliance on private tort law concepts are not compelling. But I certainly do not mean to suggest that the arguments are without merit; indeed, I find each of them plausible and have elsewhere adduced some evidence tending to support most of them. Here, however, my purpose is not to offer a full policy analysis of these arguments. It is merely to show that even to the extent that they are correct, they do not justify retaining the "official policy" requirement.

Consider, for example, the aim of limiting a municipality's exposure to damages. In order to achieve that policy goal, it is not necessary to retain the "official policy" limitation on municipal liability. One alternative would be to eliminate the "official policy" requirement but to impose a statutory ceiling on either the amount or the specific categories of damages that may be recovered under § 1983. Such an approach, which states commonly employ in wrongful death and governmental liability statutes, would assure at least partial compensation and loss-spreading, and would reduce the moral anomaly and inequity of treating victims differently depending upon the happenstance of who injured them. A more radical alternative would be to adopt a social insurance approach, requiring municipalities to compensate those whom they injure on an administrative, no-fault basis much as some communities now pay victims of certain crimes. This would facilitate prompt payment of out-of-pocket losses and should be cheaper per claim to administer. On the other hand, this approach would provide somewhat less deterrence and might also encourage more spurious claims. Many hybrid systems combining elements of tort, no-fault, and social insurance are also possible.

Suppose that none of these legislative approaches were adopted but that the Court decided to resolve municipal liability claims under § 1983 on the basis of the emergent principles of organizational responsibility—short of a rule of respondeat superior—that are today routinely applied in private tort law disputes, rather than through the "official policy" requirement. In that event, case outcomes probably would not be very different from those that a respondeat superior rule would generate. The reason for this convergence is simple. Municipalities are morally, causally, and functionally responsible for most officially inflicted injuries in precisely the same sense that private enterprises are; "official policy" is but one source of that responsibility. The Court would then face a separate—but decidedly subsidiary—question of whether it should go all the way and adopt respondeat superior or should instead persist in rejecting it. Resolution of this question would turn largely upon an evaluation of the administrative advantages of a clear, categorical rule versus the tailoring that a more fact-sensitive rule would permit, an evaluation that is outside the scope of this Article.

Whether the Court should import private law notions of enterprise responsibility into the realm of municipal responsibility under § 1983—and if it does, whether it should take the further step of adopting a rule of respondeat superior liability—are important questions. For present purposes, however, the more important point is this: it need not retain its "official policy" requirement in order to serve its jurisprudential and policy goals. There are other, better ways in which legislatures and courts can fashion remedies for municipal violations of federal law that conform both to firmly established social and legal norms of organizational responsibility and to the realities of bureaucratic decisionmaking processes.

Barbara Kritchevsky, *"Or Causes to be Subjected": The Role of Causation in Section 1983 Municipal Liability Analysis,* 35 UCLA Law Review 1187 (1988)

* * *

I. Introduction

Since 1871, the statute known as section 1983 has provided a federal remedy to those deprived of federal constitutional or statutory rights by persons acting under color of state law. The Supreme Court liberated section 1983 from almost a century of obscurity when it decided *Monroe v. Pape* in 1961. Holding that section 1983 provided a remedy supplementary to any available under state law, that state officers acted "under color" of law even if their acts exceeded their authority, and that a section 1983 action could stand without proof that the defendant specifically intended to violate a person's rights, the Supreme Court allowed persons to use the Constitution as a weapon to obtain redress and opened the doors of the federal courts to a vast wave of civil rights litigation. However, *Monroe v. Pape* also contained a restrictive element. It held that municipalities were not "persons" within the meaning of section 1983, and therefore could not be held liable for damages. As a consequence, plaintiffs were left with the prospect of recovering only from individual defendants.

In 1978, the Supreme Court appeared further to invigorate section 1983. In *Monell v. Department of Social Services*, it overruled *Monroe's* confining interpretation of "person." Municipalities were "persons" and were subject to section 1983 liability when they caused civil rights violations. However, *Monell* itself contained a restrictive element. The Court ruled that municipalities could not be held liable for their employees' actions under a theory of *respondeat superior*. Municipalities could be held liable only if they themselves, through their policies or customs, caused a constitutional deprivation. Even at the time, some sensed that *Monell* would provide a "mixed blessing." Unfortunately, this premonition appears to have been well founded.

In the years since *Monell*, the Court has been unable to agree on any but the vaguest contours of the requirements for municipal liability. More important, it has not explained how policies or customs must be causally linked to a violation if liability is to be imposed. Lower courts, accordingly, have interpreted *Monell* to require differing municipal liability inquiries, depending on their perception of the type of causal link between a policy and a violation that *Monell* requires. Some courts hold that only facially unconstitutional policies can give rise to liability; that a policy must compel a constitutional violation in order to "cause" it. Others find that a broad range of municipal policies can cause violations; their causation inquiry is guided by tort law considerations of cause in fact and proximate cause. Others adopt a third approach, allowing only policies they consider sufficiently blameworthy to give rise to liability. Accordingly, the degree of protection given civil rights now largely depends on where a victim resides.

The Supreme Court's resolution of this problem could undermine the advances of *Monell* and threaten section 1983's effectiveness as a means of deterring unconstitutional conduct and providing a remedy to individual victims. Recent decisions interpreting the *Monell* policy or custom and causation requirements show that, while the Court is deeply fragmented, some of its members are inclined to interpret the requirements in an unjustifiably narrow fashion. In *City of Oklahoma City v. Tuttle*, a plurality of the Court required a direct causal link between policy and injury that is difficult to prove and is much more stringent than that required by tort law. In *City of Springfield v. Kibbe*, four Justices said that a facially constitutional municipal policy could "cause" a constitutional violation *only* if the policy was the result of deliberate indifference or reckless disregard for constitutional rights.

The *Tuttle* and *Kibbe* plurality opinions' approach threatens section 1983's viability as a deterrent and a meaningful remedy. Importing a state of mind analysis into section 1983 would make it difficult to establish municipal liability, allowing municipalities to violate a person's constitutional rights but escape the reach of section 1983. This analysis would also undermine the statute's deterrent and remedial goals by making it impossible to hold municipalities liable for injuries caused by the interactive behavior of government policymakers who act in good faith. However, a majority of the Court has not spoken on this issue. It is thus not too late to revitalize section 1983 so that it will better serve the purposes its framers intended.

* * *

III. The Lower Courts' Struggle to Apply the *Monell* Standard: Three Models of Municipal Liability

A. *Introduction*

Monell's statements on municipal liability raised more questions than they answered, leaving the lower courts on their own to chart their way through the "foggy swampland" of liability analysis. *Monell* left them to decide, with only scant guidance, what types of policies could lead to imposition of liability and how policies had to be causally related to violations. While clearly rejecting *respondeat superior* liability, *Monell* broadcast conflicting and unclear signals on when a court could properly find that a municipal policy or custom "caused" a constitutional violation.

The Court did not define the type of policies that could impose liability, and this compounded the confusion caused by the Court's language describing the required causal link between a policy or custom and a constitutional violation. The *Monell* opinion suggested that there were two distinct approaches to liability analysis. One approach would hold a municipality liable for a custom that directed or commanded a constitutional violation, one that *necessarily* caused a constitutional violation when followed. This narrow reading was suggested by the Court's statement that the governing entity could be liable when an individual's action "implements or executes" a policy or custom. Another approach would impose liability whenever official action in accordance with a policy "caused" a constitutional violation, suggesting use of a more lenient, tort law view of causation. This approach was suggested by the Court's statement that Congress intended municipal liability when "action pursuant to official municipal policy of some nature caused a constitutional tort," and by the Court's assertion that the touchstone of municipal liability was "an allegation that official policy is responsible for a deprivation of rights." Under this view, unlike the first, a governmental policy that is itself constitutional could "cause" a constitutional violation and trigger governmental liability.

Monell, then, appeared to offer two models of municipal liability. A narrow reading of the opinion could lead courts to impose liability only when a policy or custom mandated a constitutional violation. Such a policy or custom would necessarily be unconstitutional itself. A broader reading would also allow liability for policies or customs that were "responsible" for a deprivation. Under this approach, a municipality could be held liable for injuries "caused" by its facially constitutional policies, suggesting a causation inquiry familiar from tort law. The possibility lurked, of course, that the statute's causation requirement was something between compulsion and proximate cause. If this were the case, however, the *Monell* Court did not explain it.

B. *The First Model of Liability:* Monell*'s Compulsion Model*

The facts of *Monell* provided the lower courts with a model for imposing municipal liability. The *Monell* plaintiffs, the Supreme Court said, challenged a departmental rule that, when implemented, necessarily caused a violation of the subjects' constitutional rights. The policy that the *Monell* defendants followed was clear. There was no dispute that implementation of the policy caused plaintiffs' injuries. The challenged action, forcing plaintiffs to take leaves of absence, "implement[ed] or executed[d]" a policy statement, ordinance, regulation, or decision. The only question was whether the policy and the outcome it prescribed were constitutional.

The lower courts had no trouble assessing liability in cases that fit into *Monell*'s compulsion model; that is, when plaintiffs challenged policies that compelled constitutional violations. In *Owens v. Kelley*, for example, a probationer claimed that a county probation program violated his first amendment rights. The county prescribed the content of the probation program and the program's content was claimed to be the source of the constitutional deprivation. The dispute was over the program's constitutionality.

Owen v. City of Independence illustrated a variation of the liability model shown by *Monell*'s facts. *Owen* upheld a police chief's charges that the city's lawmakers deprived him of his due process rights by discharging him without a hearing. The *Owen* situation differed from *Monell* in that the challenged policy was not designed for general application: only one person was its victim. In *Owen*, like *Monell*, however, the challenged municipal decision necessarily caused a given result. The question was whether that result violated the Constitution. The lower courts were quick to impose liability in fact situations presenting the *Owen* variation on *Monell*.

It can be difficult to determine whether a case fits into *Monell*'s compulsion model. If the challenged policy or custom is not written, or admitted, the plaintiff has the burden of proving its existence. Generally, plaintiffs seek to establish such policies by proving that many constitutional violations of the same nature have occurred and that municipal policymakers approved them or willingly allowed them to continue. If such an unconstitutional policy or custom is found, the municipality will be held liable for constitutional violations inflicted by employees acting in accordance with it. The case then falls into the *Monell* compulsion model because actions implementing the policy or custom necessarily result in a constitutional violation. In *Iskander v. Village of Forest Park*, for example, a person who was subjected to a strip-search in a windowed room sought to hold the municipality liable. She submitted evidence of similar incidents, showing that the Forest Park police customarily conducted strip-searches in such a room. A finding that an officer's actions implemented such a custom would subject the city to liability, the court agreed, because actions implementing the municipal policy or custom would necessarily violate the constitutional rights of the person being searched.

When an unconstitutional policy is proved, courts generally assume that the policy alone caused the injury. The courts assume that the violation of the plaintiff's constitutional rights occurred because the state actor was following a municipal policy so mandating, and not because of any improper personal motive. For example, the court in *Iskander v. Village of Forest Park* was willing to assume that the policy of conducting strip-searches in windowed rooms, if proved, caused the deprivation at issue. It did not consider, for example, whether the search might have occurred because of the officer's personal desire to humiliate the plaintiff. This assumption of causation is practically and legally justified in most cases and may be an important factor encouraging plaintiffs to fit even unclear cases into the model provided by *Monell*'s facts by trying to establish the existence of an unconstitutional policy.

Numerous section 1983 claims do not fit into *Monell*'s compulsion model, as plaintiffs often cannot readily establish the existence of an unconstitutional policy. Some lower courts, however, evidently believing that municipal liability can be imposed *only* when cases do fit into *Monell*'s compulsion model, seek to fit all cases into that mold. They require the plaintiff to show a municipal policy of violating the Constitution in order to establish municipal liability. In *White v. Talboys*, for instance, a Colorado district court said that a city could be held liable for a shooting death only if the plaintiffs could show "a [city] policy to have its police officers kill innocent citizens without cause or justification."

A Third Circuit case, *Kranson v. Valley Crest Nursing Home*, interpreted *Monell* to hold that actions must "implement" or "execute" a municipal policy in order to give rise to liability. Kranson's estate sued a municipally-owned nursing home, claiming that its policy, which provided guidelines for medical discretion in the use of cardiopulmonary resuscitation (CPR), caused Kranson's death. The court stated that liability could not be imposed in such a situation. *Monell*, it said, provided that a governing body could be held liable when unconstitutional action "implements or executes" a policy. Since the policy at issue did not forbid the use of CPR, a refusal to administer CPR when Kranson choked did not execute the policy. The municipality could only be held liable if its policy forbade use of CPR. The effect of focusing on *Monell*'s narrow causation language is to require that policy *command* a violation, that it be itself unconstitutional, in order to result in liability.

White and *Kranson* illustrate some of the difficulties a plaintiff will encounter when a court requires municipal liability cases to fit into *Monell*'s compulsion model in order to succeed. It will be difficult to prove the existence of an unconstitutional policy except in the rare cases in which it is written or admitted to exist. The plaintiff must try to establish such a policy or custom by introducing evidence showing past incidents of a similar nature and that policymakers allowed the violations to continue. However, some constitutional violations are so bizarre or extreme that they are unlikely to occur repeatedly. Even when there are frequent violations, the plaintiff may not learn of their existence or be able to prove that they happened. These proof requirements are virtually insurmountable for the first victim of an unconstitutional policy; there are no prior incidents to which the plaintiff can point.

Most section 1983 actions do not fit into the *Monell* compulsion model. More often, the plaintiff seeks to show that facially constitutional municipal policies, such as supervisory policies, have led to a constitutional violation, such as an instance of police brutality. A plaintiff will claim, for example, that the municipality's policy of failing to supervise officers closely actually and proximately "caused" an officer to beat him. In such cases, the vast number of possible reasons for an instance of police brutality makes it crucial to focus on the causal link between policy and injury. A police officer who beat a member of a minority group while arresting him may have done so because he wanted to take out frustrations arising from personal problems; because he hated members of that minority group; because he had a predisposition to violence; because he thought that it would make him a hero at the station; because he did not know how else to effect an arrest; or because he was following a city policy mandating such brutality. The city would clearly be liable in the last instance; municipal liability in the first situation would appear to rest on the forbidden ground of *respondeat superior*. The other situations are less clear. The city might have prevented the action if its policies of hiring, disciplining, training, or supervising had been different. Arguably, then, city policies caused the deprivation. The question when one reaches beyond *Monell's* compulsion model is what sort of causal link between those policies and the violation is required.

C. *The Second Model of Liability:* Monell*'s Tort-Causation Model*

In dicta, the *Monell* Court said that a second approach to municipal liability analysis existed, one that it did not have to apply in the case before it. It stated that liability could be imposed when "action pursuant to official policy of some nature caused a constitutional tort." Guided by this statement and by the *Monroe* Court's dicta that section 1983 liability should be assessed "against the background of tort liability," some lower courts analyzed municipal liability in terms borrowed from tort law. These courts considered established municipal courses of action to be a municipality's policies. They then asked if the policies were the actual and proximate cause of a constitutional violation, an inquiry familiar from tort law. These cases did not require that the municipality have been at fault in establishing its policies in order to be held liable.

McKenna v. County of Nassau illustrates how a court can approach a section 1983 municipal liability question from a tort law perspective. McKenna, jailed for failure to pay a $150 fine, was given a mattress and forced to sleep on the floor in a jail corridor with other inmates. That night, he was beaten continuously for over forty-five minutes, while guards failed to respond to his pleas for help. McKenna claimed that the municipality should be held liable because its policy of having inmates sleep on mattresses in the corridor "caused" his injury. A court that followed the *Monell* compulsion model of analysis would not have allowed McKenna to recover for his injuries absent a showing of a municipal policy of allowing inmates to beat each other. The United States District Court for the Eastern District of New York, however, believed that McKenna presented a proper theory for recovery.

> The jury was instructed that it was not to evaluate the policy as to whether it was wise or unwise, or good or bad, but instead was merely to determine whether the policy for housing

> prisoners had been a proximate cause of plaintiff's injuries. Under standard instructions covering proximate cause, the possibility of multiple causes, and the liability of the county for foreseeable, probable consequences of its policies, the jury found that the county's policy for housing prisoners on tier B-1 was a proximate cause of plaintiff's injuries.

Accordingly, the court based its imposition of municipal liability on a finding that the municipality's facially constitutional policy of having prisoners sleep in a corridor actually and proximately caused McKenna to suffer a deprivation of his constitutional rights.

A court that employs a tort-based causation approach may impose municipal liability even when there is no obvious connection between a policy and a violation. *Black v. Stephens* upheld a jury verdict finding the City of Allentown liable for an officer's actions in filing unwarranted charges against Black, a person he had arrested using excessive force. The plaintiff claimed that a policy of delaying disciplinary investigations until the underlying arrest was resolved "caused" the improper charges. There was no assertion that the policy was unconstitutional. Nonetheless, the court said that the record supported the jury's findings that the policy "proximately caused" a violation of plaintiff's rights. The jury reasonably could conclude that Stephens filed additional charges against Black in order to delay disciplinary inquiry into his other misconduct. The city's policy of delaying investigations caused the charges.

In *Means v. City of Chicago*, the United States District Court for the Northern District of Illinois refused to dismiss a complaint seeking to hold the City of Chicago responsible for a shooting death by a police officer, which the plaintiff claimed was proximately caused by the city's failure to train and supervise its agents. The court noted that causation was not obvious. "It may be difficult to demonstrate that the City's conduct was a proximate cause of the injury where there is an intervening intentional act by another party." The court concluded, however, that it would be possible for the plaintiff to establish causation, emphasizing the need for a careful analysis of the causal link between policy and violation.

> [T]he relevance of policy evidence will be judged by the relationship between the alleged policy and the conduct of the individual officers. Thus while evidence of a failure to train in the use of a firearm might be relevant to a charge of negligent use of a weapon, it has no relevance to a charge of a deliberate shooting. Similarly while evidence of a failure to provide crowd control training might be relevant to a charge of overreaction to crowd hostility, it would have no bearing on an incident involving a single victim. In short, the complaint, though legally sufficient, does not authorize the plaintiff to try generally the City and its police department. We are guided by the relationship between § 1983 and traditional notions of tort law. . . . Only such "policies, customs and practices" which can legally be said to be a proximate cause of Gary Lee's death are relevant.

As many types of policy can proximately cause a constitutional violation and thus impose liability under *Monell*'s tort-causation analysis, courts using that approach do not require proof of a specific type of municipal policy. Rather, they look to a municipality's routine ways of acting; these courses of action are its policies. This approach can lead courts to impose liability when the interaction between several municipal policies is responsible for a constitutional violation.

In *Garris v. Rowland*, the unconstitutional arrest of the plaintiff stemmed from the police department's policies of obtaining warrants and arresting suspects even though an investigation to determine if the facts warranted filing charges was contemplated. These policies required that investigative reports be placed in computer files, but did not provide for cross-referencing to prevent unfounded arrests. The city was held liable for the actions of various officers carrying out these policies and procedures, even though none of its policies was unconstitutional and even though there was no allegation of previous unfounded arrests.

Similarly, in *Powe v. City of Chicago*, the court was willing to assume municipal responsibility for two arrests of a person in whose name warrants were issued after a thief used his identification. The court found it "reasonable to infer that the inadequacy of the description in the warrant was systemic in nature—that is, that it resulted from the procedures followed by the defendants' law enforcement agencies in issuing warrants of the type involved here." The United States District Court for the Southern District of New York extended this approach of looking at the total sum of municipal courses of action in determining causation. In *Odal Typographers, Inc. v. City of New York*, the court suggested that the city's failure to develop a policy to prevent unlawful property seizures was a policy of "no policy" that caused the plaintiff's injury.

These cases allow imposition of municipal liability for constitutional policies and reject the idea that only cases in the *Monell* compulsion model can give rise to liability. They permit liability to hinge on a less direct causal link. While some cases do not discuss the nature of the causation requirement in any detail, most discuss causation in terms familiar from the law of torts. Concepts such as proximate causation and the existence of intervening or superVening causes guide the causation inquiry. A tort-based causation analysis by no means assures that the city will be found liable. Courts may find that a city's policies are too remotely connected with plaintiff's injuries to be considered their cause. From a plaintiff's standpoint, however, the benefit of a proximate cause analysis is obvious. As cases such as *McKenna v. City of Nassau* and *Black v. Stephens* illustrate, a policy may proximately cause injuries that it does not command. Nassau did not command beatings in the prison corridors; Allentown did not order its officers to concoct charges. Neither municipality pursued policies that were themselves unconstitutional. Following the *Monell* compulsion theory, there would be no municipal liability in those situations. The tort-based analysis also simplifies questions of proof. A plaintiff can establish municipal liability through evidence of the municipality's traditional courses of action and their link to an injury. He or she does not have to prove a policy mandating specific, unconstitutional results. As a result, plaintiffs before courts applying the tort-causation model, unlike those before courts applying *Monell*'s compulsion model, are not faced with the problem of frequently having to prove past violations to establish liability.

D. *The Third Model of Liability: The Compulsion Model Disguised in a Focus on Municipal Fault*

In a great many section 1983 cases, beginning with those cases filed shortly after *Monell*, the plaintiffs have alleged that municipal policies of supervision and training caused violations of their constitutional rights. These claims alleged policies of "inadequate training" or "inadequate supervision." Other complaints sought to show that municipal authorities had ignored a history of constitutional violations, thus making out a policy or custom of "tacit acquiescence" in misconduct or "deliberate indifference" to violations.

Claims that municipal training and supervision policies caused constitutional deprivations may fall into the second model of municipal liability, the tort-causation model. If a court simply looked to a municipality's training or supervisory policies to determine whether those policies were the proximate cause of a given injury, the case would fit into that model. Most courts, however, injected a new element into the consideration of such claims: the question of municipal fault. Those courts reasoned that a municipality could only be held liable if it was *at fault* in establishing its training or supervisory policies. Once municipal culpability became an issue, the courts began to inquire into the level of culpability required on the part of the municipality: gross negligence, recklessness, or something else. These cases form a third model of municipal liability, one based on fault. Unlike cases in the tort-causation model, they hold that the plaintiff must prove culpability in order to establish municipal liability in a section 1983 claim.

Nothing in *Monell* suggested that fault was an element of municipal liability analysis. The *Monell* Court, instead, focused on "responsibility." *Monell* did not discuss whether New York City's Department of Social Services had been negligent, grossly negligent, or deliberately indifferent in adopting its policy. Nor did the Court suggest that those questions mattered. Indeed, by reserving comment on the question of immunities, *Monell* left open the possibility that a city could be held liable even though it had acted in the utmost good faith.

Fault entered the municipal liability calculus because some lower courts misread Supreme Court cases to make state of mind an *independent element* of the section 1983 cause of action. These cases in fact made state of mind relevant only in determining whether a certain constitutional provision had been violated. This misunderstanding occurred in *Leite v. City of Providence*, one of the first post-*Monell* municipal liability cases. *Leite* considered a claim that the defendant city was liable for abuse the plaintiff suffered at the hands of five Providence policemen. Plaintiff alleged that the city had been negligent in hiring, training, supervising, and employing those policemen. The court ruled that plaintiff properly claimed "that official municipal policy was one of the direct causes of the alleged harm," but decided that the plaintiff had to show a degree of culpability greater than mere negligence in order to establish municipal liability. The court said that the plaintiff must show deliberate indifference, "that the city can fairly be considered to have acquiesced in the probability of serious police misconduct."

In reaching this conclusion, the *Leite* court improperly relied on the Supreme Court's opinion in *Estelle v. Gamble*, which held that deliberate indifference on the part of a defendant was required to establish an eighth amendment violation. In *Estelle*, state of mind was held to be necessary only to prove an eighth amendment violation, not to make out a section 1983 action generally. Despite this, and despite subsequent Supreme Court decisions holding that state of mind is not an element of the section 1983 prima facie case, many courts have followed the *Leite* court's analysis and *Leite* is considered one of the leading municipal liability cases.

By requiring "acquiescence" in constitutional violations, the *Leite* fault-based model of liability makes it harder to hold a municipality liable. Simple evidence of training policies is unlikely to be enough to establish municipal liability, as it would be if a court were applying the tort-causation liability model. Evidence of municipal response to past incidents becomes a practical necessity. In most cases, it will be impossible to persuade a fact finder that a municipality knew or should have known that its training or supervisory policies would have resulted in plaintiff's injury absent evidence of prior incidents. As courts require proof of past incidents to prove municipal culpability, they displace analysis of training or supervision policies with analysis of policies of deliberate indifference. Inadequate training or supervision policies give rise to liability only if they are also policies of indifference.

Wellington v. Daniels illustrates how this displacement can occur. In *Wellington*, the guardian of a person who was gravely injured when a police officer struck him with a Kel-lite flashlight sought to hold the city liable for "failure to train and supervise properly the police department in the use of Kel-lite flashlights as weapons." The court held that official policies inferred from municipal omissions were actionable only if they constituted "tacit authorization" of, or "deliberate indifference" to, constitutional injuries, and stated that a failure to supervise could give rise to liability only when there was a history of widespread abuse. Accordingly, it affirmed a verdict for the municipality even though its police chief knew that Kel-lite flashlights had caused injuries in other jurisdictions and that members of his force sometimes used them as weapons. The city could not be held liable because the chief was not aware that his force's use of flashlights had caused injuries. Plaintiff "could point to only the single incident during which the ward of the estate was injured on which to predicate . . . municipal liability."

Wellington failed to differentiate between policies of inadequate training and policies of deliberate indifference. Inadequate training policies were demonstrated by proof of past injuries, rather than through a focus on training. Rather than discuss police training policies to determine whether training caused the injury, the *Wellington* court looked only to past injuries. It required the plaintiff to prove that the city had a policy of injuring people with flashlights, essentially forcing the case into the *Monell* compulsion model.

Courts that require proof of culpability to establish liability usually do not discuss the question of causation clearly. After requiring a showing that training was so inadequate that there was a policy of misconduct or that misconduct was probable, these courts generally assume that the wrongful policies caused the specific constitutional violations at issue. This obviates the need to analyze the actual causal link between the policy and violation. This approach transforms the *Monell* inquiry from a question whether a municipality should be held liable because its policy or custom *caused* a constitutional violation to whether a municipality should be held liable *for having* a certain policy or custom. Liability for having a policy can properly be established only if the policy is unconstitutional. When a municipality is found liable for having a certain policy, the case has again been forced into the *Monell* model.

When courts using the culpability model to determine liability do discuss causation, they frequently confuse the causation inquiry by merging proof of a policy with proof of causation. They require the plaintiff to show past injuries not only to establish the existence of a policy, but also to establish that the policy caused the injury. Many courts that employ the fault model and discuss causation define the causation requirement neither by reference to the "executes or implements" language of *Monell* nor to tort law concepts of causation. Instead, they require that a policy be "the moving force of the constitutional violation." While the Supreme Court in both *Monell* and *Polk County v. Dodson* used the term "moving force" to define the appropriate causal link, in neither opinion did the Court attempt to define the term. Many other courts that adopt the term also do not define it, but interpret it to require encouragement or tacit approval of illegal conduct—something less than a direct command but more than proximate cause. In *Milligan v. City of Newport News*, for instance, the plaintiff claimed that the city's inadequate training policies constituted reckless disregard of citizens' constitutional rights. The Fourth Circuit affirmed a dismissal of the complaint. It said that even if the complaint described a municipal policy, it did not show that the policy was the "moving force" in causing Milligan's injuries in the sense that it was relied upon by employees as tacit approval of their conduct. Cases such as *Milligan* make the standards for proving existence of a policy and for establishing causation the same.

Fault-model decisions that discuss causation without using any particular terminology to define the required causal link often reach the same result as *Milligan*. In *Berry v. McLemore*, for instance, the Fifth Circuit ruled that a municipality's disciplinary procedures did not cause an instance of police brutality. "There was no evidence that the Town's procedure of reprimand was so inadequate as to tacitly encourage unconstitutional conduct or to give police officers the idea that the Town was deliberately indifferent to . . . such conduct." The court in *Spriggs v. City of Chicago* suggested that a government's tacit authorization of improper conduct was an implicit command, showing causation. After saying that *Monell* required the "existence of a municipal 'policy' directing the occurrence of such violation," the court said that liability could be imposed if the city recklessly disregarded blacks' right to be free from injuries. A de facto policy or custom, the court also explained, "exists only when it is highly probable that future behavior will conform to the state's informal command." Other courts assume the existence of a causal link between the policy and deprivation if the challenged misconduct was the policy's foreseeable result. In *Rock v. McCoy*, the court upheld a verdict evidently based on the city's gross negligence in failing to train officers "with the foreseeable result that beatings like those inflicted on [plaintiff] would occur." In *Herrera v. Valentine*, the Eighth Circuit first said that a city could be held liable for improperly hiring and disciplining its police force when the evidence demonstrated that the city knew of, but failed to control, rampant misconduct in its police force, with plaintiff's losses the "inevitable result."

When fault model cases such as *Herrera* and *Rock v. McCoy* do analyze causation, they tend to view the question in general terms. They assume that a policy caused a specific action because misconduct was the "inevitable result" of the policy; they do not look at evidence relating to the specific incident or attempt to determine why the offending officer acted as he did. These courts are able to avoid conducting a causation analysis in each case because they have required the plaintiffs to prove municipal toleration or encouragement of unconstitutional conduct in order to establish existence of a policy or custom. They have come close to requiring cases to fit the *Monell* compulsion model, if they do not actually do so.

The culpability model's emphasis on municipal fault, and consequent focus on policies of "inadequate training," has led some courts to force training cases into the *Monell* compulsion model in an especially dangerous way. Most courts that discuss policies of "inadequate training" use "inadequate" as a label to describe training policies; they do not require evidence that the municipality intended its training to be inadequate. Others require proof that inadequacy was intended. The court in *Gilmere v. City of Atlanta* said that it had to determine whether a policy of improper training "even existed and, if it did, which officials, if any, had established it." It was wrong to hold the city liable simply because city employees "were negligent to the point of indifference" when the evidence showed "that the City had no official policy or custom to select and train its police officers improperly." The *Gilmere* court read "inadequate training" to require that the municipality intended to train inadequately. If this interpretation were adopted, liability could be imposed solely for cases in the *Monell* compulsion model. Establishing liability would require proof of a municipal policy of causing certain harms.

* * *

VI. The Proper Understanding of the *Monell* Inquiry

The courts that attempt to fit all municipal liability determinations into the *Monell* compulsion model and that focus on municipal fault and past constitutional violations ignore that *Monell* offered a different model of liability analysis. Under *Monell*'s tort-causation analysis, a court looks to whether a municipality's established course of action was the factual and proximate cause of a constitutional deprivation. This approach enforces section 1983's mandate that liability be imposed on those who "cause" constitutional deprivations. Unlike the *Kibbe* approach, it is fully consistent with the governing precedent. It does not cause complex evidentiary problems. It applies familiar principles of tort law and recognizes the jury's proper role in determining liability. Most importantly, it effectuates the recognized purposes of section 1983: compensating the victims of unconstitutional conduct and deterring other constitutional violations.

The *Monell* requirement is rooted in section 1983's language extending liability to any person who "subject[s], or cause[s] [a person] to be subjected" to a constitutional violation. The question is how to determine when a municipality "causes [a person] to be subjected" to a constitutional deprivation. The *Monell* Court ruled that a municipality causes an injury when its acts, policies or customs, and not the independent decisions of its low-level agents, are responsible for the harm. This outline of liability was not complicated at its inception; problems were caused as the courts tried to interpret it. Instead of interpreting the meaning of the word "cause" used in the statute, courts analyzed the term "policy" used in *Monell*. The word "policy," however, does not appear in section 1983. A proper inquiry would emphasize causation, not policy.

The "municipal policy" inquiry is a proper part of the *Monell* inquiry only to the extent that it enables a court to determine if the municipality's actions caused an injury. The municipality's plans, courses of action, and systems of governing are its policies or customs. Independent and unauthorized decisions of municipal agents who lack governing authority are not. A municipality's policy of police training, then, is its course of action in training police: the sum of materials taught, including the instruction given or not given on topics such as shooting at night or using flashlights as weapons. The municipal pattern of instruction is its policy. As the *Tuttle* Court recognized, the content of such a policy cannot be proved simply by introducing evidence of the constitutional violation that the policy allegedly caused. But it is equally wrong to suggest that a given policy of training need be shown by proving incidents of police misconduct. The "policy" is properly proved by evidence of the official training program, the lesson plans, and instructional materials.

The question whether the municipality was *at fault* in establishing a given policy is both incoherent and irrelevant. It is incoherent because, as the Supreme Court has recognized, a municipality cannot have a state of mind. Focus on an individual policymaker's state of mind is improper because it incorrectly assumes that one person determines municipal policy in an area and ignores the fact that much policy is set by committees and by the interaction of various persons or branches of government. The question of fault is irrelevant because, as the Court has repeatedly held, section 1983 does not contain a state of mind requirement. Section 1983 does not base its imposition of liability on fault; it speaks in terms of causation.

When a policy is identified, the important question is whether it "caused" the challenged injury. The proper causation inquiry is one that the framers of section 1983 may reasonably be deemed to have intended when they imposed liability on one who "subjects, or causes [a person] to be subjected" to a deprivation of constitutional rights. As the Supreme Court has emphasized, section 1983 law is developed primarily through statutory interpretation undertaken with the realization that most of the statute's drafters were attorneys who intended recognized legal principles to apply. As the Court also has recognized, section 1983 creates "a species of tort liability" and should be interpreted against the background of tort law. The principles of cause in fact and proximate cause that constitute the causation inquiry in present day tort law were also applied in 1871. They form the proper causation inquiry. When the *Kibbe* dissent suggests that a municipal policy or custom need be "a material element and substantial factor in bringing about the alleged deprivation," it is consistent with traditional tort law principles. When it states that a policy must be a "moving force" behind a deprivation, and implies that this mandates a causal link other than that required by tort law principles, it ignores the language of section 1983, relies on principles with no basis in the law of torts, invents concepts of causation that were unknown in 1871, and engages in simple judicial legislation.

Reference to tort rules of proximate causation does not in itself establish the proper liability standard; proximate cause inquiries are notoriously complex and inconsistent. "Proximate cause" is a term that the courts apply "to those more or less undefined considerations which limit liability even where the fact of causation is clearly established." The proximate cause inquiry is essentially a policy question asking whether it is the law's policy to hold a person responsible for certain injuries that he in fact caused. The proper section 1983 proximate cause inquiry depends on an inquiry into the policies underlying the statute and on the scope of liability its framers intended.

The Court has recognized that section 1983's purpose was to protect the constitutional rights of all citizens against both unconstitutional laws and the nonenforcement and unequal enforcement of constitutional ones. It provided remedies for the victims of constitutional violations and aimed to deter violations in the future. As the Supreme Court has recognized, these policies mandate a broad scope of municipal liability. A damages remedy is a "vital component of any scheme for vindicating cherished constitutional guarantees, and the importance of assuring its efficacy is only accentuated when the wrongdoer is the institution that has been established to protect the very rights it has transgressed." Moreover, the threat of municipal liability will encourage officials to err on the side of protecting constitutional rights and to work to prevent unintentional deprivations. "Such procedures are particularly beneficial in preventing those 'systemic' injuries that result not so much from the conduct of any single individual, but from the interactive behavior of several government officials, each of whom may be acting in good faith." To achieve these goals, the imposition of liability should not be linked to the existence of bad faith. As the Supreme Court has stated, "[e]lemental notions of fairness dictate that one who causes a loss should bear the loss." It is proper to require a municipality to provide compensation whenever it *causes* constitutional deprivations. That approach will best achieve the statute's goals.

The proper section 1983 causation inquiry is one that will effectuate the statute's purposes. The *Kibbe* dissent's proximate cause inquiry would undermine, not promote, those goals. By refusing to hold municipalities liable for systemic injuries caused by the interactive behavior of different officials, it would allow municipalities to escape liability for numerous injuries that they in fact caused. Constitutional violations would often go uncompensated solely because they were novel or unusual; municipal officials would avoid liability by ignoring problems rather than by aiming to solve them through improved and adjusted policies and training. Moreover, a focus on the adequacy or blameworthiness of municipal policies would force the Court to second-guess the adequacy of municipal decisions, undermining the values of federalism and comity the Court has sought to promote when interpreting section 1983.

The *Kibbe* dissent is most unsettling, however, when one realizes that the proximate cause inquiry in effect determines the scope of the defendant's duty. Its narrow view of proximate causation effectively means that the only duty municipalities owe to their citizens is that their policymaking officials avoid deliberate indifference to violations of their constitutional rights. Section 1983 was not enacted solely to protect against deliberate indifference; it had broader goals. It aimed to prevent constitutional violations "by reason of prejudice, passion, neglect, intolerance, or otherwise." The proximate cause inquiry, when reached, should be broad in order to effectuate the statutory goals. The inquiry should encourage municipalities to develop policies to minimize the chance that their agents will cause injuries when doing their jobs and responding to situations that it could reasonably be assumed they would encounter in the course of their duties. A municipality that trains people to handle certain situations, to police the streets, or to run a jail, owes a duty to those with whom its agents come in contact not to cause deprivations of their constitutional rights. Section 1983, properly construed, will allow a victim to recover from a municipality that breaches this duty.

Part III
"Every person": Theories of Individual Immunity

While section 1983 on its face does not provide for any immunities, it turns out that certain individuals sued for damages are absolutely immune, while others are qualifiedly immune. In the absolutely immune category are state and local legislators who act *functionally* in a legislative capacity, judges who act *functionally* in a judicial capacity and prosecutors who act *functionally* in an advocative capacity. *See, e.g., Tenney v. Brandhove*, 341 U.S. 367 (1951); *Stump v. Sparkman*, 435 U.S. 349 (1978); *Imbler v. Pachtman*, 424 U.S. 409 (1976); *Forrester v. White*, 484 U.S. 219 (1988). All other government officials and employees are ordinarily protected by qualified immunity only, by virtue of which they escape liability for damages if they did not violate clearly settled law. *See Harlow v. Fitzgerald*, 457 U.S. 800 (1982) and *Anderson v. Creighton*, 483 U.S. 635 (1987).

Immunity issues raise difficult questions of statutory interpretation. They also raise important policy questions regarding the best immunity rules to adopt. For example, to what extent should we be concerned with overdeterring or "chilling" government officials and employees in the performance of their duties? What role should fairness to those defendants play? And what of the interests in compensating for, and deterring, constitutional deprivations?

Dean (then Professor) Matasar's article examines the Supreme Court's historical analysis in immunity cases and finds it seriously wanting. He goes on to argue that this has prevented the Court from reaching "thoughtful results" based on sound policy considerations in immunity cases.

Professor Cass's article examines immunities at a more general level. He tackles the subject from an economics perspective, focusing on the costs and incentives implicated by immunity doctrines. He is especially concerned about overdeterring government officials and employees, and suggests that a better approach might be enterprise liability for improper official conduct.

Richard A. Matasar, *Personal Immunities Under Section 1983: The Limits of the Court's Historical Analysis,* 40 Arkansas Law Review 741 (1987)

* * *

I. HISTORY AND IMMUNITY

Section 1983 seems to make all state legislators, judges, prosecutors, executive officials, and those acting under their authority liable for their unlawful actions, regardless of their mental state in committing the offense, or the government's need to insure that officials have sufficient freedom to exercise discretion in the conduct of their offices. At the time section 1983 was enacted, however, many government officials were immune under the common law from lawsuits challenging conduct within the apparent scope of their offices. Section 1983's language does not explicitly override common law immunity. Thus, one might ask: did the drafters of section 1983 intend, as the language of the statute suggests, to abrogate official immunities long available at common law?

Over the last thirty-six years, the Court's answer to this seemingly straightforward question has become increasingly complicated. First, section 1983's broad extension of damages liability does not apply at all to the unconstitutional acts of state legislators (including quasi-legislative officials of a county government), judges, or prosecutors. These officials are absolutely immune for any acts performed under color of their offices. Second, state executive officials are entitled only to a qualified immunity under section 1983: They are liable for acts that one reasonably could have foreseen as unconstitutional. Finally, despite these immunities, county and municipal governments receive no immunity for their violations of section 1983, and judges have no immunity from injunctive suits, even in suits seeking costs and attorney's fees.

The Court would have us believe that this complex mosaic is compelled by a proper historical understanding of section 1983. According to the Court, history leads to different treatment for different officials, not because there are rational distinctions between officials, or because of important social policies, but because the officials were given varying levels of immunity at common law over 100 years ago when section 1983 was drafted. The Court believes these hundred-year-old variances are critical because it assumes the drafters of section 1983 incorporated and froze common law rules current in 1871 into section 1983, despite adopting language which seemed to obliterate official immunity. Thus, the Court's historical assumptions are its justification for official immunity.

Over time, the Court's immunity decisions have wavered in their devotion to this historical methodology. The early decisions involving legislative and judicial immunities rest primarily on a strong, continuous, historical tradition of immunity that leads the Court to refuse to interpret section 1983 as broadly as its language would warrant. The Court avoided having to offer a contemporary justification for immunity because it tied immunity to historical traditions and meanings, and attributed the decision to permit immunity to the Congress of 1871. Later, in its prosecutorial and executive immunity cases, the Court could not find as strong a historical tradition of official immunity. It therefore bolstered its history with "policy" justifications. Yet, even in these cases, the Court steadfastly maintained that it was merely "interpreting" section 1983 in light of choices made long ago by Congress. Recently, the Court has once again embraced historical determinacy, not to justify requiring official immunity, but to explain its rejection. Just as members of the Court favoring immunity once emphasized that history compelled acceptance of immunities for governmental officials, those opposing immunity have discovered the powerful legitimating force provided when one can argue that history compels the Court's action.

* * *

B. Another History to be Considered

Before one can assess the legitimacy of the Court's historical methodology in its immunity decisions, one must first review the adequacy of the Court's historical analysis. Does it convince us that immunity was so deeply engrained in the consciousness of the drafters of section 1983 as to warrant the assumption that, as a matter of their historical intent in adopting section 1983, they retained common law immunities? As I suggest below, there are reasons to doubt the adequacy of the Court's historical proof. First, immunities may not have been as prevalent at the common law as suggested by the Court. Second, contrary to what the Court assumes, there are a number of indications that the drafters of section 1983, and its criminal law predecessor, might well have intended to abrogate common law immunity. Third, there are indications in both section 1983 and its precursor that the Reconstruction Congress meant to break from past conventions and create new liabilities where none previously existed. Thus, the Court's history in its immunity decisions is flawed at best.

1. Common Law Immunity Revisited

It is clear that in *Tenney* the Court accurately described the long-held common law immunity of legislators for acts within the apparent scope of their offices, although even the Court acknowledged that such immunities were far from uniform in 1871 (or 1951 for that matter). The Court's extension of absolute immunity to judicial officials is not, however, as strongly based in history.

Judicial immunity was not universally accepted at common law in England. While such immunity was available for superior court judges, justices of the peace and other lower judicial officials were subject to liability for damages. Moreover, as the Supreme Court indicated in *Pulliam v. Allen*, judges were not immune from injunctive suits (or their equivalents) under English common law.

Neither was judicial immunity uniformly applied under the common law of the United States prior to the passage of the Civil Rights Act of 1871. While it is true that the Supreme Court of the United States had held a judge immune from suit in 1868, the Court explicitly exempted from immunity judicial "acts, in excess of jurisdiction . . . done maliciously or corruptly." Under this rule, in force before the passage of the Civil Rights Act of 1871, judges apparently *were* liable for their acts in *excess* of their authority so long as the acts *appeared* to be within their authority. In contrast, under the current judicial immunity doctrine, a judge is immune from any liability unless he or she has acted in "clear absence of all jurisdiction."

The difference between the current doctrine and that in force before 1871 is not a matter of mere form. Acts in "excess" of jurisdiction encompass a wide variety of things that are not in "clear absence of jurisdiction." More significantly, the move from the "excess" to the "clear absence" test took place after the enactment of section 1983. Thus, it is hard to attribute to the drafters of section 1983 a silent acceptance of a test for judicial immunity that had not yet been in force when the drafters were acting.

As shown above, absolute immunity for judges was not firmly established either in England or the federal system before the enactment of section 1983. Thus, the Court's conclusion in *Pierson* that "[f]ew doctrines were more solidly established at common law [than immunity for judges]" is somewhat suspect. However, if such immunities were broadly accepted under *state* common law by the time section 1983 was enacted, the Court's analysis might have vitality despite its overestimation of federal and English common law. In fact, state common law as it existed in 1871 provides no better source for the Court's historical conclusion in *Pierson*. As one commentator's research demonstrates, only thirteen of the thirty-seven states in the Union in 1871 recognized absolute immunity for judges. History, contrary to the Court, does not show a "solidly established" common law immunity for judges.

The Court's extension of immunity to other governmental officials, especially executive officers, is even weaker. Under principles of agency law well-accepted by the late 1860's and early 1870's, governmental agents were held responsible in damage suits for their negligent acts, misfeasances in office, and intentional wrongs.

Private agency law of the mid-1800's provided that an agent would be liable for negligent torts, misfeasances of office, or any positive wrongs. His principal would be held responsible, under *respondeat superior*, for these acts as well, with a right of action over against the agent. Similar rules applied to public officials' misfeasances and positive wrongs, although *respondeat superior* was unavailable against the government itself because of principles of sovereign immunity. Justice Story's agency treatise of the mid-1800's makes this plain:

> . . . as to the liability of public agents for torts or wrongs done in the course of their agency. It is plain, that the government itself is not responsible for the misfeasances, or wrongs, or negligences, or omissions of duty of the subordinate officers or agents employed in the public service . . . . But although neither the government nor its superior officers are responsible to

> third parties for misfeasances, or negligences, or omissions of duty of the subordinates in office, . . . it by no means follows that such subordinates are themselves exempted . . . . On the contrary, the very consideration, that the public superiors are not responsible distinguishes the case from that of mere private agencies, and lets in the doctrine, that they shall be held personally responsible . . . .
>
> . . . *A fortiori*, the same rule applies to cases where the . . . officers . . . are guilty of direct misfeasances or positive wrongs to third persons . . . .

Because of the immunity of the government, it became essential that the official herself be liable. As one commentator, speaking to parallel English law, asserted: "[w]ith us every official, from the Prime Minister down to the constable or a collector of taxes, is under the same responsibility for every act done without legal justification as any other citizen." The equation of the private and public wrongdoer was in no sense reached merely by some formal notion of "equality." Rather, it "was the result of a deliberate effort to protect the citizen from governmental misuse of authority:"

> [Liability of public officials for their misdeeds] is founded upon a very plain principle of common sense and common justice; and that is, that no person shall shelter himself from personal liability, who does a wrong under color of, but without any authority, or by excess of his authority, or by a negligent use or abuse of his authority. Where a person is clothed with authority as a public agent, it cannot be presumed, that the government means to justify, or even to excuse, his violations of his own proper duty, under color of that authority.

This principle of public accountability insured that private individuals harmed by governmental acts would be compensated. However, the principle could lead to some harsh results for officials. Such cases gave rise to fears that public officials were being unfairly exposed to liability. Unlike private actors, against whom *respondeat superior* could be used to spread expenses, public employees were forced to bear the brunt of damage suits themselves. Moreover, exposing public employees to extensive risks was perceived not only as unfair to them, but also as a potential interference with public policy itself. Without giving public employees some room to exercise "discretion," they might be inhibited from proper administration of their offices.

It was out of these fears that official immunity for executive officials began to expand. And, it is to this expansion—and justifiably so—that the Court turned in its executive immunity decisions. The Court's decision to treat the expansion of official immunity as a common law imperative, however, clearly is not so justified. Under the Court's doctrine, a finding of immunity against an official is also a finding that an injury of an innocent third party will be uncompensated, since the state itself cannot be sued directly or indirectly under section 1983. The resulting failure to compensate innocent third parties is as unfair as punishing officials who erroneously act in "good faith," and raises policy issues as pressing as the need to protect official discretion. Yet, the Court's immunity decisions do not adequately address these results.

In contrast, the common law, as modified by legislation, adjusted the balance between protecting officials and compensating individuals. After the expansion of official immunity, several states passed state tort claims acts to protect discretionary acts of state officials from liability while at the same time giving individuals a right to recover from the whole political community. Other states began to offer indemnification to their officials to reimburse them for their errors of judgment. The Court's assessment of the expansion of official immunity in these states presents a misleading picture of the law of immunities for it treats expansion independently of other simultaneous developments in compensating individuals. The expansion of immunity was integrally related to the availability of alternative means of compensating individuals. Immunity of the officer might well be given, but only because the state itself assumed compensatory responsibility. Or, conversely, the harshness of making immunity unavailable might be mitigated by indemnification for the officer. Thus, a proper assessment of common law immunity can be made only by balancing fairness to officials with fairness to their victims, only by furthering a policy of protecting officials' discretion while simultaneously insuring compensation of victims. The Court's immunity decisions, therefore, seem to have seriously underestimated the common law's attempts to mitigate immunity by expanding other forms of compensatory relief.

2. The Reconstruction Congress Revisited

Even if one ultimately concludes that the Supreme Court's failure to address the relationship of compensatory concepts and immunities does not distort its historical analysis of immunities, one might still pause at accepting the Court's analysis if it inadequately described the Reconstruction

Congress' debates. The Court's immunity analysis rests on several key assumptions about those debates: first, that the 1871 Congress intended section 1983's plain language to be rejected; second, that the Congress in 1871 was silent on whether section 1983 abolished common law immunities; and third, that this silence should be read as an adoption of traditional common law concepts. An examination of these three assumptions reveals that the Court's analysis is suspect.

a. Plain Meaning and the Reconstruction Congress

In its immunity decisions, the Court argues that the apparent scope of section 1983 should be ignored. The Court asserts that Congress could not have intended by its silence to override common law protections of officers, and therefore, Congress did not want courts to give the language of section 1983 its plain effect. In reaching these conclusions, the Court makes no attempt to substantiate its assumptions about the Reconstruction Congress' hermeneutical understanding of the proper method for a court to interpret positive legal enactments. Had the Court made such an attempt however, the results would have undercut its assumptions about the meaning of congressional silence. Thus, the Court's failure to search for the interpretive intent of the drafters of section 1983 undermines the Court's efforts to justify its historical conclusions concerning Congress' intent.

The legislative history of important Reconstruction Era statutes shows a number of legislators who were quite aware of interpretational methodology, especially as it relates to constitutional interpretation. Some tied interpretation of provisions solely to their plain meaning. Others began with plain meaning, but accepted evidence of legislative intent as a method for resolving ambiguities in language. Others suggested that regardless of plain meaning or legislative statements, the legislation should be interpreted broadly because of its overall remedial purposes. Although there were not a great number of speakers who directly addressed proper interpretational methodology, there is absolutely no suggestion by anyone that congressional silence should be read to override either plain meaning or actual legislative statements. Therefore, the few statements that were made suggest that the Court's assumptions about congressional silence fly in the face of the hermeneutical conventions of the Reconstruction Congress.

One of the clearest statements in the Reconstruction debates concerning proper interpretive methodology was made by Senator Davis of Kentucky in his comments concerning the passage of the Civil Rights Act of 1866. As he stated:

> [W]hat is the rule of construction of our Constitution as laid down so frequently by the Supreme Court . . . ? It is this . . . : that the parties who frame an instrument give their own meaning, according to their understanding of the terms and language which they use, to that instrument, and that, therefore, in construing the Constitution . . . all we have to do is read the language, and *to ascertain from contemporaneous expositions, as well as from the force of the terms themselves*, what particular meaning the framers of the Constitution intended their language to import. Whatever meaning they intended to attach to the language of that instrument or to any of its phrases, by that light and by that rule is the Constitution to be construed and interpreted.

These comments were echoed later in the debates by Representative Thayer of Pennsylvania, who called for looking to the "words" of a document to understand its meaning, and for searching for the meaning of those words in the "definition of the general language." Far from suggesting that the Court could properly assume that congressional silence is meant to override the apparent meaning of the language chosen in a congressional enactment, Davis' and Thayer's remarks suggest that when Congress means something other than plain meaning, it says so. The only exception to this approach that might be justified, according to Senator Davis, would be when interpreting "technical" terms or "terms of art." In that situation, one might hunt for a definition of a term chosen in "its legal definition at the time [it] was adopted, how learned judges and learned lawyers understood the term . . . ." Section 1983 uses no such term of art in reference to its creation of liability for "every person"; nor is there any suggestion to the contrary in the section's legislative history.

Remarks in the passage of section 1983 itself reinforce the importance of legislative intent and plain meaning to the Reconstruction Congress. As Representative Burchard said: "the words of many distinguished gentlemen who have spoken upon this bill, and above all the legislation indorsed by gentlemen who took part in framing the amendments under which authority is claimed, will become guides in construing the extent of the new powers added to the Constitution." Even if all would not agree with Burchard that the words used in debates could give a gloss to the language chosen by its framers, no one would disagree that in arguing for an interpretation based on intent, one should at least be able to point to some evidence of that intent.

In light of these statements alone, one might seriously doubt the conclusion of the Supreme Court that Congress' silence in section 1983 must have meant that its drafters wanted to incorporate common law immunities, but nonetheless adopted language that plainly did not endorse its hidden intent. Such *sub silentio* legislating seems patently at odds with a Congress deeply concerned about plain meanings and drafters' "original" intentions.

The Court's assumptions seem even less plausible when one looks to statements of the framers of section 1983, who intended it to be given a generous reading. The remarks of Representative Shellabarger, section 1983's sponsor, on its scope are particularly apt:

> [T]here can be no rational doubt, of the right to enact the first section [section 1983] of this bill. . . . The section being . . . carefully confined to giving a civil action for such wrongs against citizenship as are done under color of State laws which abridge these rights, it goes directly to the enforcement of that provision [of the fourteenth amendment] which says that the state shall not make or enforce any law which shall abridge any privileges or franchises of citizens. . . . *I have a single remark to make in regard to the rule of interpretation of those provisions of the Constitution under which all the sections of the bill are framed. The act is remedial, and in aid of the preservation of human liberty and human rights. All statutes and constitutional provisions authorizing such statutes are liberally and beneficently construed.* It would be most strange and, in civilized law, monstrous were this not the rule of interpretation.

Senator Edmunds, the manager of the bill in the Senate, suggested an equally broad purpose to section 1983—to enforce the provisions of the fourteenth amendment:

> The first section is one that I believe nobody objects to, as defining the rights secured by the Constitution of the United States when they are assailed by any State law or under color of any State law, and it is merely carrying out the principles of the civil rights bill [of 1866] which have long since become a part of the Constitution . . . I intend to say, and this was to very simply and really reenacting the Constitution, that I supposed nobody would be opposed to it.

If, as Shellabarger and Edmunds maintained, section 1983 was a reenactment of the fourteenth amendment, and was intended to be an enforcement of the breadth of its provisions, it would be doubtful that they had any intent to incorporate, *sub silentio*, limits to the scope of the new liabilities created by the Act and the constitutional provision upon which it was based.

b. Common Law Immunities and the Reconstruction Congress

These general statements of Reconstruction legislators concerning proper interpretation of the fourteenth amendment and its supporting legislation alone make the historical analysis of the Court's immunity decisions questionable. Any assumption that the drafters of section 1983 meant to incorporate common law immunities by their silence must first justify why plain meaning should be ignored in the absence of any explicit legislative direction to do so. The Court's assumption becomes even more doubtful, however, when the legislative debates of the Reconstruction Congress are closely reviewed, because far from being silent about immunities, the debates on both section 1983 and its criminal law predecessor are replete with statements of the opponents of civil rights statutes that the legislation was overriding those immunities. Furthermore, nothing in the legislative history is said to assuage the fears of these opponents. Thus, Congress was not silent about immunities; it was only silent about *retaining* immunities.

i. The Civil Rights Act of 1871

In *Tenney v. Brandhove*, the Supreme Court asserted that the legislative debates on section 1983 did not spell out its scope, including the availability of immunities for legislators. Later, in *Pierson v. Ray*, the Court emphasized that the debates gave "no clear indication that Congress meant to abolish wholesale all common-law immunities," especially those for judges. Later yet, the Court extended its reasoning to cover executive and prosecutorial officers. If it were true that the legislative debates were wholly silent on immunities, the Court's historical justification for immunities would be understandable. But, as Justice Douglas pointed out, the Court's history cannot be found determinative since it "ignores the fact that every member of Congress who spoke to the issue assumed that the words of the statute meant what they said . . . . " Accordingly, the Court's historical assumption that Congress, by its silence, must have intended the continuance of the common law is unwarranted.

Three major speeches made in opposition to section 1983 proceeded on the assumption that it would apply to *all* officials—legislators, judges, and executive officers. Typical of these was the speech made by Representative Arthur of Kentucky. He argued not only that these officials would not be absolutely immune, but that they would have no exemption from liability, even if they acted in "good faith." As Arthur argued:

> [I]s [section 1983] expedient? [I]t . . . must fall under the sternest condemnation . . . . [I]f the Legislature [of a state] enacts a law, if the Governor enforces, if the judge upon the bench renders a judgment, if the sheriff levy an execution, execute a writ, serve a summons, or make an arrest, all acting under a solemn, official oath, though as pure in duty as a saint and as immaculate as a seraph, for a mere error of judgment, they are liable, and most certain . . . to be summarily stripped of official authority, dragged to the bar of a distant and unfriendly court, and there placed in the pillory of vexatious, expensive, and protracted litigation. . . .
>
> . . . Under the provisions of this section every judge in the State court and every other officer thereof . . . will enter upon and pursue the call of official duty with the sword of Damocles suspended over him by a silken thread . . . .

Even more significant, perhaps, are the remarks of Senator Thurman. Not only did he object to the potential reach of section 1983 against state legislators and judges, he also spoke on how the absence of protections within the legislation might be interpreted. Thus, his remarks confront assumptions about silence made by the Court eighty years later. He argued:

> I have another objection . . . . [The section] refers to a deprivation under color of law, either statute law or "custom or usage" . . . .
>
> . . . .
>
> Now . . . does that include the legislators of a State? . . . [W]here is the clause that exempts those legislators from the action that is provided in this section of the bill?
>
> But let us go a little further. What is to be the case of a judge? The Legislature . . . passes a law. It goes before a judge of the State court for interpretation. . . . [H]e conscientiously renders a decision which another man, a judge of the district court of the United States, may suppose deprives some person of a right, privilege, or immunity secured by the Constitution . . . Is that State judge to be taken from his bench? Is he to be liable in an action? . . . .
>
> Is it intended to perpetuate that? . . . That is the language of this bill. Whether it is the intent or not I know not, but it is the language of the bill; for there is no limitation whatsoever upon the terms that are employed, and they are as comprehensive as can be used.

Senator Thurman invited the sponsors of section 1983 to speak if their intent was not to abolish immunity for governmental officials. He explicitly noted the absence of such protections from the Act, thereby suggesting the need for such provisions, and pointed to the plain meaning of the language used. No one responded to his invitation. Given the 1871 Congress' significant attachment to "plain meaning" interpretative methods, the absence of *any* statement disavowing section 1983's language cuts against implying immunity. Moreover, the only explicit statements on the question seem to support the section's plain meaning; this casts serious doubts on the Court's attempt to turn Congress' supposed silence against its actual language.

There are reasons to think that Congress meant what it said. Although section 1983 was not the subject of much discussion or objection, its drafters and supporters clearly stated its broad remedial purpose. Moreover, at least some of the supporters of section 1983 believed that the only effective means to enforce federal rights would be by suits against state officers. A Congress concerned with effective legislation that intended to limit that legislation's scope would be unlikely to do so silently.

ii. The Civil Rights Act of 1866

One possible explanation for the absence of debate about immunities under section 1983 is that Congress had not adequately focused on the potential conflict between section 1983's broad language and the common law. If that were the case, the Court's interpretation of congressional silence might yet be historically justifiable. However, Congress apparently was aware of the potential conflict of section 1983's language and common law immunities, not only because a few legislators pointed out the conflict, but because it had explicitly discussed the problem during debate on the Civil Rights Act of 1866.

The significance of the legislative history of the Act of 1866 on the interpretation of section 1983 should not be underestimated. As the supporters of section 1983 frequently noted during debate on the 1871 Civil Rights Act, section 1 of that Act (now section 1983) derived from section 2 of the Civil

Rights Act of 1866; section 1 was a civil counterpart of section 2's criminal provisions. Thus, the 1866 congressional debates on section 2 are given great weight by the Court and scholars in interpreting section 1983.

Section 1 of the Civil Rights Act of 1866 declared newly freed slaves to be citizens of the United States, defined certain "civil rights" for those citizens, and voided contrary state laws. Section 2 of the Act then announced that "any person who, under color of any law, statute, ordinance, regulation, or custom shall subject, or cause to be subjected, any inhabitant of any State or Territory to the deprivation of any right secured [by the Act] shall be deemed guilty of a misdemeanor, and, on conviction, shall be punished . . . . " The parallel to section 1983 is striking.

During the debate on section 2 of the 1866 Act, several opponents of the Act criticized its applicability to government officials. Representative Kerr of Indiana, for example, stated:

> It cannot be claimed that [local governmental officials] could not be punished under the provisions of this bill because they were acting as officers and their conduct was the result of errors of judgment only. That would be no valid defense—no defense at all—against the positive terms of this law. I hold that the only persons intended to be punished by this bill are persons acting under State authority in some sort of official capacity. By its very terms, it only applies to persons who shall do these prohibited acts 'under *color* of any law, statute, ordinance, regulation, or *custom*.' Who can act under such *color* but officers of some kind?
>
> . . . .
>
> [The Act] puts the local . . . officers, executive, ministerial, and judicial, of the States, at the mercy of the petty Federal officers . . . .

Kerr's objections were shared by numerous others, including President Johnson, who vetoed the Act, in part, because it abolished immunities for state officials.

Hence, like the history of section 1983, the history of section 2 of the Act of 1866 contains indications of a Congress well aware of the broad liability for government officials despite common law immunities. However, unlike section 1983 where there is no clear rejection of common law immunity, the history of section 2 suggests that Congress explicitly rejected immunities (or at least a lessening of penalties) for state officers. No less a supporter of civil rights than Representative Bingham, the father of the fourteenth amendment, was so persuaded of the injustice of criminal liability, without a good faith defense for officers, that he offered an amendment to section 2 to turn it into a civil penalty, rather than a criminal provision. His proposed amendment was clearly perceived as being responsive to the problem of criminalizing official conduct. Yet, Representative Wilson of Iowa had a short answer to Bingham's proposal: "What difference in principle is there between saying that the citizen shall be protected by . . . civil remedy and declaring that he shall be protected by penal enactments . . . ? The House agreed with Wilson and resoundingly defeated Bingham's amendment. Even had the amendment passed, however, it would not have been a vote in favor of immunities. Bingham did not propose excepting state officers from liability; he only proposed that they be subject to civil, not criminal law.

The rejection of Bingham's amendment and the retention of criminal penalties in the Act of 1866, despite strong arguments favoring immunity, suggest that Congress in 1866 grappled with the availability of common law protections for state officials, and explicitly rejected them, five years before section 1983 was enacted. Their clear focus on the issue of immunity demonstrates that Congress knowingly rejected immunities for state officials. That this was done in a statute paralleling section 1983 further diminishes the validity of the historical determinacy argument offered by the Supreme Court for its immunity decisions.

3. The Reconstruction Congress' Break from the Past

The historical analysis of the Court's immunity decisions rests on the assumption that Congress would not have made a break from the past without explicitly saying so. Embedded in this analysis, perhaps, is an even more basic assumption: that the Reconstruction Congress was only making incremental changes in our legal fabric. This assumption, which is one some members of the Court have made in the past, is erroneous. The Reconstruction Congress undertook a fundamental reordering of American society; it was not a group hesitant to reverse traditions.

It was the Reconstruction Congress that permanently abolished the system of property that had existed in the southern states since the beginning of the nation. That same Congress, ignoring contrary Supreme Court precedent, used the narrow language of the thirteenth amendment to find authority to define United States citizenship and the rights incident to such citizenship, to hold state officials criminally liable when they enforced state laws interfering with these newly created rights, and to expand federal jurisdiction, both original and removal, to give federal courts the power to hear *state law* cases involving citizens of the same states merely because some violation of federal law lurked in the background of the dispute. This same Reconstruction Congress then constitutionalized its statutory grants of citizenship and other basic rights when it passed the fourteenth amendment, a provision that set Congress on a collision course with the states. This was the Reconstruction Congress that capped its legislative agenda in 1875 with the passage of the Civil Rights Act of 1875, legislation that went so far as to criminalize private discriminations, an arena never before entered by a federal legislature. It is this Congress that the Supreme Court "presumes" meant, by silence, to retain common law immunities that would block recovery from officials who violated citizens' constitutional rights.

Even if the legislative history of section 1983 was itself silent about whether Congress meant to break with old traditions, the broad social agenda evidenced by these other acts should cause one to be suspicious of the Court's assumptions. But, one need not rest on surmise about Congress' other acts, for it is clear that the Civil Rights Act of 1871, the very Act that gave us section 1983, was a great break from the past.

A cursory review of the legislative history of the Act shows opponents virtually apoplectic in their reaction to the legislation. As stated by Representative Swann of Maryland, the 1871 Congress' legislation showed "the utter contempt in which all State authority is held." Representative McHenry of Kentucky may best have summarized the views of opponents of section 1983, who believed the section to be a radical break from the past. As he put it:

> The first section of the bill . . . gives a civil remedy . . . and vests in the Federal courts jurisdiction to determine the individual rights of citizens of the same State, a jurisdiction which of right belongs only to the State tribunals, and to rob them of it by the power of the Federal Government is an infraction of the Constitution so flagrant that the people will hold to a strict accountability those men . . . who perpetrate the outrage.

Even if one discounts the hyperbole of Swann and McHenry, one still cannot help but believe that the 1871 Congress had more in mind than a simple tinkering with state and federal relations. Such a Congress would seem unlikely to be worried about common law niceties that would conflict with its larger legislative plan.

Only a Court bent on ignoring history (or misusing it) could fail to see these signs of an activist Congress, a Congress unwilling to silently accept common law traditions that might stand in the way of its social agenda. Together with the Court's inaccurate perception of the common law and its misreading of the explicit legislative history of the civil rights acts, this failure underscores the Court's incomplete historical analysis of personal immunities.

II. ASSESSING THE COURT'S USE OF HISTORY IN ITS IMMUNITY DECISIONS

How can we best assess the Court's immunity decisions? A persuasive case can be made that the Court's decisions are simply wrong, that Congress in 1871 meant to abrogate all common law immunities and did so by the plain language of section 1983. But, moving from questioning the Court's conclusions about immunities to accepting their converse is not that simple a progression. Even aside from the force of *stare decisis*, the evidence against the Court's position does not prove that its decisions are incorrect. At most, the evidence reveals that the Court's historical perspective inadequately accounts for a counter-history that would suggest rejecting the Court's immunity rules.

A. History and Counter-History

The Court's immunity decisions piece together various historical facts, assumptions about those facts, and assumptions about the era that generated them. In essence, the Court's historical perspective rests on the following propositions: common law immunities were extensive during the 1870's; although Congress did not explicitly acknowledge the existence of these immunities, they were so extensive that they would have been known by Congress; the civil rights acts were not a complete break with the legal traditions of the times; Congress did not address every possible legal argument or defense that might be made about its legislation; therefore, Congress assumed that silences in its statutes would be filled by reference to the traditions well-known at the time.

These arguments have a strong ring of truth to them. It is a demonstrable fact—even if one questions how widespread—that immunities were available at common law. It is true that Congress did not address every legal issue lurking in section 1983's interstices. Clearly, at least some members of

Congress knew about immunities. Thus, provided that one believes that section 1983 was a minimal incursion on generally accepted relations between state governments and federal regulation, and was merely an incremental advance on common law protections, one can readily accept the retention of common law protections as "intended" in section 1983.

The Court's resolution of the immunity problem, therefore, is not ahistorical. It is, however, somewhat one-sided. Accepting all of the "facts" underlying the Court's decisions does not lead inexorably to the conclusion reached by the Court that Congress "intended" to retain common law immunities in section 1983. That conclusion makes historical sense only if the Court correctly viewed section 1983 as a minimal additional remedy to those provided by the common law—a view that can be argued, but not proved, and that runs counter to other historical evidence.

There is a strong counter-history to the Court's version of Reconstruction and immunity. The Court's factual assertions alone may be erroneous: common law immunities were arguably substantially less prevalent than the Court asserts; and, Congress may not have been as silent as the Court suggests. Even more importantly, though, the Court's primary assumption that section 1983 was a minimalist intervention is questionable. Some legislators in 1871 clearly saw section 1983 as expansionist and revolutionary. Therefore, to one who views section 1983 as expansionist, the Court's decisions to grant immunity are historically incorrect.

At various times, the Court's immunity decisions seem to emphasize either one or the other of these historical accounts of section 1983. The Court that decided *Tenney v. Brandhove*, writing before the expansion of section 1983, saw the section as a minimal break from the past. It therefore placed the burden of demonstrating Congress' intent upon those seeking to abrogate immunities under section 1983. The Court writing after *Monroe v. Pape* found *Tenney*'s minimalist vision of section 1983 more problematic. To justify ignoring the statute's language, especially in cases involving weak common law foundations for immunity, the Court's historical explanation became more complex; the Court supplemented its views with policy analysis. By *Pulliam v. Allen* and the other recent immunity cases, the Court's historical assumptions became more complex still. The Court apparently had come to believe that section 1983 was expansionist, and therefore, shifted the burden of historical proof. Where the Court once required a showing that Congress meant to abrogate immunities, it would now require a showing that Congress meant to retain them.

From *Tenney* to *Pulliam*, the Court's emphasis shifted, but its underlying historical assumption did not: historical analysis, whether based on a minimalist or expansionist view of section 1983, would provide a "correct" answer. Differences in the outcomes of cases could be explained, not because of the discovery of different historical data, but because of different assumptions about the historical context. The Court that saw a minimalist section 1983 read historical data to favor immunities. The Court that saw an expansionist section 1983 colored the historical data to reject immunities. Yet, in neither instance did the Court seem willing to admit that history itself did not provide an answer or that history is contingent, dependent on the context of the questions asked of it. Had the Court seen history in this light, it might have made decisions based purely on judicial policy choices between equally plausible historical arguments.

B. Descriptions and Contexts

The Court's immunity decisions should be rejected, but not because their history is wrong. In order to conclude that the Court's history is erroneous, one must accept a counter-history as correct. The problem is that history is simply too complex, in most instances, to provide us with sufficient guidance to accept or reject plausible, though contradictory, historical evidence of meaning. The flaw in the Court's immunity decisions is not that they are wrong; it is that they are wrongheaded.

The Court's decisions assume that history contains but one answer to interpretational dilemmas confronting us in contemporary culture. In fact, history is so contextual that for many, if not all, questions, history's answers are multi-leveled, complex, and sometimes self-contradictory. In the Court's immunity decisions, both accepting and rejecting immunities, the Court makes a fundamental assumption about historical knowledge: "good history can accurately portray past reality." To the Court, there must be an answer—if not what Congress actually thought, at least what it would have thought, had it thought. That assumption is incorrect.

The Court sees history as a "descriptive" process, one which

> considers a historical report to be composed solely of objective evidence. Historical truth is understood to be embodied in the statements or artifacts bequeathed by the people of the

past; the historian's role is merely to assemble this objective evidence into a credible story. In so doing, he is to treat the past's legacy as a kind of sacred text; he must never tamper with, add to, subtract from, or contradict its evidentiary record, for if he does so his account will be transformed from an accurate reproduction of the past into a novelistic impression of it. Good history, according to the descriptivist, is thus a current portrait that corresponds precisely to a past reality.

Yet descriptivist historians never accept the record bequeathed by the past in its entirety, because reality is so complex that no account of it, past or present, can hope to portray it fully. Instead, descriptivist historians delete what they find unimportant in the record of the past, interpolate into the record matters that it omits, and label certain of the statements and artifacts . . . as forgeries and otherwise inaccurate representations. For a sophisticated descriptivist, the record of the past becomes good history only when sifted through and synthesized into a coherent whole . . . .

[T]he sophisticated descriptivists insist that only one correct interpretation—only one right answer—exists for any given question.

To the Court that accepted immunities, sifting through the historical records in the immunity decisions required it to discount inconsistencies of the common law, underestimate the degree of variability of common law rules, and ignore competing principles of protections for individuals. It required the Court to make certain assumptions about Congress' views toward plain meaning, to treat the broadly expansionist views of the Reconstruction Congress as irrelevant to the question of the availability of immunities, and to disregard actual statements of legislators who believed immunities had been abrogated. On the other hand, the Court that rejected immunities also ignored variability and the strength of some immunities in the common law.

Both the cases accepting and rejecting immunities use history incorrectly by treating some matters as irrelevant, ignoring other matters altogether, and highlighting some facts over others. That the Court must choose among historical data undermines its historical conclusions, for by assessing the credibility of each piece of historical evidence, counting some matters, and rejecting others, the Court's history is made to rest on the accuracy of its choices. As Professor Nelson puts it: the validity of the Court's history rests "on whether one believes credibility is a sound reason to prefer one interpretation of the . . . past to another."

There are strong reasons to doubt the "historical credibility" judgments of judges.

> While judges have fulsome experience in regard to the behavioral patterns of the sorts of people who typically appear before them, they know little about how people behaved in the distant past. They may reason anachronistically when they use their present-day behavioral assumptions to assess the accuracy of a particular interpretation of the past.

Yet, even the judge who is capable of perceiving the past with the mind-set of the past may be a poor judge of credibility, for credibility judgments are themselves the product not so much of reason as of "personal values."

Even more fundamentally, these values shape the very context in which history is perceived. To a judge who believes section 1983 is a minimal, supplementary remedy, proof of a strong common law tradition of immunity and a showing of relative silence by Congress in overcoming that tradition amounts to a historical command to retain immunity. Yet, congressional silence and a common law tradition that might not be so strong counsel a judge who perceives section 1983 as a break from the past to abrogate immunities. The Court's immunity decisions might be explained not as history at all but as a debate between minimalists and expansionists. History so contextually determined does not lead inexorably to any single answer. "[A] judge who decides . . . cases on the basis of credibility . . . mislead[s] both himself and his audience as to the ultimate basis of his decisions."

Why then do judges seek to make history definitive when it is not? In our post-substantive due process legal system, the Court is quite leery of giving the appearance of the "super-legislator." It makes common law only in limited circumstances that necessarily call for an answer. To such a Court, attribution of a policy choice to Congress is a logical, even if false, move. Moreover, by passing the blame to Congress the Court can claim that an unpopular decision is compelled, maintain the legitimacy of its decision, and yet not have to justify its result. But, as argued above, these misleading steps can backfire. When the Court's history is exposed as shallow and contingent, the Court becomes even more susceptible to the very charges of overstepping its authority that it seeks to avoid in the first place.

Should the Court disregard history completely then? I think not, for history does not have to be a search for "right" answers; it has a significance that transcends its limitations. History, even if not definitive, helps us to frame the proper issue to be decided, set out the plausible limits of debate, and maintain continuity with the past. It then becomes not a "search for *the* past meaning," but a search "for various past meanings in exploring the linguistic possibilities of the provision under discussion." So long as one places historical analysis within its proper context, one can use it instrumentally to legitimate the clear policy choices that must be made to resolve current interpretational problems.

How can one use such contextual history and still be making historical analysis rather than writing fiction. Judges must not search only for that history that best coincides with their predispositions. The whole factual record including those parts that seem inconsistent or ambiguous must be examined, credibility judgments must be justified, and assumptions must be made explicit. When historical analysis suggests only one plausible (or at least shared) understanding, this process is easy. In such cases, the Court's decision can start, and perhaps end, with its history. But, when historical data are contradictory, imperfect, or incomplete, judges no longer can use history as the primary justification for adopting a particular meaning. Where history fails, however, current policy justifications must be given.

It is not my purpose to suggest the proper policy analysis for the Court's immunity decisions. Others have already ably done so. I do not, however, stop merely to criticize the Court's flawed methodology. Whatever else might be said about the Court's decisions, if they reach justifiable results, one should not be too upset, even if the results are reached by questionable analysis. But, when the Court's flawed methodology may prevent it from reaching thoughtful results, it is incumbent to critique the methods used and suggest the consequences of reorienting the Court's approach. By altering its perception that immunity is somehow historically bound, the Court can legitimately recognize policy considerations that might alter its immunity policy. Freed from the shackles of a history that treats immunity decisions as legislatively determined, the Court can turn to principles of the common law to direct its jurisprudence.

* * *

Ronald A. Cass, *Damage Suits Against Public Officers,* 129 University of Pennsylvania Law Review 1110 (1981)

* * *

III. The Role and Costs of Official Liability

In moving from a two-tier immunity-privilege system to a one-tier qualified immunity system for executive officials, the Supreme Court has emphasized its concerns that government officials be constrained from inflicting harm on others and that the constraints not interfere with proper performance of official duties. The Court has concluded that these concerns are harmonized by allowing liability except when the official has acted from acceptable motives and not far outside the desired range of performance. Although it discussed the same concerns in cases involving legislators and judicial officers, the Court expressed the view that any liability-based constraint on their actions would entail costs (in less-than-optimal performance of their tasks) that exceed the beneficial effects of a liability constraint.

The concerns just noted are those addressed in tort litigation generally. Individual actions are presumed to respond to the actor's calculation of the costs and benefits of possible types of conduct. The calculation may be sophisticated or unsophisticated—indeed, it need not involve conscious choice with respect to each act. When there is reason to believe a class of actors will fail in their personal calculations to take sufficient account of the effect their actions have on others, damage liability presumptively can be used to induce a more socially acceptable calculus. Provided that the improvement in behavior is valued more highly than the costs of obtaining it, liability will be appropriate. Otherwise, mechanisms other than liability must be trusted to secure the desired behavior. The questions posed by these concerns are:

given some standard of desired behavior, what will damage remedies add to or detract from attainment of that behavior, and what costs will be incurred in order to accord the damage remedies? This part examines whether the solution reached by the Court meets the concerns articulated. Only the positive value of a damage remedy for official misconduct (what a damage remedy adds to attaining desired behavior) and the systemic cost of implementing such a remedy are examined. Thus, it is assumed in this part that no departure from desired behavior is induced by invocation of a damage remedy; that issue is addressed in part IV.

Analysis of the impact of damage remedies on future behavior and the systemic costs of applying them does not, of course, exhaust the list of possible inquiries respecting the propriety of affording damage relief against officials for their actions. One could inquire whether it is fair to place the cost of official action on the officer or to leave it on the plaintiff. Or one could ask whether concepts of optimal allocation of resources, as well as fairness, support transferring the costs of official action from others to the public officer. By and large, however, the Court has not spoken in terms of fairness or other reasons unrelated to behavioral considerations for preferring compensation of plaintiffs, nor is it likely that such concerns would explain the different treatment of executive and judicial officials. Nonetheless, so that these concerns may be separated clearly from the issues addressed here, it will be assumed throughout this part and part IV that some other compensatory mechanism is available to persons harmed by official misconduct if the official is held immune.

A. *Incentive Structures and Liability*

The starting point for inquiry into the value of official liability to secure appropriate official behavior is examination of the ways that personal incentives (other than avoiding liability) can be structured into official positions. To this end, it is useful to divide official activities into four highly schematic categories. These categories describe different arrangements of nonliability incentives governing official behavior. In assigning activities to the various categories, the spectrum of effects of each activity is bifurcated into costs and benefits. These terms generally carry normative connotations: costs are bad effects; benefits are good effects. When referring to an individual's view, that is how these terms will be used. But what constitutes a "benefit" to one person may be a "cost" to another. From a social standpoint, as these terms are used in defining the different categories, costs and benefits may be viewed as normatively interchangeable terms; they represent opposing considerations in structuring any activity. To enable an activity to produce more of one good, some other good must be foregone or some risk of harm incurred. Either side of the equation may be labelled "cost" or "benefit" at this point so long as the opposite side receives the other label. At the socially optimal level, an activity's marginal costs and benefits will be equal: at that level, more of the activity will decrease socially valued goods and less of the activity would mean that additional socially valued goods could be obtained by increasing the activity.

The four conceptually distinct categories are constructed on the basis of how personal costs and benefits of official decisions align with social costs and benefits. The categories are not descriptions of actual official actions but only abstract statements of the extremes possible in structuring individual officials' incentives. In this section, the effect of liability on the four hypothetical categories of activities will be considered. The next section evaluates the cost of imposing such liability standards. Although no official will fit these extreme cases, actual officials may be seen as more similar to one or another of these paradigms. Thus, section C uses these categories to classify actual official activities, suggesting the role liability might play in guiding each of these.

In category one, the official-actor personally bears all the costs and reaps all the benefits of his activity. The remaining three categories, unlike the first, involve activities the costs and benefits of which are shared by others in addition to the official. Moreover, in these categories, costs and benefits are not distributed evenly across the range of affected parties; instead, for each activity, one person or group of persons principally benefits from the activity while another person or group is disproportionately burdened with its costs. Although all three categories present this uneven allocation of costs and benefits, officials performing category two, three, and four functions differ in the way the terms of their employment induce them to take account of the interests of persons who are primarily beneficiaries of an activity and the interests of those who are primarily its costbearers. These differences in turn produce different likelihoods that activities in these categories will reflect the appropriate balance of costs and benefits. The activities comprising category two are those for which the official's job produced a personal cost-benefit calculus that leads the official systematically to favor some class of beneficiaries or costbearers in a manner inconsistent with the socially desirable result. In category three, the official's job is structured so that he has balanced incentives to consider the impact of his actions on both costbearers and beneficiaries. Category four is composed of activities for which the terms of an official's employment do not provide incentives to consider the activity's effect either on those who benefit or on those who bear its costs.

Category one, even more than the other hypothetical categories, is in reality an empty box. There are no activities within this category for which the official-actor personally bears the costs and reaps the benefits—in every case, there are external effects from official action. This category is included here, however, because it presents the limiting case for liability. If the actor and no one else is directly and immediately affected by his acts, he has all the incentives necessary to adjust the activity to produce the optimum level of costs and benefits. This does not mean that the official will never err in his attempts to strike the balance of costs and benefits. It does mean that a damage penalty for errors would not improve the official's incentives to perform his task properly. This category can be made more realistic by positing that the activities do result in external effects on some person or group of like persons, but that each cost bearer is simultaneously a beneficiary. So long as the costs and benefits are distributed in tandem, damage liability will not improve incentives for optimal behavior.

Category two is at the opposite extreme. Personal incentives are arrayed in a manner that is apt to produce consistent departures from optimal behavior because the official is encouraged by them to consider only one set of costs or benefits. Some monetary penalty for activity that imposes too many costs on society or that produces too few benefits could help balance the official's incentives. At the appropriate level, this penalty would, together with the official's other incentives, produce conduct that did not systematically depart from the ideal balance of social costs and benefits. Again, even with this penalty counterbalancing the nonliability incentive structure, some deviation from an objectively determined ideal will occur because the official has only limited powers of rationality—absent perfect officials, there always will be mistakes.

Categories three and four present intermediate cases. In category three, the official has balanced incentives to consider both costs and benefits. In contrast to category one, costbearers and beneficiaries are different classes of people. The official, consequently, will be more likely than one performing a category one activity to produce too few benefits or too many costs. The official may feel more favorably inclined to one class than to another, for instance, because of some personal affinity for that class (independent of incentives defining a category three position) or because that class has invested resources effectively in convincing the official that an outcome it favors does in fact harmonize costs and benefits. Even so, unlike category two, the likelihood of systematic errors in one direction is low—the incentives to consider both types of effects are relatively balanced and the resultant decisions should reflect that balance.

Category four presents a clearer case for liability than do categories one or three. Absent incentives to consider costs or benefits, the official might reach any result, near or far from the desirable outcome. Across a range of category four decisionmakers, one would not expect the sort of systematic bias in outcomes that category two would produce. Because the activity's incentive structure does not bias the official in one direction, any alignment of the official's personal costs and benefits with either costbearers or beneficiaries will be fortuitous and can shift from decision to decision. The problem in category four activities is not that the official is biased, but rather that the official may be uninterested. Absent incentives to consider either social costs or benefits, the official might always act in a way inconsistent with the social optimum (though the direction and magnitude of his departures will not be predictable). If category one presents the case in which all costs and benefits are internalized and liability therefore is unnecessary, category four presents the case in which no costs or benefits are internalized and liability, if available, will provide the only institutional incentive to socially optimal official behavior. Under these circumstances, liability may be useful, but if the classes of costbearers and beneficiaries are not equally willing or able to prosecute lawsuits, liability could skew the performance of category four activities in the same manner that nonliability incentives skew category two actions.

B. *The Cost of Adjudicating Liability*

The prior section evaluated the usefulness of a damage penalty for failure to perform properly official activities of four highly stylized types. No mention was made of the cost of formulating a standard to guide imposition of a damage penalty or of the cost of implementing that standard. The impact of these process costs on the four categories of official activity is considered in this section. Part IV takes up the impact of a second cost: increased performance errors resulting from liability.

Damage liability was found to be unnecessary to improve incentives of officials in category one. The existence of any cost for imposition of liability renders it unwise as well as unnecessary because resources would be consumed without social gain. Given the patent disutility of liability for category one activity, this category will not be discussed further.

Category two presented the extreme case for liability in a world where it could be imposed at no cost. Obviously, however, imposition of liability is not costless in the real world. Any gain in better performance as a result of liability will have to be measured against its cost. The major elements determining the costs of imposing liability are the clarity with which the standard of desirable performance can be defined and the ease with which departures from that standard can be identified.

Some elaboration of the sort of actions that comprise category two is necessary in order to evaluate these costs. Before doing that, one caveat is in order. In drawing separate categories of official activity so starkly, the different impact of personal liability can be seen, but only at the expense of some clear sense of actual activities that might correspond to the categorization. Rather than officials with incentives to respond wholly to one concern and not at all to the other (or to respond equally to both), the reality is likely to be officials who have significantly greater incentives to respond to one concern or relatively balanced incentives to consider opposing interests. The illustrations of category two, three, or four activities given in this section depart from the all-or-nothing definitions given in section A, and at the same time continue to abstract from a reality in which it is terribly difficult to determine what incentives guide a particular type of official in performing a specific task. In section C, an attempt will be made to integrate the conduct for which damage awards have been sought with the categories given here. For the moment, the examples are consistent with one party's view of the official's incentives but are not offered as factually correct.

With this caveat, a variety of official activities might be analogous to category two. Officials of the Food and Drug Administration (FDA) passing on applications for authority to market new drugs, for example, may be averse to adverse publicity from approval of dangerous drugs. By setting up careful, but time-consuming and costly screening procedures for testing new drugs, the FDA can reduce the chances that a drug later found to be dangerous will be approved for human use. Those who might have been prescribed a dangerous drug and who are susceptible to its dangers would be beneficiaries of such procedures. These procedures, however, will delay or prevent the marketing of beneficial drugs as well, and will increase the price of all new drugs. Producers, consumers, and a second class of potential consumers (who would have benefited from drugs not available to them) share the costs of procedural delays. Harm to these costbearers will be less obvious than harm to the beneficiaries would be. The officials thus have a strong incentive (fear of adverse publicity) for maximizing benefits of drug screening, while incentives to reduce the costs of such screening are weaker.

Police officers may have similarly imbalanced incentives. The benefits from arresting persons who may commit or may have committed crimes accrue to the members of the community who are potential victims of those crimes. Community members influential in structuring the local government may ensure that more immediate benefits accrue to the chief of police, and in turn to his subordinates, from higher arrest rates and higher "solved" rates. One of the costs from increased arrests will be an increase in the number of persons wrongfully arrested, because arrests will always be made on the basis of imperfect information, and an increase in arrests (other things being equal) will entail a reduction in the quantum of information required to make an arrest. Police officers, however, may be relatively unconcerned about this cost of increased arrests, especially if it is borne by individuals who, because of past criminality or other characteristics that are disfavored by police, are deemed undesirable.

Neither of these activities admits of a precise, easily administrable performance standard. It is difficult to specify the quantum of evidence that should be necessary to arrest, or the probabilities of benefit and of risk that should prompt licensing of a new drug. There are, however, limits that can be drawn around the range of permissible performance at relatively low cost. Some ground for suspicion beyond a previous arrest record for generally similar crimes, for instance, could be required of the police officer. That standard could be enforced without great difficulty, although it might well allow considerable scope for departure from the ideal. The police officer at least is engaged in conduct that does not differ greatly from the run of private conduct constrained by tort rules, although the occasion for engaging in that conduct does. There is a larger difference between private activities and the activities of an FDA official, and any standard constraining him risks departing from congressional intent in creating the FDA unless Congress clearly specifies the considerations that should underlie a decision to grant or withhold a license to market new drugs.

Even here, of course, some general limits can be articulated. Although it is difficult to determine whether drugs are efficacious and whether they are dangerous, the religious preferences of the drug's marketer will rarely bear on either of these questions. More generally, there is no reason to believe someone who is disliked by the FDA official for reasons unrelated to the qualities of the drug he proposes to offer for sale should be supposed less likely than anyone else to be promoting a valuable new drug. Limiting official action by penalizing these sorts of discriminations operates to check a different kind of official error than is discussed above. The first sort of error may be labelled a "performance error." The type described in this paragraph may be called an "intent error." The official commits a clear intent error when he knowingly acts to disadvantage someone on bases unrelated to his assigned task.

While standards respecting intent errors are more easily stated than standards respecting performance errors, they are not necessarily easier to administer. In many cases, the difficulty of judging performance makes ascertaining intent errors difficult as well. Suppose FDA Commissioner Jones denies a new drug license to Booker Pharmaceuticals. Booker sues claiming that its application was denied because the firm is wholly owned by blacks and Commissioner Jones discriminates against blacks. Commissioner Jones denies the allegation; he recounts the various percentage probabilities of different maladies resulting from the Booker drug and also recounts the grounds for concluding that the drug is not efficacious. The reasons for denying the license, on performance grounds, are based on extrapolations from experiments having no direct correlation with the drug's behavior in humans in recommended doses. There are no drugs for which the data yielded by experiments are identical to those for the Booker drug. Absent direct information concerning Commissioner Jones's intent or a series of relatively similar sets of circumstances from which one could draw an intuitive "regression analysis" to determine if the applicant's race seemed to be the decisive factor, it is difficult to assess the claim of intent error.

The difficulties of assessing both performance and intent errors are even greater in categories three and four than in category two. Category three activity, for which an official has nonliability incentives to respond both to interests in increasing benefits and to interests in reducing costs, is illustrated by the following situation. A legislator must vote on a bill to impose a substantial tax on the sale of fossil fuels. His constituents for the most part are either engaged in some aspect of the oil industry or in mining and purifying uranium for nuclear power plants. The costs of the tax will be borne in large measure by those with interests in oil, while the benefits will go substantially to those in the nuclear fuel industry. Both groups are likely to be influenced in their choices among competing candidates in the upcoming election by the current representative's vote on this issue. Each group will provide the legislator with information on the proposed tax's impact on society; each group will argue that the result it favors will benefit society generally. The amount each group spends on this effort, on supporting or opposing the representative in the next electoral campaign, or on similar activities, is in large measure influenced by the size of the group's gain or loss from enactment of the legislation. In responding to the interests of these groups, the legislator arguably harmonizes social costs and benefits. Indeed the legitimacy of these pressures is unquestioned; the legislator is expected to respond to them, making the formulation of a standard delineating impermissible pressures extremely difficult.

Many other official actions also could be analogized to category three. Commissioners of regulatory agencies chiefly concerned with regulation of competing industries might engage in activity allocable to category three when deciding what rules should govern that competition; zoning board members planning future growth patterns similarly might fit this pattern, as might a supervisor evaluating employees for promotion. None of these activities, of course, will necessarily be governed by incentives to balance appropriately both costs and benefits, but each could be.

The costs of evaluating category three decisions are likely to be quite high. What, for instance, is the standard by which to judge the propriety of imposing a tax on fossil fuel sales? Many activities that resemble category three are ones for which articulation of performance standards, other than in conclusory terms, is very difficult. The legislator, for example, is asked to determine which course of action among many best harmonizes costs and benefits. For those parties whose interest in the decision is strong enough, there will be ample incentive to provide information (or misinformation) supporting the position they favor; yet, it may be extremely difficult to evaluate this information in the context of a legislative information-gathering process. Furthermore, the legislator is answerable in some degree to many persons who are neither burdened nor benefited sufficiently by any course of action to warrant the costs of making their views known, but who nonetheless may be affected by the decision. Assessing the interests of these persons may be even more costly than analyzing the accuracy of information brought to the legislator's attention: costlier still would be a determination of whether the legislator had fairly assessed those interests.

Legislators are enjoined to follow perhaps the least specific of any performance standard: they are directed to harmonize social costs and benefits without any articulation of the values by which costs and benefits are to be judged. The network of constraints to which they are subject—including their party affiliation, their desire to secure votes and campaign contributions for purposes of reelection, and their ambition for higher office or for secure and remunerative future employment—may operate quite imperfectly to give legislators real incentives to strike the cost-benefit balance properly. Highly valued concerns of minority interests or concerns very widely shared that in the aggregate are of enormous social value may not receive adequate consideration by any given legislator or by all legislators. Nonetheless, constructing a standard by which to judge their performance requires some clear notion of the manner in which the social balance should be struck. In large measure, our system of governance makes the result of legislators' performance the determinant of how social concerns are balanced. To the extent the Constitution limits legislative freedom, it does so through imprecise statements that require, as well as embody, additional balancing. It seldom provides clear performance standards. Almost any constitutional decision picked at random from opinions of the Supreme Court is illustrative: if, for instance, fiscal concerns merit restriction of federal retirement benefits, are due process concerns sufficient to tilt the social balance against such restrictions?

The difficulty of assessing performance of legislative tasks and of other, similar activities that might resemble category three supports limitations on the scope of inquiry into such decisions. This is consistent with the grant of considerable discretion to officials performing category three functions. Even outside the legislative sphere, such officials often are freed from requirements that they rely upon information presented by the participating parties or that they rigorously justify a choice to shape their action in one fashion rather than another. More than the most general review of these actions would require some other official to replicate the exercise of judgment either at greater cost (in obtaining and verifying information) or on similarly ambiguous and perhaps untrustworthy information. Only greater respect for the second official's judgment would seem to justify significant review of category three actions. Were the latter official's judgment more valued, might it not be better for him simply to replace the first?

Review of category four decisions presents difficulties similar to those encountered in category three. Activity analogous to category four might be the work of a federal judge disposing of a petition, ruling on motions, or rendering judgment in a suit. For any decision, one of the litigants will bear the costs, the other will benefit; the litigants will often represent (formally or informally) those classes who will similarly bear the costs or reap the benefits. As with lobbying and related functions, the expenditures of each group on litigation will be determined in part by the value of a particular outcome to that group. Even if the investment in litigation resources were proportional to anticipated gains or losses, however, judges lack any significant incentive, intrinsic to the judicial process, for responding to the parties' (and ultimately the society's) interests in minimizing costs on the one hand and maximizing benefits on the other. The salaries of the judges are not adjusted upward or downward according to the extent to which they minimize costs, maximize benefits, or harmonize the two. Nor, at least with federal judges, is their job tenure imperilled or enhanced by their decision. Finally, judges need not be concerned about the reactions of the parties before them. It certainly is the common expectation that judges will not receive incentives to decide one way or the other directly from parties to the case.

The absence of direct incentives to adjust costs and benefits does not mean, of course, that socially disfavored action will result. To the contrary, it has been argued that decisions of Anglo-American judges tend to strike the balance of social costs and benefits fairly well and that decisions to the contrary do not long survive. Enhancing a judge's reputation among scholars or lawyers, reducing the likelihood of reversal (for judges of lower or intermediate courts), and limiting criticism by legislators and citizens have been given as reasons judges might reach appropriate solutions despite the absence of direct incentives. Ideally, these indirect (noninstitutional) incentives give judges the same impetus to balance social costs and benefits that a hypothetical category three actor would have. To perform this function, these incentives must focus less on the problem of individual erroneous decisions-ones that depart from the social ideal—than on the seriousness with which the judge takes his task. The greatest penalties, thus, are reserved for the judge who refuses to work or who is positively arbitrary in his decisions rather than for the judge whose elaborately reasoned opinion, replete with citations, reaches an outcome widely perceived to be incorrect.

Whether officials performing category four activities arrive at socially valued solutions frequently or seldom, the cost of assessing liability for their decisions is likely to be greater than in most other situations. The isolation of these officials from the pressure of interested groups reflects a belief that those groups alone cannot adequately represent societal interest. Not infrequently, difficult decisions must be rendered on the basis of complex, ambiguous, or conflicting information. In determining whether an error was made and assessing liability for it, the same difficult decisions must be repeated. If they are to be of greater accuracy than the initial decision, these decisions must be accompanied either by better information than was initially available or by better mechanisms for weighing and sifting information used initially. Imagine, for instance, a judgment in a complicated securities or antitrust case being reviewed for error to determine whether the trial judge should be liable in damages. The issues litigated initially would have to be reexamined in a trial setting with its attendant complex of procedures for eliciting and evaluating information. Repeated trials of the same issue would become phenomenally costly. That is one reason why superior courts (at least ostensibly) review a narrower range of issues than do the inferior courts. The availability of nonliability review mechanisms, of course, reflects concern over the initial decisionmaker's likelihood of ascertaining the best outcome. At the same time, availability of these mechanisms reduces the likely damage from erroneous initial decisions and offers a lower-cost alternative to liability for correcting them.

C. *The Court's Assessment of the Cost of Formulating Liability Standards*

If the analysis of individual officer liability stops at this point, still constrained by the assumption that compensation is available from other sources and only taking cognizance of the general deterrent utility of such liability and one of its costs (the systematic cost of formulating and applying liability rules), the result reached is broadly consistent with the pattern of Supreme Court decisions. The one-cost model developed thus far suggests that no liability should be imposed for category three or four activities because the gains from such alteration of incentives as liability may produce will be slight and the costs of replicating these decisions generally will be great. Development of performance standards that provide significant guidance to operating officials or to their reviewers will be extremely difficult in these categories, and the construction and implementation of performance standards for them will be costly. Checking intent errors, while less costly, also will be difficult for category three and four conduct, a difficulty derived from the problem of specifying performance standards. For category two activities, the gains from using personal liability are greater and the costs of reviewing these decisions frequently are less. Nonetheless, creation and application of precise performance standards for these activities will be costly. Allowing some range of tolerable performance within which no penalty attaches would seem to be a suitable compromise, securing a beneficial counterweight to imbalanced incentives without necessitating undue cost.

The costs of formulating even these flexible performance standards still may be high. It may, and undoubtedly would, be extraordinarily difficult to calibrate the standard and the magnitude of the damage penalty so as to create a counterweight of correct proportion to balance each official's incentives. Yet, the one-cost model would support making that effort for category two activities.

The separation of activities among the various categories also may prove difficult. How, for example, would an agency director's issuance of a press release about two employees, the conduct at issue in *Barr v. Matteo*, be characterized? To ascertain the appropriate category to which a given official action should be analogized requires consideration of the specific incentives provided an official in performing the activity at issue. In each case, it must be asked how the official's performance of that activity is likely to be affected by such incentives as income, chance of promotion, job assignments, the difficulty, duration, or pleasantness of his work, or other avenues for gratification. Although a few official actions may admit of easy categorization, it will require considerable information to answer this question with respect to most officials, information that is likely to be quite costly to acquire and evaluate.

There have been various attempts in the legal literature to divide official actions along lines that permit easier identification. Each of these alternative classification schemes may be viewed as an attempt to identify the incentives controlling broad areas of official conduct. Unfortunately, the vast numbers of different persons and actions covered by each classification prevents the classes of conduct identified by such schemes from correlating well with the nonliability incentives actually faced by officials.

Even so, it seems plausible to analogize at least "core" legislative activities to category three and "core" judicial activities to category four. The court's refusal to allow official liability for these activities, whether for performance errors or for intent errors, and even under a statute that on its face creates no exemptions from liability, then, would strike the balance properly. Similarly, it is plausible to analogize a wide range of executive functions to category two. *Pierson v. Ray* provides a good example. Police officers in Mississippi at the time that case arose were sensitive to the concerns of white businessmen but not to the interests of blacks in being served by those businesses without risking arrest. Executive functions that are fairly easily analogized to category two, notably those performed by police and prison officials, are usefully checked by liability for either significant performance errors or for intent errors. The good faith and reasonable grounds defense of *Pierson* and *Scheuer v. Rhodes*, which now is applicable to all executive officers save those clearly connected with "judicial" tasks, seems designed to give liability for these officials the contours suggested thus far for category two.

While the Court and one-cost model are thus generally in accord, the Court's uniform treatment of all executive officers sweeps into the qualified immunity fold officials whose activities seem to be more closely analogous to category three or four than to category two. The conduct in *Pierson* may be thought to fit category two fairly well, but what of the acts at issue in *Scheuer*? Among the allegations of the *Scheuer* complaint were that the Governor of Ohio called out the National Guard unnecessarily and that he and the Adjutant General of the Ohio National Guard did not ensure that Guard members were adequately prepared to handle an emergency without use of lethal force. It is difficult to argue convincingly that the chief executive of a state has inadequate incentives to weigh the benefit in protection of persons and property against the possible cost in injury or loss of life when he decides whether to call out the National Guard. The governor of a state is a person of great public visibility; most of his official activities are scrutinized by the press and by interested individuals. He likely will be asked to account both for injuries resulting from failure to call out the National Guard to control a volatile situation and for injuries resulting from actions of the Guard. Even if he is not eligible for or interested in reelection, the Governor is likely to be concerned (whether for the sake of his reputation or for the sake of his party's candidates in the coming election) with avoiding errors resulting from too little or too much use of force.

Similarly, it is by no means apparent that the Secretary of Agriculture, for whom *Butz v. Economou* found the qualified immunity defense sufficient, makes decisions under pressures more skewed than those operating on his subordinates who were granted broad immunity by the same decision. The head of a Cabinet department, directly responsible to the president, frequently examined by the Congress, and visible to the press, can be expected to fall closer to category three than to category two to the extent he is involved in setting general policies for handling revocations such as that at issue in *Butz*, and closer to category four insofar as he is involved in disposing of any particular case. It cannot be denied that intent errors, as well as performance errors, might occur at the very highest levels of government. As with category three and four activities generally, however, the need for damage liability to provide incentives to avoid such errors is slight and the cost of detecting such errors through damage suits is substantial. At least so long as it is assumed that compensation is otherwise available, it would appear that high-ranking government officers are more appropriately accorded the same immunity as legislators and judges enjoy.

In defense of the Court's integration of high-ranking officers with other executive officials, it might be argued that the Court effectively has retained the benefit of absolute immunity for such officials without the need for locating the bright line between immune executive officers and those enjoying the hybrid qualified immunity. The performance standard itself, as well as the rigor with which an official is held to it, determines the nature of the liability constraint. Insofar as courts have judged high-ranking executive officials by more lenient performance standards than might be devised for lower-ranking officers, the application of a uniform qualified immunity defense may allow treatment for the former group of officials more nearly approximating the absolute immunity accorded judges and legislators. In this regard, the paucity of damage judgments against high-ranking officials is noteworthy, suggesting that courts in fact treat their conduct in the manner suggested here for category three. Moreover, the willingness of courts in many instances to use fairly charitable performance standards in assessing the liability of even relatively low-level officials suggests a recognition that many executive officers are constrained by incentives intermediate between those described in categories two and three. Thus, the performance standards employed by the courts may reduce the impact of the disparity between the analysis presented here and the Court's decisions respecting immunity for executive officials.

IV. Overdeterrence: Effects of Liability

Although the Court's treatment of official liability fits reasonably well with a model limited to consideration of a single cost of liability (the difficulty of evaluating official decisions), there is another significant cost to official liability: the potential for overdeterring official action. The possibility that liability for one sort of official error could induce errors in the opposite direction has received considerable attention from the courts. That was the principal concern expressed by Justice Harlan in *Spalding v. Vilas* and by Judge Hand in *Gregoire v. Biddle*. It also has been offered as the main justification for absolute immunity of legislators and judges. This part examines the possible overdeterrence effects of liability and responses that might limit those effects.

A. *Assessing Overdeterrence*

The concern with overdeterrence is far from trivial. Take an activity that arguably falls within category two—arrest of suspects who have prior convictions. The police officer presumably has relatively strong incentives to arrest and relatively weak incentives to delay until he can develop additional or more accurate information linking the suspect to the crime at issue. Liability for wrongful arrest will provide a counterweight to his imbalance in incentives. This counterweight, which could be termed the "liability incentive" or the "expected damage penalty," ideally should be just enough to discourage arrest whenever the social costs of an arrest exceed the social benefit. Any greater expected damage penalty will discourage arrests in situations where the social benefits of such action exceed its cost.

A term such as expected damage penalty usually connotes the current value to an actor of a future damage judgment against him discounted by the judgment's improbability. Viewed thus, three elements are widely recognized as critical to determining the expected damage penalty: the standard for assessing liability; the defenses to liability; and the magnitude of the penalty imposed in the event of liability. It has been urged in other contexts that, despite the difficulty of the task, courts have performed well in combining these elements to produce an expected damage penalty of the appropriate magnitude to offset imbalanced nonliability incentives.

Rightly understood, however, there is a fourth element—likelihood of suit—that is also critical to calibration of the liability incentive. Generally, this element is ignored, on the assumption that if the purpose of suit for the plaintiff is to secure money damages, suits as a rule will be brought whenever the probable award exceeds the probable costs of litigating. Under this assumption, the other three elements dictate the likelihood of suit. Following this analysis, there is no need to take account of the additional penalty (beyond the expected damage award) exacted of successful defendants in the form of litigation costs. Because losing plaintiffs as well as successful defendants bear their litigation costs, each successful defendant who pays this penalty should be offset by an official who could have been successfully sued but was not, and thus was spared litigation costs.

Even if the assumptions concerning motivation for suit and irrelevance of litigation costs are generally merited, there is no reason to expect them to retain validity for the full run of litigation against officials. If litigation imposes some costs on defendants whether they win or lose, might not the desire to impose those costs on a defendant, rather than to secure financial rewards, motivate some suits? This possibility exists for all types of lawsuits, but two features of government action may make the initiation of such "spite" suits against officials peculiarly likely. First, many government officials are vulnerable to personal suit because they exercise power over others directly and visibly: the teacher who suspends a student, the policeman who arrests a suspect, and the judge who passes sentence all are clearly identifiable as individuals whose actions operate immediately against a likely complainant. In this respect, these officials differ from a wide array of employees in other large organizations whose activities, for instance in the design or manufacture of a given product, might adversely affect potential plaintiffs. Second, as the examples of official action just given illustrate, governmental action frequently is coercive in nature, intruding on individuals who may have resisted contact with those officials. It is plausible to expect anger directed against such officials to motivate suit, regardless of likely recovery, more often than would occur where the user of a commercial product, having sought contact with the producer, is disappointed with or injured by it.

If nonmeritorious suits are brought against government officials with some frequency, the expected damage penalty calculated by the courts on the basis of the liability standard, defenses, and assessed damages may be considerably smaller than the liability incentive that in fact will help shape the particular official's conduct. A liability standard, moderated by a defense of qualified immunity and by rules limiting damage calculations, and designed to reduce police incentives to overarrest, might result in a pattern of underarrest. If the nonliability incentives to overarrest were weak, and if the officer is likely to be subject to suit for any arrest, no matter how clearly within the standard of desirable performance, he may opt not to arrest in many cases for which the arrest is socially valued.

In large measure, the magnitude of the overdeterrence problem depends on the clarity of the performance standard and the scope of the official's recognized defense. At one extreme, absolute immunity reduces the cost of overdeterrence to a minimum. The official identifies himself as such, and suit against him is dismissed. The cost to the defendant, and consequently the harassment value to the plaintiff, is negligible. This is precisely the reason the Court bars suits against judges and legislators. The Court's treatment of executive officers, however, appears to leave considerable scope for harassment suits. The official must plead, and in many jurisdictions prove, both his good faith and general fidelity to the performance standard. If the burden of persuasion is on plaintiff, the vagueness of many performance standards may make it relatively difficult to demonstrate intent errors as well as performance errors. If the defendant must carry this burden, there is considerable possibility that an official could be found liable for either intent or performance errors. In any event, the imprecision of the standard allows room for costly litigation over the official's intent and over the legality of his acts.

It is easy to understand the Court's reluctance to make it difficult to impose sanctions on officials who intentionally or blatantly abuse their authority, but some of the Court's language exacerbates what under the best of circumstances may be a difficult problem. The prospects of overdeterrence would be raised appreciably if lower courts took seriously the Supreme Court's statement that officials "should have known" their actions were unlawful (and therefore will be liable) if those actions violate a constitutional proscription interpreted previously by the courts or clearly spelled out in the Constitution: "an act violating a [person's] constitutional rights can be no more justified by ignorance or disregard of settled, indisputable law . . . than by the presence of actual malice." The meaning of constitutional provisions, however, is a source of endless controversy; it is difficult to find any provision the meaning of which, as applied to a host of different factual settings, is made clear by constitutional text, history, or judicial gloss. Even where a meaning can be made out in judicial pronouncements, it is difficult to believe that officials are conversant with the myriad opinions, not infrequently conflicting, interpreting constitutional restraints. The Court's statement, hence, must either provide for liability only in situations that almost never arise or open officials to potential liability in an incredible array of circumstances in which the likelihood of being held answerable in damages is exceedingly difficult to calculate in advance. The latter possibility, if credited, might be sufficient to restrain a great deal of socially valued conduct.

One argument advanced against giving credence to concerns about overdeterrence as a result of vexatious litigation is that plaintiffs bear the same litigation costs as defendants. Even allowing that some plaintiffs may be willing to pay to satisfy a taste for harassment, the more expensive suits become for defendants (thus increasing overdeterrence problems), the more expensive suits also become for plaintiffs. Other things being equal, the quantity of harassing suits should decline as their price to plaintiffs rises. While the reasoning is sound, the premise is not. First, a successful outcome may not have equal value to both sides, and that will affect the parties' expenditures. The loss of a suit may cost the defendant not just the sum paid over to the plaintiff, but also opportunities for career advancement on which he places considerably more value. Second, the investment of time by parties to these suits may be considerable, and the alternative uses of plaintiffs' and defendants' time may have strikingly different value. Third, some classes of plaintiffs may have access to inexpensive legal services not available to defendants. These disparities often hold where the plaintiff is a prisoner or an arrestee, two groups with especially great incentives to vexatious litigation.

In combination, these distinctions between the litigation cost incurred by plaintiffs and those imposed on defendants justify considerable concern about overdeterrence even for conduct most analogous to category two. Although it is difficult to make much of these figures, the filings against police officers and prison officials are consistent with the notion that the qualified immunity defense does not discourage harassing litigation. Legal actions filed by prisoners alleging violations of constitutional guarantees, for example, have increased from less than 2,200 filings in federal district courts in 1970 to 6,606 in 1975 and 13,000 in 1980, a 491% increase in little more than a decade. The percentage of these suits that are dismissed is quite high; nonetheless, the number that proceed to trial is significant, while the instances of liability judgments against defendants are negligible. It is possible that many meritorious claims are being dismissed for inartful pleading and that other meritorious claims are being denied after trial for failure to clear a too-high burden of persuasion. It is at least equally plausible, however, that because of frustration, lack of other means for relief of related grievances, pique, or simply antipathy for the defendant, many nonmeritorious claims are being brought, consuming considerable judicial resources, entailing sizeable defense costs, yielding few damage awards, but perhaps discouraging some desirable official conduct.

B. *Preventing Overdeterrence: Individual and Institutional Responses Short of Immunity*

Given the opportunity for harassment implicit in the liability-immunity standards adopted by the Court for executive officers, it is possible that present rules respecting official liability may deter desirable, along with undesirable, official conduct sufficiently to yield net social costs. This potential for overdeterrence, however, need not automatically be realized. There are numerous antidotes to overdeterrence that may be taken by individual officials or by the enterprises for which they work. Insurance is the most obvious of these. If officials are concerned over the threat of liability, they may be willing to pay a sum certain (and some entrepreneur, an insurer, presumably would be willing to collect that sum from all risk averse officials) to avoid the risk of liability. By spreading the risk of a large financial loss over a class of similarly insured officials, insurance would reduce each official's incentives to avoid activities that might generate liability suits. To the extent that litigation costs, rather than simply liability, are a concern, insurance could pool the risk of incurring costs in defending damage suits as well as in satisfying damage judgments.

Insurance, while useful, is not a perfect antidote to rules that produce a too-high liability incentive. First, to the extent insurance is effective, it may so fully reduce the incentive to avoid liability-producing (as well as lawsuit-producing) activity that one simply replaces the imbalance of an overdeterrent liability incentive with the original underdeterrent incentive structure that prompted formulation of the liability standard. This return from overdeterrence to underdeterrence (the functional equivalent of immunity) would be accomplished at the cost of both making liability determinations and operating the insurance system. And although insurance theoretically can be structured to achieve a middle ground, retaining some of the liability incentive's effects while eliminating the risk of large losses (as "deductibles" and other limiting provisions are designed to do), there are significant practical barriers to the translation of liability incentives into insurance policies. Insofar as insurers use more easily administrable classifications as surrogates for identifying activity that should be penalized, and structure insurance policies to visit some portion of that penalty on the individual insured, the function actually performed by insurance may diverge greatly from the goals liability was intended to achieve. The magnitude of this divergence of the legal rule and the practical result will depend on the ease with which liability can be determined—the more difficult the determination, the greater the likely difference.

Second, while some officials will purchase insurance, other officials might prefer to alter their behavior so as to minimize the risk of suit rather than incur the cost of insurance. To the extent the Court's rules generate a too-great liability incentive, some of this avoidance behavior will be socially undesirable although personally beneficial. The official who is overdeterred by the liability incentive—an extreme example would be a police officer who refused to make any arrest on less than near-certain proof of the arrestee's guilt—may still be overdeterred when insurance is available. Paying the insurance premiums and acting in a socially desirable manner, even though such behavior generates some risk that the official will be sued, may be more costly to the official than engaging in liability avoidance behavior that has negative social value but that minimizes the risk of suit. The simple availability of insurance to individual officials, thus, does not eliminate the need for some other mechanism to counter overdeterrence. To avoid the problems of divergence between personal benefit and social value in the face of a too-great liability incentive, some institutional control is required.

The employing enterprises, of course, are not without means to remedy departures from optimal behavior generated by fear of liability. The enterprise can insure its employees against the costs of liability and/or providing a defense, eliminating the inducement for employees to alter their behavior in order to avoid the cost of insuring. It can, without the intermediary, produce the same result by satisfying the damage judgments against employees and by subsidizing or providing any necessary defense. Finally, it can undertake to monitor employee behavior more closely so that liability incentives do not induce undesirable behavior.

Each of these mechanisms presents some problem. Paying for the defense of the defendant-employee's choosing, for instance, could be extremely costly; sued employees would have incentives to over-invest in their defense. Conversely, actually providing the defense for employees might not fully counteract overdeterrence if employees would invest greater resources in their own defense than are provided or if they remain fearful of losing. A general problem is that each of the mechanisms that combats overdeterrence also reduces beneficial deterrence. To prevent this, additional resources must be expended to structure somewhat more complex mechanisms: for example, insuring employees except against certain types of liability or except when employees are determined to have been at fault to some specified degree, or insuring for less than the full amount of liability.

In a private, profit-making enterprise, there is a metric—profits—that makes this kind of fine tuning of incentives a plausible solution. An enterprise that pursues the goal of profit maximization will endeavor to prevent liability rules from affecting employees' conduct in ways that reduce profits. If an employee is made personally liable—for example, a designer of airplanes held liable for injuries and deaths that are caused by insufficiently safe design—and the employee then is overdeterred from the errors liability was intended to prevent, the enterprise's profits will be adversely affected. Overdeterrence here can be identified without great difficulty. Planes that are slower, more costly, less fuel efficient, or require additional maintenance—all potential responses to increasing safety—will be less desirable to buyers, other things being equal. If damage awards measure the injury costs of an activity and the price paid by buyers measures its benefits, socially optimum expenditures on safety will be to the point where an additional dollar spent in that endeavor (in reduced value of the plane or in increased costliness of its design and construction) will produce exactly one dollar reduction in the expected damage penalty. Such behavior would be synonymous with profit maximization where the enterprise is liable. Making the employee liable does not change the calculus. The airplane manufacturer should respond by insuring the employee, assuming liability, monitoring his behavior, and so on, to the point where the cost of such additional expenditures exactly equals the gain of producing more highly valued planes. This is, in fact, the way such enterprises have reacted to instances of potential employee liability.

The response of profit-making private enterprises to potentially overdeterring liability rules for employees reaches the socially desirable outcome despite the fact that corporations, like governmental entities, are composed of a variety of individuals with disparate personal interests. The differences among the interests of corporate employees, directors, and stockholders have been thought sufficient to require some legal protection for the last of these groups, although their community of interest has been deemed sufficient to severely limit the scope of legal remedies. Recent discussion of these enterprises has identified a variety of devices that operate to reduce the disparity of individual interests within the corporation and to induce the individuals comprising the corporation to act in a fashion that promotes their joint interest. The widespread practice of giving key managerial personnel ownership interests in the corporation, for example, is one mechanism by which managers' and stockholders' interests are made more congruent. Given these harmonizing devices, liability rules for corporations or corporate employees are likely to reach socially valued results if the entity or any of its component members is in a position to respond to the liability rule efficiently. The courts need not ascertain which among the various possible defendants can efficiently respond to the liability rule; so long as one of them can, they are likely to reach the appropriate outcome through a process of implicit or explicit bargaining once liability is imposed on any of the defendants.

C. *Institutional Responses to Overdeterrence: The Special Case of Governmental Enterprises*

Governmental enterprises, however, are less likely than private, profit-making entities to respond appropriately when one of their employees is subject to an overdeterrent liability constraint. Three different but related reasons impair the governmental response.

First, governmental enterprises lack the kind of clear goal that profit-making firms enjoy. Liability may be a desirable means of forcing private firms to consider costs they might otherwise ignore, but with or without liability the joint goal of the firm members is to maximize profits. The efficient response to liability for the firm (irrespective of the efficiency of the liability rules) is the response consistent with profit maximization. There is, however, no similar, easily stated goal for government. The "members" of any governmental enterprise (the citizenry of the relevant jurisdiction and the officials employed by it) may want very different goals pursued. Attempts to define an ideal for government inevitably meet a host of objections.

Second, even if we could identify a goal for government, there would be considerable difficulty determining whether the goal was accomplished. The existence of markets for the purchase and sale of private firms' products and of the ownership interests in those firms provides a useful yardstick for the firms's success. If I own stock of an airplane manufacturer, the change in stock prices and return in dividends give me relatively easy measures of management's performance; the prices buyers will pay for their planes and for their competitors' planes together with the costs of design and production give management a useful indication of the strengths and weaknesses of the firm's product. Governmental enterprises, in contrast, seldom produce products that are evaluated by a marketplace where they compete with other, similar products.

Third, the control mechanisms available to members of a governmental enterprise to regulate the conduct of other members are less useful than the control mechanisms available in a private firm. In part this reflects the greater difficulty of identifying a goal and evaluating performance in the government context. It also results from differences in how one becomes a member of the enterprise. If I own stock in a corporation, I may lack direct control over the corporation's management in any meaningful sense, but I can sell my stock if the investment is not satisfactory. If my perception of management's inadequacy is shared by others, stock prices will decline and other managers will be alerted to the likelihood that additional profits (for both stockholders and managers) could be had from improved management. Ultimately, stock sales provide the vehicle for a credible threat that poorly performing managers will be replaced. The private firm's managers, in turn, have a set of useful control devices at their disposal to ensure adequate performance by other employees. Managers generally have considerable freedom to replace personnel or alter work methods if the firm's products do poorly in the market or if the market success comes at too steep a price.

Neither "owners" nor "managers" have control mechanisms of quite the same force in governmental firms. Citizens dissatisfied with government performance can move away from the jurisdiction or they can vote to remove elected officials from office. Moving, especially if one is reacting to federal policies, is a poor parallel to selling one's stock. Voting, too, is a very imperfect means for registering a citizen's preferences. Because the citizen may have no single, overarching interest in an official's conduct (something akin to profit maximization), but instead has a number of discrete interests related to different issues, voting for or against an official who has addressed many issues over the past two, four, or six years of his term requires the citizen to balance the decisions he feels were detrimental against those he feels were beneficial. The official, however, does not learn from the vote which decisions were approved and which were disapproved by the voter. On matters of intense interest, then, a citizen may wish to express his views to elected officials more directly. Lobbying and the various expressions of interest associated with it—for example, promises of campaign contributions or voter support in exchange for a favorable position on the particular issue—may therefore play a more important role than voting in shaping official incentives respecting particular issues. But the cost of aggregating small interests to underwrite lobbying efforts may prevent the expression of some views in this manner and give officials a distorted picture of voters' preferences. When this happens, there can be "takeover" bids by another candidate or party that believes it has identified a defect in the incumbent's positions sufficiently grave that the coalition of interests he has responded to will be inadequate to secure his reelection. This only completes the circle since the takeover must be at election time and, if successful, the new "managers" must be informed by the same sort of very imperfect information that initially informed the incumbent.

The elected officials who serve as managers for the enterprise also have more cumbersome tools than their private-sector counterparts for controlling other employees. At first blush, the difference may seem slight. Most public employees are subject to a wide range of inducements to good behavior and sanctions for bad behavior, including job termination or transfer, promotion or demotion, and changes in pay and perquisites. The government's managers, however, have not been given a free hand to use these measures to reward good, and punish bad, behavior. Rather, a complex set of restrictions, most notably the civil service laws, limits the usefulness of these measures as vehicles for shaping official action either to the public's benefit or to its detriment.

These restrictions on hiring, firing, promotion, demotion, and other personnel actions were not adopted because these means of controlling employee behavior are needed less in the public than in the private sector to give employees appropriate incentives to desirable behavior. The restrictions were adopted because the managers controlling such decisions were not trusted to use them to advance socially valued, as opposed to personally desired, behavior. That mistrust follows from the difficulties of defining and recognizing socially desirable governmental action and, hence, of structuring managers' incentives to attain it. It would seem quite odd if the charter of a profit-making enterprise limited the chief executive officer's control over personnel decisions, divided authority among three officers for decisions respecting the purchase of materials and the manufacture and distribution of products, and insulated each of the officers from interference by the others in his area of decisionmaking authority. Corporations are not structured in this manner because investors know what goal they want pursued, agree on the goal, can observe whether it is attained, and can extricate themselves from involvement at reasonably low cost if it is not. Although there is, doubtless, some room for self-interested conduct by the private firm's managers, they can be trusted to make most decisions free from direct constraint—the necessity to produce profits serves as an effective check on most managerial conduct. In contrast, our whole structure of government is oriented to limiting and dividing official authority. The constitutionally mandated separation of powers among different governmental branches, as well as the host of subsidiary restraints on various officials, reflects the disbelief in our ability to give any official appropriate incentives to act in a manner that promotes the joint interests of all the enterprises' "members."

While the universal imperfection of official incentives provides the obvious impetus for liability, it also provides reason for caution in liability decisions. Because official incentives are imperfect, there always will be official errors that damage penalties might seem useful to remedy. At the same time, there is a likelihood that the socially ideal level of liability will not be found and that departures from the ideal will not be fully corrected by other mechanisms. Because judges, too, have imperfect incentives, they may err in striving to correct other officials' mistakes. Where judges believe that other officials have underestimated the cost of their actions in terms of harm to constitutionally derived values (such as freedom of speech or guarantees against unreasonable searches or seizures), officials from other branches may believe, equally rightly, that the judges have undervalued the benefit of the official conduct under review (in terms, perhaps, of public safety and health or of relief from financial burdens). Indeed, section A of this part demonstrated that the Court's qualified immunity decisions might have underestimated the impact of liability on officials.

Moreover, the difficulty of defining a goal for government, of recognizing success or failure in its accomplishment, and of structuring incentives to that end inhibits the correction of socially incorrect liability rules. Professor Coase demonstrated that in a world of zero transaction costs an incorrect liability rule would not affect attainment of the socially efficient allocation of resources. The doctor and baker in Coase's hypothetical agree to reach the highest-valued use of their adjacent properties whether the baker is or is not liable for the interference with the doctor's business by his noisy machines. The doctor represents fully society's interest in his use of the one property, the baker represents fully society's interest in his use of the other property, and there is no impediment to them striking a bargain that, in turn, fully represents society's interest in the use of both properties. The problems posed by liability rules for government officials differ strikingly from this hypothetical. At the outset, government officials do not fully represent society's interests in their particular activity. Consider the municipal police officer whose sole duty is to identify and arrest felony suspects. Does the police officer represent society's interest in arresting suspects and thus deterring crime? Does he represent society's interest in not stigmatizing or interfering with the liberty of persons who in fact have not committed crimes? Or does the chief of police represent society's interest in the first, and the city council society's interest in the second?

It seems plain that officials may represent more of one interest than another (the category two analogue) or they may represent a relatively balanced set of interests (the category three analogue), but they are not likely to represent fully any of society's interests. If all of the individuals in a community could reveal the value they place on having a suspect arrested when evidence indicates a probability between 51% and 67% that he committed a crime, and they offered a dollar equivalent of that value to official *A* to produce that result; and if all potential suspects likewise fixed a sum that represents the value to them of freedom from arrest on evidence indicating less than a 67% probability of criminality, and they offered a dollar equivalent of that value to official *B* to produce that result; and if all of this could be done costlessly, negotiations between *A* and *B* should result in agreement to produce the socially desirable amount of arresting. Unfortunately, the costs of identifying and acting on society's interest in either side of this equation are prohibitive. Very imperfect information about these values may be conveyed in city council elections. City council members may attempt to instruct the chief of police, and to structure his various employment incentives, to reflect this information. The police chief then may do the same in trying to structure his lieutenants' employment incentives, and so on down to the police officer who must decide when to arrest.

At each point, however, the difficulty of determining the appropriate level of arrests leaves room for deviation from that ideal. How will the police lieutenant or sergeant, much less the city council members, know if police officers are failing to arrest suspects who ought to be arrested? Unlike the case of an arrest that is made when it ought not to be, there is no ready complainant; and unlike comparison of firms' profit figures, there is no easy mechanic for comparing arrest figures. It is, of course, possible that police want to make arrests for reasons apart from institutional incentives. Faced with liability, the police officers may demand protection equivalent to immunity so that they will not have to alter their arresting behavior. If higher-ranking officials believe that liability rules will result in too little arresting, they may press this demand on the city council. And if the council members believe this, they may agree to pay for the police officers' defense, to hold them harmless from liability for arrest, and so on.

The point here is not that actions of this nature do not occur in governmental enterprises. Rather, the point is that they are less likely than in the hypothetical posed by Professor Coase or in the case of private, profit-making firms to result in the socially desirable amount of correction. It is possible that a liability rule's overdeterrence (here, underarrest) will go undetected. If the personally beneficial response to liability for police is, in whole or in part, a too great reduction in arresting, the impediments to communicating this perception to the relevant officials may prevent them from becoming aware of the problem, even if it is perceived by members of the public in general. If aware of the problem, those officials may be insufficiently rewarded for its correction to take significant steps to that end. The members of the city council, for instance, may derive as much personal benefit from merely issuing a public directive to increase arrests as they would from actually increasing arrests to the optimal level. If the police chief does not really believe that the council members are concerned with the level of arrests, or are only mildly and temporarily concerned, he may seek funds from the council for projects of importance to him though only pretextually related to the overdeterrence problem—funds could be used, for instance, to finance a relatively elaborate undercover operation that would be exciting to supervise.

It is difficult to predict in any instance whether the government officials ultimately responsible will undercorrect or overcorrect in response to liability rules for government officers; any empirical efforts to ascertain which response is adopted face the same problems of definition and evaluation of the socially desirable result that citizens and officials encounter. Given positive costs to securing action from the ultimate official arbiters and the difficulty of detecting some "shirking" activity (like non-arrest), however, undercorrection frequently will be the more plausible response. As just acknowledged, that supposition is not provable, and examination of the actions governments have in fact taken in response to increasing numbers of suits against officials sheds little light on this. One striking feature of these responses is that no jurisdiction has acted to grant blanket immunity to officials and few have granted immunity for an easily identified class of actions or officers. While most jurisdictions have provided some mechanism for defraying the explicit costs of defending damage actions and reimbursing officials for adverse judgments, most states make both payment of (or reimbursement for) defense costs and reimbursement for adverse judgments turn on a determination by a designated government officer or entity that the official-defendant acted in good faith and within the scope of his employment (or some variant of this formula). That test duplicates the *Scheuer v. Rhodes* qualified immunity standard. Were the standard interpreted uniformly by courts and the officers or agencies deciding when to pay defense costs or judgments, the result would be to allow for reimbursement only where there would be no adverse judgment. Payment of defense costs for nonliable officials still will be of value to potential defendants. But not all states go even this far. Some states refuse to reimburse sued employees who have insured against liability actions, and some states still require private bills from the legislature to recompense officials. It is plausible that this very tempered reaction represents an inadequate response to what probably has been too great an increase in the liability incentive faced by executive officials. Whatever conclusions one draws about undercorrection or overcorrection, however, it is relatively predictable that mechanisms for limiting the impact of expected damage penalties that are too high will not be employed to the optimal extent by governmental enterprises nearly so often as by enterprises with better defined goals and stronger incentives for managers to attain them.

In combination, the potential for judicial decisions on official excuse from liability to overdeter even official action for which liability is at least presumptively useful (category two activity) and the possible defects in the institutional response of government to such overdeterrence indicate that courts may often be faced with the choice articulated by Learned Hand three decades ago: to deny damage liability for many official errors (intent as well as performance errors) or to risk the inducement of some new errors by a liability incentive intended to correct the errors now perceived to exist. Given present abilities to describe and to attain ideals for government conduct, it is extraordinarily difficult to use damage liability to fine tune official incentives so that substantially all errors imposing demonstrable harm on identifiable individuals are prevented without inducing a substantial number of opposed errors, although these may impose a less easily observed harm on a less easily identified group. Justice Rehnquist, dissenting in part in *Butz v. Economou*, scored the majority on just this point:

> History will surely not condemn the Court for its effort to achieve a more finely ground product from the judicial mill, a product which would both retain the necessary ability of public officials to govern and yet assure redress to those who are the victims of official wrongs. But if such a system of redress for official wrongs was indeed capable of being achieved in practice, it surely would not have been rejected by this Court speaking through the first Mr. Justice Harlan in 1896, by this Court speaking through the second Mr. Justice Harlan in 1959, and by Judge Learned Hand, speaking for the Court of Appeals for the Second Circuit in 1948 [*sic*]. These judges were not inexperienced neophytes who lacked the vision or the ability to define immunity doctrine to accomplish that result had they thought it possible. Nor were they obsequious toadies in their attitude toward high-ranking officials of coordinate branches of the Federal Government. But they did see with more prescience than the Court does today, that there are inevitable trade-offs in connection with any doctrine of official liability and immunity. They forthrightly accepted the possibility that an occasional failure to redress a claim of official wrongdoing would result from the doctrine of absolute immunity which they espoused viewing it as a lesser evil than the impairment of the ability of responsible public officials to govern.

V. Enterprise Liability: An Alternative Control

In parts III and IV, it was assumed that some mechanism for compensation of persons harmed by official misconduct would be available if individual officers were immune. A variety of mechanisms, other than individual officer liability, could compensate individuals for harm. Individuals could insure against the harm; government could provide an administrative vehicle for compensation, or government could pay damages pursuant to a judicial determination of liability. The last of these alternatives is examined briefly in this part and is compared to official liability as a means of controlling officials' behavior.

A. *The Mechanics of Enterprise Liability*

To the extent compensation is embraced as a goal, enterprise liability has an obvious advantage over official liability: the governmental enterprise is much more likely than the individual officer to have the funds required to satisfy a judgment. The difficult question is whether the increase in compensation under enterprise liability would be accompanied by an increase or decrease in socially desirable official behavior. Two aspects of this question are addressed in this section: how does enterprise liability provide incentives to better behavior, and what impact might a change in defendant from individual to entity have on frequency of suit, the component of liability incentive least subject to judicial control?

In one sense, enterprise liability operates in exact opposition to official liability. The latter provides officers an incentive to modify their behavior (for better or for worse from society's standpoint depending on the courts' ability to provide a liability incentive of the correct quantum) except insofar as other officials act to alter that incentive (by paying for defense costs, for adverse judgments, etc.). Enterprise liability, in contrast, only provides officials an incentive to modify their behavior insofar as other officials choose to require. Put differently, where official liability acts immediately upon the officer whose conduct is at issue, enterprise liability generally acts only mediately upon that officer. He need not pay for the defense of the suit nor must he pay any adverse judgment. The official in all likelihood will be required to invest some time in the suit (conferring with representatives for the defense, giving testimony, and so on) and may suffer personal embarrassment from a judgment adverse to the government based on a finding that his conduct was improper. These may, of themselves, prove significant incentives to avoid conduct that could give rise to such suits or at least to adverse judgments. By and large, however, these effects seem trivial in comparison with those triggered by official liability, where the individual's purse as well as his ego are directly at issue. The more significant deterrent effect of enterprise liability is likely to come from a restructuring of incentives within the governmental enterprise. If administrative sanctions, including shifting liability and defense costs back to the employee, requiring insurance, or disciplining the employee, are imposed against officials whose conduct generates additional costs for the government, or if additional monitoring burdens are incurred by the enterprise to prevent imposition of higher costs in defense of lawsuits and payment of damage awards, these measures are likely to provide the principal incentives to alter official behavior.

In theory, these secondary incentives from enterprise liability could result in greater deterrence than official liability, less deterrence, or the same deterrence. The general imperfection of official incentives to engage in socially valued behavior, discussed in the preceding section, precludes an assumption that enterprise liability generally will induce the appropriate response. If the relevant officials decide to penalize conduct that imposes defense costs on the enterprise, whether or not that conduct is found to be improper, the same possibility for overdeterrence discussed in part IV will exist. And if the administrative penalties adopted are regarded by officials as a more severe sanction that [sic] [then] the monetary costs of the suits' defense, enterprise liability could produce a greater likelihood of overdeterrence than official liability.

While it is extremely difficult to predict what the governmental response will be in any given instance, a general pattern of underdeterrence seems a more plausible result than does overdeterrence. The initial effect of enterprise liability is the expenditure of public monies. These may come from a general fund or from an allocation to a specific bureau. Payment from a general fund requires that the initial step for altering behavior of the erring officer be taken by someone even further removed from that office than the bureau head; otherwise, the same analysis applies. If the bureau that employs the erring official provides the funds to pay for defense of lawsuits and for liability judgments, the person most immediately affected will be the head of that bureau. While each member of the bureau may suffer a reduction in bureau expenditures that benefit him personally, the whole amount of the judgment is subtracted from the funds that the bureau head has some discretion to allocate. There is considerable evidence that high-level officials are concerned about the budget for their bureaus and consistently attempt to secure larger budgets. Since liability expenditures in the short run reduce the amount of money available to be spent by the affected bureau, the bureau head is likely to attempt to protect his budget against liability costs. This can be done by seeking budget increases to cover liability expenses, by altering employees' behavior to reduce liability expenses, or by some combination of these actions.

Assuming that some effort will be made to reduce the bureau's liability costs, the extent of that effort will depend on the relative importance attached by the bureau head to the activity that generates liability and to the avoidance of the liability expense. The higher up an official, the greater the importance he is likely to attach to both. The chief of police, therefore, may be more concerned about reducing crime rates and about protecting the department's budget than the individual officer. Just as he loses more from a reduction in the department's budget, so, too, he gains a much greater share of the rewards that attach to achievement of the bureau's goals. If the individual police officer had systematically imbalanced institutional incentives to arrest in a nonliability world, the likely reason would be that his superior officers (and beyond them, the elected managers of government) believed the cost imposed on suspects wrongly arrested was outweighed by the benefit of a vigorous arrest policy. The court's judgment that there should be liability for the arrest indicates a different evaluation of these costs than is arrived at through the processes of the other two branches. To the extent officials in the other branches disagree, they may be willing to tolerate some level of liability costs in order to prevent interference with the underlying activity. Assuming that the court has identified the socially correct performance standard, then, the same incentives that caused managers and their employees to deviate from the social optimum in a world without liability would cause them to underdeter official errors when enterprise liability (but not officer liability) is imposed.

In assessing the likely response to enterprise liability, however, any extrapolation from a nonliability world must be made with considerable reticence. One reason that enterprise liability probably will alter officials' incentives is that the group burdened by departure from the socially desirable may well change—the group harmed by too many arrests, for example, is not coextensive with the group of taxpayers who must pay liability judgments against the enterprise. In a nonliability world, the arrestees bear the cost of suboptimal official conduct. In an enterprise liability world, the arrestees (theoretically) will be fully compensated for the harm imposed on them, and the cost of suboptimal conduct will shift to taxpayers. If the latter group has fewer impediments than the former to communicating with government's managers and to rewarding them for acting in a manner consistent with the group's wishes, it is reasonable to expect an increased effort by government's managers to reduce the arresting activity that courts consider undesirable once liability is imposed.

While the imposition of liability on the enterprise thus should lead to changes in the behavior of government's managers, two caveats are in order. First, if the monetary costs of liability are spread over a large number of taxpayers, causing only a very slight increase in the tax burden on each, any incentive to ascertain the cause of the increase and to take steps to limit it may for most taxpayers be less than the cost of doing so. Again, the problem of high transaction costs for diffuse groups with low individual interest prevents the translation of a substantial group interest into equally substantial incentives for government's managers. Second, the structure of government makes the translation of incentives faced by higher-level officials into similar incentives for lower-level officials difficult. As elaborated in part IV, the translation occurs, but frequently something is lost in the translation. Given positive costs to restructuring official incentives, it probably is unrealistic to expect an adjustment of each individual official's incentives that fully reflects the enterprise liability costs his actions generate. A reasonable guess, then, is that, whereas officer liability may lead to overdeterrence, enterprise liability will result in underdeterrence, but not in so much underdeterrence as prevails in the absence of any liability.

If, as posited above, liability results in some underdeterrence of official misconduct, and official liability results in overdeterrence, which is to be preferred? Although the basis of choosing between them is slim, there is one reason to believe that the level of underdeterrence from enterprise liability may be less than the overdeterrence possible with official liability. The signal provided to other officials by misconduct that results in enterprise liability is a clear one: the judicial process has valued the harm from what it has identified as misconduct at a specific dollar amount. In contrast, the signal to other officials that an officer has engaged in socially undesirable conduct that avoids some risk of liability is much less clear. Because underdeterrence of official errors will result in official misbehavior that yields too much liability, and overdeterrence will produce official misbehavior that yields too little liability, enterprise liability may produce better incentives for officials than officer liability, as well as more compensation to persons harmed by official action.

Yet, even this modest conclusion must be qualified. The greater capacity for compensation may induce some suits against the enterprise that would not have been brought against the less pecunious individual officer. To know whether suits will be brought with more frequency under one rule than under the other would require evaluation of the number of nonmeritorious "spite" suits filed against individual officers, the number of meritorious suits not filed against judgment-proof officials, and the number of nonmeritorious "deep pocket" suits filed against enterprises. This last class of suits might seem small because, by hypothesis, the plaintiffs who are motivated by monetary rather than other personal considerations should be deterred from suit except where there is at least an even probability that the award will merit the cost of suit. The costliness of litigation, however, may induce an entity that frequently is subject to suit to adopt a practice of overcompensatory settlement of small claims. Such a practice might prompt an increase in the number of such claims filed. It therefore is difficult to predict what the relative frequency of suit under these alternative liability schemes would be. Indeed, there may be too much litigation under either scheme. Still, if the likely bias of official liability is to overdeter and that of enterprise liability is to underdeter, too great a frequency of suit (although of itself a misallocation of resources) would exacerbate the problem with official liability's impact on officer's incentives and ameliorate the problem presented by enterprise liability. Granting the difficulty of assessing these various effects on official conduct, where official actions are likely to trigger a significant number of spite suits or where the imbalance in official incentives is slight, enterprise liability may entail a lower risk than official liability of substituting incentives to commit one official error with incentives to commit another.

B. *Toward Enterprise Liability: Proposed Steps*

If enterprise liability might be preferable to official liability, how can the transition from individual to institutional liability be effected? The story of judicial decisions respecting official excuse from liability presented in part II reflects an expansion of liability for some officers that may in part have been justified by the absence of enterprise liability. Yet even as official immunity has been narrowed for these officials, liability for governmental enterprises has expanded. To a significant extent, sovereign immunity from suit now has been abrogated at both the federal and state levels. Moreover, municipalities may now be sued directly under 42 U.S.C. § 1983, the principal vehicle for damage suits against public officers. It is not entirely clear what the scope of municipal liability under section 1983 will be. The Court has declared that cities will not be vicariously liable for official misconduct not sanctioned by official policy. At the same time, when conduct is found to have been sanctioned by officials of sufficient rank to trigger liability, the municipalities will not benefit from the qualified immunity defense available to officials. One possible result of these decisions could be to leave low-level officers liable for their mistakes, subject to the qualified immunity defense, while making cities absolutely liable for errors of high-level officers. If the Court adheres to its decision that the availability of enterprise liability does not abrogate official liability, that would provide plaintiffs the option of pursuing the officer or the enterprise for misconduct by higher-level officials—the very ones who are more likely to have relatively balanced incentives and for whose acts liability thus is less likely to be socially beneficial.

It may be that the difficulty of determining when an official's improper action will be attributed to the municipality will move municipal enterprise liability under section 1983 in the direction of official liability, and not in the direction of a second remedy for officials whose nonliability incentives are more closely analogous to category three than category two. If this route is taken, two more steps would substantially complete a transition to enterprise liability: congressional action, under the authority of section five of the fourteenth amendment, to extend section 1983 to suits directly against the states, and construction of section 1983 and related damage remedies as not authorizing damage actions against officials when the governmental enterprise is available as a defendant. Each step requires a brief comment.

The extension of section 1983 to suits against a state, absent the state's consent, presents a conflict with the eleventh amendment. Although that amendment bars only the exercise of federal judicial power over suits against a state by citizens of another state or nation, the Court long ago construed it also to bar suits in federal court against a state by one of its own citizens. While the amendment as written would present only a minor impediment to a shift to enterprise liability, the current judicial interpretation of the amendment constitutes a serious impediment. To an extent, innovative judicial decisionmaking, finding waivers of sovereign immunity in surprising ways, has reduced the importance of this judicial gloss. Nonetheless, a reversal of the decisions expanding the eleventh amendment would be a simple means of resolving this difficulty. To one who finds the argument for reading the amendment to mean what it does not say unconvincing, this course would produce collateral benefits by simplifying the law of federal jurisdiction.

The judicial construction of section 1983 noted here as a possible second step in the transition to enterprise liability, however, would seem at once a step toward less straightforward interpretation of that statute. That would not, of course, be the case if Congress included that interpretation in the text of the statute. Yet, even if Congress did not go so far, reading section 1983 to preclude suits against individual officers where the governmental entity is suable hardly can be thought to do more violence to the text of section 1983 than the Court has done already. Section 1983 declares that "every person" who, under color of state law, deprives another person of federally secured protections "shall be liable to the party injured in an action at law, suit in equity, or other proper proceeding." The Court has held that actions at law are, as a rule, not suitable proceedings when instituted against judges or legislators and further has suggested that for some acts by these officials, no other proceeding is proper. Moreover, the Court has interpreted the language of section 1983 to provide for liability of non-immune officials only if they have acted in bad faith or beyond the pale of reasonably authorized conduct. Finally, as noted above, the Court has declared the word "person" to include municipalities.

It quickly should be granted that the statute is not a model of clarity and its history is a fertile source of argument but not of elucidation. The point is not that the Court has gone astray in its reading of section 1983, but rather that the interpretation suggested here, refusing to hold officials personally liable for damages where the state is available as a defendant, is at least as consistent with the text as is the current construction. The Court has opted to try to reach sensible results in section 1983 litigation rather than attempt truly to divine the intent of that statute's drafters. Any attempt at the latter course is an exercise in frustration. Even at the most basic level, questions concerning section 1983's meaning and purpose are unclear. Was the statute intended to provide a federal forum for ordinary state remedies so as to assure equal protection of the laws to groups that might not receive evenhanded treatment in state courts? Or was it intended to provide a federal remedy for which there was no state analogue?

Whatever the purpose of section 1983, the Court has sought to harmonize protection of federal interests (including the interest against certain state-sanctioned discriminations) with the states' concerns over effective government. By barring actions against individuals when a state or municipality can be sued, that task will be better accomplished.

This interpretation of section 1983 would not bar states from recovering over against state officers. If states or their subdivisions believe that this course is a useful supplement to other devices for constraining employees' behavior, there is little reason for courts to distrust that judgment. Because the governmental enterprise must take an affirmative act to reach this result, it should not be expected generally to err in the direction of passing on too much of the liability burden to individual officers.

In addition to providing a better framework for adjudicating liability for government actions at the state and local levels, this interpretation of section 1983 could be expected to benefit the federal establishment. Supreme Court decisions respecting liability of federal officials over the past decade have embodied the view that, when federal rights are at issue, it is only fitting that enforcement of those rights against the federal government be no less zealous than enforcement against the states. This view was plainly expressed in *Butz v. Economou* to justify substitution of the qualified immunity test where absolute immunity had theretofore applied. So, too, this view appears in decisions, such as the delightfully titled *Bivens v. Six Unknown Named Agents of the Federal Bureau of Narcotics*, which infer rights of action against federal officers directly from the Constitution. In recently holding that such rights of action can be implied against officers even where statutory damage remedies against the United States are available, the Court again was simply paralleling the course of liability for state officials. The distinctions between the position—practical and legal—of state and federal officers may well militate against this sort of parallelism. But if the Court followed this pattern by restricting suits against federal officers where alternative remedies are available, a result parallel to the proposed reading of section 1983, it might increase the likelihood that damage suits would improve rather than diminish those officials' incentives to behave in a socially desirable manner.

* * *

Part IV
"Secured by the Constitution": The Fourteenth Amendment and Due Process

Section 1983 encompasses the provisions of the Fourteenth Amendment, and makes their violation actionable for damages. The Fourteenth Amendment contains the privileges or immunities clause, the equal protection clause and, finally, the due process clause, which has been held to incorporate most of the Bill of Rights.

However, a considerable amount of section 1983 litigation revolves around the due process clause in its procedural and substantive aspects (apart from incorporation). In part, this is because the due process clause is an open-ended provision whose meaning and application are capable of significant expansion and contraction. Due process often functions as a kind of lightning rod whereby differing theories of constitutional interpretation and federalism are worked through in a section 1983 context. Many observers (I among them) believe that the Court's interpretation of the due process clause is directly influenced by the availability of a damages remedy under section 1983.

The articles by Professor Monaghan and Professors Wells and Eaton analyze important due process issues as they arise in the section 1983 context. Professor Monaghan's article, dealing with procedural due process, criticizes the Supreme Court's controversial 1981 decision in *Parratt* v. *Taylor*, 451 U.S. 527 (1981), *overruled in part, Daniels v. Williams*, 474 U.S. 327 (1986), as inconsistent with Fourteenth Amendment state action theory. He argues that if *Parratt* is not overruled, it ought at least to be recast in non-Fourteenth Amendment terms.

In contrast, the article by Professors Wells and Eaton discusses substantive due process. In it, they maintain that the Supreme Court has failed to confront what they call the central issue in *Parratt* and related cases: "whether a government-inflicted injury to life, liberty, or property violates the substantive protections of the due process clauses and thereby warrants a constitutionally derived tort remedy." They suggest that *Parratt* be abandoned and that the "shock the conscience" standard of *Rochin v. California*, 342 U.S. 165 (1952), be used instead. Their analysis is insightful even though, in cases involving alleged police use of excessive force in making arrests, the Supreme Court has since rejected the applicability of substantive due process and held that the Fourth Amendment alone governs. *Graham v. Connor*, 490 U.S. 386 (1989).

Henry Paul Monaghan, *Comment, State Law Wrongs, State Law Remedies, and the Fourteenth Amendment,* 86 Columbia Law Review 979 (1986)

Parratt v. Taylor is among the most puzzling Supreme Court decisions of the last decade, and the lower federal courts have been thrown into considerable confusion in their efforts to implement it. In large part, this confusion stems from the fact that *Parratt* decided two independent points: first, the negligent loss or destruction of property by state officials could constitute a "deprivation" thereof for purposes of the due process clause of the fourteenth amendment; and second, the existence of an adequate state remedy to redress the wrong meant that the deprivation was not "without due process of law." In this Comment, I hope to show that this second, or "state action," holding contradicts long-embedded understandings of *when* a denial of due process occurs for fourteenth amendment purposes.

The state action issue remains important even after this term's decision in *Daniels v. Williams. Daniels* expressly overruled *Parratt*'s first holding. In *Daniels*, the Court held that, ordinarily, negligently inflicted injuries to "liberty" and "property" are not the kind of "deprivations" with which the due process clause is concerned. But *Daniels* left undisturbed *Parratt*'s state action theory. Indeed, the *Daniels* Court cited with approval *Hudson v. Palmer*, which had extended *Parratt*'s state action holding to intentional deprivations of property by state officials.

Parratt's state action theory is best seen in a larger context. *Parratt* is one part of an ongoing effort by the Supreme Court, particularly Justice Rehnquist, to reorient fourteenth amendment jurisprudence. The goal is to keep the lower federal courts out of the business of monitoring the routine day-to-day administration of state government in areas that only marginally implicate constitutional values. Philosophically, this development embodies a belief that a clear distinction can be drawn between constitutional violations and state law wrongs. Linguistically, it stresses a close parsing of section 1983 and the due process clause. Analytically, it generates two decisional lines: cases like *Board of Regents v. Roth* and *Paul v. Davis* narrow the domain of constitutionally protected "liberty" and "property," while decisions like *Daniels v. Williams* and *Parratt v. Taylor* limit the state action that constitutes a "deprivation" or a "denial of due process" of interests admittedly entitled to constitutional protection.

The vagaries and gossamer distinctions of *Roth* and its progeny have been examined by numerous commentators. The important point here is that in denying the presence of a "liberty" or "property" interest, these decisions suggest that the state need not justify some state-inflicted injuries to important interests of individuals. So far, however, this line of authority is limited in reach and is largely confined to the area of public entitlements. Unlike *Roth*, *Parratt* deals with "property" interests concededly entitled to constitutional protection. As limited by *Daniels*, *Parratt* concerns one category of intentional interferences with such interests: the conduct challenged under the fourteenth amendment is also misconduct under state law, and the state provides an adequate remedy for the wrong. The crucial question is the constitutional relevance of either of these facts.

In the past, these facts have been irrelevant. The landmark decision in *Home Telephone and Telegraph Co. v. City of Los Angeles* established that any intentional conduct of state officials that, prima facie, contravened the fourteenth amendment is open to challenge in the district courts without regard to whether that conduct also violates state law or whether the state provides adequate corrective process. *Monroe v. Pape* confirmed *Home Telephone*, and as a matter of statutory construction, also held "that section 1983 presently occupies and exploits all of the constitutional space that *Home Telephone* permits." In *Monroe*, the Court held that section 1983's "under color of [state law]" requirement embraces conduct by state officials that violated state law, and that the section 1983 remedy is "supplementary" to any state judicial remedy.

Despite the apparent sweep of *Home Telephone* and *Monroe*, *Parratt*'s state action holding is designed to exclude one form of intentional misuse of state authority from the federal trial courts: misconduct that, unlike the conduct in *Home Telephone*, is "random and unauthorized," and that, unlike the conduct in *Monroe*, does not infringe upon a "fundamental" constitutional right. As yet, this exclusion applies only if the state provides adequate corrective process.

Parratt's limited compass does not diminish its practical importance. With the exception of police brutality cases, *Parratt* excludes from the federal courts all low-level intentional official misconduct resulting in losses of property or nonfundamental liberties where state law provides a remedy. *Hudson v. Palmer* is the paradigmatic illustration. In *Hudson*, a prison officer, acting without authority, intentionally destroyed an inmate's property during a shakedown search. After denying that any fundamental right was implicated, the Court characterized the officer's conduct as "random and unauthorized." *Parratt* was then invoked to bar the inmate's section 1983 due process claim because the inmate had an adequate remedy in the state courts.

This Comment contends that *Parratt* is ultimately grounded in a theory of "state action" that cannot be reconciled with the more general constitutional understandings contained in *Home Telephone* and *Monroe*. Moreover, *Parratt* has consequences that arguably are beyond the power of Congress to alter. These results are unfortunate and unnecessary. Either the remaining aspects of *Parratt* should be overruled, or the decision should be recast. The Court's goals—which are certainly defensible—can be achieved by viewing *Parratt* as abstention doctrine, or alternatively, by statutory construction: by limiting the scope of section 1983 so that its requirement of "under color of [state law]" does not include random and unauthorized wrongs for which the state provides adequate corrective process.

I. *PARRATT* V. TAYLOR

While *Parratt* arose in a prison setting, it presented a common problem: low-level misconduct in the routine administration of state government that results in the loss or destruction of the plaintiff's property. The conduct violates state law, and the state law provides a remedy for the wrong. But the plaintiff also insists that this conduct also violates the due process clause of the fourteenth amendment, and he brings a section 1983 action in federal court. More specifically, in *Parratt* the plaintiff alleged that he had ordered by mail a hobby kit worth $23.50. Upon its receipt at the prison, the kit was not processed according to established mail procedure and was negligently lost by prison officials. As a result, the plaintiff claimed a "deprivation" of his property "without due process of law." The district court gave summary judgment for the plaintiff; the court of appeals affirmed.

The Supreme Court reversed in an opinion by Justice Rehnquist. The Court began by setting out the language of section 1983:

> Every person who, *under color of* any statute, ordinance, regulation, custom, or usage of any State or Territory, subjects, or causes to be subjected, any citizen of the United States or other person within the jurisdiction thereof to the *deprivation* of any *rights*, privileges, or immunities *secured by the Constitution* and laws, shall be liable to the party injured in an action at law, suit in equity, or other proper proceeding for redress.

After concluding that the defendant's conduct satisfied section 1983's "under color of [state law]" requirement, the Court decided two very different points.

First, the Court held that defendants' negligence could work a "deprivation" of "property" within the meaning of section 1983 and the fourteenth amendment. On this point, *Daniels v. Williams* explicitly overrules *Parratt*. *Daniels* held that while section 1983 has no state of mind requirement, at least some parts of the fourteenth amendment do. The Court insisted that negligent injuries are far removed from the evils of arbitrary governmental oppression that are the concern of the due process clause. Strong federalism principles, reflecting a belief in a distinction between ordinary state law wrongs and constitutional violations, drove the holding:

> Our Constitution deals with the large concerns of the governors and the governed, but it does not purport to supplant traditional tort law in laying down rules of conduct to regulate liability for injuries that attend living together in society. We have previously rejected reasoning that "would make of the Fourteenth Amendment a font of tort law to be superimposed upon whatever systems may already be administered by the States . . . . "

Second, the *Parratt* Court held that the "deprivation" did not infringe upon any "rights . . . secured by the Constitution" within the meaning of section 1983, because the deprivation was not without due process of law. *Daniels*' approving citation of *Hudson v. Palmer* seemingly confirms that *Parratt*'s state action holding remains good law for some forms of intentional official misconduct. Thus, *Parratt*'s reasoning requires careful attention.

II. False Starts: Procedural and Jurisdictional Accounts of *Parratt*

Several quite different accounts of *Parratt* can be given, each of which has significantly different implications for the principles of federal jurisdiction and, more importantly, for substantive constitutional law. In order to understand *Parratt*, it seems helpful to discuss first what the case is not about.

A. *Parratt as Procedural Due Process*

In *Parratt*, the Court concluded that the plaintiff had received all the process that was due. Postdeprivation process was constitutionally sufficient where, as here: (1) the plaintiff did not challenge the established procedures for processing mail; (2) the defendants' conduct was "random and unauthorized," and thus predeprivation process was impracticable; and (3) state law provided adequate postdeprivation corrective process. Focusing on this aspect of *Parratt*, several federal appellate courts have understood the case to be simply a procedural due process decision, concerned only with the timing of any constitutionally required process. Recently, the Second, Eighth, and Ninth Circuits have taken this position, and after *Daniels* other courts might be encouraged to so view the case. In a categorical manner these courts insist that *Parratt* has no applicability to *any* substantive due process challenge, and that such challenges can be brought immediately in the federal courts. This is an attractive position. A procedural due process interpretation accords with the great bulk of the *Parratt* opinion, which is quite plainly concerned with the constitutional sufficiency of postdeprivation process, and with the views expressed in several concurring opinions.

But this limited conception of *Parratt* will not work. This becomes apparent once the concept of "substantive due process" is unpacked. Insofar as the concept refers to fundamental rights, such as those contained in the Bill of Rights or those accorded fundamental status under the *Roe v. Wade* line of cases, *Parratt* has no relevance. But insofar as substantive due process refers simply to the general substantive freedom from arbitrary and unreasonable restraints on "liberty" and "property," *Parratt* is relevant.

My conclusion rests on two grounds. First, if *Parratt* has no substantive import, why was the judgment for plaintiff reversed? One would have expected that, having rejected the procedural due process claim, the Court would then address the plaintiff's substantive constitutional claim. And here the result appeared clear: the facts were not in dispute; the Court had already decided that the defendants' conduct had worked a "deprivation" of the plaintiff's property; and no immunity rule shielded the defendants from damages. Accordingly, unless the plaintiff had asserted *only* a procedural due process claim—a point nowhere suggested in the Court's opinion—the judgment below should have been affirmed, not reversed.

Second, a procedural due process interpretation cannot plausibly account for *Parratt*'s final paragraphs. The Court does not say that the judgment for damages was reversed because the plaintiff had alleged only an unsound procedural due process claim. Rather, reversal seems premised on the belief that the plaintiff was in the wrong forum. In concluding that the plaintiff "has not alleged a violation of the Due Process Clause," the Court abandons its prior discussion of due process in a plainly procedural sense. Instead, the traditional distinction between substantive and procedural due process is collapsed, and due process is discussed as though it were a unitary concept:

> Although he has been deprived of property under color of state law, . . . there is no contention that the [established state] procedures themselves are inadequate nor is there any contention that it was practicable for the State to provide a predeprivation hearing . . . . This [state] procedure was in existence at the time of the loss here in question but respondent did not use it . . . . [Even though not identical to § 1983, the state] remedies provided could have fully compensated the respondent for the property loss he suffered, and we hold that they are sufficient to satisfy the requirements of due process.
>
> Our decision today is fully consistent with our prior cases. To accept respondent's argument that the conduct of the state officials in this case constituted a violation of the Fourteenth Amendment . . . "would make of the Fourteenth Amendment a font of tort law . . . ."

During *Parratt*'s heyday—when negligence could constitute a "deprivation" of property—these paragraphs were widely understood to require that a plaintiff vindicate any substantive damage claim in the state courts.

B. *Parratt as Abstention Doctrine*

As modified by *Daniels*, *Parratt* might be viewed as a special abstention doctrine applicable to certain cases in which plaintiffs seek damages for "deprivations" of constitutionally protected "property" or "liberty" resulting from intentional official conduct that also violates state law and for which the state provides corrective process. Official misconduct can come in different forms. For example, in *Home Telephone*, the officials were enforcing a municipal rate ordinance, but if the ordinance constituted a deprivation of property without due process of law, it also would have conflicted with the state constitution. *Monroe v. Pape* involved a constitutionally offensive search and seizure that was unauthorized by any level of state law. The conduct in *Parratt* was not authorized by state law, and it did not impinge upon any specific "fundamental" right. Excluding cases like *Parratt* from the federal trial courts is certainly a defensible policy. Those courts seem ill-used if their task is to superintend the routine administration of state government where the states are themselves willing to correct abuses and no fundamental rights are involved.

Treating *Parratt* as a special abstention doctrine for this narrow category of federal claims would be a bold move. The Court has often spoken of the district courts' "virtually unflagging obligation" to exercise their statutory jurisdiction. Surely, the propriety of such a massive, judicially fashioned curtailment of statutorily mandated jurisdiction is open to doubt. Yet, employed here and in other areas of "routine" state administration, abstention doctrine has the considerable advantage of recognizing that the point in time at which a substantive constitutional violation takes place is not necessarily determinative of the point in time at which entry to the federal courthouse is obtained. On the latter point, the existence vel non of state corrective process is a relevant consideration.

But *Parratt*'s reasoning is not captured by abstention doctrine. For the Court, something quite different underlies the decision.

C. *Parratt as Ripeness or Exhaustion of Remedies*

The Court has also suggested that *Parratt* rests on principles akin to ripeness, a doctrine that concerns the timing of access to the federal courts. Ripeness principles require that controversies be sufficiently focused to ensure a clear presentation of the issues.

In *Williamson County Regional Planning Commission v. Hamilton Bank*, a landowner filed a regulatory taking challenge in the district court. The Court gave two reasons for its conclusion that the challenge was "premature." First, the Court found that further administrative relief to the landowner was possible by way of variance. Second, the Court held: "The taking claim is not yet ripe [because the landowner] did not seek compensation through the [judicial] procedures the State has provided for doing so." This second ground is of concern to us, for here the Court shuts the federal courthouse door even if all state administrative remedies have been exhausted.

From the settled premise that the takings clause itself does not require pre-taking process or pre-taking compensation, the Court somehow generated another conclusion: any substantive takings claim is "premature" until the landowner "has used the [state provided judicial] procedure and been denied just compensation." The Court believed that this result was "analogous to the Court's holding in *Parratt*," and added:

> In . . . a situation [such as *Parratt*], the Constitution does not require predeprivation process because it would be impossible or impracticable to provide a meaningful hearing before the deprivation. Instead, the Constitution is satisfied by the provision of meaningful postdeprivation process. . . . Thus, the State's action is not "complete" in the sense of causing a constitutional injury "unless or until the State fails to provide an adequate postdeprivation remedy for the property loss." Likewise . . . the State's action here is not "complete" until the State fails to provide adequate compensation for the taking.

This passage indiscriminately mixes jurisdictional, procedural due process, and substantive taking concepts. The Court is quite wrong in thinking that the point in time at which a substantive deprivation occurs is a function of the point in time at which the state can reasonably provide corrective process. The relationship runs the other way: discussion about the timing of any process due presupposes independent criteria for specifying the point at which the substantive deprivation has occurred. Moreover, the Court's reliance on ripeness concepts is in error. No authority supports use of ripeness doctrine to bar federal judicial consideration of an otherwise sufficiently focused controversy simply because corrective state judicial process had not been invoked.

Hamilton Bank might be defended, as a footnote in the opinion suggests, as a special rule for takings cases—a rule grounded in the perception that it is not the taking but the refusal to compensate that constitutes the violation. The difficulty here is that the argument cannot be so limited. Assuming that some intentional property deprivations are not to be viewed as takings, these "non-taking" property "deprivations" cannot be accorded readier access to the district courts for substantive relief than are takings claims. Thus, it would seem that all substantive property claims, whether takings or not, must be pursued in the state courts, so long as an adequate corrective process exists. While this analysis yields a distinction between claims of liberty and of property, the distinction is not consistent with *Hamilton Bank*'s general ripeness, which posits that the constitutionally relevant state action is not "complete" until the state court acts. That view of ripeness seems equally applicable to deprivations of "liberty" and of "property." In any event, *Hamilton Bank*'s ripeness rhetoric fails to capture *Parratt*'s basic premise. Ripeness is concerned only with the *timing* of access to the district courts; but *Parratt* completely *bars* access, if the state corrective process is adjudged "adequate."

III. Explaining *Parratt*

Parratt is concerned with interests that owe their existence to state law but that constitute "property" for due process purposes. *Parratt* seeks to distinguish sharply between injuries to this category of constitutionally protected interests and injuries to "fundamental" constitutional rights. While hard to capture in a phrase, this distinction seems best expressed in "state action" terms. The heart of the distinction is the moment in time at which the constitutionally decisive state action is thought to occur.

With respect to fundamental rights, the Court continues to assert, as it did in *Monroe v. Pape*, that section 1983 "makes a deprivation . . . actionable independently of state law." The injured plaintiff has immediate access to federal courts whether or not the complained of conduct contravenes state law and whether or not the state provides corrective process. Thus, in fundamental rights cases, the constitutionally offensive state action occurs when the state official acts or threatens to act.

But where only a "property" interest is involved, as in *Parratt*, the analysis is more complex. If the deprivation is pursuant to some official policy, then the *Monroe v. Pape* approach is followed. However, if the official conduct is "random and unauthorized," the crucial constitutionally offensive state action *may* shift. This is because the focus is not on the specific official act, but on the overall design of the legislative scheme. If adequate corrective process exists, the conduct of the state official is not of constitutional dimension; it is only a state law wrong. If adequate corrective process does not exist, anyone injured as a result of *that* omission has suffered a constitutional deprivation. The specific act that causes the loss is not of constitutional significance except to create standing to complain.

On this analysis, *Parratt*'s premises seem as applicable to "liberty" as to "property." If that is true, *Parratt* will require that intentional but random and unauthorized state misconduct be sorted into two categories: injuries to fundamental rights and "straight" substantive due process claims, which involve challenges to state conduct that "arbitrarily" or "unreasonably" interferes with liberty or property. The need to classify certain actions, such as police brutality, will present some boundary uncertainty. At first glance, the category of "fundamental" rights seems coterminous with those provisions of the Bill of Rights held applicable to the states, as well as any judicially-created fundamental rights. But this line may not quite capture the distinctions made in the cases, particularly in the opinions of Justice Rehnquist. Seemingly, he distinguishes between rights, such as first and fourth amendment rights, whose sole origin is in the Constitution, and rights with origins in state law and which are simply protected by the Constitution. This distinction subjects at least some takings claims to the *Parratt* regime, even though protection against uncompensated takings is a specific textual guarantee. On the other hand, for Justice Rehnquist the federal content of "liberty" includes a root freedom from the imposition of new legal disabilities, even though that "liberty" cannot be fitted into a Bill of Rights mold.

The complex distinctions spawned by *Parratt* reflect the Court's deep-seated belief that a sufficiently stable line exists between constitutional torts and simple state law wrongs. But in fact, many state-caused constitutional violations necessarily retain much of the substance of common law torts. In any area where a "specific" constitutional provision has a common law tort counterpart, any effort at positing a strong distinction between constitutional and non-constitutional torts is not likely to succeed. In these situations, a section 1983 litigant will allege the substance of a common law tort and perhaps some additional aggravating circumstances.

The Court's recent efforts to fashion a general theory of state wrongs under the fourteenth amendment is incomplete. Indeed, as *Daniels* shows, this project is open to continuous revision. But at present, we have a rather complicated three-tiered structure:

1. *Fundamental rights.* This category includes most of the Bill of Rights plus judicially posited fundamental rights. The focus here is on the specific act of official misconduct, which gives rise to an immediate right under section 1983 to sue in the federal court for damages and injunctive relief. This section 1983 claim stands whether the defendant's conduct is authorized or unauthorized under state law or wheth-

er the state provides adequate corrective process. *Monroe v. Pape* is the classic illustration.

2. *Liberty or property invasions.* The focus here is on intentional (and perhaps reckless) interference with interests that originate in state law but that amount to "liberty" or "property" within the meaning of the fourteenth amendment. So long as the challenge is not to an official state policy, but only to random and unauthorized misconduct, the state wrong is not in the interference but only in the denial of the corrective process. *Parratt v. Taylor* provides the theoretical underpinning for this model, although *Hudson v. Palmer* is the best illustration.

3. *Other injuries.* The focus here is on a set of state harms to specific individuals that do not implicate either "liberty" or "property." In principle, such harms do not seem to require any justification under the due process clause. So far this is a quite limited area, largely involving public sector entitlements such as welfare and jobs. Moreover, the Court has spoken only of the lack of need for predeprivation process, and it has hinted that the availability of some state law remedies is important. *Board of Regents v. Roth* is the standard bearer here.

IV. UNDERSTANDING *PARRATT*

Parratt's state action theory is a deeply problematic aspect of the Court's complex three-fold classification. My submission is that *Parratt* is not tenable, and it should be either overruled or recast.

A. *Of Intentional Injuries*

The line between "random and unauthorized" official conduct and "authorized" conduct is unstable, as the recent decision in *Regents of the University of Michigan v. Ewing* illustrates. There, the Court rejected on the merits a substantive due process challenge to the dismissal of a student from a special medical degree program. The student alleged that his dismissal was contrary to both the announced policies and the actual practices of the university for students experiencing academic difficulty in this program. The complaint alleged state law contract and estoppel theories, and a section 1983 claim. The Court did not consider *Parratt*, but the case can be understood in those terms: the heart of the student's complaint was that he was dismissed as a result of the "unauthorized" conduct of state officials. Perhaps, however, the dismissal was not "random" because it was made at a high enough administrative level. If that be the explanation, "random" is a term of art, and *Parratt* collapses into little more than a distinction between acts of "lower echelon state employees . . . and high ranking officials." If, however, *Ewing* holds that a plaintiff can *always* make a substantive due process challenge for arbitrariness, *Parratt* and *Hudson v. Palmer* are overruled completely.

But difficulties in understanding what constitutes "random and unauthorized" conduct are not the heart of my concern. *Parratt*'s asymmetric treatment of different kinds of official conduct cannot be adequately rationalized in state action terms. No distinction can turn on the adequacy of state corrective process, because that factor can be held constant in all situations. *Parratt* provides no basis for a distinction between injuries to fundamental rights and injuries to other constitutional interests. As commentators have noted, *Monroe* and *Parratt* have the same structure: state officials have interfered with a constitutionally protected interest under circumstances in which their conduct is illegal under state law and for which state law provides adequate corrective process.

More fundamentally, as a means for determining the time when a constitutional violation occurs, *Parratt*'s state action theory is in direct conflict with principles thought to be settled by *Home Telephone and Telegraph Co. v. City of Los Angeles.* There, the company filed a bill to enjoin the enforcement of a city rate ordinance, alleging that the rates were confiscatory and thus the ordinance contravened the due process clause of the fourteenth amendment. The district court dismissed the bill, reasoning that, if confiscatory, the rates were also illegal under the state constitution, and since the state law provided corrective process, the "state" could not be said to have deprived the company of property without due process of law. The Supreme Court unanimously reversed, rejecting the view that the fourteenth amendment applied to the state only in its collective capacity and reached only wrongs "authorized" by the state. "[I]n truth," the amendment "contemplates the possibility of state officers abusing the powers lawfully conferred upon them by doing wrongs prohibited by the Amendment." Stressing the amendment's "completeness" and "comprehensive inclusiveness," the Court continued:

> [W]here a state officer, under an assertion of power from the State, is doing an act which could only be done upon the predicate that there was such power, the inquiry as to the repugnancy of the act to the Fourteenth Amendment cannot be avoided by insisting that there is a want of power . . . . [W]hen it is alleged that a state officer in virtue of state power is doing an act which if permitted to be done prima facie would violate the Amend-

ment, *the subject must be tested by assuming that the officer possessed power* if the act be one which there would not be opportunity to perform but for the possession of some state authority.

Under *Home Telephone*, the fourteenth amendment reaches any executive or administrative conduct that contravenes the fourteenth amendment. It makes no difference whether the state provides corrective process. More importantly, it makes no difference whether the state official is using or misusing state power. Under *Home Telephone*, the constitutionally offensive state action occurs at the point at which the state official acts. This has been the standard understanding in constitutional law for many decades. Yet, under *Parratt*, some forms of intentional conduct that "prima facie" would violate the amendment, standing alone, cannot constitute constitutional violations.

Parratt makes no effort to reconcile its conclusion with *Home Telephone* or *Monroe v. Pape*. Without reflection, the Court simply assumes that the situations are different. There are plausible differences between fundamental rights and other rights, between challenges to state and local policies and challenges to unadorned official misconduct, and between situations in which the state provides adequate corrective process and those in which it does not. These factors have relevance in legislative and judicial determinations as to the appropriate point at which federal trial court intervention should occur. But they are not relevant in determining the point at which a substantive violation has occurred. *Parratt*'s state action theory is fundamentally wrong, at least so long as *Home Telephone* and *Monroe v. Pape* are thought to be sound.

B. *Of Adequate Corrective Process*

Additional difficulties emerge once we focus on *Parratt*'s apparent premise that access to the federal courts is available if the state does not provide some "adequate" corrective process for an intentional interference with a constitutionally protected "liberty" or "property" interest. Does this mean that the state cannot abolish or sharply modify its common law of torts so as to create a special immunity from damages for state officials? If the general fourteenth amendment standard of reasonableness is the test, a plausible argument can be advanced for at least some such immunities. Both *Daniels* and *Davidson* presented this issue, but the Court's disposition of both cases left it unresolved. Perhaps eventually the Court will hold that *Parratt* does not require actual relief. But then what would *Parratt* mean?

C. *Congress and Parratt*

Parratt's potential is quite startling once Congress is brought into the picture. Consider an example suggested by *Hudson v. Palmer*, which extended *Parratt* to bar a section 1983 challenge to the intentional misconduct of state officials who destroyed an inmate's property. As in *Parratt*, the Court seems to have assumed that no substantive violation had been made out so long as the state court provided adequate corrective process. Suppose that, after *Hudson*, the United States indicted the offending officials under a criminal statute that proscribed the "intentional deprivation of rights secured by the Constitution of the United States." Seemingly, *Parratt*'s logic requires dismissal: the random and unauthorized official misconduct does not constitute a violation given the existence of adequate state corrective process. This result runs strongly against our intuitions.

Could Congress overrule *Parratt*? With a single arguable exception, no Supreme Court decision has departed from the understanding of the *Civil Rights Cases* that section five of the fourteenth amendment authorizes "remedial" legislation only—that is, legislation designed to correct state wrongdoing. To be sure, in the race area the remedial conception has been given such an expansive gloss that any distinction between remedial and primary legislation has been drained of substance. But this development has evoked strong dissents and is not likely to be pressed beyond the race area. If that is true, it is doubtful that Congress could overrule *Parratt*: there would be nothing to "remedy" since the official misconduct is not itself a violation where the state legislative scheme has adequate corrective process. Of course, one can readily imagine the countermoves. Congress could "find" that, though fair on its face, the state remedial scheme will not work in practice and that a federal cause of action is therefore necessary to vindicate fourteenth amendment rights. Whether this "prophylactic" argument would prevail outside the race area, or whether congressional power under artcle I, section 8 might support federal legislation, is not important for my purposes. The difficulties cast doubt on *Parratt* simply because the decision makes so complex our understanding of the fourteenth amendment. In constitutional law, as elsewhere, needless complexity should be eschewed.

V. Overruling or Recasting *Parratt*

The appropriate role of the federal courts in cases of misuse of authority by state officials is a problem with a very long history. Leaving aside differing conceptions of what amounts to "authorization," the view that only "authorized" state conduct can offend the fourteenth amendment has been espoused before. As a theory of "state action" it was categorically rejected in *Home Telephone*. However, in Justice Frankfurter's dissenting opinion in *Monroe v. Pape*, it resurfaced, this time as a theory of statutory construction. Justice Frankfurter insisted that an unreasonable search and seizure by police officers did not occur "under color of [state] law]" for purposes of section 1983 where the conduct violated state law unless it was in fact supported by some custom or usage.

Parratt resurrects this tradition. *Parratt* asserts that some forms of official misconduct do not fall within the ambit of the fourteenth amendment so long as the state provides corrective process. *Parratt*'s push to embrace some such position is understandable—indeed, in practical terms, imperative—if negligence could amount to a "deprivation." But, after *Daniels*, the practical need for this remaining aspect of *Parratt* is far less clear, particularly given the difficulty of its application.

But my real concern is at the level of theory. The lines drawn by *Parratt*, however defensible they may be when viewed as a sensible use of the federal trial courts, render the decision incoherent as a theory of state action. That result is quite unnecessary, even accepting the Court's policy objectives. The Court could find a far less controversial basis for its results in abstention doctrine. This would be my preference. But, alternatively, the Court might, as Justice Rehnquist has suggested, re-examine *Monroe*'s holding that section 1983's reach is coextensive with the reach of the fourteenth amendment. Of course, the two can be read as perfectly congruent, but such a reading is not necessary. *Parratt* could be rationalized as a construction of section 1983 under which wholly unauthorized official misconduct with respect to interests whose origins are in state law and where adequate state corrective process exists does not occur "under color of [state law]" within the meaning of section 1983. Whether this reading comports comfortably with the language or the original intention of section 1983 is another matter. For me, the decisive point is that if *Parratt* is not overruled, it is far better to charge its narrowing results to abstention principles or to section 1983 than to the fourteenth amendment.

Michael Wells & Thomas A. Eaton, *Substantive Due Process and the Scope of Constitutional Torts,* 18 Georgia Law Review 201 (1984)

* * *

II. The Supreme Court Cases

The Supreme Court cases bearing directly on the scope of constitutional tort are *Parratt v. Taylor*, *Baker v. McCollan*, *Ingraham v. Wright*, and *Paul v. Davis*. These cases have presented the Court with opportunities to develop a coherent body of doctrine for resolving the boundary issue, as they all concern claims of harm to life, liberty, or property inflicted by government actors. The Court has purported to address this issue, but actually has disposed of the cases on other grounds or has written opinions that are too incoherent to provide any guidance. As a result, the scope of constitutional tort is still unclear, and the issue remains open for debate.

A. *Parratt and its Antecedents*

The Supreme Court's first effort to deal with the scope of constitutional tort was *Paul v. Davis*. A police chief, seeking to control shoplifting, circulated a flyer containing photographs of persons arrested for shoplifting and which identified them as "active shoplifters." The plaintiff's photograph was included; he had been arrested but never convicted, or even tried, for shoplifting. He sought damages for harm to his reputation, and relied on an earlier Supreme Court decision for the proposition that reputation is an aspect of constitutional liberty protected by the due process clause of the fourteenth amendment. The Court, rejecting his claim, ruled that reputation, standing alone, is not an aspect of fourteenth amendment liberty. The Court distinguished the cases cited by the plaintiff on the ground that in them harm to reputation was accompanied by some other deprivation, like the loss of a job or the right to buy liquor.

The opinion itself indicates why the Court strained to limit the reach of its prior decisions. *Paul* presented allegations of defamation that would ordinarily be brought as a common law tort in state court. The plaintiff was able to frame his claim as a constitutional tort only because the defendant was a state actor. The Court feared that, if this circumstance could convert common law defamation into a constitutional tort case, constitutional status could not be denied to suits by "the survivors of an innocent bystander mistakenly shot by a policeman or negligently killed by a sheriff driving a government vehicle . . . . " Under that broad view of life, liberty, and property, the fourteenth amendment would become "a font of tort law to be superimposed upon whatever systems may already be administered by the States." Such a result, thought the Court, "would come as a great surprise to those who drafted and shepherded the adoption of that amendment."

The plaintiffs in *Ingraham v. Wright* were public school students who had been severely paddled for misbehavior. They claimed violations of the cruel and unusual punishments clause of the eighth amendment and deprivations of liberty without due process of law. The Court, denying the first claim, ruled that the eighth amendment does not apply to public schools. The Court did agree with the plaintiffs that personal security against physical harm is an aspect of constitutional liberty. The Court pointed out, however, that every state provides tort remedies for excessive corporal punishment and held that these, "[i]n view of the low incidence of abuse, [and] the openness of our schools," provided due process of law. As in *Paul*, the Court was concerned that recognizing a constitutional tort in such a case "would . . . entail a significant intrusion into an area of primary educational responsibility."

In *Baker v. McCollan* the plaintiff had been mistakenly named in an arrest warrant and as a result spent several days in jail. The Court denied his constitutional tort claim because the arrest was made pursuant to a constitutionally valid warrant and he was held for only a few days. In these circumstances, his deprivation of liberty was brought about pursuant to due process of law. The Court distinguished constitutional tort from common law false imprisonment and stressed that the plaintiff may have a good claim "under a tort-law analysis," but that this would not be enough for a constitutional claim. The Court never indicated what additional factors might give a false imprisonment claim constitutional dimension.

The most recent and the most important Supreme Court case is *Parratt v. Taylor*. The plaintiff was a prison inmate who sued prison officials on the ground that they had lost some hobby materials belonging to him. In the lower courts the plaintiff successfully argued that the defendants' negligence deprived him of property without due process of law. The Supreme Court agreed that the plaintiff had shown a deprivation of property under the fourteenth amendment, but nonetheless denied his claim because he had not shown that the deprivation was without due process. Relying in part on *Ingraham*, the Court held that due process was served by a state law remedy available to the prisoner. Echoing *Paul*, the Court said that granting constitutional status to the plaintiff's claim "would almost necessarily result in turning every alleged injury which may have been inflicted by a state official . . . into a violation of the Fourteenth Amendment." As in *Paul*, the Court resisted making the due process clause such a "'font of tort law to be superimposed'" on state systems.

B. Understanding Parratt

The foregoing discussion illustrates the Supreme Court's determination to maintain a distinction between common law and constitutional torts. The need to define clearly the boundary between the two stems from two related considerations. The first of these is the concern that courts not ignore principles of federalism. Most constitutional tort actions are brought in federal court and seek to impose federal constitutional obligations on state and local officials. Constitutional tort necessarily intrudes upon the traditional sovereign prerogative of a state to define for itself the tort rules governing its conduct. Maintaining the boundary between common law and constitutional tort, and keeping the latter within narrow limits, helps to reduce federal intrusions upon state autonomy.

Respect for the principles of federalism, however, provides only a partial explanation for the Court's holdings. Federal officials are also subject to constitutional tort liability. While federalism plays no significant role in this context, the importance of separating common law from constitutional tort remains. The importance of making the separation may be understood as part of the broader concern for preserving discretion and diversity in the development of tort law. The due process clause, fears the Court, could engulf all torts committed by all government officials. Such a development would unduly infringe upon the legitimate exercise of legislative and judicial discretion in the shaping of tort rules since constitutional tort cannot be modified by state law. For that reason alone, constitutional tort is inherently less flexible. Furthermore, the extent to which government should be held liable for torts is a matter over which there is considerable disagreement. States with differing positions on the issue are free to adopt different tort rules under common law, but would be bound by a national standard under constitutional tort.

In counterbalance to these concerns for federalism and state discretion lies the plaintiff's interest in being made whole for government-inflicted injuries. By focusing on the similarities between the common law and constitutional claims, however, the Supreme Court has implicitly concluded that common law tort can adequately protect this interest. When there are state law mechanisms for dealing with such claims, the effect of permitting constitutional tort recoveries would be to abrogate state prerogatives and arguably expand the fourteenth amendment further than necessary. Accordingly, the Court in *Parratt* held that constitutional tort will not be available when an "adequate" state remedy is available.

This approach to constitutional tort is superficially plausible because it appears to make an appropriate compromise between the conflicting interests. Problems become apparent, though, upon closer scrutiny. While the *Parratt* solution is potentially an innovative step toward an accommodation, it is fatally flawed as presently articulated. The innovation is in allocating the bulk of decision making to state courts. The objection is that the Court has not yet indicated what, if any, constitutional restrictions it will place on the state tort rules used to decide these cases. The opinion fails to distinguish adequately between the forum in which due process constitutional tort claims will be heard and the substantive law that will govern such claims. For this reason, *Parratt* does not speak at all to the scope problem.

1. Parratt and the Supplemental Remedy Doctrine. In order to place our objection to *Parratt* in proper perspective, it is useful to examine the Court's innovation in funnelling cases to state courts. The cardinal principle of constitutional tort, established twenty years ago in *Monroe v. Pape*, is that an injured person can sue in federal court under section 1983 even if state law provides a remedy for the government conduct of which he complains. The plaintiffs in *Monroe* brought a constitutional tort action against several policemen who had broken into the plaintiffs' home without a warrant and forced them to stand naked while the officers ransacked the house. One of the plaintiffs was taken to the police station and interrogated for ten hours before being released. He was never charged with a crime. The defendants' conduct violated state law as well as the dictates of the fourth amendment. It was also clear that state tort law provided a "simple remedy" that would give "that full redress which the common law affords for violence done to a person."

In his dissent, Justice Frankfurter urged that state law alone should control this action. He foresaw that treating the claim as a constitutional tort would mandate the establishment of a federally generated body of tort law. This development, he warned, would greatly intrude on a traditional domain of state sovereignty. The values of federalism would be better served if this claim were left to state courts and state law for redress. Justice Douglas, speaking for the majority, was undeterred. "It is no answer that the State has a law which if enforced would give relief. The federal remedy is supplementary to the state remedy, and the latter need not be first sought and refused before the federal one is invoked."

Parratt is seemingly inconsistent with *Monroe*. *Monroe* finds co-existing state remedies irrelevant to the constitutional claim, while *Parratt* finds them dispositive. While the tension between the two cases is clear, they may be reconciled with one another. In *Monroe*, the plaintiff asserted a violation of a specific provision of the Bill of Rights, the fourth amendment. The plaintiff in *Parratt*, on the other hand, relied solely on the due process clause of the fourteenth amendment. The danger of constitutional tort taking over matters best left to the common law is greater when the claim asserts a general injury to life, liberty, or property than when a more specific constitutional right like freedom from illegal searches and seizures is at issue.

This difference with respect to constitutional tort policy can be stated in terms of a more technical distinction between the cases. The ruling in *Monroe* was a construction of the Civil Rights Act, 42 U.S.C. § 1983. The *Monroe* Court held that, if the plaintiff alleged a constitutional violation by a state officer, that violation was committed "under color of" state law within the terms of the statute, even though state law made it illegal and provided a remedy. In *Parratt* the Court held that deprivations of property are not constitutional violations at all when a state remedial scheme is provided. For in that event, there is no deprivation "without due process of law" within the terms of the fourteenth amendment. In short, the *Parratt* Court brings its holding into harmony with *Monroe* by taking state remedies into account in determining whether the plaintiff has shown a constitutional violation, and not whether an established violation is "under color of" state law under the statute.

2. *Parratt : Allocative or Substantive?* Holding that the existence of state remedies will preclude constitutional tort appears to limit the scope of constitutional protection provided to life, liberty, and property interests. But the extent to which *Parratt* has that effect depends on what the Court decides adequate state remedies include. Consider the facts of *Parratt.* Nebraska provided redress for negligent loss of property by the state, and the Court deemed this to be an adequate state remedy. If the Court meant to imply that a state is constitutionally required to make the plaintiff whole upon his proving that the state negligently lost the plaintiff's property, then the primary effect of *Parratt* would be allocational. It would route claims to state courts to be decided under state law meeting federal standards of adequacy. If these standards compel a recovery, then state tort law would provide just as much protection as constitutional tort. Under this reading of *Parratt,* the due process clause would shape state tort law in a fashion analogous to the role played by the first amendment in state libel law. Just as the first amendment restricts the protection provided public figures under state libel law, so would the due process clause expand state law protection against government-inflicted injuries to life, liberty, and property.

On the other hand, if *Parratt* does not require that the plaintiff be made whole, then its effects are more substantive. Several lower courts have interpreted *Parratt* to mean that a state remedy is adequate even if it grants immunities to all the defendants. If these cases are correct, then the scope of constitutional protection of life, liberty, and property could be very narrow. *Parratt* would not only allocate cases to state forums, but would also constitutionally sanction the formulation of substantive state tort law that could leave uncompensated those injured by government action.

The scope of constitutional tort thus depends on what state remedies the Court will require to meet the "adequacy" test of *Parratt.* The problem with the opinion is that the Court provided no standards, and gave no hints, on how this question should be answered. The Court approved of Nebraska's torts claims procedure, but that is the easy case for adequacy. The Court never declared that a state *must* grant redress to a plaintiff who can prove a deprivation of life, liberty, or property. Nor did it examine the scope a state might give to sovereign, municipal, and official immunities against suit. In *Parratt,* the Court never came to grips with the question of whether the due process clause places substantive limitations on a government's power to injure life, liberty, or property without recompense.

C. Substantive and Procedural Due Process

The ambiguity resulting from the *Parratt* Court's failure to elaborate on its adequate state remedies rule can also be described as a failure to articulate whether the holding is a ruling on procedural due process or substantive due process or both. This failure makes the opinion virtually worthless as a guide to the scope of constitutional tort. The Court stated its decision as a ruling on due process, but the due process clauses of the fifth and fourteenth amendments have both a procedural and a substantive component. Procedural due process concerns the method by which government deprives a person of life, liberty, or property. Due process in this context is designed to insure that governmental intrusions upon constitutionally protected interests are accompanied by fair procedures. As recognized by the Court, the objective of "procedural due process is to convey to the individual a feeling that the government has dealt with him fairly as well as to minimize the risk of mistaken deprivations of protected interests."

Substantive due process is a more stringent limit on state power. It protects the individual against certain government actions regardless of the fairness of the procedure used to implement them. Just as the first amendment renders the federal government powerless to prohibit peaceful picketing in front of the Supreme Court, the due process clause prevents states from imposing criminal sanctions for the performance of first trimester abortions. Criminal abortion laws are unconstitutional not because they are attended by unfair procedures, but because the Constitution does not grant government the power to interfere with this aspect of liberty.

The Court in its scope cases often has left unclear which aspect of the due process clause it was examining. Some parts of the opinions read as though the only issue before the Court was whether proper procedures were followed in depriving the plaintiff of liberty or property. *Ingraham v. Wright* is the clearest example. There the plaintiff, having lost in the Fifth Circuit, petitioned for certiorari on three grounds: that severe corporal punishment in public schools violated the eighth amendment cruel and unusual punishments clause, that the absence of any hearing before being punished violated the fourteenth amendment guarantee of procedural due process, and that the punishment itself offended substantive due process. The Court granted review on only the first two issues. The Court's subsequent rejection of the plaintiff's due process claim therefore must be understood in strictly procedural terms. What the Court decided was that a student need not be accorded any prepaddling procedural safeguards to assure that the punishment is justified. Rather, in view of the openness of the public schools and the low incidence of abuse of students, state tort remedies were a sufficient check on the unjustified imposition of corporal punishment. The Court did not decide that there were no substantive constitutional limits on the infliction of corporal punishment in public schools.

In *Paul v. Davis* the Supreme Court rejected constitutional protection for the plaintiff's interest in reputation. To attain constitutional status, the Court said, an interest must "have been initially recognized and protected by state law," and reputation did not meet that standard. This reasoning strongly suggests that the Court's holding is a substantive decision denying any constitutional protection to reputation. In a footnote, however, the Court stated that the decision "is limited to the procedural guarantees of the due process clause" and does not address "those substantive limitations on state action which may be encompassed within the concept of 'liberty' expressed in the Fourteenth Amendment." The Court apparently meant that there is no constitutional requirement of notice or a hearing before the police can defame someone, but that it was not deciding whether or not there are any substantive constitutional limits on government power to ruin someone's reputation. While the Court never openly stated its holding in these terms, it is hard to see how the footnote can be reconciled with the rest of the opinion on any other basis.

The holding in *Baker v. McCollan* was that a person held in jail for three days because of mistaken identity was not deprived of liberty without due process of law. While the opinion did not distinguish between procedural and substantive due process, many of the reasons the Court gave to support the decision suggest that the Court was concerned with procedure. The Court pointed out that "[t]he Fourteenth Amendment does not protect against all deprivations of liberty," but only against those "accomplished without due process of law." This distinction is important only to the procedural side of the doctrine, for the import of a substantive due process ruling is that certain aspects of liberty cannot be taken under any circumstances, no matter what process is followed. The Court noted that the confinement was pursuant to a valid warrant under the fourth amendment and that both the speedy trial provisions of the sixth amendment and the bail clause of the eighth amendment would help prevent lengthy incarceration without a determination of guilt. This reasoning suggests the Court was holding that the plaintiff's deprivation of liberty was in accordance with constitutionally valid procedures.

Notice, however, that the plaintiff also could have made a substantive due process claim on the facts of *Baker*. His case can be stated not only as a claim that bad procedures were responsible for his confinement, but also that the Constitution requires that he be made whole for *any* mistaken incarceration regardless of the procedures used. The Court's ruling against the plaintiff seems implicitly to reject this claim. Since the Court did not directly address the issue, however, *Baker* should not be viewed as holding that a mistaken imprisonment could never support a substantive due process claim. Indeed, Justice Blackmun's concurring opinion explicitly noted that the majority did not address the substantive due process issue. Accordingly, the scope of substantive constitutional protection of liberty remains an open question after *Baker*.

In *Parratt v. Taylor*, the Court once more confused the procedural and substantive due process issues. The plaintiff's claim was first phrased by the Court in terms sufficiently broad to address both procedural and substantive due process. The Court stated the issue as "the correct manner in which to analyze claims . . . which allege facts that are commonly thought to state a claim for a common-law tort . . . but instead are couched in terms of a constitutional deprivation . . . . " Shortly thereafter, however, the issue was recast as "whether the tort remedies which the State of Nebraska provides as a means of redress for property deprivations satisfy *procedural* due process." Justices White, Blackmun, and Powell separately expressed their understanding that *Parratt* is limited to questions of procedural due process.

Despite the Court's characterization of the issue, it is exceedingly difficult to see any procedural element in the plaintiff's claim in *Parratt*. Procedural due process is required when the state attempts to advance its interests by intruding upon an individual's life, liberty, or property. It is conceded in these cases that the state may constitutionally interfere with liberty to achieve certain ends. As suggested in *Ingraham v. Wright* and *Paul v. Davis*, for example, corporal punishment may help maintain order in the classroom, and warning merchants of suspected thieves may help reduce levels of crime. Various safeguards might be required, nevertheless, under the rubric of procedural due process in order to reduce the risk of unjustifiable paddling or labeling. By contrast, the defendants in *Parratt* did not take the prisoner's property to achieve some state interest, and the issue was not whether proper procedural safeguards were followed in deciding to take that property. Rather, the defendants negligently lost the property with no claim of justification, and the only genuine question was whether such a negligent deprivation of property stated a claim in constitutional tort to be made whole for the loss. To speak of procedural due process in this context is to do violence to the common understanding of that term and lose sight of its function in constitutional law.

Even so, the Court's reasoning in *Parratt* makes use of procedural due process caselaw. An understanding of those cases and why they are inapposite requires a bit of background. Procedural due process usually demands that the government grant "some kind of hearing" to the individual before deliberately depriving him of liberty or property. Thus, some process is required before firing a tenured professor, suspending a student from school, or cutting off such government benefits as social security. There are, however, exceptional cases where predeprivation hearings are impractical. For example, the immediate need to stop poisoning justifies confiscating suspect food without a prior hearing. In such instances, the Court has held that due process has been satisfied by a post-deprivation hearing. In *Ingraham v. Wright* the Court pushed this principle a step further. It held that a state tort remedy could provide adequate procedural protection for the student's interest in avoiding unjustified corporal punishment. The Court's rationale appears to be that the threat of tort liability encourages school officials to act more carefully in deciding whether to paddle students. Potential tort liability thus acts as a surrogate for a prepunishment hearing to reduce the risk of unwarranted punishment.

Parratt relies on *Ingraham* and the more conventional post-deprivation remedy cases in holding that a post-deprivation tort remedy satisfies the due process clause when the plaintiff claims negligent loss of property. This rationale strongly indicates that the Court conceived of the issue as a procedural one. The problem with the Court's approach is that the plaintiff's claim in *Parratt* was fundamentally different from the claim in *Ingraham* and the other cases. In those cases, the underlying premise was that the state is constitutionally authorized to take the plaintiff's property or bodily security, if the state does so upon a proper showing of justification. The procedural due process issue was deciding what process is constitutionally required in order to determine whether a sufficient justification exists. In *Parratt* the claim did not proceed from the premise that the deprivation might be justified on proper facts, but that a negligent loss of property is always a constitutional wrong. It is as if, on the facts of *Ingraham*, the plaintiff argued that paddling, or paddling of a certain severity, could never be administered because it is a violation of his personal security guaranteed by the substantive fourteenth amendment right to liberty. The plaintiff made just this claim in *Ingraham*, but the Court declined to consider it.

When one focuses on the substantive due process deprivation of property issue in *Parratt*, it becomes apparent that the hard question is whether the state is constitutionally required to compensate a plaintiff who can prove that the state negligently lost or destroyed his property, or whether the state instead can avoid liability by adopting immunity rules or other principles similar in effect. As explained earlier, the Court was able to avoid dealing with this issue because the state law in question did provide a remedy in such circumstances. The effect of the case, therefore, is to leave the scope issue just as clouded as it was before the decision.

III. A Substantive Due Process Approach to the Boundary Problem

The Court in *Paul*, *Ingraham*, *Baker*, and *Parratt* never squarely faced the problem of determining the scope of constitutional tort. The Court's procedural due process analysis and cautionary footnotes enabled it to dispose of the cases without addressing the questions of whether and in what circumstances a government defendant must compensate a victim for physical or other injuries in constitutional tort, even though that defendant has violated no specific provision of the Bill of Rights. Lacking guidance, the lower federal courts have had to cope with the problem on their own and have failed to reach a consensus on how these questions should be answered.

The remainder of the Article puts aside the Supreme Court's opinions and examines the scope problem from a fresh perspective. In Part III we argue that substantive due process is the appropriate doctrinal category for defining the scope of constitutional tort. Taking substantive due process as our starting point, we identify the questions that must be addressed and the competing values that must be ranked or accommodated in resolving the scope issue.

A. *Substantive Due Process and Tort Damages*

The inmate whose property is destroyed, the mistakenly imprisoned suspect, and the paddled student all assert claims that are more accurately characterized as substantive rather than procedural. These plaintiffs contend that the physical, emotional, or dignitary harm they suffer is itself a constitutional wrong, however proper is the procedure used to inflict that harm. For this reason, the appropriate constitutional doctrine for considering their claims is not procedural but substantive due process.

At first this may seem a surprising conclusion, for constitutional torts appear to bear little resemblance to the typical substantive due process case. That doctrine is ordinarily invoked as a defense against criminal prosecutions or similar government actions. Substantive due process is the Supreme Court's instrument for invalidating statutes that do not violate any of the express prohibitions listed in the Bill of Rights, but that threaten fundamental values, including personal autonomy "in making certain types of important decisions," that the Court deems worthy of constitutional protection. Thus, the Court has struck down laws forbidding abortions or the use of contraceptives and certain laws regulating marriage and family life. The right that is recognized in these decisions is rooted in the due process clause, but it is not a procedural right. The "right" to an abortion, like the first amendment right to publish a newspaper, is a substantive right against government interference in one's activities. Although it is verbally awkward to employ the due process clause as the foundation for these rules, the Court plainly believes that they are important enough to warrant this contortion of language.

Our assertion is that claims for damages in tort can also appropriately be viewed as substantive due process cases because here too the party challenges the constitutional validity of some government action. There are two differences between constitutional tort damages and traditional substantive due process, but neither of these is strong enough to overshadow the fundamental similarity between them. First, a distinction may be drawn on the nature of the remedy sought by the plaintiff. In the traditional cases, the government is trying to imprison or otherwise penalize the individual by using the legal process, and the plaintiff invokes substantive due process as a defense to the threatened government action. The defensive use of constitutional rights is adequate in this context to protect him against government overreaching. In the tort context, the government actor has already hurt the plaintiff, and the only possible remedy (apart from criminal or administrative penalties) is to award damages to make him whole for his injury. The difference, then, is that in tort the individual is *made* whole, while in the traditional case he is *kept* whole. This distinction merely reflects the different ways in which government might improperly harm someone.

The other difference relates to the type of analysis that is employed in the two areas. The terms of the debate in traditional substantive due process analysis are familiar to all students of constitutional law. The state by its legislature seeks to impose some obligation on the individual in pursuit of the public good. It argues that in a democracy its accountability to the voters is all the justification the program requires, in the absence of conflict with the specific substantive provisions of the Bill of Rights. The individual responds that substantive "liberty" in the due process clause embraces more than the Bill of Rights and includes the right of autonomy in personal decision making and the right of families to be free of certain forms of state regulation. Broadly stated, the court's task is to choose between democratic values and the competing claims of personal or familial autonomy.

The analytical structure of a constitutional tort case varies from this pattern because of the differences in the factual circumstances that give rise to tort suits. In the tort context the government actor has already injured the individual in some way, as by defaming, or physically attacking, or imprisoning him. Unlike the criminal defendant, the tort plaintiff does not assert autonomy in personal decision making as the counterweight to government discretion. Rather, he claims that the government has invaded his interest in physical or emotional well-being, or reputation, or personal privacy, or property. The task of the court is to identify the circumstances in which these interests warrant constitutional protection.

The Supreme Court decision in *Rochin v. California* links traditional substantive due process doctrine with this new strain. In *Rochin*, the defendant had been suspected of selling narcotics. When confronted by the police he swallowed a number of capsules. After unsuccessfully attempting to retrieve the capsules by hand, the police forcibly extracted them from the defendant's stomach and introduced them as evidence at the defendant's trial. The Supreme Court, reversing the conviction, held that the government's conduct in obtaining the evidence violated the due process clause. Due process was denied because the forced stomach pumping "offend[ed] those canons of decency and fairness which express the notions of justice of English-speaking peoples even toward those charged with the most heinous offenses." In a phrase that has endured as a shorthand for the holding, the Court said that the government's conduct "shocks the conscience."

Here, then, is a hybrid case. The government's conduct involves the infliction of physical, emotional, and dignitary injury ordinarily remedied in tort, yet the Court permitted *Rochin* to use that conduct as a due process defense to a criminal prosecution. It seems even more appropriate to allow a suit for tort damages based on the constitutional violation, for then the remedy is more directly tied to the breach and society's interest in criminal punishment is not denied on account of the policemen's errors. Only the absence of this last step separates *Rochin* from our substantive due process approach to harm to life, liberty, and property.

The usual differences in context between tort and defensive cases mean that most traditional substantive due process precedents will be inapposite in the tort context. Yet the essential unity of the two variants of substantive due process remains. In both areas, the basic question is the same: Within the universe of state actions that harm individuals, which of those actions should the Court proscribe as deprivations of constitutionally protected life, liberty, or property, and which should be left for the states to grant or deny remedies for at their discretion? Stated in institutional terms, the issue in both kinds of cases is when, if ever, should the courts make constitutional rules that nullify the choices of politically responsive governments with regard to social policy and when should courts leave those choices standing.

B. *Asking the Right Questions*

Recognizing that substantive due process is the appropriate doctrinal category is only the first step toward resolving the boundary problem. The next step is to identify the competing individual and governmental interests at stake in these tort suits, rank them in order of importance, and search for ways to accommodate them. This is a contemporary instance of the classic problem in constitutional law of individual liberty against the state. The plaintiff's interest in support of liability is compensation for physical, emotional, or dignitary harm inflicted by the government actor. The government counters that its financial resources would be unduly strained by the imposition of liability. Moreover, if individual officers are held liable, argues the government, they will be reluctant to take actions that might risk tort liability, and they, therefore, might become too cautious in carrying out their duties. Finally, as in other conflicts over the scope of constitutional rights, government defendants can invoke the principle that, in a representative democracy, policy conflicts generally should be resolved by politically responsive legislatures rather than by courts. Some special justification is needed to warrant judicial intervention under the Constitution since such decisions cannot be overturned by legislation.

A strong proponent of either set of values can resolve the scope problem without much further analysis. By giving great weight to the individual's interest in recovery, constitutional tort can be justified for any personal injury caused by government. Similarly, advocates of government discretion and strong legislatures can defend a narrow scope for constitutional tort. It is likely, however, that neither of these extreme positions would receive wide support. In our view, a better approach, therefore, is to adopt a more pragmatic view, to acknowledge that both individual and government concerns are valid and should be accommodated. The task thus becomes one of identifying the kinds of cases in which the plaintiff's interests are strong enough to overcome the countervailing government interests. By focusing on this inquiry, it is possible to fashion decisional guidelines that permit some of these injuries to be treated as constitutional torts, while leaving others to state tort systems.

1. The Plaintiff's Interest. The plaintiff's interest in recovery for damage to his property and for physical, emotional, and dignitary harm is a concept familiar to every first-year law student. It is the basis for the plaintiff's claim in virtually all areas of common law tort. If, however, the plaintiff's interest is taken into account by ordinary tort law, why should a plaintiff ever be allowed to sue in constitutional tort? The problem with this question is that it rests on a faulty premise. The question assumes that the interests at stake in substantive due process constitutional tort litigation are identical to those at issue in common law tort suits. Compensation for the kinds of harm cognizable in common law tort is only one of the plaintiff's interests in constitutional tort suits, and the common law might not give adequate respect even to this interest in traditional tort damages.

One difference between governmental and private tort flows from the special role of government as the keeper of public order. Because of that role, statutes and common law rules accord government actors broad discretion to use force without fear of civil or criminal liability. Individuals generally acquiesce in governmental threats and use of force in circumstances where they might either resist or flee or turn to government for help if similarly threatened or harmed by some private person. For this reason, victims are more vulnerable to the exercise of illegitimate or excessive force by government actors. The individual will often be less willing and less able to resist or escape a beating inflicted by a police officer than, for example, a beating inflicted by a drunk in a bar.

There is another, more subtle, reason why governmental injuries sometimes warrant the imposition of constitutional tort liability. A government actor can violate a different kind of duty from that owed by a private defendant. Individuals in our society are largely left free to pursue their own ends without regard for others, save a general duty not to hurt others by negligent conduct. The relationship between government and the individual is radically different. In a free society government is neither an autonomous actor nor a master to whom the people must acquiesce. The function of government is to serve the people and to enhance the conditions of life. The broad purpose of all constitutional limits on government power is to try to ensure that government does not stray from that role.

A fundamental aspect of the concept of government as servant is that the government must treat individuals with some minimal level of concern and respect for their well-being, even when it has good reason for doing them some harm. Abusive conduct by a government actor violates this duty, and it is, therefore, appropriate to employ constitutional law to impose sanctions for such conduct. *Rochin v. California* is the Supreme Court case that most clearly supports this proposition. Recall that there the Court cited "those canons of decency and fairness which express the notions of justice of English-speaking peoples even toward those charged with the most heinous offenses" as constitutional grounds for striking down a conviction.

Other substantive due process cases deal with a different kind of problem and are only obliquely relevant to constitutional tort. Even so, there are echoes in them of this emphasis on governmental sensitivity toward persons. For example, in *Meyer v. Nebraska* the Supreme Court struck down a statute forbidding the teaching of foreign languages in private schools on the ground that constitutional liberty embraces "not merely freedom from bodily restraint but also the right of the individual to . . . enjoy those privileges long recognized at common law as essential to the orderly pursuit of happiness by free men." Among those privileges, the Court concluded, is the right to study what one pleases. *Griswold v. Connecticut* invalidated laws forbidding the sale of contraceptives because the marital relationship is "intimate to the degree of being sacred" and the law sought "to achieve its goals by means having a maximum destructive impact on that relationship."

These considerations persuade us that the courts should recognize a constitutional right against some harms inflicted by governments and their officers. Even so, a critic of our proposal might point out that state law often provides adequate protection to these concerns and argue that this protection renders the constitutional right superfluous. An illustration is the common law rule that permits police officers to use force in apprehending suspects, but holds them liable if the force used is excessive. Given the availability of such a remedy, the argument goes, constitutional tort is a redundant and unnecessary intrusion upon an area of the law ordinarily left to the states. One response to this argument is that the general adequacy of state remedies is open to question. Dissenting in *Ingraham*, for example, Justice White questioned the efficacy of Florida's state law remedies for excessive corporal punishment. Furthermore, a formally adequate state rule may be devalued by onerous procedural rules and unsympathetic fact-finding.

Suppose, however, that a state's tort law does permit recovery for abuse of government power, both in principle and in practice. This may be a good reason to require the plaintiff to pursue his remedy in state court under state law, but it does not defeat the proposition that those courts should recognize a constitutional right to recovery and be subject to Supreme Court review of state judgments for compliance with the constitutional standard. The assertion that state law is "adequate" implicitly recognizes that state law must be measured by its effectiveness in meeting the constitutional concerns we have identified. It confuses ends with means to go further and argue that the state remedy renders the constitutional right itself superfluous.

2. *Limitations on the Reach of the Plaintiff's Interest.* Of course it does not follow that constitutional tort is appropriate for every injury that might be recognized by the common law of torts. On the contrary, the plaintiff's interest in concern and respect from government is both a justification for constitutional tort and a limit on its reach. In defining the boundary of constitutional tort, courts should not focus their attention exclusively on the plaintiff's interest in recovery for physical harm. Rather, courts should ask whether the circumstances of a given case indicate a threat to concern and respect. Only an affirmative answer to this question will justify imposing constitutional tort liability.

This requirement sharply distinguishes constitutional tort from traditional tort law. Common law courts and legislatures may consider a wide variety of policy considerations in fashioning liability rules.

They may take as their guiding concern, for example, the compensation of victims and the widest possible spreading of losses. In that event the scope of recovery will be broad, with few defenses available to defendants, such as governments, who can spread losses. On the other hand, decision makers may choose to adopt tort rules that minimize the cost of accidents and encourage accident avoidance. Lawmakers with this aim might come up with a radically different set of rules that grant or deny recovery in order to give the plaintiff or defendant an incentive to take a cost-justified precaution.

Determining the scope of constitutional tort requires the identification of cases in which statutory and common law policy choices should be abrogated and replaced with constitutional rules establishing a right to recovery that is largely beyond political change. The only appropriate justification for rejecting statutory and common law liability rules is that they do not adequately respect the individual's claims to have and to hold life, liberty, and property against intrusions by the state. This standard places significant limitations on the permissible scope of constitutional tort. A constitutional tort obligation should not be adopted because it facilitates loss spreading or cost reduction since these goals do not bear on the individual's rights of autonomy against the state.

3. The Defendant's Conduct. What matters in constitutional tort, then, is whether the defendant's conduct has passed the boundary of acceptable governmental behavior toward individuals and not merely whether the plaintiff has been harmed, or how severely. The Supreme Court in *Rochin v. California* intuitively understood this point, although it did not develop the underlying analysis. The Court articulated a "shock the conscience" standard for invalidating convictions under the due process clause and held that the forcible stomach pumping in that case met the standard. As our analysis suggests, the *Rochin* approach focuses the inquiry on whether the defendant's conduct is bad enough to justify a constitutional sanction. The only difference between the Court's holding and constitutional tort is that in *Rochin* the sanction involved permitting the individual to use the government's conduct as a defense in a criminal proceeding, while constitutional tort allows the individual to sue for damages.

The Supreme Court has never formally taken that last analytical step, but several lower federal courts have done so. The most influential decision is the Second Circuit's ruling in *Johnson v. Glick*. In *Glick*, the plaintiff was a pretrial detainee who allegedly was attacked by a correctional official and then denied medical attention. The court held that, while these allegations did not state a claim under the eighth amendment, they stated a good substantive due process violation and could support an award of tort damages. Judge Friendly, writing for the court, explained that *Rochin* "must stand for the proposition that, quite apart from any 'specific' of the Bill of Rights, application of undue force by law enforcement officers deprives a suspect of liberty without due process of law." The challenge of *Rochin* and *Glick* is to articulate the precise guidelines for determining when a substantive due process violation exists. It is to this task that we now turn.

IV. Four Principles for Deciding Boundary Cases

Rochin is right to focus on the defendant's conduct in deciding whether constitutional tort should be available, but the Court's "shock the conscience" test is too vague and subjective to provide guidance for lower courts deciding particular cases. The development of more concrete standards has been retarded in the Supreme Court by the Court's continued refusal to confront the scope issue directly. Although lower courts have not evaded the problem, their efforts to deal with it suffer from the Supreme Court's lack of leadership. Their standards in constitutional tort cases, therefore, are often as vague as the *Rochin* test. Courts state that constitutional tort should be available not for every injury cognizable at common law, but only when there is an "abuse" or "misuse" of power, or when the governmental defendant's conduct was "severe," "reprehensible," or "egregious." Using these characterizations to explain their rulings, the courts have held that constitutional tort is appropriate when a passive arrestee is shot, beaten, or threatened, when a prison guard deliberately permits a group of prisoners to attack another inmate, or when a prison guard intentionally destroys the prisoner's radio. They have rejected constitutional tort liability for a government's negligently designed streets, for slippery prison floors, and for breach of contract. Yet even this vague "egregiousness" standard is not uniformly followed. Some courts rule that mere negligence is enough for liability, while others say that even malicious or severe intentional harm is not cognizable in constitutional tort.

We propose four specific standards for resolving the boundary issue. Constitutional tort should be available: (1) when the defendant acts with an impermissible motive or ill will toward the plaintiff, (2) when his intrusion on the plaintiff is unreasonably disproportionate to the legitimate goal that intrusion serves, (3) when the defendant's recklessness causes injury to a plaintiff under substantial control by the state, or (4) when a defendant recklessly harms a plaintiff not under state supervision. In our view, these standards identify the cases in which the defendant's conduct is bad enough to justify overriding statutory and common law to recognize constitutional tort.

Our confidence in these principles is bolstered by our examination of the lower court caselaw. Many of the results in the cases can be squared with our proposals, even if the opinions themselves often offer little or no reasoning to support those results. Some of the more thoughtful opinions do articulate these or similar standards, but even those opinions do not offer a very elaborate defense for the standards. An example is the opinion in *Johnson v. Glick*, the often-cited case in which the Second Circuit relied on *Rochin* to permit a pretrial detainee to maintain a constitutional tort action for abusive treatment. Writing for the court, Judge Friendly declared:

> In determining whether the constitutional line has been crossed, a court must look to such factors as the need for the application of force, the relationship between the need and the amount of force that was used, the extent of injury inflicted, and whether force was applied in a good faith effort to maintain or restore discipline or maliciously and sadistically for the very purpose of causing harm.

Note that these standards are similar to the first two of our proposed principles, except for the court's use of "the extent of the injury inflicted" as a criterion for recovery. The problem with the opinion is that Judge Friendly does not explain how he got from the "shock the conscience" test of *Rochin* to these more specific standards. As a result, the merits of the *Glick* approach can easily be overlooked by courts that lack Judge Friendly's intuitive perception and do not have the time or inclination to develop an analytical defense of the standards. The analysis presented in Part III supporting substantive due process and in Part IV concerning specific rules for deciding cases demonstrates that the *Glick* standards do not rest on intuition alone.

At the same time, the *Glick* guidelines are themselves open to two criticisms. First, the court's "extent of the injury inflicted" test should be rejected. Second, and more important, the standards should not be viewed as "factors" to be weighed on a case-by-case basis. Rather, a bad motive should by itself be a sufficient condition for a court to apply constitutional tort, as should disproportion between force and justification. Recklessness should also suffice for liability, at least in situations where the government has control over the plaintiff, and perhaps more generally. This recklessness standard is not mentioned by *Glick*. As one court recently noted, the *Glick* formulation is not much of an improvement over *Rochin* when the criteria are viewed as "factors." It "does not instruct the factfinder as to how much weight should be given to each factor." Instead, the question whether "the constitutional line has been crossed . . . is left ultimately to the discretion of the factfinder." We explain each of these objections in the course of defending our own approach in the ensuing sections.

Our principles not only identify cases that ought to receive constitutional status; they also exclude from constitutional tort many cases that are actionable under the common law by denying constitutional status to harms caused by mere negligence. Before discussing cases that should be accorded constitutional treatment, we explain why negligence and strict liability are not sufficient justifications.

A. *Negligence and Strict Liability*

The common law ordinarily imposes liability when a private defendant negligently causes harm and sometimes even holds him strictly liable, as when he employs a negligent worker, or manufactures a defective product, or engages in an abnormally dangerous activity. Often, however, government officials are effectively shielded from liability for negligence by state law good faith immunity rules as well as other obstacles to recovery. This scheme raises the question of whether constitutional tort liability should be imposed on the defendant under a negligence, or even a strict liability standard in order to guarantee that the injured plaintiff can recover in spite of state law. One reading of the ambiguous opinion in *Parratt v. Taylor* is that the negligent defendant must pay damages because a state tort remedy which does not permit recovery will be deemed "inadequate" to satisfy due process. Justice Powell, concurring in the result, read the opinion this way and so have a number of lower federal courts. Relying on *Parratt*, they have ruled that negligence is sufficient to establish constitutional tort liability.

Viewed from the perspective of substantive due process, the case for a constitutional tort claim for negligent harm is unconvincing. One of the major arguments for negligence (and strict liability) is that such a standard is necessary to give the defendant proper incentives to take cost-justified, economically correct precautions. This rationale lacks independent force in constitutional tort since the policy of minimizing accident and accident-avoidance costs has no constitutional underpinning. The case for constitutional tort must be based on the plaintiff's interest in freedom from government intrusions onto his person or property. This interest is present whenever he suffers an injury, but it is not *especially* strong when the defendant is merely negligent.

Consider some of the principles of negligence law. Negligence is an objective standard of care that is met whenever the defendant's conduct does not measure up to that of the mythical reasonable person. Typically, it does not imply a moral judgment of blameworthiness. It does not denote ill will or subjective lack of concern for the plaintiff's welfare, and it cannot support an award of punitive damages signifying societal disapproval of the defendant. When the plaintiff carelessly disregards his own safety, recovery of even compensatory damages will be diminished or barred entirely. More or less arbitrary rules of proximate cause and concededly arbitrary limits on damages for emotional harm further restrict recovery for negligence. All of these principles operate even when the plaintiff's injuries are severe. Taken together, these principles show that negligence is not commonly viewed as a particularly grave intrusion on the victim. Mislaying an inmate's property, failing to enforce the speed limit, and building dangerous streets are rather far removed from the Constitution's focus on individual autonomy against abuse of government power. This kind of government conduct shows no particular lack of concern and respect for the individual.

At the same time, there is a strong argument against negligence liability for government officials. Unlike private individuals, public servants cannot capture for themselves the benefits of efficient government. They will likely be paid the same whether or not they save money by cutting out wasteful safety measures. For this reason, their incentives will be skewed toward taking too many precautions. They know that if they do not take a reasonable precaution, they can be held liable for damages. This consequence gives them an incentive to take every safety measure that a jury, acting with hindsight, might decide a reasonable person would take. Government officials, however, feel a much weaker incentive to stop taking precautions when they are no longer cost-justified, as the officials themselves neither pay the cost of the safety measure nor capture the efficiency gained if it is eliminated. They will probably take too many precautions, and government will be less effective than it should be in pursuing wholly legitimate aims. Whether or not this "overdeterrence" argument is empirically true, it is plausible enough to warrant leaving the policy judgment on negligence liability to legislators and common law judicial decisions and not to decide it by an inflexible constitutional tort rule.

B. *Recklessness and Deliberate Indifference*

In the common law, where negligence is almost always enough for liability, courts usually pay little attention to precise formulations of the more extreme forms of negligence—gross negligence, recklessness, and wilful and wanton misconduct. The difference is usually important only in such questions as whether punitive damages can be recovered, or whether a guest statute limiting liability to gross negligence is applicable in a given case. In constitutional tort, these standards take on greater importance. If liability is denied for negligence because negligence is not enough of an affront to the plaintiff, perhaps liability can be justified for reckless conduct on the ground that the affront to the plaintiff is greater.

In this section we argue that recklessness should suffice for liability. At the same time, we acknowledge that the argument for recklessness is stronger in cases when the government exercises control over the plaintiff. Accordingly, a court that values the government's interest in discretion somewhat more highly than we do (but not highly enough to preempt constitutional tort entirely) might impose liability for recklessness only in control cases while denying it in other situations.

1. Control. The government differs from private defendants in that it may legitimately exercise control over individuals against their will, a privilege rarely accorded private actors and then only for brief periods in narrow settings. When the government exercises such control, notably by imprisoning convicted criminals, it significantly alters their ability to protect themselves from danger. The prisoner is surrounded by dangerous people from whom he cannot escape. The prison environment affecting his health and well-being is wholly beyond his control. This circumstance significantly affects the balance of equities between plaintiff and defendant. When the government makes the individual more vulnerable to harm by imprisoning him, fairness demands that the government take some measures to protect him from the risks.

The Supreme Court has recognized that government control warrants imposing constitutional duties to protect and provide for the incarcerated. This duty is variously articulated in terms of "recklessness," "callous indifference," or "deliberate indifference." The particular label is relatively unimportant. The principle is that serious disregard for the medical and security needs of those over whom government exercises control crosses the boundary of common law tort and becomes a matter of constitutional concern. This principle was first clearly stated in *Estelle v. Gamble*. A prisoner sued in constitutional tort claiming that his inadequate medical treatment amounted to a violation of the cruel and unusual punishments clause of the eighth amendment. The Supreme Court held that he could not recover by showing ordinary medical malpractice. That was a matter for state tort law. But constitutional tort would be available if the prison officials showed "deliberate indifference" to his medical needs because "such indifference [would] . . . offend 'evolving standards of decency' in violation of the Eighth Amendment." More recently, in *Smith v. Wade*, the Supreme Court affirmed an award of punitive damages against a prison guard whose "callous indifference" resulted in the beating and sexual assault of an inmate. In the course of its opinion, the Court made clear that a "reckless or callous indifference to" an inmate's need for protection can support a constitutional tort claim.

While *Estelle* and *Wade* were argued and decided under the eighth amendment, the "recklessness" or "deliberate indifference" standards articulated in those cases can also support a claim under the due process clause. The Supreme Court has repeatedly noted that the constitutional protections afforded prisoners under the eighth amendment may be available to others as a matter of substantive due process. The most recent example is *City of Revere v. Massachussetts General Hospital*, in which a criminal suspect named Kivlin was shot by police in the course of his arrest. Unlike the prisoner in *Estelle*, Kivlin could not base his constitutional claim for medical care under the eighth amendment because "there had been no formal adjudication of guilt." Yet the Supreme Court agreed that his "due process" right to medical care was "at least as great as" those afforded prisoners under the eighth amendment.

Taken together, these cases strongly support the principle that, when a person is under government control, recklessness defines the boundary between common law and constitutional tort. The element of control extends, of course, beyond persons being arrested or detained for trial. Another obvious group of persons within government control are inmates of public mental health institutions. A less obvious case of control is illustrated by *White v. Rochford*. There the police stopped a car on an expressway, took the driver away, and left two small children stranded in the car for several hours. The court held that the officers could be liable for the harm the children suffered, even though the harm was not deliberate.

Since the vulnerability argument is equally applicable to all these situations, the same rule for liability should apply. If a deliberate indifference or recklessness standard is appropriate for prisoners, it should also be applied to others under government control. Yet the eighth amendment roots of the current rule for prisoners does not permit its extension to those other situations. This doctrinal limitation, however, has not deterred the Supreme Court and some lower courts from treating the other control cases like prisoner cases, although the courts have not adequately explained the logical basis of their decisions. We think these courts reach the correct results and that the right way to defend those results is to employ the substantive due process argument presented here.

2. *No Control.* The case for applying a recklessness standard in the absence of government control is less compelling since the element of government-induced vulnerability is not present. There are good reasons, nonetheless, why this standard should apply here as well. The less care the government defendant takes, the more persuasive is the plaintiff's claim that the dereliction of duty violated not only his common law claim to physical safety but also a constitutional right to personal respect from government officers. As the common law recognizes by awarding punitive damages for extremely careless conduct, the reckless defendant not only physically injures his victim but insults him as well. This insult is all the greater when the agent of the harm is a government officer who supposedly is a servant of the people. In addition, the countervailing policy against overdeterrence of beneficial government action diminishes in strength as the degree of care diminishes. It is harder to maintain that government officers will not vigorously perform their jobs for fear that they will be successfully sued for gross negligence than when the threat is a suit for simple negligence. The risk to the officer that his conduct will be viewed as reckless is less than the risk that it will be found negligent.

The overdeterrence argument, nonetheless, is not without force even here and, coupled with a strong preference for legislative decision making, might still carry the day. The heart of the overdeterrence argument lies in the fear that courts and juries will be unable or unwilling to distinguish between simple negligence and recklessness. Admittedly this distinction is often difficult to articulate, and there are instances in which seemingly simple negligence has been deemed wilful and wanton misconduct.

The Supreme Court's recent approval of a recklessness standard for awarding punitive damages suggests, however, that the term is not "too vague to be fair or useful." The Court's confidence in the standard is shared by many lower courts that hold defendants liable for reckless conduct, but take pains to distinguish between ordinary negligence and recklessness. Thus, a policeman who carelessly fires his gun is not liable to those he injures in constitutional tort, while one who does so with callous disregard of the risk to the plaintiff may be liable. A supervisor or government that should be, but is not, aware of its employees' transgressions will not have to pay damages, but one that does know about them and fails to act will be held liable.

C. Intent to Harm

The common law generally holds that an unconsented touching coupled with an intent to touch are sufficient to establish a prima facie case of intentional tort, subject only to reasonable self-defense and sometimes defense of others and defense of property. This is the rule for private individuals, but for government actors there are a variety of other privileges that reflect the government's virtual monopoly on the routine use of legitimate force to carry out its aims. For example, policemen are allowed to use force to stop fleeing suspects and to control arrestees, and school authorities may confine or paddle students who misbehave.

In constitutional tort the issue is what substantive due process limits should be placed on government officers' discretion to harm individuals intentionally. What constitutional limits are appropriate depends upon whether the actor's motive for harming the victim is constitutionally legitimate. In the case where the motive is not legitimate, a strong, and we think conclusive, argument can be made for constitutional tort. On the other hand, if the defendant acts in good faith pursuant to a constitutionally permissible state policy, the issue of constitutional tort liability should turn on the relationship between the force he uses and the objective he is trying to achieve.

1. *Bad Motive.* The best case for liability arises when the defendant acts under the pretext of a legitimate state purpose but his true motive is to achieve some personal goal such as revenge, or some constitutionally illegitimate public goal, like punishing a criminal suspect without a trial. The policeman who treats a suspect roughly may use force because he believes such force is necessary to the arrest, or his reason may be improper. In such a case, the argument for constitutional tort is at its strongest. Government officers cannot persuasively maintain that their vigor in acting for the public interest will be diminished by a rule that holds them liable when the plaintiff can show a bad motive. Such defendants must therefore fall back on the argument that the threat of litigation by itself will deter them from vigorously discharging their obligations. Admittedly, even under a bad motive standard of liability, the officer may be forced to defend meritless and perhaps even frivolous law suits. Moreover, the risk of erroneous judgments is always present.

We find this argument unpersuasive. There are other ways of combatting frivolous law suits, such as requiring losing plaintiffs to pay attorney's fees when the facts are clear enough to support a finding of harassment. In addition, the state can diminish the harm from harrassment by providing its officers with legal services, or even indemnification. It is fairer to cope with harassment through measures such as these than to deny relief to plaintiffs with meritorious claims.

In any event, the plaintiff's interest in recovery in bad motive cases is strong enough to outweigh the potential deterrent effect of litigation costs. A victim might incur the same physical injuries from properly motivated government action, but wrongly motivated harm results in dignitary injuries as well. The individual must expect that he will be treated roughly by government when there is good reason for it and that he will sometimes be the victim of mistakes. The suspect who is physically harmed when he refuses to submit to arrest and the prisoner who is mistaken for someone else suffer physical and emotional harm, but their injuries include no element of insult. When the motive for those injuries is bad, however, the victim is not accorded the concern and respect due him from the government. In a nation of free people, government officers must be permitted to use force, but they are still our servants and not our masters. A tort remedy can be an effective economic reminder to them of their proper role, as well as a symbolic affirmation of the limits of governmental power.

2. *Severity of Injury.* Many of the lower courts have acknowledged that bad motive is relevant to constitutional tort liability under an "egregiousness" test, although they do not articulate their reasons. Perhaps because they grasp the point intuitively and not analytically, they do not give motive quite the force it deserves. Applying the factors set forth in *Johnson v. Glick*, they often hold that even a bad motive will not be sufficient justification to apply constitutional tort if the harm suffered is not too great. But the argument for liability based on motive does not rest on the severity of the measurable harm.

The argument turns on the lack of any good reason to tolerate badly motivated harm and the personal affront suffered by the plaintiff. An illustrative case is *Howse v. DeBerry Correctional Institute*. Two guards had attacked an inmate, who sued in constitutional tort for damages. The court correctly reasoned that the issue was one of substantive due process and quoted the "articulate discussion" of the problem in *Johnson v. Glick*. The *Howse* court conceded that the actions of the guards "were not an effort to maintain discipline." Rather, they were a reaction to the inmates' assertion, "in each defendant's presence, that each had engaged in a variety of homosexual practices at the prison." Nevertheless, because the attacks "were not totally unprovoked" and because "plaintiff actually suffered no physical harm whatsoever, aside from momentary physical discomfort," the constitutional tort action could not be maintained.

To the extent this decision relies on the principle that the severity of the physical harm should be considered, we think it is wrong. The measurable damage from a constitutional violation may be only a small part of the actual harm. The dignitary injury suffered from physical coercion by government power and the intangible harm to constitutional values are often of more constitutional significance than physical damage. An uncompensated violation of the body or of freedom of movement can suggest, both to government officials and individuals, that personal autonomy is not in itself very important and should be taken seriously only when substantial physical damage is done. The individual's interest in a remedy when government officials use force for personal ends, under color of government authority, does not depend on measurable harm for its vitality. Recovery should not be limited to cases in which such harm can be proved.

3. Legitimate Force and Disproportion. Suppose, however, that the defendant is not motivated by a personal grudge, or by a desire to punish the plaintiff summarily, or by some other constitutionally illegitimate reason. The defendant instead uses force or otherwise intentionally harms the plaintiff in pursuit of a constitutionally permissible government policy. The police chief who publicizes the plaintiff's shoplifting arrest in order to warn merchants, the teacher who paddles a student to discipline him, and the jailor who uses force to subdue an uncooperative prisoner all fall into this category. When, if ever, can the plaintiff make out a case in constitutional tort under such circumstances?

The balance of interests is closer here than in bad motive cases. The plaintiff cannot maintain, as he can in bad motive cases, that the intentional harm is not justified and hence should be actionable. Nor can he show that he has not received the respect due him from government. He should expect to be subjected to intentional harm when he provokes it, like the unruly student or prisoner or suspect. For these reasons, it would be unwise to adopt a general rule that any intentional harm is cognizable in constitutional tort, and it is not surprising that courts have rejected that alternative.

It does not follow that constitutional tort should *never* be available when the actor's purpose is legitimate. Even when the use of force or other intentional harm is permissible, limits on the extent of intentional intrusions on the plaintiff's body, emotions, reputation, and other interests may be appropriate. Corporal punishment of students is an appropriate use of force, but a severe beating is not. The same is true for policemen's treatment of arrestees and treatment afforded inmates by prison guards. The factor that distinguishes proper from improper force in these cases is the relation between force and justification. Harm that is grossly disproportionate to the legitimate government aim should be cognizable in constitutional tort.

Under this standard there will be some cases in which a great deal of government force is acceptable, as in quelling a prison riot, or in dealing with a rowdy arrestee. In others, hardly any force will be tolerable. In *Shillingford v. Holmes*, for example, the court held that a single blow with a nightstick was excessive force against someone who was trying to photograph the police making an arrest, not only because the motive was probably illegitimate, but also because of the disproportion between any legitimate need to maintain order and the use of a nightstick.

The policy justification for such a rule is straightforward. The presence of a legitimate governmental interest justifies the use of force or other action to harm the plaintiff, but it does not wholly obliterate the plaintiff's interest in government respect for his physical and emotional well-being. The obvious compromise is to permit the use of force, but to avoid giving government officers an unlimited discretion. A disproportion test accomplishes that aim. It requires an examination of the facts in every case to determine just what the victim might have done to warrant the force used. Short of a rule that either hamstrings the police or leaves the individual defenseless, it is hard to see any alternative to case-by-case adjudication in this area.

There is ample case law in the lower federal courts to support such a disproportion rule. The egregiousness test often reaches the right result because disproportionate force, like badly motivated government action, can often be characterized as egregious. But disproportion and motive are better standards than egregiousness because they identify more precisely the circumstances to look for in analyzing a fact situation. We also can support them with concrete reasons why they should be controlling principles. Egregiousness, abuse, and outrage are intuitively appealing terms for describing cases in which constitutional tort should be available, but in the development of workable doctrine they are no substitute for specific criteria and specific reasons to support those criteria.

V. Conclusion: The Supreme Court Decisions Reexamined

Defining the scope of constitutional tort in terms of substantive due process invites a reexamination of the Supreme Court's leading decisions. The application of our proposed decisional guidelines suggests that the claims raised in *Parratt v. Taylor* and *Paul v. Davis* lie outside the scope of constitutional tort. They are to be addressed solely within the framework of a state tort system. By contrast, *Ingraham v. Wright* presents a proper constitutional tort claim. *Baker v. McCollan* is, in many ways, the most difficult test for our analysis. The facts alleged in *Baker* illustrate the difficulty in distinguishing between simple negligence and recklessness.

Parratt is the easiest case to resolve. The negligent loss of a hobby kit is the weakest case for constitutional tort. Perhaps for this reason the Supreme Court selected *Parratt* as its vehicle for defining the scope of constitutional tort. In *Parratt*, there was no evidence of any intent to injure or recklessness. The most the plaintiff could prove was that his property was misplaced while it and he were under the defendant's custody. Under our guidelines, such claims of simple negligence are properly restricted to the common law tort system, in which states are free to decide for themselves whether to provide compensation.

Paul is a case that should be analyzed under the disproportion principle. There was no indication that the defendant police chief acted from an improper motive when he circulated the list of "active shoplifters." There was no allegation that Chief Paul harbored any personal animosity toward Davis or desired to injure him in any way. The apparent objective was to reduce the incidence of shoplifting. Circulating the names of persons arrested for that crime allows merchants to maintain a particularly watchful eye and thus advances this legitimate goal. There is, without question, a cost to the plaintiff in publicizing his arrest. The arrest may have been the result of error and the charge unfounded. The plaintiff may suffer embarrassment or other injury as a result of the publication. Yet, to some extent, such risks inherently attach to any arrest. While the matter is not beyond debate, given the limited circulation, publicizing the names of persons arrested for shoplifting is not a disproportionately intrusive means to combat crime.

The case for treating *Paul* under constitutional tort is strengthened, however, by the defendant's use of the phrase "active shoplifters." There was no evidence that the plaintiff was an active shoplifter at the time the flyer was distributed. Had the circular read "persons recently arrested for shoplifting" or "suspected shoplifters," it would have been entirely accurate. The defendant's misuse of words, though not trivial, does not alter the basic flavor of the case. The defendant's conduct was properly motivated by a desire to advance a legitimate function of government. The publication was restricted to those most directly concerned with shoplifting. Under these circumstances, the defendant's conduct lacks the elements of abusiveness necessary to give rise to a constitutional tort action.

Ingraham illustrates how the concept of disproportion can support a claim for constitutional tort. The plaintiff complained of the severity of the corporal punishment inflicted by public school officials. Normal punishment was "one to five 'licks'" on the buttocks with a wooden paddle. One student, however, was paddled fifty times for skipping school. Another was paddled fifty times for allegedly making an obscene phone call. A different student later confessed to having made the call. Ingraham himself earned twenty licks for being too slow to respond to his teacher's instructions. Many of these incidents produced injuries requiring medical attention. While the goal of maintaining classroom decorum is laudable, there are constitutional limits on its attainment. Severe physical punishment is disproportionate to the offense of playing hookey or slowly responding to instructions. Post-*Ingraham* courts have recognized that, if sufficiently severe or improperly motivated, corporal punishment in public schools may be unconstitutional. We believe that the allegations in *Ingraham* demonstrate a sufficiently disproportionate use of force to warrant recourse under constitutional tort.

The most troublesome case is the mistaken arrest of the plaintiff in *Baker*. The defendant sheriff did not act out of an improper motive, nor was the arrest and confinement disproportionate to the suspected offense. But the plaintiff was within the defendant's custody. We have argued that, when the defendant has custody of the plaintiff, the defendant's recklessness can support a claim in constitutional tort. Whether *Baker* should have proceeded in constitutional tort thus depends on whether the defendant's conduct amounted to recklessness as opposed to simple negligence.

The majority characterized the mistaken arrest as a case of simple negligence. The plaintiff was the person named in the arrest warrant issued in Amarillo, Texas. His name was listed in the warrant because the person sought by the police was using the plaintiff's name on an altered driver's license. Under this view of the facts, the defendant's confinement of the plaintiff was, at most, simple negligence. Yet, as argued in the dissent, there was also evidence that the defendant's conduct was more blameworthy. The defendant had reason to know that the person sought was using an alias and therefore was not the individual named in the warrant. Moreover, the defendant did not disclose the risk of misidentity to the arresting officers in Dallas, Texas. At the time the defendant took custody of the plaintiff, he failed to follow customary identification procedures that would have revealed that he had the wrong person. Whether these allegations transcend simple negligence is admittedly a matter of opinion. It is, however, the type of opinion that juries are customarily called upon to give. Indeed, the Court recently approved submitting such a question to the jury in the context of awarding punitive damages. Eight days of wrongful confinement is a serious intrusion upon one's liberty. Given the importance of the interest invaded and the defendant's awareness of the risk, we believe a reasonable jury could conclude that the defendant was reckless. Therefore, the plaintiff should have been permitted to present his claim in constitutional tort.

The fundamental problem with the Supreme Court's efforts to date is the failure to think clearly about the boundary problems the cases present and to fashion appropriate standards for resolving. *Ingraham* and *Paul* evade the issue by a combination of expansive states' rights rhetoric and footnotes that render the holdings quite narrow, and the *Baker* opinion distorts the facts to make the case easier. *Parratt* is the most disappointing of the lot. The opinion is an analytical maze that leads the reader down one blind alley after another. The Court held that claims of negligent deprivations of property must be raised in state court if there is an adequate state remedy. But it left open all the hard questions: whether this rule extends to intentional or reckless harms, whether it extends to deprivations of life and liberty, what criteria a state remedy must satisfy in order to be deemed adequate, and whether the Court's rule is directed only to procedural due process claims or to substantive due process claims as well.

The Court should abandon *Parratt*, begin again with *Rochin v. California* as its leading case, and use the concepts of recklessness, motive, disproportion, and control to decide scope cases. These are the factors that distinguish tort claims that warrant constitutional protection from those that do not. In addressing the boundary problem, the Court could learn much from the judges of the lower federal courts. As our discussion demonstrates, there is a wealth of authority supporting our approach in the caselaw of the circuit and district courts.

Part V
"[S]ecured by the . . . laws": Federal Statutory Violations

On its face section 1983 makes violations of *all* federal statutes actionable for damages. Indeed, the Supreme Court's first "laws" decision, *Maine v. Thiboutot*, 448 U.S. 1 (1980), seems to have taken this position, albeit over a sharp dissent that criticized the majority for "creat[ing] a major new intrusion into state sovereignty under our federal system." Shortly thereafter, however, the Court retreated in *Middlesex County Sewerage Authority v. National Sea Clammers Association*, 453 U.S. 1 (1981), and imposed certain conditions on such "laws" actions. Subsequent Supreme Court decisions have interpreted and applied these conditions. *Compare Golden State Transit Corporation v. City of Los Angeles*, 110 S.Ct. 444 (1989) *with Suter v. Artist M.*, 112 S.Ct. 1360 (1992).

Professor Monaghan's article analyzes the Court's approach to "laws" actions, particularly in connection with the *Golden State* case. He then compares this "laws" approach to judicial review of the conduct of federal officials under section 702 of the federal Administrative Procedure Act, 5 U.S.C. sec. 702 (1988). Professor Monaghan concludes that the Court has adopted a parallel framework for each which "reflect[s] the distinction between primary and remedial law that runs back to well before Hohfeld."

Henry Paul Monaghan, *Federal Statutory Review Under Section 1983 and the APA,* 91 Columbia Law Review 233 (1991)

* * *

I. The *Golden State* Decision

Although the Court in *Golden State* decided that a federal preemption claim was enforceable under section 1983, the dissent was troubled that a federal immunity could constitute a "right" within the meaning of section 1983. But the weaknesses inherent in the dissent's analysis raise important issues that are fundamental to any inquiry into the availability of rights of action under section 1983. *Golden State* is usefully approached, therefore, by first examining the dissenting opinion of Justice Kennedy and then turning to the opinion for the Court authored by Justice Stevens.

A. *Justice Kennedy's Dissenting Opinion*

For Justice Kennedy, a claim of immunity from state action based solely upon a federal statute's preemptive effect does not create a "right" within the meaning of section 1983 because section 1983 does not include immunities resulting "solely" from the division of power in the federal system. His analysis is problematic, however, because he assumes that the district court in *Golden State* had the authority to grant injunctive relief, but not damages. Yet unless a right of action arose under section 1983 or was implied from the NLRA, it is not clear that the district court had "arising under" jurisdiction, and thus any authority to enjoin the federally preempted conduct.

Drawing upon the celebrated analytical framework constructed by Professor Hohfeld in his series of articles beginning with *Some Fundamental Legal Conceptions as Applied in Judicial Reasoning*, Justice Kennedy characterized the preemption claim as a simple claim of a federal "immunity":

> The city's lack of power gives rise to a correlative legal interest in [plaintiff] that we did not discuss in [our previous decision]. The majority has chosen to call the interest a right. I would prefer to follow the familiar Hohfeldian terminology and say that Golden State has an immunity from the city's interference with the NLRA. This terminology best reflects Congress' intent to create [a] free zone of bargaining . . . .

Justice Kennedy recognized that, in terms, section 1983 embraces "'the deprivation of any rights, privileges, or immunities secured by the Constitution and laws.'" But, for him, the "immunity" conferred by the NLRA was not one "secured" within the meaning of section 1983 because this statute does not protect "those interests merely resulting from the allocation of power between the State and Federal Governments."

Justice Kennedy's appeal to the Hohfeldian distinction between rights and immunities cannot carry him very far. The Hohfeldian categories (as we shall see) lack resolving power; they are entirely formal and descriptive. Accordingly, they cannot inform the crucial substantive decision whether a federal immunity claim can be asserted affirmatively. Because that determination turns solely on the wishes of Congress, Justice Kennedy was quickly forced to undertake a detailed examination of section 1983's legislative history and the Court's cases construing the statute. The necessity for examination of the meaning of the relevant statute, not Hohfeld, is clarified by analogy to other federal statutes that are concerned with federal immunities. For example, the statute that governs the Court's appellate jurisdiction over state courts authorizes review when "any title, right, privilege or immunity is specially set up or claimed" under federal law. Surely, Justice Kennedy would not believe that a Hohfeldian "immunity" claim would not qualify for the purposes of section 1257.

Justice Kennedy's rejection of the section 1983 claim left him with deep difficulties. What was the source of the district court's authority to enjoin the federally preempted conduct? Did the district court have "arising under" subject matter jurisdiction; and even if so, did the court have the authority to award an injunction? Justice Kennedy moved so quickly that he did not separate these issues.

Early in his opinion, Justice Kennedy stated that an "injured party does not need § 1983 to vest in him a right to assert [in the federal district court] that an attempted [state] exercise of jurisdiction or control violates the proper distribution of powers within the federal system." He cited without elaboration such great decisions as *Gibbons v. Ogden*, *Willson v. Blackbird Creek Marsh Co.*, and *Cooley v. Board of Wardens*. But none of these decisions involved the nature of the district court's "arising under" jurisdiction; each was rendered on appellate review of a state court judgment rejecting a federal defense and thus fell squarely within section 25 of the Judiciary Act of 1789, the predecessor of present 28 U.S.C. § 1257. Only at the close of his opinion did Justice Kennedy seek to ground his claim that the district court could award equitable or declaratory relief:

> Our omission of any discussion of § 1983 [when *Golden State* was first before the court] perhaps stemmed from a recognition that plaintiffs may vindicate *Machinists* pre-emption claims by seeking declaratory and equitable relief in the federal district courts through their powers under federal jurisdictional statutes. See 28 U.S.C. § 1331 (1982 ed.); 28 U.S.C.A. § 2201 (Supp. 1989); 28 U.S.C. § 2202 (1982 ed.); *New York Tel. Co. v. New York Labor Dept.*, 440 U.S. 519, 525, 99 S.Ct. 1328, 1332, 59 L.Ed. 2d 553 (1979) (plaintiff sought declaratory and injunctive relief on a *Machinists* pre-emption claim). These statutes do not limit jurisdiction to those who can show the deprivation of a right, privilege, or immunity secured by federal law within the meaning of § 1983.

This analysis fails. To begin with, it does not explain why the district court could have awarded declaratory and injunctive relief but not damages under the cited statutes. But the difficulties run deeper. Section 1331 is simply the general "arising under" jurisdictional statute; the statute merely confers jurisdiction when a plaintiff has a right of action—it does not itself create a right of action. Justice Kennedy's references to the Declaratory Judgment Act, are even more inapposite. That act is remedial only; it is not designed to confer any "jurisdiction," let alone to dispense with the need to establish a right of action. Finally, *New York Telephone*, the only decision cited by Justice Kennedy, simply observes that (like *Golden State*) the case arose as a suit to enjoin conduct preempted by the NLRA, without commenting on the source of the federal court's jurisdiction.

Perhaps because he thought the district court's jurisdiction to award equitable and declaratory relief to any preemption plaintiff so clear, Justice Kennedy made no mention of several recent decisions that seemingly did so hold. For example, in *Shaw v. Delta Air Lines*, the Court said that a "plaintiff who seeks injunctive relief from state regulation, on the ground that such regulation is pre-empted by a federal statute which, by virtue of the Supremacy Clause of the Constitution, must prevail, thus presents a federal question which the federal courts have jurisdiction under 28 U.S.C. § 1331 to resolve." But if *Shaw* and similar decisions are read to establish the district courts' authority to award relief to nondamages-seeking, federal preemption plaintiffs, they provide no explanation for their result.

The difficulty with both *Shaw* and Justice Kennedy's dissent in *Golden State*, is the source of subject matter jurisdiction. *Shaw* did posit a distinction between plaintiffs claiming preemption, for whom jurisdiction was available, and plaintiffs seeking a declaration of nonpreemption. Congress could, of course, draw precisely such a jurisdictional line, and such a line possesses intuitive appeal. But whether that line reflects existing "arising under" doctrine is another matter. Under the "well-pleaded complaint" rule, the existence of a federal immunity to a state law claim does not confer "arising under" jurisdiction. The result should not be different simply because the immunity holder is the plaintiff. Under *Public Service Commission v. Wycoff Co.*, federal court jurisdiction is not available if the plaintiff simply alleges a claim of a right to be let alone because federal statutory or constitutional law so requires. There, the Court said:

> If the cause of action, which the declaratory defendant threatens to assert, does not itself involve a claim under federal law, it is doubtful if a federal court may entertain an action for a declaratory judgment establishing a defense to that claim. This is dubious even though the declaratory complaint sets forth a claim of federal right, if that right is in reality in the nature of a defense to a threatened cause of action. Federal courts will not seize litigations from state courts merely because one, normally a defendant, goes to federal court to begin his federal-law defense before the state court begins the case under state law.

The tension between *Wycoff* and *Shaw* is obvious, and has already been noted in the courts of appeals. *Shaw* seems wrong, if read to permit any federal immunity holder automatic access to federal courts for declaratory and injunctive relief. Unless Congress otherwise directs, as it has in various removal statutes, generally the plaintiff must assert a right to sue in order to establish "arising under" jurisdiction. That is, a plaintiff asserting a substantive federal immunity—or even a federal primary right—must also assert a remedial right of action. This rule has been relaxed to the extent that the Court seems willing to permit declaratory judgment suits without insisting upon a right of action when the defendant could have maintained a coercive suit under federal law. But, of course, even if the Declaratory Judgment Act permits party realignment and alteration in the timing of an otherwise proper federal court suit, that exception is not broad enough to explain jurisdiction in cases such as *Shaw* in which plaintiffs seek access to federal courts based solely on their own federal immunities.

The plaintiff in *Golden State* surely satisfied the standard established under *Bell v. Hood* and its progeny that a *colorable* claim of a federal right of action suffices to establish "arising under" jurisdiction. But even if subject matter jurisdiction would exist for the plaintiff to seek an injunction, Kennedy's assertion that a remedy other than relief under section 1983 would be available seems unjustified. To obtain injunctive relief, the plaintiff must do more than establish a colorable claim: a right of action must actually be established before injunctive relief is appropriate. For example, *California v. Sierra Club* was a suit by an environmental organization and several of its members to enjoin construction of a state water project as a violation of a federal statutory prohibition on unauthorized waterway obstructions. Presumably, the complaint satisfied the requirements of *Bell v. Hood*. After extended analysis, though, the Court concluded that the relevant federal statute did not confer a private right of action on the plaintiffs. The Court then declined an invitation to address the merits of the controversy notwithstanding this defect: "we cannot consider the merits of a claim which Congress has not authorized [plaintiffs] to raise." Unless Justice Kennedy assumed that the *Golden State* plaintiffs possessed an implied right of action under the NLRA, his denial of a right of action under section 1983 would have left the plaintiffs without a remedy in the federal courts, despite his assertions to the contrary.

B. *Justice Stevens' Opinion: The Search for a Federal "Right"*

The Court's opinion in *Golden State*, written by Justice Stevens, deserves careful attention from three perspectives: first, its emphasis on the importance of an underlying federal right; second, its rejection of any attempt to formulate a general exclusion from section 1983 of interests that are the "sole result" of preemption; and finally, the extended reach of section 1983 confirmed, if not established, by the decision.

Analytically, the Court's opinion contains much that is satisfying. The entire opinion is cast in terms of a judicial hunt for a "federal right," which is consistent with section 1983's focus on the "deprivation of any rights" secured by federal law, and the statute's provision of a "remedy [that] encompasses violations of . . . [such] rights." The Court recognizes that while section 1983 "must be broadly construed," the preemption plaintiff nonetheless "must assert the violation of a federal right." Apparently, section 1983's additional references to "privileges or immunities" secured by federal law refer to claims that in some important way also possess the structure of "rights." This concern with the contours of a federal right is quite understandable and has its roots, in part, in article III's "case or controversy" requirement. Courts do not confer discretionary benefits; a case requires that the plaintiff assert a claim of right. This means, as the Court correctly recognized, that a plaintiff seeking access to a federal court must assert more than that the federal statute expresses a congressional "preference"; the plaintiff must assert an interest sufficiently specific to be capable of judicial enforcement.

If violation of a federal "right" can be established, section 1983 is available, the Court said, unless Congress has "'specifically foreclosed a remedy [thereunder].'" The Court then undertook an inquiry for the requisite right. In a single sentence the Court denied that the supremacy clause itself could constitute a general source of rights enforceable through section 1983. That clause simply states a rule of priority: valid federal law prevails over conflicting state law. By itself the clause provides no algorithm for determining when concededly valid federal law can be asserted only as a defense, or when it can be employed also as a sword.

The heart of the Court's opinion is contained in the sentences that immediately follow its rejection of the claim under the supremacy clause. The Court first noted that

> [g]iven the variety of situations in which preemption claims may be asserted, in state court and in federal court, it would obviously be incorrect to assume that a federal right of action pursuant to § 1983 exists every time a federal rule of law preempts state regulatory authority. Conversely, the fact that a federal statute has preempted certain state action does not preclude the possibility that the same federal statute may create a federal right for which § 1983 provides a remedy.

This reasoning led to the following formulation:

> In all cases, the availability of the § 1983 remedy turns on whether the statute, by its terms or as interpreted, creates obligations "sufficiently specific and definite" to be within "the competence of the judiciary to enforce," *Wright*, 479 U.S., at 432, . . . *is intended to benefit the putative plaintiff*, and is not [specifically] foreclosed . . . .

Turning to the task of applying these principles, the Court found that the "nub of the controversy" turned on whether the NLRA created "rights" in labor and management that are "protected . . . against governmental interference," and it answered that question affirmatively.

The Court is surely correct that federal statutory preemption of state action "does not preclude the possibility that the same statute may create a federal right for which § 1983 provides a remedy." But care must be taken to see the precise work that the concept of "right" does here. Congress could confine assertion of a federal immunity claim to a defense in a state law enforcement proceeding; indeed, federal preemption claims often work precisely that way. But *Osborn v. Bank of the United States* long ago established that Congress also can invest the federal immunity shield with the character of a sword—unconstrained by legal abstractions such as "rights" and "immunities." Congress need only make clear its will.

As section 1983 itself shows, terms such as "rights" are the familiar staples of the legal structure and are frequently employed by Congress. Without contrary Congressional direction, courts should be expected to interpret legislation within the familiar framework. But more specifically, when a section 1983 action is filed in a federal court, that court's recognition of a federal "right" will be important in two ways: in *Golden State*, for example, the existence of a federal "right" under the NLRA meant jurisdictionally that "arising under" jurisdiction was incontestable; substantively, it allowed for the award of damages and attorneys fees.

C. *Scope of the* Golden State *Decision*

1. *Of Personal Rights and Federalism.*—In *Golden State*, the Court stated that "it would obviously be incorrect" to conclude that section 1983 is available "every time a federal rule of law preempts state

regulatory authority." This conclusion followed, the Court said, because of "the variety of situations in which preemption claims may be asserted, in state and in federal court . . . . " Seemingly, this perception would instruct the Court that in each case judicial consideration must be focused upon context-specific factors such as the extent to which affirmative challenges would disrupt state programs and the need for affirmative enforcement. Instead, however, the Court immediately fashioned a general approach that is unconnected to any of the restrictive implications of its reasoning: unless specifically displaced, section 1983 is available to any plaintiff with a federal right to enforce federally established legal duties. Put differently, despite its disclaimer, the Court does *not* treat preemption claims differently from any other claims raised by a section 1983 plaintiff.

At the center of the difference between the dissent and the Court is Justice Kennedy's effort to distinguish the treatment of preemptive claims from other section 1983 claims. For him, section 1983 requires that the plaintiff assert some identifiable "plus" apart from the simple existence of the preemptive federal law—federal property entitlements would qualify, such as the right to a particular rent calculation or to social security benefits. Justice Kennedy also believed that section 1983 embraced cases like *Monroe v. Pape*, because the official conduct challenged in these cases "constitutes only an element in the primary wrong that the injured party seeks to vindicate." But section 1983 would not include federal statutory interests that are "the sole result of the [federal] statute's preemptive effect." These interests reflect only the appropriate distribution of power between the nation and the states; they do not establish the kind of "personal interest" secured by section 1983.

To my mind, Justice Kennedy's attempt to isolate interests that are "the sole result" of preemption is unconvincing. He cited no convincing historical support for his analysis, and without such a basis no other principled difference between *Monroe* and *Golden State* appears. In each case, the plaintiff seeks damages complaining that state officials have interfered with a federally secured right to be let alone. Justice Kennedy seems to have unconsciously assumed that the interests protected by the common law of torts (at issue in *Monroe*) implicate section 1983 but not those protected by the common law of contracts (at issue in *Golden State*). Why that should be so is never made clear in his opinion. More fundamentally, in seeking to identify interests that are "the sole result" of federal preemption, Justice Kennedy fails to recognize that every claim against state officials based upon federal regulatory or entitlement law is, in the end, "the sole result" of federal preemption. If the otherwise applicable state rule (a rule of no recovery) is displaced, it is only because it has been displaced by valid federal law.

Stripped of historical support, Justice Kennedy needs some theory to support his distinctions. That theory will be hard to come by; indeed no coherent theory seems plausible. Consider in this context the question to be argued in *Dennis v. Higgins*: whether section 1983 is available to vindicate a dormant commerce clause claim. Presumably, for Justice Kennedy the "immunity" conferred by the clause is not "secured" by section 1983; the commerce clause is concerned with the appropriate distribution of power between the nation and the state and thus does not involve the kinds of personal rights embraced by section 1983. But the "and thus" is a *non sequitur*; the purported dichotomy between distribution of power and personal rights issues is illusory. For the Framers and well into the nineteenth century the power-allocating provisions of the national constitution (federalism and separation of powers) were thought to be important structures for maximizing individual liberty.

If section 1983 does not embrace commerce clause claims, another round of analysis will be called for: for what rights secured by the Constitution does section 1983 make available a remedy? The Court then also must consider the full implications of its decision in *McKesson Corp. v. Division of Alcoholic Beverages & Tobacco* on the duty of the states to provide adequate remedies for state violations of federal constitutional commands.

2. *Scope of Section 1983.*—In *Golden State*, the Court does not suggest that the NLRA itself satisfied the four criteria established by *Cort v. Ash* for judicial recognition of implied rights of action. If it had, "arising under" jurisdiction (and the award of an injunction and compensatory damages) could have been predicated on that basis alone, without need for any reference to section 1983. In *Wilder v. Virginia Hospital Association*, both the Court and the dissent render explicit what *Golden State* assumed: section 1983's availability turns only on whether federal statutory law creates a "primary" right, even though the federal law does not otherwise establish a "remedial" right (i.e., a right of action). In a footnote in *Wilder*, the Court noted that the availability of section 1983 presents "a different inquiry" from that involved in implied right of action analysis. Chief Justice Rehnquist, dissenting, agreed on this point. He observed that the Court's section 1983 jurispru-

dence in effect reduced *Cort v. Ash*'s four factors to its first: did the "statute[] contain a right 'in favor of' the particular plaintiff." This observation serves to highlight *Golden State*'s importance because judicial resistance is hardening against implication of rights of action.

Golden State thus "completes the process of divorcing section 1983 from its historical [and rights] roots and directs the focus of future cases away from the availability of a section 1983 cause of action and toward the scope of the right asserted under a particular constitutional or statutory provision." Section 1983 is, of course, unavailable if Congress has "specifically" foreclosed the remedy. But both *Golden State* and *Wilder* shore up the intimations in prior case law that this limitation is exceedingly narrow. Implied preemption of a section 1983 remedy on the basis of the assertedly comprehensive nature of the remedial scheme created by the federal legislation is not favored; indeed, *Wilder* pointedly observed that "only on two occasions" had the Court held that the section 1983 remedy was foreclosed on these grounds.

Golden State closes any Hohfeldian gap between primary federal statutory rights and section 1983 rights of action. The latter follows simply from the existence of the former. Apart from article III's requirements of injury in fact, causation, and redressability, the only limiting principle on the apparent sweep of section 1983 in enforcing federal legal obligations is the Court's statement in *Golden State* that section 1983 "may not be available" when the plaintiffs are benefited "only as an incident of the federal scheme of regulation." "May not" is more than that; as *Wilder* demonstrates, whether a plaintiff is categorized as an intended or an incidental beneficiary determines whether or not that plaintiff has a primary federal right.

> We must therefore determine whether the Boren Amendment creates a "federal right" that is enforceable under § 1983. Such an inquiry turns on whether "the provision in question was intend[ed] to benefit the putative plaintiff." . . . If so, the provision creates an enforceable right unless it reflects merely a "congressional preference" for a certain kind of conduct rather than a binding obligation on the governmental unit, . . . or unless the interest the plaintiff asserts is "too vague and amorphous" such that it is "'beyond the competence of the judiciary to enforce.'"

The term "right" contained in section 1983, therefore, expresses the crucial conclusions with respect to whom are owed the legal duties created by federal statutes.

II. Of Primary and Remedial Law

Golden State's search for an underlying "federal right" draws not only on section 1983's explicit language but on currents deeply embedded in our legal and political culture. Apostolic authority instructs us that "the province of the court is, solely, to decide on the rights of individuals." More important here, the judicial fixation on a search for and articulation of the relevant "federal right" is an analytic approach that not only has powerful cultural appeal but also is quite useful for the concrete needs at hand. Nonetheless, uncertain use of familiar legal terms can cause unnecessary confusion. For example, "cause of action" is a term thought to possess such intractable difficulties that it was banished from the Federal Rules of Civil Procedure. Of course, the effort failed; the term persists in the working vocabulary of lawyers and judges with the tenacity of original sin. More to the point here, the term "right" is susceptible to particular uncertainty because it is "incorrigibly multifarious in actual usage." For example, to state that *A* has no right against *B* may carry either of two different meanings: *A* lacks a primary right against *B*, or *A* has such a primary right but no remedial right. Thus, an important distinction exists between primary and remedial law.

A. *Primary Law*

Primary law concerns the "authoritative directive arrangements"—or more simply, the legal rules—that govern persons independently of litigation. In this domain, concepts such as "rights," "duties," "immunities," and "powers" simply describe the various "characteristic positions" held by persons in relationship to one another. "Duty" plays a pivotal role: active in character, this term describes the position of a person who is legally required to act, not to act, or to act only in a certain way. Surprisingly, perhaps, at first blush "primary right" seems to be a theoretically uninteresting concept: wholly passive, it simply mirrors the primary duty. "[A] 'right,' if spoken of with Hohfeldian accuracy, is a position which a person has because someone else has a duty in the performance of which the right-holder is . . . *interested*." This perception contains much that illuminates. *Golden State* itself makes apparent the passive, reflective character of a primary right. For all its emphasis on the need to establish the existence of a "right," the Court's description of what that meant was repeatedly cast in terms descriptive of the kind of obligations imposed on the putative duty holder:

> In deciding whether a federal right has been violated, we have considered whether the provision in question creates obligations binding on the governmental unit or rather "does no more than express a congressional preference for certain kinds of treatment." The interest the plaintiff asserts must not be "too vague and amorphous" to be "beyond the competence of the judiciary to enforce." We have also asked whether the provision in question was "inten[ded] to benefit" the putative plaintiff.

The Court's reasoning correctly assumes the need to establish both (a) the existence of a legal obligation, and (b), the "persons" to whom the obligation is owed: the "what" and the "to whom." The latter can be one person, several, or the entire population. From this perspective, the judicial concern with primary right draws attention to the "to whom" issue—the persons who *in a legally cognizable sense* are "interested" in the duty holder's discharge of his obligations. The effort (exemplified in both *Golden State* and *Wilder*) is to capture a distinction between those who are "incidental" beneficiaries of federal programs imposing duties and those who are intentionally protected. To be sure, this inquiry can be, and has been, extracted from the concept of duty—*A* owes a duty to *B* but not to *C*—but the Court's inquiry into the federal "right" is a way of highlighting the important fact that duties imposed by federal law are not necessarily owed to the public at large.

The word *federal* is properly underscored, at least initially. One could argue that the American political tradition supports, even though it may not require, a theory of judicial recognition of federal primary rights more restrictive than that applied at the state law level. This position might be defended as a residual aspect of our constitutional tradition of a national government of (theoretically) limited powers, or, perhaps more persuasively, as expressive of an appropriate federal judicial role grounded in separation of powers concerns. Any such contention is, however, misplaced. Claims of excessive judicial lawmaking made in the context of criticizing the propriety of implying rights of action seem unpersuasive: perhaps judicial establishment of new primary duties invades the legislative prerogative, but fashioning remedial rights hardly seems to rise to that level. In any event, whatever the merits of implying a right of action, this dispute has no relevance to deciding whether the legislature has created a primary right.

When both the duty and a general right of action (section 1983) have been established by Congress, no persuasive claim of excessive lawmaking exists because the Court discharges an ancient task in determining whether *A* is an intended, rather than an incidental, beneficiary. In the area of primary rights, there seems to be no reason to impose unusual restrictions on the courts that interpret the will of Congress.

B. *Remedial Law*

Section 1983 is, of course, an express right of action, and *Golden State* and *Wilder* close the gap between primary right and remedial right, making the existence of the former determinative of the existence of the latter. This development is important because the existence of a primary right entails no necessary conclusion that the right holder can sue. To sue, a plaintiff must establish the existence of a remedial right, a right of action in the traditional language:

> A right of action is a species of power—of remedial power. It is a capacity to invoke the judgment of a tribunal of authoritative application upon a disputed question about the application of preexisting arrangements and to secure, if the claim proves to be well-founded, an appropriate official remedy.

But the beneficiary of a primary right may not possess a right of action: there may be no express action and one may not be implied; alternatively, any right of action may inhere only in a public official.

Distinguishing among rights, rights of action, and remedies helps illuminate some issues, particularly issues arising in the context of "Our Federalism." For example, in a diversity case how shall we understand the respective relationship between state and federal law? Clearly, both the underlying duty and the right of action are drawn from state law. But what of the remedy? It is possible, but rather awkward, to conceive of the federal court as awarding a "state law remedy." For me, the federal court simply supplies a federal remedy to enforce a state-created right of action. This formulation better captures our understanding that state law cannot authorize the award of remedies beyond those authorized by Congress, but Congress may enlarge remedies beyond what state law authorizes. Similarly, section 1983 simply provides a minimum remedy, available in federal and state courts, to enforce many federally-created rights.

III. Section 1983 and the APA

Golden State should be compared with developments that have now taken hold in the area of standing under section 702 of the Administrative Procedure Act ("APA") to obtain judicial review of the compliance of federal officials with federal statutory commands. There is, however, a natural resistance to undertaking such a comparison. Our reflex is to think of section 1983 as involving trial oriented litigation in which plaintiffs seek damages caused by "constitutional torts" like assault, battery, and defamation, with issues of sovereign and official immunity sharply arising. On the other hand, APA review appears to involve the quite different task of judicial review of the compliance of federal officials with federal norms. In fact, however, as both *Golden State* and *Wilder* illustrate, much section 1983 litigation after *Maine v. Thiboutot* is at bottom no more than judicial review of the compliance of state (rather than federal) officials with federal statutory norms. And in both cases the Court distinguishes between "intended" beneficiaries, who may sue, and "incidental" beneficiaries, who may not.

A. *A Comparison Between Section 1983 and APA Section 702*

To the extent that section 1983 functions like section 702, a methodological comparison is warranted. The most important barrier to that undertaking is the differences in the operative vocabulary. Section 702 replaces familiar section 1983 (Hohfeldian) terminology such as right, duty, and right of action with a provision stating that any "person suffering legal wrong . . . or adversely affected or aggrieved by agency action within the meaning of a relevant statute, is entitled to judicial review thereof." But the language differences mask important structural similarities between section 1983 and section 702. In Hohfeldian terms, like section 1983, section 702 provides a general "right of action." Like section 1983, it, too, is available even though there is no other express or implied right of action. Also like section 1983, it embodies the important distinction between primary and remedial law. And, as *Lujan v. National Wildlife Federation* shows, section 702, like section 1983, ultimately requires distinguishing between intended and incidental beneficiaries.

Lujan originated as a challenge by an environmental group to federal agency decisions permitting increased mining on public lands. After noting that no claim of an implied right of action had been made, the Court said that plaintiff's standing depended upon a demonstration that it was "adversely affected or aggrieved by agency action . . . . ":

> the plaintiff must establish that the injury he complains of (*his* aggrievement, or the adverse effect *upon him*) falls within the "zone of interests" sought to be protected by the statutory provision whose violation forms the legal basis for his complaint. See *Clarke v. Securities Industry Assn.*, 479 U.S. 388, 396-397 . . . . Thus, for example, the failure of an agency to comply with a statutory provision requiring "on the record" hearings would assuredly have an adverse effect upon the company that has the contract to record and transcribe the agency's proceedings; but since the provision was obviously enacted to protect the interests of the parties to the proceedings and not those of the reporters, that company would not be "adversely affected within the meaning" of the statute.

This inquiry is substantially parallel to that required by *Golden State*: the section 1983 plaintiff must establish the existence of a duty of which she is an intended beneficiary. *Clarke*, cited by the Court in *Lujan*, had noted that the APA standing test is more liberal than the standard for implying a private right of action in cases in which the APA is inapplicable; the latter requires the plaintiff to show membership in a "class for whose *especial* benefit the statute was enacted." Although "especial" is not a requirement under section 702 of the APA (or of section 1983), section 702 only confers standing to intended and not incidental beneficiaries. *Lujan* also imposed a causation requirement for APA standing comparable to the same inquiry in section 1983 actions. The Court found that although the litigants asserted the sorts of aesthetic and recreational use interests that the relevant federal statutes were designed to protect, and thus the plaintiffs were "intended beneficiaries," the record failed to show that those interests were affected by the specific agency action challenged. Proof that the defendant's conduct caused injury to the plaintiff is, of course, also a long-recognized standing requirement in section 1983 actions.

The convergence of the two lines of decisions appears from another aspect of *Lujan*. The APA's "finality" requirement and settled rules governing ripeness bar premature challenges to governmental conduct. More specifically, as the Court said in *Lujan*, ordinarily plaintiffs cannot bring wholesale challenges to agency misconduct or mismanagement; in most cases those who seek "*wholesale* improvement of [a governmental] program" must resort to "the offices of the Department or the halls of Congress, where programmatic improvements are normally made." Here, too, APA review parallels developments in section 1983 litigation. The Court has some—but by no means complete—reluctance to permit plaintiffs to invoke section 1983 to bring systemic challenges to state governmental agencies on the ground that the agency is being mismanaged contrary to federal law.

Other symmetries exist. For example, the Court's requirement that a plaintiff's section 1983 claim assert more than a congressional preference and not be too open-ended for judicial enforcement resonates with APA cases refusing judicial review when "agency action is committed to agency discretion by law." Furthermore, the case law shows a presumption of reviewability under the APA, but Congress can specifically foreclose review of federal agency action just as it may foreclose a section 1983 remedy.

Of course, some differences remain, at least so far: section 702 does not itself authorize suits for damages without the consent of Congress, or for punitive damages. This distinction is not crucial when the real relief sought is declaratory or injunctive, and, in addition, the case turns on the meaning of the underlying federal statutes. But the distinction can matter. To be sure, doctrines of sovereign and official immunity make damages of any kind hard to obtain from public officials under section 1983 when the gist of the complaint is no more than that state officials have transgressed federal statutory commands. But public bodies below the state and its subdivisions hold no immunity from damage claims, and they may be held liable for the consequences of their seemingly official policies.

Other differences also exist, most significantly with respect to the scope of review. The *Chevron* doctrine, which requires judicial deference to reasonable agency constructions of ambiguous statutes, is not directly applicable to section 1983 actions. But in section 1983 actions based on violations of federal statutory law, I believe that courts should review actions by state officials who adhere to the construction given to federal statutes by the responsible federal administrative officials with the same deference under *Chevron* that would be applied in section 702 proceedings to review the federal official conduct. Nor is there any reason to believe that section 1983 actions against state officials for the violation of federal statutes would require a disregard of any administration record or of the APA's substantial evidence test, if otherwise appropriate.

B. *Intended and Incidental Beneficiaries*

Whatever the differences between section 1983 and section 702, *Golden State* and *Wilder* bring section 1983 criteria closer to APA standing rules when the issue is who may sue. Under both statutes not everyone can sue; something more than "injury in fact" must be established, however that term is defined. The availability of section 1983 turns on the distinction between direct and incidental beneficiaries. While at first blush the APA's "adversely affected" language may suggest a more pragmatic and generous attitude toward permitting access by plaintiffs than that suggested by section 1983's "a federal right" language, that difference is, at best, likely to be marginal. The section 702 litigant must still show that she is adversely affected "within the meaning of a relevant statute," a requirement that, after *Lujan*, seems identical to the Court's insistence in *Golden State* that the section 1983 plaintiff must establish that she is more than simply an "incidental" beneficiary of a federal statute. That symmetrical approaches are taken in the two contexts is entirely justified because (so far as is relevant here) both are concerned with the same issue: determining who is a proper plaintiff when public officials (federal or state) have transgressed norms imposed by federal law.

The distinction between intended beneficiaries and bystanders has the appearance of a conventional legal question: what did Congress intend? No doubt there is much truth to such a characterization of the problem, but there is more to the matter than that. Judicial attitudes, often formed by deep but imperfectly conscious intuitions, will play a role, at least at the margins, in making this distinction. We can, accordingly, expect to see similar divisions in both section 1983 and APA section 702 cases over just who, legally, is only a "bystander." My own bias is toward ready access to the courts. I have never been persuaded that deep separation of powers concerns exist every time courts entertain suits by those hurt by administrative agencies to determine whether the injury-causing agency conduct was wrongful.

My bias aside, precedents developed under section 702 and section 1983 will, I suspect, prove to be interchangeable. Thus, persons who are subject to state regulation (as in *Golden State* and *Wilder*) contrary to federal law will readily be found to be right holders. It seems unlikely, though, that the ultimate "beneficiaries" of federal regulatory and entitlement programs will be able to invoke section 1983 to compel state officials to comply with the federal obligations imposed on them; they are likely to be treated as "incidental beneficiaries." In *Wilder*, for example, it is doubtful that the patients dealing with the health care providers would be treated as appropriate plaintiffs to assert that the state rates transgressed federal law. This seems to be the teaching of the APA cases, which frequently deny standing to the ultimate beneficiaries of federal statutes, typically on the grounds of "causation" and "non-redressability." Only beneficiaries asserting something that looks like a "property" right will be able to seek review. Thus, in *Golden State* Justice

Kennedy had no doubt that persons asserting a "property" claim—for example, to social security benefits or a particular rent calculation—could properly invoke section 1983. Curiously, however, he dissented in *Wilder*, even though the plaintiffs were asserting what could be seen as a federal property entitlement comparable to a particular rent calculation. Perhaps this was based on an unexpressed intuition that judicial review could not work in the health care area with any effectiveness, or on a view that corporate public contracts were troublesome in this regard.

A commentator recently has insisted that the Court's refusal to confer standing upon beneficiaries of programs reflects a return to an older private rights or Hohfeldian model of administrative law in which the only proper litigant is a person asserting interests protected by the common law. But this characterization seems overdrawn. Judicial review is now available to whole categories of litigants who would have been barred by at least the early version of the private rights model. Moreover, APA section 702 and section 1983 review are open to plaintiffs asserting not only the traditional common law property interests but also, as Justice Kennedy acknowledges, the "New Property" interests created by the welfare state. In addition, *Lujan* is inconsistent with this characterization; there the Court seemed quite willing to assume that aesthetic and recreational use interests were protected by the relevant federal statutes.

Part VI

"[S]hall be liable to the party injured in an action at law": Corrective Justice and Damages

How should compensation for the violation of constitutional rights be measured? At one level, the answer depends on whether and to what extent the damages rules of the common law of torts are applicable. At a deeper level, though, the answer calls for the articulation and application of a theory of justice, particularly corrective justice. *See* Aristotle, *Nicomachean Ethics*, Book V, Chs. 2-4, on corrective and distributive justice.

Professor Jeffries's article deals with these matters. He asserts, in reliance on Weinrib, *Causation and Wrongdoing*, 63 Chi-Kent L. Rev. 407 (1987), that corrective justice theory requires both causation and wrongdoing for noninstrumental compensatory damages liability. Borrowing from proximate cause theory, he then goes on to argue for a risk-rule approach to compensatory damages liability in section 1983 cases under which "the relation of risk to injury helps determine the appropriate measure of compensation for constitutional violations."

In response, I accept Professor Jeffries's approach to corrective justice as grounded on Weinrib's theory. However, I disagree strongly with the application of the risk-rule to section 1983 compensatory damages. In my view, "compensatory damages are normatively justified for all foreseeable harm resulting from unconstitutional conduct."

While not explicitly addressing such issues of corrective justice, the Harvard Law Review Note does so implicitly in its focus on the proper measure of compensatory damages for constitutional violations in section 1983 cases. The Note criticizes the Supreme Court's reliance in *Carey v. Piphus*, 435 U.S. 247 (1978) on the "background of tort liability" with respect to damages. In the view of the author of the Note, damages are not only compensatory in purpose but should "redress for the abridgement of the constitutional right itself." The Note argues for awarding damages without proof of actual injury and discusses the possibility of implementing such an approach judicially.

John C. Jeffries, Jr., *Damages for Constitutional Violations: the Relation of Risk to Injury in Constitutional Torts,* 75 Virginia Law Review 1461 (1989)

. . .

I. Of Compensation and Deterrence

Damages for constitutional violations may be sought under either 42 U.S.C. section 1983 or the parallel common-law remedy based on *Bivens v. Six Unknown Named Agents of Federal Bureau of Narcotics.* These actions are commonly called "constitutional torts," and they are in many respects analogous to ordinary torts.

Both constitutional tort law and ordinary tort law are an uneasy amalgam of regulation and compensation. That is, both regimes share an instrumental concern to inhibit undesirable conduct and a noninstrumental desire to compensate injured persons. In constitutional tort law, at least, the regulatory aspect predominates. Discussion of the incentive effects of damages liability pervades both judicial opinions and academic comment. Compensation is routinely celebrated, but rarely decisive. As a result, it is hard to think carefully about compensation for constitutional violations. The goal of compensation is so often displaced by the concern for incentive effects that a kind of thought experiment is required to imagine what an appropriate compensatory remedy would include.

The issue of appropriate compensation for violations of constitutional rights may be inaccessible, but it is not unimportant. Recently, the Supreme Court has vindicated compensation as the controlling value in a particular context. *Owen v. City of Independence* held that a local government, unlike every other "person" sued under section 1983, has no immunity against award of damages. This unusual resort to strict liability was based chiefly on noninstrumental concerns. The Court cited the "injustice" of not compensating victims of municipal malfeasance and invoked "[e]lemental notions of fairness dictat[ing] that one who causes a loss should bear the loss." One swallow does not make a spring, but *Owen* suggests that, at least in one context, the Court is prepared to take noninstrumental concerns seriously.

More pervasively, assumptions about appropriate compensation for violations of constitutional rights form the background for debates about deterrence. Typically, some assumed level of compensation for injury resulting from government unconstitutionality is taken as a kind of natural starting point — a baseline charted by ideas of justice and fairness, from which departures can be justified (if at all) by more or less weighty concerns for incentive effects. Simply stated, the idea of compensation influences our perception of what is right, even as that perception is compromised in the debate on what is sound policy. Focusing on the relation of risk to injury identifies the appropriate measure of compensation for violations of constitutional rights and thus clarifies the starting point at which the debate on deterrence should begin.

II. The Relation of Risk to Injury in Nonconstitutional Torts

In the traditional language of tort law, actors have a duty to avoid unreasonable risk of harm to another. When breach of the duty causes such harm, the actor must make good the loss. The extent of that obligation depends, ordinarily, on the extent of injury. Thus, the actor has a duty to avoid unreasonable risk of harm to another and, where that duty is breached, the obligation to pay for the resulting injury.

The obligation to compensate, however, does not extend to all consequences of the actor's conduct. The obligation is curtailed by the requirement of a certain relation between harm risked and injury caused. The required connection is often, although incompletely, expressed in terms of foreseeability. Doctrinally, the limitation of liability is usually accomplished in the name of "proximate" or "legal" cause. Alternatively, the relation of the risk created to the injury sustained may be said to fix the scope of the actor's duty. Under either formulation, risk and injury are directly related. The actor has a duty to avoid risking certain harms (or harms to certain persons), and it is injury of that sort (or to those persons) that supports the claim for compensation.

Of course, the link between creation of risk and realization of risk is partly fortuitous. Conduct posing unreasonable risk of harm may cause injury or not, or injury more or less severe, depending on the circumstances. There is great variation in the extent of liability that may flow from a breach of duty. Liability differs *in degree* from one situation to the next. But usually there remains a relation *in kind* between duty owed and injury caused. The actor's freedom is restricted in the first place in order to avoid risk of certain harms, and it is the occurrence of those harms that triggers the obligation to compensate. Wrong and injury derive from the same risk.

It happens, however, that sometimes wrong and injury do not coincide. That is, sometimes conduct deemed wrongful because it creates an unreasonable risk of a particular harm, causes injury of an entirely different sort. In such cases, there is a *qualitative* disparity between the reason that the act is wrong and the specific injuries that result from its commission.

This kind of disparity is important in tort theory, but uncommon in the cases. Scholars usually resort to hypotheticals, such as the following from Robert Keeton:

> The proprietor of a restaurant places an unlabeled can of rat poison beside cans of flour on a shelf near a stove in the kitchen. The can explodes and kills someone. If the restaurateur was negligent because of the risk of poisoning, but had no reason to know of the risk of explosion, is she liable for the death?

Keeton's answer is "No." The negligent actor is liable only for injury "within the scope of the risks by reason of which the actor is found to be negligent." In other words, liability extends only to injury caused by the negligent aspect of the defendant's conduct. In Keeton's hypothetical, the restaurateur was negligent in disregarding the risk that the rat poison would be eaten. That risk did not occur. The risk that did occur (explosion) was one with respect to which the restaurateur was not negligent. Therefore, no liability.

Keeton calls this the "risk rule" and treats it as fundamental to negligence theory. Others would frame the point differently, but the general argument that liability for negligence should be limited to the kinds of risks that made the conduct negligent is widely familiar. That is not to say that the limitation is uniformly observed. In fact, the precedential basis for the risk rule is far more variegated than this discussion suggests. Nevertheless, this brief summary may suffice to show that the relation of risk to injury as a way of fixing the scope of compensation is a concept well known in ordinary tort law.

The same idea surfaces in antitrust law. The Supreme Court has held that private antitrust plaintiffs must show more than injury caused by an antitrust violation. Rather, they must prove *antitrust* injury — that is, injury specifically related to the anticompetitive effect of the antitrust violation. In the language of this Article, antitrust plaintiffs must show injury within the risk that the antitrust laws seek to avoid. Other sorts of injury, although caused by the antitrust violation, are not compensable. This result does not differ in kind from the principle described above; it is simply a particularly well-defined application of the relation of risk to injury as a boundary of appropriate compensation.

III. Constitutional Torts and the Premise of Fault

Damages actions for violations of constitutional rights are in many respects analogous to ordinary tort actions. The two regimes are similar in structure. Both rely on private claimants. Both are enforced by the threat or fact of civil litigation. Both reward successful claimants with compensatory judgments. Most importantly, both regimes are based on fault.

The last point requires explication. Nominally, damages actions for violations of constitutional rights do not require proof of fault, except as dictated by the definition of the underlying right. That is, proof of the defendant's negligence is not a necessary part of the plaintiff's cause of action under section 1983. Of course, section 1983 does not create rights; it only provides a mechanism for their enforcement. Proof of fault may be required by the definition of the underlying right, and many constitutional rights are so defined that their violation requires some form of culpability. In such cases, the particular motivation underlying government conduct may determine constitutionality. Other constitutional violations are defined without regard to culpability. In these cases, the plaintiff's case under section 1983 or the analogous *Bivens* remedy will not require proof of negligence or any other kind of culpability. In short, the cause of action is not itself fault based, even though the underlying right may have a fault component.

Looking at the plaintiff's case, however, tells only half the story. Nearly every defendant subject to a damages action for violation of constitutional rights has a defense of qualified immunity. Originally framed in the context of false arrest, the defense was said to require a showing of "good faith and probable cause" for the unlawful action. Recent cases have deemphasized the subjective branch of the defense, so that today, the defendant need only show that the conduct was objectively reasonable. This defense is quite generally available in damages actions for violations of constitutional rights.

Thus, despite the circumlocution of qualified immunity, damages actions for violations of constitutional rights are, very generally, negligence-type actions. With rare exceptions, the damages remedy for constitutional violations requires some finding of fault. Of course, it is perfectly possible to think that it should not. Some have endorsed strict enterprise liability for violations of constitutional rights. I have explained elsewhere why I think this suggestion misguided, but the merits of that question will not be canvassed here. For present purposes, it is enough to say that the existing damages remedy for violations of constitutional rights *is* predominantly fault based. I intend to explore the appropriate measure of damages in a fault-based regime for redressing violations of constitutional rights.

The premise of fault is important to this argument. It explains why the relation of risk to injury in constitutional torts has normative significance apart from supposed incentive effects. In my view, the normative case for compensation does not rest on the mere fact of injury. Injury is an inevitable part of life and of living in an organized society; there neither is, nor could there be, any generalized moral claim that all injury should be set right. The normative case for compensation rests, rather, on *wrongful* injury. It is the relation of wrong to injury — not merely the relation of act to injury — that justifies compensation. Of course, act and injury may be linked by causation, but causation itself is morally neutral. Wrongdoing is required to show why *this* causal agent — as opposed to all the others that invariably exist — is morally obliged to make good the loss. In short, fault supplies to causation the moral dimension essential to a noninstrumental case for compensation.

The relation of risk to injury tracks the moral dimension of causation. It links the injury for which compensation is sought to the fault that justifies compensation. Not all injury counts, because not all injury is constitutionally relevant. Sometimes, conduct violative of a constitutional right will cause injury unrelated to the kinds of risks that constitutional prohibitions were designed to avoid. In such cases, there is a disjunction between the reason the act is wrongful and the specific injury that results from its commission. When this occurs, "but for" causation lacks moral significance. Whatever considerations of deterrence may suggest, the noninstrumental case for compensation for constitutional torts reaches only those injuries caused by the wrongful — i.e., unconstitutional — aspect of the government's behavior. Injury outside the constitutionally relevant risks is morally indistinguishable from the very broad range of injury caused by lawful government action. Unless a contrary answer is indicated by consideration of incentive effects, such injury is appropriately noncompensable.

IV. The Relation of Risk to Injury in Constitutional Torts

The relation of risk to injury in constitutional torts is surprisingly varied. Some constitutional provisions are much like ordinary tort duties. They guard individuals against specified harms by directly prohibiting the infliction of such harms. Violation of these provisions is likely to cause exactly the kind of injury that the prohibition was designed to avoid. In these cases, radical disparity between harm risked and injury caused is exceedingly unlikely.

A good example of a tort-like constitutional right is the takings clause. Private citizens are secured against private "takings" by ordinary tort law. The government's power of eminent domain threatens the same harm, but traditional sovereign immunity would preclude a remedy. The fifth amendment fills the gap by requiring compensation. The result is a constitutional remedy for government "takings" (as that term is narrowly defined) that roughly parallels the ordinary tort remedy for private misconduct. The constitutional provision directly bars specified harm to individuals, and violation of that provision gives rise to damages claims by those individuals for the constitutionally relevant injury. The case for compensation is exactly met.

Other constitutional provisions are not like ordinary tort duties. They prohibit conduct that is wrongful only, or differently, if done by government. Some of these provisions are not aimed directly at preventing specified harms to identifiable individuals. Rather, they seek to prohibit certain government actions. These actions may be thought unacceptable for reasons not easily captured by a focus on specified harms to individuals. Of course, at some level of generality, all constitutional rights may be seen as duties imposed on government to avoid injury to the people. But the link between such duties and the occurrence of particular harms to particular individuals may be exceedingly indirect.

Disparity between risk and injury is especially likely where constitutional doctrine is prophylactic. In modern constitutional law, many rules have that focus. They are not aimed directly at conduct causing a particular harm, but at antecedent or related conduct that is easier to monitor or suppress. This is true not only of overtly prophylactic requirements, such as *Miranda* warnings, but also of many nominally substantive doctrines. The fourth amendment warrant requirement is an important example. In these and other instances, modern constitutional law prohibits conduct not immediately productive of constitutionally relevant harms. Rather, the relation between the conduct proscribed and the harm ultimately feared is strategic and indirect.

This characteristic of modern constitutional law explains the importance of the relation of risk to injury in constitutional torts. The point is not merely that the prohibited conduct may not cause the kind of harm that the prohibition aims to prevent; the failure of causation is altogether commonplace. The point is rather that violation of a constitutional prophylaxis often produces constitutionally irrelevant injury. The greater the distance between conduct proscribed and harm ultimately feared, the greater the prospect that proscribed conduct may cause injury of a different sort. The more constitutional doctrine is prophylactic and strategic in its structure, the more likely it is that unconstitutional conduct will cause injury unrelated to constitutional concerns. And because constitutional prohibitions are far more likely to be prophylactic and strategic than are ordinary tort duties, constitutional torts are correspondingly more likely to yield injury unrelated to risk. While it requires some imagination to come up with examples of ordinary tort injuries unrelated to perceived risks, examples abound in constitutional law.

It should be emphasized that disparity between the reason an act is wrongful and the kind of injury that may result from its commission is by no means an invariant feature of constitutional torts. Rather, it is an attribute of some constitutional guarantees, to a greater or lesser extent, under some conceptions of their content. Thus, a limitation of damages liability to constitutionally relevant injury — that is, to injury of the sort that the prohibition aims to prevent — will be more or less consequential, depending on the right in issue. What is needed is individuated analysis of the appropriate measure of damages for various constitutional rights. Two examples will reveal the kind of inquiry that I have in mind.

A. *Unreasonable Search and Seizure*

Few constitutional rights seem more suited to ordinary compensatory damages than the fourth amendment guarantee against unreasonable search and seizure. At least, so the *Bivens* Court thought. Justice Brennan described award of damages for fourth amendment violations as "hardly . . . a surprising proposition." Indeed, the aptness of the traditional tort remedy seems to have been thought so obvious as to require little argument. The Court contented itself with noting that "[h]istorically, damages have been regarded as the ordinary remedy for an invasion of personal interests in liberty." Justice Harlan agreed; he thought it "clear" that injury from an unlawful search was "a claim . . . that, if proved, would be properly compensable in damages." He noted that the fourth amendment protects "personal interests" in "privacy" and that those interests are closely analogous to the interests involved in traditional tort claims of trespass and false imprisonment. The judicial experience in dealing with the common-law torts indicated to Harlan that the courts were "capable of making the types of judgment concerning causation and magnitude of injury necessary to accord meaningful compensation for invasion of Fourth Amendment rights." Harlan therefore endorsed a compensatory remedy, but with characteristic caution, also noted that damages might not be equally suitable for other rights.

Both Brennan and Harlan referred to, but did not stress, the fourth amendment's protection of "personal" interests. The word suggests something important. Measuring damages for these violations seems straightforward in part because the fourth amendment is so easily understood as a "personal" constitutional right. It is "personal" in the sense that it directly and immediately protects privacy interests held by individuals. Individuals are protected as such, not as proxies for society at large. An unlawful search invades chiefly the rights of the person searched. Of course, all wrongs to individuals have aggregate effects, but here it is at least meaningful to say that the wrong is done *to* an individual and that resulting harm is suffered *by* that individual. Strategic concerns seem distinctly secondary.

This means that, at least in one dimension, the relation between risk and injury is immediate and direct. The fourth amendment protects personal interests in privacy; damages claimants are those persons whose privacy interests have not been respected. The amendment guards against risks to identifiable individuals, and violations give rise to damages claims by those same individuals. There is a match between the incidence of risk and the incidence of actionable injury. The "personal" nature of the fourth amendment right is simply a way of labeling this congruity. It is the same congruity that exists in ordinary tort cases, and it supports compensatory damages for injury caused by unlawful search and seizure.

In another respect, however, the issue is problematic. From a purely noninstrumental perspective, routinely awarding damages for *all* injuries caused by fourth amendment violations would go too far. Although there is a correspondence between the incidence of risk and the incidence of injury, there is a potential mismatch between the kind of risk against which the fourth amendment guards and the kind of injury that may result from its violation. Injury caused by unlawful search may be qualitatively unrelated to constitutional concerns, even though it is "but for" caused by the constitutional violation.

Suppose, for example, that a police officer conducts an unlawful search and finds nothing. This is an actionable wrong, and the person searched would have a claim for damages to the extent of his or her injury. The injury, however, would likely be insignificant. A search that uncovers nothing (unless accompanied by some additional wrong such as assault) is likely to be little more than an inconvenience. Of course, consequential damages would be available if the victim suffers "pain and suffering" from the invasion of privacy, but the unsuccessful search ordinarily does modest harm.

Compare the case of the unlawful search that uncovers incriminating evidence. The wrong is the same, but the injury is considerably more severe. The person searched would face the prospect of criminal charge, trial, conviction, and punishment. In some circumstances the exclusionary rule would bar use of the illegally obtained evidence, but that is not invariably so, and in any event the accusation is in itself injurious. Harms associated with criminal accusation and trial would certainly be foreseeable (indeed, desired) consequences of an unlawful search. If all such injury were compensable, however, the result would be a radical disparity between the kind of harm against which protection is desired (unreasonable invasion of privacy) and the kind of harm for which compensation would be sought (criminal prosecution and trial). A regime compensating individuals for all injury caused by government unconstitutionality would end up awarding money damages to offset losses that should be attributed to (and that are also "but for" caused by) the claimant's own misconduct. The result would be a wealth transfer from society generally to those guilty of criminal wrongdoing. The prospect is peculiar, if not perverse.

The limitation of constitutional tort liability to constitutionally relevant risks would avoid this result. It would measure damages by the kind of injury that the fourth amendment was designed to prevent. The victim of an unconstitutional search could recover damages for invasion of privacy. Monetary compensation would not extend to harms flowing from the discovery of incriminating evidence and consequent criminal prosecution. This result would accord with the conceptual structure of a fault-based regime of compensation for constitutional torts and also, I think, with common sense. After all, injury from criminal prosecution can scarcely be considered a societal wrong. Enforcement of the criminal laws is a good thing. The costs imposed on violators are not constitutionally disapproved, but morally right and socially useful. The concern of the fourth amendment is not to curtail criminal prosecution, but to avoid unfounded (and therefore abusive) invasions of privacy. Compensation for violations of the fourth amendment should redress the invasion of privacy, not the costs of criminal prosecution.

If any argument is to be made against so tailoring compensation, it is likely to be based on instrumental concerns. For instance, the objection might be raised that limiting damages to constitutionally relevant harms would invite unlawful searches by allowing the police to "buy" fourth amendment violations at too low a price. This might be true, if there were no alternative sanctions (exclusion of evidence, administrative discipline, civil fines, or punitive damages) to discourage such behavior. Obviously, analysis of the optimal deterrence of fourth amendment violations would require consideration of all these approaches. No such comprehensive analysis can be made here, but it may be useful to point out some implications that might flow from focusing on the relation of risk to injury.

Suppression of illegally seized evidence is desirable because it creates incentives to avoid illegal searches. Suppression may also be objectionable, however, for at least two reasons. First, suppression benefits only the guilty; it has no application to unlawful searches that uncover no incriminating evidence. Second, suppression is vastly overcompensatory. Letting the murderer go free because the constable blundered seems incommensurate with the wrong done. The windfall benefit to the guilty offender will rarely be viewed with satisfaction; to most observers, it will be an occasion for regret. The Supreme Court's response to these tensions has been not only to curtail the remedy of suppression, but also to adopt both substantive and institutional restrictions on the right itself.

A money damages remedy for fourth amendment violations would ameliorate the objections to suppression, but only at some cost in vitiating deterrence. Money damages would be preferable to suppression in that the remedy would be available to all victims of unlawful searches, not merely to those found to possess incriminating evidence. This would be a good thing. If, however, compensation were limited to constitutionally relevant injury (i.e., the invasion of privacy), recoveries might be so modest that law enforcement authorities would tend to regard them merely as a cost of doing business. At least in serious cases, the authorities might willingly pay the fine for invasion of privacy as a means of securing criminal conviction. Ultimately, the question is empirical, but risk seems great that a strictly compensatory remedy would be instrumentally inadequate.

Progress might be made if compensation were combined with a narrowly tailored exclusionary rule targeted to the deterrence shortfall. Perhaps there might be a scheme of presumed or liquidated damages, calculated to redress the dignitary injury of abusive invasion of privacy by unlawful search. The prospect of such awards would create a useful disincentive for casual disregard of fourth amendment precedent. And quite apart from incentive effects, such awards would have a salutary role in affirming for all citizens, not just for criminal wrongdoers, the constitutional values underlying the fourth amendment. Suppression would be reserved for situations where a compensatory regime of liquidated damages might predictably yield inadequate deterrence — chiefly, cases of intentional fourth amendment violations in the investigation of serious crimes.

Obviously, this sketchy suggestion leaves many questions unanswered, but the point of these remarks is not to pretend to a comprehensive solution to fourth amendment law. It is, rather, to support a single observation: Whatever the criteria of judgment —whether deterrence or compensation or some blend of both — there would be no plausible reason to award money damages for *all* injuries caused by unlawful searches. Damages for costs of defending criminal charges would effect a wealth transfer most would find more perverse and more objectionable than the suppression of evidence. Consulting the relation of risk to injury indicates why such damages are not required by any noninstrumental theory of compensation. To put the point differently, I hope to have shown that there is no *non*deterrence rationale for awarding damages for injuries unrelated to fourth amendment concerns. This simple statement seems to me a useful clarification of, even though not a complete solution to, the problem of fourth amendment enforcement.

B. Free Speech

More difficult problems attend the appropriate measure of damages in free speech cases. Unlike the fourth amendment, the first amendment guarantee against laws abridging the freedom of speech is not usually understood as a strictly "personal" right. Of course, there is an aspect of free speech ideology based on the protection of personal autonomy in matters of belief and expression. Often phrased in terms of self-realization and self-fulfillment, this conception treats free speech as a right held individually by individuals. Some version of this idea surfaces in many first amendment theories and predominates in a few. More commonly, however, theorists recognize an instrumental relation between freedom of speech and societal decisionmaking. This idea is expressed most generally in Holmes's metaphor of the "marketplace of ideas." More narrowly, the instrumental conception relates freedom of speech to representative democracy. Under this view, freedom of speech is secured to make democracy work. This premise suggests that the kind of speech with which the constitutional guarantee is most concerned is speech relevant to self-government — or, more briefly, "political" speech. This emphasis on the relation of free speech to the constitutional process of self-government has many adherents, including some who insist on its exclusivity and others who merely recognize its strength.

For present purposes, this divergence among theorists is unimportant. Whatever one's conception of the organizing principles that *should* guide first amendment adjudication, this much is clear: Existing first amendment doctrine is strongly, albeit incompletely, oriented toward a systemic rationale. In its rhetoric and in its decisions, the Supreme Court emphasizes societal concerns and systemic solutions. Indeed, many important lines of cases make sense only under this conception. The most obvious example is the overbreadth doctrine, which invites facial invalidation of a law because of its effect on third parties. The concern for preserving the systemic functions of free speech also underlies the familiar conclusion that a would-be listener can claim a constitutionally protected interest in another's speech. The same approach explains many other first amendment doctrines, including the law of obscenity, campaign finance, corporate speech, and other areas. That is not to say that the universe of first amendment cases is consistent, or to deny that there are counterexamples to the observations made above. The point is simply that substantial parts of existing first amendment doctrine are unmistakably grounded in an appreciation of the systemic value of free speech in a democratic society.

When "systemic" rights are at issue, measuring damages for constitutional violations becomes problematic. The trouble is that the risk to society against which such prohibitions are designed to guard is not necessarily congruent with the kinds of injuries that may result to individuals. Stated in terms of this Article, there is a disparity between the incidence of risk and the incidence of actionable injury. In some situations, the unconstitutional act will have no measurable impact on any identifiable individual. In those cases, a strictly compensatory remedy would not function. In other circumstances, government unconstitutionality will cause injury to individuals, but injury of a sort quite different from the risk at which the constitutional prohibition is aimed. In those situations, the connection between the constitutionally relevant risk (of harm to society) and the injury actually caused (to individuals) may be mere coincidence.

Suppose that *A*, an entrepreneur, operates an "adult" bookstore, selling magazines, video cassettes, "marital aids," and the like. Additionally, *A* offers a live show featuring a nude dancer. Patrons enter small booths equipped with coin-operated timers. Upon deposit of a coin or token, the dancer can be viewed for a few minutes, after which a panel or curtain slides back into place. From these activities, *A* turns a handsome profit. Suppose further that the locality tries to shut down these operations under a zoning ordinance prohibiting all "live entertainment" in the town. The bookstore is closed, litigation results, and eventually the ordinance is held unconstitutional. In the meantime, however, *A*'s business has been destroyed. Perhaps the lost income prevented timely mortgage payments, or the clientele has been attracted to a similar facility in a neighboring town; in any event, *A* no longer has a profitable enterprise.

If damages were unconstrained by the relation of risk to injury, *A* could recover from the locality an amount sufficient to offset the loss resulting from closing the business. The locality acted unconstitutionally, and the action caused injury. Moreover, the locality's action would likely be found in negligent disregard of existing overbreadth precedents. Thus, even without regard to the rule of strict liability for the official policy of local governments, the locality would have to pay money damages for *A*'s loss.

The trouble is that the damage to *A*'s business enterprise is not the sort of injury that the first amendment is concerned to prevent. In free speech terms, the relevant harms are (1) primarily, the contraction of social discourse resulting from the inhibition of "live entertainment," and (2) secondarily, the consequent restriction on individual self-fulfillment. For the former, it is society at large that has suffered the relevant harm, not *A* personally. Indeed, it seems likely that the societal harm feared by the Court would not flow from the unavailability of nude dancing but from the prospect of suppressing other "live entertainment" of greater value. The connection between *A*'s lost profits and the potential systemic damage of other possible applications of the zoning ordinance is truly obscure. In terms of individual self-fulfillment, the connection is not much better. In this view, the relevant injuries are suffered by the expressive nude dancer and the self-fulfilling patrons, or perhaps by the unidentified and unidentifiable individuals elsewhere in society who might suffer a restriction in self-realization if other forms of "live entertainment" were suppressed. Again, the relation of these noninstrumental concerns to *A*'s business injury is exceedingly indirect.

The disparity between constitutionally relevant harms and actionable injury can also be seen from another perspective. Not only is *A*'s injury unrelated to concerns that can plausibly be assigned to the first amendment, it is also the sort of harm to which modern constitutional interpretation is notoriously indifferent. Zoning laws routinely restrict the use of property, often in ways costly to owners. The takings clause provides little protection. Unless there is a physical invasion of the property, zoning restrictions are typically upheld, even though the economic injury to the owner is anything but de minimis. Thus, if *A*'s business had been destroyed by an ordinance regulating set-backs, requiring off-street parking, or doing anything else that did not happen to intersect the first amendment, there would be little likelihood of a plausible claim for damages. The injury to *A* could be exactly the same, both in nature and magnitude, but it would not be actionable under section 1983. Only the coincidence of *A*'s economic injury and an essentially unrelated first amendment concern makes the claim work.

Here, the implications of this analysis are dramatic. If damages were limited to constitutionally relevant concerns, *A* would have no plausible claim for compensation. Act and injury are linked by "but for" causation, but wrong and injury are not. There is a complete disjunction between the risk at which the constitutional prohibition is aimed and the injury for which compensatory damages are sought. To put the point more simply, the government's fault is unrelated to *A*'s injury. Compensation is not required.

Again, this is not to say that awarding damages to *A* would serve no purpose. An instrumental rationale might well exist. The prospect of damages no doubt would help deter unconstitutionality and would encourage government to take great pains to know (or anticipate) the law. Presumably, a larger award, however calculated, would increase deterrence. Reasoning of this sort may well justify penalties apart from, and additional to, compensatory damages. But the difference in rationale may be consequential. It is hardly inevitable that a deterrence rationale would focus on the economic value of the claimant's injury to fix the amount of damages. Indeed, given the unusual incentive structure of overbreadth cases, it is entirely plausible to believe that *no* recovery of damages would be required from a strictly deterrence point of view.

This rather surprising conclusion rests on the following observations. Overbreadth doctrine invites facial attack and categorical invalidation of overbroad laws. Repeated challenge to the law's case-by-case application is not required. This means that injunctive or declaratory relief is peculiarly potent in overbreadth cases; it allows one litigant to vindicate the claim of an entire class. As a matter of deterrence, therefore, it is not necessary to create incentives for repeated litigation; one injunction is enough. Given this situation, it seems unlikely that there would be a failure of deterrence, even if no money damages were available. Many litigants likely have sufficient incentive, either economic or ideological, to challenge overbroad laws, and their ability to mount such challenges is greatly augmented by the availability of attorney's fees.

Of course, these observations might be modified by closer inspection. The point here is not to attempt comprehensive analysis of the overbreadth doctrine, but to bring into sharper focus the significance of the noninstrumental rationale for awarding money damages in such cases. If, as has been suggested, there is no strong deterrence justification for money damages in overbreadth cases, the compensatory rationale would control. In my view, there is a compelling, noninstrumental reason to compensate overbreadth plaintiffs for all first amendment injury, without regard to whether such damages are needed for incentive effect. But it seems to me equally clear that there is no noninstrumental case for constitutionally irrelevant injury that happens to be caused by the government's act. If that conclusion is sound, it refines and clarifies the appropriate measure of compensatory damages in such cases.

Sheldon H. Nahmod, *Constitutional Damages and Corrective Justice: A Different View,* 76 Virginia Law Review 997 (1990)

. . . I propose to criticize *Jeffries's* risk-rule approach on several grounds. I argue that wrongdoing is inherent in unconstitutional conduct, not in qualified immunity. Consequently, the use of a risk-rule approach to compensatory damages is not normatively compelled. Rather, compensatory damages are normatively justified for all foreseeable harm resulting from unconstitutional conduct. In the course of making my argument, I criticize Jeffries's distinction between constitutional rights that protect individual interests and those that protect systemic interests.

I further contend that *Jeffries's* application of the risk rule to section 1983 is flawed because section 1983 is better analogized to intentional dignitary torts, where the risk rule does not govern, than to negligence where Jeffries asserts that the risk rule does govern. However, what ultimately is most troubling about his position is the extent of his willingness to allow tort doctrine and its accompanying rhetoric to determine the scope of a federal civil rights statute intended to vindicate fourteenth amendment interests. Significantly, the disagreements between Jeffries and myself are of more than academic interest because the issues raised are beginning to emerge explicitly in the circuits.

. . .

II. Critique and Analysis

A. *Section 1983 Qualified Immunity and Wrongdoing*

I assume that Jeffries is on solid ground in claiming that, based upon Weinrib's corrective justice view, both causation and wrongdoing are necessary to make out a normative case for compensation. This claim is indispensable for Jeffries's risk-rule conclusion that "the noninstrumental case for compensation for constitutional torts reaches only those injuries caused by the wrongful — i.e., unconstitutional — aspect of the government's behavior." However, in arriving at this conclusion, Jeffries is constrained for several reasons to discover the presence of negligence-type fault in section 1983 doctrine. Inasmuch as Keeton derives the risk rule from, and articulates it for, negligence law, the fit between the risk rule and section 1983 wrongdoing is more comfortable for Jeffries to the extent that section 1983 wrongdoing is similarly identified with negligence. Also, and more fundamentally, there is for Jeffries no normative basis for applying the risk rule to section 1983 compensatory damages cases in the absence of such negligence.

Unfortunately, Jeffries's reliance on qualified immunity doctrine for the proposition that section 1983 liability is negligence-based is not convincing. It is true that the Supreme Court ruled in *Anderson v. Creighton* that a "law enforcement officer who participates in a search that violates the Fourth Amendment may [not] be held personally liable for money damages if a reasonable officer could have believed that the search comported with the Fourth Amendment." However, the reference to reasonableness in *Anderson* is misleading because the Court intended something very different from negligence. It announced that a law enforcement officer is not liable unless she violated *clearly-settled* fourth amendment law, determined as of the date of the challenged conduct. This inquiry into the existence of clearly-settled law must be made in a somewhat particularized and fact-specific manner. Thus, the reference to reasonableness is a shorthand way of saying that where there is clearly-settled law, a police officer *is held to that standard* irrespective of what the officer actually knew.

It may be suggested that the clearly-settled-law inquiry, even as I have described it, still is an inquiry into the existence of wrongdoing. After all, since the defendant should have known clearly-settled law (whether she did or not), she was a wrongdoer in not acting accordingly. However, this is to misapprehend profoundly the nature and function of qualified immunity. Its primary purpose is not to deny the wrongdoing of a section 1983 defendant who acted in the absence of what Jeffries calls negligence. Its primary purpose is to promote independent decision-making by persons who might, when confronted with the spectre of section 1983 liability, refuse to act professionally and properly.

While the Supreme Court made this point clear in the first qualified immunity case decided in 1967, it was expressed more recently by the Court in *Harlow v. Fitzgerald,* when the Court eliminated the subjective component of the qualified immunity test:

> Where an official could be expected to know that certain conduct would violate statutory or constitutional rights, he should be made to hesitate; and a person who suffers injury caused by such conduct may have a cause of action. But where an official's duties legitimately require action in which clearly established rights are not implicated, the public interest may be better served by action taken 'with independence and without fear of consequences.'

Qualified immunity is thus essentially instrumental in nature and does not connote wrongdoing or its absence. A defendant who causes a constitutional deprivation which does not violate clearly-settled law is exonerated for public policy reasons. Conversely, a defendant who causes a constitutional deprivation in violation of clearly-settled law is liable because there are no public policy reasons that demand a contrary result.

This view of qualified immunity derives considerable support from several additional observations. First, the doctrine of qualified immunity itself is not grounded in the text or legislative history of section 1983 but is instead a creation of instrumental policy. The Court acknowledged as much in *Pierson v. Ray,* its seminal qualified immunity decision, when it applied what it erroneously called a "good faith" defense to police officers accused of making unconstitutional arrests. The Court reasoned that "[a] policeman's lot is not so unhappy that he must choose between being charged with dereliction of duty if he does not arrest when he has probable cause, and being mulcted in damages if he does."

Second, when the Court eliminated the subjective component of the qualified immunity test, and thereafter allowed defendants immediately to appeal denials of motions for summary judgment based on qualified immunity, it did so for the explicit purpose of allowing such defendants to avoid, to the extent possible, the need to proceed to trial. In effect, the Court went far in the direction of converting qualified immunity into absolute immunity, an affirmative defense which similarly is not fault-based. Rather, absolute immunity reflects the policy that an absolutely immune defendant who causes a constitutional deprivation is exonerated even where clearly-settled law is violated so as to protect her not only from liability but from the need to defend at all. In short, both qualified immunity and absolute immunity tell us little or nothing about wrongdoing in section 1983 cases.

B. The Section 1983 Prima Facie Case and Wrongdoing

We are thus brought back to the section 1983 prima facie case and Jeffries's rejection of the argument that every constitutional violation itself constitutes wrongdoing. Recall that "fault supplies the moral dimension to the causal relationship." Hence, the presence of what Jeffries calls negligence-type fault in section 1983 cases (through qualified immunity) is crucial to his position that corrective justice warrants the application of a risk-rule approach to compensatory damages. In order to adhere to his risk-rule approach, he must argue that constitutional violations are not in themselves wrongdoing. If Jeffries is wrong about this, as I shall argue he is, then even those constitutional provisions to which he refers as systemic can normatively and noninstrumentally give rise to compensatory damages broader in scope than he considers defensible.

Jeffries correctly observes that section 1983 does not have its own state-of-mind requirement, that it does not create rights but is a vehicle for enforcing them, and that different constitutional provisions have varying state-of-mind requirements ranging from impermissible motivation to nonnegligence. Because he equates fault and wrongdoing and identifies them with states of mind which "vary from right to right," he is forced to find wrongdoing elsewhere than in the prima facie case. Jeffries finds it in the qualified immunity doctrine. This explains why he critically characterizes the Court's decision in *Owen v. City of Independence* as an unwise strict liability case. He refuses to accept the "intuition" that "fault is inherent in unconstitutionality," so that "the reasonableness of an official's conduct is irrelevant, and every constitutional violation, regardless of circumstance, is presumptively appropriate for rectification by money damages."

His justifications for this refusal are intriguing but unconvincing. First, he observes that qualified immunity negligence-type fault derives from the law of "constitutional torts," not constitutional law itself. He considers this derivation advantageous because "it does not imply a redefinition of the rights themselves nor any limitation of their traditional application." But even if it is true that qualified immunity is not derived from constitutional law, so what? The identical statement about advantage can be made even if one takes the position that wrongdoing is inherent in unconstitutionality. Qualified (and absolute) immunity can still play important and instrumental policy roles regardless of which of these positions is taken.

Jeffries's second argument is that viewing wrongdoing as inherent in unconstitutionality is "more responsive to the traditional rhetoric of constitutional law than to much of its current doctrine." While "[t]raditionally, constitutional rights are described as fundamental and timeless[, i]n fact, some are neither." He notes that in many cases the Supreme Court has refused to give retroactive effect to declarations of new constitutional rights. He again criticizes *Owen,* but this time as an example of a case in which a governmental actor was held liable for damages even though the procedural due process requirements violated were apparently declared for the first time in *Owen* itself. Jeffries maintains that "[i]n these circumstances, it is surely odd to describe the municipality's action as intrinsically wrongful."

There are several difficulties with this argument. Jeffries sets up a straw man when he asserts that constitutional rights traditionally are described as "fundamental and timeless." I know of no one who so describes them in the sense he means. Constitutional rights are derived from textual or historical sources through interpretation by the judiciary. They are not "out there" simply waiting to be discovered. Moreover, after constitutional rights are derived through interpretation, there may be instrumental or other policy reasons *independent of their existence* which compel only prospective application. For example, the doctrine of nonretroactivity that Jeffries mentions has its most frequent application in cases involving criminal procedure and convicted defendants. If all newly declared rights automatically were applied retroactively, state and federal criminal proceedings frequently would be disrupted, extensive resources, having been already expended, would have to be expended once again on retrials and many guilty defendants could go free. This does not mean, though, that such unconstitutional conduct does not constitute wrongdoing.

One does not have to view constitutional rights as "fundamental and timeless" in the way Jeffries seems to mean in order to maintain that wrongdoing is indeed inherent in all constitutional violations.

But it probably is not the kind of wrongdoing that he has in mind. Jeffries uses fault and wrongdoing interchangeably and defines them "in the conventional legal sense as culpability, including culpable inadvertence, as in the violation of a legal norm of which the actor should have been aware." His repeated emphasis on negligence-type fault suggests that he envisions some sort of state-of-mind requirement which he identifies with negligence and more generally with wrongdoing. However, this conflation of fault and wrongdoing is seriously questionable. Fault connotes state of mind, but wrongdoing, while including fault in *Jeffries'* sense of the term, is considerably broader in scope.

Even where wrongdoing is grounded on negligence, it frequently turns out that no particular state of mind is required beyond volitional conduct. This is because the negligence standard primarily is objective in nature. There are many situations in which a defendant is held liable for negligent conduct even though that particular defendant could not realistically have acted otherwise. As the famous tort case of *Vaughn v. Menlove* demonstrates, defendants often are held to a socially created standard of reasonable care even though they have done all that could be expected of them (short of not engaging in the activity altogether) given their mental capacity. In a very real sense, we announce that because such defendants live and operate in our society, they are held at their peril to know certain things and to act accordingly. When they do not, they are negligent and liable for the harm caused.

Consequently, it is not exclusively negligence or any particular state of mind that constitutes wrongdoing. Rather, wrongdoing is a social construct that does not necessarily include states of mind or fault. So long as there is a judicial declaration that a given constitutional provision articulates a given standard of conduct — with or without any particular state of mind added, as the case may be — then there is wrongdoing of the kind that normatively makes out the noninstrumental case for compensation. Under this approach to wrongdoing and constitutional violations, there is no need to resort to qualified immunity, as Jeffries does. Thus, his argument for a risk-rule approach that limits section 1983 compensatory damages is considerably weakened, if not altogether undermined.

III. A Different View

A. *Wrongdoing as Inherent in Unconstitutionality*

1. *Consistency with Weinrib*

Jeffries' analysis of wrongdoing and qualified immunity is flawed because it identifies qualified immunity with wrongdoing and rejects the plausible claim that wrongdoing is inherent in unconstitutionality. Significantly, this claim also appears consistent with Weinrib's view of causation and wrongdoing in tort law. It is true that Weinrib, whose normative views are relied on so extensively by Jeffries, focuses on tort law in general and negligence in particular in his discussion of the moral need for both causation and wrongdoing. However, this is only because tort law is the subject at hand in the article in question.

As I read his article, Weinrib maintains that both causation and negligent wrongdoing are normatively required for tort law compensation: causation explains why *this plaintiff* is entitled to recover and negligence explains why *this defendant* is obligated to compensate. His purpose is to "vindicate . . . tort law as the expression of a single normative [noninstrumental] conception integrating the plaintiff's injury and the defendant's negligence." To quote Weinrib:

> In institutional terms, [the] relationship [between injury and negligence] is expressed by the lawsuit between the parties, with its assumption that the transference of a single sum can simultaneously satisfy the plaintiff's entitlement against the defendant and discharge the defendant's debt to the plaintiff. If a parallel doctrinal relationship exists, particularization of the plaintiff through causation must allow for linkage to the defendant, and particularization of the defendant through wrongdoing must similarly allow for linkage with the plaintiff.

Weinrib's conclusion, in short, is that "wrongdoing and causation [are] the interpenetrating aspects of a unified conception of tort."

The law of section 1983 compensatory damages liability comfortably can be fit into Weinrib's normative model. Causation explains why *this plaintiff* is entitled to recover and unconstitutional conduct explains why *this defendant* is obligated to compensate, although it may imply more. This captures the institutional relationship between a section 1983 plaintiff and defendant, whether the defendant is an individual or a local government: both causation and unconstitutional conduct exemplify that relationship. Indeed, one might describe the section 1983 relationship in right/duty terms in a manner parallel to Weinrib's description of the tort relationship: "The plaintiff's [constitutional] right to be free of wrongful [unconstitutional] interferences with his person and property is correlative to the [constitutional] duty on the defendant to abstain from such [unconstitutional] interferences."

Important advantages flow from my position that the normative implications for section 1983 encompass all damages attributable to constitutional wrongdoing. It is no longer necessary to distinguish, as Jeffries does, between individually and systemically focused constitutional rights. There are other principled ways of drawing lines around damages liability. Additionally, *Jeffries*'s position compels the trial judge to distinguish, for damages purposes, among various constitutional interests, and thus to reach difficult constitutional questions in order to resolve what ought to be straightforward damages issues. In contrast, my position that wrongdoing is inherent in unconstitutionality does not compel such distinctions.

2. *The Questionable Distinction Between Individual and Systemic Rights*

Under *Jeffries*'s risk-rule approach, it is important that there be a meaningful distinction between those constitutional provisions that "guard individuals against specified harms by directly prohibiting the infliction of such harms" and "provisions . . . seek[ing] to prohibit certain government actions." In the latter instance, because "the relation between the conduct proscribed and the harm ultimately feared is strategic and indirect, . . . violation of a constitutional prophylaxis often produces constitutionally irrelevant injury." Consequently, for Jeffries it makes considerable sense — indeed, it appears necessary — to apply a normatively derived risk-rule approach derived from qualified immunity in order to exclude "constitutionally irrelevant" damages from section 1983 liability.

However, that the distinction is as clear cut as Jeffries wants to make it is questionable. Indeed, attempting to make the distinction tends to lead to disjunctive thinking in which a particular constitutional right is primarily either individual or systemic. Constitutional rights, however, are more complex than that. The "takings" clause, which Jeffries characterizes as a tort-like constitutional right, surely is systemic as well. It is directed at government conduct of the sort that affects many. Conversely, the fourth amendment's warrant requirement, which he characterizes as systemic and prophylactic, also is directed at protecting individuals.

Yet Jeffries is compelled for theoretical reasons to attempt such a determination for *all* constitutional rights in order to decide in individual cases whether there exist "constitutionally irrelevant" damages which normatively should be excluded from section 1983 liability. In contrast, if wrongdoing is inherent in all constitutional violations, there is no normative need to draw *this* distinction (although other lines may have to be drawn) in connection with section 1983 compensatory damages for constitutional violations. Perhaps the best way to demonstrate this is to consider the fourth and first amendment hypotheticals that Jeffries uses in support of the application of a risk-rule approach.

a. *The Fourth Amendment Hypothetical*

Jeffries's fourth amendment hypothetical is one in which a police officer's search violative of the fourth amendment uncovers incriminating evidence, and it turns out, as sometimes happens, that the exclusionary rule does not bar the use of this evidence. The criminal defendant is charged, tried, convicted, and punished. Since all that occurred is reasonably foreseeable, according to Jeffries, this defendant, when he becomes a section 1983 plaintiff suing for damages for the violation of his fourth amendment rights, would be entitled to compensatory damages for all the harm stemming from that violation in the absence of a risk-rule approach. Jeffries argues against such a "peculiar, if not perverse" result on the grounds that the plaintiff's own misconduct contributed to the harm and that liability for all such damages "would be a wealth transfer from society generally to those guilty of criminal wrongdoing." He allows recovery only for invasion of privacy, the interest protected by the fourth amendment, while disallowing recovery for harm resulting from the discovery of incriminating evidence and the criminal prosecution.

But it is not necessary to adopt *Jeffries*'s risk-rule approach and its normative qualified immunity underpinnings in order to deal with this unusual hypothetical sensibly. We might concede that from a normative point of view — premised on the position that wrongdoing is inherent in unconstitutionality — the plaintiff is at least prima facie entitled to all damages resulting from the fourth amendment violation and still avoid what might be considered an unpalatable result. In addition to the defendant, various independent decisionmakers are causally responsible for plaintiff's damages as well, including the prosecutor, the trial judge, and the jury. It may thus be possible to deal with the compensatory damages issue not through *Jeffries*' risk-rule approach, but rather by focusing on causation in fact or superseding cause.

Suppose, for example, that the incriminating evidence unlawfully seized is not the only evidence used against the section 1983 plaintiff as the basis for his prosecution, conviction, and imprisonment. If the defendant can prove by a preponderance of the evidence that the plaintiff would have been prosecuted, convicted, and imprisoned even in the absence of the incriminating evidence, then the defendant is absolved from damages liability *for those events* on cause-in-fact grounds. There is thus no need to reach the proximate cause issue.

In the alternative, suppose the unlikely situation in which the incriminating evidence is indeed the primary, if not the only, evidence used in the decisions of the prosecutor, the judge, and the jury. Here, the proximate cause issue must be reached and, when it is, it plausibly can be dealt with in superseding cause terms. Under such an approach, it could be argued that the "intervening acts of the prosecutor, . . . judge and jury . . . each break the chain of causation unless plaintiff can show that these intervening acts were the result of deception or undue pressure by the defendant [police officer]." That is, even if we assume that the defendant is normatively responsible for all damages resulting from the incriminating evidence unlawfully seized, we can take the position that for instrumental reasons, such as a concern with overdeterrence, we do not want to award all damages to the plaintiff in the absence of deception, undue pressure, or misrepresentation by the defendant police officer.

Consequently, there is no real need to use the risk-rule approach in order to avoid a compensatory damages result which may be considered instrumentally unwise. Money damages can be limited in many cases through the use of causation in fact or superseding cause without artificially limiting to privacy alone the interests protected by the fourth amendment.

b. The First Amendment Hypothetical

According to Jeffries, first amendment cases pose even more difficult compensatory damages problems because "theorists recognize an instrumental relation between freedom of speech and societal decisionmaking." That is, "first amendment doctrine is strongly, albeit incompletely, oriented toward a systemic rationale." His first amendment hypothetical, intended to show that the harm resulting to an individual is different in kind from the harm at which the first amendment is directed, concerns the operator of an adult bookstore which provides live shows featuring nude dancers in addition to books and magazines. A local government attempts to shut down the bookstore by passing a zoning ordinance prohibiting all live entertainment. Ultimately, the ordinance is held unconstitutional but, in the meantime, the plaintiff's business is completely destroyed.

Jeffries contends that if damages were not limited by the risk rule, the plaintiff could recover for the entire loss resulting from closing the business. However, this is problematic for him for several reasons. To the extent that a relevant harm is the "contraction of social discourse," then it is society that has suffered the harm. Also, to the extent that individual self-fulfillment is a relevant harm, the nude dancers and the patrons have suffered the harm. Finally, Jeffries asserts that since "[z]oning laws routinely restrict the use of property, often in ways costly to owners," what happened to plaintiff's business "is also the sort of harm to which modern constitutional interpretation is notoriously indifferent." He concludes that, because the local government's fault is unrelated to the plaintiff's harm, the plaintiff would thus not be entitled to compensatory damages as a normative matter. Jeffries even goes on to question whether *any* compensatory damages in this case are necessary to serve the instrumental function of deterrence inasmuch as the successful assertion of the overbreadth doctrine could provide the basis for injunctive relief.

I disagree with *Jeffries*'s characterization of the relevant first amendment harms. He is too quick to assert that the relevant harm in the contraction of social discourse is only to society. Whatever we think of the plaintiff bookstore owner, he suffers from this contraction as a member of society (whether he knows or cares about it) and because it is his bookstore that can no longer contribute to social discourse. In addition, his interest in individual self-fulfillment has been harmed, because he can no longer sell books and magazines as well as provide nude dancing. Thus *Jeffries*'s characterizations are far too narrow, in part reflecting his initial distinction between individual and systemic harms.

I also find troubling his observations that "modern constitutional interpretation is notoriously indifferent [to the sort of harm suffered by the plaintiff]" and that "[o]nly the coincidence of [plaintiff's] economic injury and an essentially unrelated first amendment concern makes the claim work." Even though many constitutional challenges to zoning regulations lose in litigation, some do not. In addition, it surely is no "coincidence" that the defendant's unconstitutional conduct in this hypothetical is both the cause of plaintiff's business losses and constitutes wrongdoing. Indeed, it is for this very reason that the application of Weinrib's corrective justice approach to this hypothetical normatively justifies damages liability for all of the plaintiff's business losses.

c. *An Administrative Difficulty with* Jeffries's *Position*

In order to apply his risk-rule approach to the hypotheticals, Jeffries is forced, or at least considers himself forced, to discern just what the particular fourth and first amendment interests are. If I understand him correctly, a trial judge applying this approach for damages purposes must similarly articulate and separate these interests for the jury. However, a requirement that these interests be identified raises issues about the nature of the particular constitutional provision being considered that are even more difficult in most cases than the question whether the constitutional provision has been violated in the first place. For example, determining whether there has been a constitutional violation in the fourth amendment hypothetical is considerably easier than deciding thereafter, for damages purposes, just which individual and systemic interests the fourth amendment is intended to protect, and then distinguishing among them. Similarly, deciding in the first amendment hypothetical whether there has been a constitutional violation is easier than deciding which individual and systemic interests the first amendment is intended to protect, and then distinguishing among them as well.

In the case of the first amendment, this question is a deeply theoretical one about which judges and scholars differ, and one which should only be answered when it is necessary to do so. Yet because Jeffries insists on the normative presumption that such section 1983 plaintiffs are entitled only to compensatory damages for the harm to their individual interests, his risk-rule approach dictates that we confront this kind of question head on even after the threshold constitutional violation has been found. I contend that in so doing, he overloads the compensatory damages issue, an issue which ought to be relatively straightforward, both at the section 1983 interpretation level and in application.

In contrast, the identification of unconstitutional conduct with wrongdoing normatively justifies awarding compensatory damages for all foreseeable harm resulting from unconstitutional conduct. That is, I insist on the normative presumption that section 1983 plaintiffs who prove a constitutional violation are entitled to compensatory damages for all such harm. This avoids the need to distinguish among compensable individual interests and uncompensable systemic ones. When it becomes necessary to draw lines limiting awards for compensatory damages, that is better done, as I suggest, through the application of causation-in-fact doctrine or superseding cause doctrine. Except for those cases in which there is no causal connection whatever between the defendant's unconstitutional conduct and the plaintiff's harm, these doctrines do not affect the initial normative basis for awarding compensatory damages for unconstitutional conduct.

By way of summary, then, Jeffries and I differ significantly in our respective views of the relationship between section 1983 liability and wrongdoing, which he grounds in qualified immunity doctrine and I ground in unconstitutional conduct. Even though, like Jeffries, I assume that Weinrib is correct about corrective justice and its requirement of both causation and wrongdoing, Jeffries and I reach different conclusions respecting section 1983 and wrongdoing. My view leads me to conclude that compensatory damages liability for all foreseeable harm resulting from unconstitutional conduct is normatively justified. His view leads him incorrectly to apply a risk-rule approach to such compensatory damages.

However, there is considerably more than this that separates Jeffries and me. First, even under *Jeffries'* view that qualified immunity supplies the requisite wrongdoing in section 1983 cases, it does not necessarily follow that the risk rule should be applied. Indeed, it turns out that the risk rule is misplaced. Second, Jeffries and I have very different positions on the proper role of tort law and its accompanying rhetoric in section 1983 interpretation.

B. *The Flawed Risk Rule-Section 1983 Analogy*

Robert Keeton's risk rule for negligence is:

> A negligent actor is legally responsible for the harm, and only the harm, that not only (1) is caused in fact by his conduct but also (2) is a result within the scope of the risks by reason of which the actor is found to be negligent.

The application of this rule to Keeton's hypothetical, involving an exploding can of negligently unlabeled rat poison which injures a nearby person, results in a finding of no liability because the risk that did occur, the explosion, is not one with respect to which the defendant's conduct is negligent.

The risk rule, as applied in this example and in most, although not all, other negligence cases, arises in situations in which the issue is *liability*. However, Jeffries instead describes the risk rule "as a way of fixing the scope of *compensation* [which] is a concept well known in ordinary tort law." Liability and compensation are certainly intertwined, but they also are analytically distinguishable. That he does not distinguish between them obviously facilitates his later attempt to use the risk rule in a section 1983 compensatory damages context. But this move blurs an important distinction between section 1983 liability and compensatory damages. There can be, at one and the same time, liability for nominal damages of one dollar and no compensatory damages at all. In contrast, the prima facie case for negligence requires actual damages; nominal damages are not allowed.

That nominal damages are not allowed for negligence but are allowed under section 1983 suggests that, even assuming with Jeffries that qualified immunity supplies the requisite wrongdoing for normative purposes, the more appropriate analogy is between section 1983 and intentional dignitary torts such as assault, offensive battery, and false imprisonment. This analogy is more appropriate than that between section 1983 and negligence because it recognizes the dignitary nature of constitutional violations and such intentional torts. Just as compensatory damages in dignitary tort cases can include damages for physical, emotional, and economic harm, so too can compensatory damages in section 1983 cases.

If the better analogy for damages purposes is between section 1983 and intentional dignitary torts, then the rationale of the risk rule is inapplicable to section 1983 cases. Consider that Robert Keeton rejects as "untenable" the argument that "by analogy to the Risk Rule in negligence cases, the scope of liability for an intentional tort should be limited to results within the intent" because "it would produce a narrower scope of liability for the more blameworthy type of tort." If the focus is on the scope of liability for unintended harm resulting from intentional conduct, then, according to Keeton, "the course of decisional development appears to have been one of somewhat broader liability . . . ." Indeed, the Restatement of Torts permits liability for all damage resulting from intentionally tortious conduct unless, through hindsight, the resulting harm appears extraordinary.

In short, applying a negligence-based risk rule to section 1983 compensatory damages issues is seriously questionable even if one grants *Jeffries*'s premise that qualified immunity supplies the requisite wrongdoing. However, I believe that there is an even more fundamental theoretical difference between us — one that is grounded in our respective views of the appropriate role of tort doctrine in section 1983 interpretation.

C. *The Dangers of Tort Rhetoric in Section 1983 Litigation*

I recently argued at some length that the Supreme Court increasingly has moved from emphasizing constitutional rhetoric in section 1983 cases to using tort rhetoric. This strategic shift has profound implications for section 1983 and related constitutional doctrine. The use of tort rhetoric tends to determine the doctrinal outcomes in many section 1983 cases and, perhaps more subtly, also tends to encourage a certain way of thinking about section 1983 on the part of judges and lawyers. Such tort rhetoric allows the Court to remove certain state conduct from fourteenth amendment coverage. In addition, it enables the Court to use tort doctrines to decide section 1983 cases and to manipulate those doctrines and related cost-benefit analyses to limit section 1983. Moreover, it masks classical liberal theories of federalism, of the state-citizen relationship, and of political society.

It is against this background of the Court's increasing use of tort rhetoric to limit section 1983, and to structure the way in which we think about it, that *Jeffries*'s position should be understood. He candidly states that he thinks that the "law of section 1983 has transcended the original statutory authorization" even though he is forced to recognize that "the long tradition of attribution to the statutory text continues to constrain flexibility." Because of the "apparent categoricalness" of section 1983's language, he cannot justifiably distinguish among constitutional rights. Instead, he offers his "conceptual limitation of damages liability" as a way around section 1983 language and tradition. *Jeffries*'s purpose is thus clear.

His method for limiting the scope of section 1983 liability is similarly transparent: to use tort law's risk-rule doctrine and its accompanying rhetoric, even though the risk rule is derived from, and applied to, negligence, not constitutional law, and even though the determination of negligence requires cost-benefit analysis, unlike most constitutional violations. It is this strategy that is most troubling to me in the final analysis. It marginalizes the constitutional core of section 1983 by forgetting, or choosing to ignore, that section 1983 is a federal statute enacted to promote the policies implicated in the fourteenth amendment.

Note, *Damage Awards for Constitutional Torts: A Reconsideration After* Carey v. Piphus, 93 Harvard Law Review 966 (1980)

* * *

II. The Inadequacy of the Common Law Model

A. *The Roots of the Common Law Model:* Monroe v. Pape *and the "Background of Tort Liability"*

The pattern of dependency on common law tort concepts to interpret section 1983 began with *Monroe v. Pape*. Despite enactment of the Civil Rights Act in 1871, section 1983 lay dormant for almost a century. Then, in the 1961 *Monroe* decision, the Court held that state officials could not avoid liability by asserting that their actions were also illegal under state law. In making clear that section 1983 was created to provide a supplement to whatever relief might be obtained in state courts, the *Monroe* decision opened the door for the explosion in civil rights litigation. While *Monroe* envisioned special federal protection for those whose constitutional rights had been violated, it also provided the first reference to the background of tort liability which would eventually limit that protection. In explaining that the "wilfull intent" required in criminal prosecutions was not a prerequisite for section 1983 recovery, Justice Douglas said the section "should be read against the background of tort liability that makes a man responsible for the natural consequences of his actions."

From this modest original purpose of distinguishing civil from criminal actions, "the background of tort liability" emerged as a general principle through which section 1983 was to be interpreted—often without due regard for the context of the original statement. Six years after *Monroe*, in *Pierson v. Ray* , this background of tort liability previously invoked to impose liability was relied on to restrict section 1983 liability through the common law defense of good faith. The concern for uniform treatment of state and federal officers led to an identical immunity doctrine for federal officers. Decisions on whether a constitutional tort claim can be predicated on negligence have similarly relied on the common law.

The development of constitutional tort doctrine, however, has not always mirrored common law tort concepts. At times courts have eschewed the "background of tort liability" when it appeared to conflict with the letter and intent of the statute. Thus, in *Monell v. Department of Social Services*, the Court rejected the respondent superior theory of liability for section 1983 actions. *Monell* implies it was improper for *Carey* presumptively to employ the common law model to measure damages. Rather than simply assuming it should apply common law principles, the Court should have considered whether those principles would serve the statutory purpose: providing special federal protection for constitutional rights. Since *Monroe* refused to allow the *existence* of parallel state remedies to bar 1983 actions, it was ironic for *Carey* to work from the assumption that the doctrinal limits on state tort remedies should restrict the scope of 1983 relief. Because courts have extrapolated the background of tort liability with too little attention to its context in *Monroe*, its incantation in judicial opinions does not substitute for an analysis of whether the common law tort model is appropriate in constitutional tort actions.

B. *The Compensatory Interest*

. . . [T]he common law tort model authorizes compensation for tangible injuries and such intangibles as emotional distress. The occurrence of such harms bears only a coincidental relationship to the violation of constitutional rights. Clearly, a victim of unconstitutional conduct does not always suffer "actual injury." And the amount of consequential harm incurred is only fortuitously related to the constitutional deprivation. Yet, under the common law model, if a book is seized in violation of the first amendment, the author would recover the value of the printed material, but not the value of his right to express his views. Law enforcement officials who break into a citizen's home and place a wiretap would be liable for the proven physical damage to his property or for personal embarrassment but not for the loss of his fourth amendment expectation of security in his home and possessions. A person tried, but not convicted, on evidence obtained in violation of the fifth amendment would be entitled to no compensation whatever for the violation of his privilege against self-incrimination.

These concerns have been borne out as courts have relied on *Carey v. Piphus* to maintain that it would be inappropriate to award more than nominal damages for discriminatory failures to enter into good faith labor negotiations, denial of the right to a speedy appeal, confinement of a prisoner in a "Behavior Adjustment Unit" without full procedural due process, an unconstitutional refusal to allow an expelled student to call his accusing teacher as a witness, termination of supplemental food benefits for four-year-old children without due process, and the illegal impoundment of an automobile for nearly two weeks. Where actual injuries have been found and compensated, no additional award has been allowed for the constitutional deprivation itself.

This paradigm depends upon acceptance of the proposition that the deprivation of a constitutional right is merely a technical violation whose significance is entirely instrumental and can be measured by the "actual injury" produced. But constitutional guarantees have an important intrinsic dimension entirely apart from the injuries to person or property that may or may not accompany their violation. The first amendment protection of free speech and assembly is an entitlement of personal liberty secured to all persons by the due process clause of the fourteenth amendment. The fourth amendment creates an expectation of privacy; the fifth an assurance of government regularity. That damages are a uniquely appropriate remedy for the violation of such rights was recognized as far back as 1903, when Justice Holmes pointed out that "the deprivation of a man's political and social rights properly may be alleged to involve damage to that amount, capable of estimation in money."

While recognizing the intrinsic value of substantive constitutional rights, some courts and commentators suggest that procedural due process serves only an instrumental function. Thus violations of substantive guarantees in the Bill of Rights would receive compensation, while recovery for deprivations of procedural due process would depend solely on the coincidental presence of consequential injury. This perspective is myopic. An individual who becomes the focus of lawless official action loses the assurance that the government affords all its citizens a degree of security for their basic interests. This loss of security in one's entitlements is inherent in the deprivation of due process; the arbitrary taking is itself an element of damages separate from the value of the property taken. Even the instrumental function of procedural due process is undercut when a court may refuse a plaintiff's claim for damages by concluding that plaintiff would still have suffered the same consequential injuries even if prior notice and a hearing was provided. Retrospective reconsideration of the decision, bounded by the principles of judicial review, cannot substitute for the broader discretion in decisionmaking, experimentation in policy formulation, or consideration of individual circumstances which may be provided in an administrative determination. A district court cannot bring to the dispute the same expert knowledge that enlightens the deliberations of the hearing officer.

Thus, with respect to both substantive and procedural rights, the common law tort model has the courts find value in the sometimes insignificant collateral consequences of the violations of constitutional rights, but ignores the primary value of the right itself. The random relationship between compensation of actual injury and meaningful protection of constitutional rights was recognized by Justice Harlan in his concurrence in *Monroe*:

> Even the remedy for such an unauthorized search and seizure as *Monroe* was allegedly subjected to may be only the nominal amount of damages to physical property allowable in an action for trespass to land. It would indeed be the purest coincidence if the state remedies for violation of common-law rights by private citizens were fully appropriate to redress those injuries which only a state official can cause and against which the Constitution provides protection.

Certainly the nominal one dollar award granted in *Carey* is insufficient to compensate for the loss of a constitutional right. Nominal damages are in no sense compensatory, but merely symbolic, and even as a symbol clearly unable to convey the importance of a constitutional right.

C. The Deterrence Interest

The legislative history of section 1983 makes clear that the statute was primarily intended to deter violations of newly created fourteenth amendment rights. Recent legislative proclamations have reemphasized this objective. The focus, seen in *Monroe*, on the official nature of the act rather than the harm to the plaintiff supports this interpretation. Indeed, some circuit courts have held that section 1983 liability does not apply to undeterrable conduct. Moreover, the "custom or usage" phrase in the statute has been interpreted with an eye to deterrable conduct. In *Imbler v. Pachtman*, Justice White noted that deterrence was "precisely the proposition upon which § 1983 was enacted," and commentators have generally concurred.

The traditional tort model, embraced in *Carey v. Piphus* , treats compensation as the guiding principle for measuring damages. Although deterrence has been recognized as a valuable purpose of the civil damage mechanism in its own right, the traditional model views deterrence as a byproduct to be achieved through the extension of awards for consequential injury. But even under this common law model, achieving a proper level of deterrence depends upon the granting of full compensation. Yet, for constitutional torts, awards limited to collateral injuries necessarily undermine the deterrence function since consequential harm does not always accompany a violation of constitutional rights. In the due process context, for example, there is less incentive to extend a prior hearing if damages will be awarded only when a court determines after the fact that an administrative hearing would have led to a different result. Similarly, the incentive offered law enforcement officers to abstain from electronic surveillance diminishes if it is made a function of their confidence that little actual injury will be inflicted. The prospect that valuable entitlements to privacy will be compromised may be safely ignored.

This need for substantial damage awards is not met by suggestions that deterrence can be achieved through the possibility of recovering either attorneys' fees or exemplary damages. Attorneys' fees are not always available and can hardly provide an incentive for the plaintiff who recognizes that the lack of compensable injury will prevent the recovery of meaningful damages. Punitive damages generally require the presence of malicious intent. Some jurisdictions insist that the punitive award bear a "reasonable relation" to the damages for actual injury. Nor do other alternatives suffice. While helpful, injunctive relief and criminal prosecution are severely handicapped as means of deterrence by extraordinary proof requirements and federalism concerns.

Indeed, federalism interests may be better served by an effective damage remedy which would reduce the necessity for more direct forms of intervention into state and local affairs. Reforms initiated because of fear of civil liability are far less intrusive than the structural reform that has characterized judicial efforts in the school desegregation, prison and mental health fields. Given a renewed emphasis on federalism in the Supreme Court, the ability to induce changes in state and local protection of constitutional rights through a revitalized damage award should be attractive. The obvious tension between the desire for full effectuation of constitutional rights and for less federal intervention in state affairs can be resolved only through a civil damage remedy large enough to deter potential violations of the Constitution.

III. Using the Voting Rights Model to Measure Damages in Constitutional Tort Actions

An appropriate system for measuring damages for constitutional violations requires sensitivity to the right that has been abridged and the need for deterrence. Although the broader use of the voting rights model represents an extension of existing legal doctrine, it is consistent with and fulfills the purposes of the civil rights acts. By providing substantial compensation for the inherent value of the right violated it redresses the primary deprivation rather than coincidental consequential injury. By assuring compensation whenever a violation occurs it enhances deterrence even when a constitutional violation does not produce provable actual injury.

A. The Permissibility of Judicial Implementation of the Voting Rights Model

The use of the voting rights paradigm could obviously be mandated by Congress. Short of legislative action, the judiciary itself may implement the voting rights model through the development of federal common law. As discussed in Part I, *Carey v. Piphus*' instruction that the nature of particular constitutional interests should dictate damage standards is sufficiently broad to permit adoption of the voting rights cases in measuring damages. For procedural due process claims, of course, this option has been foreclosed.

This implicit authorization in *Carey* for the development of a federal common law of damages is justifiable. The federal courts have often utilized federal common law to effectuate the purposes of federal statutes. In *Textile Worker's Union v. Lincoln Mills*, the Supreme Court concluded that the need to provide "necessary legal remedies" for the Labor Management Relations Act, despite the fact that the statute made no reference to an applicable body of substantive or remedial law, authorized "federal courts to fashion federal law where federal rights are concerned." Similarly, given the purposes of section 1983 discussed in Part II, it is appropriate for federal courts to implement a voting rights paradigm for damages.

Before formulating an independent federal rule of decision, courts normally look first to state law. In the landmark *Clearfield Trust* case, the desirability of a uniform rule was sufficient to give the federal courts authority to create a federal common law for commercial paper. Certainly, uniform protection of constitutional rights is at least as important as a uniform law of commercial paper. Indeed, in *Adickes v. S.H. Kress & Co.*, Justice Brennan postulated that section 1983 relief "should not depend on the vagaries of the general common law but should be governed by uniform and effective federal standards."

Furthermore, section 1988 may be read to invite the development of federal common law. This section has been interpreted by the Supreme Court to require those federal and state rules of damages used in civil rights cases to serve "the policies expressed in the federal statutes." Last Term, however, in *Robertson v. Wegmann*, in refusing to apply section 1988 to allow a survivorship claim where Louisiana law did not provide for one, the Court instructed that success of the section 1983 action was not the only benchmark by which to determine the appropriate remedy. Section 1988 was read to require that state law should play a role in the remedy selection process, regardless of whether state law would provide a remedy for the particular plaintiffs before the court. *Robertson* should not stifle the development of a federal common law for damages. The Court expressly limited its holding and asserted that deterrence purposes of section 1983 would not be compromised by the absence of a survivorship cause of action. Moreover, *Robertson*'s emphasis on state standards is in apparent conflict with *Carey* , where the Court did not refer to Illinois law.

Alternatively, courts need not rely upon statutory interpretation to establish the appropriateness of the voting rights model of measuring damages. *Bivens* stands for the proposition that courts may imply a damage action directly from the Constitution when appropriate to effectuate constitutional rights. It would be less drastic for the Court to adopt a damage measure necessary to protect constitutional rights than it was in *Bivens* to imply the existence of an entire cause of action.

B. Need for a Fixed Minimum Recovery

Assessing the monetary value of intangible injuries is an inherently uncertain endeavor. Juries will find it difficult to quantify the loss of a constitutional right in dollars and cents. In the voting rights cases, juries were simply instructed to award compensation for the loss suffered by the defendant's deprivation of his right to vote. The openendedness of such an instruction can only marginally be reduced by suggestions for the jury to look at "what proportion of its value has been destroyed," or by setting the award with respect to the "defendant's motives and behavior" and perhaps even the "wealth of the defendant." Yardsticks developed by appellate courts are even more ambiguous, as typified by the Seventh Circuit's maxim that the awards be "neither so small as to trivialize the right nor so large as to provide a windfall." Judge Leventhal admonished that "compensation . . . should not be approached in a niggardly spirit. It is in the public interest that there be a reasonably spacious approach," which Judge Wilkey operationally defined as "an amount which will assure [the plaintiff] that [constitutional] rights are not lightly to be disregarded and that they can be truly vindicated in the courts."

The antimajoritarian nature of constitutional guarantees further suggests that a jury reflecting community standards may not fairly value the unpopular exercise of constitutional rights. In addition, many plaintiffs who bring section 1983 and *Bivens* actions do not possess the status and reputation that will appeal to a traditional jury. These concerns are only partially mitigated by the plaintiffs' ability to dismiss potential jurors or request a change in venue.

A fixed minimum recovery would reduce the danger of arbitrary awards. Such a scheme would not be without precedent. The Omnibus Crime Control and Safe Streets Act, the Foreign Intelligence Surveillance Act, and California's Civil Rights Act, have liquidated damage provisions. Proposed amendments to the Federal Tort Claims Act, in addition to providing an exclusive remedy against the government in *Bivens*- type actions, would establish a minimum damage award of $1,000 for a constitutional violation. A number of commentators agree with the suggestion that a floor for section 1983 recovery be established.

Judicial establishment of a fixed minimum recovery is problematical. First, the setting of a liquidated amount exemplifies "judicial legislation," fears of which have led courts to rely on the "background of tort liability" and import state statutes of limitations. Despite the availability of liquidated damage provisions in wiretapping statutes as a source of analogy, most judges will be reluctant to take such a step. Second, judicial fiat of a minimum recovery may impermissibly infringe upon a defendant's seventh amendment right to trial by jury. For these reasons, it is probably necessary for Congress to establish a minimum recovery for victims of constitutional violations.

* * *

Part VII

"[S]hall be liable to the party injured in . . . [a] suit in equity": Federalism and Public Law Litigation

Even though section 1983 provides on its face for equitable relief, the Supreme Court has imposed significant obstacles to its availability. In the course of interpreting the standing requirements of Article III of the Constitution, for example, the Court dramatically limited the availability of equitable relief under section 1983 in *City of Los Angeles v. Lyons*, 461 U.S. 95 (1983). Similarly, in the name of "Our Federalism," the Court announced the doctrine of *Younger v. Harris*, 401 U.S. 37 (1971), whereby federal courts ordinarily do not have jurisdiction to enjoin pending state criminal proceedings. This doctrine has since been expanded to include certain pending state civil administrative proceedings as well. *See Middlesex County Ethics Committee v. Garden State Bar Association*, 457 U.S. 423 (1982) and *Ohio Civil Rights Commission v. Dayton Christian Schools*, 477 U.S. 619 (1986).

In his article, Professor Fallon maintains that the Court in *Lyons* misused the doctrines of standing and equitable restraint for the purpose of limiting federal court public law litigation under section 1983. He also argues that the Court's approach is inconsistent with section 1983 policy. Professor Fallon proceeds to set out an alternative approach which distinguishes between justiciability and the question of appropriate remedies and between "non-Hohfeldian" and institutional litigation. He further proposes a role for Congress.

Professor Nichols deals with federal judicial intervention directed at pending state judicial proceedings. He suggests "a method of interpreting the demands of section 1983 as it applies to state judiciaries that respects the aims of the provision without debilitating local decisionmaking."

Richard H. Fallon, Jr., *Of Justiciability, Remedies, and Public Law Litigation: Notes on the Jurisprudence of* Lyons, 59 New York University Law Review 1 (1984)

INTRODUCTION

In the broad sense, this is an essay about the future of public law litigation. The era of the public lawsuit began with *Brown v. Board of Education.* Responding initially to the massive injustice of racial discrimination, federal courts in the years following *Brown* began to involve themselves increasingly in the oversight, and sometimes in the management, of various state and local institutions. But judicial innovation was not animated by race alone. The desegregation cases inaugurated a judicial revolution not easily cabined. Since *Brown*, novel classes of

---

litigants routinely have sought judicial resolution of novel issues. Courts increasingly have granted relief once thought extraordinary. Too, Congress has given to the judicial branch expansive mandates to oversee the behavior of federal, state, and private actors.

Commentators have disagreed about the defining features of "public law litigation" — a term often used to refer generally to the diverse phenomena of modern, nontraditional litigation. But it seems mistaken to seek a set of necessary and sufficient criteria to link, for example, class actions, taxpayer suits initiated to challenge the lawfulness of government expenditures, and suits to restructure state institutions such as schools, mental hospitals, and police departments. For purposes of this Article, two forms of public law litigation are especially important.

One important category of public lawsuits involves "non-Hohfeldian plaintiffs." In contrast with the classic plaintiffs of American legal history, non-Hohfeldian plaintiffs invoke the judicial power to redress injuries not easily definable in terms of personal, financial loss or other harms actionable at common law. Nor do they claim that the defendant has breached a legal duty running personally to them. Undertaking to represent shared interests in enforcing lawful conduct by large institutions, non-Hohfeldian plaintiffs initiate legal action to redress legal wrongs that offend their moral or ideological sense of right. Sometimes ideological plaintiffs can plead an injury to a traditionally recognized interest. For example, plaintiffs challenging the lawfulness of government expenditures under the first amendment might attempt to demonstrate economic injury in their capacity as taxpayers. But the economic injuries, if any, are trifling. Nor do they differentiate the plaintiffs, as affected rights holders, from the class of all other taxpayers. Non-Hohfeldian plaintiffs aspire to secure the enforcement of legal principles that touch others as directly as themselves and that are valued for moral or political reasons independent of economic interests.

A second important category of public lawsuits involves "structural" or "institutional" litigation. Structural litigation departs from the classic lawsuit of the "received tradition" mostly in the remedy sought — an injunctive decree reordering the policies or structures of an institution of government. *Mills v. Rogers* exemplifies the concept. The plaintiffs in *Mills* all were present or former patients of a state mental institution. As the predicate for their action, they alleged an injury easily assimilable into a traditional legal category: the involuntary administration of medical treatment. If the involuntary treatment of mental patients was substantively illegal — the principal "merits" issue in the case — then the facts would have supported a battery action cognizable at common law. The plaintiffs in *Mills*, however, did not request only money damages for past harms; instead they sought an injunction reforming the institutional practices of the Boston State Hospital. The lawsuit asked the federal court to address its remedy to the institutional structure that led to the plaintiffs' injuries and to decree structural alterations that would prevent recurrence of illegal acts.

The future of public law litigation, including lawsuits by non-Hohfeldian plaintiffs and actions seeking structural remedies, currently is much in doubt. However erratic its pattern, the Supreme Court's drift has been unmistakable. In recent Terms, the Court insistently has demanded judicial "restraint" from the lower federal courts. Yet, apparently without sense of paradox, over the same period the Court has wielded doctrine more and more innovatively to achieve desired substantive outcomes.

City of Los Angeles v. Lyons exemplifies both trends: the hostility to the phenomena of public law litigation, and the unrestrained reworking of doctrine to obtain a "restrained" result. The plaintiff in the case, Adolph Lyons, had been choked to unconsciousness by Los Angeles police. Alleging a departmental policy of applying unnecessary and life-threatening chokeholds, Lyons asked a federal district court to enjoin the practice. The district court granted a preliminary injunction, and the Ninth Circuit affirmed. But the Supreme Court reversed the lower courts and ordered the suit dismissed.

The Supreme Court held first that Lyons lacked standing — the required personal stake in the outcome of the controversy — to seek an injunction against the asserted chokehold policy. This holding effectively barred the possibility of federal injunctive relief; if Lyons lacked the requisite interest to sue for an injunction, then no one else would possess it either. But the Court did not limit its holding to the law of standing. Even if Lyons's standing were upheld, the Court ruled that principles of comity and deference to state law enforcement agencies would require dismissal under the doctrine of equitable restraint. As construed by the Court, equitable restraint, like the doctrine of standing, mandated dismissal of the lawsuit based on a very narrow conception of the plaintiff's "personal stake." Omitted from the equitable calculus were the culpability of the defendant, the nature of its existing policies, the burdensomeness of the requested remedy, and the substantive policies of Congress in authorizing injunctive relief against state officials.

Lyons is an important case for the future of public law litigation. First, the *Lyons* majority both expanded the requirements of standing law and extended the doctrine's terrain. As a result of *Lyons*, standing analysis apparently has displaced the more flexible doctrine of mootness as the applicable justiciability hurdle in much federal litigation predicated on past injuries. Second, because the Court's opinion is framed in constitutional terms, *Lyons*'s standing analysis raises questions about the capacity of Congress to authorize standing for non-Hohfeldian plaintiffs. Finally, the Court's construction of "equitable restraint" stretches that concept beyond its reasonable justifications and mistakenly ignores congressional statutory policy.

In the narrow sense, this is an Article about *Lyons*: the case's implications are explored and its logic critiqued. But the Article also aims at more general insights concerning public law litigation — particularly the distinctive phenomena of non-Hohfeldian and structural lawsuits — and its future. While the main effort of critique and reconstruction must await later discussion, some recurring themes can be anticipated.

The first theme involves a distinction between threshold questions of justiciability — questions of the Court's constitutional power even to entertain a lawsuit — and final decisions whether to award particular remedies. In *Lyons*, the Supreme Court treated as an element of standing the question whether an injunction would alleviate the specific personal injury on which the plaintiff's standing was predicated. This approach, which views the issue of remedial efficacy as part of the standing inquiry, is unnecessary and unfortunate. It forecloses a federal court from obtaining pertinent information about the lawfulness of the defendant's conduct and from balancing the various interests, before deciding whether relief ought to be provided. This Article will argue that an inquiry into the effectiveness of a particular remedy should play no part in article III standing analysis.

A second theme concerns the legal foundations of justiciability doctrines. In *Lyons*, the Court's standing analysis sounded almost entirely in constitutional terms. Although standing and other justiciability doctrines are traceable ultimately to article III, recent cases wisely have acknowledged a role for Congress in defining the boundaries of the judicial function. In contrast with this deference to congressional judgments, *Lyons'* constitutional pronouncements regrettably undermine Congress's ability, through the conferral of standing, to use the federal courts to protect federal rights. In our increasingly bureaucratic age, large institutions frequently dominate individual lives. The scope of judicial oversight of institutional behavior therefore implicates questions of enormous practical and political significance. On such questions the Court should not claim too quickly for itself the final word.

A third theme holds that the Supreme Court has failed to appreciate an important distinction among issues encompassed by the term "public law litigation." One set of issues involves the appropriateness of adjudication in cases brought by non-Hohfeldian plaintiffs. Other issues, which are conceptually distinct, are raised by "institutional litigation." The claim here is not that non-Hohfeldian and institutional litigation are always, or even usually, distinct in practice; non-Hohfeldian plaintiffs sometimes seek injunctions reordering government institutions. The much more limited argument is that suits brought by non-Hohfeldian plaintiffs characteristically give rise to one set of issues concerning the scope of judicial power, institutional litigation to another. The former present issues as to the appropriateness of parties — whether a particular plaintiff can sue, and possibly whether a particular defendant should be subject to suit. In contrast, structural lawsuits raise concerns about the appropriateness of particular forms of relief, especially whether particular injunctive remedies are too intrusive or beyond the courts' practical competence or constitutional authority. Given this difference, courts would do well to address the issues separately, even when both are involved in a single lawsuit.

Had this distinction between non-Hohfeldian and institutional litigation been recognized in *Lyons*, it would have suggested that remedial restraint becomes less appropriate as the relief sought becomes less intrusive and coercive. Also relevant to the appropriateness of equitable restraint, and also ignored by the *Lyons* majority, are the substantive policies underlying Congress's decision to authorize equitable relief under 42 U.S.C. § 1983.

* * *

III

Remedial Standing

The majority and dissenting opinions in *Lyons* did not join the standing debate at the level of ultimate principle. The majority held that the plaintiff's requests for various remedies must be assessed separately for purposes of standing analysis. The dissent contended that they should not be separated. But the argument over whether Lyons's remedial requests should have been aggregated or disaggregated ought to be pursued only insofar as it illuminates, rather than obscures, the deeper issues at stake. The fundamental concern presumably is whether article III ever would allow Lyons to obtain a federal injunction. If article III limitations on judicial remedies would prevent Lyons from winning an injunction on the facts as pleaded, the aggregation or disaggregation of his remedial requests would matter little. The underlying concerns thus emerge more clearly if the facts are modified. Although he could have asked for damages, assume that Lyons requested only an injunction. Had he done so, would he have had standing to sue?

A. *The Implications of* Lyons

In *Lyons*, the Supreme Court held that article III standing to seek an injunction requires a showing of remedial efficacy: The plaintiff must establish that the requested relief will alleviate a present injury sufficient for personal interest standing. Although other cases also have stated that article III imposes remedial standing requirements, the constitutional policies supporting remedial standing all are embodied in, and amply protected by, doctrines of personal interest standing, nexus standing, and mootness. When the relationship of remedial standing to these doctrines is clarified, arguments of precedent and constitutional policy establish that remedial standing should not be regarded as a mandatory precondition of judicial relief under article III. The constitutionalization of remedial standing intrudes into the domain of mootness. Defying implicit policies of emerging public law, it also diminishes the power of courts, and potentially the capacity of Congress, to protect federal rights and to provide remedies for their violation.

1. *Whither Mootness?*

In holding that Adolph Lyons lacked standing to seek an injunction, the Supreme Court reasoned from the premise that article III imposes a stringent standing requirement that the requested remedy, or at least an injunctive remedy, should redress either the actual injury on which standing is predicated or some other actionable injury. This premise did not appear on the surface of the Court's opinion. But it is needed to explain the Court's application of standing's personal injury requirement: "The plaintiff must show that he 'has sustained or is immediately in danger of sustaining some direct injury' as the result of the challenged official conduct, and the injury or threat must be both 'real and immediate' not 'conjectural' or 'hypothetical.'" When Lyons's claims are tested under this formulation, there is a clear sense in which he had "sustained . . . some direct injury." He had suffered a collapsed larynx, caused by his being choked to unconsciousness by the Los Angeles police. A more palpable injury is hard to imagine. In the Court's usage, however, Lyons's was a "past" injury; in a suit for injunctive relief, the Court held, past injuries drop from consideration. Because they cannot be remedied by a present injunction against future conduct, the Court found that such injuries fail to establish a present case or controversy.

Although it embodied familiar elements, the *Lyons* Court's analytical approach by no means was dictated by established doctrine. An injury's past character traditionally has raised questions of justiciability in actions for injunctions. But the issue arising from the passage of time after an acknowledged injury, sufficient at some moment to confer standing, easily could have been analyzed as one of mootness instead of standing. Mootness is the justiciability doctrine concerned specifically with the relevance or irrelevance of an injury's temporal passage.

The Supreme Court plainly was aware that *Lyons* invited a mootness analysis. By the time the case reached the Supreme Court, the Los Angeles police had instituted policies different from those in force at the time of Lyons's injury. Citing this change, Lyons himself argued that the case was moot and need not be decided. But the Court held expressly that the case was not moot. Because the City still might resume its past practices, the Court reasoned, "[i]ntervening events" had not "'irrevocably eradicated the effects of the alleged violation.'" Yet this conclusion extended only to the issue of mootness. Though not sufficiently dissipated to moot the case, the "effects of the alleged violation" were so eradicated as to deprive Lyons of standing.

Lyons's disparate conclusions as to standing and mootness could have major implications for the future of mootness doctrine. It means nothing to say that Lyons's case was not moot if, because his injury was "past," he lacked standing nonetheless. Moreover, *Lyons* by no means appears to be an anomolous case. Under the majority's reasoning, no plaintiff ever would have standing to sue for an injunction based on a past injury, even though the case might not be moot.

By displacing mootness with standing analysis, *Lyons* apparently erects a heightened barrier to the protection of federal rights in suits for injunctive relief. Mootness and standing serve similar functions. But while both employ concepts of concrete adverseness to ensure that issues are framed properly and to establish that judicial intervention is warranted, and both limit judicial involvement in the functions of political institutions of government, there are important differences between the doctrines. First, the Supreme Court has viewed mootness as much more flexible than the article III aspects of standing. This flexibility is lost under the reasoning of the majority in *Lyons*. Second, although the Court often has said that plaintiffs must retain their personal interest in the outcome throughout a controversy, examination of the Court's decisions suggests that the personal interest needed to defeat mootness may be different from, and less than, that required initially to establish, standing.

A familiar mootness paradigm illustrates some of the disparities of mootness and standing analysis. In actions to enjoin a defendant from repeating conduct that caused a past harm, mootness analysis typically has assumed the existence of standing, predicated on the past injury. The operative inquiry then has focused on the likelihood of future harm to the same plaintiff. Often the Court has suggested that there must be a "reasonable expectation" of recurrence — a formulation similar to that used by the *Lyons* Court to identify the applicable standing requirement. But where the defendant has suspended challenged conduct, the Court's mootness cases instead have established a powerful presumption favoring adjudication. Before a case will be dismissed as moot, the Court has imposed a burden on the defendant to prove that there exists no reasonable expectation of recurrence. In at least some cases, the Court has held that a case should not be held moot if it was "not absolutely clear" that the defendant's challenged conduct would not again result in injury to the plaintiff.

Also illustrative of the Court's less restrictive approach to mootness than to standing are cases "capable of repetition, yet evading review." Decisions within this category have established that a plaintiff, injured by the defendant's conduct in the past, must show some likelihood of incurring further injury in order to escape a mootness bar. But while the Court sometimes has required a "reasonable expectation" of recurrence, on at least one occasion it has stated no requisite likelihood at all. In *Roe v. Wade*, the Court considered whether a woman, who no longer was pregnant when the case reached the Supreme Court, was entitled to challenge a statute prohibiting abortions. In light of public policy concerns militating in favor of judicial resolution, the Court in *Roe* was satisfied to recognize that "[p]regnancy often comes more than once to the same woman." On that basis, it found the case not moot.

Mootness cases involving secondary or "collateral" injuries provide another example of the difference between standing and mootness analysis. When a plaintiff alleges some present injury in addition to the "past" harm sustaining standing, the secondary injury may overcome mootness even if it would not have sufficed independently to support standing. In lawsuits challenging criminal convictions after the challenger's sentence had been served, the evident injury supporting federal standing, the Court has "acknowledged the obvious fact of life that most criminal convictions do in fact entail adverse . . . consequences. The mere 'possibility' that this will be the case is enough to preserve a criminal case from ending 'ignominiously in the limbo of mootness.'"

The Court gave perhaps its most striking application of collateral effects analysis in *United States Parole Commission v. Geraghty* — a decision in which the Court also appealed directly to the "flexible character of the Art. III mootness doctrine" in cases presenting issues of continuing significance and satisfying the functional requisite of justiciability. In *Geraghty*, a federal prisoner filed a class action challenging the guidelines governing release on parole. The district court rejected the claim on the merits and denied class certification. Geraghty then appealed, but completed his sentence before the appellate court rendered a decision. Nonetheless, when Geraghty took his case to the Supreme Court, the Court held squarely that the plaintiff's case was not moot, even though he no longer retained a personal stake in the outcome of the lawsuit. His live interest in the procedural motion for class certification sufficed to forestall mootness. Such an interest plainly could not have established standing at the threshold.

Several policy considerations underlying the case or controversy requirement justify allowing a lesser interest to preclude mootness than would be necessary to establish standing initially. An actual injury, even if past, continues to frame litigation in a factual context that illuminates and delimits judicial decisionmaking. The occurrence of injury, past as well as present, establishes a moral warrant for judicial intervention; having caused injury, a defendant has no just claim to freedom from judicial process. Finally, absent judicial intervention, a defendant who has caused injury remains free to repeat or continue injurious conduct. In such a case, a judicial decision is not clearly nugatory or merely advisory.

Where an injury is past, other settled premises of the judicial system do counsel reticence. Justiciability doctrines reveal a deep, systemic antipathy to judicial coercion that is unnecessary to protect rights actually in danger. Equally established policies urge courts to avoid unnecessary constitutional decisionmaking. These policies suffice to justify the existence of a mootness bar to federal adjudication; nevertheless, with the defendant's claim to noncoercion diminished, and with an issue of continuing significance posed for judicial resolution, the decision whether to allow a suit to continue should depend at least in part on flexible policy considerations about the desirability of resolving a particular dispute. The widespread effects of institutional practice and policy should not be ignored.

Remedial standing fails to consider the factors justifying a lower personal interest threshold to preclude mootness than to establish standing. Moreover, when a plaintiff also can seek damages, remedial standing simply overlooks the reality that the merits issues — concerning the constitutional lawfulness of the defendant's conduct — may be unavoidable. The policy against unnecessary constitutional decisionmaking therefore should impose no bar. Especially in such a case, remedial standing represents an unnecessary and unjustified doctrine that reduces judicial capacity to protect constitutional rights.

2. *The Stake of Congress*

Lyons's remedial standing analysis also may jeopardize the protective powers of Congress. By characterizing its remedial standing inquiry as mandated by article III, the Supreme Court implied that Congress could not authorize injunctive relief based solely on past injuries. But this conclusion, which subverts prior recognitions of congressional authority, is unwise if not untenable.

To assess *Lyons*'s implications for congressional power, it may be helpful to hypothesize a congressional enactment prescribing the award of equitable remedies. As part of a regulatory or civil rights statute, imagine a provision for mandatory injunctions: upon proof of a defendant's violation, the statute directs that a federal court "*shall* issue an injunction" against further violations of the law. The statute does not authorize the exercise of remedial discretion, but instead expresses a clear intent that the likelihood of future injury to the plaintiff — the dispositive variable in remedial standing analysis — is not to be weighed as a precondition to relief. *Lyons*'s constitutionalization of remedial standing suggests that such a statute would exceed the bounds of congressional power. But previous decisions of the Court, as well as accepted practice and constitutional policy, indicate a contrary view.

Under article I, Congress possesses broad legislative discretion to prescribe a wide variety of civil and criminal penalties, as well as injunctive relief, for violations of federal law. Remedial standing questions do not arise in criminal cases or in suits for damages, nor in some suits for injunctions. Congressional power to prescribe schemes of punishment and deterrence therefore confronts no remedial standing limitation in such cases. But if Congress can require a court to impose criminal penalties, or to assess fines or damages of a specified amount, there is no compelling reason why it could not direct issuance at least of prohibitory injunctions solely upon proof of unlawful activity. It is no persuasive objection that the historic function of equity was to deter rather than to punish. Under the constitutional scheme of separation of powers, decisions to adopt particular schemes of punishment and deterrence appropriately are invested in Congress. If Congress should determine that mandatory injunctions afforded the best feasible balance of punishment and deterrence under a statute, the legislative judgment should be respected.

Heedful of congressional prerogatives, practice under existing statutes has reflected an acceptance of Congress's power to authorize suit where remedial standing does not exist. Various civil rights statutes permit the Attorney General, either as a plaintiff or as an intervenor, to seek injunctions against unlawful conduct by state institutions. Prior to *Lyons*, the Court had not held that injunctions under such statutes must be remedially effective in curing particular wrongs to identified parties. In *Pasadena City Board of Education v. Spangler*, for example, the Court allowed the Attorney General to continue to prosecute a lawsuit, despite the facts that all the original student plaintiffs had graduated and that the pleaded standing injuries all were past in the *Lyons* sense. Since the suit could not possibly have remedied any of the past injuries about which the plaintiffs had complained, any requirement of remedial standing was not satisfied.

It is unclear how far *Lyons* might undermine Congress's capacity to authorize access to federal courts for litigants who might lack remedial standing. It could be argued that the requirement of remedial standing, though constitutional, tolerates exceptions in those cases, but only those cases, in which the United States appears as a party seeking injunctive relief. This argument, however, invites two objections. First, past decisions have not made clear that the Attorney General enjoys a unique exemption from remedial standing requirements. Even in cases in which the United States is not a party, courts have framed remedial orders to prevent lawbreakers from committing new violations in the future. Second, the presence of the United States in a lawsuit generally depends directly or indirectly on the authorization of Congress. If Congress can authorize the Attorney General to sue without remedial standing, then article III should not bar congressional authorization of suit under similar conditions by a "private attorney general." After *Lyons*, however, Congress's capacity to prescribe injunctive relief would seem to be in doubt.

Restrictions of congressional power would be unfortunate. Where the functional requirements of adjudication are satisfied, and where concern about the separation of powers provides no impediment, the contours of judicial power should be open to evolution and adjustment. In particular those contours should be open to expansion, at least at the margins, when Congress, with its political sensitivity to changed social conditions and perceived public needs, seeks to secure the vindication of federal rights.

Several lines of authority support Congress's power to adjust doctrines of justiciability to allow private parties to enforce constitutional rights. Congress's decision to adopt the Declaratory Judgment Act, an apparent loosening of the ripeness doctrine, was upheld by the Supreme Court. Congressionally enacted rules for class actions also have altered the historical contours of the "case" requirement and have undermined the mootness doctrine substantially. The Court even has determined that Congress may confer personal interest standing where none otherwise would exist. These decisions reflect both a principled hesitation to rigidify the Constitution and a prudent respect for congressional prerogatives.

When it elevated the requirement of remedial standing to the constitutional level, the *Lyons* Court couched its holding in the language of judicial "restraint." But that term is ambiguous and unhelpful. Although they sometimes may be mandated by the Constitution, judicial decisions undermining congressional authority cannot be justified as acts of *self*-restraint. Because the remedial standing requirement places into doubt the powers of another branch of government, the crucial issue is whether remedial standing is required by article III.

* * *

C. *Toward a More Equitable Resolution*

Conceived as a solution to the problems of public law litigation, remedial standing imposes heavy costs by limiting both Congress's and the federal courts' ability to protect federal rights. On the other hand, there also may be a cost, in diminished public perception of judicial legitimacy and in possible exhibitions of practical ineptitude, in reposing broad discretionary powers of institutional reorganization in a single federal district judge. Assessment of costs and benefits therefore is needed. But it is important that the range of possible choices is not limited to polar alternatives. Perhaps the most powerful objection to *Lyons*'s constitutionalization of remedial standing is that the Court failed to adopt an available calculus more sensitive to the various concerns at stake. Provided that mootness doctrine imposed no bar, *Lyons* should have been decided within the familiar framework of equity.

Although remedial standing traditionally has not been applied as a constitutional requirement, the policies that would support it are represented in settled law. Even when jurisdiction exists, courts always have exercised discretion in determining the appropriateness of equitable relief; from the identification of an injury to a legal right, entitlement to an injunction never has followed automatically. Pertinent public and private interests must be weighed to determine whether and in what form equitable relief ought to issue.

Compared with the constitutionalization of remedial standing, the law of equitable remedies may seem the less effective tool for preventing excessive judicial involvement in the affairs of government institutions. But even if great weight is assigned to the interests protected by remedial standing, this instrumental justification should be rejected. First, the constitutionalization of remedial standing fails to acknowledge adequately the federal constitutional interests that sometimes may require institutional reform. Second, the impulse to erect threshold barriers ignores the reality that not every lawsuit affecting a public institution stretches judicial competence or intrudes too deeply into institutional management.

There was a considerable difference between the relief requested in *Rizzo* on the one hand and in *Lyons* on the other. The plaintiffs in *Rizzo* sought a substantial restructuring of police department procedures. The plaintiff in *Lyons*, by contrast, asked the district court to do no more than what courts traditionally have done and have done effectively: to enjoin the defendant from continuing a particular course of unlawful conduct. Lyons asked the court to undertake no management responsibilities plausibly regarded as beyond the bounds of practical judicial competence.

Although some forms of equitable relief might overreach those bounds, a more reasonable response to the problem would focus directly on the precise form of evil to be avoided. Such a response would assess how far judicial competence would be strained by a particular form of equitable remedy and would not apply per se rules at the threshold. Located at the remedial level, reasonable accommodations in the law of equitable relief would trench less heavily on important constitutional values than does resolution of the problem through the doctrine of standing.

Among the vices of standing analysis is that it allows no opportunity to assess the interests served by adjudicating a dispute. Stationed at the threshold, standing analysis overprotects defendants. Even if standing is upheld, a plaintiff always must show that the defendant has violated his rights as a further prerequisite to obtaining judicial relief. To gauge the appropriateness of dismissing a lawsuit, this "merits" question may require more careful consideration than remedial standing analysis allows. A court also may need more information about institutional policy and structure before it knows how seriously individual rights are threatened and how deeply into institutional autonomy judicial relief would need to intrude to be effective. The availability of relief should depend partly on these factors.

Although the task may be formidable, appellate courts should undertake to craft enforceable remedial principles that respect qualitative differences in various types of equitable relief. Until a range of plausible choices emerges from the courts of appeals, the Supreme Court reasonably might hesitate to pronounce too broadly. While reticence is not exactly a virtue, it is preferable to creating overbroad threshold requirements that preclude vindication of federal rights.

Provisional principles, responsive to the Court's concerns about competence and intrusiveness, are readily imaginable. If troubled by a perception that district courts have entered excessively intrusive remedial orders, the Supreme Court — based on a reasoned assessment of pertinent sources of law — undoubtedly has authority to prescribe standards narrowing the range of permissible remedial choices. Such standards might establish a presumption in favor of less coercive relief. For example, declaratory judgments and negative decrees, forbidding or limiting unconstitutional practices, generally should be preferred to a court's affirmatively restructuring the operation of some state or local institution.

Such a presumption should not be irrebuttable. If the defendants seem especially unlikely to adapt their behavior to constitutional standards, or if they have failed to do so in the past, a trial judge should retain flexibility to enter a more comprehensive judicial order. Even then, however, appellate courts could identify factors that a trial judge would be obliged to weigh. Moreover, an appellate panel should be entitled to examine the judicial record closely to ensure that all of the relevant factors have been taken into account. The more extensive and intrusive a judicial decree, the more rigorous and exacting appellate scrutiny should become.

In comparison with remedial standing analysis, decisionmaking through this equitable approach would diminish the Supreme Court's capacity to reverse all perceived remedial excesses by the lower federal courts. This truth should not be blinked. Standards of remedial propriety probably never should be cast as determinate rules; trial court discretion seems unavoidable within the law of remedies. Nonetheless, the law of equitable remedies should be preferred to constitutional doctrines of remedial standing as an instrument of judicial restraint. Recognizing the Constitution's function as a document to span the ages, the Court should avoid constitutionalizing doctrines that are broader than their functional or historical justifications. The Court should exercise restraint, but restraint of a kind different from that sometimes invoked under pressure of present frustrations — the restraint to preserve in the Constitution a fair degree of openness for the future, and to reserve to Congress as well as itself a role in defining the contours of a properly evolving judicial function.

* * *

V

Equitable Restraint

Although its decision on the standing issue rendered unnecessary further consideration of remedies, the *Lyons* majority proceeded to consider the appropriateness of equitable relief. Its reasoning on this issue accorded insufficient heed to the legislative policy underlying section 1983. Propounding bright-line principles of remedial restraint, the Court also demonstrated too little of the sensitivity to particularized facts that forms the moral core of equity jurisprudence.

A. *Congressional Intent and the Scope of Section 1983*

Although little-discussed in *Lyons*, the history and policy of section 1983 have been canvassed frequently by the Supreme Court. Injunctive actions under section 1983 almost invariably request the federal judiciary to enter domains traditionally reserved to state authorities. Yet the plain language of the statute suggests that Congress intended this result: The statute provides that state officials engaged in civil rights violations "shall be liable to the party injured in an action at law, suit in equity, or other proper proceeding for redress." Relying on this language and on the legislative history, the Court found in *Mitchum v. Foster* that "the very purpose of section 1983 was to interpose the federal courts between the States and the people, as guardians of the people's federal rights . . . ." This purpose departed fundamentally from the traditional understanding of appropriate federal relationships. But the Court concluded in *Mitchum* that

> Congress clearly conceived that it was altering the relationship between the States and the Nation with respect to the protection of federally created rights; it was concerned that state instrumentalities could not protect those rights; [and] it realized that state officers might, in fact, be antipathetic to the vindication of those rights. . . .

Nor does *Mitchum* stand as an aberration in Supreme Court jurisprudence under section 1983. Other cases have expressed a similar understanding of the congressional purpose and have relied on that purpose to uphold plaintiffs' claimed right of access to a federal judicial forum.

Despite the line of Supreme Court authority that has viewed section 1983 as intended to promote liberal access to the federal courts, the Court held in *Lyons* that doctrines of equitable restraint required dismissal of the suit for an injunction. Three strands of argument supported the Court's conclusion. The first invoked traditional equitable principles prescribing that an injunction will issue only to alleviate a "substantial and immediate irreparable injury," for which there is no adequate remedy at law. The issues pertinent to this strand of argument — whether the harm to the plaintiff is imminent and substantial, whether the legal remedy is adequate, and whether the threatened injury is irreparable — generally have been resolved contextually. Indeed, they often have been characterized as questions of fact. This strand of the Court's argument, holding that the plaintiff had failed to satisfy requirements of imminence, substantiality, and irreparability, therefore might not be considered of broad significance, were it not conjoined by the Court with broader remedial principles.

The other two strands of the Court's reasoning merit more extended discussion. The first, inherent in the structure of the majority's analysis, affirms the traditional maxim that equitable remedies are discretionary. The other strand relies on cases counseling that principles of "equity, comity, and federalism" require special restraint — more stringent than that ordinarily required in suits for injunctions — in actions for "injunctions against state officers engaged in the administration of the states' criminal laws." These two strands of argument will be considered in turn.

1. *The Scope of Judicial Discretion*

Judicial discretion traditionally has been defined in terms of limits on, or lacunae within, governing legal standards. Under this view, applicable rules confine permissible legal choices within a range of alternatives, but do not determine "correct" legal outcomes. A judge remains free to choose among limited alternatives. So explicated, the concept of discretion contains a central ambiguity. Even if it is assumed that ascertainable standards confine judicial discretion, the question remains whether applicable law guides or structures decisionmaking within the discretionary range. One view would regard discretion as absolute: a judge exercising discretion might decide as he or she wishes for whatever reasons he might fancy. Another conception, however, would hold that discretion requires that "'something is to be done according to the rules of reason and justice, not according to private opinion. . . . It is to be not arbitrary, vague, and fanciful, but legal and regular.'" Under this latter view, judicial decisionmakers exercising discretion must seek guidance from available legal materials. Moreover, the determinacy of applicable authorities can increase over time, as accumulating decisions assert controlling force over similar cases.

Viewed as archetypes, these two conceptions of discretion — one stronger, one weaker — may help to elucidate the nature of the equitable discretion involved in *Lyons*. The Supreme Court has established that the district courts' range of discretionary choices is subject to narrowing over time through the issuance of controlling opinions. This pattern suggests that the Court regards judicial discretion to award equitable remedies as approximating the weaker form. When discretion is used in this sense, Supreme Court decisions under section 1983 eventually could narrow to nonexistence the range of choices. Despite the general principle that equitable remedies are "discretionary," the district courts might be prohibited from awarding equitable relief in defined classes of cases. But the question would persist, to what standards, if any, the Supreme Court should conform its own section 1983 decisionmaking.

Under other statutes authorizing equitable remedies, the Court generally has insisted that the judicial obligation is to effectuate Congress's purposes in enacting the substantive legislation pursuant to which relief is sought. Similar reasoning might have been applied in *Lyons*. In adopting section 1983, Congress — or so the Court has taught — expressed a policy of making federal forums readily accessible for the vindication of federal rights. Moreover, section 1983 explicitly announces a congressional policy allowing equitable actions. Within the terms of the Court's own jurisprudence, judicial departure from these congressional policies thus requires an explanation that relates the policy concerns cited by the Court in denying equitable relief to the intent of Congress in enacting section 1983.

Supreme Court decisions under section 1983 have not always explained the Court's jurisprudence of remedies in these terms. But it is not difficult to construct a theory that would provide a link between the policy considerations of "equity, comity, and federalism" and the purposes of section 1983. Consistently with the traditions of equity, the Court might assume that Congress meant to invest the federal courts with responsibility to develop judicially the law of equitable remedies under section 1983. Under this view, the Court's obligation generally would be to effectuate section 1983's protective policies, but to do so conformably with the traditional standards of equity: balancing the interests of plaintiffs under the statute against the competing claims of other national policies, especially insofar as those policies can be accommodated through the traditional canons of equity.

This view of the judicial mandate under section 1983 has broad support in the case law, and it can be explicated by reference to *Younger v. Harris*, the leading case in the development of the policies of equity, comity, and federalism on which the *Lyons* Court relied. The Court's invocation of these policies represents the third strand of its justification for applying an especially stringent form of equitable restraint in *Lyons*. But this strand of argument fails to justify the Court's conclusions. In his dissent, Justice Marshall revealed with admirable succinctness the deficiency in the majority's reasoning:

> With the single exception of *Rizzo v. Goode* all of the cases relied on by the Court concerned injunctions against state criminal proceedings. The rule of *Younger v. Harris*, that such injunctions can be issued only in extraordinary circumstances in which the threat of injury is "great and immediate," reflects the venerable rule that equity will not enjoin a criminal prosecution. . . .
>
> . . . [T]he concerns [governing the injunction of] a state criminal proceeding simply do not apply to an injunction directed solely at a police department.

A brief historical survey will clarify Justice Marshall's argument, and also expose deeper flaws in the Court's remedial jurisprudence under section 1983.

2. *Younger and Its Progeny: The Appropriate Limits of Equitable Restraint*

The Supreme Court's decision in *Younger* frequently is identified with the broadening doctrine of equitable abstention law in actions under section 1983. But *Younger*'s facts framed a narrower legal issue. Already a defendant in a state criminal proceeding, the plaintiff Harris challenged the constitutionality of the criminal statute in federal court and sought an injunction against the pending state proceedings. On these facts, traditional canons of equity supported the Court's conclusion that an injunction was improper. One such canon — though subject to important exceptions — provides that equity generally will not interfere with an ongoing criminal prosecution. *Younger* illustrates the rationale behind this rule. With a criminal prosecution already pending against him, Harris had available an "adequate" legal remedy in state court: he could challenge the constitutionality of the statute as a criminal defense. Lacking were any of the exceptional circumstances that might have triggered equitable intervention, such as prosecutorial harassment, multiple prosecutions, or interruption of a "continuing course of conduct." Thus, under the *Younger* facts, the Court could have decided the case exclusively through application of traditional standards of equity — standards of which Congress presumably was aware when it provided for equitable relief under section 1983.

The Court, however, was not content to rest on this narrow rationale. Although *Younger* did invoke traditional equity standards, Justice Black's opinion for the Court also undertook to develop broader justifications for withholding injunctive relief. First, Justice Black invoked the "national policy" of the Anti-Injunction Act, which generally bars federal injunctions of state judicial proceedings. This was a curious appeal to statutory authority. Although suggesting that the statute commanded deference, Justice Black explicitly assumed that Congress had not intended the Anti-Injunction Act to apply to cases such as *Younger*. Having stated this assumption, however, he found that the underlying policy of the inapplicable statute — indeed, one assumed to have been made inapplicable by Congress — should be taken into account by a court of equity.

Beyond the Anti-Injunction Act, Justice Black advanced a second policy in support of equitable restraint. Again without direct support from congressional intent or identifiable statutory policy, he invoked

> the notion of "comity," that is, a proper respect for state functions, a recognition of the fact that the entire country is made up of a Union of separate state governments, and a continuance of the belief that the National Government will fare best if the States and their institutions are left free to perform their separate functions in their separate ways.

Once again, context renders the argument incongruous. It seems fair to assume that comity was not among the foremost concerns of the Reconstruction Congress that adopted section 1983 — the Congress that the Court has viewed as having undertaken to "interpose the federal courts between the states and the people, as guardians of the people's rights."

Nevertheless, the sweeping rationale having been propounded, Justice Black concluded in *Younger* that federal injunctive relief must be withheld in virtually all cases involving pending state prosecutions. As Professor Laycock has argued, *Younger* thus redefined the bounds set by the general equitable principle of noninterference and its accompanying set of exceptions. In particular, by forcing plaintiffs to remain in criminal proceedings, *Younger* and its progeny made unavailable the protections of interim, prospective, and class remedies that previously would have been available from a federal court.

Post-*Younger* decisions that have invoked its rationales of comity and federalism seem even harder to justify. They find less suport in traditional principles of equitable restraint. Furthermore, the recurring equitable calculus, for which *Younger* provided the model, accords no substantial weight to the protective purposes of section 1983.

Extending the reasoning of *Younger*, the Court now has established that federal courts must abstain during the pendency of a variety of state civil proceedings. In these civil contexts, the traditional equitable maxim against enjoining state criminal prosecutions plainly has no application. Other decisions have applied the *Younger* doctrine to state litigation filed subsequent to a federal lawsuit, but before "proceedings of substance on the merits" in the federal case. These cases are in tension with the traditional tenet that a court of equity, having taken jurisdiction of a case, need not surrender that jurisdiction.

The Supreme Court further extended *Younger* in *O'Shea v. Littleton* and *Rizzo v. Goode*, cases in which the Court for the first time relied on decisions in the *Younger* line to impose demands for extraordinary equitable restraint in actions challenging the policies and behavior of local police departments. These cases presented no plausible application of the equitable doctrine, which underlies *Younger*, against enjoining pending criminal proceedings in which the asserted claim can be litigated fairly. Moreover, given the historical policy of the 1871 Civil Rights Act to protect individual rights threatened by coercive state behavior, and especially by the corruption of state institutions, the application of extraordinary deference in this area ignores congressional policy.

A similar distension of *Younger* occurred in *Fair Assessment Real Estate Association v. McNary*. In *McNary*, the majority invoked *Younger* to justify federal judicial abstention from a suit to recover damages from a state official under section 1983. However unsettling to relations of comity, suits for damages are actions at law to which equitable principles, by definition, do not extend. *McNary* seems irreconcilable both with cases holding that Congress intended section 1983 to provide litigants with access to a federal forum and with the venerable maxim that a court possessed of jurisdiction may not lawfully decline its exercise.

3. *Judicial Activism and Ante-Bellum Federalism*

In retrospect, it seems clear that *Younger* launched the Supreme Court on an enterprise of unilaterally redefining the contours of judicial federalism. There are obvious dangers in such an independent approach. First, by unhinging its remedial jurisprudence from substantive congressional policy, the Court deprives its decisionmaking of statutory warrants of lawfulness and legitimacy. Indeed, the Court invites the criticism that it has impinged on Congress's policymaking prerogatives.

Another danger inheres in the tendency of judicial lawmaking, when it strays too far from statutory policies, to acquire both a logical and a psychological momentum of its own, and ultimately to produce conflicts among judicial decisions. *Mitchum v. Foster*, interpreting section 1983 as intended to interpose the federal courts between the states and the people, coheres uneasily at best with the tenets of "Our Federalism." Later decisions in the *Younger* line, applying an equitable calculus largely divorced from substantive statutory policy, also are hard to reconcile with pronouncements that courts must exercise their equitable discretion under substantive federal statutes chiefly to advance statutory policy.

Lyons's principal significance for the doctrine of equitable restraint may lie in its failure to interrupt the self-enforcing momentum of "Our Federalism." Although recognizing that *Rizzo* had included broad language forbidding federal injunctions against state agencies of law enforcement, the court of appeals in *Lyons* had distinguished *O'Shea* and *Rizzo* as cases involving requests for "massive structural" relief. If the Ninth Circuit's approach had been adopted, *Lyons* would not stand for the proposition that federal courts generally should show extraordinary deference to state institutional processes — a proposition incompatible with the judicially recognized purpose of section 1983. *Lyons* instead might have affirmed the principle that a particular institutional remedy must be justified by a threat commensurate with its intrusiveness. The Supreme Court, however, rejected this approach. *O'Shea* and *Rizzo* , the Court explained, "cannot be so easily confined to their facts." As construed by *Lyons*, however, neither *O'Shea* nor *Rizzo* can be justified. Nor can *Lyons*.

B. *Of Rights and Remedies: The Calculus of Equity*

Lyons deployed the doctrine of equitable restraint to preclude litigation not only of the plaintiff's claims but also of a broad range of analogous lawsuits. First, *Lyons* wielded *Younger* principles of comity and federalism to establish that a federal injunction could issue against state law enforcement officials only in the most extraordinary circumstances. The previous section argued that this doctrine of extreme judicial restraint properly should apply only in actions to enjoin pending state criminal proceedings.

Second, the *Lyons* majority reiterated a requirement established independently in its treatment of remedial standing and held that, as a precondition of any form of injunctive relief, applicable remedial doctrines require a showing equivalent to that required for remedial standing — causal efficacy of the remedy in alleviating an injury sufficient for standing. This condition cannot be satisfied by past injuries. As argued in Part III, the Constitution imposes no such standing requirement. Nor should the law of remedies embrace such unyielding demands. Once standing is established and a constitutional violation identified, the availability of an injunction, as well as the form of injunctive relief, should depend on a calculus more complex than that employed by *Lyons*. The Court should weigh attentively the relevant statutory policy. In balancing statutory policy against competing interests, the Court also should attend more closely to particular facts to identify how deeply the various asserted interests are implicated.

The desirability of a more fact-specific, balancing approach — as distinguished from *Lyons*'s door-closing conception of equitable restraint — can be explicated by the following heuristic model of constitutional rights. Constitutional rights can be thought to have initially only an abstract character. The fifth and fourteenth amendments, for example, establish a right not to be deprived of life, liberty, or property without due process of law. But the practical meaning of this right remains undetermined by the constitutional text. Assume, for example, that a municipal police department systematically encourages its officers to apply unconstitutional chokeholds to a certain class of suspects, such as black males. To a black male in that community, the meaning of the due process right is a practical rather than an abstract question. In *Lyons*, the majority suggested that the due process right minimally would represent an entitlement to recover damages. Less minimally, the abstract right might represent an entitlement to a federal injunction, at least preventing repetitions of unlawful behavior.

Although initially abstract in nature, constitutional rights acquire substance in two, relatively concrete dimensions. The first is what can be considered the right's "procedural instantiations," a term that refers to the kinds of legal proceedings specifically available for enforcing a particular right. For example, possible procedural instantiations of a due process right would include a right to sue for an injunction, a right to sue for a declaratory judgment, and a right to sue for damages after the fact. Distinct from a right's procedural instantiations is the set of "remedial entitlements" that the right may entail. Remedial entitlements are dependent upon, yet distinct from, procedural instantiations. While the holder of an abstract right may be entitled to sue for a particular remedy, a plaintiff who prevails on the merits may be entitled only to a remedy less intrusive than the one requested, or perhaps to no equitable remedy at all.

Part of the moral core of equity jurisprudence lies in an aspiration never fully realized: to achieve a particularized balancing of interests that would be affected by granting or denying a particular remedy. From the violation of a legal right there follows no necessary entitlement to an injunction at all, and certainly not to a particular form of injunction. Yet, while it would exert precedential significance in similar future cases, the denial of a remedy in an individual case would not deprive prospective plaintiffs of procedural instantiations of their rights. Future plaintiffs still would be entitled to a balancing of the public and private interests unique to the circumstances of their situations.

The role of the Supreme Court is in tension with this idealized goal, as, indeed, are the traditional canons of equity. One of the Court's important functions is to develop doctrine and to provide guidelines for future decisions; guidelines for the future tend to foreclose particularized balancing. This tension demands that the model be heuristic, rather than descriptive, or even wholly prescriptive.

Nonetheless, particularized balancing remains an ideal, and the ensuing tension with judicial hierarchy frequently may prove salutary. Broadly framed doctrines of equitable restraint, imposed by the Supreme Court, jeopardize this tension. Depending on the breadth of their formulation, the Court's evolving and expanding doctrines effectively negate procedural instantiations of federal constitutional rights. Lost in the Court's jurisprudence is sensitivity to particularity, and with it important, concrete dimensions of constitutional rights.

As suggested earlier, the Supreme Court's enlargement of doctrines of restraint may derive mostly from concerns about the intrusiveness of institutional litigation and structural remedies. If so, resolution should occur on the level where the problem exists — the level of remedy formulation. Such a resolution would differ in kind as well as in effect from the door-closing prescriptions of *Lyons*. It would adjust remedial entitlements, not withdraw procedural instantiations, and would accord respect to the congressional policy to protect rights under section 1983.

Conclusion

City of Los Angeles v. Lyons reveals a Supreme Court in confusion about the role of the federal courts and of Congress in an era crucial to the future of public law litigation. As in other recent cases, the Court responded to important concerns. Increasingly, federal courts have been asked to undertake remedial supervision of institutions of state and local government. Novel classes of plaintiffs have brought to the federal courts disputes that invite expanded judicial supervision of state and federal executives. The resolution of these disputes raises fundamental questions of judicial power.

In *Lyons*, the Supreme Court provided an answer not tailored analytically to the specific problem at hand. The Court used the jurisdictional doctrine of standing to decide questions better addressed at the remedial stage of litigation. It unwisely elevated to the constitutional level — beyond the control of Congress — politically controversial questions concerning the future of public law litigation. When answers cannot be derived from the foundational principles of justiciability doctrines, such questions should not be foreclosed judicially from political debate. The *Lyons* majority failed to appreciate the importance of congressional policy to the law of equitable remedies. Defining the relations of federalism is not exclusively a judicial function.

This Article has offered an alternative approach to some leading problems of public law litigation. Two main distinctions have been urged. The first involves the separation of questions of justiciability from questions of appropriate remedies. Enforced at the threshold of litigation, standing doctrine — and especially the *Lyons* doctrine of remedial standing — precludes a federal court from obtaining relevant information concerning the appropriateness and desirability of adjudication. It rigidifies the constitutional framework and prevents the evolution of legal forms. A second distinction, also unheeded by *Lyons*, separates the issues posed by non-Hohfeldian and institutional litigation. The former may expand the number of issues presented to the federal courts, but it otherwise does not strain practical judicial competence. Where Congress has granted authorization, there should be no separation-of-powers objection to non-Hohfeldian lawsuits. By contrast, institutional litigation may impose formidable strains on the resources and the capacities of the federal courts, and it may invite them into the traditional provinces of political decisionmakers. To the extent that constitutional problems exist, however, they arise not from the adjudication of discrete issues but from the scope of requested remedies. Solutions ought to be introduced at that level.

This Article's recommended approaches would require finer distinctions than the Court recently has attempted, and there is no denying the potential attendant costs. A more complex calculus could be misapplied more easily; it would reduce the capacity of appellate courts to correct summarily all perceived errors by the lower federal courts in nontraditional lawsuits. With all its costs, however, complexity should be preferred to the ossification of judicial forms — especially when those forms may be unsuited to evolving needs of the legal and political culture. The future of public law litigation should not be the Court's alone to determine.

Gene R. Nichol, Jr., *Federalism, State Courts, and Section 1983,* 73 Virginia Law Review 959 (1987)

* * *

III. Interpreting Section 1983

The legislative history of section 1983 clearly indicates that its drafters were untroubled by such niceties as solicitude for local jurists. It is also clear, however, that this attitude was shaped by their perceptions of emergency in the Reconstruction South. The severity of the moment called for a remedy that was effective, not deferential. But over a century later, the exigencies of Reconstruction no longer exist. If the draftsmen of the Civil Rights Act of 1871 could reasonably worry that state judges were in league with the Ku Klux Klan, or fundamentally antithetical to civil liberties, we need not. Accordingly, some have argued that section 1983 should be interpreted to take this change of circumstance into account. It seems doubtful, however, that change of condition alone merits the judicial creation of a large exception to a broadly phrased statutory mandate. Deciding when a regulatory scheme is no longer needed is a particularly legislative function. The overt judicial authority to modify or update archaic statutes remains, at present, but a glimmer in Dean Calabresi's eye.

But our remove, constitutionally speaking, from 1871 is not so easily dismissed. Change of circumstances is perhaps common to all statutes — at least all old ones. And updating statutes to conform with the times should be done by legislatures, not courts. But the degree of commitment to the federal Constitution exhibited by state judges is not the only alteration the intervening century has wrought. The "rights, privileges, and immunities" secured by the United States Constitution — and thus the scope of section 1983 — have undergone a massive transformation. The cause of action under the Civil Rights Act, therefore, has been subject to more than mere changing times. The scope of the provision has been so broadened that construing it in line with the framers' intent could threaten the dual judicial system.

Though section 1983 was designed as an extremely intrusive tool, in comparative terms, its scope was exceedingly narrow. In 1871, the liberties assured by the constitution against the states did not include, for example, the provisions of the Bill of Rights. As a result, the typical practices of local criminal process did not implicate federal guaranties. States could not violate the first amendment's speech, press, or religion clauses. Decisions recognized no fundamental right to travel or vote, nor any right to privacy. The equal protection clause carried no weight outside the race context, and precious little even there. In short, none of the cornerstones of our modern system of constitutional review was yet in place. And this distinction is reflected in the legislative history of section 1983.

The character of constitutional injury that the Civil Rights Act sought to remedy was hardly subtle. As Congressman Coburn explained: "The arresting power is fettered, the witnesses are silenced, the courts are impotent, the laws are annulled, the criminal goes free, and the persecuted citizen looks in vain for redress." Given the threatened outrage, the proponents of the statute claimed a willingness "to go to the extreme verge of fair construction that will justify Federal intervention." But the harshness of the exercise of power was tempered by the perceived ease of avoiding liability. As one supporter claimed, speaking of the statute as a whole: "Every man can escape the stringency of [the bill's] action by remaining a quiet and peaceful citizen, and not infringing the rights of person, property, or liberty of another . . . ." Today, with the tremendous expansion of the substantive scope of the federal Constitution brought about in the last several decades, any local law enforcement official, public university president, state agency administrator, school board member, prison warden, or other government actor finds it considerably more difficult to avoid the rigors of section 1983. But, as I argue below, state judges are placed in a particularly exposed position. In 1871, section one of the Civil Rights Act could be violated primarily by the continued enforcement of some of the more egregious examples of overtly racist legislation or, perhaps, by manipulating legal process to harass blacks and Union sympathizers. A constitutional infraction by a local judge, therefore, was regarded as an intentional flouting of federal authority. Now it may be no more than a mistake.

In one sense, this tension between the concerns of the Reconstruction era and our own is a reflection of what Professor Eisenberg has characterized as "two competing visions of section 1983." As he puts it, in "one perspective, section 1983 addresses a limited historical problem in post-Civil War race relations. In another, it is the primary civil mechanism for vindicating . . . constitutional rights." But if the section 1983 cause of action is not to be limited to the particular evils that brought it into being — which I argue below would be an inappropriate turn — the potential for conflict between federal and state judiciaries under the "modern" statute is markedly increased. The flowering of the incorporation doctrine has resulted in the constitutionalization of a substantial segment of the work of state courts. The demands of the fourth, fifth, sixth, and eighth amendments play a predominant role in state criminal process. The standards of procedural due process and equal protection of the laws, to name but two obvious choices, pervade local civil process. It is hardly the case, therefore, that a state jurist can with ease "escape the stringency" of section 1983 by not "infringing the rights of person, property, or liberty of another." A section 1983 cause of action that literally calls local judges to task for the "deprivation of any rights, privileges, or immunities secured by Constitution and laws" of the United States is much closer to a system of complete federal supervision over state courts now than it would have been in the late nineteenth century. If section 1983 were to be given its full intrusive power, the frictions resulting from federal supervision would be unmitigated by protections from injunctive obstruction, immunities from damage claims, and the respect afforded through collateral estoppel. Like it or not, interference with even the good faith decisionmaking of state courts under an expansive section 1983 would pose problems that are potentially crippling to both judiciaries.

A. *Addressing the Dilemma*

Correctly interpreting section 1983 thus presents something of a dilemma. The statute was intended to be intrusive. Yet the scope of its original mission, at least if we tie it to the concerns of the framers, was quite limited. As its purview has expanded to conform to the provision's language, the potential for interference with local judicial process has expanded dramatically. If the section is applied with the full intrusive force that its drafters envisioned, complications that the framers would perhaps have rejected, or at least did not contemplate, arise.

There are a number of ways one might propose to deal with the dilemma. The first, and probably the least satisfactory, is the tack the Supreme Court has chosen. The Court's decisions on section 1983 and state courts deal with the tensions of section 1983 interpretation by pretending that they do not exist. When the Justices opt for intervention, they cite passages of legislative history to support federal intrusion. When deference carries the day, opinions typically maintain that "nothing in the legislative history of section 1983" demands a contrary conclusion. Even if the results of the various decisions can be supported on one ground or another, the methodology is indefensible.

The claim that the scope of section 1983 should be tied to its origins is more plausible. This argument has two principal variants. The first is that *Mitchum v. Foster* and, by implication, *Pulliam* and *Monroe* were wrongly decided. Those cases, authorizing strong federal intervention, cannot be supported, because the framers of the 1871 Civil Rights Act sought to remedy a very specific and dramatic evil — racial suppression in the South. To root the modern section 1983 cause of action, which is the conduit for a broad system of constitutional adjudication, in an emergency Reconstruction measure is erroneous. The tension between the broadened scope of the statute and the intrusive nature of its original design is thus cured by returning the Act to its earlier confines. The second claim is closely related to the first. If the legislative history of section 1983 demonstrates that it was designed to be strongly interventionist, its full power should be reserved for the circumstances the framers had in mind — actions alleging racial discrimination. Accordingly, section 1983 litigation would develop along two tiers. In race cases, no deference to local judicial officers would be afforded. In the great bulk of other disputes now falling under section 1983's broad mantle, traditional solicitude for state government actors would be mandated.

The primary shortcoming of these suggested alterations, of course, is the language of the statute. Section 1983 unambiguously affords relief for the "deprivation of *any* rights, privileges, or immunities secured by the Constitution and laws" of the United States. The text of the statute thus provides an insurmountable barrier to at least the stronger of the two claims. The scope of the rights embraced by the Act could simply not be clearer. "Reasonably well-informed people" could hardly conclude, from the language of the statute alone, that the evils addressed are limited to race discrimination. As a result, the legislation must be "held to mean what it plainly expresses." Moreover, if the scope of section 1983 were to be dramatically reduced, a new set of even more intractable problems would result. Without the benefit of the spaciously worded statute, the federal courts would be forced to develop a body of decisions outlining the causes of action against state actors created directly by the fourteenth amendment. At the federal level, this has proven to be a particularly thorny problem. The confusion should be compounded only as a last resort.

The two-tiered approach at least conflicts less dramatically with the wording of the Act. Under its premises the scope of section 1983 would be unchanged. Only in cases of "racial [discrimination] and Klan . . . violence" would the full intrusion of federal power be employed. An accommodation of sorts is thus achieved between the broad terms of the Act and a legislative history that calls for strong federal intervention. Of course, tension with the language of the Civil Rights Act remains. The provision suggests no hierarchy of rights. The phrase "deprivation of any rights," in fact, seems to represent the strongest declaration possible to the contrary. Functionally, the two-tiered methodology would leave the section 1983 cause of action out of step with the fourteenth amendment — the provision it was primarily designed to enforce. No doubt we are far removed from the time when that amendment's protections provided special scrutiny only for claims of racial inequality. Ultimately even this strategy suffers from a failing more familiar to the most rigid originalist doctrines of constitutional interpretation. Section 1983, like the fourteenth amendment itself, embraces a principle that is substantially broader than the evils that brought it into being.

There is also a significant practical problem with a two-tiered vision of section 1983. Commentators have rather easily characterized the core concern of the statute as race discrimination. The legislative history of the Civil Rights Act, however, indicates that the provision is not so easily cabined. No doubt protecting the newly freed slaves from the abuses of hostile southerners was a central goal of the 1871 statute. The Congressional Globe also reveals, however, a related and substantial concern for the plight of Republicans and Unionists. As Senator Pratt complained, for example, redress in the state courts "only fail[s] . . . when a man of known Union sentiments, white or black, invokes their aid." The hearings that preceded the passage of the Act "demonstrated that the Negro was not alone in his tribulations; white persons who had supported the Union cause or who were bold enough to advocate civil rights for the Negro were also the victims of terrorism in the South." Any core of section 1983 defined by the circumstances that led to the statute's passage, then, would need to encompass a broader universe than racial injustice. "Causal" wrongs include, at a minimum, manipulation of legal process to punish political opposition, to suppress freedom of speech, and apparently, to discourage the exercise of the right to travel. But once that door is opened, the effort to define the heart of the expansive provision is lost.

It has also been suggested that the friction between section 1983's intrusive intention and its modern scope should lead to a very different conclusion — that the legislative history of the statute is no longer relevant to its appropriate interpretation. To any reader of the Supreme Court's section 1983 decisions, this proposal carries obvious appeal. At a minimum, it calls for the end of the inconsistent and haphazard use of legislative intent. It also recognizes that judicial opinions have on occasion attributed more to the framers of the Civil Rights Act than their century-old deliberations can reasonably be asked to bear. The Supreme Court's flipflop on the applicability of the statute to municipalities provides a ready example. If governmental entities carrying out the responsibilities and exercising the prerogatives of modern cities did not meaningfully exist at the local level in 1871, it is hardly fruitful to scour the debates in search of references to municipalities. The drafters' intentions are simply unhelpful on many of the issues of modern section 1983 jurisprudence.

Courts should be reluctant, however, to disregard the intention of the statute's proponents when it is both ascertainable and capable of being carried forward under our existing litigation framework. Rejecting legislative intent in favor of a complete system of common law development poses several problems. First, section 1983 does not furnish the apparent textual warrant to construct judicially a set of freestanding principles for decision of the sort that some other federal statutes have been held to provide. Section 301(a) of the Labor Management Relations Act, for example, has been determined to authorize "federal courts to fashion a body of federal law for the enforcement of . . . collective bargaining agreements." But 42 U.S.C. § 1988 indicates that in cases under the Civil Rights Act "the laws of the United States," or, if they are "deficient," the "common law, as modified and changed by the constitution and statutes of the State wherein the . . . cause is held, so far as the same is not inconsistent with the Constitution and laws of the United States" shall apply. Section 1988 has hardly proven a model of clarity. It does at least indicate that judges, in measuring the demands of section 1983, are not simply to make it up as they go.

A freewheeling common law process poses legitimacy dangers from the other direction as well. If judge-made section 1983 standards result in a more restrictive cause of action than the framers contemplated, the judiciary apparently usurps legislative mandate. *Mitchum*, for example, declares that the Civil Rights Act was designed to afford injunctive relief against state judiciaries. *Younger* largely takes away what *Mitchum* grants. If we are to characterize *Younger* as an exercise in common law decisionmaking, it is hard to comprehend the judicial warrant for rejecting, as Professor Redish has put it, "the product of the congressional balancing process" reflected in section 1983.

This point hints at yet a third approach to the interpretation of section 1983. Under this theory, the courts should allow both the intrusive design of the statute and its expansive modern scope to be given full play. The legislative history of the Civil Rights Act demands that the statute be read to penetrate traditional concepts of state sovereignty. The language of the provision, meanwhile, requires that it be applied broadly. This analysis leads Professor Redish to claim that *Younger v. Harris* is illegitimate "judicial lawmaking of the most sweeping nature." *Younger*'s premise, Redish correctly indicates, "rests largely on the desire to avoid insulting state judiciaries by questioning their competence or good faith." Given *Mitchum*'s ruling that section 1983 was designed to provide injunctive relief against distrusted state courts, however, Congress appears to have left little room for a contrary judicial conclusion.

Professor Redish's logic is unassailable. The problem with his position, however, flows from carrying his premises to their natural conclusion. It is true that *Mitchum* calls into question *Younger*'s legitimacy. But for exactly the same reasons, *Mitchum* and the legislative history of section 1983 cast doubt on *Allen v. McCurry* and *Pierson v. Ray*. And, as I shall argue below, a section 1983 cause of action that provides federal relief for the "deprivation of any rights" at the hands of state judges without the implementation of immunities, freedom from injunctive interference, or the safeguard of collateral bar would necessarily result in a debilitating clash between the two judicial systems. If this claim is true, then there are reasons apart from sheer judicial willfulness to interpret section 1983 to avoid such friction.

B. Section 1983 and Deference to State Courts

A number of conclusions may be drawn on the basis of this reading of the legislative history of section 1983. First, regardless of the intricacies of proper interpretation of the Anti-Injunction Act, *Mitchum*'s conclusion that the framers of the Civil Rights Act would have authorized equitable relief against state courts is correct. Second, the 1871 Congress had grave misgivings about the reliability of state court process. It is very unlikely, therefore, that the statute's proponents would have considered the possibility of presenting a constitutional defense to the state courts an appropriate substitute for a section 1983 cause of action. *Younger*, as a result, seems to be at odds with legislative intention. Third, state courts played a central role in the evil the Civil Rights Act was designed to abate. Given the broad language of the statute, it is very difficult to make a case based on framers' design for *Pierson*'s grant of absolute judicial immunity from damage claims. Nor, for that matter, would the 1871 Congress have been likely to demand the exhaustion of state remedies or to apply principles of collateral estoppel to limit the issues cognizable under section 1983. In short, the circumstances of the Civil Rights Act's passage lead reasonably to its characterization as a fully intrusive assertion of federal power, designed to ensure the protection of basic civil liberties even at the cost of displacing, and offending, traditional state prerogatives. *Mitchum, Pulliam*, and at least the nonexhaustion rule of *Monroe*, therefore, are supported by the intent of section 1983's drafters. *Younger, Pierson*, and *McCurry* are not.

The inquiry, however, cannot stop there. Given the tremendous expansion in substantive scope that the "rights, privileges, and immunities" protected by the statute have undergone in the past three decades, a fully intrusive section 1983 would lead to ramifications unforeseen in 1871. The gradual constitutionalization of a substantial portion of the state judicial process has led to a considerable overlap, and thus to considerable opportunity for friction, between the two court systems. Consider a simple example.

Suppose that a Virginian is indicted in the courts of his state for possession of cocaine. In his defense, along with declaring his innocence, he claims that the drugs were the subject of an unreasonable search, that a statement was introduced against him in violation of his *Miranda* rights, and that his right to confront his accusers was breached by the admission of certain hearsay testimony. The motions he files to present the challenges are denied in both pretrial and trial rulings. Eventually, he is convicted. If the section 1983 cause of action provides the strongly interventionist remedy the framers probably intended, the defendant's federal options are numerous.

As soon as the state judge denies his pretrial motions to suppress, he could move to the federal forum seeking an injunction to stop the state prosecution. The claim could easily be made that the trial judge is a "person" acting "under color of" state law who has deprived the new federal plaintiff of a right secured by the Constitution of the United States. As *Mitchum* suggests, injunctive relief against a state tribunal is envisioned by section 1983. Nor would *Younger* stand as a bar to interference with the local prosecution: the legislative history of section 1983 offers strong rebuttal to the assertion that the framers of the statute would have considered the possibility of presenting a constitutional defense to the state court an adequate remedy at law.

If the criminal defendant should choose to wait until he is convicted to seek federal relief, he might again find a hospitable forum. After final judgment, a section 1983 damages action could be filed against the convicting judge. Alleging wrongful admission of the evidence contested under the fourth, fifth, and sixth amendments, the new plaintiff could seek actual and punitive damages, as well as attorney's fees. *Pierson* would no longer stand as a bar to retroactive monetary claims because it is inconsistent with the language and intent of section 1983. Of course, the constitutional issues would have been given a full and complete airing in the convicting court. The rejection of the constitutional defenses by the local judge, however, would carry no weight in the federal tribunal. *McCurry*'s determination that collateral estoppel applies to civil rights actions cannot be squared with the framers' distrust of state judiciaries. Accordingly, the fourth, fifth, and sixth amendment issues would be retried in the federal suit. If the federal district court disagreed with the local judge's disposition, an award of damages and attorney's fees would be mandated.

Under a fully intrusive version of section 1983, this hypothetical scenario would hardly be aberrant. Theoretically, this ping-pong adjudication could transpire daily in every jurisdiction in the nation, at least until both judicial systems broke under the pressure. Section 1983, if given both its complete scope and its full mandate of intervention, would serve to extinguish the separate existence of the state courts and massively overburden the federal courts. Such a result would hardly be the product of reasoned statutory construction.

It is hard to disagree with the claim that a piece of remedial legislation like section 1983 should be "construe[d] in such a way as to make it a more rather than a less effective cure" for the ills it set about to address. In the broadest terms, section 1983 was designed to provide a federal cause of action that assures state constitutional compliance. It is certainly possible, however, that *if* the statute is interpreted in too intrusive a fashion, the final result would be a remedy that is less rather than more effective. The easiest example is the question of judicial immunity. It is certainly plausible that a state judge would be debilitated from carrying out her appointed tasks if she should be adjudged liable for damages, without benefit of immunity, for any deprivation of constitutional rights resulting from her actions. The sheer volume of "constitutional" decisions made by trial courts, especially criminal trial courts, would engender a level of risk that even the most learned, and the most solvent, jurist would find unacceptable. In addition, the flood of section 1983 claims would likely overwhelm the federal docket, thus impeding those with serious constitutional claims from obtaining swift redress through the federal courts. Is it possible to conclude, therefore, that regardless of the designs of the framers, section 1983 can be read to embrace an absolute immunity for state judges?

Curiously, it may be that a body of decisions interpreting the provisions of an antitrust statute is instructive. The Sherman Act provides that "every contract . . . in restraint of trade or commerce . . . is . . . illegal." But as Justice Brandeis pointed out in *Chicago Board of Trade v. United States*, "every agreement concerning trade . . . restrains. To bind, to restrain, is of their very essence." If a buyer closes a deal with a seller, the contract ties both to a particular course, limiting options and restraining the efforts of others who might offer different bargains. Surely, the argument goes, the Sherman Act does not render all contracts that affect interstate commerce illegal. Accordingly, "some mode of confining the generality of the language" of the act must be sought. To that end, in *Standard Oil Co. v. United*

States, the Supreme Court announced that the Sherman Act would be interpreted pursuant to a "Rule of Reason," forbidding only contracts that constitute "undue restraint[s]" of trade.

The majority position in *Standard Oil* was not achieved without a fight. The first Justice Harlan dissented vehemently, proclaiming that the opinion of the Court "may well cause some alarm for the integrity of our institutions." It was his position that the adoption of the "Rule of Reason" was nothing more than "judicial legislation"; it altered the Sherman Act with an "exception" that was "not placed there by the lawmaking branch of the Government." The statute, in short, says every contract in restraint of trade, not only unreasonable ones.

Of course, Chief Justice White's opinion, the majority opinion in *Standard Oil*, has carried the day. And its theory is useful in addressing the dilemma presented by the disjunction between section 1983's genesis and its modern application. *Standard Oil* suggests that the Sherman Act cannot be read to proscribe every contract because it simply would not work. The statute's drafters could not have intended for such a result to transpire. Or if they did, they clearly failed to think the problem through. A statute should not be interpreted in a manner that will render it impossible to carry out.

If we focus for the moment on the question of judicial immunity from damage claims under section 1983, it is possible to see the problem in a similar light. The Civil Rights Act applies, by its terms, to "every person." Judges are persons. The legislative history of the provision, if anything, actually bolsters the claim that no immunities for judges were contemplated. Thus both the statute and its legislative circumstances suggest full judicial liability. Yet surrounding circumstances, as well as the scope of section 1983, have changed. But these changes have not merely rendered the statute less useful or necessary. Rather, the Civil Rights Act, like the Sherman Act, cannot be interpreted in accord with its language. It simply will not work. It might well have been possible in 1871 to hold state judges fully accountable under section one of the Civil Rights Act. Without an incorporated Bill of Rights and invigorated substantive visions of the various clauses of the fourteenth amendment, a state judge could perhaps have conscientiously performed his duties without the paralyzing specter of threatened federal damage claims. Very likely, however, that is no longer the case. State adjudication involves the determination of too many constitutional questions, too many potential deprivations. A cautious, or perhaps wise, judge would, at the least, steer far clear of deciding any constitutional issues against a criminal defendant. Her pocketbook would be threatened only if she erred on behalf of the state. It is possible, one might counter, that local judges could survive under a mere qualified immunity — thus the case I make is overstated. But that only moves the debate back a step. The language and history of section 1983 support no judicial immunities, no matter what their degree. The recognition of any shield for state courts, strong or weak, results from necessity, not intention. But the necessity is real. Accordingly, it is reasonable to conclude that section 1983 should be read to countenance judicial immunity so that the statute remains possible to effectuate. By embracing immunity, the statute is construed "to make it a more rather than less effective" tool of constitutional supervision.

This methodology suggests a model for the interpretation of section 1983 as it applies to state courts. The language and history of the Act imply full accountability, both in law and in equity, for state judges. Because the statute provides no grant of authority to create a common law of federal-state judicial relations, especially a common law that is at odds with the terminology and design of the statute, the full breadth of federal supervision countenanced by the Act should, as a general matter, be exercised. Given the dramatically increased opportunities for friction between state and federal courts that result from the modern expansion of constitutional decisionmaking, however, it is necessary to incorporate some key aspects of deference to local judiciaries into the section 1983 cause of action regardless of the attitudes of the framers. The "exceptions" to section 1983's regime of supervision should thus be measured by necessity. Deferential rules should be adopted only if the application of the statute's intrusive original design would render it a less effective tool of constitutional enforcement by debilitating state judicial actors or overwhelming federal oversight capacity.

There would be several advantages to such an approach. First, it would pay continued respect to the language and mission of the Civil Rights Act. Legitimacy questions that arise from the unexplained recognition of limitations on section 1983 liability — typified by cases like *Younger* and *Pierson* — would be mitigated. Judicial decisions could recognize and implement one consistent, rather than two diametrically inconsistent, visions of the legislative history of section 1983. Finally, and perhaps most importantly, the debate over whether to afford deference to local courts would be altered. In making the determination to embrace injunctive oversight, to allow the estoppel of claims, or to recognize immunities, for example, the decisive factor would be the necessity that such protections be provided for state tribunals. The harms resulting from federal intrusion would be made an overt, and largely determinative, aspect of the section 1983 decisionmaking process. And only if a clear and compelling case for state protection, one rooted in necessity, were made, would a departure from section 1983's mandate be called for.

C. Application

The series of Supreme Court decisions that set the present contours of the relation between section 1983 and state courts would, at least in some particulars, receive different treatment under the interpretive strategy suggested above. *Mitchum*, as already noted, provides an essentially accurate vision of section 1983's legislative intent. The Civil Rights Act was designed, at least in part, to afford injunctive relief against state jurists. Nor can the demands for independence by state courts justify a total proscription of equitable intervention. Certainly patterns of harassment, systematic constitutional abridgements, or dramatically erroneous interpretations of federal law can be envisioned that mandate federal intrusion, and yet pose no overwhelming dangers to state judiciaries. As a result, a section 1983 methodology that gives credence to original intention, tempered by the essential demands of local judicial prerogative, would reject an across the board no-injunction rule.

Monroe's principle of nonexhaustion is even more easily justified. The historical case against exhaustion of judicial remedies is very strong. Intrusion upon local process, on the other hand, is minimal and indirect. At the other end of the spectrum, *Pierson* presents an undeniable argument for deference. Accordingly, I think that in ruling that state judges are absolutely immune from damages, the Supreme Court made the right decision — but for the wrong reason. Judicial immunity should be recognized under section 1983 not because the framers contemplated it, but because local judiciaries would be crippled without it.

Pulliam, the recent decision refusing to apply the *Pierson* rule to actions for prospective relief against state jurists, initially appears to conform to the approach I suggest. The decision, however, strikes me as more complex. I start from the premise that the draftsmen of the Civil Rights Act envisioned no judicial immunity. And, as the Court has recognized in other contexts, prospective remedies tend to prove considerably less debilitating than the possibility of looming damage actions. As I have just claimed, it is difficult to justify a complete ban on injunctive intervention. Yet something troubles me about a ruling that a successful action for an injunction against a state judge can be accompanied by an award of attorney's fees under 42 U.S.C. § 1988. To my mind, Justice Powell's claim in dissent is difficult to counter: "[T]he availability of injunctive relief under § 1983, combined with the prospect of attorney's fees under § 1988, poses [a] serious threat of harassing litigation with . . . potentially adverse consequences for judicial independence." It may well be, as the majority concluded, that *Pulliam*'s result is compelled by the clear intention of the Civil Rights Attorney's Fees Awards Act of 1976. As a matter of section 1983 interpretation, however, the threat of a fee award can intimidate as easily as the threat of a damage claim.

Under the interpretive scheme I propose, *Younger v. Harris* takes on something of a different cast. It seems clear that the "national policy" on which "Our Federalism" is based was rejected by the framers of the Civil Rights Act of 1871. Had they been acting according to its dictates, one doubts that the section 1983 cause of action would have been deemed necessary. Nor, for that matter, would they have been apt to violate traditions of state sovereignty so rudely by authorizing the employment of the national militia or the suspension of habeas corpus. The tenor of the debates over sections one and two of the Act also engenders a firm conviction that the forty-second Congress would have spurned the notion that the opportunity to present a federal defense to a state court constitutes an adequate remedy at law, thus precluding section 1983 relief. The essential premises underlying *Younger*, therefore, are at odds with the language and legislative history of the Civil Rights Act.

At least some aspects of the intrusiveness claim that justifies *Pierson*, however, are relevant to *Younger*. Direct injunctions against state court process can obviously be highly disruptive. Not only are proceedings interrupted midstream, but the state judicial system is subjected to an inference that it cannot be trusted to run its course. Granted, this "insult" to state jurists and the costs of possible obstruction of state proceedings were perceived by the framers of section 1983, but were thought to be outweighed by the need to further state constitutional compliance. Still, the opportunities and the obligations of federal injunctive oversight of state process are dramatically expanded under the modern section 1983 cause of action. From the state courts' viewpoint, federal interference is perhaps less daunting than potential liability for damage claims. At least injunctions operate prospectively, and compliance, even if reluctant, can be achieved. But the possibility of federal intervention as the result of "any deprivation" sustained at the hands of state courts would be debilitating both for the federal intruder and the local victim of national supervision.

The *Younger* question seems to turn, therefore, on the extent to which the normal requisites for equitable relief should be bolstered by the requirement of deference to state courts. Justice Black concluded that federal interference ought to be barred unless the state case is brought in "bad faith," or pursuant to a statute "flagrantly and patently violative of express constitutional prohibitions in every clause, sentence and paragraph." The bad faith or harassment exception, with its apparent demand for ill-motivated or repeated prosecutions, surely poses no great threat to state judicial independence. For purposes of section 1983 jurisprudence, however, the "flagrantly and patently violative" standard is of greater interest.

Given the central premise of the *Younger* decision — trustworthiness of state judicial decisionmaking — the patently violative exception is anomalous. Surely if state judges can be trusted, they can be trusted to handle the most clear-cut cases. And if the deferential doctrine is based on an unwillingness to assume the worst about state courts, why construct an exception that anticipates that judges might intentionally violate the Constitution's demands? Perhaps the standard represents, therefore, an unelucidated compromise between the goals of section 1983 and the unfettered operation of state judiciaries. A legal standard that exposes state courts to easy and repeated injunctive interference threatens local judicial independence. But if principles of federal jurisdiction prohibit both equitable and legal claims against judicial process, a major segment of section 1983's mission has been lost. The "patently violative" standard, then, can be seen as an effort to temper the original designs of the Civil Rights Act with the concessions to necessity. If injunctive relief against state courts is available under section 1983, but only in cases of clear and obvious mistake, the constitutional oversight envisioned by the statute's framers is at least partially saved without crippling local adjudicators.

This, however, is hardly the way the "patently violative" standard has been implemented. The Supreme Court's view of the exception is so rigid that it has never been deemed satisfied. *Trainor v. Hernandez* presented the Court with a viable opportunity to explore the standard, and the results were not encouraging. The trial judge had found the state attachment provision challenged in *Trainor* to be "patently violative of the due process clause of the Fourteenth Amendment." The Supreme Court overturned the conclusion, maintaining (somewhat surprisingly given the language of the trial opinion) that "even if such a finding was made below, which we doubt, . . . it would not have been warranted in light of our cases." *Trainor*'s curt treatment of the exception has led commentators to conclude, not unreasonably, that it "has become meaningless."

Under the reading of section 1983 that I propose, the Supreme Court's effective interment of the *Younger* exceptions is unfortunate, and wrong. It is true, of course, that if *Younger*'s stated rationale is dispositive, the exclusions are misguided from the outset. But "Our Federalism," whatever its content, cannot be defined without reference to the demands of section 1983. If the *Younger* exceptions are in fact not that, but mere illusory components of an absolute bar to injunctive intervention, then, at a minimum, *Mitchum* has been buried. A central tenet of the Civil Rights Act of 1871 — that the actions of state jurists are federally cognizable — is lost as well.

A handful of federal trial courts have treated the exception in a meaningful way. In one case, for example, the court found that a statute clearly violating the first amendment and recently upheld by the highest court of the state "appear[ed] to be patently unconstitutional," thus excusing the rigors of *Younger*. In another, the district judge determined that a pending state action presented dangers of an "appalling infringement of the rights of free speech and free exercise of religion," and thus concluded that the *Younger* doctrine "must give way." Such an approach secures a core of federal supervision so that the intentions of the Civil Rights Act are given at least some vitality. And unlike an open balance of federal and state interests, a "patent" unconstitutionality standard leaves state judiciaries a broad range of unencumbered operation. With the implementation of meaningful exception, therefore, *Younger* itself can be justified as an effort to bend the intentions of section 1983 to accommodate modern necessity.

Allen v. McCurry is a harder case. As an interpretation of section 1983, the opinion is simply wrong. Justice Stewart concluded that "nothing in the language or legislative history of § 1983 *proves* any congressional intent to deny binding effect to a state court judgment." "[P]roves," of course, is the operative word. It is literally true that the framers never mentioned collateral estoppel in express terms. Given the restrictive state of the doctrine in 1871, it would have been unnecessary for them to have considered the question had they desired to do so. But the demand for such proof is hardly a fair way to read the intention of section 1983. The Civil Rights Act of 1871 was rooted in distrust for state officials, including state judges. If the *McCurry* Court had asked simply, "Would the drafters of section 1983 have foreclosed federal consideration of any issues that were presented, or could have been presented, in a prior state trial?," the legislative history reveals that the response would have been an unequivocal "no."

But the Supreme Court has now apparently followed Professor Currie's lead and ruled that preclusion, even in section 1983 cases, is demanded by the Federal Full Faith and Credit Statute, 28 U.S.C. § 1738. That conclusion may be the correct one, though it seems a strange way to treat a federal cause of action that was designed, at least in part, to operate against state tribunals. It would also appear that the analysis of legislative history that rendered section 1983 an exception to the Anti-Injunction Act would go a long way toward a determination that the Civil Rights Act is not bound by the normal dictates of section 1738. Still, the question is hardly an easy one. It should be added, though, that when this decision is added to *Younger* and *Pierson*, the result is striking. If *Younger* completely bars injunctive oversight of pending claims, *Pierson* obviates damage actions, and principles of collateral estoppel prevent even subsequent equitable or declaratory review of state judicial process, the sweep is clean. A cause of action that was designed in no small measure to ensure state judicial accountability essentially has no applicability to state courts. If section 1738 does demand preclusion in section 1983 cases, therefore, the call for a meaningful exception to the *Younger* principle is heightened, rather than diminished.

Part VIII
Federalism, Section 1988 and the Relationship Between Federal and State Law

What is the relationship between section 1983 *federal court* litigation and state law? In one sense, the answer is straightforward: by virtue of the Supremacy Clause of the United States Constitution, the federal substantive law of section 1983 surely governs despite conflicting state law. Thus, section 1983 local government liability and individual immunity doctrines are applicable to section 1983 claims regardless of the law of the forum state. However, what of those areas of substantive law—limitations and wrongful death, for example—that are not covered by either the language of section 1983 or its legislative history?

The answer, which raises issues of section 1983 interpretation as well as federalism, is made more complicated by the existence of 42 U.S.C. sec. 1988. This statute provides in relevant part that jurisdiction of the district courts for the protection of civil rights

> shall be exercised and enforced in conformity with the laws of the United States, so far as such laws are suitable to carry the same into effect; but in all cases where they are not adapted to the object, or are deficient in the provisions necessary to furnish suitable remedies and punish offenses against law, the common law, as modified and changed by the constitution and statutes of the State wherein the court ... is held, so far as the same is not inconsistent with the Constitution and laws of the United States, shall be extended to and govern the said courts in the trial and disposition of the cause ....

The significance of section 1988 for section 1983 litigation in federal courts is addressed in articles by Professors Eisenberg, Kreimer and Steinglass.

Professor Eisenberg argues against the conventional reading of section 1988 as "a choice-of-law provision instructing federal courts hearing civil rights cases to fill the inevitable gaps in federal statutes with compatible state law." In his view, not only was this not the purpose of section 1988, but it has led to inconsistencies in section 1983 doctrine. Professor Eisenberg contends that section 1988 was intended to be applicable only to actions removed from state court to federal court pursuant to civil rights removal provisions. For him, an advantage of this interpretation is that, depending on their view of the policies of section 1983, federal courts are free to determine in each case whether to borrow a particular state rule.

Professor Kreimer's article identifies two lines of cases dealing with section 1983 interpretation which stem from the very broad language of section 1983 and the limited assistance provided by its legislative history. The first is based on federal common law, while the second is based on section 1988. Professor Kreimer argues that the Supreme Court will one day have to resolve these two differing approaches to section 1983 "and reach the question of where the mandatory incorporation of state law leaves off and the domain of independent federal statutory interpretation begins." In his view, based on *Swift v. Tyson*, 41 U.S. 1 (1842), section 1988 plausibly can and should be understood as referring to the applicability of federal common law, as modified by state statutes, but only where the latter are not inconsistent with section 1983 policy. Professor Kreimer's position is, of course, very different from that of Professor Eisenberg.

Professor Steinglass's article deals with these questions in the specific context of section 1983 wrongful death actions. He argues that courts should not blindly rely on state survival and wrongful death law but should rather develop federal wrongful death policies consistent with the purposes of section 1983. He proposes as a framework an "independent" section 1983 wrongful death action.

Theodore Eisenberg, *State Law in Federal Civil Rights Cases: The Proper Scope of Section 1988,* 128 University of Pennsylvania Law Review 499 (1980)

The Constitution is not what it used to be. In the 1960s vindication of individual rights through expansions in constitutional doctrine became commonplace. Although the Berger Court slowed that trend, it has continued and in some respects expanded another trend in federal law—the protection of individual rights by means of federal civil rights statutes. Today, the cutting edge of substantive civil rights doctrine consists of comprehensive modern civil rights legislation and of revitalized civil rights statutes of the Reconstruction era. Given the prominence of federal legislation in the civil rights field, a statute that threatens to defederalize the national civil rights program is of great significance. This Article concerns such a provision, 42 U.S.C. § 1988.

Section 1988 is now known primarily for the civil rights attorney's fees provision appended to it in 1976, but the corpus to which the 1976 amendment was fastened is of substantial interest and potential influence in its own right. Superficially, section 1988 appears to be a choice-of-law provision instructing federal courts hearing civil rights cases to fill the inevitable gaps in federal statutes with compatible state law. That seemingly straightforward reading, however, has embroiled the courts in continuing controversies. Section 1988's interpreters have been unable to agree on criteria for deciding when federal law is in need of supplementation, or when state rules, once examined, nevertheless may be ignored as undermining federal civil rights policy. The Supreme Court and the lower federal courts have espoused inconsistent interpretations: one approach threatens to place important aspects of federal civil rights litigation at the mercy of state law, while others appear to render section 1988 meaningless.

These difficulties reflect a widespread misunderstanding of section 1988. Despite its appearance, that section was not meant to be a general instruction to fill gaps in federally created causes of action with state rules, and it makes little sense when it is so used. In this Article, I sketch the existing anomalies in section 1988 doctrine before attempting to show that current approaches to section 1988 suffer from one of two problems. They either are logically flawed or require federal courts in civil rights cases to apply state rules of decision that are both unrelated to federal civil rights policy and inconsistent with nationwide uniformity in the adjudication of civil rights actions. I then argue that section 1988, when viewed as part of the larger provision from which it derives—section 3 of the Civil Rights Act of 1866—makes sense today only when it is applied to actions that are removed from state to federal court pursuant to civil rights removal provisions. In such cases section 1988 is an instruction, perhaps unneeded, to apply the state's substantive law when that law is the basis for the action removed to federal court. But when the cause of action is federal, as it is, for example, in cases brought under section 1983, the central statutory vehicle for vindicating constitutional rights, section 1988's instruction to apply state law is inapplicable.

Relegating section 1988 to a deserved obscurity does have a cost. At present, courts may at least mumble something about section 1988 before filling gaps in federally created civil rights actions. What guidance do they have once section 1988 is out of the picture? One need only recall the interstitial nature of federal law, which regularly obliges federal courts to flesh out federal statutory programs. Whatever principles courts follow in choosing law to round out these other federal statutes should provide adequate guidance for filling the interstices of federally created civil rights actions. The important point is that section 1988 is not a command by Congress to fill those gaps by reference to state law. Although federal courts may choose to follow state law, they do have a choice. Courts erroneously have believed that in section 1988 Congress expressly or impliedly meant to restrict or influence that selection.

I. Inconsistencies, Paradoxes, and Section 1988

Little of what follows will be comprehensible without some effort by the reader to parse section 1988, which provides in pertinent part:

> The jurisdiction in civil and criminal matters conferred on the district courts by the provisions of this Title, and of Title "CIVIL RIGHTS," and of Title "CRIMES," for the protection of all persons in the United States in their civil rights and for their vindication, shall be exercised and enforced in conformity with the laws of the United States, so far as such laws are suitable to carry the same into effect; but in all cases where they are not adapted to the object, or are deficient in the provisions necessary to furnish suitable remedies and punish offenses against law, the common law, as modified and changed by the constitution and statutes of the State wherein the court having jurisdiction of such civil or criminal cause is held, so far as the same is not inconsistent with the Constitution and laws of the United States, shall be extended to and govern the said courts in the trial and disposition of the cause, and, if it is of a criminal nature, in the infliction of punishment on the party found guilty.

The courts' failure to interpret section 1988 consistently is understandable for it is difficult to divine its meaning merely by reading it. This difficulty is not solely a problem of communication between section 1988's nineteenth-century drafters and contemporary lawyers. Almost one hundred years ago Justice Clifford termed the provision "a mere jumble of Federal law, common law, and State law, consisting of incongruous and irreconcilable regulations, which . . . amounts to no more than a direction to a judge [to conduct proceedings] as well as he can."

One might guess that much of the perplexity surrounding section 1988's interpretation could be dispelled by thoughtful and detailed analysis. Indeed, at least four neglected questions emerge in parsing section 1988, none of which has been satisfactorily answered and some of which have been completely ignored. When is federal law "deficient" or "not adapted to the object" within the meaning of section 1988? What follows when federal law is found to be deficient? What is section 1988's role in criminal prosecutions? Why is section 1988 limited to civil rights cases? Surely, one might think, serious study of these questions would substantially further progress towards a solution of the problems of interpreting section 1988.

Yet attempting to understand section 1988 solely by examining its entrails is fundamentally misguided. Although, following a brief introduction to the case law, I shall address those four questions in more detail than any court has done, I do not claim that focusing on them will explain away the inconsistency of section 1988 law or lead to some irrefutable interpretation. Detailed analysis of the language of section 1988 will lead not to "good" answers, but to even greater complexity and frustration, a result that suggests the courts have been working in the wrong frame of reference. To make sense of section 1988 an entirely new approach must be ventured, one that interprets the current wording of the statute in its original context.

A. *Section 1988 in the Courts*

Robertson v. Wegmann, the Supreme Court's most recent encounter with section 1988, is a useful starting point for study because it raises typical section 1988 issues and resolves at least some of them in a questionable manner. *Robertson* did not originate as a battle between obscure figures that wound its way to the Supreme Court to enshrine unknown litigants in the annals of American jurisprudence. It started as a dispute between Jim Garrison and Clay Shaw, two prominent figures in the turmoil following President Kennedy's assassination. In 1969, Garrison, then district attorney for the Louisiana parish containing New Orleans, prosecuted Shaw on charges of conspiracy to assassinate the President. Soon after his acquittal, Shaw was arrested on charges of having committed perjury at his conspiracy trial. In a section 1983 action in federal district court, Shaw obtained an injunction against the pending state prosecution and sought damages against Garrison and others, including Robertson, an alleged financial backer of Garrison's investigations. Shaw died before the scheduled trial on his damage action. When Shaw's executor, Wegmann, was substituted as plaintiff, Garrison and the other defendants moved to dismiss on the ground that the action abated upon Shaw's death. The case thus squarely posed the issue whether a section 1983 action survives the death of the plaintiff.

Had the Court ignored section 1988, it might have followed the traditional common law rule that tort actions do so abate, or it might have construed the language and purpose of section 1983 to evidence a congressional desire to have such actions survive. The Court believed, however, that it was bound to follow other guidance, and it therefore did not choose either of these relatively straightforward lines of analysis. Instead it rested its decision upon an interpretation of section 1988.

An inquiry into section 1988's origins might have shed some light on the statute's perplexing syntax, for section 1988 has a revealing past. The Court chose, however, to interpret section 1988 primarily by reading it. By its terms, the section applies in civil rights cases adjudicated in federal court. In such cases, section 1988 becomes relevant only when federal laws are "not adapted to the object, or are deficient in the provisions necessary to furnish suitable remedies." In *Robertson*, there was little doubt that the case involved civil rights, and the district court, the court of appeals, and the Supreme Court all concluded that federal law was deficient or not adapted to the object. The Supreme Court reiterated prior observations that federal law does not cover every issue likely to arise in a civil rights action and that survival of actions was one such neglected area. In cases of federal law deficiency, section 1988 instructs a court to employ "the common law, as modified and changed by the constitution and statutes of the State" in which the federal court sits. Under Louisiana's survivorship statutes, which provided that actions like Shaw's survive only in favor of certain relatives, all parties agreed that Shaw's claim would abate. The dispute centered on whether adherence to the Louisiana statutory scheme was permissible in light of the caveat at the end of section 1988, that state laws be applied only when they are "not inconsistent with the Constitution and laws of the United States."

Both the district court and the court of appeals concluded that abatement under Louisiana law was inconsistent with the policies of section 1983, and noted that adoption of a federal rule in favor of survival would generate uniformity in applying section 1983. The Supreme Court reached a different result. The Court indicated that the policies underlying section 1983 include compensation for victims of official misconduct and prevention of abuse of state power, but it believed that neither of these policies would be seriously damaged by application of Louisiana's survivorship laws. The Court observed that, on the whole, Louisiana's law was not hostile to survival of actions, and in no way was it specifically hostile to survival of federal civil rights actions. Shaw just happened not to be survived by the right class of relatives. The Court rejected the notion that a state rule causing a plaintiff to lose a federal civil rights action could, without more, be deemed inconsistent with federal law. Having found Louisiana's laws not inconsistent with section 1983, the Court held that Louisiana's rule of survivorship governed and that Shaw's executor's action should be dismissed.

Although in *Robertson* the Court read section 1988 as a command to apply state law in the face of federal statutory silence, the Court has not always adhered to that reading. In *Sullivan v. Little Hunting Park, Inc.*, the Court relied on section 1988 in implying the existence of a damage remedy under 42 U.S.C. § 1982, a provision barring private racial discrimination in the sale and rental of property. The *Sullivan* Court viewed section 1988 as giving the federal courts freedom to choose between state and federal rules rather than binding them to follow state law: "Compensatory damages for deprivation of a federal right are governed by federal standards, as provided [in] . . . § 1988. . . . This means, as we read § 1988, that both federal and state rules on damages may be utilized, whichever better serves the policies expressed in the federal statutes."

Whether or not the Court's interpretation is a fair statement of the content of section 1988, that interpretation is not consistent with the Court's approach in *Robertson*. According to *Robertson*, when federal law is silent section 1988 binds federal courts to apply the common law as modified by state rules unless those rules conflict with federal mandates. In *Sullivan*, *Robertson's* approach would have led the Court to inquire whether the common law as modified by state law allowed a private damage action. Furthermore, under *Robertson*, the mere fact that application of a state rule would defeat the action would not necessarily render the state rule inconsistent with federal law. Although the Court in *Sullivan* might have gone on to find the state rule inconsistent with federal law for other reasons, the primary inquiry would have focused on state standards. Conversely, if the Court had followed the *Sullivan* approach in *Robertson*, the inquiry would not have been whether section 1988 mandates adherence to the state survivorship rule, but whether the state rule or a federal rule would better serve the policies expressed in federal civil rights statutes.

The lower courts have not achieved greater success in formulating a uniform approach to section 1988. In *Basista v. Weir*, the Court of Appeals for the Third Circuit faced two questions—whether punitive damages could ever be awarded in a section 1983 action, and whether, if they could, recovery of at least nominal damages was a prerequisite. The court concluded that federal law was not deficient on these points and that it allowed punitive damages even in the absence of other damages. Yet a district court interpreting section 1988 intimated that the availability of punitive damages in civil rights actions would turn on whether state law allowed punitive damages in similar cases. A second area of inconsistency concerns the issue of a superior officer's liability for the acts of a subordinate. The Court of Appeals for the Ninth Circuit, applying section 1988, held in *Hesselgesser v. Reilly* that the answer turns on the superior's liability under state law. Yet many circuit courts, without alluding to section 1988, have found no vicarious liability for supervisors in section 1983 cases.

These cases demonstrate not only that conflicts exist in the courts' approaches to section 1988, but that the proper interpretation of the statute cannot turn on a desire to expand or contract the scope of liability for civil rights violations. Depending upon the state rule to be applied in the federal action, section 1988 may increase the number of cases in which liability is found, as in *Hesselgesser*, or decrease it, as in *Robertson*. The need for a more stable approach to section 1988 is thus independent of differing views on the proper reach of federal civil rights remedies.

B. *Sources of Inconsistency: Interpretive Problems Raised by Section 1988*

It seems rather late in section 1988's checkered life to offer in print a detailed reading of the statute, but no one has yet done so. Courts dealing with section 1988 seem preoccupied with the result it produces and do not pause to give opinion readers the benefit of the intermediate analytical steps that must precede a conclusion that state law is or is not applicable. Commentators have all but ignored section 1988. In this subpart, I attempt to penetrate the thicket that surrounds the section by focusing first on two issues that must be resolved before section 1988 can be read as commanding deference to state law and then on two larger questions about its structure. The unsatisfactory results of this analysis suggest that a major shift is needed in our thinking about section 1988.

One threshold issue, largely neglected by the courts that rely on section 1988 to apply state law in civil rights cases, is the determination that federal law is "deficient" or "not adapted to the object." Unless such a finding is made, section 1988 does not command resort to state law. The courts' implicit tests for determining deficiency—there are no explicit tests—lead to troublesome results. A second thorny problem arises once federal law is deemed deficient, thereby triggering section 1988's instruction to apply state law. State law seems inappropriate as a mandatory guide for settling many issues that arise in civil rights cases, even those that are purely remedial. But can one neglect state law without rendering section 1988 meaningless? The dilemma of a federal statute containing instructions seemingly at odds with federal policy lies at the heart of judicial confusion about section 1988.

In addition to these problems of interpretation that surface in the typical section 1988 case, another pair of questions concerns two puzzling aspects of the statute that have eluded judicial attention. Although section 1988 traditionally has been used to resolve questions arising in civil actions, on its face the statute purports to operate as well in the criminal sphere. In criminal cases, in which the remedy—the criminal penalty—is prescribed by statute, the remedial issues that *Sullivan* and other cases have found suitable for resolution under section 1988 are absent. What conceivable role can section 1988 play in criminal prosecutions? Finally, the statutory language invites inquiry into section 1988's limitation to civil rights cases. If Congress thought it appropriate to fill the gaps in federal civil rights legislation with state law, why did it choose not to extend section 1988's choice-of-law rule to remedy similar gaps in non-civil rights statutes?

* * *

II. The Proper Scope of Section 1988

Because analysis reveals no attractive reading of section 1988, each unappealing alternative begins to grow in plausibility. It is possible, after all, that Congress passed an essentially meaningless statute. And the Republic would no doubt survive even if Congress did enact a federal statute that places many federal civil rights questions at the mercy of state law. These views, however, ought to be embraced only as a last resort, in the absence of any plausible alternative. In this part, I propose an approach that avoids the objections to either extreme view of section 1988. This new reading of section 1988 provides a simple test for determining when federal law is deficient, gives a plausible meaning to the inconsistency clause, and offers insight into why Congress included criminal cases within the ambit of section 1988 but excluded cases not involving civil rights.

Courts have misinterpreted section 1988 because they have been asking the wrong questions about it. Instead of seeking the circumstances under which section 1988 should influence issues in federal civil rights cases, courts should be asking whether Congress intended section 1988 ever to incorporate state rules in federally created actions. That Congress did not so intend follows from viewing section 1988 in its historical context. As enacted, the precursor to the present section 1988 played a rational but limited role in the structure of the federal civil rights legislation. That role, an instruction to federal courts to apply substantive state rules when adjudicating cases arising under state law, remains section 1988's only appropriate sphere of operation.

A. *Section 1988 in Original Context*

Section 1988 derives from section 3 of the Civil Rights Act of 1866, and its original role can be gleaned by study of the 1866 Act's first three sections. Although the Act is lengthy, its structure, and section 1988's place in that structure, cannot be understood without reference to these sections, which provide:

> [Sec. 1] . . . [A]ll persons born in the United States . . . are hereby declared to be citizens of the United States; and such citizens, of every race and color . . . shall have the same right . . . to make and enforce contracts, to sue, be parties, and give evidence, to inherit, purchase, lease, sell, hold, and convey real and personal property, and to full and equal benefit of all laws and proceedings for the security of person and property, as is enjoyed by white citizens, and shall be subject to like punishment, pains, and penalties, and to none other, any law, statute, ordinance, regulation, or custom, to the contrary notwithstanding.
>
> Sec. 2. . . . [A]ny person who, under color of any law, statute, ordinance, regulation, or custom, shall subject, or cause to be subjected, any inhabitant of any State or Territory to the deprivation of any right secured or protected by this act . . . shall be deemed guilty of a misdemeanor, and, on conviction, shall be punished by fine not exceeding one thousand dollars, or imprisonment not exceeding one year, or both, in the discretion of the court.
>
> Sec. 3. . . . [T]he district courts of the United States . . . shall have, exclusively of the courts of the several States, cognizance of all crimes and offences committed against the provisions of this act, and also, concurrently with the circuit courts of the United States, of all causes, civil and criminal, affecting persons who are denied or cannot enforce in the courts or judicial tribunals of the State or locality where they may be any of the rights secured to them by the first section of this act; and if any suit or prosecution, civil or criminal, has been or shall be commenced in any State court, against any such person, for any cause whatsoever . . . such defendant shall have the right to remove such cause for trial to the proper district or circuit court . . . . The jurisdiction in civil and criminal matters hereby conferred on the district and circuit courts of the United States shall be exercised and enforced in conformity with the laws of the United States, so far as such laws are suitable to carry the same into effect; but in all cases where such laws are not adapted to the object, or are deficient in the provisions necessary to furnish suitable remedies and punish offences against law, the common law, as modified and changed by the constitution and statutes of the State wherein the court having jurisdiction of the cause, civil or criminal, is held, so far as the same is not inconsistent with the Constitution and laws of the United States, shall be extended to and govern said courts in the trial and disposition of such cause, and, if of a criminal nature, in the infliction of punishment on the party found guilty.

Reading the statute without the benefit of later gloss, one might gather that it functioned in the following manner: section 1 defines a set of rights that cannot be denied on account of race; section 2 imposes criminal sanctions against those who, under color of law, deny the rights guaranteed by section 1; and section 3 provides further information about federal court vindication of the rights set forth in section 1. Not surprisingly, section 3 provides, in the initial clause ending with the words "this act," for exclusive federal jurisdiction of section 2 criminal cases. The next clause, ending with the first semicolon, seems to give the federal courts original jurisdiction over all cases, civil and criminal, in which section 1 rights are denied or cannot be enforced in state courts. In the remaining language of its first sentence, section 3 allows for federal jurisdiction in cases commenced in state courts by giving the state-court defendant the right to remove to federal court when his section 1 rights are not enforceable in the state court. Finally, in what is now section 1988, the second sentence of section 3 sets forth guidance as to what law should govern in the actions over which the federal courts have been given jurisdiction by the preceding language. The operation of this last sentence can best be appreciated through the use of examples.

Assume that it is 1866 and Mr. X, a black man in a southern state, is charged by the state with criminal trespass. At his trial in state court, Mr. X wishes to testify in his own defense, but he is barred from testifying because state law deprives blacks of the power to testify in court. How would the three quoted sections of the 1866 Act function in such a case?

Clearly the law preventing Mr. X from testifying is unlawful under section 1 of the 1866 Act. Those enforcing the disqualifying statute seem criminally liable under section 2. What happens to the state court action in which Mr. X is being prosecuted? Under section 3, the state's failure to give Mr. X a trial at which he can testify, a violation of section 1, invests Mr. X with the right to remove the criminal proceedings against him to the local federal district or circuit court. But after removal, nothing in the 1866 Act precludes the prosecution of Mr. X for the crime. Presumably, Mr. X's trial will go forward in federal court.

In contemplating how that trial is to proceed, the language of section 1988 originating in the second sentence of section 3 begins to make sense. Here there is a deficiency in federal law not merely because a federal statute fails to outline every detail of a federally created cause of action. The deficiency arises instead because the substantive rule sought to be vindicated by the court proceedings against Mr. X is not even a creature of federal law. In short, the action "arises under" state law. Even in the days of a general federal common law, it made no sense for Mr. X to be tried in federal court on anything other than the charge for which he was being tried in state court prior to removal. The instructions of section 1988's predecessor are clear—in the prosecution removed from state court pursuant to section 3 of the Act, state substantive rules defining the crime must govern. With one exception, any other result would be nonsensical.

The exception arises when the crime for which Mr. X is being prosecuted is itself violative of section 1. Suppose that the southern state also makes it a crime for a black man to enter into a contract with a white man and that Mr. X is being prosecuted for having done so. Mr. X is unable to enforce a section 1 right in state court—the right to make and enforce contracts. But now removal to federal court and continued prosecution pursuant to state criminal law will not afford Mr. X much relief. When his problem was merely that state law disqualified him from testifying, removal to federal court could eliminate the disqualification, and the prosecution could continue in a manner not violative of Mr. X's section 1 rights. But when the statute under which he is being prosecuted itself violates section 1 of the 1866 Act, it will not do merely to remove to federal court and allow the prosecution to go forward. A prosecution in any forum under a law that violates section 1 is prohibited. This is the purpose of the inconsistency clause of section 3, which ensures that state law (or, more accurately, the common law as modified by state law) will be used to cure deficiencies in federal law only if the state law is "not inconsistent with the Constitution and laws of the United States." Thus, although the prosecution of Mr. X for criminal trespass might go forward in federal court after removal, with state substantive criminal law defining the proscribed behavior, the inconsistency clause of section 3 prevents a state criminal law that violates section 1 from having force in the removed proceedings. In such cases, dismissal of the removed action seems the only appropriate course.

Under the first three sections of the 1866 Act, incorporation of state substantive law is not limited to criminal cases. If Mr. X is a defendant in a civil action in state court and state law denies him the right to testify because of his race, section 3 again authorizes removal and state substantive civil rules govern in the removed proceeding.

Under section 3 of the Civil Rights Act of 1866, it appears that section 1988's precursor was also intended to function in some cases originally brought in federal court. Assume that Mr. X is the victim of some tortious behavior and that he wishes to bring a civil action under state tort law. Assume further that Mr. X must testify on his own behalf if his tort case is to succeed, but that, as in the preceding hypothetical cases, state law bars Mr. X from testifying. There will not be much point to filing his tort claim in state court because Mr. X's inability to testify will assure the claim's failure. The language in the first sentence of section 3, providing federal courts with original jurisdiction over all cases affecting persons who are either denied or cannot enforce their section 1 rights in state court, here comes to Mr. X's rescue. Because he is denied his section 1 right to testify by state law, Mr. X can bring his tort action originally in federal court without wasting his time in state court. In the federal court action, the precursor to section 1988 instructs the federal court to apply the state's law of torts.

By viewing section 1988 in the context of the 1866 Act one may give content to what is now section 1988 without having to read it as allowing state law to modify federally created rights. In all of the examples just discussed, section 3's reference to state law becomes relevant either when an action is removed from state to federal court or, as in the last example, when an original federal court action seeks to enforce state law. According to this view of section 3, it permits substantive state law to operate in a federal forum only in cases arising under state law, a situation that occurs if state law denies to black persons the rights secured by section 1 of the 1866 Act.

In addition to conferring removal and original federal jurisdiction for state-created causes of action, the first sentence of section 3 of the 1866 Act conferred upon federal courts exclusive jurisdiction of prosecutions brought under section 2 of the Act. This third basis or jurisdiction raises a final possible class of cases in which section 3 might be read to require resort to state law in a federally created action. Section 2 criminal cases constitute actions arising under a federal law; that section is followed in the text of the statute by section 3, authorizing resort to state law. Even if one accepts that section 1988's precursor in the second sentence of section 3 did not contemplate use of state law in actions arising under other federal laws, the question remains whether it mandated resort to state law in the federal criminal actions created by the 1866 Act itself. For a number of reasons, it seems unlikely that Congress intended to do so.

First, section 3's grant of jurisdiction over section 2 criminal prosecutions to the federal district courts "exclusively of the courts of the several States" indicates that Congress perceived these cases as having a uniquely federal nature. If anything, one would expect these cases to be less dependent than other cases upon state law. Second, for the reasons canvassed in part I, it is unlikely that section 3 was meant to have any application to federal criminal cases. Third, it is possible to give a plausible interpretation to the second sentence of section 3 without having it require resort to state law in criminal prosecutions under section 2. That sentence begins by stating that the federal jurisdiction conferred by the 1866 Act "shall be exercised and enforced in conformity with the laws of the United States, so far as such laws are suitable to carry the same into effect," and goes on to provide for the use of state law when federal law is deficient. If the first part of the sentence, that requiring exercise of jurisdiction in conformity with federal law, is read to refer to section 2 as well as to other federal laws, and the rest of the sentence is read to refer only to state-created causes of action, then section 3 would never mandate applying state law to criminal prosecutions under federal law. If, as in the case of section 2 criminal cases, one finds an applicable federal law to interpret, one need not resort to state law. In such cases, section 2 is "the law of the United States" in conformity with which federal jurisdiction shall be exercised. State law is irrelevant because federal law is not deficient. Thus, nothing in this third basis for federal jurisdiction requires federal courts to use state law in actions arising under federal law.

Assuming for the moment that subsequent statutory developments have not altered the original understanding of section 1988's antecedents in section 3 of the Civil Rights Act of 1866, the reading that emerges—that section 1988 requires resort to state law only in cases arising under state law—avoids all of the seemingly insurmountable difficulties raised by other interpretations. First, the difficult problem of deciding when federal law is deficient disappears. One need no longer apply an artificial magnifying glass to section 1983 or to other federal civil rights statutes to determine whether they address an issue. Federal law is deficient within the meaning of section 1988 only when a substantive state rule, civil or criminal, is the source of the action. This limited interpretation eliminates the awkwardness of having a federal law mandate resort to state rules in cases involving primarily questions of federal policy. Under this interpretation, section 1988 never mandates adherence to state rules in actions arising under section 1983, or any other federal law. Indeed, as originally enacted, section 1988 could not have been meant to influence section 1983 actions because the initial version of section 1983 did not become law until five years later.

Second, the new approach to section 1988 supplies a reading of the inconsistency clause that does no violence to ordinary meaning; state laws are inconsistent with federal law only if they violate it. And because the inconsistency clause is not activated unless the action arises under state law, there is no longer any need to stretch the definition of "inconsistent" to include state laws that significantly restrict the federal cause of action, or to find state laws inconsistent on one set of facts but not on another.

Third, the new approach solves the puzzles of section 1988's inclusion of criminal cases. Section 1988 neither authorizes creation of a mysterious new class of crimes based on state law nor mandates use of state procedural rules in federal criminal prosecutions. It simply instructs federal courts to apply state criminal law when state criminal prosecutions are removed to federal court.

Finally, the mystery of section 1988's limitation to civil rights cases is resolved. In addition to providing exclusive federal jurisdiction over federal criminal prosecutions brought against persons who violated the civil rights guaranteed by section 1, the Civil Rights Act of 1866 also took the unusual step of conferring federal jurisdiction over cases arising under state law in which section 1 rights were implicated. The provisions in section 3 concerning the law to be applied in the exercise of those jurisdictional grants were naturally limited to these civil rights actions, there being no need or reason to formulate a rule for any other kind of case.

B. *Legislative History of Section 1988*

I do not pretend that the text of the 1866 Act and the previous discussion prove conclusively that section 3's command to apply state law was meant to operate only in cases arising under state law. It is possible, consistently with the English language, to read the second sentence of section 3 to apply to federal claims as well. But the case for a new interpretation of section 1988 rests on more than the investigation of section 1988's original context and on the weakness of alternative readings; the argument draws modest but important support from the legislative histories of the 1866 Act and of later relevant provisions. Nowhere in those histories do members of Congress suggest that section 1988's progenitor required application of state law in any case other than one arising under state law.

Understandably, section 3 did not receive the lion's share of attention during Congress's consideration of the 1866 Act. The substantive rights set forth in section 1 were hotly debated, and the criminal sanctions in section 2 drew much fire from opponents. Section 3's significance was dwarfed by the importance of the preceding sections. When it was mentioned, however, the discussion supported the view that section 3 imported state law into federal court only in cases arising under state law.

Senator Trumbull, who introduced the bill that became the 1866 Act, made the following preliminary remarks about section 3:

> [The third section of the bill] provides further that no person whose equal civil rights are denied him in the State courts shall be tried by those courts for any offense, but that he shall have a right to remove his cause into the courts of the United States, and be there tried if it be for an offense against the laws of the United States, according to those laws, and if it be for an offense which is not provided for by the laws of the United States, then according to the common law as modified by the statutes and constitution of the State where the offense is committed, so far as they are not inconsistent with the Constitution and laws of the United States.

Senator Trumbull's description alludes to the use of state law only in cases removed from state court in which the offense was not provided for by federal law. There is no hint that section 3 might mandate application of state law in federal causes of action.

Opponents of the act seemed to agree that section 3's references to state law operated in cases of removal. Senator Saulsbury, in challenging the constitutionality of the 1866 Act, pointed to cases similar to those of Mr. X:

> Suppose that an action of ejectment is instituted in any State where free negroes are denied the right to testify, and suppose that action of ejectment is against a free negro. He wishes to prove that he has not been guilty of trespass in ejectment, and he proposes to prove it by a negro, and the court say [*sic*], "No; under the law of this State that negro is not a competent witness." In such a case as that, this bill authorizes the circuit or district court of the United States to take cognizance of that action of ejectment, and the State courts are excluded from its consideration.

In hearing the ejectment action, there could be little choice but to apply state ejectment rules. Senator Saulsbury also objected to the fact that the Act allowed for removal of criminal cases.

> Take another case. A free negro commits murder in the State of Kentucky. He is indicted under the laws of Kentucky in the State courts . . . He calls up a negro . . . The judge in Kentucky . . . would say under their law that this negro could not be a witness. What does this bill provide? It provides that that case of murder shall be taken from the jurisdiction and control of the State courts, and that the district

> and circuit courts of the United States shall have exclusive jurisdiction of it.

Whatever objections Senator Saulsbury had to removal of the criminal case, he assumed that the murder trial would go forward in federal court under the state's substantive law of murder. President Johnson's message vetoing the 1866 Act also indicated that state law would determine the outcome of cases removed under section 3 in which the offense was not within the purview of federal law.

It is tempting to overread this admittedly sparse legislative history. The conclusive, positive statement always yearned for by future generations is missing. But omissions may be as instructive as positive statements. No member of Congress mentioned cases in which section 3 would mandate incorporation of state law other than in cases arising under state law and removed to federal court.

An irony emerges in contrasting the reason that today's Court gives for its interpretation of section 1988 with the reasons given in 1866 for opposing section 3. In *Robertson v. Wegmann*, the only cogent reason the Court gives for applying section 1988 to incorporate Louisiana's survivorship law is that if section 1988 does not mandate use of state law in that case, it might never do so. Yet opponents of section 1988's predecessor objected that the provision was part of a section, one providing for removal, that would operate in too many cases. How can both of these positions have been entertained? The answer, of course, is that in 1866 several states had provisions that, on their face, violated section 1 of the 1866 Act. Saulsbury and others referred to them in the debates. In such states removal was expected to be a frequent occurrence, and section 3's invocation of state law would be frequently called upon in the removed cases. Today, there are no state laws comparable to the Black Codes which section 1 was designed to overcome. In the absence of such blatantly unlawful provisions, civil rights removal has become exceedingly rare, and the instruction to resort to state law in removed cases has suffered a corresponding reduction in importance. Section 1988, as the successor to the second sentence of section 3, deserves a similar fate. This is not to say, however, that the provision was passed without a purpose, but only that the problems it was intended to remedy are no longer real. Contrary to the Supreme Court's assertion in *Robertson*, one need never apply section 1988 to fill gaps in section 1983 or other federal civil rights statutes in order to avoid rendering section 1988 meaningless. If states were to pass statutes similar to the Black Codes, both the removal provisions and section 1988 would again be of central importance.

Because the words now constituting section 1988 were originally part of the 1866 Act the major focus in divining their meaning from secondary sources should be on the history of that Act. The post-Civil War burst of federal civil rights legislation, however, extended well beyond 1866, and some of the later developments bear upon section 1988. The 1866 Act was followed by proposal of the fourteenth amendment in 1866, its ratification in 1868, and ratification of the fifteenth amendment in 1870. With these new sources of power Congress embarked upon a civil rights program that included the Enforcement Act of 1870 and the Ku Klux Klan Act of 1871. Both Acts incorporate by reference provisions of the 1866 Act, including section 3, and it is therefore necessary to consider their effect on that portion of section 3 from which section 1988 derives.

In the 1870 Act, Congress dealt primarily with voting rights. Passed only two months after ratification of the fifteenth amendment, the Act was intended to guarantee in practice the right to vote that the new amendment secured in theory. Given that Congress's primary concern was with voting rights, and that the provisions of the 1870 Act relating to the 1866 Act were not the focus of substantial discussion, it is unlikely that in enacting those provisions Congress meant to work substantial changes in section 1988's precursor. Nor does anything in the 1870 Act suggest a contrary result.

Section 18 of the 1870 Act reenacted the 1866 law and provided that two new sections, analogous to sections 1 and 2 of the 1866 Act, were to be enforced according to the earlier Act's provisions. In reenacting the 1866 statute, the 1870 Act created no situations in which reference to state law in federal causes of action would be any more necessary than it had been under the 1866 Act. All the removal cases that could have arisen under the 1866 Act could arise as well under the 1870 Act. Thus, the passage of the 1870 Act in no way requires adjustments to the interpretation of section 3 of the 1866 Act advanced here.

The structure of the 1870 Act contains subtler evidence bearing on the likely intended scope of section 3 of the 1866 Act. Section 1 of the 1870 Act states a general principle outlawing discrimination in voting. Sections 2 through 6 of the Act define a series of federal crimes for interfering with federally protected rights. Section 8, which outlines the role of the federal courts in vindicating the rights established by the new Act, a function identical with that of section 3 of the 1866 Act, provides:

> [T]he district courts of the United States, within their respective districts, shall have, exclusively of the courts of the several States, cognizance of all crimes and offences committed against the provisions of this act, and also, concurrently with the circuit courts of the United States, of all causes, civil and criminal, arising under this act, except as herein otherwise provided, and the jurisdiction hereby conferred shall be exercised in conformity with the laws and practice governing United States courts; and all crimes and offences committed against the provisions of this act may be prosecuted by the indictment of a grand jury, or, in cases of crimes and offences not infamous, the prosecution may be either by indictment or information filed by the district attorney in a court having jurisdiction.

It is instructive to contrast this provision with the related provision set forth in section 3 of the 1866 Act. The first few lines of the two sections are identical. Yet in the remaining language there are differences significant for this inquiry. First, Congress omitted from section 8 of the 1870 Act any reference to removal such as that contained in section 3 of the 1866 Act. This omission is understandable because the provisions preceding section 8 in the 1870 Act create federal crimes or rights of action. Given the exclusive federal jurisdiction provided for in the first clause of section 8, there are no state law claims to be removed to federal court. Second, unlike the 1866 Act, the 1870 Act gives federal courts neither original nor removal jurisdiction over any state law claims. More importantly, the absence from section 8 of those jurisdictional grants is accompanied by the absence of the language in section 3 from which section 1988 derives. This omission supports the view that such language was meant to operate when actions arising under state law were removed to or originated in federal court. Where there was no possibility that a state law claim would be adjudicated in federal court, there simply was no need for language equivalent to section 1988.

The Ku Klux Klan Act of 1871 was the last significant civil rights provision to incorporate portions of the 1866 Act. After creating a federal civil action for violations of federal rights in language substantially the same as that found now in section 1983, section 1 of the 1871 Act provides in part: "[S]uch proceeding [is] to be prosecuted in the several district or circuit courts of the United States, with and subject to the same rights of appeal, review upon error, and other remedies provided in like cases in such courts, under the provisions of [the Civil Rights Act of 1866] . . . ." Given the 1871 Act's reference to the remedial structure of the 1866 Act, one might ask whether Congress meant to apply the choice-of-law provision contained in section 3 of the 1866 Act to the federal cause of action created by the 1871 Act. If so, then section 3's directive that state law govern would apply to actions arising under federal law, and the thesis advanced here would be undermined.

It is doubtful that Congress's reference to the 1866 Act was so intended. Initially, as suggested by the interpretation offered above of the application of section 3 to section 2 criminal cases, Congress expressly limited resort to state law to cases arising under state law. The same reference in section 3 to the exercise of jurisdiction "in conformity with the laws of the United States" that rendered section 3's invocation of state law inapplicable to section 2 criminal prosecutions could be viewed as rendering state law inapplicable to cases arising under all other federal laws. If Congress entertained different notions with respect to the cause of action set out in section 1 of the 1871 Act, one would expect the change to have been expressly noted in statutory language or reflected in the congressional debates. Yet nothing in the text or the legislative history of the 1871 Act indicates that the reference to the 1866 Act was meant to require federal courts to fill the gaps in section 1983's progenitor with the law of the state in which they sat.

In addition, section 2 of the 1866 Act was a model for section 1 of the 1871 Act. The latter was in part intended to add civil remedies to the criminal penalties already provided by the former. Viewed in this light, the language of the 1871 Act, referring to "like cases" under the 1866 Act, acquires a special significance. Of the three classes of cases over which federal jurisdiction was granted in the 1866 Act—section 2 criminal cases, cases arising under state law brought originally in federal court, and cases removed from state to federal court—the first of these three was most "like" the cases to be brought under section 1 of the 1871 Act. Therefore, the reference in section 1 to "like cases" under the 1866 Act could be interpreted as singling out those cases arising under section 2 of the 1866 Act. If so, then section 1 of the 1871 Act need not be viewed as ever requiring that state law govern actions arising under it. In them, just as in criminal actions arising under section 2 of the 1866 Act, federal law would always be "adapted to the object" and never deficient.

The last significant step in section 1988's transformation from its foundations in the 1866 Act to its current isolation in Title 42 consists of what were supposed to have been nonsubstantive revisions of the United States Code. In 1866, Congress authorized an organizational revision of all United States statutes. The task, completed in 1874, separated substantive civil rights provisions, such as section 1 of the 1866 Act, from their jurisdictional and procedural counterparts. In the course of those revisions, section 3 of the 1866 Act was separated from the rest of what was originally the 1866 Act, and splintered into a removal provision, section 641 of the Revised Statutes, and a choice-of-law provision identical to section 1988, section 722 of the Revised Statutes. This separation of section 3 into separate removal and choice-of-law provisions may have been the most significant development in section 1988's history. For viewed in its original context, as part of the 1866 Act, there is little doubt that section 1988 was meant to function primarily in removal cases arising under state law. Yet when viewed in isolation, section 1988 becomes sufficiently ambiguous to deceive courts into believing that it dictates a choice-of-law rule in civil rights cases arising under federal law. Cut adrift from the only provision with respect to which it made any sense, section 1988 seems to take on a life of its own, and the attempt by courts to define the limits of that artificial existence predictably has led to great confusion.

III. Consequences of a Limited View of Section 1988

The realization that section 1988 mandates application of state law only in state-created causes of action gives rise to two series of questions, each leading in turn to new doctrinal paths. The first involves the doctrine of *Erie Railroad v. Tompkins* . When substantive state law governs the claim being tried in federal court, may judges, in the light of the *Erie* doctrine, tolerate a different result in the federal forum than would be reached by a state court trying the same action? Of course, if the substantive state law itself violates federal law, then the inconsistency clause of section 1988 mandates a different result in the federal forum. But apart from such cases, the question whether to follow federal or state rules persists. To illustrate, assume Mr. X is a defendant in a civil case in a state court in a state that prohibits blacks from testifying. Mr. X, in 1866 and today, may remove the state court civil case to federal court. Except for the federal rule substituting for the state's testimonial disqualification, are federal rules to be applied in the removed proceeding when they might lead to results different from those that would be reached by the state court using state rules? Although it is tempting to plunge ahead with what, in the *Erie* tradition, might turn out to be an endless analysis of this question, demanding appropriate sensitivity to the particular federal rule in question and the true meaning of the Rules of Decision Act, I trust I will be forgiven for not doing so. Today, the cases in which section 1988 will give rise to a federal court trial of a state cause of action are virtually nonexistent. Civil rights removal is all but a dead letter, and the state statutes, the Black Codes, that might have enabled a Reconstruction era litigant to bring state law claims as an original matter in federal court no longer exist.

The second series of questions generated by new insight into section 1988 is of more immediate relevance. With section 1988 out of the picture there seems momentarily to be a void in the federal civil rights program. If section 1988 provides no guidance, how should courts deal with issues they have been handling or mishandling by reference to section 1988?

The answer is not surprising. Federal courts should fill out the federal civil rights program by the same techniques used to fill out other federal programs. These techniques are not reducible to facile formulae but they have been explored with sophistication by others, a process I see no reason to repeat here. The result may be that state law will govern some matters, but this in no way discredits the limited interpretation of section 1988. For once section 1988 is restricted to its proper scope, the decision whether to apply state law is no longer coerced by congressional command. The new approach leaves federal courts room to maneuver, while undertaking a careful analysis of the propriety of borrowing the state rule in the particular case. And in deciding whether to adopt or reject the state rule, the courts need no longer embarrass themselves by mangling or ignoring section 1988.

Seth F. Kreimer, *The Source of Law in Civil Rights Actions: Some Old Light on Section 1988*, 133 University of Pennsylvania Law Review 601 (1985)

* * *

I. The Problem

A. *Sources of Law in Civil Rights Cases*

Section 1983, the keystone of modern constitutional litigation, declares with majestic simplicity that

> [e]very person who, under color of any statute, ordinance, regulation, custom, or usage, of any State . . . subjects, or causes to be subjected, any citizen of the United States . . . to the deprivation of any rights, privileges, or immunities secured by the Constitution and laws, shall be liable to the party injured in an action at law, suit in equity, or other proper proceeding for redress.

Although section 1983 obviously provides a cause of action, the extent and conditions of this liability are entirely unclear. The problematic definition of "color of law" has bedeviled a generation of constitutional litigators. The difficulties of causation are no more tractable here than in other areas of tort law. Nor is the substantive scope of "rights, privileges, or immunities" protected by section 1983 without difficulty. Once a relevant deprivation has been established, moreover, courts must find guidance on issues of the measure of damages, available defenses, the applicability of vicarious liability, provisions for contribution, applicable statutes of limitations, the requirement of exhaustion of state remedies, and the burden of proof concerning these matters. In regard to these matters, section 1983 is silent. The statute directs that rights be vindicated, yet it fails to erect any remedial structure.

In the search for guidance on these issues, one might turn first to the statute's legislative history. But two decades of excursions into the Congressional Globe of 1871 have convinced most observers that the legislative history of section 1983 is, in the main, unhelpful. Given the passions raised by Reconstruction and the breadth of the issues addressed, few lawyers are unable to find support for their position in those turbulent debates. To take one indicative example, both the abrupt establishment of municipal immunity in *Monroe v. Pape* in 1961 and, seventeen years later, its sudden replacement by a scheme allowing liability on a showing of a link between the violation and some municipal policy in *Monell v. Department of Social Services* rested nominally on readings of legislative history. Both cases, however, had less to do with new-found insight into the mood of the 1871 Congress than with emerging perceptions of the proper scope of government responsibility in the twentieth century. If each nuance of the elaboration of section 1983's remedial structure must be rooted in explicit legislative discussion, the courts face an impossible task. But this task is one that the Court has, in fact, eschewed. Although most opinions still mention the legislative history of section 1983, such references are, in large measure, ceremonial. More often, neither the debates nor the context of the legislative record can be said to provide solid ground for decision.

Forsaking the thickets of legislative history, courts interpreting section 1983 have often attempted to erect a structure of presumptions based on the law as it stood in 1871. Justice Frankfurter argued in *Tenney v. Brandhove*, and subsequent cases have regularly reiterated, that if the Congress had intended to impose liability incommensurate with the common law of 1871, it would have said so. Absent statements or statutes to the contrary — runs the argument — the nineteenth century law of government immunities, damages, and torts should govern.

But implication from silence is a risky business. Given the unqualified language of section 1983, one might argue with equal force that had Congress intended to limit the scope of liability it would have voiced that intention. There is, moreover, some incongruity in suggesting that a statute adopted to redress a failure of existing legal remedies for violations of constitutional rights should be defined by the scope of those very remedies.

Nor is the case for the assimilation of the jurisprudence of 1871 compelling on policy grounds. At least Justice Frankfurter's argument in *Tenney* for the incorporation of legislative immunity into section 1983 was bolstered by contentions regarding the continued centrality of legislative immunity to the democratic process and by Justice Frankfurter's professed doubt regarding the constitutional ability of Congress to impose liability. In contrast, in some recent cases the Court has treated section 1983 as automatically incorporating by reference all of the answers found in the law of 1871.

This increasing attention to contemporaneous common law has generated a boom in law-office history in recent Terms. The pages of the *U.S. Reports* fill with the smoke of battle over how many of the thirty-seven states in 1871 required intent as opposed to recklessness as an element of the case for punitive damages, over whether an action against a police officer for testifying falsely and thereby denying due process is more closely analogous to the nineteenth century action of defamation or to the common law writ of *crimen feloniae imposuit*, and over whether a federal injunction against a magistrate who insists on incarcerating defendants charged with nonjailable offenses pending trial is properly analogized to prerogative writs issued by the King's Bench against the ecclesiastical courts in 1691. In similar fashion the Court has disavowed the power to "establish immunities from section 1983 actions in the interests of what we judge to be sound public policy" and denied immunity to public defenders "because there was, of course, no such office or position in existence at that time."

In contrast to the Court's claims of fidelity to the common law as it stood in 1871, from early in its development constitutional tort doctrine in fact looked to modern policy as decisive. Nearly twenty years ago, in *Pierson v. Ray*, Chief Justice Warren referred to modern rather than nineteenth century tort doctrine in defining the scope of good faith immunities under section 1983. Warren relied on the "prevailing view" of the good faith immunity of law enforcement officials under the common law as it stood in 1967, citing *Restatement (Second) of Torts* and *The Law of Torts* by Harper & James, although the scope of official immunity in the nineteenth century may well have been considerably narrower than the good faith immunity accorded by any branch of current doctrine.

Expansions and refinements of section 1983 immunities have continued this trend away from reliance upon nineteenth century tort law. Immunity doctrine under section 1983, moreover, has increasingly become divorced from any body of law outside of federal civil rights cases. The Court elaborates doctrines conferring quasi-legislative immunity on judicial and regional administrators, quasi-judicial immunity on administrative officials, and administrative liability on judicial officials, without references to either the common law of 1871 or, for that matter, of the twentieth century.

A recent and revealing example of Court-created civil rights law was the elimination, in *Harlow v. Fitzgerald* , of the requirement of subjective good faith as a prerequisite for official immunity. Not only did the Supreme Court fail to examine the law of 1871 on the point, but it enunciated the alteration of section 1983 immunity in the context of a federal common law action grounded directly on the first amendment. After a "balancing of competing values" as a matter of federal common law, to which the intent of the 1871 Congress was entirely irrelevant, the Court announced a new test for official immunity. Acknowledging that no issue under section 1983 was before it, the Court, without elaborating, incorporated the new test into the jurisprudence of section 1983 in a footnote. This incorporation cannot be read as mere dictum, for last Term, in *Davis v. Scherer*, — a case brought under section 1983 — the Court relied on *Harlow* and the federal common law decision in *Butz v. Economou* to elaborate this immunity doctrine without reference to the history or context of section 1983. In light of this development, it is clear that what the Court undertakes in most immunities cases is not a search for century-old legislative intent or common law context but the enunciation of a federal common law that the Court regards as appropriate to modern social and political realities.

This analysis is not unique to immunities issues. With respect to the calculation of damages, the Court has decided that "over the centuries the common law of torts has developed a set of rules to implement the principle that a person should be compensated fairly" and that these rules are the "starting point for the inquiry." In the absence of a specific statutory mandate, the Court "look[s] first to the common law of torts (both modern and as of 1871), with such modification or adaptation as might be necessary to carry out the purpose and policy of the statute." The Court has apparently decided to incorporate a proximate cause test into section 1983 as a matter of federal common law. And it is perhaps most accurate to characterize the doctrine limiting municipal damage liability to violations pursuant to municipal policy as an evolving common law quasi-immunity that will be developed and elaborated on a case-by-case basis as courts gain experience with the doctrine.

B. *The Dissonance of Section 1988*

After issues of immunities, damages, and municipal liability, the most frequently litigated question of law in section 1983 actions may well be that of the applicable statute of limitations. Because section 1983 contains no more mention of statutes of limitations than of immunities or damage calculations, one might expect the Court to employ the federal common law process described above to govern this area as well. In the statute of limitations cases, however, as in the field of survival of actions, the Supreme Court does not view this question as a matter of federal common law but as an issue governed by section 1988, the choice of law provision incorporated into the ancestor of section 1983 itself.

Section 1983 was originally a part of section 1 of the Ku Klux Klan Act of 1871. In addition to creating a cause of action for the violation of federal constitutional rights, section 1 provided for federal jurisdiction over the civil actions it authorized, a grant made necessary by the absence of general federal question jurisdiction. As part of a series of Reconstruction statutes stretching from 1866 to 1875, the Ku Klux Klan Act incorporated by reference the procedures adopted by the Civil Rights Act of 1866 to govern federal civil rights actions.

The entire body of civil rights statutes was reorganized and codified in the Revised Statutes of 1875. One element of the 1866 Civil Rights Act became section 722 of the Revised Statutes, which was drafted to govern all remaining civil rights actions, both civil and criminal. Recodified as section 1988, section 722 is the statute to which the Supreme Court looks in deciding statute of limitations questions in actions brought pursuant to the Reconstruction Statutes.

It is worth reproducing section 1988 *in extenso* to remind readers of the full scope of its obscurity:

> The jurisdiction in civil and criminal matters conferred on the district courts by the provisions of this Title, and of Title "CIVIL RIGHTS," and of Title "CRIMES," for the protection of all persons in the United States in their civil rights, and for their vindication, shall be exercised and enforced in conformity with the laws of the United States, so far as such laws are suitable to carry the same into effect; but in all cases where they are not adapted to the object, or are deficient in the provisions necessary to furnish suitable remedies and punish offenses against law, the common law, as modified and changed by the constitution and statutes of the State wherein the court having jurisdiction of such civil or criminal cause is held, so far as the same is not inconsistent with the Constitution and laws of the United States, shall be extended to and govern the said courts in the trial and disposition of the cause, and, if it is of a criminal nature, in the infliction of punishment on the party found guilty.

The Supreme Court has informed us that in section 1988 "Congress ha[s] plainly instructed the federal courts to refer to state law when federal law provides no rule of decision . . . ." Where state law applies, says the Court, such law is to be treated as "binding rules of law," which the federal courts are "obligated . . . to apply."

Indeed, so forceful is the Court's reading of a mandate to apply state law to statute of limitations questions that recently, in *Chardon v. Fumero Soto*, it disregarded the existence of a clearly-established federal rule regarding tolling in class action practice and applied the local rules instead. The state rule may be disregarded only if it is "inconsistent with the Constitution and laws of the United States."

This is, in isolation, a plausible reading of the words of section 1988. In practice, however, we confront an anomaly. If section 1988 requires deference to state law in the absence of governing federal rules, it would seem that each time a federal court encounters a situation not covered by the terms of section 1983, it should survey the entire field of potentially applicable state law, choose the appropriate state rule, and measure it against the Constitution and laws of the United States. One rule of law may be applicable in New Jersey, another in Texas, and a third in Minnesota. The jurisprudence of section 1983 would resemble a patchwork quilt laboriously constructed in each of the fifty states.

Yet, as we have seen, in addressing the important questions of damages and immunities, the federal courts appear to establish rules of decision in section 1983 cases as a matter of federal common law without even a passing reference to the state rules to which section 1988 is thought to direct attention. As the Supreme Court continues to resolve open issues, a substantial degree of national uniformity increasingly prevails. How can this state of affairs coexist with a statute that directs federal courts to treat state rules as "binding rules of law" in civil rights cases?

On the other hand, one might just as plausibly ask why section 1988 should be read as mandating the binding nature of state law. The tortuous syntax of the statute, read in light of its opaque legislative history, leaves substantial room for interpretation. And there is but a limited case to be made for local experimentation with the protection of civil rights under a federal statute. Yet the Court in recent Terms, in resigned deference to what is apparently regarded as the inscrutable will of Congress, has foresworn the virtues of a uniform federal rule in areas in which it reads section 1988 as governing the choice of law.

This resignation is problematic, for the alleged congressional intent is anomalous. Not only is it difficult to provide persuasive justifications for deference to state law as the basis for the rules of federal civil rights actions today, but such deference is also questionable in light of section 1988's historical context. It requires an incongruous historical vision to picture the Reconstruction Congress establishing the local law of the recently-rebelling states as the linchpin of an avowedly nationalist enforcement program.

As originally adopted, section 1988 formed a part of the Civil Rights Act of 1866, a statute that, as Justice Marshall has reminded us, "was the first federal statute to provide broad protection in the field of civil rights." The purpose of the Civil Rights Act was to "guarantee the newly emancipated Negro equality with whites before the law," and its means included provisions for direct federal military intervention, removal of cases from hostile state courts, direct civil actions under the newly-conferred civil jurisdiction, and the establishment of federal criminal penalties, along with federal enforcement mechanisms against those who denied others equal rights under color of state law. As was true of other weapons of Reconstruction, the Civil Rights Act "was aimed directly at the State judiciary."

This aim was well warranted. During Reconstruction the judiciary of former confederate states served both as a means of resisting and harassing federal officials and as a way of attempting to reestablish white hegemony over the recently emancipated Negro. In the early period of Reconstruction, occupying federal forces responded by establishing parallel judiciary systems, in the form of Army provost courts and Freedman's Bureau courts, to provide more sympathetic forums. By 1866, however, the emphasis had begun to shift to establishing more permanent federal forums by providing access to federal circuit and district courts. In this context it seems unlikely that the local common law elaborated by the very judiciary that the federal courts were designed to supersede was to be given primacy.

So, too, the Ku Klux Klan Act of 1871, which contained the predecessor of section 1983, was crafted to provide an alternative to a hostile and ineffective state judiciary. The Act provides that civil actions for violations of constitutional rights are "to be prosecuted . . . with and subject to the same rights of appeal, review upon error, and other remedies provided in like cases in such courts, under [the 1866 Civil Rights Act] and the other remedial laws of the United States which are in their nature applicable in such cases." But this is hardly a clearcut congressional mandate that remedies are to vary from state to state in accord with the practices of the local judiciary. If a more plausible interpretation is available, both historical and practical considerations support its adoption.

II. Remembering History

A. *A First Look*

In fact, such an interpretation is available with the recognition of a single historical fact: section 1988 was originally enacted more than seventy years before *Erie Railroad v. Tompkins.* In light of this recollection, section 1988 can be parsed as follows. Congress directs courts in civil rights cases to begin by looking at the "laws of the United States," and under *Swift v. Tyson* , the "laws" of the several states were thought to comprise primarily their statutes. If the federal statutes are not "adapted" or are "deficient" — if there is no controlling statutory rule — a court should look to "the common law, as modified and changed by the constitution and statutes of the State" in which the court sits.

Note that section 1988 does not say "the common law of the state" in question but "the common law." The Reconstruction Congress lived in the era of *Swift* and, as Justices Brandeis and Holmes told us, *Swift*

> rests upon the assumption that there is "a transcendental body of law outside of any particular State but obligatory within it unless and until changed by statute," that federal courts have the power to use their judgment as to what the rules of common law are; and that in the federal courts, "the parties are entitled to an independent judgment on matters of general law" . . . .

Federal courts were wont to expound the common law in diversity cases, and section 1988 is explicit statutory authority to do the same in the newly-created civil rights jurisdiction. As noted above, in elaborating the infrastructure of civil rights enforcement under section 1983, the Supreme Court refers ultimately either to principles of tort law distilled from contemporary precedents and commentary or to the common law evolution of its own recent cases, influenced by the felt necessities of the time. The Supreme Court need not be embarrassed in adopting this approach, for, under the interpretation of section 1988 advanced here, the Reconstruction Congress has made good any want of authority in the Rules of Decision Act, and there is no lack of constitutional warrant to legislate under the fourteenth amendment.

Nor is the Court tied to the common law of 1871. Under *Swift*, courts sitting in diversity acknowledged the necessity of the evolution of the common law. And, far from establishing a clear congressional mandate that rights and remedies under the civil rights statutes vary from state to state, this reading of section 1988 suggests that the norm is uniformity. In areas not directly governed by federal statute, a uniform "general common law" should be the centerpiece of enforcement.

Only local statutes and state constitutions impinge on the otherwise uniform body of federal civil rights law. Section 1988 instructs federal courts to apply the general common law, as modified by local statutes. This in turn explains the particularly deferential treatment accorded to statutes of limitations and survival statutes. In the cases treating state law as binding, the Supreme Court has deferred to local statutes, pursuant to the mandate of section 1988. In cases announcing federal common law, on the other hand, no state statute applies.

Finally, even where state statutes appear to modify the common law, a court must still evaluate whether that modification is inconsistent with the Constitution and laws of the United States. Not content with establishing a general common law parallel to the diversity law as the fulcrum of civil rights enforcement, the Reconstruction Congress was aware of the possibility that state statutory modifications adopted by the same legislatures that promulgated the Black Codes might prove inimical to effective vindication of federal rights. Congress thus provided a federal veto of such inconsistent provisions; they would be treated as ineffective, and general common law would govern.

This interpretation has the virtue of being consistent with the words of section 1988, current practice under section 1983, and the statute's historical context. It has, moreover, the advantage of leaving opportunities for federal courts to craft sensible and uniform solutions to contemporary problems based on contemporary values. The question remains, however, is it correct?

B. *Remembering History More Carefully*

The interpretation set forth above is consistent with current judicial practice and with intimations in a number of Supreme Court cases interpreting section 1988. Nonetheless, some authorities have rejected reference to the common law of *Swift* as not only antiquarian but inaccurate. Although decidedly mixed, the historical record on balance appears to support the view proposed here.

The crucial determination for the viability of the proposed reading is the nature of the "common law" to which section 1988 mandated reference in the absence of controlling federal statutory law. Although Professor Fletcher has recently assured us that "in early nineteenth century usage, 'common law' was a general common law shared by the American states rather than a local common law of a particular state," it appears that, at least by the middle of that century, courts and commentators were well aware of the possibility of ambiguous usage and took cognizance of the possibility of a common law of each individual state. The question of what the 1866 Congress intended by the words "common law" simply cannot be answered by consulting the contemporaneous plain meaning of the statute.

Neither do the relevant legislative materials resolve this question. Although there is support for the "general common law" reading in the directly applicable legislative history, other legislative materials lend plausibility to a reading of the "common law" as that of the individual states.

Referring to section 1988 in debate over the 1866 Civil Rights Act, Congressman Kerr, in opposition to the bill, objected that

> the things attempted to be prohibited are in themselves so extraordinary and anomalous, so unlike anything ever attempted before by the Federal Government, that the authors of this bill feared, very properly too, that the system of laws heretofore administered in the Federal courts might fail to supply any precedent to guide the courts in the enforcement of the strange provisions of this bill, and not to be thwarted by this difficulty, they confer upon the courts . . . the power to make such other laws as they may think necessary. Such is the practical effect of [section 1988] . . . .
>
> That is to say, the Federal courts may, in such cases, make such rules and apply such law as they please, and call it *common law.*

In Kerr's view the "common law" in question was a common law at the mercy of federal interpretation, which was a reasonable prediction, given recent developments under *Swift*.

Similarly, Senator Saulsbury, who opposed the enactment of the 1866 act, characterized the predecessor of section 1988 as obligating courts "to render [their] decisions conformably to the common law as modified by State law." So, too, the marginal note in the official version of the *Statutes at Large* that identifies section 1988 reads "Jurisdiction to be enforced according to the laws of the United States, or the common law, &c." Reference to "the common law," standing alone, has a strong flavor of a general common law.

By contrast, the report of the Revision of Statutes commission in 1872 viewed the predecessor of section 1988 as an "anomalous provision," providing for "variable punishment" from state to state according to local common law and hence open to "serious constitutional question." Although there are reasons to discount this interpretation, it nonetheless lessens the force of any argument based on legislative history for interpreting "common law" as general common law.

Perhaps the best source of guidance in determining what Congress intended when it enacted section 1988 is the functioning of the federal jurisdiction already in existence at that time. In 1866 a general federal question jurisdiction was still a decade in the future. Diversity jurisdiction, the major source of private federal cases, was the primary precedent for the functioning of the federal judiciary. Thus one might plausibly argue that, in conferring jurisdiction under the Civil Rights Act and the Ku Klux Klan Act, Congress used the diversity experience as a model. And in 1866 the paradigm for federal diversity cases was *Swift*.

Professor Eisenberg is dubious of references to *Swift* in construing section 1988, in part because "*Swift*, even in its heyday, seemed only to bless a federal common law of commerce." His factual premise, however, is almost certainly incorrect. Although early application of the *Swift* doctrine was arguably limited to commercial matters, the province of federally enunicated general law had expanded substantially beyond those boundaries before the adoption of the precursors to sections 1988 and 1983.

Discussions in contemporaneous treatises refer to no limitatin of the *Swift* doctrine to commercial law issues. In the field of tort actions, the Court stated that "where private rights are to be determined by the application of common law rules alone, this Court . . . does not feel bound by [state] decisions." And in 1866 the most recent and outstanding application of the *Swift* principle was the Court's determination in *Gelpcke v. City of Dubuque* that, in matters affecting municipal bonds, a federal diversity court was not bound by a state supreme court's interpretation of its own constitution. In such an environment it seems unlikely that a reference to the common law would require deference to local rules as a binding source of decision. A more reasonable inference is that Congress intended to allow federal courts in civil rights cases at least the same freedom that those courts enjoyed in diversity cases.

Nonetheless, a mystery remains. If the governing interpretation of the Rules of Decision Act under *Swift* would allow federal courts so much discretion, why should Congress adopt an additional choice of law statute to govern civil rights cases? The answer, I suggest, is that the precise scope of the *Swift* doctrine at that time was, and was to remain, unclear. In matters of local law, state rules governed; in matters of general law, federal courts were free to follow their own interpretations. And the boundary between local and general law was a matter in substantial dispute.

In such a climate, absent explicit congressional direction, newly-established causes of action for individuals seeking to vindicate their civil rights might, in the view of states-rights advocates, be classed as local. To avoid such a result, as well as to guarantee the application of general law to removed cases, Congress provided that the common law would be the primary source of law. Moreover, because the *Swift* doctrine mandated deference to state statutes, regardless of whether the statutes conflicted with federal policy, Congress added the final inconsistency proviso.

III. Implications

If I am right and section 1988 is properly to be read in light of *Swift v. Tyson*, it seems to me that there are two major implications that the courts and civil rights litigators should heed. The first pertains to the proper role of federal courts and the second to the rule of state law in civil rights litigation.

A. *The Development of a Federal Common Law in Civil Rights Actions*

In section 1983 litigation the system cannot function as Congress originally intended. Federal courts have gone out of the business of making general common law, and there is no contemporary body of nationally uniform common law to fill in the gap. Given this fact, three responses are possible, as long as the Supreme Court wishes to retain section 1988 as an active piece of the enforcement system of civil rights legislation. The Court may look to the pre-*Erie* federal common law; it may look to the common law of the state that allegedly violated the Constitution; or it may craft a new set of rules for section 1983 actions.

Reliance on the pre-*Erie* common law would sacrifice the ability of courts to mold civil rights jurisprudence in response to changing times and values. There is no indication that Congress contemplated such an ossified system, and its defects are manifest. The rules forged by common law courts of three and four generations past bear no necessary relation to modern problems. And, indeed, the lesson would not be foreign to a Congress on the verge of replacing static with dynamic conformity in federal procedure.

A focus on state common law would repudiate the congressional intent to look to a uniform body of law as the infrastructure for civil rights litigation. Such repudiation is hardly compelled by policy. Whatever the merits of allowing state courts to determine the boundaries of causes of action created by their domestic law, the norm of equal treatment suggests that identically injured plaintiffs should not be treated differently in federal court on federal claims because of the vagaries of local law. The fourteenth amendment is as valuable in Utah as it is in New York.

Nor are concerns of federalism vindicated by a state-to-state variation in the scope of federal remedies. *Monroe v. Pape* tells us that section 1983 is designed to supplement the remedies provided by state law, not to mirror them. It is neither an infringement of state sovereignty nor an arrogation of judicial authority to suggest that state officials who violate federal constitutional rights have no claim to retain state law immunities or to rely on state damage rules attuned to state rather than federal interests. Moreover, the importance of providing a clear set of guidelines for civil rights claimants suggests a federal interest in uniformity. Any search among state precedents for rules governing federal causes of action is likely to be a choice among parallels of dubious salience. Today, in advance of a decision, there is no real way for litigants to predict, for example, whether the state rules applicable to libel, negligence, or contract will be held to govern an action for disparaging discharge without due process. A uniform federal rule would make it less likely that federal rights will be forfeited by a plaintiff's incorrect but plausible analogy to state practice.

Federal courts should naturally turn to the third route and undertake to establish a common law of civil rights actions. Such federal common law loses the discipline that reference to a general common law evolving in other areas would have imposed on the federal courts of 1866 and 1871. Nonetheless, the large number of current civil rights cases suggests that federal courts will have ample opportunity to evolve a structure of civil rights law on a case-by-case basis. Of the three options, this one seems the closest to what Congress originally intended, and it is the one that best characterizes the Court's approach in recent cases.

Under section 1988 the lack of a binding federal statute does not mean that a court must survey the entire field of potentially applicable state law. Section 1988 directs the federal courts in the first instance to proceed as a matter of federal common law. State rules may be persuasive, but they are certainly not binding. And, similarly, the courts need not be concerned with uncovering the arcana of nineteenth century tort doctrine. The search is for the best current common law rule in light of federal policies. Let us admit freely that federal courts can and do make law in civil rights litigation. In making such law courts must remember that, in adopting section 1988, Congress has not foresworn an interest in national uniformity. Rather it has put its imprimatur on a federal common law.

B. *The Significance of State Law*

The second implication of my analysis is that federal courts cannot ignore state law. Congress intended that the common law rule tentatively arrived at be modified by applicable state statutes; courts and litigants must be on the lookout for these statutes. Although this modification is a considerably narrower constraint than a general rule of deference to state law, the proliferation of state statutes will generate escalating difficulties. Courts will increasingly be faced with the problem of classifying rules of mixed origin and addressing the impact of aging, ambiguous, or obsolete statutory systems. In applying state statutes, therefore, federal courts cannot be content with a simple literal reading. Rather, the elaboration of the statute at issue must be sensitive both to the construction state courts have given and are likely to give the statute and to federal civil rights policies.

Indeed, this has been the Court's approach in its two most recent ventures into the interpretation of section 1988. In *Chardon v. Fumero Soto* the Court approved the First Circuit's extrapolation of the way in which a Puerto Rican court would mesh Puerto Rico's rules on class actions and the tolling of statutes of limitations. Puerto Rico's tolling rule, unlike most federal provisions, causes the statute of limitations to begin running anew when the tolling event ceases. The Puerto Rican class action procedure is modeled after Rule 23 of the Federal Rules of Civil Procedure. Although the Puerto Rican courts had not addressed the issue, the First Circuit concluded that, when a class action in a federal court located in Puerto Rico is decertified, the Puerto Rican rule applicable under section 1988 would cause the statute to begin running anew for the benefit of the unnamed class plaintiffs. The Supreme Court approved this exegesis, despite the contrary federal common law rule adopted for antitrust cases in *American Pipe & Construction Co. v. Utah.* As long as federal interests are not adversely affected, even a tentative prediction of the state court's interpretation of domestic statutory rules can function as the basis for statutory determinations.

On the other hand, where state law provides a variety of statutory analogies for the rule of decision question, a federal court should feel free to choose the analogous provision that best serves federal interests. The court should defer to the most appropriate state statutory analogy, bearing in mind that "[a] state law is not 'appropriate' if it fails to take into account practicalities that are involved in litigating federal civil rights claims and policies that are analogous to the goals of the Civil Rights Acts." Thus, in *Burnett v. Grattan*, the Supreme Court held that a section 1983 action for employment discrimination was to be governed by the three-year residual state statute of limitations rather than the six-month statute of limitations for the filing of administrative complaints with the state equal employment agency. The Court reasoned that the three-year statute better furthered the goals of section 1983:

> To the extent that particular state concerns are inconsistent with, or of marginal relevance to, the policies informing the Civil Rights Act, the resulting state statute of limitations may be inappropriate for civil rights claims.
>
> The divergence between the goals of the federal civil rights statutes and of the state employment discrimination administrative statute is clear in the present case.

This process of construing state statutes consistently with federal interests was, by 1871, a regular feature of the *Swift* regime, and it is a reasonable concomitant of the interpretation of section 1988 advanced above.

Finally, whatever alterations state statutes make in the underlying federal rule must still be measured against the policies of federal legislation. States cannot immunize themselves from section 1983 actions by passing statutes to that effect, and federal courts should be reluctant to allow restrictive procedural prerequisites to accomplish the same thing by less direct measures. Application of state law must be contingent on the full availability of the federal remedy.

Nonetheless, in most situations, it is not inconsistent with the policies underlying section 1983 for a state statute to impose a higher level of responsibility or damages than is available under federal law. State statutes that augment the effectiveness of the section 1983 remedy may not be immediately obvious, but courts and counsel should be alert for their existence.

Conclusion

I realize that there is something anachronistic, perhaps antiquarian, in bottoming modern statutory interpretation on a case that has been overruled for almost half a century. Nonetheless, the elaboration of section 1983 is an anachronistic enterprise. The statute was originally adopted over a century ago, and, because it languished unused until its 1961 resurrection in *Monroe v. Pape*, there is no history of continuous interpretation to link today's perceptions of section 1983 to those of the statute's framers. Indeed, these many years of inactivity prompted one of Justice Frankfurter's objections to the revival of section 1983 in *Monroe*: "We cannot expect to create an effective means of protection for human liberties by torturing an 1871 statute to meet the problems of 1960."

If the interpretation advanced in this essay is valid, no torture is necessary. The 1871 Congress itself manifested a preference for the common law power of federal courts to adjust the framework of the law to meet the problems of the changing society. To take that preference at face value allows us to justify the otherwise unsupported but sensible approach that the Court has largely adopted toward elaboration of section 1983 in the last decade. It permits courts to direct civil rights practitioners in most instances to a single and uniform body of precedents from which to seek guidance. The proposed interpretation provides a basis for elevating contemporary policy concerns above both the fruitless search for direct legislative evidence of specific remedial intentions and the interminable excavation of fossilized contemporaneous tort law. It is, I submit, preferable to either willfully ignoring an apparently applicable statute or finding oneself adrift in a raging sea of state law. Until Congress decides to remedy the predicament, it is the best we can do.

Steven H. Steinglass, *Wrongful Death Actions and Section 1983,* 60 Indiana Law Journal 559 (1985)

* * *

III. Statutory Construction, § 1983 and the Use of State Law

Given the absence of Supreme Court decisions directly addressing the availability of § 1983 as a wrongful death remedy, it is necessary to look to decisions involving other aspects of § 1983. This is not a simple task. Although all cases involving interpretations of § 1983 can be reduced to matters of statutory construction, the Court has often failed to develop clear and consistent approaches to interpreting federal statutes, and § 1983 is no exception. Moreover, it has often not attempted to justify or even explain the approach it has followed, particularly with respect to the role of state law in § 1983 litigation.

There are many possible approaches to the use of § 1983 as a wrongful death remedy, all of which involve the need to construe § 1983 and to determine its relationship to state law. The Supreme Court, when it reaches this issue, will have to decide whether § 1983 — independently, through the federal common law, or through the incorporation of state law — is available as a wrongful death remedy. It will also have to address the applicable damage policies and, if state wrongful death causes of action are incorporated into § 1983, whether state damage limitations, such as ceilings on recoveries or prohibitions on awards for nonpecuniary losses, are also incorporated. Finally, if § 1983 incorporates state wrongful death actions and their damage policies, the Court will have to address whether the state policies are consistent with the purposes of § 1983. State law is relevant to these inquiries. A review of state law in 1871 may help explain what members of the 42d Congress, almost two-thirds of whom were lawyers, intended in enacting the predecessor to § 1983. In addition, current state law may give meaning to § 1983 when it was contemplated that particular elements of the § 1983 cause of action would evolve over time. Finally, federal law may require use of the law of the forum state to fill any gaps in § 1983 concerning its availability as a wrongful death remedy.

The search for an applicable policy in § 1983 litigation is made difficult because of the limited legislative guidance, but this is not unique. Federal law is interstitial and federal courts often look to the law of the forum state to fill gaps in federal statutes, usually under the general mandate of the Rules of Decision Act. What is unique about § 1983 and other surviving Reconstruction-era civil rights acts, however, is the existence of 42 U.S.C. § 1988, a choice of law statute that may limit the power of federal courts to use the federal common law to supply missing details in § 1983 and other civil rights actions. Under § 1988, federal courts look to state law where federal law is deficient; the most analogous state policy is then applied as the federal rule unless it is inconsistent with § 1983's purposes of compensation and deterrence.

Despite the surface simplicity of these steps, its application is more complex. Section 1988 defies a simple construction, and the Supreme Court has provided only minimal guidance as to when courts should develop a uniform federal rule or resort to the law of the forum state. Although the Court has provided answers to many specific questions, courts facing new issues are often uncertain whether to forge ahead to construe ambiguous aspects of § 1983 or to look to state law. Moreover, the Court has not developed standards to be used in selecting the appropriate state policy. Finally, the Court has only begrudgingly applied § 1988's inconsistency clause and has never rejected an otherwise applicable state policy once it made the initial decision to resort to state law.

A. *Statutory Construction*

The task of construing § 1983 has been made difficult for at least three reasons. First, § 1983 is a threadbare statute and the Court has often been unable to find answers in its language to issues that arise in § 1983 litigation. Second, § 1 of the Civil Rights Act of 1871, unlike some of its other provisions, was relatively uncontroversial, and members of the 42d Congress did not discuss it in great depth. Finally, the breadth of the cause of action that would result from a literal interpretation of § 1983 was unacceptable to members of a Court sensitive to considerations of federalism and influenced by a tradition of historiography that found suspect much work of the Reconstruction Congresses. Thus, the construction of § 1983 has often involved a search for limiting principles so that it would not override traditional common law and equitable defenses and would not provide a private right of action against all state and local officials and the governmental entities that employed or elected them.

The threshold question in construing § 1983, although rarely addressed expressly, is whether to give § 1983 a uniform interpretation. The Court has generally approached § 1983 with a view toward developing uniform policies without regard to the law of the state in which the federal court sits but has rarely discussed why. Where the language or legislative history of § 1983 directly addresses a particular issue, the Court has had no difficulty requiring a uniform interpretation of § 1983. In addition, where the language of the statute was literally applicable, the Court has applied it uniformly, although it has often limited the statute's reach. Finally, the Court has often looked to the broad purposes of § 1983 to develop uniform policies where the language and legislative history did not address the particular issues or addressed them only obliquely.

The relationship between § 1983 and state law has raised few problems where there are federal standards otherwise applicable in federal court litigation, or where it is necessary to construe § 1983 or other federal statutes. In such cases the Court has developed uniform interpretations of § 1983 and has not looked to state law. Thus, the Court has resolved issues as diverse as the applicable pleading requirements and equitable principles through the development of uniform policies. Likewise, where the interpretation of § 1983 required construction of statutory language for which there is no state counterpart, the Court has looked to the legislative history and purposes of § 1983 to develop a uniform interpretation. Finally, the task of reconciling § 1983 with other federal statutes that create rights or authorize remedies has also resulted in uniform definitions of the scope of § 1983. On the other hand, where § 1983 was enacted against a background of well-developed state law governing litigation and where there was little legislative guidance, the Court has not always made clear how it decided whether to develop a uniform interpretation of § 1983 or to defer to state policies. Thus, issues involving matters such as statutes of limitations, survival, immunities, and damages have presented the Court with the most difficult issues concerning the construction of § 1983 and the use of state law.

Statutes of limitations are the archetypical area for borrowing state law, and the Court has relied on state policies of repose in § 1983 litigation. Prior to looking to state law, however, the Court considered whether there was an available policy based on federal law. In *O'Sullivan v. Felix*, the case in which the Court first applied a state statute of limitations to § 1983, the Court rejected the argument that the federal statute of limitations for suits for penalties or forfeitures applied to all § 1983 actions. Having concluded that § 1983 neither contained a specific limitations period nor provided for a penalty, the Court turned to state law for the applicable period. Nonetheless, the Court has not treated all questions relating to statutes of limitations as being governed initially by state law. Although the Court has looked to state law for the choice of the limitations period as well as for the related rules on tolling and on revival, it has treated the question of which state statute of limitations to borrow as a federal question and has required use of the state limitations period for personal actions. It has also considered the accrual of a cause of action to be a uniquely federal issue even though state law is not silent on such matters and even though the date selected has a direct impact on the limitations period.

In addressing the survival of § 1983 actions, on the other hand, the Court has departed from the approach used under other federal statutes in which it searched for the applicable policy in the statute authorizing the action and in the federal common law. Thus, in *Robertson v. Wegmann*, the Court followed a borrowing approach to § 1983 survival issues without considering whether an answer might be available in the language, legislative history, or purposes of § 1983 or in the federal common law.

The willingness of the Court to search for uniform interpretations of § 1983 where the language and legislative history provide little or no guidance is best seen in immunity cases in which the Court provides state and local governmental officials either absolute or qualified immunity from liability for damages. The language of § 1983, if taken literally, creates a broad damage action that allows no immunity. The Court, however, has been uncomfortable with the prospect of imposing what might amount to strict liability on state and local officials for violations of federal law. In developing official immunities under § 1983, the Court has been guided by a test ostensibly based on statutory construction and has developed uniform policies without regard to the policies followed in the forum state. In reaching this result, the Court has not addressed directly why it has rejected state policies but has suggested that the use of state immunities could affect the substance of the § 1983 action.

Even where the Court has determined that a uniform interpretation of § 1983 is required, it has often had difficulty determining what that interpretation should be, particularly where it would lock the cause of action into an 1871 model. In construing § 1983, the Court has generally begun with the language of the statute, but has rarely stopped there. When a provision is not vague, the Court has occasionally relied on its plain meaning to provide an expansive interpretation of the scope of the action. In other cases, the Court has been reluctant to give the broad general language its full meaning, at least where it qualifies policies generally applicable in federal courts. Thus, the Court was unwilling to interpret § 1983 literally to impose liability on "every person" who violates another's constitutional rights.

When a phrase is vague or the contours of a doctrine are unclear, the Court has looked to the legislative history and purposes of § 1983 but has not always been consistent in identifying what it was seeking. In some cases, the Court has searched for specific evidence that members of the 42d Congress intended a particular result. In other cases, the Court has looked to the broad purposes of the Civil Rights Act of 1871 and construed § 1983 despite the absence of guidance in its language or evidence that the issue was addressed in the debates. For example, in the immunity cases the Court looked for specific evidence of congressional intent to create liability when the immunity in question was well established in 1871. On the other hand, when an immunity did not exist or was not well established, the Court has been willing to construe the statute literally and deny the immunity despite the absence of guidance in the legislative history. This approach, however, has not been consistently followed in other areas. For example, despite the absence of guidance in the language or legislative history on the duty to exhaust administrative remedies, the Court has relied on the broad tenor of the legislative debates to conclude that § 1983 provides litigants direct access to a judicial forum without exhausting administrative remedies.

In looking to the legal background against which the Civil Rights Act of 1871 was enacted, the Court has often focused on the state of the law in 1871. This has invariably involved reviewing case law because official immunities were rarely codified, but the Court has never suggested that it would not consider state statutes that abolished or modified traditional immunities, and has looked to state positive law in determining whether an immunity was well established.

Although the Court has generally asked whether a particular immunity was well established in 1871, it has sometimes considered immunities that appeared later. For example, in *Imbler v. Pachtman*, the Court relied exclusively on post-1871 state court cases to conclude that prosecutors' absolute immunity from suit was well established and extended them an absolute immunity for acts taken as prosecutors. On the other hand, in considering the immunity of public defenders, the Court observed that no such office existed in 1871 and refused to provide them an absolute immunity.

The role of policy in the immunity cases has also been confusing. In developing official immunities for § 1983 cases, the Court has reviewed considerations of public policy and has suggested it would reject an immunity not supported by policy considerations even where the immunity was well established in 1871. The Court, however, has never rejected an immunity solely on policy grounds, and the policy analysis invariably comports with the conclusion based on the legislative history. Moreover, the Court has maintained parity with *Bivens* actions, despite the absence of any historical or statutory constraints, and has relied on § 1983 and *Bivens* cases interchangeably in determining which public officials are immune and in defining the immunity. Thus, although the year 1871 remains a touchstone in addressing immunities in § 1983 cases, the Court has retained the flexibility to avoid locking itself into the policies followed in 1871.

The Court's unwillingness to adopt a methodology that too tightly ties § 1983 to the state of the law in 1871 is most apparent in the treatment of damages. Although § 1983's language and legislative history provide little guidance as to the available damages, the Court has tied the availability of damages to the principles of compensation and has allowed for the evolving nature of the law by not limiting damages to those available in 1871.

In *Carey v. Piphus*, the leading § 1983 damage decision, the Court refused to award substantial damages for a procedural due process violation without actual proof of damages. The Court ruled that the plaintiff, an Illinois high school student challenging a procedurally defective suspension, could not recover unless he could show he would not have been suspended after a hearing or that he had suffered a mental or emotional injury; such damages, however, would not be presumed, although the Court left open whether damages for the violation of a substantive constitutional right could be awarded where the underlying violation was not procedural.

In addressing these issues under the principles of compensation, the Court identified the source of the principles in the policies followed by the common law. The Court, however, did not look to the Illinois common or statutory law of damages, nor did it look to the damages generally available at common law in 1871. Rather, it identified an evolving body of common law that courts must adapt to provide fair compensation for injuries caused by deprivations of constitutional rights.

In *City of Newport v. Fact Concerts, Inc.*, the Court held that a municipality may not be held liable for punitive damages under § 1983. In addressing the availability of this element of damages, the Court cited *Carey* only in passing and relied on the methodology of the immunity cases. Because the immunity of municipal corporations for punitive damages was settled in 1871, such damages were not available in § 1983 actions absent evidence that the 42d Congress intended to override the immunity. The Court also considered whether the immunity was good public policy and concluded it was. Thus, although *Fact Concerts* involved an element of damages, the Court treated the case as an immunity case and never considered whether evolving principles of compensation justified a different result.

The Court's most recent § 1983 damage case, *Smith v. Wade*, involved the standards that govern awards of punitive damages. *Carey* had suggested that punitive damages were available in § 1983 actions, and *Fact Concerts*' immunization of municipalities did not undercut that. Still, it was unclear as to the applicable standards and role, if any, of state law. In upholding the use of a "recklessness" standard for punitive damages in § 1983 cases, Justice Brennan, writing for the Court, looked to state law in 1871 and found that the majority of states did not limit punitive damages to cases of intentional misconduct. Justice Brennan, however, also relied on post-1871 cases, and defended this reliance by suggesting that the 42d Congress intended to permit the availability of damages to change as the law evolved.

Despite the Court's willingness to approach damage issues in light of evolving principles of compensation, the policies followed in 1871 have special significance. When it was well established in 1871 that a specific element of damages was unavailable, those damages are unavailable in § 1983 actions unless the law has evolved or considerations of public policy dictate otherwise. Moreover, a curious feature about the § 1983 damage cases is the almost total disregard of § 1988, which the Court had once suggested required damages in civil rights litigation to be based on the state or federal damage policies that best serve the purposes of the federal statutes. *Carey*, *Fact Concerts* and *Wade*, however, all stand for the proposition that issues of the available damages in § 1983 litigation will be based on uniform federal standards.

In construing § 1983, which was enacted by § 1 of the Civil Rights Act of 1871, the Court has also been willing to seek guidance from debates on other sections of the Act. For example, the Court has looked to the debate on the Sherman Amendment to support a construction of § 1983 as not imposing vicarious liability based on the doctrine of respondeat superior. It has also looked to § 6 of the Act, which was the compromise that resulted from the controversy over the Sherman Amendment, for support for the principles of compensation it found equally applicable to § 1983. Similarly, in concluding that police witnesses had an immunity under § 1983 for testimony given in trials, the Court considered the debates of the 42d Congress on the conspiracy and criminal actions created by § 2 of the Civil Rights Act of 1871.

What is present in varying degrees in all these areas is the Court's reliance on traditional tools of statutory construction — the language, legislative history and purposes of the statute in question — to give meaning to the statute. Even where neither the language nor the legislative history of § 1983 addressed specific issues, the Court has not hesitated to search for a uniform federal definition of elements of the § 1983 cause of action, and state law has played only a limited role. Although the Court rejected early the argument that only federal law could limit federally created § 1983 actions, there is no support in the language or legislative history of § 1983 that Congress prohibited the Court from using the full range of statutory construction tools to resolve issues not specifically addressed in the language or legislative history of § 1983.

B. Section 1988 — The Civil Rights Choice of Law Statute and Wrongful Death Actions

Section 1988 of Title 42, which is derived from § 3 of the Civil Rights Act of 1866, requires federal courts entertaining certain civil rights actions to look to state law to fill gaps in federal law. This provision was incorporated by reference into § 1 of the Civil Rights Act of 1871 and was made generally applicable to civil rights actions in the 1874 codification of the revised statutes. The argument has been made that § 1988 does not apply to original actions filed in federal court, but applies only to state court actions removed to federal court. But the Court has continued to rely on § 1988 to restrict the power of federal courts to develop a uniform federal common law where the civil rights acts are silent. The Court has also rejected a construction of § 1988 that would permit federal courts to select the procedures that enabled plaintiffs to prevail, but § 1988 has had only a minor impact on § 1983. For the most part, the issues on which state policies have been borrowed would have also resulted in borrowing absent § 1988, and the Court has developed uniform national policies on many elements of § 1983 despite the minimal guidance available from its language and legislative history.

Section 1988 is relevant to the use of § 1983 as a wrongful death remedy in three ways. First, § 1988 might be expected to provide guidance on how federal courts should approach the use of § 1983 as a wrongful death remedy and on whether they may look to the federal common law if they determine that no answers are provided by § 1983's language and legislative history. Second, in cases in which neither § 1983 nor the federal common law provides an applicable policy, § 1988 could be the vehicle for engrafting appropriate state wrongful death policies into § 1983. Third, if § 1988 requires the incorporation of state wrongful death policies into § 1983, including damage and other limitations on the cause of action, it also provides explicit authority for scrutinizing borrowed state policies in light of the purposes of § 1983.

1. Section 1988 — The Deficiency Clause and the Use of State Law

What is most noteworthy about § 1988's deficiency clause is the limited attention it has received from the Supreme Court. The clause requires courts hearing civil rights actions to follow "the laws of the United States" except "where they are not adapted to the object, or are deficient in the provisions necessary to furnish suitable remedies and punish offenses against law." Where federal law is "deficient," courts are required to follow the "common law, as modified and changed" by the law of the state in which the court is sitting.

This clause constitutes the linchpin of § 1988 and should govern the threshold determination whether a court initially looks to state law or follows federal law. Yet, aside from a cryptic comment in a 1969 decision suggesting an open-ended process of looking to state and federal law for the most suitable policy to govern the availability of damages in civil rights actions, the Court has not construed the deficiency clause in any of the § 1983 and other civil rights actions in which it relied on § 1988 to require initial resort to state law. Moreover, the Court has often ignored § 1988 and the deficiency clause in cases in which it developed uniform federal policies to govern various elements of § 1983 despite the absence of specific guidance in the language and legislative history of § 1983.

The failure of the Court to construe the deficiency clause may have resulted from the fact that despite the volume of § 1983 litigation there have been few close questions concerning whether federal courts should initially look to the state law. Moreover, because the Court has been willing to construe even vague provisions of § 1983 based on its broad purposes, it has rarely had to look to the deficiency clause for guidance.

In approaching § 1988, the Court has never made clear whether a court making a deficiency finding should consider the federal common law. Professor Eisenberg has argued against such an interpretation in attempting to demonstrate the incoherence of § 1988 and its inapplicability to § 1983 and other actions filed under the original jurisdiction of the federal courts. In addition to a textual argument, he has suggested that the federal common law bears no necessary relevance to § 1983 and that reliance on it gives courts the opportunity to manipulate results. Finally, Eisenberg points out that, absent § 1988, federal courts entertaining § 1983 actions will still be able to look to state law for guidance.

An interpretation of § 1988 that considers the federal common law before making a deficiency finding is also subject to the criticism that it deprives § 1988 of independent meaning by making it applicable to § 1983 and other civil rights actions only where no other sources of federal law — the statute, legislative history, statutory purposes, and federal common law — provide an answer. In such cases, however, state law would be relied upon anyway, and the deficiency clause would somewhat lamely only require the use of state law where state law is otherwise applicable.

In applying the federal common law, however, courts do not proceed independently of the underlying federal statutory or constitutional provisions they are enforcing. In fact, in many ways the federal common law represents a set of guidelines for construing federal statutes that have gaps, but the reference point is still the federal statute at issue. Thus, federal courts applying a federal common law of survival to statutory actions may reach different conclusions based on the character of the causes of action and the relief sought, but such an approach is closely tied to the underlying statute. Moreover, given the Court's awareness of the concerns of the 42d Congress and the need to engage in a parallel analysis in *Bivens* actions, courts should be permitted to fill gaps in § 1983 through the use of a common law of § 1983 that seeks to effectuate its dual purposes of compensation and deterrence.

In addition, even if the deficiency clause has no independent force in expanding the issues on which state law is initially looked to, § 1988 taken as a whole still establishes the framework for determining which state policies to borrow and when they should be rejected. Finally, in light of the remedial purposes of the Civil Rights Act of 1871, § 1 of which contained a reference to the predecessor to § 1988, it would be inappropriate to construe § 1988 to preclude federal courts from engaging in the lawmaking that is incidental to adjudicating cases. Whether this is characterized as developing the federal common law or, more narrowly, the common law of § 1983, it can be reduced to a question of statutory construction. In fact, in approaching § 1983, the Court has been reluctant to characterize its actions in terms of the federal common law and has subsumed under the rubric of statutory construction decisions that in other areas have been treated as being governed by the federal common law. Thus, questions of the scope and definition of official immunities and the damages available in federal court litigation are often viewed as matters of federal common law in *Bivens* actions, but in § 1983 litigation, these issues are approached as matters of statutory construction.

Nonetheless, the question remains as to what impact, if any, § 1988 has on limiting the ability of federal courts to develop a federal common law of § 1983. This can be addressed less abstractly by asking how decisions in which § 1988 was relied upon would have been resolved in its absence. Clearly when § 1983 itself — through its language, legislative history, and purposes — requires a particular remedial policy, federal law is not deficient and § 1988 does not alter the outcome. Likewise, if, absent § 1988, federal courts would look to state law, § 1988 is not relevant to the initial issue of whether state law should be borrowed. The difficult question, however, is whether § 1988 precludes or limits the power of courts to look to the federal common law to resolve issues not addressed by the language, legislative history, or purposes of § 1983.

The statute of limitations cases would probably be resolved similarly absent § 1988, as the Court required the use of state law in § 1983 actions more than seventy years ago without even considering § 1988. The survival issue, however, is more complex. Under an approach based on federal common law, federal courts permit nonpenal federal actions to survive despite the absence of relevant statutory provisions or legislative history. This suggests that § 1983 actions should survive, but the Court in *Robertson v. Wegmann* treated federal law as being deficient and borrowed a state no-survival policy. The *Robertson* Court, however, did not seek an answer to the survival issue in either § 1983 or in the federal common law. This failure to consider whether federal common law permitted the action to survive could mean the Court believed the action would have abated under federal common law, or that the survival of the action under federal common law was not relevant as § 1988 precluded resort to federal common law. In any case, the parties did not argue that federal common law applied, and the Court did not address it independently. Thus, *Robertson* does not provide a clear answer as to whether § 1988 denies or limits the power of federal courts hearing § 1983 actions to exercise their normal discretion to fill the interstices of federal statutes with federal common law.

The confusion in the Court's approach to the § 1988 borrowing issue is also seen in the damage cases. In *Sullivan v. Little Hunting Park*, a § 1982 case arising in state court, Justice Douglas found § 1988 applicable and suggested a construction that would have permitted courts entertaining civil rights actions to look to state and federal law for the most suitable damage policy. Such a construction, however, alters the nature of the § 1988 inquiry and permits courts to reject otherwise applicable federal policies. Moreover, although it is not free from doubt, *Sullivan* appears to require courts to look to the law of the forum state in developing the policy that then becomes the federal policy. This open-ended approach to § 1988, however, has not been followed, and the Court has all but ignored § 1988 and the law of the forum state in its damage cases.

There often have been sharp divisions within the Court on particular constructions of § 1983, but the threshold decision of whether uniform interpretations should be sought has rarely resulted in major disagreements. Although not framed in these terms, the Court has generally developed uniform federal policies on issues that go to the substance of the § 1983 cause of action and that affect the underlying conduct § 1983 was intended to control; but where the policy at issue does not affect this primary conduct, the Court has permitted initial resort to state law. Thus, issues involving the application of official immunities or the elements of damages influence primary conduct, and the Court has consistently applied federal definitions. On the other hand, statutes of limitations and survival policies generally have little effect on the underlying conduct, and initial resort to state law is acceptable, especially given the Court's treatment of the choice of the most analogous state policy as a federal issue and the availability of the inconsistency clause to reject borrowed state policies that are inconsistent with § 1983's purposes.

The failure of the Court to provide adequate guidance when federal law is deficient leaves unclear the proper approach to § 1983 wrongful death claims. Lower federal courts, however, influenced by the Court's treatment of the closely related survival issue, have generally looked to state law for the applicable policies. Thus, the Court's failure to articulate the standards it has been following to determine whether federal law is deficient has led lower courts to take the path of least resistance and borrow state wrongful death policies rather than to look closely at the language, legislative history, and purposes of § 1983 to see if § 1983 independently or through the federal common law constitutes a wrongful death remedy.

2. Section 1988 — The Incorporation of State Wrongful Death Actions

Where federal law is deficient on a particular issue, § 1988 requires federal courts to adopt the most analogous state policy. Often this involves difficult questions as to which competing state policy to use, but the choice of a particular policy is a federal issue. Competing policies are less likely to exist, however, with respect to state wrongful death remedies, but there still may be limitations on the extent to which courts may use § 1988 to incorporate state wrongful death policies into § 1983. Moreover, even if § 1988 can be used to engraft state wrongful death policies that authorize the cause of action, it is unclear whether state damage limitations accompany the wrongful death cause of action and must also be used.

The Supreme Court has construed § 1988 as not permitting the incorporation of new and independent state causes of action. In *Moor v. County of Alameda*, the plaintiffs, who sought damages based on allegations of the improper use of force by county law enforcement officials, argued that § 1988 permitted the use of state law to impose vicarious liability on the county. At the time this case arose, counties had an absolute immunity from § 1983 liability by virtue of their not being within § 1983's definition of "person." Nonetheless, Justice Marshall's opinion for the Court found a more basic reason to dismiss the vicarious liability claim. Even assuming a deficiency in federal law, § 1988 did not permit federal courts to borrow entire causes of action from state law. Section 1988 did not authorize an independent cause of action but only addressed the choice of remedies to be applied in actions arising under the civil rights acts. In so holding, however, the Court distinguished, but did not disapprove, two courts of appeals decisions that used § 1988 to borrow state law and to impose vicarious liability on supervisory law enforcement officials in § 1983 damage cases. These cases were distinguishable because § 1983 actions were independently available against the individual defendants; thus, the vicarious liability claims were not based on § 1988 alone. Although this distinction is not altogether clear, the Court seems to have suggested that if a particular defendant is independently amenable to suit under § 1983, § 1988 can be used — state law permitting — to expand the scope of liability.

In *Runyon v. McCrary*, the plaintiff relied on § 1988 to seek attorney fees on a private attorney general theory, but the Court further limited the availability of § 1988 to authorize new remedies. Although state law did not authorize fees, the plaintiff argued that § 1988 independently provided the necessary authority. The Court, however, refused to allow this use of § 1988 as it would incorporate a new and independent remedy as well as conflict with the prevailing policy preventing federal courts from awarding fees absent specific statutory authority.

The application of these principles to wrongful death claims is a close question. Traditionally, wrongful death claims were not available at common law, which did not recognize an actionable interest of survivors in their continued relationship with a decedent. This was changed in this country by the adoption of new and independent statutory causes of action patterned largely after Lord Campbell's Act. The purpose of wrongful death statutes was to avoid the harshness of the prevailing common law rules against the survival of actions, but the statutes did not address directly the issue of whether a decedent's cause of action would survive. Rather, they gave survivors an actionable interest that they did not have at common law.

Wrongful death statutes permit survivors to sue when a killing violated their decedent's rights, but the defendants in such actions are already amenable to survival actions based on the same wrongful acts. Moreover, both survival and wrongful death actions assert the identical legal rights of the decedent. Thus, the effect of using state law to incorporate wrongful death actions into § 1983 is to create new plaintiffs who can seek relief against defendants already amenable to suit as well as to expand the relief available against those defendants.

At one time wrongful death claims were viewed as new and independent actions, and they must still be distinguished from survival claims to keep clear the different interests at stake and the different measure of damages. Nonetheless, the claims are integrally related, and a number of states do not even maintain independent wrongful death remedies; rather, they simply permit wrongful death claims to be pursued in enlarged survival actions. Finally, nothing in § 1983 expressly or by implication precludes wrongful death claims from being heard through § 1983, and, although it is not free from doubt, the better view is that courts should be able to use § 1988 to incorporate state wrongful death actions into § 1983.

Assuming courts may use § 1988 to incorporate state wrongful death and survival policies into § 1983, there is an independent question of whether state limitations on damages are also incorporated. These issues will arise with regard to state ceilings on the amount of damages, state definitions of the elements of compensatory damages, and state policies on the availability of punitive damages.

Most state and federal courts that have addressed this issue assumed that state damage limitations accompany the cause of action and are initially incorporated into § 1983. Moreover, the Supreme Court has required the attributes of the cause of action to accompany the cause of action when federal admiralty courts borrow state causes of action and has also required state courts entertaining federal causes of action to utilize the entire cause of action. Nonetheless, strong arguments can be made to permit courts entertaining § 1983 claims to look to state law on the threshold issue of the availability of the survival or wrongful death action, yet allow those courts to apply federal policies as to the available damages.

Courts entertaining § 1983 actions that involve wrongful killings have looked initially to state law for survival and wrongful death policies because they have implicitly or explicitly concluded that federal law is deficient. The federal law of damages, however, is not similarly deficient, and courts entertaining § 1983 actions have developed a full body of § 1983 damage law. Moreover, courts borrowing causes of action generated by other jurisdictions have often been under a special obligation to borrow the entire cause of action, including its remedial attributes. For example, state courts entertaining federal causes of action are obligated by the supremacy clause and the interpretation of the federal statute being enforced to borrow the entire cause of action and all of its attributes. Similarly, federal law often expressly requires federal courts to borrow an entire cause of action from state law. On the other hand, § 1988 has a more limited borrowing requirement and contemplates the use of state law only where federal law is deficient. Thus, state and federal courts entertaining § 1983 survival and wrongful death actions should be able to rely on state law to authorize the action but ignore state limitations on the available damages.

3. Section 1988 — The Inconsistency Clause

Even when courts look to state law for the appropriate policy, the requirement that state law be used is not absolute. The language of § 1988 qualifies that obligation by requiring the use of state law only "so far as the same is not inconsistent with the Constititution and laws of the United States." The inconsistency clause has been interpreted by the Supreme Court to permit courts to reject a borrowed state policy when its application would either conflict with federal law or be inconsistent with the purposes of § 1983 — compensation and deterrence.

As with the deficiency clause, the interpretation of the inconsistency clause is far from clear. If an inconsistency arose only when a federal law expressly or implicitly conflicted with a state policy, the clause would have little meaning. Federal courts applying § 1988 already follow federal law as a threshold matter, and a second requirement — after resort to state law — seems unnecessary. In addition, the Court hardly needs the inconsistency clause to justify a refusal to borrow state policies that violate federal law.

When there are direct conflicts between borrowed state law and federal law, the Court has had little need to construe the inconsistency clause. Thus, in *Moor*, the Court relied on the inconsistency clause as an alternative basis for refusing to permit the state law of vicarious liability to support a § 1983 claim against a municipality that was outside the § 1983 definition of "person." Similarly, in *Runyon*, the Court refused to permit § 1988 to authorize an award of attorney fees, in part, because to do so would violate the long-established American rule.

The Court's major interpretation of the inconsistency clause came in *Robertson v. Wegmann*. After concluding that federal law was deficient and that the action would abate under applicable state law, the Court addressed whether such a result was inconsistent with federal law. In interpreting the inconsistency clause, the Court went beyond the literal language of the clause and held that the use of state law would be improper when it would be inconsistent with the underlying purposes of § 1983 — compensation and deterrence.

Despite this construction, the Court's application of it was timid, and the Court concluded that abatement of the action was consistent with compensation and deterrence. The goal of compensation was disposed of almost summarily. Because the original plaintiff had died, he no longer had an interest in compensation that justified the survival of his action; his estate's interest in obtaining compensation was ignored, but the Court observed that survivors pursuing wrongful death claims based on their own injuries would have an interest in compensation. The deterrence analysis, however, was more complex. The Court embraced a theory of marginal deterrence by reasoning that the purposes of § 1983 would not be undermined if survival of the action was conditioned on the existence of particular relatives. Since defendants would rarely be aware of the composition of their victims' families, it was unlikely that their conduct would be influenced by knowledge that an action would not survive. On the other hand, if state law was hostile to the survival of personal actions, a different assumption would be warranted. Thus, a state policy that required all personal actions to abate would be rejected because of its adverse effect on deterrence. Similarly, a state policy that required actions to abate when death resulted from the complained-of conduct would be inconsistent with the deterrence rationale of § 1983.

Issues involving the inconsistency clause have arisen in the Supreme Court most frequently with respect to state statutes of limitations and related policies. The Court, however, has never rejected an otherwise applicable state policy on the basis of its being inconsistent with the purposes of § 1983. For example, when the Court rejected a six-month statute of limitations borrowed from state employment discrimination administrative procedures, it did so on the basis of the statute's not being the analogous state policy. Thus, although the Court suggested that it would reject an unreasonably short limitations period, it did not have to reach the final step of the borrowing process to determine whether the policy in question was inconsistent with § 1983's purposes.

In *Board of Regents v. Tomanio*, however, the Court reached the inconsistency issue after borrowing a state policy under which the statute of limitations was not tolled during the pendency of a related cause of action. The plaintiff had split her claims and pursued a state claim in state court and a § 1983 claim in federal court, but the statute had run when the latter was filed. In reviewing this policy under the inconsistency clause, the Court disposed of plaintiff's arguments in a single sentence. Neither compensation nor deterrence were significantly affected because the plaintiff only had to have commenced her suit within the three-year limitations period to avoid the state rule.

Despite the development of a test of inconsistency based on the broad purposes of § 1983, the Court's approach to these issues has been timid, and this may have significant implications for the use of § 1983 as a wrongful death remedy. If the Court holds that § 1983 may be used as a wrongful death remedy only through the incorporation of state law and that state damage limitations accompany the action, the validity of these state damage limitations will become a major remedial issue in § 1983 litigation involving wrongful killings. Thus, the fact that the Court has never rejected an otherwise applicable state policy as inconsistent with the purposes of § 1983 suggests that the Court may require deference to state policies except in unusual situations.

* * *

2. Section 1983 Wrongful Death and Damages Policies

Courts entertaining § 1983 wrongful death claims by incorporating state wrongful death actions and their damage policies must address many of the issues that arise in survival actions. Because every state permits wrongful death actions, however, courts have not had to consider the availability of survival actions in determining whether § 1983 wrongful death actions are available. Nonetheless, these issues arise when states limit the survivors who can bring wrongful death actions and the available damages, but courts have often constitutionalized these issues and have not approached them as matters of statutory construction.

In addressing state limitations on the availability of wrongful death actions, courts should examine the state policy in light of the purposes of § 1983, and it is necessary to sort out the different interests involved. Although the Court in *Robertson* viewed compensation solely from the perspective of the decedent, in § 1983 wrongful death actions, survivors have an interest in compensation independent of the interest of the decedent or his estate. Similarly, the need for deterrence when the complained-of conduct causes death supports reviewing the availability of wrongful death actions without regard to whether the state would allow an action to survive. The marginal deterrence approach of *Robertson*, however, suggests that a court might rely on the state survival policy because a defendant contemplating an illegal act would unlikely be more deterred knowing that survival actions were available but wrongful death actions were not. Nonetheless, the possibility of eliminating substantial categories of damages for surviving relatives can significantly affect the deterrence purpose of § 1983.

Courts entertaining § 1983 wrongful death actions have generally found statutory ceilings on damages and limitations on the elements of damages to be inconsistent with the purposes of § 1983. To the extent a purpose of § 1983 is to compensate survivors of wrongful killings as well as to deter the wrongful conduct, these decisions seem correct. In reaching these conclusions, however, these courts have not considered the implications of the Court's holding in *Robertson* that § 1983's purpose of compensation is for the individual whose rights were violated, not for his estate.

Courts reviewing the use of state damage restrictions in § 1983 wrongful death cases have generally not addressed whether § 1983 was intended to compensate survivors. Nonetheless, in following the borrowing approach sanctioned by the Court for survival issues, these courts have assumed that § 1983 itself was intended to compensate survivors. Likewise, courts have rarely addressed the extent to which specific limitations on damages reduce the deterrence goal of § 1983. Instead, they have often approached the issue in conclusory terms and have come close to assuming that all state limitations on wrongful death damages are inconsistent with § 1983's purposes. Such an approach, however, may be at odds with the marginal deterrence approach of *Robertson*. Further, as more difficult § 1983 wrongful death cases arise involving state policies denying damages for losses not generally compensated under state law, such as mental anguish and punitive damages, the short-comings of the borrowing approach become more apparent. These problems, however, are avoided when courts treat § 1983 itself as a wrongful death remedy. In such cases, the inquiry is not whether to reject a state damage limitation but how to construct a federal policy of damages in light of the purposes of § 1983.

Because the interests at stake in § 1983 wrongful death actions differ from those in survival actions, courts entertaining the former should be able to consider the interest of survivors in being compensated in addition to the role of compensatory and punitive damages in deterring prohibited conduct.

The traditional damages available under state wrongful death actions — loss of support, inheritance, services and society — are intended to make survivors whole by providing full compensation. State policies that deny these damages or that place dollar ceilings on them deny survivors full and fair compensation and fail to deter misconduct by prospective defendants. Thus, courts that have reviewed these limitations in § 1983 wrongful death actions have generally rejected them as inconsistent with § 1983's purposes.

More difficult questions, however, are suggested by the increasing number of states that make available wrongful death damages for mental anguish, grief, and sorrow. These damage policies also serve the goal of compensation, albeit more generously, and courts have not hesitated to incorporate them into the borrowed § 1983 wrongful death remedy. The harder question, however, arises when states deny those damages by defining damages narrowly in terms of pecuniary losses. If a central purpose of § 1983 is to provide full compensation to survivors, courts should reject this limitation. Nonetheless, the fact that a state limitation is rejected does not mean that federal courts must allow such damages; rather, their availability should depend on the federal common law of § 1983 damages that the courts have developed in light of the purposes of § 1983.

The interest in compensation may be a stronger basis for rejecting some state limitations on wrongful death damages than the concern for deterrence. For a state limitation on the availability of damages to violate *Robertson*'s marginal deterrence approach, it may be necessary for the prospective defendant to not only be aware of the limitation but also to have some idea how it would affect the intended victim. Of course, when limitations are well known and broadly applicable, the interest in deterrence requires the limitation to be rejected. Thus, state policies that deny wrongful death damages for mental anguish and grief should be rejected. Although a defendant may not have specific knowledge about whether a decedent has survivors who can claim such losses, defendants can generally assume that there will be some survivors who can do so. Likewise, defendants can often assume that certain victims have limited earning potential and are not likely to be providing financial support to dependents at a sufficiently high level to support a large damage award. Finally, Alabama's rejection of all compensatory damages gives prospective defendants the clear message that they only need to avoid reckless conduct to be safe from § 1983 damage awards.

On the other hand, state policies defining the loss of support or prospective inheritance differently or limiting damages for some classes of survivors may encourage prohibited acts only when a prospective defendant is aware of the policy and the impact it will have on the awards to potential survivors. Thus, a technical state policy of deducting personal living expenses from an award measured in terms of an estate to be inherited is unlikely to have even a marginal impact on deterrence, and a court would be justified in not rejecting such a method of calculating damages under § 1988. Likewise, a borrowed state policy that only denied damages for mental anguish and grief to siblings might be consistent with *Robertson*'s narrow approach to deterrence.

State limitations on the availability of punitive damages in § 1983 wrongful death actions, however, raise different issues. Punitive damages are available in § 1983 actions as a matter of federal law for the purpose of curbing malicious or reckless behavior. Because compensation is not one of the purposes of punitive damages, it is not necessary to separate the respective interests of the decedent and his survivors in such damages. The availability of punitive damages, whether in the survival or wrongful death action, serves the identical purpose of deterring otherwise culpable defendants from engaging in extreme conduct. Thus, the deterrence purpose of § 1983 is served by a state policy that made punitive damages available in either the survival or wrongful death action but not in both. On the other hand, a state policy that denied punitive damages in both actions would single out § 1983 actions involving wrongful killings for less favorable treatment than other § 1983 actions and would be inconsistent with the federal law of § 1983 damages and with the purposes of § 1983.

V. Section 1983 as a Wrongful Death Remedy: A Proposed Construction

It is not necessary to look to state law to fill gaps in the § 1983 cause of action when federal law provides the relevant policies. Thus, when no answer is immediately apparent from the language of § 1983, the language, legislative history, and purposes of § 1983 should nonetheless be examined to determine whether the statute itself constitutes a wrongful death remedy. The Supreme Court has not undertaken this inquiry, and most lower courts that have reviewed the legislative history of § 1983 in this context have done so to determine whether state wrongful death remedies may be incorporated into § 1983, or whether state limitations on wrongful death remedies, once borrowed, should be rejected as inconsistent with the purposes of § 1983.

A. *Proposed Construction*

There is a clear and simple answer to the question of the availability of § 1983 as a wrongful death remedy independent of state law. That answer, which is applicable uniformly throughout the country, is suggested by § 1983's "party injured" language, which has never been reviewed by the Supreme Court. Although most courts have assumed that the plaintiff — the "party injured" in § 1983 — is identical to the "person" whose rights are violated, that is not necessarily the case. A textual argument can be made that § 1983 itself authorizes parties injured by the death of another to recover damages suffered from that injury. Thus, § 1983 may be read as permitting the third-party standing of survivors suing because they were injured by conduct that not only violated the decedent's constitutional rights but also took his life.

Such a proposal may seem bold. It is consistent, however, with the usage in the other sections of the Civil Rights Act of 1871 and with the civil actions created by the other Reconstruction-era civil rights acts. It is also supported by § 1983's legislative history and purposes. Moreover, the use of § 1983 to pursue a wrongful death claim is consistent with the state of the law in 1871 when the predecessor of § 1983 was enacted. Although the common law did not recognize a wrongful death action, the adoption of statutory wrongful death actions by the majority of American jurisdictions demonstrates that in 1871 it was well established that survivors had wrongful death remedies available to them. Finally, the use of § 1983 to authorize third-party standing in cases in which the decedent can no longer seek redress for the violation of his rights is consistent with the Court's willingness to authorize third-party standing in other limited circumstances as well as with the prudential limitations on the case or controversy requirement. Thus, § 1983 can be read as ex proprio vigore establishing a wrongful death remedy, and it is not necessary to consult state law to determine whether § 1983 can be used to pursue a wrongful death claim.

B. *Legislative History*

The legislative history of the Civil Rights Act of 1871 supports the view that the cause of action created by § 1 should be available to permit survivors to recover damages they suffered as a result of an unconstitutional killing. The 42d Congress was vitally concerned with wrongful killings, and the argument that the new civil actions they created only reach wrongful killings when state law so provides must be rejected.

The Supreme Court has reviewed the legislative history of § 1 of the Civil Rights Act of 1871 many times to answer questions concerning the scope of § 1983. Although the Court has considered the definition of "person" to determine who may be a defendant in § 1983 actions, it has never reviewed the legislative history for the purpose of addressing who is a "person" with rights secured by § 1983 or a "party injured" under the statute. Nor has the Court considered whether the legislative history and purposes of § 1983 shed any light on the statute's availability as a wrongful death remedy.

The Civil Rights Act of 1871 was a congressional response to widespread lawlessness in the southern states and the inability and unwillingness of state and local officials to curb it. Prior legislation had dealt with official abuses directed towards blacks and Union sympathizers by creating federal criminal remedies and expanding the president's police power. The Civil Rights Act of 1871, however, focused on the private lawlessness and atrocities of the Ku Klux Klan and similar organizations. As ultimately passed, the Act increased the power of the federal government. The president was given expanded power to use the military to protect federal rights and temporary power to suspend habeas corpus; the federal criminal law was expanded to reach private conspiracies; and, a civil cause of action against such conspiracies was created. The far-reaching proposals of Senator Sherman to impose an affirmative duty on counties to prevent private violence were rejected, but a compromise civil action for nonfeasance was created. Finally, the Act included a relatively uncontroversial provision creating a civil remedy against persons who acted under color of state law to violate the constitutional rights of persons within the United States.

On March 23, 1871, President Grant had sent an urgent message to Congress describing conditions in the southern states that rendered "life and property insecure" and urging the passage of legislation to "effectually secure life, liberty, and property, and the enforcement of the law in all parts of the United States." At the time the message arrived, Congress had been considering a number of proposals to enforce the fourteenth amendment and had recently received a lengthy investigative report describing the widespread lawlessness in a number of the southern states, particularly North Carolina, and the complicity of state and local officials in that lawlessness.

President Grant's message appears to have been a catalyst for the Republicans who controlled Congress, and on March 28, 1871, five days after that message was received, Representative Shellabarger, the chair of the select committee to which the *President's* message was sent, presented a bill to the House of Representatives.

Despite the proposal's focus on private lawlessness, it also expanded the available sanctions against state and local officials who acted to deprive persons of their constitutional rights. This was accomplished by creating a civil counterpart to earlier criminal legislation that prohibited actions taken under color of state law violative of federal rights, including actions that involved wrongful killings.

In presenting the proposal, Representative Shellabarger informed the House of Representatives that § 1 of the Act was modeled after the criminal provisions of § 2 of the Civil Rights Act of 1866. Aside from differences concerning the broader reach of the civil remedy, which was not limited to former slaves, Shellabarger stated that the earlier statute "provides a criminal proceeding in identically the same case as [§ 1] . . . provides a civil remedy." Because § 2 of the Civil Rights Act of 1866 had extended the criminal sanction to situations in which persons acting under color of state law deprived others of their life, there can be little doubt that § 1 of the Civil Rights Act of 1871 was also intended to provide a civil remedy in such cases. Moreover, in defending the constitutionality of legislation to secure the rights of citizens, Shellabarger noted how "plainly and grossly absurd" it would be to deny such power to the national government and "leave all the protection and law-making to the very States which are denying the protection."

The debate on the Civil Rights Act of 1871 makes clear that its proponents were vitally concerned with the unlawful killings that characterized the reign of terror in the southern states. They repeatedly referred to wrongful killings in identifying the evils they were addressing, and they relied extensively on the investigative report that vividly described the state of lawlessness. Representative Lowe of Kansas, a Republican proponent of the Act, stated as follows:

> While *murder* is stalking abroad in disguise, while whippings and *lynchings* and banishment have been visited upon unoffending American citizens, the local administrations have been found inadequate or unwilling to apply the proper corrective. Combinations, darker than the night that hides them, conspir-

> acies, wicked as the worst of felons could devise, have gone unwhipped of justice.

In summarizing the concern about the actions of the southern states, Representative Beatty of Ohio noted that

> certain States have denied to persons within their jurisdiction the equal protection of the laws. The proof on this point is voluminous and unquestionable . . . [M]en were murdered, houses were burned, women were outraged, men were scourged, and officers of the law shot down; and the State made no successful effort to bring the guilty to punishment or afford protection or redress to the outraged and innocent.

Finally, Congressman Butler, although disappointed by the failure to obtain an even stronger bill, remarked as follows:

> This, then, is what is offered to the people of the United States as remedy for wrongs, arsons, and murders done. This is what we offer to a man whose house has been burned, as a remedy; to the woman whose husband has been murdered, as a remedy; to the children whose father has been killed, as a remedy.

Although some of these comments refer to the private lawlessness to which the civil and criminal remedies created by § 2 of the Act were addressed, there is no indication in the legislative debates that Congress intended to create remedies for killings that resulted from private conspiracies but not from official lawlessness. Moreover, the criminal sanction from which § 1 was derived was clearly available when the perpetrator acted under color of law, and the tie-in between the new civil remedy and its criminal counterpart is unmistakable. Thus, there is strong support for the conclusion that wrongful killings under color of law were not only actionable in the courts of the United States through the criminal sanction, but also gave rise to a civil claim under § 1 of the Civil Rights Act of 1871.

The absence of detailed discussion on the reach of § 1 is not surprising given the lack of controversy concerning the provision. Its proponents accepted that it did not confer new rights, but only a new civil remedy available in federal court. On the other hand, § 2, which created a civil and criminal remedy against private conspiracies, was controversial, and the debate on it was intense. As originally introduced, § 2 was only a criminal provision, but it proscribed private conspiracies to perform acts that violated the "rights, privileges, or immunities" of other persons. The criminal acts were then enumerated, and expressly included murder.

Opponents of the legislation argued that Congress lacked power under the fourteenth amendment to regulate private conduct and that only the states could enact criminal codes. Even some Republican supporters objected to the breadth of the original formulation, and eventually Representative Shellabarger offered an amended version of § 2 to create a civil remedy and to more closely tie the underlying rights to the fourteenth amendment. In doing this, the amended bill dropped all references to specific crimes, but there is no indication of any intent to exclude from the proscribed conspiracies those that achieved their prohibited evils through murder, or to create a civil remedy under § 2 that was not as broad as the criminal one. The controversy involved federalizing responsibility for enforcing what opponents viewed as state law, and no suggestion was made that the new remedies would be available when the conspiracy maimed its victims but not when it killed them.

Thus, Judge Brown in *Brazier v. Cherry* concluded:

> [I]t defies history to conclude that Congress purposefully meant to assure to the living freedom from such unconstitutional deprivation but that, with like precision, had meant to withdraw the protection of the Civil Rights statutes against the peril of death. The policy of law and the legislative aim are certainly to protect the security of life and limb as well as property against these actions. Violent injury that would kill was not less prohibited than violence which would cripple.

Although this statement was made in the course of holding that a § 1983 action, in conjunction with state law, survived the death of a victim and could be used as a wrongful death remedy, the conclusion that the 42d Congress intended § 1 to reach wrongful killings is relevant to the question of how to construe § 1983 in the first place.

This analysis is also consistent with a textual review of the other surviving Reconstruction-era private civil rights actions, including the civil actions created by other provisions of the Civil Rights Act of 1871. Section 1981 of Title 42, which is derived from the Civil Rights Acts of 1866 and 1870, provides "persons within the jurisdiction of the United States" the same right to make contracts, and to participate in judicial proceedings for the security of person and property, as is enjoyed by white citizens. Section 1982 of Title 42, which is also derived from the Civil Rights Act of 1866, limits its protection to "citizens of the United States" and provides them the same property rights as are enjoyed by white citizens. Neither of these sections contains any reference to the appropriate remedy or to the party who can seek redress for their violation. Thus, the text of these sections does not shed any light on the proper interpretation of the "party injured" language of § 1983, and whether persons other than those whose rights are violated may sue depends on an analysis of the language and purposes of § 1983.

However, § 1985, which is derived from § 2 of the Civil Rights Act of 1871, also contains the phrase "party injured," and the textual argument made under § 1983 is similar to that made under § 1985. Section 1985 proscribes five separate classes of conspiracies and contains a single remedial section providing that "the party so injured or deprived may have an action for the recovery of damages, occasioned by such injury or deprivation, against any one or more of the conspirators." Under these provisions the "party injured" either by an act under color of state law or pursuant to a proscribed conspiracy can be a person other than the person whose underlying rights were violated. Moreover, there is persuasive legislative history that supports interpreting § 2 of the Civil Rights Act of 1871 as being available to survivors in cases that involve wrongful killings.

There is, however, a provision of the Civil Rights Act of 1871 that expressly provides survivors a legal remedy, and the argument has been made that its presence negates any congressional intent to permit § 1983 actions to be available as a wrongful death remedy.

Section 6 of the Civil Rights Act of 1871 was the watered-down version of Senator Sherman's amendment that was rejected twice by the House. As ultimately enacted, however, § 6 created a civil remedy against persons who are aware of conspiracies under § 1985 and who have the power to prevent them or aid their prevention but neglect or refuse to do so. The section made such persons "liable to the person injured, or his legal representatives, for all damages caused by any such wrongful act which such . . . person . . . by reasonable diligence could have prevented." It then went on to contain the only explicit survival or wrongful death provision in the civil rights acts:

> [I]f the death of any person shall be caused by any such wrongful act and neglect, the legal representatives of such deceased person shall have such action therefor, and may recover not exceeding five thousand dollars damages therein, for the benefit of the widow of such deceased person, if any there be, or if there be no widow, for the benefit of the next of kin of such deceased person.

This provision supports the arguments that the "party injured" throughout the Civil Rights Act of 1871 is the party whose rights were violated, and that when Congress intended to provide remedies to other "legal representatives" it did so explicitly. These arguments, however, must be rejected. The inclusion of an actionable interest in specified legal representatives when death resulted from the illegal conduct can best be explained as an effort to limit the unusual form of liability imposed by § 6 of the Civil Rights Act of 1871, and not as a limitation on the actions available under other sections of the Act. Likewise, the inclusion of a ceiling on the damages available in actions under § 6 for nonfeasance in no way supports the conclusion that Congress intended that ceilings be used in the more traditional actions for misfeasance under § 1, even when such actions are brought on behalf of survivors.

Further support for the use of § 1983 as a wrongful death remedy is available from a review of the state law against which the 42d Congress legislated. Although the common law in 1871 denied the existence of a cause of action for wrongful death, most states rejected the common law rule by enacting general wrongful death statutes patterned after Lord Campbell's Act. Thus, by 1871 there was no well-established state policy of denying wrongful death remedies to survivors, and the availability of state wrongful death remedies was the rule, not the exception. The existence of wrongful death statutes had become part of American jurisprudence, and it is likely that members of the 42d Congress were aware of the expanding right of survivors to bring wrongful death actions.

Although other aspects of the law of wrongful death, especially those involving damages, were in a state of flux in 1871, the immunity from civil suit previously given those whose illegal actions resulted in a killing was no longer well established. Thus, the widespread availability of wrongful death actions makes it inappropriate to condition the use of § 1983 as a wrongful death remedy upon the existence of express legislative history, and any ambiguity from the language of § 1983 and the use of the phrase "party injured" should be resolved in light of the purposes of the legislation. It is simply not convincing to argue that Congress, in making civil remedies available under § 1 of the Civil Rights Act of 1871, chose to exclude from the phrase "party injured" persons whose injury resulted from the wrongful killing of a family member.

C. *Third-Party Standing*

The traditional policy of the federal courts is that parties may not assert the rights of others, and some courts have rejected the use of § 1983 as a wrongful death remedy because they have been reluctant to transform § 1983 into a third-party standing statute. These concerns, however, are misplaced.

The case or controversy requirement of article III of the Constitution does not prohibit third-party standing, but the Supreme Court has developed prudential limitations on when it will permit an injured party to assert the rights of others. When Congress has created a statutory action on behalf of a third party, the Court has deferred to this judgment. In addition, when there is a special relationship between the party injured and the person whose rights have been violated, the Court has been willing to allow the injured party standing to advance the rights of the third party.

Although the Court has not addressed the issue of third-party standing in terms of the text of § 1983, it has permitted parties who have been injured to assert the rights of others in actions authorized by § 1983. Typically, such cases have involved the assertion of constitutional claims on which the legislative history of § 1983 had little relevance, but the availability of § 1983 in such circumstances demonstrates there is no constitutional or prudential bar to § 1983's being used as a third-party standing statute.

When § 1983 is used to raise wrongful death claims, however, its legislative history and purposes have a special significance that justify its use as a third-party standing statute. Moreover, as Professor Currie recently noted, many standing questions, especially those involving statutory actions, are really questions as to the definition of the cause of action and require determinations of what action is authorized and who may bring it.

Permitting survivors to obtain damages for losses they suffered as a result of the unconstitutional killing of a close relative is also consistent with the prudential doctrines that govern when the Court allows third-party standing. In *Warth v. Seldin*, the Court denied city taxpayers standing to advance the rights of low-income persons allegedly excluded from a suburban community by restrictive zoning ordinances. Unlike the city taxpayers who had no special relationship with those whose rights they were seeking to enforce, survivors pursuing wrongful death actions are, by definition, claiming a close relationship with the decedent. The termination of that relationship by the wrongful killing and the resulting damages to the survivor provide the survivor with the constitutionally required "injury in fact" as well as with a special relationship that justifies permitting the survivor to pursue the rights of the decedent. Moreover, unlike the circumstances in *Warth* in which the low-income persons were at least in theory able to pursue their own rights, decedents will have only rarely been able to do so.

The doctrine of third-party standing has often been criticized, and it has been argued that courts should not extend that doctrine to cases involving damage claims. Nonetheless, federal courts commonly award damages to injured parties asserting the rights of third parties in diversity cases under state wrongful death statutes, in special damage actions under federal statutes, and under general maritime law. Such cases clearly meet the prudential limitations on third-party standing. The plaintiff — the survivor — is injured because of the death of the decedent; the rights enforced by the plaintiff are those of the decedent. More importantly, the availability of these third-party damage actions further supports the observation that the issue of third-party standing can often be reduced to a question of defining the cause of action. Thus, the availability of § 1983 as a wrongful death action ultimately turns on the issue of statutory construction and the strength of the argument that the language, legislative history, and purposes of § 1983 support its use as a wrongful death remedy.

VI. The Contours of the § 1983 Wrongful Death Action

If the Supreme Court interprets § 1983 as a wrongful death remedy regardless of state law, it will still have to answer questions typically addressed in wrongful death statutes, such as who may sue, what elements of damages are available, and how to distribute any awards. In fact, the difficulty of some of these issues and their legislative nature has made some courts reluctant to develop nonstatutory wrongful death remedies. Nonetheless, there are tools available to address these problems. The Federal Rules of Civil Procedure provide guidance for managing litigation and determining who is a proper plaintiff, and damage issues that arise are governed by the same principles of compensation used in determining available damages in other § 1983 cases. Moreover, the damages available may help define both who is a proper party and how to distribute the proceeds from successful suits. Finally, there may be room for a limited use of state law to address some of these questions.

Although the emergence of § 1983 as a wrongful death remedy independent of state law will raise a number of unique damage and other issues that do not typically arise in § 1983 litigation, this is not a basis for rejecting the use of § 1983 as a wrongful death remedy. The federal common law that governs damage issues and other aspects of § 1983 is capable of responding to the requirements of the § 1983 wrongful death action. Finally, if the problems of determining what damages are available in § 1983 wrongful death actions and these related questions prove too difficult or if the Court's resolution of them is unacceptable, Congress can address them through legislation as it has in other statutory wrongful death actions.

A. Proper Parties

The question of who can bring a § 1983 wrongful death action involves a determination of both the party in whose name a case may be filed and the identity of the party for whose benefit it is brought. The latter issue is one of substance and its resolution depends initially on the language, legislative history, and purposes of § 1983.

Regardless of whether state or federal law is used to identify the parties for whose benefits wrongful death actions are brought, there will be technical issues of who is a proper party. With state law no longer the starting point, federal courts can address these issues by looking to the Federal Rules of Civil Procedure and by considering the nature of the claim and the damages being sought.

Rule 17(a) of the Federal Rules of Civil Procedure requires that actions be pursued in the name of the "real party in interest." Nonetheless, executors, administrators or other representative parties with duties to the decedent under state law, or the decedent's beneficiaries may also sue. Thus, state law may identify the nominal party.

The duties of statutory representatives are also defined by state law, and those representatives may file wrongful death actions under § 1983. Their ability to pursue such § 1983 wrongful death claims in federal courts, however, will be determined by federal rules, but the Federal Rules of Civil Procedure incorporates state law. Thus, statutory beneficiaries may have wrongful death claims pursued on their behalf only by their statutory representatives, and they will not be able to proceed independently.

The borrowing of state procedures to govern issues involving the real party in interest and capacity to sue, however, does not prevent nonstatutory beneficiaries from pursuing wrongful death actions independently. Thus, parties with no rights under a state wrongful death statute may nevertheless file actions in their own name under § 1983 to seek damages that result from the wrongful killing of their respective decedents.

The identity of the beneficiaries of § 1983 wrongful death actions is a function of the losses those beneficiaries have experienced and the relief they seek. Thus, family members legally dependent on the decedent should have little difficulty becoming plaintiffs in § 1983 wrongful death actions. Likewise, family members who were not legally dependent on the decedent but who were receiving actual financial support prior to the killing should also be able to claim that the death denied them support. Finally, persons claiming loss of services or loss of society may have suffered a palpable injury and, if such damages are available in § 1983 wrongful death actions, they should be able to recover them.

Problems may arise, however, where nonstatutory beneficiaries file § 1983 wrongful death actions. Without the constraints of a comprehensive state law, there may be no limit on the number of persons claiming that their relationship with the decedent resulted in compensable injuries. Initially, however, the ability to claim damages will depend on the element of damages available in § 1983 wrongful death actions. There are also a number of other sources of guidance that courts could follow to develop limiting principles. For example, courts entertaining § 1983 wrongful death actions could rely on Roscoe Pound's observation about wrongful death statutes having become part of the general law and look to see how states generally limit the beneficiaries who could pursue claims. Similarly, courts could look to the beneficiaries under federal wrongful death statutes.

The Federal Rules of Civil Procedure also provide some assistance in making § 1983 wrongful death litigation more manageable. Given the absence of a comprehensive federal statute, there are many unresolved questions as to the scope of the § 1983 wrongful death action, and defendants may be subject to multiple or successive suits arising out of the same death. Although this may currently happen in states that permit survival and wrongful death suits to be pursued simultaneously, the use of § 1983 as a wrongful death remedy without the constraints of settled state law may expand the number of potential beneficiaries and potential law suits. In such cases, however, defendants may be able to rely on Rule 19, which creates a mechanism whereby indispensable parties may be joined.

B. Damages

Damage issues in § 1983 wrongful death actions require courts to look to federal common law and to the general principles of compensation applied in non-wrongful death § 1983 cases. In addressing such issues, courts should look to the state of the law in 1871 to determine whether there was a well-established policy precluding the availability of particular elements of damages. If an element of damage was clearly unavailable in 1871, courts may still consider the evolving law of damages, public policy, and the purpose of § 1983 in deciding whether to make that element available. In such cases, however, there must be a strong showing before a well established policy would be rejected. On the other hand, when elements of damages were not clearly precluded, courts should search for the most appropriate damage policy without any presumption in favor of using state law. In any case, it should not be necessary to demonstrate affirmatively that an element of damage was available in 1871 to support making it available today. Thus, when particular elements of damages were not generally available in 1871, courts should look to the broad purposes of § 1983 — compensation and deterrence — to determine which policies best meet these ends.

Section 1983 actions involving wrongful killings also raise survival issues, and the Court has required courts to look to the state law of survival. In addressing the availability of survival actions under § 1983, federal courts have often had to address whether specific state limitations on the damages available in survival actions are inconsistent with the purposes of § 1983. For example, some states expressly prohibit the survival of punitive damages as well as damages for pain and suffering. However, the framework that the Court has developed to determine the consistency of state policies with the purposes of § 1983 has been used to reject such limitations.

Federal courts entertaining § 1983 survival actions have also had to address the appropriate measure of damages when state law was silent. For example, states that do not permit personal actions to survive provide little guidance as to the appropriate measure of damages. In such cases, there is little difficulty in concluding that the decedent's estate is entitled to damages for the losses the decedent suffered during his lifetime. Thus, loss of income or medical expenses during the period between the time of injury and death should be available in the § 1983 survival action even if state law required the action to abate. The more difficult question, however, is whether an award should be made for the illegal killing and for the violation of the constitutional right itself. These issues often arise because the circumstances of persons whose deaths result in § 1983 survival and wrongful death actions often preclude significant damages under the state wrongful death statute. Thus, the question often arises whether the survival action will be able to award damages for injuries that may not be described as actual injuries, and some courts have been willing to award damages in such cases for the loss of life and for the violation of the rights despite the absence of consequential damages.

C. Distribution

The distribution of the proceeds of § 1983 wrongful death and survival actions depends on the nature of the damages awarded and the identity of the plaintiffs who obtained them. When survival claims are made under § 1983 for the wrongful killing, the estate would typically bring the action, and either the decedent's will or state law on intestate succession will govern the distribution of the proceeds of any litigation.

In § 1983 wrongful death actions, on the other hand, the distribution of damages will depend on the nature of the damages awarded, and the allocation will generally not pose significant questions. When damages are awarded for loss of support, loss of inheritance, loss of services, loss of society, or mental grief or anguish, the parties experiencing those losses are the ones to whom the awards will be distributed. When punitive damages are obtained in wrongful death actions, the question of distributing the award will be more difficult, but courts should be able to resolve such issues based on the identity of the parties bringing the suit and, when necessary, state law.

Conclusion

The use of § 1983 as a remedy in cases involving wrongful killings has undergone a significant expansion in recent years. Originally tied to the provisions of state law, such actions are on the increase as the personal representatives and survivors of decedents seek federal remedies that avoid the limitations of state law. Although courts have been willing to reject state law limitations that are inconsistent with the purposes of § 1983, courts should break away from their initial dependence on state law and develop an independent § 1983 wrongful death action. Such a development is supported by this analysis of § 1983 ex proprio vigore as a wrongful death remedy.

Part IX

Federalism, State Courts, Parity and "Converse-*Erie*"

The Supreme Court declared in *Monroe v. Pape*, 365 U.S. 167 (1961), that a section 1983 plaintiff may sue in federal court without first pursuing a state law remedy. Moreover, there is no exhaustion of state remedies requirement even though state courts are almost certainly required by the Supremacy Clause to entertain section 1983 actions. This suggests a preference for federal court adjudication of section 1983 actions.

Apart from the 42nd Congress's evident distrust of the states when it enacted section 1983 in 1871, does anything else account for this preference for a federal forum in connection with the enforcement of federal constitutional rights? Professor Neuborne's article on parity deals with this question at a level going beyond section 1983 litigation but equally applicable to it. Professor Neuborne argues that federal courts are institutionally more competent forums for the decision of federal constitutional claims than are state courts. For this reason, constitutional litigators should, to the extent possible, be able to choose a federal forum.

Nevertheless, there could be reasons for a section 1983 plaintiff in a particular case to choose a *state forum.* Where that occurs and there is no removal by the defendant to a federal forum, what is the relation between section 1983 state court litigation and state law? The answer is simple in one sense: the Supremacy Clause mandates the applicability of the federal substantive law of section 1983 to all section 1983 claims, even where filed in state court. For example, a state law rule conferring absolute immunity on police officers sued for using excessive force in making an arrest may not be applied to a state court section 1983 claim that a police officer engaged in such conduct.

Suppose, though, that a state law rule does not conflict with the explicit substantive law of section 1983 but instead arguably conflicts with its *policies.* This raises a "converse-*Erie* " issue, so-called because of the classic case of *Erie Railroad v. Tompkins*, 304 U.S. 64 (1938). In *Erie*, the Supreme Court held that in a diversity of citizenship case, a federal court enforcing state law must apply the substantive law of the forum state. In contrast, in converse-*Erie* cases, a state court is enforcing federal law. The question is the extent to which, if at all, section 1983 *preempts* state law.

Professor Herman's article deals with this question in connection with state court procedures. After offering several choice of law principles, she urges that state courts not use procedures that adversely affect civil rights plaintiffs. State courts, moreover, should affirmatively "develop procedures that would enhance their role in civil rights litigation." Professor Herman concludes that if this were to happen, and state courts were to become the preferred forum for section 1983 litigation, "what a wonderful irony it would be."

The Harvard Law Review Note addresses the complicated issues arising out of section 1983 state tax challenges filed in state court. Section 1983 state tax challenges may not be filed in federal court where a "plain, speedy and efficient" remedy is available in state court under the terms of the Tax Injunction Act, 28 U.S.C. sec. 1341 (1982). Furthermore, the Supreme Court has ruled that the Tax

Injunction Act's principle of comity prohibits a federal court in such cases from awarding damages as well. *Fair Assessment in Real Estate Ass'n v. McNary*, 454 U.S. 100 (1981).

Inasmuch as federal courts cannot hear section 1983 state tax challenges, the question is whether and to what extent state courts should adjudicate them. The Note argues that state courts are under an obligation to do so. While issues of equity and fiscal autonomy may be considered by state courts in such cases, "neither concern should be applied to undercut the federal rights protected by section 1983."

Burt Neuborne, *The Myth of Parity*, 90 Harvard Law Review 1105 (1977)

* * *

II. Parity: Contemporary Institutional Considerations

As a civil liberties lawyer for the past ten years, I have pursued a litigation strategy premised on two assumptions. First, persons advancing federal constitutional claims against local officials will fare better, as a rule, in a federal, rather than a state, trial court. Second, to a somewhat lesser degree, federal district courts are institutionally preferable to state appellate courts as forums in which to raise federal constitutional claims. I know of no empirical studies that prove (or undermine) those assumptions. Yet, they frequently shape the forum selection strategy in constitutional cases today as they have in the past.

The Supreme Court, however, presently seems bent on resolving forum allocation decisions by assuming that no factors exist which render federal district courts more effective than state trial or appellate courts for the enforcement of federal constitutional rights. I hope to challenge the Court's present assumptions, and to support my own, by focusing on institutional characteristics relevant to assessing the relative competence of state and federal courts as constitutional enforcement mechanisms.

Admittedly, since forum allocation choices implicate concerns for federalism, judicial economy, and the federal courts' caseload, it is not surprising that there has been an increasing tendency to channel constitutional challenges to state action into the state courts. And, of course, even if federal district courts were conceded a comparative advantage in constitutional enforcement, those concerns might militate in favor of routing certain constitutional cases into state forums. However, by uncritically assuming parity, the Supreme Court has avoided the difficult, but critical, issue of whether concerns for federalism, efficiency, and caseload outweigh the importance of having constitutional claims heard by the more sympathetic and competent forum.

A. *An Institutional Comparison: Some Preliminary Observations*

The first step in assessing the relative institutional capacity of state and federal courts to enforce constitutional doctrine requires agreement on which state forum should be compared with the federal district courts to determine whether a comparative advantage exists. Generally, when the parity issue is discussed, it is in the context of a comparison that tends to measure the federal district courts against state appellate courts. While such a comparison makes sense in the context of habeas corpus, where the petitioner first will have pursued his federal claims unsuccessfully through the state court system, it is inappropriate in most constitutional cases. Even if one concedes parity between state appellate and federal district courts, corrective state appellate work does not adequately substitute for vigorous constitutional protection at the trial level. The expense, delay, and uncertainty which inhere in any appellate process render ultimate success after appeal far less valuable than speedy, accurate resolution below. Especially in the context of first amendment rights, by their nature fragile, the possibility of a lengthy, problematic appeal in order to reverse an adverse criminal or civil judgment may deter many individuals from effectively exercising their rights. Moreover, in many constitutional cases, the factfinding process plays a critical role in resolution of the controversy. These two factors combine to render the trial forum often the most critical stage, and thus the appropriate institutional comparison should be between federal district courts and their state trial counterparts.

A second preparatory step is to dispel the notion that acknowledging a comparative advantage to federal courts need imply that state trial judges violate their oaths by consciously refusing to enforce federal rights. We are not faced today with widespread state judicial refusal to enforce clear federal rights. When the mandates of the Federal Constitution are clear, most state judges respect the supremacy clause and enforce them. Constitutional litigation is, however, rarely about clear law. The disputes which propel parties raising constitutional questions into court frequently pit strong legal and moral claims against each other and resolution of those competing "legitimate" claims is the real stuff of constitutional litigation. Thus, one need not intimate that state trial judges act in bad faith. Our comparison need only suggest that given the institutional differences between the two benches, state trial judges are less likely to resolve arguable issues in favor of protecting federal constitutional rights than are their federal brethren.

As a final preparatory step, another notion—that federal district judges, when called upon to enforce the fourteenth amendment against local officials, resemble an alien, occupying army dispatched from Washington to rule over a conquered province-must be dispelled. Federal judges are chosen from the geographical area they serve. Generally, they are appointed with the consent and often at the behest of a senator representing the state in which they will sit, frequently after local officials and citizen groups have had the opportunity to make their views on the nominee known. To characterize federal judges as carpetbaggers, unaware of, and insensitive to, local concerns is thus inaccurate and serves to deflect attention from the relative efficacy of state and federal forums in enforcing constitutional norms.

Concentrating, therefore, on an institutional comparison at the trial level, disclaiming any intent to cast aspersions on the good faith of state judges, and recognizing that both state and federal trial judges have roots in the communities they serve, three sets of reasons support a preference for a federal trial forum. First, the level of technical competence which the federal district court is likely to bring to the legal issues involved generally will be superior to that of a given state trial forum. Stated bluntly, in my experience, federal trial courts tend to be better equipped to analyze complex, often conflicting lines of authority and more likely to produce competently written, persuasive opinions than are state trial courts. Second, there are several factors, unrelated to technical competence—which, lacking a better term, I call a court's psychological set—that render it more likely that an individual with a constitutional claim will succeed in federal district court than in a state trial court. Finally, the federal judiciary's insulation from majoritarian pressures makes federal court structurally preferable to state trial court as a forum in which to challenge powerful local interests.

B. Technical Competence

Merely because federal judges feel constrained by legitimate considerations of comity from explicitly recognizing that a competence gap exists between the state and federal courts, that gap does not become any less real. It stems in part from the relative capacities of the judges themselves and, in part, from institutional factors unrelated to personal ability.

Because it is relatively small, the federal trial bench maintains a level of competence in its pool of potential appointees which dwarfs the competence of the vastly larger pool from which state trial judges are selected. There are about twice as many trial judges in California as in the entire federal system. As in any bureaucracy, it is far easier to maintain a high level of quality when appointing a relatively small number of officials than when staffing a huge department. Additionally, there is a substantial disparity between state and federal judicial compensation which allows the federal bench to attract a higher level of legal talent than state trial courts can hope to obtain.

The selection processes utilized to staff the respective judicial posts also incline toward a federal bench of higher professional distinction. While the federal selection process is not without flaws, it does focus substantially on the professional competence of the nominee. The selection processes for state trial courts are generally less concerned with gradations of professional competence once a minimum level has been attained. Neither elections nor an appointment process based largely on political patronage is calculated to make refined judgments on technical competence.

The competence gap does not stem solely from the differences in the native ability of the judges. While it is often overlooked, the caliber of judicial clerks exerts a substantial impact on the quality of judicial output. Federal clerks at both the trial and appellate levels are chosen from among the most promising recent law school graduates for one- to two-year terms. State trial clerks, on the other hand, when available at all, tend to be either career bureaucrats or patronage employees and may lack both the ability and dedication of their federal counterparts. Moreover, while the caseload burden of the federal courts is substantial, it pales when compared to the caseload of most state trial courts of general jurisdiction. Thus, even if state and federal judges were of equal native ability, the advantages enjoyed by federal judges would probably result in a higher level of performance. When those institutional advantages are combined with the differential in native ability, the competence gap becomes pronounced.

It is fair to ask why a civil liberties lawyer is particularly concerned about the relative competence of the possible forums. Even if a competence differential exists, would not an allegedly less competent state judge be as likely to err in favor of the lawyer's position as against it? Apart from esthetics, the answer is twofold. First, since constitutional decisions serve to guide third persons seeking to conform to constitutional norms, the clarity and persuasiveness of judicial opinions in constitutional cases assume great importance. A randomly correct decision by an inarticulate court, while welcome, is of far less value to the general protection of constitutional rights than the same decision by a court which can produce an eloquent and technically precise opinion to guide similarly situated persons.

Second, a technically less competent judge is not as likely to err on the side of the constitutional claimant as against him. Constitutional litigation generally involves an assault on an existing state of law or facts which enjoys the imprimatur of democratic decisionmaking, with the party asserting a constitutional claim bearing a substantial burden of explaining why the status quo should be changed. Since judicial failure to comprehend his claim renders it impossible to satisfy that heavy burden, the constitutional claimant will be generally disadvantaged in a forum of limited technical capacity.

More specifically, for the past two decades constitutional litigators have sought to implement principles inherent in a series of expansive constitutional interpretations by the Warren Court. Much of that effort has involved explaining to skeptical lower court judges why those decisions have altered much of the law they remember from law school. Our success has depended not only on our skill as advocates, but also on the technical proficiency of the trial court.

Clearly, if the Supreme Court retrenches from those expansive decisions, superior technical competence at the trial level may be as troublesome to future civil liberties lawyers seeking to enforce eroded precedents as it is currently attractive to those seeking to enforce viable ones. A possible future preference for a mistake-prone tribunal as an antidote to a less libertarian Supreme Court, of course, hardly constitutes a serious forum allocation argument. However, it does emphasize that technical competence is not synonymous with victory for a constitutional plaintiff. Yet, despite gloomy predictions, the current Court does not appear to be engaged in a wholesale reversal of the Warren Court's legacy. Thus, while trial level competence may be a future adversary of expansive constitutional enforcement, it remains a current ally.

C. Psychological Set

Even if state and federal forums were of equal technical competence, a series of psychological and attitudinal characteristics renders federal district judges more likely to enforce constitutional rights vigorously. First, although intangible, an elite tradition animates the federal judiciary, instilling elan and a sense of mission in federal judges and exerting, as Judge Friendly has noted, a palpable influence on the quality of the judicial product. As heirs of a tradition of constitutional enforcement, federal judges feel subtle, yet nonetheless real pressures to uphold that tradition. State trial judges, on the other hand, generally seem to lack a comparable sense of tradition or institutional mission.

Second, federal judges often display an enhanced sense of bureaucratic receptivity to the pronouncements of the Supreme Court. State judges, of course, almost always recognize that they too are bound not to disregard the Supreme Court's interpretation of the Federal Constitution. Their bureaucratic relationship with the Supreme Court is, however, more attenuated than that of a district court judge. Although the effects of this difference are difficult to isolate with certainty, in my experience federal judges appear to recognize an affirmative obligation to carry out and even anticipate the direction of the Supreme Court. Many state judges, on the other hand, appear to acknowledge only an obligation not to disobey clearly established law. While this distinction is subtle, in the doubtful case it can exert a discernible impact on the trial level outcome. Since civil liberties lawyers frequently are engaged in urging judges to recognize Supreme Court precedent, which, while not clearly dispositive, implies judgment for the constitutional plaintiff, the forum's recognition of an institutional duty to anticipate the as yet unexpressed views of the Supreme Court is critical.

Third, in seeking a federal forum, civil liberties lawyers hope to benefit from what can be described as an "ivory tower syndrome." The scope of federal jurisdiction, even taking account of that over federal crimes and habeas corpus, is such that federal judges are insulated from the more cynicism-breeding dimensions of constitutional law. State trial judges, conversely, especially at the criminal, family, and lower civil court levels, are steadily confronted by distasteful and troubling fact patterns which can sorely test abstract constitutional doctrine and foster a jaded attitude toward constitutional rights. The fourth amendment's exclusionary rule, for example, will command greater allegiance from a judge who has not been repeatedly exposed to the reality of the social harms inflicted by some felons whom the rule requires to be freed. Similarly, the right to hold a political demonstration or a union organizing rally will seem more obvious to a judge who need not face the disorderly conduct arrests which may arise from them. Distance from the pressures and emotions generated by the application of constitutional doctrine is conducive to a generous reading and vigorous enforcement of constitutional rights. For state trial courts, which ordinarily must be responsible both for law enforcement and the day to day implementation of constitutional rights, no such distance is possible. Federal trial judges, on the other hand, because of the limited nature of their jurisdiction, enjoy a degree of distance enhancing the likelihood that they will liberally and assiduously perform their function of enunciating constitutional norms.

Finally, the differences in the backgrounds of the state and federal trial judges make it more likely that a federal judge will possess certain class-based predilections favorable to constitutional enforcement than will his state court counterpart. The federal bench is an elite, prestigious body, drawn primarily from a successful, homogeneous socioeducational class—a class strongly imbued with the philosophical values of Locke and Mill (which the Bill of Rights in large measure tracks). As such, when a plaintiff asserts a constitutional claim against a state official whose socioeducational background does not include obeisance to that libertarian tradition, a federal judge generally will protect the threatened constitutional value.

This is not to say that judges consciously shape rulings in constitutional cases according to the defendant's social class. Rather, I suggest only that if the defendant and the judge are of the same socioeducational class, a judge will tend to trust that the defendant shares his values and thus will not feel compelled to enforce them vigorously. If the defendant deviates from the judge's class, however, no assumption of shared values will exist—and indeed a suspicion of contrary values may exist—leading to stronger enforcement of the judge's values in the guise of constitutional adjudication.

Most of the constitutional rights which civil liberties lawyers seek to protect fit snugly within nineteenth-century liberal thought. And since a class disparity between federal trial judges and the individual targets of constitutional enforcement is more likely than one between state trial judges and constitutional defendants, this class phenomenon will assist the constitutional plaintiff more often in the federal courts.

D. Insulation from Majoritarian Pressures

Constitutional adjudication inherently involves persuading a judicial forum to counter the will of the majority as expressed through its representatives. To the extent that the forum is itself subject to the political pressures which shaped the judgment it is asked to review, its capacity to provide sustained enforcement of countermajoritarian constitutional norms will be diminished. When one compares the institutional structure of the federal trial bench with state court structures, the functional superiority of federal courts as checks on majoritarian excess is pronounced.

Federal district judges, appointed for life and removable only by impeachment, are as insulated from majoritarian pressures as is functionally possible, precisely to insure their ability to enforce the Constitution without fear of reprisal. State trial judges, on the other hand, generally are elected for a fixed term, rendering them vulnerable to majoritarian pressure when deciding constitutional cases. Thus, when arguable grounds supporting the majoritarian position exist, state trial judges are far more likely to embrace them than are federal judges. This insulation factor, I suggest, explains the historical preference for federal enforcement of controversial constitutional norms. While the level of hostility towards any given constitutional decision varies from locality to locality, from issue to issue, and over time, constitutional adjudication still frequently involves issues which raise strong political passions. Insulation from political pressures may not be necessary in all constitutional cases; yet, where such pressures are strong, insulated judicial forums are necessary if constitutional rights are to remain viable.

E. Some Costs of the Federal Forum Preference

Opting for a federal forum in constitutional cases admittedly entails some costs. First, an insulated federal judge may be less sensitive to the social milieu into which his decisions must fit and thus less successful in shaping decisions and remedies to the reality of that milieu. That danger, however, is minimized by the fact that "insulated" federal judges are typically drawn from, and well acquainted with, the locality in which they sit. Even so, the decisions of a politically insulated federal judge may encounter greater public resistance than the same decisions rendered by a politically accountable state judge. Clearly, to the extent that constitutional norms are enforced by a forum sensitive to the majority will, the chances of public acceptance are enhanced. Conversely, by entrusting constitutional adjudication to federal trial forums perceived as free from majoritarian influence, a measure of public acceptance is lost. That loss, however, seems necessary to insure the existence of a forum capable of protecting individual rights in the face of local political dissatisfaction.

Second, by urging a broad option to invoke federal jurisdiction in constitutional cases, civil rights lawyers exacerbate an already difficult caseload burden in the federal courts. One factor rendering federal courts desirable is their superior technical competence. Yet a failure to remedy the overburdening of the federal trial courts threatens precisely that capacity for excellence. While the caseload problem cannot be dismissed, several responses do exist. Although its small size is important in maintaining both a high level of professional ability and an elite sense of institutional mission, the current federal bench could be substantially enlarged without compromising either attribute. More fundamentally, the major justification for a system of lower federal courts is the protection of federal rights. Before that basic function is curtailed, substantial savings of federal judicial time could and should be effected by eliminating archaic heads of federal jurisdiction which lack contemporary social purpose. Moreover, barring a given case from the federal courts does not mean its disappearance. Rather, it likely will reappear on an already overcrowded state court docket. Limiting access to the federal courts, therefore, does not really solve the problem of overburdened judges. The burden is merely shifted to institutions which are often even less able to cope with the caseload.

Third, by assuming state court inferiority and by seeking to funnel important constitutional cases into federal trial courts, civil liberties lawyers may be engaged in self-fulfilling prophecy which helps perpetuate the second-class status and performance of state trial courts. Clearly, if significant constitutional cases were forced into state courts more frequently, state judges would acquire greater expertise and sensitivity in the area and would probably develop an enhanced sense of institutional responsibility for the enforcement of constitutional rights. Moreover, over time the competence gap might diminish, since such a regime would likely engender pressure from the bar and the public for upgrading the quality and the prestige of state trial benches. That, of course, would be all to the good. Channeling more cases into the state courts, however, would have no impact on their vulnerability to majoritarian pressures. Indeed, it would be likely to increase (and certainly cannot decrease) the extent to which state trial judges are exposed to such pressures. And even if state courts could be upgraded by a force feeding of constitutional cases, such an avenue of judicial reform may well require the sacrifice of several waves of litigants in the hope of achieving subsequent improvements. Where constitutional rights are at stake, that is, to my mind, too great a risk to run in order to improve the state courts.

* * *

Susan N. Herman, *Beyond Parity: Section 1983 and the State Courts,* 54 Brooklyn Law Review 1057 (1989)

State court is the new frontier of civil rights litigation. As the Supreme Court has been cutting back on the substance of federal constitutional rights and the availability of federal court relief, prospective plaintiffs have been turning to the state courts for vindication of their rights. These federal court refugees rely on state constitutional claims if they need a haven from restrictive federal constitutional doctrine, but, more and more frequently, they simply bring their federal claims to state court under the aegis of 42 U.S.C. section 1983.

The rapid proliferation of section 1983 actions brought in state rather than federal court is easy to understand. Although state courts might not be required to entertain section 1983 actions, they do have concurrent jurisdiction to do so, and most states have agreed to exercise this concurrent jurisdiction. Plaintiff's attorneys now frequently add a section 1983 claim to what would otherwise be a state tort action — adding a fourth amendment based police misconduct claim to a battery action when police brutality is alleged, or a due process claim to a wrongful discharge action when a government employee has been fired — because in this way they can consolidate related state and federal claims in one action, because state court may be more familiar or convenient to the attorney than federal court, and because a victory on a section 1983 claim brings with it the coveted right to collect attorney's fees.

A federal statute in state court is an awkward guest. Two different sets of governing rules compete, each with a strong argument for its own applicability. Should a state court hearing a federal section 1983 claim seek to mimic the procedures a federal court would have followed in hearing the same claim, or should it follow the procedures it would have followed (or possibly will be following) in hearing the state law analogue of the claim? It is clear that the state courts must follow the "substance" of section 1983 and, at least in some circumstances, may follow their own "procedure," but long experience in diversity cases and in other areas of concurrent jurisdiction teaches that this distinction is more a restatement of the problem than a resolution of it. Are strict pleading rules procedural? Are allocations of burdens of proof or the relative responsibilities of judge and jury procedural?

Other issues, less familiar from the past, also arise. May a state court apply a state notice of claim statute which would not have been applied in a parallel federal court section 1983 action in that jurisdiction? May a state court, following its usual court rules, refuse a section 1983 plaintiff a jury trial in a category of case in which a jury trial would have been available in a parallel federal court proceeding? On the other hand, may a state court apply an unusually generous standing doctrine and hear the section 1983 claim of a plaintiff the federal courts would have turned away? Does it matter whether the federal court would have denied the plaintiff standing on the basis of prudential concerns, or because of the restrictions of article III, in which case the state court's decision on a matter of federal law would be unreviewable by the Supreme Court?

These questions and many others like them are inevitable. They are also inevitably difficult for two reasons. First, the answers to these questions depend on the intent of Congress in an area in which Congress has been particularly inscrutable. Second, even if Congress wished to create a new statute to address these questions, it is not easy to resolve the conflicting policies at stake or to draw clear lines in this area. The Supreme Court, working in the absence of articulated congressional intent, has provided answers to several questions about what collateral law state courts may or must use in section 1983 actions, but has not provided a cogent theoretical basis for answering the questions remaining. Thus, the brunt of the problem of deciding what procedures and principles to apply to state court section 1983 actions is being borne by state court judges and litigators, who have been discovering the truth of Hart's observation, in a similar context, that "[p]eople repeatedly subjected, like Pavlov's dogs, to two or more inconsistent sets of directions, without means of resolving the inconsistencies, could not fail in the end to react as the dogs did."

* * *

B. *Congress, Concurrent Jurisdiction, and Section 1983*

Congress has not explicitly addressed the issue of the role of the state courts in section 1983 litigation. However, several sources provide some basis for judging Congress's views on the interests section 1983 was intended to further, the role of state law, and the significance of uniformity: the history of section 1983 itself and its presumptive grant of concurrent jurisdiction to the state courts; 42 U.S.C. section 1988, which provides for choice of law in federal court section 1983 actions; and 28 U.S.C. section 1441, which permits civil rights defendants to remove section 1983 actions to federal court. The legislative history of section 1983 supports an inference that the 42nd Congress not only wished to promote civil rights, but also would have wished to encourage the state courts to litigate their own civil rights disputes. Section 1988, at least as interpreted by the Supreme Court, shows a Congress not unwilling to allow diversity in section 1983 litigation and expressly advocating the use of some state law in adjudication of this federal right. The removal statute, surprisingly and probably accidentally, enhances the role of the federal forum by allowing civil rights defendants to undercut plaintiffs' choice of forum when a plaintiff has made the choice Congress did not expect, and remitting to the federal courts cases that both the plaintiff and the state court wish the state court to hear.

1. The Purposes of Section 1983 and Concurrent Jurisdiction

It is accepted gospel that Congress's main aims in enacting the Civil Rights Act of 1871, the predecessor of section 1983 and its companions, were three: (1) to override certain kinds of state laws when those laws prevented the vindication of civil rights; (2) to provide a remedy where state law was inadequate, as where blacks were incompetent to testify against white men who committed crimes against them; and (3) to provide a federal remedy where the state remedy, although adequate in theory, was not available in practice. The third aim has been characterized by the Supreme Court as the broadest and the most important of Congress's goals.

The question of whether Congress intended federal justiciability principles and procedures to apply to state court section 1983 litigation is complicated by the fact that most members of Congress apparently did not "intend" the state courts to entertain section 1983 actions at all, at least not in the usual sense of the word. When the 42nd Congress created section 1983 and its companion civil rights statutes, state court was part of the problem rather than the solution. As the fourteenth amendment already provided sufficient ammunition for dealing with restrictive state laws, it does seem fair to say that the chief impetus for section 1983 was to provide a federal court forum and federal remedies for those unable to vindicate their federal civil rights in state court. Among the obstacles to state court relief cited in the legislative debates were the biases of state prosecutors, juries, and even judges. Federal court, where judges enjoyed life tenure and, hence, better insulation from political pressure, and where discriminatory state statutes and procedures could be sidestepped, provided an opportunity to overcome these obstacles.

Because the Supreme Court operates on a presumption of concurrent jurisdiction, state court jurisdiction over section 1983 actions derives from what Congress did not say. The legislative history of section 1983 bears only several passing references to the awareness of particular congressmen that the state courts might be able to entertain section 1983 actions, and no discussion of why or how section 1983 actions were to be treated in state court.

There are many compelling reasons for assuming that Congress, had it considered the issue, would have decided to allow, indeed to encourage, state court litigation of section 1983 actions. One common justification for conferring exclusive federal jurisdiction is a desire for nationwide uniformity of result, a goal inapposite in section 1983 litigation where the issues involved concern the intrastate conduct of state and local officials. Permitting concurrent jurisdiction provides for greater availability of relief in civil rights actions and, thus, generally promotes the purposes underlying section 1983. Section 1983 was created to provide a forum for those who could not obtain relief from their state courts. If the state courts are in fact available, and even preferable to a civil rights plaintiff, there is no reason why that plaintiff should be denied the opportunity to bring such an action in state court, or the state court denied the opportunity to hear it.

This result also promotes interests of comity and federalism. Because section 1983 provides a cause of action against state officials alleged to have deprived individuals of their federal civil rights, federal court adjudication of section 1983 claims is frequently seen as potentially or actually intrusive upon the states' power. Federal judges and their critics alike have often felt uncomfortable about the prospect of federal courts sitting in judgment on state officials or implementing decrees compelling state officials to take or refrain from certain actions. It was the experience of federal judges intimately involved in the day-to-day operations of state institutions, such as prisons and hospitals, that led the current Supreme Court to fashion doctrines curtailing federal court intervention. Rightly or wrongly, the Supreme Court has been very sensitive to the urgings of comity and federalism in decisions cutting back the scope of federal court involvement with state officials' civil rights violations, and Congress has acceded.

These same concerns favor encouraging the state courts to police their own state's errant officials if they will do so. There is no comity or federalism problem if a state court finds a state official guilty of a civil rights violation, or if it enforces a detailed decree concerning the operation of a state prison or hospital. The federal courts would be liberated from part of what many view as a burdensome caseload, while the state courts would accept responsibility as guardians of the federal Constitution.

Encouraging state court civil rights litigation also serves the important function of allowing more efficient litigation of civil rights cases. The substantial overlap of section 1983 actions and state tort actions has already been noted, as has the fact that a plaintiff who wishes to consolidate state and federal claims arising out of a single incident may only be able to do so in state court. In light of the ever increasing number of restrictions on the availability of federal relief, encouraging plaintiffs to litigate in state court may be the only way to avoid duplicative litigation.

Given all of these rationales for concurrent jurisdiction — comity, efficiency of adjudication, plaintiff's choice of forum, and expansion of remedies for civil rights violation — and the fact that Congress only created a federal remedy to address what it saw as the states' abdication of the responsibility to entertain civil rights litigation, it seems clear that the state courts should be encouraged to exercise their concurrent jurisdiction as much as possible.

* * *

II. The Theoretical Structure

The subject of this section is how the choice of collateral law issues in state court section 1983 actions should be handled. The previous section demonstrated that expressed congressional intent does not resolve this question. If Congress wished to become more explicit about its views, it could enact a new statute, select a standard (favoring Hart or Neuborne, for example) or address some particular issues, like those previously discussed in Section I. Whether Congress elucidates its intent or not, these issues will have to be addressed by the courts on a case-by-case basis.

In *Felder v. Casey*, the Supreme Court began the process of formulating its own approach to these questions. Despite the Court's misleading portrayal of its decision as a simple matter of implementing congressional intent, what the Court actually did in *Felder*, as it must do in any similar case, was to balance the relative state and federal interests involved. Because the *Felder* Court did not acknowledge this, it did not discuss the state and federal interests actually at stake, and in fact appeared to adopt a cavalier attitude toward the state's interest, finding that the state's interest is "not material" in a supremacy clause inquiry. Both the federal and state interests involved are more complex than the Court's opinion suggests and deserve a much more open and honest appraisal. In addition, the Court has posited that uniformity is an important interest that weighs heavily in the balance. If this preoccupation with uniformity abates, as I argue it should, the real question is whether the relative state and federal interests warrant an approach closer to Hart's, allowing the states to use their own procedures unless they are distinctly in contravention of federal purposes, or an approach closer to Neuborne's, requiring the states to use federal procedures whenever plaintiffs' prospects in civil rights litigation would thereby be enhanced.

My conclusion, somewhere in the middle, but probably closer to the position I have characterized as Hart's, is that the states should be permitted to use their own neutral procedures so long as those procedures are not so inconsistent with the purposes of section 1983 as to warrant judicial exercise of the supremacy clause, regardless of whether those procedures are more or less generous to plaintiffs than federal procedure would have been.

In this section, I will discuss the federal and state interests in the balance, and how they are served or disserved by each of these paradigms. I will then address to what extent other considerations, such as the need for uniformity or concern with efficiency of adjudication, should enter the balance. In the following section, I will discuss the validity of answering the questions posed here by referring to precedent in two purportedly analogous areas of the law — the FELA concurrent jurisdiction cases, and the "mirror image" *Erie* cases.

A. *The Balance of Interests*

1. Defining the Federal Interest and Choosing a Standard

The initial question is how the federal interest at stake should be defined: in terms of the ultimate goal of deterring civil rights violations, or in terms of the broader instrumental goal of enabling more plaintiffs to win civil rights cases? Is the federal interest at stake here an interest in preventing the states from applying state laws that defeat federal rights, or in compelling the states to apply federal laws that enhance federal rights?

In *Felder*, the difference between these two inquiries was not significant because the notice of claim provision falls into the former category — a state law that tended to annihilate the federal right by disabling plaintiffs from bringing suit at all. Examples of procedures falling into the other category include Professor Neuborne's example of class action rules, or discovery rules and rules of evidence. If a state has restrictive class action rules, civil rights plaintiffs would certainly benefit if the state court were to adopt more generous federal class action law. But is it fair to say that less generous state class action rules defeat the rights protected by section 1983? It may be that fewer plaintiffs will prevail in section 1983 claims due to a state court's refusal to certify a class, but it is unlikely that state or local officials will thereby be encouraged to more freely violate civil rights, especially given the fact that those plaintiffs could have circumvented the state rules by going to federal court.

Given Congress's silence, I think the Court should opt for the more modest definition of the federal interest at stake, which yields more room for accommodating the state courts' interests and general concerns of federalism. If a state law can be fairly characterized as inconsistent with section 1983, as was the case in *Felder* and in *Martinez*, then it is proper for the Supreme Court to use the supremacy clause to prohibit the state from applying that law. Further, if Congress has specified a particular procedure it wishes to compel the state courts to use — as the Court believed Congress had done in singling out the attorney's fees provision of section 1988 — then it is proper for the Court to compel the state court to use that procedure. But if Congress has not specified that a particular collateral rule is to be considered part of section 1983, and if it cannot be fairly said that a state collateral rule is inconsistent with the deterrent goal of section 1983, then I do not think the Supreme Court should exercise the power of supremacy clause to compel the states to follow federal collateral law simply because that law would benefit civil rights plaintiffs. To that extent, I find Hart's theory that concurrent jurisdiction assumes a choice between two different procedural systems persuasive. As long as a fair federal forum is available, there is little risk that illegal conduct by the class of potential defendants will be encouraged by procedural disadvantages plaintiffs might encounter in state court.

2. The State's Interests

The Court's remark in *Felder* that the state's interests were "not material" must be read in the context of that case. The state's principal interest in the notice of claim statute was in protecting its subdivisions and officials from the very liability section 1983 imposes. If Congress wishes to impose liability, and the state's interest is to avoid liability, then the state's interest may be disregarded as illegitimate. This is apparently what the Court meant by declaring the state's interest to be immaterial to the supremacy clause inquiry.

If the state's interest is not legitimate, or if the state's use of an apparently neutral procedural rule does in fact discriminate against federal claim plaintiffs, the balance is clear and the federal interest must prevail. But what of a case in which the state has legitimate interests that do not join issue with congressional intent? If, for example, a state wishes to use its usual restrictive class action rules, discovery rules, or rules of evidence only because they are efficient and familiar (and perhaps because these rules are being followed with respect to another claim in the same case), should that state interest be deemed "not material'? The Court in *Felder* several times distinguishes the notice of claim provision from a "neutral and uniform applicable rule of procedure." Presumably, the state's interest in following its own procedural rules is cognizable and should enter the balance when the Court is considering whether to override a state procedure. These interests include the state court's interest in following its own rules because those rules are familiar, because they are the rules possibly being applied to other claims in the same case and, therefore, will promote efficient litigation, because the rules may be well adapted to that particular state or court, and because of the dignitary interest the states have in making their own procedural decisions.

It is difficult to predict how heavily the Supreme Court would weigh these state housekeeping interests and correlative federalism concerns as against the federal interests involved. The Court's attitude toward the significance of such procedural interests has been wildly inconsistent, varying from context to context. Federalism concerns do argue for allowing the state courts some leeway to use their own procedures, and efficiency argues for allowing the states to use their accustomed rules in multiclaim litigation. But these concerns must yield when a state procedure actually is inconsistent with the purposes of section 1983.

3. Uniformity

Prominent in the Court's opinion in *Felder*, as in the section 1988 cases discussed previously, is the notion that collateral law followed in federal and state court section 1983 actions should be identical for the sake of intrastate uniformity. The Court deplores the possibility that the same case might turn out differently in state or federal court because of a difference in the two jurisdictions' collateral law. This concern too should be confined to its context. If the reason the cases would turn out differently is that the state has an outcome-determinative law that prevents plaintiff from bringing a claim, then it has already been established that the state should not be permitted to apply that inconsistent law. But if the case turns out differently because a seemingly neutral procedure has in fact disadvantaged the plaintiff — or, for that matter, disadvantaged the defendant — is that a problem? Is there really some independent value to parity of procedure between state and federal court in section 1983 actions? I doubt it.

Uniformity is both served and disserved whichever choice of procedure is made. If state court section 1983 actions look like federal court section 1983 actions, they achieve that uniformity at the price of uniformity with other state court actions (often including a tort claim joined in the same case). If state court actions follow state procedure, the price is sacrificing some procedural uniformity with actions in the federal court sitting within that same state. The value of applying uniform procedures in a state court case containing section 1983 and other state law claims is obvious. Litigation is simplified and the possibility of contradictory commands is avoided. Borrowing federal procedure on one out of two or three claims in a case might lead to a situation in which the federal claim is entitled to class action treatment, or a jury trial, and the state claims are not. Must there be two trials, or might the plaintiff get a jury trial on a state law issue simply because section 1983 was invoked in the complaint? These issues are troubling to the state courts, as well as to attorneys confronting these procedural imbroglios.

The virtues of federal/state uniformity are somewhat more elusive. Disparity in procedure has several possible negative effects. First, defendants might feel encouraged to violate the civil rights of potential plaintiffs if state procedure makes it too difficult for a plaintiff to succeed in a civil rights action. As noted previously, it would be foolish for defendants to change their behavior if plaintiff could avoid procedural difficulties by simply choosing federal court.

Disparity of procedure might itself be considered problematic. If a plaintiff in a state court section 1983 action could not bring a class action when a plaintiff in a federal court section 1983 action with the same claim could, is this asymmetry more than an aesthetic concern? The Supreme Court suggests that such disparity may threaten interests of federalism. If state procedures are less favorable than federal procedures, plaintiffs will bring their section 1983 actions in federal rather than state court, despite the earlier conclusion that state court adjudication of section 1983 actions should be encouraged. But uniformity trims the good as well as the bad. Plaintiffs may be tempted by state court procedures as well as repelled. The central aim of federalism is to give the states enough room to follow their own paths. If a state is offended by the fact that too many plaintiffs are turning to federal court to litigate their section 1983 actions, the solution is simple. The state courts or legislatures may offer procedures as attractive as they wish — unless they are constricted by federally imposed uniformity.

Another reason to be concerned about federal/state uniformity is fear of forum shopping. Deploring forum shopping is a principal activity of some diversity cases, on the apparent assumption that forum shopping is an unmitigated evil. But what is wrong with forum shopping? Section 1983 was enacted to provide plaintiffs with an opportunity to shop for a forum in a situation in which the states had an unwholesome monopoly. Even in diversity cases, the evil reputation of forum shopping has been questioned. The opportunity to select a forum is an integral feature of any concurrent jurisdiction statute. Concurrent jurisdiction in this context is, as Professor Neuborne says, a "self-correcting constitutional compass," because plaintiffs will choose the forum they consider more promising. The abhorrence of forum shopping in the diversity cases derives from comity concerns not present in this context. It may be undesirable to divert litigation of state law disputes to federal court by promising procedures advantageous to plaintiffs, but there is no comity problem if advantageous procedures attract civil rights plaintiffs with federal claims to state court.

Furthermore, the prospect of eliminating forum shopping is illusory. Total uniformity between federal and state court in section 1983 litigation is unachievable. Even if Congress were to make clear its desire to apply federal collateral rules broadly, there would still be significant differences between the state and federal forum that Congress would be unable or unlikely to do anything about. Among the features of federal court that might continue to attract plaintiffs are the life tenure of federal judges, and some of the other institutional characteristics Professor Neuborne has enumerated. Among the unique features of state court section 1983 litigation are the inapplicability of the eleventh amendment, which might enable a state court plaintiff to sue the state or to collect money unavailable in a federal court proceeding; the inapplicability of restrictions like the tax anti-injunction statute, which leaves the state court as the only possible forum in some cases challenging state tax systems or decision; the inapplicability of the equitable restraint doctrine of *Younger v. Harris* and succeeding cases; and the probable inapplicability of other federal doctrines limiting injunctive relief. There will and should be forum shopping, so the desire for federal/state uniformity as an antidote does not provide a strong reason to modify state procedures or collateral rules.

Professor Neuborne, the chief proponent of procedural parity between state and federal courts, rests his argument not on the inherent desirability of parity, and certainly not on any dislike of forum shopping, but rather on the assumption that federal collateral law generally is superior to state collateral law in ways that will promote civil rights litigation. Professor Neuborne draws this conclusion because of his focus on examples, like the federal class action rules, in which federal collateral law would be more attractive to plaintiffs. It is certainly true that in particular instances federal law will favor civil rights plaintiffs, but I do not think that the superiority of federal collateral law provides a strong basis for arguing for procedural parity with federal court generally. Whatever may have been the case in earlier decades, federal collateral law is now less notable for its favorable attitude toward civil rights litigation. Professor Neuborne's self-avowed preference for federal court as an institutional matter is more and more under siege as the Supreme Court riddles federal court civil rights litigation with doctrines limiting federal relief. Standing, the *Pennhurst* doctrine, the expanding *Younger v. Harris* doctrine, and many more developments in a list that could consume pages, plague federal court section 1983 plaintiffs. If the true goal is not parity but promotion of civil rights by advantaging civil rights plaintiffs, wholesale imposition of federal collateral law is becoming a less productive means of serving that goal.

Given that state court section 1983 plaintiffs have a choice of forum and that imposing procedural consistency with federal court will mean sacrificing consistency within the state courts as well as the prospect of state courts developing procedures beneficial to plaintiffs, the desirability of federal/state uniformity should not shift the balance of the relative state and federal interests at stake. Even if the Court's section 1988 decisions do not misconstrue congressional intent in their urge for uniformity in federal court section 1983 litigation, the concern for the type of uniformity reflected in those cases is not a valid goal in the state court context. A more worthwhile goal, cited by the Supreme Court as a desirable consequence of uniformity, is eliminating the prospect of unnecessary litigation over which procedure to use. Serving this goal requires not uniformity but predictability. Any approach providing predictability will serve this goal, regardless of whether it dictates results uniform among state courts, among federal and state courts, or some combination of the two.

If uniformity is read out as an important goal, if the federal interest at stake is defined as deterring civil rights violations, and if the state interest in using its own procedure is factored into the balance, the Court should tend to allow the states to use their own collateral law in areas like class action rules and rules of evidence. The Court so far has not seemed to indulge in any presumption in favor of allowing the states to use their own procedure, in part because of its generous view of the propriety of creating federal common law under section 1983, and in part because of its reliance on cases in areas of the law in which the need for uniformity and the relative state and federal interests at stake are different.

* * *

III. Getting Down to Cases

Previous sections discussed the extent to which Congress or the Supreme Court should impose federal collateral law on the state courts in section 1983 actions. This section will consider the perspective of state court judges, who have a freer choice in evaluating the same concerns. Just as Congress can decline to exercise its presumed power to compel the state courts to adopt federal collateral law, the state courts or legislatures are free to borrow as much federal collateral law as they wish, at least where that federal law would benefit civil rights plaintiffs.

It is easy to conclude that if disparate state collateral law benefits plaintiffs, the state courts are free to use that law. The federal interest in serving the goals of section 1983 and the state's interest in following its own procedure coalesce, with only the previously discredited interest in uniformity on the other side of the scales. The problem arises when neutral state collateral law is less favorable to plaintiffs, and the state courts view a legitimate state interest in using accustomed procedure as strong enough to warrant using the state law anyway.

State court judges can prevent such crises from arising by selecting procedures that will make state court at least as hospitable a forum for civil rights litigants as federal court. This posture will better serve the state's interests in the long run because if state courts become plaintiffs' primary choice for conducting civil rights litigation, the friction of federal court intervention into state affairs will be eased. However, if a state procedure is neutral, not inconsistent with the goals of section 1983 and serves a strong enough legitimate state interest that the state courts wish to insist on its application, allowing the state courts to apply a procedure plaintiffs might dislike may be simply the other side of the coin of allowing state court generosity.

A. *Differences in Federal/State Justiciability Doctrine*

When the state collateral law at issue is a justiciability doctrine, which will generally be easily categorized as favoring or disfavoring plaintiffs, application of these principles is fairly simple. If a state wishes to confer standing on a plaintiff the federal courts would not have heard, it should certainly be allowed to do so; if it wishes to deny standing to a plaintiff the federal courts would have heard, the state's doctrine is likely to be inconsistent with federal law. There are also several exceptional situations that deserve comment. May a state follow its own generous justiciability doctrine if it would then be rendering a decision not subject to review by the Supreme Court? On the other hand, may a state apply an unfavorable justiciability doctrine in a case in which a federal forum would have been unavailable for other reasons?

1. State Doctrine Tending to Benefit Plaintiffs

a. *Collateral Law*

Only a fanatical advocate of intrastate uniformity would suggest that the state courts should follow all of the collateral restrictions applicable to federal courts in section 1983 litigation. By their very terms, constitutional provisions like article III's case or controversy requirement or the eleventh amendment apply only to the federal courts. Limitations derived from these provisions, like the restrictions on the availability of federal injunctive relief declared in *Pennhurst State School & Hospital v. Halderman*, and *City of Los Angeles v. Lyons*, or the standing restrictions of *Warth v. Seldin*, therefore need not apply in state court. Neither should restrictions on federal injunctive relief based on prudential concerns of federalism and comity that, like the eleventh amendment, are simply inapplicable in state court. The only basis for arguing that state courts should follow these federal principles would be the urge for uniformity. But even the argument for uniformity is undercut where a federal forum is unavailable, because disparate results in identical cases are as impossible in this situation as forum shopping. In contexts, like *Felder*, in which state courts are required to adopt more generous federal law, the compulsory uniformity serves federalism in one way by ensuring that the state courts will continue to attract a fair share of civil rights litigation, even as it disserves another conception of a federalist model by preventing the states from employing their usual procedures. To prevent a state from using its own more generous collateral law would not serve any purpose.

What if a state court does not wish to afford the benefit of a more generous state justiciability doctrine to section 1983 plaintiffs? One New Jersey court, for example, seemed to suggest that its state's generous standing doctrine in exclusionary zoning cases might be available in claims under the state but not the federal Constitution. I think this is another example of the well-intentioned but misguided striving for uniformity with federal court, even in an instance where plaintiffs would benefit from disparate treatment. There is no reason, uniformity aside, for a state court adjudicating federal claims to adopt a limiting justiciability doctrine that arose out of the federal courts' concern with their proper role in a federalist system. If the state shared the federal courts' concerns — perhaps as a matter of state separation of powers principles — presumably its justiciability doctrine would not be so generous to plaintiffs, and there would be little choice to make.

In fact, there is some basis for arguing that not only *may* the state court apply its own more generous doctrine, but it *must*. Failure to do so might be considered discrimination against a plaintiff with a federal claim. If the state courts must worry that by failing to apply federal collateral rules in section 1983 actions they might run afoul of the supremacy clause, the antidiscrimination doctrine is a constitutional Charybdis. An old line of cases establishes, presumably also on the authority of the supremacy clause, that a state court may not refuse to hear a federal cause of action when it has jurisdiction over analogous causes of action. If a state court may not be less generous to plaintiffs with federal claims than to those with state claims, should this principle extend to prohibit a state court from denying federal statutory litigants the benefit of procedures it would afford litigants with a state cause of action? Under this theory, once it is determined that a particular doctrine, such as a standing doctrine, is not part of the substance of section 1983, the state courts would be required to apply their usual doctrine, at least where that doctrine is more favorable to section 1983 plaintiffs than federal law would be.

While I doubt that the Court would extend the antidiscrimination doctrine to compel state courts to afford civil rights plaintiffs the benefit of more generous state justiciability principles, the state courts nevertheless should be wary of such discrimination and should offer their own more generous collateral law to federal claim plaintiffs rather than pursue a foolish consistency with federal court.

b. *Noncollateral Law*

The foregoing discussion has focused on doctrines, like standing, presumed to be extrinsic to section 1983 and, therefore, offering the state courts room to maneuver. The Supreme Court has posited that once federal common law has been created in a given area, the states may be neither more nor less generous than federal law provides. This was the explanation, in *Monessen Southwestern Ry. Co. v. Morgan*, for refusing to allow a state court to afford an FELA plaintiff prejudgment interest on a damages claim. If a state court hearing a section 1983 action wished to award prejudgment interest, the existence of federal common law on damages under section 1983 presumably would stymie that generous impulse also.

The more expansively the Court interprets section 1983 and its concomitant common law, the less opportunity the state courts have to afford civil rights plaintiffs the benefit of advantageous state law. Even doctrines now considered collateral, like standing, might be federalized if the Court were to decide to interpret the availability of injunctive relief, for example, as being a matter of "statutory interpretation" of section 1983. *Lyons*, for example, could be characterized as a restriction on the availability of injunctive relief rather than as a doctrine derived from article III or prudential concerns only applicable in federal court. The nationalized doctrine would then bind the state courts. This situation is undesirable because the interests of both the state courts and civil rights plaintiffs are disserved.

There are two approaches the Court might take to avoid glorifying uniformity above all other interests. First, the Court could exercise restraint in "interpreting" section 1983 and make more liberal use of section 1988's direction to use hospitable state law in *federal* court section 1983 actions. This would leave space for the state courts to create plaintiff oriented law concerning justiciability and remedies. Decisions restraining state court generosity could be narrowly construed. Further, decisions resting on uniquely federal considerations could be restricted in their applicability to *federal* court section 1983 actions. The cases creating a federal common law of damages and immunities were, for the most part, decided in the context of federal court section 1983 actions, where providing a uniform federal common law is less intrusive and more desirable than in the context of state court. These cases might be distinguished in the state court context.

The other possible solution is truly radical. The state courts could be given license to apply even the "substance" of section 1983 in any way at least as generous to plaintiffs as federal doctrine. The state courts would then be permitted to use a more generous damages rule, immunity doctrine, or statute of limitations, and perhaps even to expand the scope of section 1983 by entertaining actions based on a theory of *respondeat superior*, or permitting suits against entities not considered "persons" under section 1983. Professor Sager has proposed that state courts be permitted to be more generous in interpreting federal constitutional provisions underenforced by the federal courts. The same proposal could be applied to section 1983, as an underenforced federal statute.

This is not a proposal the Supreme Court is likely to adopt. Awareness of the problems created by blanket federal rules, however, should lead the Court to consider carefully whether there really is a need to federalize any more of the collateral law surrounding section 1983 litigation, and whether it would indeed be desirable to federalize less.

2. Article III and Supreme Court Review

If the state courts do hear cases the federal courts would be unable to hear, however broadly that power is defined, an additional problem is posed if the state courts hear a case deemed not to present a case or controversy under article III. This was ostensibly the case with the standing doctrine of *City of Los Angeles v. Lyons*. Should a state court be free to reject the restrictive views of *Lyons* despite the fact that its decision would be unreviewable by the Supreme Court?

The Supreme Court has been unwilling to review cases not presenting a case or controversy, but also has been unwilling to vacate state court decisions in such cases simply because of the unavailability of Supreme Court review.

In *Doremus v. Board of Education*, a state taxpayer was initially granted standing in state court to challenge a state statute providing for Bible reading in the schools. The Supreme Court declared itself unable to review the case in light of its previous determination that such taxpayer standing is insufficient to satisfy article III. The Court then dismissed the appeal, remarking, "We do not undertake to say that a state court may not render an opinion on a federal constitutional question even under such circumstances that it can be regarded only as advisory."

I think that the Court was right in *Doremus* and that there is no good reason for resolving that a state court cannot hear a federal claim simply because the Supreme Court will be unable to review it. Why should there not be "advisory" state court opinions about the constitutionality of a Bible reading statute, or of an affirmative action program in that state? Uniformity of state court results with federal court results is not, for the reasons already described, a good reason to impose the limitations of article III on the state courts.

A state's highest court already has the final word in interpreting the provisions of its own constitution. Because of the adequate state ground doctrine, these state constitutional rulings are not subject to Supreme Court review. Why should the lack of availability of Supreme Court review of similar cases for a different reason — article III — prevent the state courts from rendering advisory opinions to the officials of its own state as to what the federal Constitution would require in circumstances the federal courts would have difficulty considering?

If states were permitted to hear section 1983 claims unreviewable under article III, it is unlikely that the power would be abused. Section 1983 was created precisely because most states were perceived as being unreceptive to civil rights claims. Commentators are still deploring restrictive state justiciability doctrine and its impact on federal civil rights litigation. The state court would have the opportunity to render an unreviewable federal constitutional decision only if the state's usual justiciability doctrine were more beneficial to plaintiffs than federal doctrine. A state adventurous enough to have created a generous standing doctrine would, in all likelihood, have reached a similar result on the basis of a state law claim. Is it likely that permitting New Jersey courts hearing section 1983 exclusionary zoning cases to utilize a broader theory of standing than *Warth*, or California courts hearing police misconduct cases to entertain a claim for injunctive relief that would be barred by *Lyons*, would significantly change the law in those jurisdictions? The potential defendants are not likely to be affected, and the prospective plaintiffs will be encouraged to bring their actions in state rather than federal court.

2. State Court Doctrine Tending to Disadvantage Plaintiffs

In the previous section, benefits to civil rights plaintiffs lined up with the state's interest in the integrity of its own procedures and other interests to present a very strong case for permitting a state to use its own generous justiciability doctrine in section 1983 actions. But what if state justiciability doctrine is different in a way that disadvantages plaintiffs?

a. *Preclusive Justiciability Doctrine*

If a state's unique justiciability doctrine prevents a state court section 1983 plaintiff from bringing a case the federal courts would have heard — if the state has a special standing requirement, or a restrictive mootness doctrine, for example — it might be said, as the Court suggested in *Felder*, that the doctrine is "outcome-determinative," imposes an inordinate burden on federal rights and may not be used. This is a relatively easy rule when applied to justiciability doctrines, which will tend to be outcome-determinative, and is probably preferable because of its predictability. But there could be room to reach different conclusions on a case-by-case basis.

Suppose that a state has a particularly harsh mootness doctrine, for example. The Supreme Court has announced that mootness of a federal question is itself a federal question, but this decisive sounding pronouncement only asserts federal power to displace state law if necessary to serve federal interests. The question to be asked, as described in the preceding section, should focus not only on whether the federal right is burdened, but also on the nature, weight, and legitimacy of the state interest involved. If a state had a strong legitimate interest in its doctrine — if, for example, the state had a particular need to keep moribund cases off its crowded docket and applied this doctrine equally to state and federal claimants alike — then it could be said that the doctrine was not an "unnecessary" burden on the federal right, that the state had a "valid excuse," or that the doctrine is not so inconsistent with federal law as to require the state to forego a neutral procedure, even if it would be outcome-determinative.

In areas like justiciability in which negative state doctrine is so likely to be inconsistent with the purposes of section 1983 — which was enacted on behalf of plaintiffs who had difficulty getting their claims heard in state court — I think a blanket rule is justifiable. This is particularly true in light of the fact that the state doctrines falling into this category are uncommon and subject to the self-restraint of state court judges. The issue-by-issue balance just described is more appropriately used in the area of procedure, where it is not always clear whether it is plaintiffs or defendants who are favored.

b. *The Unavailable Forum — Exhaustion and the Tax Cases*

The Court's decision in *Felder* that the outcome-determinative requirement of exhaustion of state administrative remedies may not be applied in a state court section 1983 action was simply an extension of a prohibition previously applied in the federal courts. According to the Court, Congress had more or less explicitly viewed an exhaustion requirement as repugnant to the goals of section 1983. The state courts were required to make themselves no less readily available than the federal courts.

There are circumstances, however, in which the federal courts are permitted to impose various doctrines remitting would-be federal court section 1983 plaintiffs to state judicial remedies. One good example of this situation arises in federal court section 1983 litigation involving the constitutionality of state tax decisions; another is state prisoner challenges to the length or fact of custody. May a state court impose an exhaustion of administrative remedies requirement, despite *Felder*, in a case in which the federal courts are permitted to impose a judicial exhaustion rule? Is it the goal of state courts to replicate federal court, even in its unavailability, or to open its doors to civil rights plaintiffs precisely because the federal courts are unavailable?

There are compelling reasons why the state courts have become the primary forum for constitutional challenges to a state or local government's system of taxation. Congress, showing a particularly strong concern for comity when a state's finances are involved, prohibited federal courts from enjoining a state's collection of its taxes "where a plain, speedy and efficient remedy may be had in the courts of such State." In *Fair Assessment in Real Estate v. McNary*, the Supreme Court then held, on the basis of similar comity concerns, that plaintiffs seeking damages should also be precluded from a federal forum if the state provided adequate remedies. Thus, the federal courts will not consider a constitutional challenge to a state tax system or decision in a section 1983 action, but only the adequacy of existing state remedies.

In many jurisdictions, plaintiffs wishing to challenge the constitutionality of a particular tax system arrive in state court only to be confronted with the state's requirement that they exhaust administrative remedies. It seems clear that the tax anti-injunction act should not be held to bar injunctions issued in section 1983 taxpayer actions in state court, and that *McNary* should not be held to bar state court actions for damages. But does *Felder* prevent a state from applying its administrative exhaustion doctrine in this context?

In contrast to the usual situation governed by *Felder*, the Supreme Court has already weighed the significance of the availability of a federal forum for taxpayers under section 1983 against considerations of comity, and found that comity should prevail. The *McNary* opinion is cast as resolving a conflict between the policies of section 1983 and the policies of the tax anti-injunction act (albeit in a broadened application). If Congress agrees with the Supreme Court's preference for the comity interests and with the concomitant exception to section 1983 jurisdiction, why should a state not be able to create a comparable exception to the exhaustion doctrine in order to implement its own similar concerns with the proper balance of power between state administrative agencies and state courts? Some state courts have reasoned that if *McNary* gives federal courts permission to carve out an exception to section 1983 jurisdiction, it must give similar permission to the state courts. If Congress were to become concerned with the lack of an immediately available forum, it could overrule *McNary* and make federal court more available, at least for damages actions, or even go so far as to amend the tax anti-injunction statute.

The existence of a general exhaustion doctrine reflects a state policy concerning state separation of powers or possibly even a jurisdictional bar. Given that it is presumably Congress's will that providing a forum for such tax litigation is less important than federal prudential concerns, I think that a state would not be unwarranted in taking *McNary* as permission to impose a requirement of exhaustion of administrative remedies in the tax cases described. I do not agree with the Court's conclusion in *McNary* that the tax cases are so unique as to warrant an exception to section 1983, but since this conclusion has created exceptional treatment of these cases in federal court without Congress demurring, the state courts should not have to shoulder a burden the federal courts have been instructed to decline, at least in the absence of any evidence that this is what Congress desires, and therefore should not be required to suspend any exhaustion requirement generally applicable to state cases, regardless of *Felder*, in the tax cases.

The same reasoning would apply to allow the state courts to apply an exhaustion requirement in other areas where the federal courts are effectively permitted to do so. As suggested earlier, however, the fact that the states have the power to impose limits on section 1983 cases does not mean that they should do so, any more than the fact that Congress may have power under the supremacy clause to void those limits means that that power should be exercised. Discretion is involved in both instances.

Subject only to a few exceptions, like article III, Congress may remedy any situation it finds insufficiently receptive to civil rights — like the holes in section 1983 created by *McNary* and *Preiser* — by making the federal forum more available. This is a more appropriate first step than flexing the muscles of the supremacy clause to require the states to do what Congress will not or cannot require the federal courts to do.

B. *Federal/State Disparities in Procedure*

While with justiciability doctrine, it is usually clear which of two different doctrines will favor the plaintiff, with many procedural rules that is not the case. If a state procedure differs from a federal procedure — if, for example, a state permits a nonunanimous jury verdict — plaintiff's counsel would need to be clairvoyant to know before the litigation begins whether that rule would help or hinder plaintiff's chance of prevailing. Other procedures may be easier to categorize — liberal class action rules, for example, or a generous right to a jury trial will generally be attractive to civil rights plaintiffs, while strict pleading rules will not. The state should be permitted to apply its own procedures as long as, balancing the relevant factors, the procedure is not so inconsistent with the purposes of section 1983 as to warrant an exercise of the supremacy clause.

1. Procedures Favoring Plaintiffs

For the same reasons discussed in connection with justiciability, if a unique state procedure does favor plaintiffs, there is no doubt that the state should be permitted to use that procedure in section 1983 litigation. In one FELA case in which the state had attachment procedures far more attractive to plaintiffs than federal court procedures, Justice Brandeis had no difficulty in concluding that the plaintiff should be given the benefit of the state rule. If other state procedures are similarly generous to plaintiffs — if, for example, the state does not require that a bond be posted as a prerequisite to injunctive relief — all interests other than uniformity combine on the same side of the balance.

2. Procedures Disfavoring Plaintiffs

A procedure that is generally and predictably adverse to plaintiffs might be impermissible. One example, familiar from the FELA cases, is strict state pleading rules. Courts declaring that it is a federal question whether state pleading rules are so exacting as to be inconsistent with federal policy are correct. This does not necessarily mean that the conclusion in the FELA cases rejecting strict local pleading rules should apply to section 1983 cases. State courts differ on whether the federal rules on construing pleadings should apply in this context. Are strict pleading rules so inconsistent with federal interests that they should be displaced? This depends on the particular rule involved. On some pleading issues, like construction of the pleadings, or the relation back of amendments to the complaint, either party might suffer from state restrictions.

At least as I see the balance of interests on some of these questions, the particular results reached in the FELA cases and the *Erie* cases need not apply here. In contrast to the conclusion in the diversity cases, the forum's law should, I think, apply on issues like the relation back of amendments or when a suit is deemed to have commenced. These procedures, which do not generally disadvantage plaintiffs, are not inherently inconsistent with the purposes of section 1983.

Some pleading issues are so entwined with the elements of the case the plaintiff must prove that federal law clearly should govern. If the issue is specificity of the pleadings, however, I think the state should be probably permitted to apply its usual rules, even though it is predictable that some plaintiffs might be discomfited by the rule. Unlike restrictive standing requirements, or a state court's misapprehension over plaintiff's burden of proof, strict pleading requirements may be overcome by competent counsel, and, thus, are not inherently inconsistent with the goals of section 1983.

Other disparities between federal and state court, such as issues concerning the scope and nature of the right to a jury trial, and class action rules, must also be examined carefully. If a procedure cannot be characterized as advantaging or disadvantaging plaintiffs, outside the context of a particular case, the state should not be prohibited from using its own neutral rules. If a rule might be thought to be disadvantageous to plaintiffs, that does not end the inquiry into whether the state may be permitted to use its own procedure, but is the beginning of a process of analysis and balancing.

My balance of the relevant interests maintains a presumption in favor of state court procedures, plaintiff-oriented or not, that is overcome only if the procedure is inherently hostile to section 1983 plaintiffs. The result of this approach would lead to less uniformity between federal and state court, or among state courts, than would Professor Neuborne's position. I do not find this result troubling. Uniformity trims the good as well as the bad. While the availability of a federal forum does not give the state courts license to eviscerate the remedies of section 1983, it is, as Hart argued, relevant when debatable questions concerning the applicability of state collateral law arise.

The state courts and legislatures have the power to minimize any disparities in justiciability or procedure between state and federal court. The ideal result would be for the state courts or legislatures to maintain a posture at least as generous as the federal courts, particularly with regard to justiciability doctrine. But when the states find a neutral but restrictive procedure important enough to force the issue, in many cases the Supreme Court should permit the state courts their choice in exchange for those instances in which the states' choice will favor civil rights plaintiffs.

Note, *Clarifying Comity: State Court Jurisdiction and Section 1983 State Tax Challenges,* 103 Harvard Law Review 1888 (1990)

* * *

I. The Tax Injunction Act and the Federal Courts

The Supreme Court has repeatedly described the Tax Injunction Act as rooted "in equity practice, in principles of federalism, and in recognition of the imperative need of a State to administer its own fiscal operations." When called upon to interpret the Act, the Court has relied on these general concerns of equity, comity, and fiscal autonomy, and sometimes has even declined to construe the Act itself. By freely drawing from among these strands, the Court has woven an almost impenetrable barrier to state tax challenges in federal court.

A. *State Tax Cases and Federal Equitable Restraint*

Even before the Tax Injunction Act was enacted, a federal court could not enjoin an illegal or void tax unless the prerequisites of equity were satisfied. Equitable relief was not available unless the plaintiff could prove that there was no adequate remedy at law and that enforcement of the tax would result in irreparable injury, a multiplicity of suits, or a cloud on title to real property. This rule of equitable restraint in tax matters derived from the broader limitation on equity jurisdiction contained in section 16 of the Judiciary Act of 1789, which prevented federal courts from sustaining suits in equity "in any case where plain, adequate and complete remedy may be had at law."

Historically, section 16 applied only when the remedy at law was available in federal courts; an adequate state remedy was insufficient to defeat federal jurisdiction. Because a suit for damages against a state would be barred by the eleventh amendment, some taxpayers successfully invoked federal equity powers by arguing that there was no adequate remedy at law.

The rule that only federal court remedies were sufficiently "adequate" to bar equity jurisdiction was changed as to tax cases in the 1932 case of *Matthews v. Rodgers*. In *Matthews*, the Supreme Court unanimously held that a federal court could not enjoin a state tax if an adequate remedy was available through state channels. Writing for the Court, Justice Stone maintained that the "guiding principle" of equitable restraint was of "peculiar force" in cases in which the plaintiff sought to enjoin the collection of state taxes. First, he argued that restraint was dictated by notions of comity, which he described as "[t]he scrupulous regard for the rightful independence of state governments which should at all times actuate the federal courts." Second, Justice Stone pointed to the narrower consideration of fiscal autonomy, "a proper reluctance to interfere by injunction with [a state's] fiscal operations." The three themes of equity, comity, and fiscal autonomy continue to pervade Supreme Court jurisprudence in the area of federal court jurisdiction over state tax challenges.

B. Congress and the Concern for State Fiscal Autonomy

Despite the restraint advocated by the Supreme Court in *Matthews*, lower federal courts remained "readily amenable to persuasion that the state remedy was inadequate." At the same time, the states were adopting a variety of taxes in an attempt to counteract escalating expenditures and declining revenues resulting from the Depression and the New Deal. Five years after the *Matthews* decision, Congress enacted the Tax Injunction Act and thereby prohibited federal courts from interfering with the collection of state taxes as long as a "plain, speedy and efficient remedy may be had in the courts of [the] State." The legislative history of the Act concentrates on preserving state access to tax revenues during litigation. The Senate Judiciary Committee argued that the bill would enable "States . . . to survive while long-drawn-out tax litigation is in process." It noted that the federal power to enjoin state tax collection allowed taxpayers "to withhold . . . taxes in such vast amounts and for such long periods of time as to disrupt State and county finances." Senator Homer T. Bone, the bill's sponsor, suggested that one reason taxpayers brought suit was to force local governments, "hard-pressed for money," to "thr[o]w up their hands" and accept a lower tax than originally was assessed.

Broader comity concerns — the "scrupulous regard for the rightful independence of state governments" invoked in *Matthews* — are less apparent in the Act's legislative history. Apart from the undesirable impact on state finances, Congress gave no indication that the federal courts had been unduly interfering with state sovereignty. The only hint of more general comity concerns appears in the recurrent criticism of the problems caused by diversity jurisdiction.

The legislative history reveals that curtailing diversity jurisdiction was Congress' principal concern, even though the Act by its terms applies to nondiversity cases as well. Diversity jurisdiction was repeatedly criticized for the unfair advantage it gave to out-of-state taxpayers, usually foreign corporations doing business in the state. For example, the Senate Report remarked on the unfairness of requiring "the citizen of the State . . . to pay first and then litigate, while those privileged to sue in the Federal courts need only pay what they choose and withhold the balance during the period of litigation." The emphasis on the problems created by diversity jurisdiction suggests that Congress sought only to restrict access to a federal forum and may not have considered how the Act would affect the operation of federal law.

C. The Supreme Court and the Rise of Comity

Although comity concerns played a minor role in the adoption of the Tax Injunction Act, the Supreme Court has emphasized these concerns in construing the Act's provisions. The Court most clearly articulated the Act's principle of comity in *Fair Assessment in Real Estate Association v. McNary*, in which it prohibited taxpayers from bringing section 1983 damage actions in federal court. Faced with conflicting precedents on the role of comity in section 1983 actions, the Court held that comity concerns should influence state tax matters. It found that a damage action "would be no less disruptive of [a state's] tax system than would the historic equitable efforts to enjoin the collection of taxes, efforts which were early held barred by considerations of comity."

Despite the Court's claims that it was also drawing from traditional equitable principles and a concern for state fiscal autonomy, *McNary* represents the first time that the doctrine of comity was essential to the Court's denial of jurisdiction in a state tax case. Prior to *McNary*, even the most stringent criteria for equity jurisdiction contemplated that actions at law could be brought in federal court. Furthermore, arguments for fiscal autonomy had previously been limited to cases that obstructed state access to disputed tax revenues. Because the plaintiff in *McNary* was seeking damages for taxes already paid, the holding extended the concern for fiscal autonomy exhibited in the legislative history beyond its former bounds.

The decision in *McNary* generated a moderate amount of controversy. Although commentators generally found the *McNary* result acceptable because of the need to protect state fiscal health, they disagreed with the Court's reliance on notions of comity to reach its decision. One of the more vehement critics of the application of comity concerns to section 1983 actions is Justice Brennan, who is also the Court's most faithful proponent of fiscal autonomy concerns. His separate opinion in *McNary* rejected the majority's premise that the Court could decline to hear the damage action "by applying a 'principle of comity' grounded solely on [a] notion of an appropriate division of responsibility between the federal and state judicial systems." Justice Brennan argued instead that the case should have been dismissed because the exigencies of state fiscal management required the prior exhaustion of state remedies.

Justice Brennan's exclusive focus on fiscal autonomy concerns is consistent with his earlier majority opinion in *Rosewell v. LaSalle National Bank*. In *Rosewell*, the Court held that the "plain, speedy and efficient" language of the Tax Injunction Act required that state remedies meet certain minimal procedural criteria but did not impose any substantive standards of adequacy. Thus, as long as the state procedure provided the taxpayer with a "'full hearing and judicial determination'" at which she might raise her claim that the substance of the state remedy was constitutionally deficient, a federal court should not interfere with the state proceeding. Justice Brennan argued that such a narrow interpretation of the Act was supported by the "dependency of state budgets on the receipt of local tax revenues."

In sum, the Court has alternately emphasized traditional rules of equity, a specific concern for state fiscal autonomy, and broader comity considerations to bar most challenges to state taxation from federal district court. It has never made clear, however, whether state courts must hear the federal claims that are thus barred from federal court or whether they too may rely on equity, comity, and fiscal autonomy to defer to remedies available under state law. The Court's use of varying rationales to support federal abstention in state tax cases has led to a confusion among state courts regarding which cases they must hear and which they may dismiss.

II. Section 1983 and the State Courts

Section 1983 creates a legal entitlement to relief against any person who violates the Constitution or laws of the United States while acting under color of state law. If it were not for the Tax Injunction Act and the *McNary* comity doctrine, a plaintiff challenging state taxes could get into federal court by bringing an action under section 1983. Barred from federal court, some plaintiffs have tried to bring their section 1983 claims in state courts. Although the Supreme Court has held that state courts have concurrent jurisdiction over section 1983 claims, it has never decided whether this jurisdiction is compulsory. The issue is particularly important in state tax litigation, because a state court is the only forum in which the section 1983 claim can be raised.

A. *State Tax Litigation and the Section 1983 Cause of Action*

With a few exceptions, state courts have not confronted the fundamental question whether state tax challenges present a valid cause of action under section 1983. Such an inquiry must be approached in several steps. First, what causes of action for unconstitutional state taxation did the federal courts traditionally recognize? Second, were these traditional causes of action subsumed by section 1983? Third, in what way, if any, were these causes of action affected by the enactment of the Tax Injunction Act in 1937?

1. *Implied Rights of Action.*

— The federal courts traditionally recognized implied rights of action for constitutional violations that varied according to whether the plaintiff sought damages or injunctive relief. When taxpayers sought *refunds* of taxes, federal courts recognized an implied federal remedy. For example, in *Ward v. Love County*, the Supreme Court held that it would violate the fourteenth amendment for a county to "collect . . . unlawful taxes by coercive means, and not incur any obligation to pay them back." *Carpenter v. Shaw* reached the same result with respect to taxes paid to the state.

Unlike the availability of damage actions, the existence of a federal cause of action for injunctive relief depended on the adequacy of the state remedy. Under the doctrine of equitable restraint set out in *Matthews v. Rodgers*, federal law would not grant relief as long as state channels provided a "plain, adequate and complete" remedy. Thus, as long as state law provided an adequate remedy as defined by federal equity practice, there was no federal cause of action. If there was no adequate remedy at law, however, the federal court would hear claims for equitable relief.

2. *The Effect of Section 1983.*

— The early cases seeking relief from unconstitutional taxation were brought directly under the Constitution. Since the Court's 1961 decision in

Monroe v. Pape, however, section 1983 has been the principal mechanism for remedying constitutional violations by state and local officials. Because of the availability of this statutory cause of action, some courts have dismissed suits seeking implied constitutional remedies in favor of the expressly authorized remedy of section 1983. Thus, the continued vitality of cases such as *Ward* and *Carpenter* is not entirely certain.

In some ways, section 1983 is not as broad as the early remedies implied directly under the Constitution. For example, the decision allowing recovery against the state in *Carpenter* conflicts with the Supreme Court's recent holding that, for purposes of recovering retrospective relief under section 1983, states are not "persons" and therefore are not liable under the statute. If section 1983 has supplanted directly implied remedies against state governments, as it appears to have done in the case of municipal governments, then a federal cause of action against a state may not be available in state court.

Although in some ways section 1983 may have limited the remedies available to plaintiffs, in other ways it may have expanded them. Early due process cases such as *Ward* involved suits for refunds only, and whether damages beyond refunds were available is unclear. The standard of "actual damages" under section 1983, in contrast, probably encompasses any consequential damages resulting from unconstitutional taxation.

When injunctive relief is sought, *McNary* suggests that section 1983 absorbs the standard of equitable relief adhered to in *Matthews v. Rodgers*. In *McNary*, the Court barred section 1983 actions from federal court, "provided . . . that [state] remedies are plain, adequate and complete." Federal courts applying rules of equitable restraint to section 1983 actions in other contexts have also assumed that the statute left these traditional rules intact. Although state courts may argue that the availability of a cause of action under *federal* equity practice does not bind *state* equity practice, state courts cannot apply their rules of equity to undercut a federal right.

3. The Effect of the Tax Injunction Act.

— The third part of the inquiry — whether the Tax Injunction Act eliminates the federal cause of action — is complicated by the Act's use of the terms "plain, speedy and efficient" rather than the traditional equitable standard of "plain, adequate and complete." If a state remedy does not meet the Act's "plain, speedy and efficient" standard, the taxpayer clearly has both a valid federal cause of action and access to a federal forum. The legislative history and early interpretation of the Act, however, suggest that, by its choice of "plain, speedy and efficient," Congress meant to restrict federal jurisdiction to a greater degree than would the traditional equitable standard. Thus, it is possible that there could be a federal *cause of action* (if the state remedy were not "plain, adequate and complete") but no federal *jurisdiction* (if the remedy were nonetheless "plain, speedy and efficient").

For those cases that satisfy the procedural standard of "plain, speedy and efficient" but fail to satisfy the substantive standard of "plain, adequate and complete," one must determine whether the Tax Injunction Act was intended to eliminate federal causes of action as well as federal jurisdiction over these claims. If Congress were satisfied that a "plain, speedy and efficient remedy . . . in the courts of [the] State" could supplant federal jurisdiction, perhaps it intended the statutory standard to supplant federal claims as well.

Nothing in the text of the Tax Injunction Act, its legislative history, or its subsequent interpretation by the Supreme Court suggests that Congress intended the statute to do anything more than restrict forum choice. First, the language of the statute specifically refers to the *courts*, not the *laws*, of the states. Moreover, the legislative history indicates that Congress was concerned primarily with curtailing diversity jurisdiction and not with eliminating any underlying federal causes of action. Finally, the Supreme Court has never suggested that a section 1983 state tax challenge brought in state court would be inappropriate in light of the congressional purposes behind the Act.

Against this evidence that the Tax Injunction Act is at best ambivalent in choosing between state law and federal law, courts must weigh section 1983's unambiguous preference for federal remedies over state remedies. The Court has repeatedly emphasized the "uniquely federal" nature of the section 1983 remedy. It has stressed that "[i]t is no answer that the State has a law which if enforced would give relief" because "[t]he federal remedy is supplementary to the state remedy." In sum, there is no indication that the Act was meant to eliminate the historical federal cause of action for state tax challenges or to prevent the use of section 1983 as its modern equivalent.

B. The Advantages of Pursuing a Section 1983 Claim

Even if state law provides a "plain, speedy and efficient" remedy, taxpayers may prefer to pursue a section 1983 action for several reasons. The most significant advantage is the availability of attorneys' fees under the Civil Rights Attorney's Fees Awards Act of 1976. Under the Act, state courts as well as federal courts have the power to award fees in civil rights actions. The provision of fees increases the incentive to bring suit, particularly when a tax may be unconstitutional but the amount exacted does not justify incurring substantial litigation costs. Other advantages of challenging a state tax under section 1983 are the collateral rules governed by federal law regardless of the forum. For example, taxpayers suing under section 1983 have tried to take advantage of the longer limitations period for personal injury actions and of section 1983's preemption of state notice-of-claim statutes. These policies are integral to the federal claim and must be applied by state courts hearing those claims.

In addition to attorneys' fees and collateral rules, a further advantage of pursuing section 1983 claims in state court is the possibility that a federal remedy would be more complete than the remedy available under state law. The possibility that section 1983 may require a more comprehensive remedy is significant because many states adhere to the common law rule that a refund is not available under state law unless the state has waived its sovereign immunity through a statute allowing refunds. For example, some state courts have held that their states have not waived immunity for class action refund suits or for suits seeking interest payments on tax refunds. Even when a state does permit refunds, however, state officials sometimes will grant only prospective relief.

There are two possible sources for a federal remedy. First, section 1983 itself embodies a federal standard of damages that may require a refund remedy in state court. Although the statute does not specify what level of damages may be recovered, federal courts have relied on principles of compensation and deterrence to construct a standard that aims to compensate civil rights plaintiffs for all actual damages incurred. It is not clear whether the measure of damages used by federal courts also applies in state court litigation, but state courts that have addressed the issue have generally used the federal standard. Under the federal standard of actual damages, payment of unconstitutional taxes is a readily identifiable and easily quantifiable harm that can be fully compensated by refund of taxes paid.

The second possible avenue to a federal refund remedy under section 1983 arises out of the common law right to a refund of illegal taxes, which appears to have secured constitutional status in *Ward v. Love County* and *Carpenter v. Shaw*. In light of these cases, some plaintiffs may argue that there is a right to a refund obtainable only under federal law. Such a constitutional right to a refund, however, would also operate to prohibit state remedies from falling short of the standard required by the due process clause of the fourteenth amendment. The refund claim therefore would not have to be raised in a separate section 1983 action, but would be independently binding on state-law remedies.

Both Congress and the Court have invoked section 1983's fundamental goal of protecting constitutional rights to justify the creation of auxiliary procedural and remedial policies. These policies are designed to encourage plaintiffs to bring their claims to court and to take advantage of the "uniquely federal" remedies provided by the civil rights statutes. Even more fundamental to the section 1983 remedy is a willingness of courts to exercise jurisdiction over the federal claim. Because the Tax Injunction Act and the *McNary* doctrine of comity preclude federal courts from hearing section 1983 tax challenges, this responsibility falls squarely on the state courts.

III. State Tax Litigation in the State Courts

State courts that have considered the relevance of the Tax Injunction Act in deciding whether to hear a section 1983 state tax claim have reached conflicting results. Courts in eight states, including the highest courts in six of those states, have refused to hear these challenges. These courts have reasoned that they have the discretion to refuse to hear section 1983 tax challenges if a "plain, speedy and efficient" remedy is available under state law. Courts in four states, including two state supreme courts, have concluded that they are obligated to hear these claims. In addition, a number of state courts have entertained section 1983 actions challenging state taxes without considering the impact of the federal policies on their power or discretion to hear these claims.

The courts that have refused to hear section 1983 suits challenging state taxes by relying on the principles behind the Tax Injunction Act have interpreted the Act to mean not only that a federal *forum* is unavailable whenever there is a "plain, speedy and efficient" remedy under state law, but also that federal *law* is inapplicable. In so holding, they have erroneously applied comity interests to cases implicating the laws and courts of a single sovereign. There is no role for "comity" in the relationship between a state court and the administration of that state's tax system. If comity were removed from the state court calculus, those courts would be forced to confront their obligation to hear claims brought under federal law.

A. *Clarifying Comity*

Many of the state courts that have dismissed section 1983 state tax actions have cited *McNary*, but not all have relied explicitly on *McNary*'s principle of comity. A close inspection, however, reveals that all of these courts assume that they may follow the pattern of federal court deference to state tax administration exhibited in *McNary* by declining to hear federal claims. For example, in *Stufflebaum v. Panethiere*, the Supreme Court of Missouri held that "the teaching of *McNary* is that, given a plain, adequate and complete remedy [under state law], taxpayers may not seek relief under § 1983." Similarly, in *Zizka v. Water Pollution Control Authority*, the Supreme Court of Connecticut, citing *McNary*, stated that "[state law] furnishes a remedy that forecloses the plaintiffs' § 1983 claims . . . in state court." If *McNary* were extended to allow state courts to dismiss section 1983 state tax challenges in this fashion, that decision would burden federal rights to a considerably greater extent than any other federal abstention doctrine. Other abstention doctrines suggest that although comity may require a plaintiff to litigate in a state forum, it does not deprive a plaintiff of federal remedies.

Because state tax statutes generally provide that suits may only be brought after administrative remedies have been exhausted, *McNary*'s principle of comity most closely resembles the federal abstention doctrine established in *Burford v. Sun Oil Co. Burford* instructs federal courts to dismiss complex cases that affect an important state interest and involve a comprehensive system of state administrative and judicial review. Under *Burford*, the plaintiff cannot reserve any claims for later hearing in federal court. In holding that the federal forum was unavailable, however, the *Burford* Court noted that "[the state] courts can give *fully as great relief* . . . as the federal courts." In contrast, tax challenges under state law may not provide "fully as great relief" as challenges under section 1983, which provide a plaintiff with auxiliary procedural and remedial benefits.

The *McNary* opinion gives no indication that it was meant to extend to state courts. In *McNary*, then-Justice Rehnquist referred to "the need for federal-court restraint," "the fundamental principle of comity between federal courts and state governments," and "the . . . respect that should be accorded state tax laws in federal court." Quoting Justice Brennan, he further argued that "'questions of state tax law . . . , like issues of state regulatory law, are more properly heard in the state courts.'" None of these comity concerns survives the shift to a state forum, because *state* courts present no danger of *federal* court interference in state affairs or misunderstanding of state law.

The "principle of comity" that the Supreme Court has identified as inherent in the Tax Injunction Act, and that was so crucial to the decision in *McNary*, is not a factor that state courts should consider when deciding whether to hear section 1983 suits challenging state taxation. "Comity," as used by the Supreme Court, refers to the relationship between federal and state *institutions*, not federal and state *law*. More specifically, "comity" as used in the tax injunction cases refers to a policy decision to keep federal courts from interfering with state tax systems.

B. *State Court Obligation To Hear Section 1983 Claims*

The Supreme Court has twice reserved the general question whether state courts must exercise jurisdiction over section 1983 claims. In the particular context of state tax litigation, which is complicated by the foreclosure of access to the federal courts, the Court's pronouncements on section 1983 jurisdiction have been especially cryptic. In *McNary*, the Court found it significant that "the Missouri Supreme Court has expressly held that plaintiffs such as petitioners may assert a § 1983 claim in state court." However, in *Spencer v. South Carolina Tax Commission*, an equally divided Court affirmed without opinion a state case refusing to exercise jurisdiction over a section 1983 tax claim. Most recently, in *Arkansas Writers' Project, Inc. v. Ragland*, the Court admitted that "[w]hether state courts must assume jurisdiction over [section 1983 suits challenging state taxation] is not entirely clear."

Courts and commentators who argue that state courts must hear section 1983 state tax challenges have relied on the Supreme Court's decision in *Testa v. Katt*. Although the actual *Testa* holding is quite limited, the Court's reasoning might suggest a comprehensive duty of state courts to hear federal claims. Compulsory jurisdiction over tax challenges has been justified under both narrow and broad readings of the case.

The narrow reading of *Testa* confirms the "nondiscrimination principle" first articulated in *Mondou v. New York, New Haven, & Hartford Railroad. Mondou* held that state courts of general jurisdiction could not refuse to hear federal claims if they opened their doors to analogous state claims. *Testa* expanded *Mondou*'s holding to encompass claims that were "generically similar" and not just "factually identical." The Court has specifically endorsed *Testa*'s holding with respect to section 1983 claims. Applying *Testa* to section 1983 state tax cases, some commentators have argued that, as long as state courts are open to tax challenges under state law, they must also be open to tax challenges under federal law. State tax cases will almost always involve analogous state claims because by the very terms of the Tax Injunction Act, state courts must provide "a remedy . . . in the courts of [the] State."

Testa also suggests a much broader state court responsibility than can be fulfilled by simply hearing federal claims that are loosely analogous to state claims. In *Testa*, the Court maintained that the supremacy clause compelled the state court to exercise jurisdiction over a claim brought under a federal statute because "the policy of the federal Act is the prevailing policy in every state." Any other result, the Court argued, "flies in the face of the fact that the States of the Union constitute a nation." The state courts that have held themselves obligated to hear section 1983 state tax challenges have based their decisions on this broad reading of *Testa*. These courts have argued that because the supremacy clause requires state courts to hear all federal claims, they do not have the option of refusing to hear state tax challenges brought under federal law.

C. *Equity and Fiscal Autonomy in the State Courts*

The Tax Injunction Act is best interpreted as a forum-shifting provision that does not eliminate federal causes of action challenging state tax schemes, but only displaces them from federal court. Consequently, the Act does not excuse the state courts' obligation to hear federal causes of action. Once they have asserted jurisdiction over section 1983 state tax challenges, state courts must still decide what kinds of federal remedies they are required to provide. Only at the remedial stage may state courts give weight to concerns of equity and fiscal autonomy.

As noted above, traditional rules of equitable restraint counseled that federal courts could not enjoin tax collections or assessments as long as an adequate remedy at law existed. By statute, this remains the operative rule in both federal and state courts, and the fact that a claim is brought as a section 1983 action need not change existing practice. In addition, as the Court held in *Great Lakes Dredge & Dock Co. v. Huffman*, the same principles that limit injunctive relief also apply to actions for declaratory judgment.

Fiscal autonomy considerations should concern a state court adjudicating a section 1983 action only to the extent that they do not undercut the compensation and deterrence goals underlying the federal civil rights statutes. If fiscal autonomy concerns were allowed to negate refund remedies and attorneys' fees, constitutional violations could go unremedied. Thus, section 1983 may require a refund remedy that may not otherwise be available through state channels. The statute also requires that the state accept a longer statute of limitations for these claims, even though this may make budget estimations more difficult. Furthermore, under the Civil Rights Attorney's Fees Award Act, the state will have to pay attorneys' fees to a successful plaintiff.

Although fiscal autonomy considerations do not allow a state to dilute a plaintiff's right to full recovery under section 1983, they may permit state courts to require exhaustion of administrative remedies before hearing a section 1983 claim. Even though exhaustion of state administrative remedies is not normally required for section 1983 actions under *Patsy v. Board of Regents*, *Patsy* should not apply to state tax challenges. As Justice Brennan argued in his *McNary* concurrence, the Court has long recognized that fiscal autonomy concerns may require exhaustion of administrative remedies in state tax challenges, and section 1983 did not create an exception to this rule. Therefore, fiscal autonomy considerations may allow state courts to impose an exhaustion requirement in state tax litigation that is not generally required in section 1983 litigation.

* * *

Part X
Critical Perspectives

Most assessments of section 1983 are grounded on traditional notions of statutory and constitutional interpretation, federalism and the like. These assessments typically assume a distinction between law and politics and, with the exception of economic approaches to section 1983 (and possibly also theories of justice), they tend not to be interdisciplinary. The following two articles take a critical approach and, in so doing, provide provocative overviews of section 1983 doctrine in its entirety.

Professor Beermann's article claims that traditional ''legalistic'' analyses of section 1983 are not only indeterminate, but they also mask what are in reality political questions. *See generally* on critical approaches to law, M. Kelman, *A Guide To Critical Legal Studies (1987).* Professor Beermann wants courts that decide section 1983 issues to reject the usual ways of interpreting section 1983. Rather, they should engage in overtly political dialogue that ''opens up the policy debate to competing theories and data'' so as to evaluate ''more pragmatically'' the results of their decisions.

My article has a different focus. Examining the rhetoric used by the Supreme Court in its section 1983 decisions, I notice that constitutional rhetoric tends to predominate in earlier cases while in later cases it is tort rhetoric that is increasingly more prominent. After briefly setting out post-structuralist theories of language and discourse by way of background, I suggest that the shift to tort rhetoric reflects the current Court's view of the diminished stature of section 1983 and, at the same time, directly influences the ways in which we and the court think about it.

Jack M. Beermann, *A Critical Approach to Section 1983 with Special Attention to Sources of Law,* 42 Stanford Law Review 51 (1989)

The Civil Rights Act of 1871 ("§ 1983") establishes a tort-like remedy for persons deprived of federally protected rights "under color of law." While the statute's broad language provides a remedy for violations of federal constitutional and statutory rights, the statute itself provides little or no guidance regarding important subjects such as the measure of damages, the availability of punitive damages, the requirements for equitable relief, the statute of limitations, survival of claims, proper parties, and immunities from suit.

The Supreme Court has mined several sources of law to fill these gaps in § 1983. Besides the usual sources of statutory language and legislative history, the Court has looked to the state law of the forum jurisdiction; the general common law as it existed in 1871, when Congress passed the Civil Rights Act; the general common law as it exists today; federal common law developed in light of the federal policies

---

that are implicated in § 1983 cases; and federal common law developed in actions brought against federal officials directly under the Constitution. Furthermore, the Court has used an array of constitutional and structural principles not explicit in § 1983 to limit the reach of the statute's remedy.

Commentators have long attacked the Court's method of construing § 1983, charging the Court with ignoring congressional intent; applying false history as a smokescreen for the Justices' personal views; having inconsistent theories concerning § 1983's relationship to the preexisting common law and federal structure; and, in general, lacking a theory under which to develop the statute. To these allegations I would add the charge that some Justices are outright hostile to § 1983 and to § 1983 plaintiffs, and veil their hostility only thinly beneath the most rudimentary, unelaborated "policy arguments." The Court has thus limited the scope of § 1983 without ever seriously evaluating the arguments for and against rigorous or lax enforcement.

The confusion over § 1983 is a symptom of a larger problem, one that Gary Peller has called the "impoverishment" of political arguments in our law. We do not have a developed language for addressing the political questions that lurk behind legalistic discussions of § 1983; instead we apply history that can be manipulated to justify any result, statutory "constructions" that are never quite convincing, and policy arguments that are more like incantations of magic formulae than descriptions of consequences in the real world. We argue within a set of reified conceptions with no genuine attempt to fix their referents in the outside world.

The indeterminacy of legalistic analysis of § 1983 should send us back to political discussion over the function and consequences of federal civil rights enforcement. My point is not that political discussion is more determinate than legal argument, but that the sole justification for replacing overt political argument with formal legal discourse is that the latter is supposedly determinate and politically neutral. Thus, once the legal arguments surrounding § 1983 are exposed as indeterminate and politically charged, the reasonable method for the courts is to turn back to the political dialogue that legal argument was designed to replace. And by "political dialogue" I mean something more substantial than what has traditionally passed for "policy analysis" in the law: Courts, I will argue, should open up the policy debate to competing theories and data, and assess more pragmatically all available evidence of the consequences of their policy-based decisions.

The first part of this article examines the narrowly "legal" analysis of § 1983 in the cases and commentary, with particular attention to the sources of law from which § 1983 cases have drawn. Neither the Court nor most commentators, I shall argue, have squarely admitted how little the methods of interpretation have constrained the choices made. And the attempt to buttress legal argument with "policy analysis," I argue in the second part, has also failed, because the cases and commentary display no vision of how one would go about evaluating what is at stake in § 1983 cases. The third part of the article tries to develop such a vision, taking a preliminary look at the value choices that must be made in civil rights cases and raising the moral and political questions that might enable a conversation about them. The debate should center on what rights should be created and how they should be enforced. The final part of the article suggests a pragmatic approach to § 1983 that would open the courtroom doors to detailed studies of the effects that § 1983 litigation has had on plaintiffs and defendants, actual and potential. Does § 1983 litigation really vindicate constitutional rights? Whose rights? And what are its effects on state and local government officials? At present, these questions are either answered tacitly, when the Court and commentators purport to decide cases by relying solely on text, history, and other sources of law, or they are assumed away with facile policy analyses and elementary lectures on "our federalism." While we may not know the answers to these questions, we must discuss them realistically, and admit when our knowledge is lacking or incomplete.

I. Sources of Law in Section 1983 Cases

While many recent commentators have agreed that the Court's "method" in § 1983 cases seems ad hoc, designed to allow the Court to rationalize any outcome in any case, none of the proposed solutions avoids this problem. The text and history of § 1983 cannot themselves establish the boundaries of the statute's enforcement, nor can the various statutory and common law sources that commentators and courts have suggested. In every case, a decisive choice must be made between opposed rules, policies, and principles; the weakness of narrowly "legal" approaches, I argue, is that they fail to face this choice squarely.

A. *The Text and Legislative History of Section 1983*

Section 1983 provides that any person who, "under color of" state or local law, "subjects" or "causes" a citizen of the United States or other person within the jurisdiction of the United States to be subjected to a deprivation of a federal legal or constitutional right, "shall be liable to the party injured" in law, equity, or "other proper proceeding for redress." From these words the Court has decided, for example, that only "persons" are the proper defendants to § 1983 actions, that the statute's causation requirement precludes vicarious liability, that action is "under color of" state law even if contrary to that law, and that both federal statutory and constitutional rights are protected under § 1983. These decisions are not compelled by the language of § 1983, and often, as is discussed in more depth in later sections, the Court avoids the effect of the literal words of the statute when it suits the Court's purposes.

The controversy over the meaning of "under color of" is an interesting example of the way the Court and commentators have manipulated text and history to achieve their desired results. The phrase "under color of" is ambiguous, and the alternative meanings have different consequences for the scope of § 1983. In holding that action can be "under color of state law" even if it violates state law, the Court purportedly relied on clear legislative history. Eric Zagrans, on the other hand, argues that the "clear weight" of the same legislative history suggests that action in violation of state law could not be "under color of law." Both the Court's and Zagrans's reading of the legislative history are plausible, but for that very reason, both are open to dispute. The key analytical weakness in each case is that neither Zagrans's nor the Court's argument is particularly convincing. Because each argument depends on a controversial version of the statute's legislative history, neither position is compelling.

This conflict between opposed readings, perhaps unsurprising in arguments based on legislative history, comes to pervade the text itself. The Court interprets the text with the classical array of interpretive canons; as is often the case, two of these canons lead to opposite results. On one hand, the Court reasons, since the statute changes the common law, it should be construed narrowly. But on the other hand, since the statute grants a remedy, it should be construed broadly. Indeed, the Court sometimes applies both canons in the same case. For example, in *Gomez v. Toledo*, the Court explicitly stated that "[a]s remedial legislation, § 1983 is to be construed generously to further its primary purpose." But in ruling on the affirmative defense of immunity, the Court expressed its "unwillingness to infer from legislative silence a congressional intention to abrogate immunities that were . . . 'well-established at common law.'" Which canon of interpretation should be chosen is, of course, a question that the text itself cannot answer.

The Court's manipulation of text and history has predictably led some commentators to recommend abandoning altogether the Court's search for legislative intent. Decisions, they argue, should be a matter of "tort policy," discovered by a test that balances "the twin concerns of protecting officers and insuring compensation to the victims of their misdeeds." Dean Nichol has proposed what amounts to a pure policy analysis under which courts should construe § 1983 "'to make it a more rather than less effective' tool of constitutional supervision." Professor Eskridge has put forward a "dynamic" model of statutory interpretation under which § 1983 would be interpreted "in light of [its] present societal, political, and legal context." These proposals have the virtue of directing the discussion away from fruitless searches through legislative history. But because they do not tell us which substantive values should guide our choice of interpretations and why, they provide no real guidance toward answers to problems arising under § 1983. A call for "policy analysis" and an invocation of the present "context" are empty, when clearly there are competing policies to be analyzed and conflicting values within the present "context."

Proposals like Nichol's and Eskridge's are thus no more than a beginning. But at least they have discredited the idea that one can answer important questions just by reading the text and legislative history of § 1983. These approaches are inevitably selective — as when Zagrans dismisses contrary legislative history as aberrant or unreliable. In interpreting § 1983, text and history answer so few questions that the Court is forced to look elsewhere, as it sometimes admits. The rest of this section examines the sources that the Court and commentators have used to fill the gaps in § 1983.

B. *Statutory Direction to Apply State Law in Section 1983 Cases*

Three statutes direct the federal courts, in at least some instances, to look to state law to fill gaps in the statutory language of § 1983. These are the statute[s] governing "Proceedings in Vindication of Civil Rights" ("§ 1988"), the Rules of Decision Act (the "RDA"), and the "Full Faith and Credit" Statute. In a few cases the Court follows the apparent command of these statutes, but in many other cases, it simply ignores them altogether.

The most important statute of the three is § 1988, because it applies specifically to civil rights actions and because it has been interpreted (at least in some instances and by some commentators) to require federal courts to "borrow" state law to fill gaps in § 1983. Where federal law is not "suitable," or "not adapted," or is "deficient in the provisions necessary to furnish suitable remedies," § 1988 directs the federal court to apply "the common law, as modified and changed by the constitution and statutes" of the forum state. The statute also presumably empowers the federal court to create federal common law to fill the gaps in § 1983 where the state gap-filler would be inconsistent with the Constitution or federal law.

While the text of § 1988 appears to direct the Court at least to look at state law *whenever* § 1983 is silent on a subject, in practice, the Court has applied state law to § 1983 actions in only two situations: state survival statutes and state statutes of limitations governing federal § 1983 actions. And in the case of state statutes of limitations, the Court has partly federalized state law: The federal interest in "uniformity, certainty and the minimization of unnecessary litigation," according to the Court, requires that each state's personal injury statute of limitations apply, whether or not the state itself would characterize the particular § 1983 action as a personal injury claim.

The Court has not made clear whether § 1988 *requires* it to apply state law, even in the limited circumstances where it has done so. It has said, for example, that application of state statutes of limitations is "settled practice" which Congress "implicitly endorsed" in § 1988. Apparently the Court is unwilling to admit that § 1988 *compels* any result, although it may "instruct" courts in the results that they reach.

An extensive scholarly debate has taken place over the meaning of the choice of law provisions in § 1988. The views of the various scholars are surprisingly diverse. At one end of the spectrum, Jennifer Coleman has argued for an expansive role for state law under § 1988. She argues that § 1988 requires federal courts to fill gaps in § 1983 with the common law, statutes and constitutional law of the forum state, unless federal law outside § 1983 can fill the gaps, or unless the state law would frustrate the purposes of the statute. At the other end of the spectrum, Theodore Eisenberg has argued that § 1988 never requires federal courts to resort to state law in § 1983 cases, and that its gap-filling provisions apply only in a narrow class of cases commenced under state law in state court and removed to federal court by the defendant. Seth Kreimer has argued that § 1988 requires federal courts to fill the gaps in § 1983 with "general common law" a la *Swift v. Tyson*, not state common law; state statutes and constitutional provisions may be relevant, but only so far as they modify the "general common law." Another commentator has suggested that § 1988 requires federal courts to apply state law in civil rights cases only where the state law bears a "peripheral relationship to the scope and definition of federal rights." Still other commentators have either altogether ignored § 1988 in discussing choice of law for § 1983 or argued that federal courts *should* ignore § 1988 and apply general tort principles, the history of § 1983, or its purposes, to fill its textual gaps.

Coleman's proposal for expansive application of state law under § 1988 is inviting in its simplicity. Her proposal tracks the language of § 1988: The courts, she argues, should look first to the language and history of § 1983 to make sure there is a gap, then fill any gap with applicable federal law outside § 1983. If no federal law can fill the gap, then state law of the forum jurisdiction applies, unless it is inconsistent with the purposes of § 1983. In that case, the federal court should create federal common law.

Coleman's chief criticism of the Court's current practice is that it allows the Court to proceed in an ad hoc manner, choosing from text, history, federal law, federalist principles, and state law without constraint. In my view, however, her proposal for § 1988 would allow the Court the same freedom. Indeed, the Court's method is perfectly consistent with Coleman's recommendations: It has exercised considerable discretion without even reaching the choice of law provisions of § 1988, and it has avoided the "constraints" of § 1988 by purporting to find all that it needs in the words and history of § 1983 itself. If the words and history of § 1983 provide the answer, there is no gap and, thus, no need to resort to state law at all.

The Court has avoided the § 1988 procedure, however, only with quite creative constructions of § 1983's text and history — interpretations that reflect a narrow reading of the statute's potentially broad remedial language. For example, the Court has construed § 1983 to incorporate features of the common law that were well-established in 1871, on the theory that Congress was aware of that common law and would have realized that any intention to alter it would have to be quite explicit: As the old statutory construction canon goes, "statutes in derogation of common law should be construed strictly." Of course, an opposite reading of § 1983 is perfectly possible: The plain meaning of the statute's explicit language implies an expansive liability with no common law defenses. The Court has chosen the first of two alternative readings and has pretended that only its chosen interpretation is consistent with § 1983's text and history. Thus, the Court has exercised considerable discretion without even reaching the second step of Coleman's procedure. Section 1988, it would seem, is hardly a solution to the problem of judicial discretion.

Coleman, of course, denies that the Court's method is consistent with her view of § 1988. In many of its opinions, she correctly points out, the Court has supplemented the common law of 1871 with modern common law principles. Thus, rather than interpreting § 1983 for gaps and ambiguities, she argues, the Court has simply engaged in judicial policymaking.

One problem with this response is that Coleman's notion of "interpretation" is controversial. As noted above, theorists like Eskridge have argued that statutory interpretation is not necessarily a matter of recapturing authorial intentions. And even if we were to identify the meaning of a statute with the intentions of those who enacted it, the Court's practice could still be justified on Coleman's principles. Because Congress knew that tort rules would evolve, one could argue, it intended that current tort principles continually replace the common law of 1871 as such common law became outdated. In that case, the Court would be true to congressional intent in relying on contemporary common law principles. Whether or not (as Coleman thinks) these "constructions" are strained, as long as the Court claims it is construing § 1983 and not making federal common law, it can remain consistent with Coleman's method without ever applying state law.

Moreover, under both its procedure and Coleman's recommendations, the Court can exercise considerable discretion when it does find a gap or ambiguity in § 1983. The text of § 1988 suggests that where the civil rights statutes are not "suitable," "adapted to the object," or are "deficient in the provisions necessary to furnish suitable remedies," courts may consider other applicable federal law. Thus, the Court could incorporate doctrines from other federal statutes and from federal common law developed in other areas. The suitability requirement gives the Court power to borrow law it likes and disregard law it does not, limited only by its understanding of what is "suitable." And § 1988 does not define "suitability." While some commentators have suggested that the test for suitability is that the borrowed law advance the plaintiff's claim, it is unclear why this should be so. For example, a borrowed statute of limitations will bar some claims, but no one has argued that § 1988 means that there can be no statute of limitations for § 1983 actions.

If the Court should find no "suitable" federal law, § 1988 requires federal courts to fill gaps in the civil rights statutes with "the common law, as modified and changed by the constitution and statutes of the State" in which the court is sitting as long as such law is "not inconsistent with the Constitution and laws of the United States." Here, too, courts have considerable latitude of interpretation. For one thing, the expression "the common law" could mean either "the general common law" (as modified by statutes and constitutional provisions of the forum state) or "the common law of the forum state" (as that state has modified its own common law by statute or constitution). Both meanings find support in the commentary, and which interpretation one should choose is not clear from the text or history of § 1988. The proviso that state law applies only insofar as it is "not inconsistent with the Constitution and laws of the United States," opens the door further to judicial policymaking. One might assume, at first glance, that the word "inconsistent" would require that the state law be contrary to federal law, i.e., in direct conflict with it, to be deemed inconsistent. But in fact, the view which the commentators and the Court have adopted is that state law is inconsistent with federal law whenever it conflicts with the purposes of § 1983.

This appeal to the purposes of § 1983 seems peculiar for two reasons. First, if the Court were so clear on the purposes of § 1983, it could simply appeal to those purposes directly when construing the statute, and bypass § 1988's law-finding process altogether. Second, the purposes of § 1983 are controversial, and thus it would seem no less controversial to appeal to those purposes in the context of § 1988. Whatever the function of § 1988 may be in this one connection, one thing it clearly does *not* do, given the disagreement on § 1983's purposes, is guide judicial discretion. To require courts to balance the purposes of § 1983 against the justifications given for state law is nothing if not a call for judicial policymaking. In each situation, the state interests in pursuing its policies will run up against the urge to provide broader remedies. Within our legal discourse, there are good arguments directing us in each direction. The federalist doctrine holds that federal law should be sensitive to state interests and state autonomy, while the contrary nationalist view holds that state interests are always inferior to federal enforcement of civil rights. In accepting either of these arguments, a judge will be influenced by her ideological opinion of the appropriate balance between federal and state power.

The other statutes that refer federal courts to state law, the RDA and the Full Faith and Credit Statute, are less directly related to § 1983, and thus can be discussed more briefly. The RDA instructs federal courts, in actions at law, to regard state laws as "rules of decision" in civil actions "where they apply." The Court, however, never applies or even adverts to this statute in § 1983 cases, perhaps because it believes that state rules never "apply" in federal civil rights actions, or perhaps because the issue has never been raised.

In its opinions concerning the preclusive effect of state court judgments on federal civil rights actions, on the other hand, the Court applies the Full Faith and Credit Statute literally, without considering whether its application subverts the purposes or policies of the federal civil rights statutes. This literalism contrasts dramatically with the Court's open-ended construction of § 1983 and its policy-based reading of § 1988. The Court does not explain why it is compelled to literalism on preclusion questions but not on other matters relating to § 1983 and § 1988.

Faced with the Court's silence as to why its interpretive strategies differ from one statute or factual setting to another, commentators have sought to develop an unarticulated rationale that would weld seemingly disparate decisions into a coherent whole. These attempts usually fail even on their own terms. According to Kreimer, for example, the Supreme Court has covertly applied his theory that § 1988 never requires courts to apply state common law, but only state statutes; that, he claims, explains why the Court has applied state law only on the issues of limitation periods and survival of actions. The Court has not only never articulated anything like Kreimer's reasoning, but has effectively rejected it by completely ignoring state statutes in the process of creating federal common law to cover immunities or damages issues. Another commentator explains the Court's practice in terms of the nature of statutes of limitations and survival statutes: State law can resolve these issues because they are supposedly not "bound up with" the rights and remedies under § 1983, while federal law should resolve other issues, such as the measure of damages, because they are "bound up with" the rights. The distinction between an issue being "bound up with" or "not bound up with" federal rights is slippery even in principle: It is unclear why whether a § 1983 action survives the victim, or the passage of time, is not "bound up with" the rights and remedies that § 1983 would guarantee.

When a scholar argues that a court's decisions can be explained only by departing from the terms of its opinions, what she has really said is that the court has done a poor job of writing its opinions. The point of a court's written opinion is not simply to announce the result in the case and to leave the reasoning to others; for that a single sentence would do, and the government could save the salaries of the law clerks who write the opinions. Rather, the opinion is supposed to reveal the court's reasoning in the case, the factors that led to its decision, and the factors the court rejected or chose to ignore. If the Court's reasoning is bad, commentators should criticize it and perhaps propose new reasoning; if an unstated rationale is motivating the Court, commentators should bring forward evidence of that fact, evaluate the secret rules, and criticize the Court for not revealing its true reasoning.

The commentary on § 1983, certainly no less than other legal commentary, too often expends its energy in constructing theories that attempt to make consistent all the seemingly inconsistent things the Court has done. If the Court's cases are inconsistent on the reasoning the Court itself has offered, perhaps scholars should seek not just to rationalize the inconsistencies, but to replace the legal paradigm that produced them.

C. *Non-Statutory Choice of Law in Section 1983 Cases*

As suggested above, the Court does not always decide the choice-of-law question in § 1983 cases by referring to one or another federal choice-of-law statute. Sometimes it selects its source of law even more eclectically. In these cases, the Court has relied on four sources to fill the gaps in § 1983: the general common law as it stood in 1871, when Congress passed the Civil Rights Act; the general common law as it is currently understood; federal common law developed in light of federal policies implicated in § 1983 cases; and federal common law developed not in § 1983 cases but rather in actions brought against federal officials directly under the Constitution. The Court's choice of law seems to be determined by the issue it is considering: It relies on one source to decide immunities questions and another to fix the measure of damages. In what follows, I outline a few examples of the various sources of law and illustrate the confusions in the Court's extrastatutory method of choosing its sources.

1. *Immunities: The common law of 1871 and federal common law in* Bivens *cases.*

The Court relies on the common law of 1871 to grant immunities to many potential defendants, again applying a modernized version of the old canon that statutes in derogation of the common law should be construed strictly. The Court's theory is not so much that the common law is the embodiment of true reason, but rather that since Congress knew about the important aspects of that common law, it intended to incorporate all aspects of the common law that were not explicitly changed by § 1983.

We saw earlier that in some cases the Court interprets statutory silence to trigger § 1988's choice-of-law provisions. The Court never explains why, in the immunities context, statutory silence should lead it to the common law. The Court is therefore either confused about the importance of statutory silence or it is deciding on some other basis what source of law it should consult. Despite commentators' valiant efforts to explain how the Court chooses between § 1988 and other sources, the Court itself articulates no theory, and seems unaware that something is amiss. Without some explanation of why silence leads it to the common law of 1871 when considering immunities, the Court's claim that it is compelled to apply that law rings hollow.

The earliest § 1983 immunity cases deny that Congress intended to abolish the well-established common-law immunities with the "general language" of § 1983, which makes all "persons" potential defendants and which contains no immunities. But while these cases often purport to follow the contours of 1871 common law in deciding the scope of the immunity granted to each official, modern principles of tort law always seem to have influenced the Court's decisions. In *Pierson v. Ray*, for example, the Court relied on nineteenth century cases to justify absolute judicial immunity, but also cited cases and other materials from the 1950s and 1960s in support of its decision on the scope of immunity for police officers. Some theories, such as the view that the framers of § 1983 intended the statute to develop along with the common law, could explain the Court's reliance on contemporary law. But the Court offers no such theory, perhaps because then its reliance in the first half of this opinion on nineteenth century opinions would have been wrong.

The Court has stated in some cases that it looks to a combination of nineteenth century common law and contemporary common law to fill gaps in § 1983. It has not, however, explained how this combination relates to Congress's intent, even though the Court insists that its only function is to "interpret the intent of Congress in enacting § 1983, not to make a freewheeling policy choice." The Court, in filling the gaps in § 1983, is engaged in just that freewheeling policy choice which it claims it lacks authority to do. Indeed, this is nowhere more clear than in the immunities area, where the early reliance on 1871 common law has given way to a body of law that can be accurately characterized as a pure federal common law of immunities.

Recent developments regarding the qualified immunity demonstrate this shift to federal common law. In *Wood v. Strickland*, the Court held that an official — who at common law held a qualified immunity — would be subject to damage liability only if either the constitutional right at issue were clearly established (the objective element) or if the official acted with malicious intent (the subjective element). While the Court relied on nineteenth century common law for its conclusion that the school board members in *Wood* were entitled to a qualified immunity, the pedigree of the two-pronged test establishing the scope of the immunity is uncertain, and the Court cited no authority to support it. The Court did discuss the policy of allowing school boards to function free of the constant threat of damages for every constitutional mistake, and one can only conclude that the Court created the test as a matter of federal common law.

Without even a nod to the history of common law immunities, the Court later modified the *Wood* test to make it more difficult for victims of civil rights violations to recover damages. In *Harlow v. Fitzgerald*, the Court eliminated the subjective element of the test because, in its opinion, bare allegations of malice permitted too many cases to get past summary judgment. *Harlow* was not a § 1983 case, but a *Bivens* action brought against federal officials directly under the Constitution — a cause of action created by the Court as a matter of federal common law — and, consequently, the intent of the framers of § 1983 was not relevant. However, the Court has applied this new qualified immunity in § 1983 cases without discussing its authority to modify a test that was supposedly faithful to Congressional intent. And the Court continues to insist that it is not making policy.

Defenders of the Court's practice might argue that while the Court does make policy when determining the *scope* of the immunity, it applies history to determine *who* is immune. Officials absolutely immune at common law are entitled to absolute immunity from civil rights damages. Officials who historically enjoyed qualified immunity may still receive qualified immunity; only the scope of their immunity is determined by federal common law developed in light of underlying policies. The Court, however, has never said anything like this. And even if it did, the Court would still have to justify its departure from the historical method of interpreting § 1983.

In fact, the Court grants absolute immunity to officials without really considering whether they would have had such immunity at common law. The Court looks at the function that the official performs, not the official's title; it has held, for example, that administrative law judges are entitled to absolute judicial immunity even though they are technically executive officials. The Court developed this "functional approach" without considering whether courts at common law would have applied it. While perhaps in 1871 the problem might not have arisen, the Court spared itself any historical investigation of this issue — despite its willingness to consider historical evidence in other circumstances.

The functional approach to absolute immunity remains indefinite in two ways. First, the Court's judgments as to the functions an official performs are indefinite and allow for manipulation. For example, the Court recently held that members of prison disciplinary committees — prison officials who determine whether the evidence establishes that a prisoner has violated a prison rule — are not "adjudicators" entitled to the traditional judicial immunity, because the usual judicial safeguards do not exist in the prison disciplinary setting. However, the Court has not applied a similar analysis to whether members of local legislative bodies perform a legislative function for purposes of absolute legislative immunity. The Court has granted absolute legislative immunity to local officials, even when they are unfettered by the normal checks on legislative authority, such as election, public meetings, and open deliberations of the legislative body. The Court has never explained why the lack of traditional checks on power abrogates immunities for adjudicative, but not legislative, officials.

Second, in the case of presidential advisers, the Court has simply disconnected absolute § 1983 immunity from the common law immunities altogether. While *Harlow v. Fitzgerald* denied automatic absolute immunity to presidential advisers, it suggested that on remand the defendants might be able to establish that their function is so sensitive that they are entitled to absolute immunity. The Court's suggestion that some officials may receive absolute immunity because of the importance of their function to the national interest was made without any common law support.

The primary sources of law in the immunities area are thus the common law of 1871 and the federal common law developed in *Bivens* actions brought directly under the Constitution. The text of the statute plays no role, since it does not mention immunities. Contemporary tort theory has popped up only in a citation or two, but has never been invoked explicitly as a source of immunity from § 1983 damages.

2. *Legal remedies: The common law of 1871 and contemporary federal common law.*

The Court's wavering between the common law of 1871 and federal common law in the immunities area is repeated in the legal remedies area, with the added twist that the federal common law is generated not by *Bivens* cases brought directly under the Constitution, but from the general principles of common law. The two primary issues in legal (as opposed to equitable) remedies are the measure of damages and the availability of punitive damages. The statute itself does not address these issues. In the face of this silence, the main source of law for damages rules has been contemporary common law, although the Court has not undertaken a thorough review of contemporary damages rules. For punitive damages, the Court has looked to a mixture of the common law of 1871 and contemporary common law. The Court, of course, has never explained why statutory silence should direct it to contemporary common law rather than to the common law of 1871 or to the § 1988 sources invoked by silence in other contexts.

The most important damages rule for § 1983 limits recovery to injuries compensable at common law. This rule excludes damages based only on the "importance" of the right that was violated: Common law principles, the Court claims, rarely presume damages and never grant substantial compensatory damages merely because an important right has been violated. Without a recognized common law injury, a plaintiff can recover only nominal damages.

The Court claims that its limitation of damages recovery to common law injuries is justified because this limitation is consistent with the purposes of § 1983. The Court reasons that since Congress intended to create "a species of tort liability," it must have intended that the damages rules be based on common law tort rules. And these rules, according to the Court, do not allow recovery for the "importance" or "abstract value" of a right. The primary purpose of § 1983, the Court argues, is to compensate victims for tangible, not abstract, injuries.

This reasoning is problematic for several reasons. First, the Court assumes that there is some objectively existing body of law known as "the common law" which provides a set of damages rules. This view is inconsistent with current theories that interpret the common law as the creation of particular jurisdictions, each of which chooses a common law for itself, with substantial freedom to choose the interests it will protect and to define what constitutes a compensable harm. Furthermore, even assuming that there were a coherent body of law called "the common law" with a unitary conception of appropriate damages rules, none of the evidence the Court has cited demonstrates that Congress wished to limit the definition of compensable harms to "concrete" or "tangible" injuries as the Court conceives of them. One might reasonably assume that a Congress granting a damages remedy for the violation of constitutional rights would define the denial of those rights as compensable harms. Finally, the Court seems to forget about other standard common law justifications for damage recoveries, most obviously, deterrence theories. Why it has fixed upon "compensation" is hardly clear. If its theory is that compensatory damages provide exactly the amount of deterrence that the authors of § 1983 intended, its reasoning is inconsistent with its theories in other areas. The entire immunities jurisprudence, for example, rests on the assumption that Congress wanted *less* deterrence than a uniform regime of compensatory damages would provide, since the immunities prevent compensation from most defendants.

This criticism of the Court's reliance on common law damages rules is arguably irrelevant: A careful reading of the opinions suggests that perhaps the Court doesn't really rely on the common law for its damages rules. *Carey v. Piphus*, for example, despite its references to the common law, can be interpreted as creating a completely federal rule of damages. While the Court's articulated analysis requires it to look at analogous common law actions for damages rules, the Court did not identify a common law claim analogous to the *Carey* plaintiffs' procedural due process claim. Nor did it cite common law authority for its refusal to grant substantial damages; its reasoning that substantial damages were inappropriate because the procedural violation had no effect on the substantive outcome is a purely federal rule. Thus it may be that reliance on "the common law" in § 1983 damages cases is a sham to cover federal common law.

In any event, whether the source of law is common law or pure federal policy, the effect of the damages rules the Court has constructed is to limit § 1983's deterrence value. Indeed, the emphasis on compensation appears to be intended to deny that § 1983 should be employed as a broad deterrent or preventative measure.

The Court acknowledges that one purpose of § 1983 is to deter future violations, just as one purpose of damages at common law is to deter injuries. However, in both cases they do so only to the extent that liability for compensatory damages is a deterrent. Significant damages awards in cases like *Carey*, which involve no common law injuries, could make § 1983's deterrent effect more widespread. Furthermore, the Court has not made a persuasive case against such a role for the statute.

As for punitive damages, § 1983's silence has once again led the Court to modern and old common law. But contrary to the more contemporary focus for compensatory damages, the Court's punitive damages analysis focuses obsessively on nineteenth century cases. In *Smith v. Wade*, the leading case on the standard for punitive damages under § 1983, both the majority and Justice Rehnquist's dissent cite dozens of cases from the late nineteenth century to support their respective views on the proper standard for punitive awards, on the theory that the framers of § 1983 intended to incorporate the rule that prevailed at that time. And the terms of the disagreement between the majority and the dissent concern what the nineteenth century rule was. There is no discussion of why the Court departs from *Carey*'s focus on contemporary common law.

3. *Injunctions: The "federal common law" of equitable remedies.*

The final set of remedies issues — standards for injunctive relief — is still more confusing. Here the Court often mixes together traditional equity issues, federalist limits on equitable relief, and constitutional issues regarding the justiciability of the case as a whole. Section 1983 provides for suits in equity, but is silent on the requirements for equitable relief. The Court fills this gap with equity rules of its own making without giving much attention to the source of its doctrines. Instead, it relies exclusively on contemporary federal equitable standards, a sort of federal common law of equity.

The Court has employed equity doctrines in many different contexts to limit the reach of § 1983. For example, despite the Court's holding in *Mitchum v. Foster* that the statute is an exception to the Anti-Injunction Act, the Court has erected a heightened irreparable harm requirement for § 1983 injunctions against unconstitutional state proceedings. The Court bases this decision on the special nature of federal-state relations. The Court has similarly imposed, as a matter of equitable restraint, limits on federal court power to intervene into unconstitutional practices by local government agencies. In these cases, as in § 1983 equity cases generally, the Court is less than clear as to its source of law.

One reason the Court may be less attentive to choice of law issues in equity cases is that federal equity practice has traditionally assumed a body of law, derived from English Chancery Court practice, that functions independent of state law. The statutory scheme for federal equity practice, both generally and with specific regard to civil rights actions, has supported this assumption, since it has not explicitly required the federal courts to apply state law. Early versions of the RDA, dating back to the Judiciary Act of 1789, required federal courts to apply state rules of decision only to actions "at common law" in the federal courts. And while amendments in 1945 substituted the words "civil actions" for "trials at common law," thus requiring federal courts to apply substantive state law in equity actions as well, the law establishing the proper conditions for injunctive relief has been deemed "jurisdictional" and is still exclusively federal, even in diversity cases.

The Court never mentions the possibility of applying the equity doctrines of 1871, or the law of the forum state, to decide whether an injunction should be granted under § 1983. As discussed above, in damages issues the Court sometimes holds that the law of 1871 is vital, because Congress intended to incorporate that law into § 1983, while for other issues state law is incorporated under § 1988. The failure to focus on either the law of 1871 or the particular state's law in equity cases seems to leave the Court with more discretion in granting equitable relief than in granting legal relief. Since the 1871 and state law focuses constrain the Court very little, there is an inconsistency here, in form if not in substance.

4. *Exhaustion of remedies: Federal common law.*

The usual practice in the United States is for governments and government agencies to require claimants to exhaust intra-agency remedies, and sometimes other administrative remedies, before filing a court action against government. The Supreme Court rejected such a rule for § 1983 cases, on historical and policy grounds. The Court reasoned that an exhaustion requirement would be inconsistent with Congress's intent to provide an immediate federal remedy for § 1983 violations, and that such a requirement might prove harmful to the interests of civil rights plaintiffs. The Court thus concluded that the exhaustion requirement was not appropriate in § 1983 cases.

Notice the terms on which this argument was conducted. The Court did not ask what the state rules for exhaustion are (as might be required under § 1988) or what the prevailing rule in 1871 was (as is sometimes done to determine Congressional intent). If there were a well-established practice of exhaustion in 1871, then the Court should perhaps take statutory silence on the matter as an intent to incorporate widespread practice. The mere fact that the rule would frustrate § 1983's central policy of providing an immediate federal forum should not itself defeat the exhaustion requirement, since a similar argument does not prevent immunities from defeating another central policy of § 1983 — that of compensating victims. There may or may not have been a settled practice in 1871; the point is that the Court has never even posed that question.

The objection might be raised that when the Court held that Congress intended to provide an immediate federal forum for § 1983 plaintiffs, its focus was on the legislative history, and that it was therefore simply construing the statute, not making common law. Obviously, the difference between statutory construction and making federal common law is a matter of degree. The Court, however, is not pointing to statutory language to justify its result, but looking at more general policies it finds behind the language. And across the spectrum of § 1983 cases it has not only interpreted what is apparently the same phenomenon — statutory silence — in different ways, it has never bothered to explain why § 1983's silence should lead it to four different bodies of law.

* * *

There is no developed body of law governing choice of law in § 1983 cases, just a hodgepodge of different approaches. But this uncertainty actually exists at two levels, that of choosing law and that of applying the law once chosen. Thus, even if the Court were to develop doctrines that could determine which body of law to consult in any particular case, each source of law would still provide little if any guidance in the application.

The greatest difficulty in construing § 1983, particularly but not exclusively at the level of application, is that there is no agreement on the purposes of § 1983 and how broadly it should be read and applied. The consensus in the commentary has been that the history of § 1983 is too indefinite to give real guidance on most questions, and that the Court should admit that it is making policy and not engaged in statutory construction.

The Court itself has been made aware of this view. In *Smith v. Wade*, after examining the hundreds of citations in the majority and dissenting opinions to nineteenth century punitive damages cases, Justice O'Connor argued that the Court should admit that history gave no clear answers for that case; the Court, she argued, should instead look to the policies underlying § 1983 for guidance.

The policies, however, are as indeterminate as the history. In the next section, I examine the typical policy arguments made in § 1983 cases and seek to expose the weaknesses of traditional policy analysis.

II. Frivolous Cases Make Bad Law: Policy and Limits on Section 1983

The unmistakable undertone of hostility in many Supreme Court opinions suggests that some Justices think § 1983 cases are often frivolous, presenting controversies that are of no legitimate federal concern, and holding state officials and programs hostage to federal civil rights liability. This hostility is at least partly self-generating: As the Court tightens up on § 1983 liability, the plaintiffs appear more and more to be reaching for a legal theory, and to be going against the grain of the Court's restrictive civil rights jurisprudence.

The Court cloaks its hostility with the standard policy arguments that are familiar to every first-year law student. Policy analysis in § 1983 cases purports to weigh the value of greater enforcement against the consequences for government that such enforcement entails. The spectrum of the Court's policy arguments here is narrow, not encompassing the more explicitly normative questions behind § 1983 enforcement. Nor does the Court adequately examine its empirical assumptions as to the effects that vigorous (or lax) civil rights enforcement might have. It simply rehearses its familiar arguments, most of which concern the nature of "our federalism."

These "policy arguments" have become the new formalism in our law. Although their proponents may use the realist-sounding word "policy," these arguments have little to do with the policy analysis that the legal realists sought to substitute for doctrinal analysis. The realists hoped that social science could provide a window between the legal system and the world, but their followers have not incorporated serious empirical research into legal analysis. In any event, the window the Court has installed in its § 1983 cases is opaque.

Policy analysis in § 1983 jurisprudence, as we will see, is infected with the same problems as doctrinal analysis. In this section, I examine closely the policies that the Court espouses in § 1983 cases. Because its "policy" constructions of § 1983 place little constraint on the Court, I will conclude, they are illegitimate surrogates for the political analysis they assume away. As analysis, the Court's reasoning is insufficiently empirical; as policy, it is insufficiently political.

A. *The General Purposes of Section 1983*

Compensation for injuries related to constitutional violations, deterrence of future violations, and vindication of constitutional rights are the most frequently cited purposes of § 1983. One could argue from the history underlying § 1983 and from the Court's early opinions construing the statute that the most important purpose the statute could serve would be prevention, either direct, through injunctions, or indirect, through the deterrence of damage awards. But the Court's remedies rules make prevention a secondary goal at best. Throughout the history of § 1983 enforcement, which began in the 1960's, the Supreme Court has stressed § 1983's tort-law pedigree and has identified the primary policy of § 1983 as compensation for those denied their federal rights. While initially the tort analogy served to justify an expansive reading, lately it has limited the scope of § 1983 to only those constitutional violations which cause, or threaten to cause, injuries recognized by common law.

Nor does the Court freely grant a damages remedy in all cases of common law constitutional injury. On the contrary, it has left most such injuries uncompensated, often on the ground that federal intervention would disrupt the operation of local government. As Professor Whitman points out, by granting immunities, imposing strict causation requirements, and forbidding vicarious liability against governmental entities, the Court ensures that § 1983 will not even be an effective compensatory device.

The identification of compensation as the primary purpose has suppressed another set of purposes: the vindication of rights and maintenance of constitutional limits against the intrusions of state government. That is not to say that a determinate set of rights exists that the Court refuses to enforce. The Court has, itself, identified rights that § 1983 is to enforce, as well as limits on state government activity that the statute is to maintain, but its decisions allow these rights and limits to be violated without the imposition of any serious liability under § 1983. Many potential constitutional violations cause little or no injury cognizable in tort, but still seriously transgress constitutional limits. The Court has recognized that deterrence of constitutional violations is a goal of § 1983. But since punitive damages are rarely available, a plaintiff's recovery will be limited in most cases not involving common law injury to nominal damages plus attorney's fees. This gives potential plaintiffs little incentive to sue. Thus, while the legislative history on which the Court relies for its compensation theory also suggests that Congress sought to deter constitutional violations, the Court has created a whole class of cases in which § 1983 creates almost no incentive to comply with the Constitution and federal law.

If the Court were to grant injunctions freely, it might prevent some violations that its damages rules leave undeterred. Again, the legislative history cited in several § 1983 opinions suggests that the statute's framers intended to prevent as many constitutional violations as possible. The Court, however, has repeatedly stated that the requirements for an injunction under § 1983 should be stricter than in other contexts, because federal court injunctions against state officials pose special problems of federalism. In the most notorious of these cases, *City of Los Angeles v. Lyons*, the Court refused to enjoin a police practice that had actually killed people, on the ground that the plaintiff could not establish that he was likely to encounter the practice again. The Court relied, in part, on the fact that Lyons would be allowed to challenge the constitutionality of the practice in his damages suit based on the same conduct. This ruling prompted Justice Marshall to characterize the Court's attitude toward constitutional violations as a "pay as you go" system in which local governments were free to violate the Constitution, even if the victims died, as long as they would pay the toll afterwards.

While the Court often pretends that the statute itself compels these limits on § 1983's reach, the text and legislative history of § 1983 clearly permit different interpretations. The Court sometimes seems to recognize this point and adduces policy arguments to support its interpretations of § 1983. In what follows, I discuss the policies that, according to the Court, justify the restrictive readings the Court has given to § 1983.

B. *Federalism and the Intrusiveness of Remedies*

The primary policy justification which the Court invokes for its restrictive reading of § 1983 is "federalism." The word "federalism" is, in one sense, neutral, merely describing a political system in which local governments and a centralized national government coexist. In common usage, however, "federalism" signifies a theory that would limit the power of the federal government, ostensibly in favor of local control. I intend the second usage in this discussion.

The Court invokes federalism to support significant restrictions on § 1983 protections that both limit § 1983's compensatory remedy and ensure that the statute cannot effectively prevent constitutional violations. While in particular cases the Court is often unclear as to precisely what policy it means to promote by respecting federalism, over the years it has given several justifications for limiting the reach of § 1983 based on this concept. Its most general justification has been the policy of avoiding needless friction between federal courts and state governments. Federal intervention has also been discouraged because it seems in some instances to threaten a state's ability to formulate and execute its own policies, and some programs, the Court reasons, can best be pursued at a local level. The Court has only rarely defended federalism on the ground that it enhances democracy or that it allocates functions to the agency that can best perform them, even though such reasoning is a staple of federalist ideology.

Sometimes, the Court's reasoning has appeared to be purely nonconsequentialist: The Court has relied on principles of federalism for their own sake, without considering their consequences. The Court's struggle to keep ordinary tort cases against states and state officials out of the federal courts is an example of this strategy. The Court has repeatedly stated that tort cases against state officials do not belong in federal courts because, on federalism grounds, the Court should not allow § 1983 to displace state tort law. The opinions do not contain a hint of the social consequences that the Court is seeking to avoid. Rather, federalism is treated as a self-evident principle.

When the Court does explicitly advert to its favorite federalist policies — the avoidance of needless friction and the worry that states will be unable to perform their functions — it sometimes looks for an alternative, less disruptive way to enforce federal rights. The alternatives include raising the federal issue as a defense in a state court action, or suing for damages, rather than injunctive relief, in the federal courts. In some cases, however, the Court's solicitude for the states' ability to function has left the victim not only without a federal forum, but also without any remedy whatsoever.

When the Court worries that a *federal* remedy will cripple a state's ability to carry out its programs, federalism plays only a small role in the reasoning against granting relief. After all, under the supremacy clause, state courts should grant the same remedies in § 1983 cases as federal courts, and state officials are presumably indifferent to the name of the court that grants an injunction or damages award against them. If state courts do not grant the same remedy, then from the perspective of federal interests the problem is state recalcitrance, not the existence of a federal remedy.

As for avoiding friction between federal and state governments, it is unclear what this friction is and why it is something that should concern the federal courts. Perhaps the Court worries that it will anger state officials, for instance state judges, if it halts unconstitutional court proceedings. No doubt states may regret the restraints that the federal government places on them, but once a federal rule is in place or a federal right has been recognized, the supremacy of federal law should resolve struggles between § 1983 and inconsistent state law in favor of federal law. Of course, if there is uncertainty about the proper boundaries of federal and state power or the proper reach of the § 1983 remedy, then federalism arguments become meaningful and important. But in these situations, the Court needs much more information about the state policies allegedly threatened than its current opinions would indicate that it seeks. Further, a more efficient method of safeguarding federal rights which would minimize the disruption of state activities and reduce the friction between federal and state governments should be adopted, all other things being equal. But the Court makes no such argument; in fact, it is difficult to find anything in its opinions beyond philosophical displeasure at federal enforcement of federal law against the states.

The Court's acceptance of these arguments with little or no evidence of any alleged undesirable consequences reveals two things about its attitude toward § 1983. First, the Court is clearly not interested in vigorous enforcement of § 1983 or an expansive definition of the rights it protects; otherwise, friction between the states and the federal government would be the price the Court would pay for aggressive enforcement. "Federalism" in this context cannot be dissociated from the Court's substantive preferences for a narrow construction of § 1983. Second, the Court has converted an ideological image once called "states' rights" into a reified picture of social life, supported not by evidence, but by arguments that resemble incantations of belief more than descriptions. The Court's acceptance of the states' rights picture not only reflects its devaluation of civil rights enforcement, but establishes the criteria against which all arguments for greater civil rights enforcement will be judged.

The Court's statements about the policy concerns behind damages and injunctions are hopelessly confused. In keeping with its general preference for compensation over prevention, the Court has often declined to grant injunctions against state officials on the ground that injunctions are more intrusive than damages. The Court has, for example, withheld equity relief when damages relief would be available, following the familiar requirement that a party seeking an injunction establish that no adequate remedy at law exists. But in other cases, the Court has apparently concluded that damages are equally as intrusive as, if not more intrusive than, injunctions, and has denied damages on the ground that they are too intrusive in situations where equitable relief might be available. For example, the Court has refused to grant a damages remedy against unconstitutional state tax collection, on the ground that federal injunctions against state tax collection are barred by the Tax Anti-Injunction Act, and under the circumstances damages would be as intrusive as an injunction. Similarly, since the Court has held that some officials who are partially or completely immune from damages liability have no immunity from injunctions, it again appears that the Court thinks damages might be more intrusive than injunctions. Remember, these are both examples of recognized rights which the Court has decided not to enforce through the § 1983 action. Without a theory that evaluates the intrusiveness of particular remedies in specific situations, I can only conclude that if the Court believes the plaintiff should lose, whichever remedy the plaintiff seeks will, for the time being, be too intrusive.

C. *Timidity of Officials Threatened with Liability*

The policy analysis underlying the immunities provides the clearest example of the incoherent Court policies limiting § 1983. As discussed above, once one discards the dubious statutory justifications for the immunities, what remains is a set of policies concerned with the degree to which damages awards interfere with local governmental functions. The Court states that the immunities are intended to advance the public interest in freeing local officials from the threat of litigation and liability. Local officials will be unable to advance the public interest effectively, the Court reasons, if they must constantly worry about personal liability for constitutional error.

I agree with the Court, and with commentators, that the more damages liability an official is threatened with, the greater the tendency toward timidity. However, neither the Court nor the commentators have any information about the magnitude of the effects of increased damages liability. It may be that under the current regime officials are vastly overdeterred, or it may be that much greater liability could be imposed without threatening the effective administration of government. Further, there is very little, if any, analysis of the costs of the immunities: How much compliance with the Constitution and compensation for violations is sacrificed each time an immunity is expanded? By readily accepting the arguments for personal immunities and making enterprise liability more and more difficult, the Court appears to place a low value even on the compensatory purposes it endorses for § 1983.

The policy arguments used to justify the immunities are the purest examples of the Court's failure to link its image of social life to the world. The Court continually asserts that local officials could not function if they were under a constant threat of liability, or even the threat of having to defend a suit. But it cites no facts or figures to establish that any particular level of civil liability would cripple government, and the opposite possibility is never discussed — that government and official immunity might underdeter unconstitutional conduct. While the harm to the plaintiff from not being compensated is occasionally acknowledged, the costs of decreased compliance with the rights enforced through § 1983 are not considered at all. The Court has created a distorted and incomplete picture of the world of civil rights enforcement.

D. *Clearing the Federal Docket and Avoiding Frivolous Cases*

A final policy that the Court appears to pursue is docket-clearing. Although research has revealed that the increase in the number of § 1983 suits has not been much greater than the increase in litigation generally, some members of the Supreme Court have claimed that the federal courts are buried under an avalanche of frivolous § 1983 suits. While the Court has stated that § 1983's goals outweigh the danger of frivolous litigation, the desire to eliminate frivolous cases has moved members of the Court to advocate strict limits on punitive damages and to expand the reach of the immunities.

Frivolous cases make bad law, and so do cases the Court perceives to be frivolous. So many "frivolous" cases are still brought because the Court itself sends mixed signals about what constitutes a proper § 1983 case. The case law, policies and principles of § 1983 are so hopelessly contradictory that litigants and their attorneys cannot rationally predict the Court's response to their claims.

Some commentators have suggested that, frivolous or not, a type of claim that produces a great deal of litigation in the federal courts should, for that reason alone, be limited. For example, Dean Nichol argues that state judges should be absolutely immune from damages, because otherwise § 1983 cases against them would inundate the federal courts. The theory seems to be that if the federal courts are overrun with cases against state judges, § 1983 will become generally a less effective statute. But there must be more to the argument. Unless the cases lack merit — e.g., because the plaintiffs don't really need judicial relief, or because any relief would be too disruptive of the state judiciary — then the logical solution would be to expand the courtroom, not close the door.

III. *Politics and Pragmatism in Applying Section 1983*

Legal doctrine and policy arguments in the narrow sense fail to answer the hard questions about § 1983 enforcement. In this section, I argue that the alternative to these indeterminate doctrinal and policy arguments in § 1983 cases is a combination of an explicitly political discussion of § 1983 and a more pragmatic policy development. First, I contend that political argument may legitimately replace doctrinal argument. Next, I develop the contours of the political arguments over § 1983, and apply those arguments to a few specific situations. Finally, I return to the policy problems surrounding the application of § 1983 and develop a pragmatic method for adjusting the statute to resolve policy issues as they arise.

A. *Section 1983, Indeterminacy and Political Arguments*

My principal criticism of the legal arguments made concerning § 1983 is that they are indeterminate — i.e., that they require choices made on extralegal and, presumably, political grounds. The Supreme Court, I have argued, hides behind doctrinal and policy arguments that constrain their authors no more than the political views that motivated their construction. In this section I argue that courts and commentators should give up the charade and replace legal argument with political argument.

Courts and commentators participate in this charade in different ways. Commentators are far more likely than judges to admit that doctrine is pliant enough to permit doctrinal choices. And most commentators on § 1983 are motivated to write by their political views. Surprisingly, however, the literature contains little explicit discussion of the writers' views of the statute: The legal scholarship is short on principled defenses of either an expansive or narrow scope for § 1983. In some cases, the author's views can be inferred: If *Parratt v. Taylor* is praised for eliminating many § 1983 cases, or damned because it allows too many cases to remain, then the reader knows where the writer stands. In other cases, the author's views remain completely obscure, as where the author simply advocates an "effective" enforcement of § 1983 without many specifics. In neither case, however, does the author explicitly argue for one or another political view. Professor Eisenberg may be right that there are two fundamentally conflicting views of § 1983 — one which confines it to remedying the racist and lawless conditions in the post-Civil

War South, and another which presents it as a tool of enforcement to be used against constitutional violations everywhere. But even where an author clearly holds one or the other view, his reasons for doing so are very rarely discussed explicitly.

My argument that judges and commentators should make explicit the political views that motivate their interpretations is an argument both for political discussion and for candor. Arguments for candor have often been made, usually focusing on judicial candor, and usually resting either on a moral preference for honesty in the legal system or on policy grounds such as predictability. For example, David Shapiro rests his argument for judicial candor on a moral preference for honest judicial decisions. By contrast, Robert Leflar has argued for candor primarily on utilitarian grounds: Honest judicial decisions, he claims, not only make the law more predictable, but they create better policy as well because they explicitly consider the potential consequences of the rule they adopt.

My argument for candor in § 1983 analysis rests on both moral and utilitarian premises. I share the moral preference for honesty in judicial decisions and believe that academic writing should explicitly address the political views that motivate even technical doctrinal work. I also think that if the political premises of the arguments for and against liberal enforcement of § 1983 were made explicit, the legal community would find the Supreme Court's limitations on § 1983 liability inconsistent with American constitutional ideals. This last belief may be mistaken, and, indeed, a consensus might form against civil rights enforcement. But given the existing trend in that direction, the risk is worth taking.

Arguments against candor in legal writing have focused mainly on adjudication. For example, critics of legal realism warned that talk of how judges' political views influenced their decisions would threaten legal stability and judicial legitimacy. No doctrine, they objected, would be safe from political manipulation, and the public would lose confidence in judicial decisions if it doubted that judges apply objective, neutral legal rules. More recently, Critical Legal Studies scholars have been accused of threatening the stability of the legal system and the rule of law through their attacks on the alleged neutrality and determinacy of legal rules.

The problem with these arguments against candor is that they blame the messenger who bears the bad news. Those who would prefer a § 1983 jurisprudence that safely relied on the intent of Congress are uncomfortable with suggestions that text and history do not answer all the relevant questions, and they fear the results of "political" judging. The argument against candor in these matters asserts that judicial discretion *does not* exist because it *should not* exist. Critics of candor, however, have no effective solution to the problem of general statutes like § 1983. In some circumstances, the intent of Congress (or at least its practice) has been to pass general legislation and delegate to the federal courts broad discretion in interpretation. Because "political" judging may be perfectly consistent with congressional intent, the argument against candor, at least with respect to general statutes like § 1983, should as much be addressed to Congress as to the federal courts.

A more plausible argument against candor is that, against a background of political disagreement, it would be difficult to write generally acceptable opinions which relied explicitly on political views. Even arguments from general legal and constitutional principles are likely to be controversial, and unless we confine ourselves to the narrow arguments from principle that appear as adjuncts to doctrinal argument, we will be treading on terrain that is unfamiliar to lawyers. Explicit political discussion in legal opinions seems inconsistent with the role of a judge as many have long understood it.

I have argued, however, that at least with respect to general statutes like § 1983, there is no alternative to "political" judging: Text and history provide such meager guidance that the issue is whether political reasoning will be candid or covert, not whether politics can be excluded from judging altogether. In full recognition of the difficulty of this task, I think it is time to develop a vocabulary that can open a moral and political discussion of how much enforcement of civil rights there should be — a vocabulary that frankly recognizes the uncertainty inherent in policy judgments as to the effects of § 1983 enforcement.

In what follows, I discuss the political and policy judgments that must be made in § 1983 cases. I attempt to illustrate that the real grounds for the debate over civil rights enforcement lie in the political disagreements between liberals, conservatives, and radicals. I do this by outlining the ways in which each group frames the issues important to § 1983 litigation. Finally, I return to policy arguments, attempting to combine political awareness and skepticism about policy into a pragmatic approach to § 1983 litigation.

B. *Three Political Images of Section 1983 Litigation*

It would be impossible to describe separately all of the political views of § 1983 that have been articulated (or just assumed) since 1871. But that would be unnecessary for my present purpose of orienting the political discussion of § 1983. Just as one can, as a first approximation, classify general political theories as conservative, liberal, and radical, so too can political views of § 1983 be sketched in these dimensions. The accounts of the various political stances that follow are not intended to exhaust all possible views or to describe precisely any particular set of views; I recognize that many people will hold views from different sets. However, in social theory, and particularly in social criticism, the use of ideal types has long been considered a useful method of investigation. The way these various sets of views should be understood here is as an attempt to create typologies of viewpoints about § 1983, and to use them to open up discussion of the issues along the lines presented, not to describe the views of any particular judge or theorist. Because these "ideal types," "paradigms," or "images" are rarely found in pure form, they highlight the themes that do appear frequently, thus providing useful perspectives, points, and orientation for the discussion that follows.

1. *The liberal, rights-based reformist perspective.*

Persons taking the liberal, rights-based approach to § 1983 believe the statute to be a potentially effective tool of civil rights enforcement. Section 1983 plaintiffs, in this view, are powerless victims of abusive state and local government. These abuses threaten the set of rights that § 1983 is designed to protect — the rights enshrined in the liberal's view of the Constitution. With some play at the margins, these rights are relatively determinate, and the liberal insists that they be interpreted correctly. Limiting § 1983, whether by narrowing rights or restricting remedies, is thus an attack on the true constitutional order.

One paradigm victim of governmental power is the state prisoner. The liberal sympathizes with the prisoner on several grounds. First, the liberal senses that whatever their misdeeds, most criminals have themselves been victims of social injustice, and that without that injustice they would probably not be prisoners. Second, the liberal believes that the procedural rights of criminal suspects, defendants, and convicts are both important in themselves and inextricably linked to other individual rights that the Constitution guarantees. Third, the liberal believes that the conditions in prison are, in fact, terrible and that absent constitutional guarantees, prison guards and officials would have virtually unrestrained power to abuse their prisoners. If anyone in our society is treated the way blacks were treated in the post-Civil War South, it is prisoners. Finally, even if the plaintiff is not a sympathetic character herself, it would be impossible to construct rules that would exclude the bad plaintiffs without also eliminating the deserving ones.

By contrast, this vision suspects local officials of possible incompetence, unconcern, or corruption, and sees the local political system as factional, fractious and subject to capture. The background narratives of the liberal approach are stories of police brutality and official insensitivity, together with the history of local government's resistance to desegregation. The only way to prevent repeat episodes is for the federal government to protect constitutional rights from state and local attacks. The liberal hears in contemporary federalism an echo of states' rights rhetoric of the segregationist past.

The liberal believes strongly in the rule of law and in the Constitution. The liberal approach values individual rights over federalist principles, and thus would narrow the immunities and limits on justiciability: Violations of individual rights and state overreaching, the liberal maintains, must not go unremedied. This approach sees the genius of the Constitution in its establishment of real limits to government power over individuals, and thinks that this value would be undermined if § 1983 litigation were curtailed.

The liberal approach sees § 1983 litigation as at least one way of vindicating these rights. Liberals differ on the effectiveness of § 1983, however, with some preferring a system of administrative remedies that would spare plaintiffs the uncertainties and delay of litigation. But even if § 1983 is procedurally imperfect, and even if a deterrent effect on civil rights violations is difficult to establish, the liberal finds symbolic value in strict federal enforcement, and is confident that the symbolism is not entirely lost on potential law-breaking local officials. This view sees the federal courts as the forum of principle, insulated from the political pressures that turn other government institutions into civil rights violators.

In sum, the liberal supports the expansion of constitutional rights and the increased legislative protection of civil rights over the past few decades. The liberal approach may recognize that the judicial activism of the sexual and reproductive privacy decisions is difficult to defend, but as long as the activism is in line with proper political views, the liberal will leave well enough alone.

2. *The conservative, authority-defending perspective.*

What I am calling the "conservative" perspective sees the prevailing distribution of wealth and power as generally benevolent, or at least benign. In this view, state and local government officials conscientiously do their best to respond to the local community, but they stagger under the crushing burden of governing, and are often encumbered by federal interference. While occasionally they make good faith mistakes, the cause of the problem is not official abuse of power, but the pressure of a difficult job made more difficult by federal meddling. In the criminal justice system, for example, police and prosecutors by and large respect criminals' rights in substance, even if they sometimes make technical mistakes; their efforts to combat crime are too often thwarted by a judiciary that has failed to understand the real needs of law enforcement. Officially sanctioned segregation is from the distant past, and accusing local governments of racism is like accusing the government of West Germany of responsibility for Nazi crimes. State and local officials have been unjustly insulted by the liberal attack.

The conservative image of the civil rights plaintiff is quite different. Most prisoner plaintiffs are looking for a diversion from the routine of prison life, and their constant litigation is usually frivolous, unfounded and a nuisance: They clog the courts with their endless attempts to escape punishment. Other civil rights plaintiffs, in this view, make federal cases out of things that are essentially local matters, often trying to win a fight in federal court that has already been lost in the local executive or legislative forum. These plaintiffs are lured to federal court by the prospect of attorneys' fees and a sympathetic judge. And the decisions they protest were probably correct to begin with; for example, fired employees who allege civil rights violations were probably fired for good reason. The only legitimate civil rights plaintiffs are victims of racial discrimination and, perhaps, victims of violations of some of the Bill of Rights. Even these cases should be viewed with suspicion, however, because they do not happen very often.

The conservative image of the Constitution and its enforcement is complicated. On the one hand, it presents the United States Constitution as the embodiment of the most enlightened government in the history of the world; its genius lies in the limits it places on government. While government must be restrained from undue interference with individual rights, the individual rights the conservative has in mind are more likely to be property and contract rights than, for example, the free speech, criminal procedure, and privacy rights which the liberal celebrates. The conservative takes the indeterminacy of "privacy" rights in particular to be different in kind from the inevitable blur at the boundaries of other rights. This indeterminacy, together with the undemocratic character of judicial review and the perceived gulf between the federal courts and local needs, makes the conservative quite suspicious of using federal law to promote the liberal agenda.

These mixed feelings about the Constitution lead the conservative to presumptions against justiciability and judicial enforcement of most individual constitutional rights, and presumptions in favor of defenses such as the immunities that protect state and local administration from federal attack. Federalist limits are of constitutional pedigree too, the conservative reminds us. And not only federalist principles, but also practical reasons counsel narrow § 1983 liability. These practical reasons are that § 1983 litigation wastes resources, puts distant federal judges in charge of local administration, sacrifices the greater good to claims of a few individuals, and may even fail on its own terms by making local governments lazy about constitutional matters because they expect the federal courts to step in and correct any constitutional mistakes.

3. *The radical, "tool of oppression" perspective.*

The keystone of the radical approach to § 1983 is its demand that the statute be applied substantively, empowering people to control their own lives. Within the context of the current liberal/conservative dominance, however, this demand leads the radical toward ambivalence regarding § 1983. On the one hand, the radical views § 1983 litigation as a tool of oppression which helps maintain the existing distribution of power. By correcting some highly visible problems, the legal system creates the false impression that constitutional enforcement protects individuals from oppression, and thus it diverts attention from potentially fruitful methods of social change. The radical deplores the formalistic terms of the debate between liberals and conservatives that depoliticize political issues and foreclose the possibility of radical reform.

On the other hand, the radical agenda for reform resembles the liberal scheme in some ways. Both advocate greater recognition of some personal rights and greater participation in important decisionmaking. And on many particular issues, the radical position is close to the liberal, rights-based view. Both distrust state and local government officials; they agree further that § 1983 combats state and local governments' abuse of power, the frustration of participation, and the evasion of limits on governmental action. But the radical hardly trusts the federal government: Both the federal and local governments, according to the radical, abuse their citizens all the time. And one problem with § 1983 is that its inevitably selective style of reform may empower federal officials as much as the victims of governmental abuse.

The radical dilemma arises from the apparent choice between recognizing the plaintiff's rights or not: While the radical will choose to recognize them, she will still worry that successful civil rights litigation will pacify victims of social injustice and divert resources away from more productive methods of social change, such as community organizing. Thus, the radical sympathizes with individual plaintiffs against government officials, but shares the conservative's skepticism about social change through litigation, albeit for different reasons.

The radical distrusts federal judges, but not for the conservative's reasons. To the radical, doctrines such as the immunities and limits on justiciability demonstrate judicial hostility toward victims' claims and the inevitable limits on even modest change within the American constitutional order. In the radical view, federal judges are privileged members of the ruling class no more likely to further radical change than the Joint Chiefs of Staff. While the expansion of constitutional rights in recent years might be good in theory, in practice it has brought little if any benefit for the less fortunate. The radical has very little hope for genuine change without the radical redistribution of wealth, but believes that § 1983 litigation is not likely to produce significant redistribution.

The radical's views about reform through law are colored by context. The rule of law, while preferable to unrestrained governmental terrorism, at present looks like a powerful conservative force. Thus, while the radical favors more protection for the powerless, she doubts that judicial activism will fundamentally democratize social institutions. And only this democratization, the radical thinks, could make the changes that the radical political agenda requires. The radical would like, therefore, to redirect the rights debate toward recognizing the kinds of rights connected to radical change. And here, where the discussion turns to long-term goals, the radical and liberal part company, with the radical looking toward institutional reform that would create a much more democratic society in which people radically increase their control over their lives.

C. *The Effects of Section 1983 Litigation*

Each of the political views described above presupposes a view of the policy effects of § 1983 enforcement. This is true despite our near-total ignorance of the magnitude of these effects, both on the ability of state and local government to function and on the degree of constitutional compliance. The legal literature contains no substantial empirical studies of these issues. While we can logically assume that greater liability will tend to increase compliance with the Constitution and make local government more expensive, the magnitude of those tendencies is not similarly predictable.

The failure to distinguish between tendencies and magnitudes is perhaps the central weakness of policymaking under § 1983 and elsewhere. Reasoning about tendencies without considering magnitudes creates a false consensus, since widespread agreement about the former does not imply agreement on the latter. For example, the proposition that legislative liability would make local legislators more cautious about trying new programs is uncontroversial, but how much they would be inhibited — not to mention how we should evaluate their inhibition — is much more difficult to determine. Perhaps other factors make them so timid already that liability would not make much difference; perhaps all but the most courageous legislator would avoid introducing any new programs, or perhaps widespread insurance or government indemnification would ameliorate the effect. General political views, in their relationship to legal policy views, influence which conjecture we choose, and how much of the private interest in compensation we think should be sacrificed.

The policy discussions in the § 1983 literature have generally confined themselves to tendencies, not magnitudes. This weakness is crucial, since so many important issues in § 1983 litigation are said to turn on a trade-off between governmental effectiveness and compensation for (or deterrence of) constitutional violations. As one commentator put it in the immunities area, the issue is "how to balance the twin concerns of protecting officers and insuring compensation to the victims of their misdeeds." But we have no real empirical evidence of the effects that expansive liability would have on local administration, and, thus, no way to "balance" the competing tendencies rationally. Stating the issue as one of "balancing" opposed tendencies of uncertain magnitude invites unreflective conjectures that will predictably correlate with one's prior political views on the subject. Further, the "balancing" metaphor deflects attention from the political issues that lurk just below the surface.

The Court's analysis suffers from the same weakness. Its emphasis has recently been on the potential costs that § 1983 imposes on government. These costs range from the immediate dollar cost of a damages judgment paid out of public funds, to the loss of governmental services whose funding has been diverted to pay the judgment, and, finally, to the expense of litigation even if the local government or official wins the case. The potential costs also include the "costs" of official timidity that the threat of litigation presumably induces. However, nothing in the Court's opinions suggests the magnitudes of these costs, or even a method by which to calculate them. Nor does the Court compare these costs to the private losses from constitutional violations.

The political views of an author, whether judge or commentator, influence which costs appear more real and more important. The liberal is likely to see high costs from constitutional violations and potentially large gains from increased enforcement. Further, the liberal is likely to discount the costs to government administration either as small, or as clearly outweighed by the benefits of imposing the costs of unconstitutional conduct on government and ensuring constitutional compliance. The conservative, on the other hand, views the potential costs to local government as crippling and the gains to victims as either small or undeserved, because of the phoniness of many claims and the illegitimacy of many "rights." Because no empirical evidence is available, only the ideology of the author appears to influence which costs and benefits the author finds most important.

The fact that the empirical questions raised in § 1983 cases are difficult does not mean that these issues should be ignored. But neither should the policy issues be decided as they have been in both cases and commentary. A better approach would be pragmatic, opening the discussion to empirical evidence of the effects different rules would have, and inviting reassessments if the results were not as anticipated. This pragmatic approach should not be aimed at establishing certainty regarding social reality. Rather, it has the more modest goal of making a serious attempt to investigate the effects of legal rules, recognizing that these effects are always contextual, and, thus, subject to change with the passage of time and the modifications of circumstances.

A pragmatic approach to § 1983 litigation would base decisions on empirical arguments — such as the argument that police liability for false arrests would dangerously chill enforcement — only if data supported these arguments. The Supreme Court might even allow disagreements among circuits to remain, so that it could assemble comparative data. The Court should not cast its decisions in terms of congressional intent, so that it will feel more free to reverse itself if its empirical judgments are proven wrong. And it should admit when it is uncertain, so that parties will be encouraged to offer data and arguments for reversal. Because many § 1983 litigants would be unable to afford the expense of conducting detailed studies, the courts should encourage others to do so. Government agencies, advocacy groups, private interest groups, and universities all could be called upon to do research and offer the results to courts through publications and as *amici*.

Courts and commentators should also assess more closely the effects of nonenforcement on victims of civil rights violations. Until now, neither the victim's interest in compensation nor the potential victim's interest in deterrence has often entered the Court's calculus as to the proper scope of § 1983. Organizations and individuals advocating civil rights enforcement should, thus, be encouraged to come forward with data on the costs of nonenforcement.

I recognize that labeling the Court's approach to policy "pragmatic" will not magically transform its method. But the recharacterization of policy arguments in terms of pragmatism is meant to be more than a semantic change. Rather than simply the old balancing of the plaintiff's interest in compensation against the government's interest in effective functioning, the discourse should be open to broader political and empirical questions. The constitutional norms that § 1983 enforces should be established by the same consequentialist analysis I have recommended; once the Court has identified a constitutional norm, its commitment to constitutional limits should not be sacrificed without hard evidence that granting a remedy would seriously hamper the greater good. And even then the diminution of remedies should be narrowly tailored and open to reassessment. Because the Court's judgments would have a broader focus and be explicitly revisable, the Court would be free to make decisions in light of all relevant factors, without focusing narrowly on government interests and enshrining those interests as statutory intent.

The objection may be raised that opening court proceedings to expert testimony and studies regarding the likely effects of various statutory interpretations makes the court look more like a legislature. On this familiar view, the legislature makes policy, and the courts simply defer to that policy judgment. But as I have argued, courts commonly engage in policy reasoning when they apply general statutes — including not only the civil rights statutes, but also antitrust and copyright laws, just to name a few examples. If fault lies anywhere, it is with the Congress that writes statutes which plainly call for judicial policymaking. Unless Congress suddenly decides to write a detailed code of civil rights enforcement, instead of general statutes like § 1983, the federal courts must make policy and political judgments if the statutes are to have any application at all. I argue only that they should do so explicitly and self-consciously.

D. *Moral, Political and Pragmatic Aspects of Civil Rights Enforcement*

The politics of the different images of § 1983 — not text, history, or policy in the narrow sense — explain the differences among judges and commentators. Neither group, however, has forthrightly addressed the political questions involved. Judicial opinions rely on false history and policy, while commentators tacitly assume their political views about § 1983 rather than argue for them explicitly. In this subsection, I attempt to explain how politics influences § 1983 analysis, and to show how positions on some central issues — immunities, remedies, amenability to suit, and "color of law" — can be better understood in light of political arguments.

1. *Immunities.*

The argument over immunities captures many of the political differences over the proper scope of § 1983. The liberal's opposition to immunities is consistent with her general views about § 1983 litigation. Immunities threaten the statute's role in pursuing social change and combating abuses of government power. Immunities increase the powerlessness and alienation of civil rights victims by denying a remedy even where there has been a violation. The liberal may acknowledge that constant § 1983 litigation could hamper local government's ability to function, and perhaps he might allow some narrow immunities in particularly sensitive areas, such as judicial immunity from damages. But generally the liberal will view the costs of § 1983 litigation as part of the cost of maintaining constitutional government — something the liberal believes we should be willing to bear. The liberal's real philosophical objection to the immunities is that they are inconsistent with the rule of law and recent constitutional developments: The immunities place official conduct above the law, and subvert the expansive readings of the Bill of Rights and the fourteenth amendment that have become established over the past few decades. To recognize rights without granting effective remedies, the liberal argues, is plainly inconsistent.

The conservative's sympathy for expansive immunities is also consistent with his general views about § 1983. The conservative is suspicious of § 1983 plaintiffs, and believes that § 1983 suits only harass, distract, and discourage local officials who are trying in good faith to serve the public. Litigation, the conservative thinks, is an ineffective tool for social change, and judicial activism threatens the only legitimate avenue for social change — the legislative process.

The conservative may acknowledge in principle the *Marbury v. Madison* dictum that all rights have remedies, but she will still argue that this dictum should have no effect in § 1983 cases. First, many of the rights potentially protected under § 1983 are illegitimate, the product of judicial activism that has gone far beyond the Constitution. Second, even where the "rights" claimed are legitimate, the realities of government have made it impractical to enforce all rights through damages actions, and the courts should trust the political process to correct important deficiencies in the observance of rights.

The radical's reaction to this debate is twofold. First, because they make officials less accountable and more likely to transgress democratically established limits, the immunities should be criticized as impediments to radical social change. Second, the radical sees the immunities as an illustration of the contradictions in the liberal theory of American constitutional government. The irony of conservative defenders of the Constitution favoring broad immunity for constitutional violations only supports the radical's general views about the system. And the liberal's willingness to compromise by allowing narrow immunities is, if anything, more confused than the conservative view.

Part of the disagreement between the liberal and the conservative is about government's ability to function under the threat of liability and how the immunities for governmental bodies affect the enforcement of the constitutional guarantees of § 1983. Commentators and courts should try to discover the effects of the immunities. Local governments should put forth data on the effects of liability. Civil rights groups should produce evidence of the costs of looser enforcement of civil rights. Courts should take a pragmatic approach to the policy questions surrounding the immunities. They should be willing to experiment with different levels of immunity, to admit when they are uncertain about policy, and to encourage the parties to bring forth data on the effects of the immunities.

2. *Remedies.*

Remedies issues are treated extensively above, but a few comments here will illustrate the political nature of the controversy. The liberal view favors broad injunctive relief to help prevent as many § 1983 violations as possible, while the conservative views injunctions as undesirable judicial interference with the political system. The liberal may favor a more generous measure of damages, because civil rights victims deserve compensation, and because damages relief will deter violations. The conservative favors narrow measures of damages, lest civil rights plaintiffs receive windfall recoveries and innocent local officials be punished for honest mistakes.

The radical view here is close to the liberal view, but it more closely connects the issue of remedies to the cause of increased democracy and self-determination. Courts should interpret the Constitution to guarantee, and should grant remedies to advance, institutions that allow for local, democratic control and eliminate illegitimate hierarchies.

3. *Persons.*

The liberal favors expanding the definition of "persons" subject to suit under § 1983 to include state and local governments and their officials, for all of the reasons that she desires more effective § 1983 enforcement. Governmental bodies should be deemed "persons," the liberal thinks, because they are more able than individual officials to pay damages and prevent violations. The conservative, in contrast, would limit the definition of "person" to protect government from suit, hoping that victims will not bother to sue judgment-proof officials. The conservative would not include states and state agencies as persons, so that federal courts, or state courts applying federal law, would not meddle in state affairs.

The radical would define "person" by comparing the substantive consequences of different interpretations. Because government institutions oppress people in ways that a § 1983 remedy might combat, the radical would define them as "persons." But to the radical, the whole debate is symptomatic of mainstream relapses into formalism and renewed indulgence of the long-discredited public/private distinction.

Here again, no definition of "person" can be discovered in the language or history of § 1983. The issue is largely one of politics and, to a lesser extent, policy. The policy involved is minimizing federal court intervention into the affairs of state government. But before accepting a narrow definition of "person," the federal courts should demand some evidence of the effects that different definitions would have on government agencies. Talk about tendencies toward friction and interference is no substitute for realistic assessment of the actual consequences.

4. *Under color of law.*

Section 1983 grants a remedy only if the defendant has acted under color of state "statute, ordinance, regulation, custom, or usage." The big issue here is whether conduct that is contrary to state law can nonetheless be "under color of" state law if performed by a state official. The liberal favors an expansive definition of "under color of" that would allow § 1983 to attack a broader category of unconstitutional conduct, thus preserving constitutional values and the rule of law. The liberal sees government officials as involved in a significant amount of illegal conduct, and § 1983 as a necessary weapon against the renegade official. The liberal sees great symbolic value in allowing a federal remedy even where a state remedy is also available: The federal court, in the liberal view, is the guardian of civil rights. But the weakness in the conventional liberal argument is the absence of any but symbolic reasons for a redundant remedy.

The conservative, on the other hand, thinks that it makes sense to limit "under color of" to conduct authorized by state law, because if the state official acts illegally under both federal and state law, a remedy will probably be available in the state courts. The conservative image of § 1983 generally is that if it does anything, it overrides state laws that are unconstitutional, thus granting a remedy against action taken pursuant to unconstitutional state laws. Arguments based on conservative federalism favor as little federal intervention as possible: If the state grants a remedy of its own, the civil rights plaintiff should be required to pursue that remedy before suing in federal court. The embarrassing aspect of the conservative position, however, is that it would subject to § 1983 liability those officials who follow, in good faith, a state law that turns out to be unconstitutional, yet exonerate officials whose conduct violates both state and federal law.

While the radical sympathizes with the liberal desire to bring more official conduct under § 1983 scrutiny, she scorns this argument over the meaning of the words "under color of" law, which reenacts the public/private distinction that was exploded long ago. For the radical, almost all action involves state power, and private abuse of contractual rights is as much under color of law as police brutality. The state defines the contours of power, and § 1983 should be used to attack any concentration of power that prevents people from controlling their own lives. The radical views the argument between the liberal and the conservative as an example of how both are still stuck in formalism.

IV. Conclusion

There is no excuse for retaining the traditional methods of construing § 1983. The court's manipulation of text, legislative history and policy is transparent, especially when it jumps merrily from one source of law to another. The indeterminacy of the Court's choice of law rules has led commentators to seek a definitive construction or application of § 1983. Commentators who have recognized the indeterminacy of the text and history of § 1983 would replace doctrinal analysis with political analysis, in the form of conjectures about the effects of proposed applications of § 1983. The political motivations for the various suggestions, however, have remained hidden, impoverishing the debate and dooming the analysis to a new formalism, in which policy arguments are made and accepted with no real attempt to determine their truth through research or testing.

The way to understand the controversy over § 1983 is to understand its political and ideological aspects, and to open the process to real assessment of the facts rather than stylized policy arguments. What is needed are data regarding the social costs of more or less enforcement, and straight talk about a political vision for § 1983 — a vision that explains the author's preference for more or less expansive liability.

Section 1983 can be a helpful tool for reform, but only if it is freed from its troubled history. The statute can be used, together with progressive constitutional doctrine, to move toward greater democratization of local institutions and to maintain official accountability. But § 1983 will not become useful in this way through better legal reasoning. Rather, such change will only happen through a social movement that will reshape legal consciousness along progressive lines.

Sheldon H. Nahmod, *Section 1983 Discourse: The Move From Constitution to Tort*, 77 Georgetown Law Journal 1719 (1989)

* * *

I. An Overview of § 1983 Discourse

By virtue of its language, § 1983 does in some ways resemble a tort statute, and the Court has always taken that into consideration when deciding § 1983 cases. However, the Court's recent tendency to liken § 1983 to a simple tort cause of action has allowed it to limit the range of "rights, privileges, or immunities" protected by the section. It is important to see how this recent tendency differs from the Court's initial focus with respect to § 1983, when it merely made reference to tort law. The increasing use of tort rhetoric has allowed the Court to transform § 1983, thereby diluting the protection it offers to persons whose constitutional rights have been violated.

A. Constitutional Rhetoric

This section examines three § 1983 cases in which the Court was especially solicitous of the plaintiffs. Although the Court in these cases occasionally referred to tort law in its constitutional analyses, such references were incidental and did not limit the relief granted.

In 1961, the Court in *Monroe v. Pape* gave life to § 1983 in holding that § 1983 provides a remedy for persons deprived of their fourteenth amendment rights by a state official's abuse of his position. The Court thereby interpreted the phrase "under color of [law]" to include acts of state officials that are illegal under state law. This decision was in large measure responsible for the treatment of § 1983 as the equivalent of a fourteenth amendment action for damages.

In *Monroe*, constitutional rhetoric dominated. The Supreme Court emphasized that even if a state law remedy existed for the § 1983 plaintiffs, the drafters of § 1983 meant to provide a supplemental federal remedy for cases in which states are either unwilling or unable to enforce fourteenth amendment rights. In addition, the Court held that § 1983 does not require plaintiffs to exhaust state remedies before bringing a § 1983 action.

Justice Harlan said it best when he asserted that § 1983 reflects the view that "a deprivation of a constitutional right is significantly different from and more serious than a violation of a state right and therefore deserves a different remedy even though the same act may constitute both a state tort and the deprivation of a constitutional right."

Implicit in this view is the idea that § 1983 was enacted to enforce the fourteenth amendment, and that in many cases persons deprived of fourteenth amendment rights should receive relief different from and additional to what state courts would award for trespass or other common law torts. States could not be relied on to ensure compliance with the fourteenth amendment, and a federal remedy was necessary in cases in which states were unwilling to prosecute state officials who had violated the fourteenth amendment. However, *Monroe* did not use constitutional rhetoric exclusively: tort rhetoric also played a role in its § 1983 interpretation. In particular, the Court insisted that § 1983 was to be interpreted against a "background of tort liability that makes a man responsible for the natural consequences of his actions." Tort doctrines enabled the *Monroe* Court to conclude that the allegedly intentional conduct of the defendants was covered by § 1983.

The Court also emphasized constitutional rhetoric in *Monell v. New York City Department of Social Services*, a 1978 decision in which the Court, overruling part of *Monroe*, held that local government entities may be sued under § 1983. Most of Justice Brennan's majority opinion focuses on § 1983's legislative history in an effort to determine whether Congress intended local governments to be immune from suit under § 1983. In its discussion of legislative history, the Court emphasized constitutional rhetoric. For example, the Court quoted Representative Shellabarger's statement that the function of § 1983 was to provide a civil remedy for all persons "'where, under color of State law, they or any of them may be deprived of rights to which they are entitled under the Constitution by reason and virtue of their national citizenship.'"

In addition, the Court stated that the municipalities in question could not assert that they acted in reliance on the prior law of absolute immunity. The court affirmed that "municipalities simply cannot 'arrange their affairs' on an assumption that they can violate constitutional rights indefinitely since injunctive suits against local officials under § 1983 would prohibit any such arrangement." Moreover, the Court emphasized that "there can be no doubt that section 1 of the Civil Rights Act was intended to provide a remedy, to be broadly construed, against all forms of official violation of federally protected rights."

It is true that the Court in *Monell* described § 1983 as a "constitutional tort" and discussed the policies underlying the tort doctrine of respondeat superior. Nonetheless, the Court did not allow its use of tort language to determine the substantive result in the case; it ultimately ruled against the applicability of respondeat superior to § 1983 actions on two grounds. First, the Court considered § 1983's "subjects, or causes to be subjected" language to be incompatible with respondeat superior liability. Second, the Court reasoned that the policy objectives underlying respondeat superior liability in the tort setting had been rejected by the 42nd Congress. Consequently, this tort doctrine was found by the Court to be inapplicable to § 1983.

Constitutional rhetoric was similarly dominant in *Owen v. City of Independence*, in which the Court held that local governments are not protected by an immunity based on the good faith of their officers and agents. After determining that there was no tradition at common law of qualified good faith immunity for local governments, the Court emphasized the significance of § 1983 as a remedy for the vindication of fourteenth amendment rights. It stated: "A damages remedy against the offending party is a vital component of any scheme for vindicating cherished constitutional guarantees, and the importance of assuring its efficacy is only accentuated when the wrongdoer is the institution that has been established to protect the very rights it has transgressed." The Court went on to observe that § 1983 was designed not only to compensate for past constitutional deprivations but "to serve as a deterrent against future constitutional deprivations, as well." It also pointed out that local government liability without a qualified immunity protection "may encourage those in a policymaking position to institute internal rules and programs designed to minimize the likelihood of unintentional infringements on constitutional rights." Finally, the Court explained its individual qualified immunity cases as not understating the significance of constitutional compliance but rather as recognizing that "overriding considerations of public policy" require individual government officials to be afforded qualified immunity protection. Those concerns, however, were either inapplicable or not compelling with regard to local government liability.

Even *Owen*, also authored by Justice Brennan, was not free of tort language. The Court at the end of its opinion maintained that insofar as doctrines of tort law had changed since § 1983 was enacted in 1871, "our notions of governmental responsibility should properly reflect that evolution. No longer is individual 'blameworthiness' the acid test of liability; the principle of equitable loss-spreading has joined fault as a factor in distributing the costs of official misconduct." The Court concluded by asserting that its decisions in this and other immunity cases properly allocated the costs of constitutional violations among the victim, the officer causing the injury, and the public at large. In so doing, the Court expressly sanctioned the use of cost-benefit analysis in § 1983 interpretation.

B. TORT RHETORIC

In *Monroe*, *Monell*, and *Owen*, the Court placed constitutional rhetoric in the foreground of § 1983 interpretation. In contrast, in the individual immunity cases that followed on the heels of *Monroe*, the Court increasingly used tort rhetoric to shape the outcome. The Court also used tort rhetoric extensively in a case presenting the question of whether presumed damages are available in a § 1983 suit, and in § 1983 cases involving alleged due process violations, particularly those with prisoner plaintiffs.

Pierson v. Ray, decided in 1967, involved the question of individual officer immunity. In *Pierson* plaintiffs sued a justice of the peace and police officers for arresting and convicting them under an unconstitutional statute. The Court held that the justice of the peace was protected by absolute judicial immunity and further held that the police officers could defend on the ground that they acted in good faith and with probable cause in making an arrest under a statute they believed to be valid.

Pierson is noteworthy because the Court relied exclusively on doctrines of common law tort immunity. In concluding that the justice of the peace was protected by absolute judicial immunity, the Court relied on an earlier legislative immunity decision and asserted that § 1983 must be interpreted against a common law tort background of absolute judicial immunity. The Court reasoned that had Congress intended to abolish wholesale this common law immunity when it enacted § 1983, it would have done so explicitly. In ruling on the police officers' defense of good faith immunity, the Court similarly looked at § 1983's common law tort background and concluded: "Part of the background of tort liability, in the case of police officers making an arrest, is the defense of good faith and probable cause."

Consequently, a clear pattern emerged: the Court would begin its inquiry with the common law of torts and proceed to use tort law as the basis for the § 1983 officer immunity rules it would ultimately apply. Indeed, with few exceptions, the Court has accepted defenses of immunity in § 1983 actions. Thus, absolute immunity protects prosecutors from damages liability under § 1983, just as it does under common law, provided that the conduct at issue was advocative. The same is true for legislators who engage in legislative conduct. As at common law, however, school board and prison officials are protected only by qualified immunity from § 1983 damages liability.

In 1978 the Court held in *Carey v. Piphus* that presumed damages are not available in § 1983 procedural due process cases. This case similarly reflects the change in emphasis from constitutional rhetoric to tort rhetoric. The *Carey* Court first asserted that the basic purpose of § 1983 liability was "to compensate persons for injuries caused by the deprivation of constitutional rights." It then went on to declare: "Rights, constitutional and otherwise, do not exist in a vacuum. Their purpose is to protect persons from injuries to particular interests, and their contours are shaped by the interests they protect." The Court's characterization of compensation as the basic purpose of § 1983 tends to understate the significance of complying with the fourteenth amendment. In addition, its assertion that constitutional rights do not exist in a vacuum suggests that they do not have intrinsic value. Further, the comparison between constitutional and "other" rights implies that constitutional rights do not occupy a place higher than those other rights.

The Supreme Court's view that § 1983 "creates a species of tort liability" is especially apparent in § 1983 cases alleging violations of due process. In its 1976 decision in *Paul v. Davis*, a significant due process case, the Court moved tort rhetoric to the foreground of its analysis. In *Paul* the plaintiff alleged that the defendant law enforcement officers had damaged his reputation by publicly branding him as an "active shoplifter." Writing for the Court, Justice Rehnquist ruled that injury to reputation, standing alone, is not a liberty or property interest for procedural due process purposes. It is the Court's reasoning, however, that is especially pertinent. The Court responded to the plaintiff's fourteenth amendment interpretation by observing that such an interpretation "would make of the Fourteenth Amendment a font of tort law to be superimposed upon whatever systems may already be administered by the States." The Court went on to characterize the plaintiff's interest in reputation simply as one of the many interests that states could protect through tort law, "providing a forum for vindication of those interests by means of damages actions."

At first blush, the Court appears to have been concerned in *Paul* that § 1983 *not* become a kind of tort statute. That is, one might read *Paul* as upholding the special status of § 1983 as different in kind from tort law. However, this is not an accurate reading of the decision. The Court told the plaintiff that his proposed § 1983 action was not different from a defamation action. With this holding, the Court revealed a strategy that would later dominate its § 1983 procedural due process jurisprudence. The Court first described the proposed § 1983 action as the functional equivalent of a state tort action and then declared that state remedies were adequate, sending the matter to state courts where it belonged. The Court was not really saving § 1983 for important cases but was rather using tort rhetoric to undermine § 1983.

In later § 1983 due process cases, the Court has explicitly relied on tort rhetoric to achieve the results it wanted. In particular, the Court has attached significant weight to potential state court remedies and to tort states of mind. For example, in *Parratt v. Taylor*, a prisoner claimed that prison authorities negligently lost certain hobby kit materials he had ordered, thereby depriving him of his property without due process of law. Treating this claim as alleging a procedural due process violation, the Court, again through Justice Rehnquist, agreed with the prisoner that the hobby kit materials, worth $23.50, amounted to a property interest, and that the alleged negligence on the part of the defendants was enough to constitute a deprivation of that property interest. However, the Court ruled that an apparently adequate state post-deprivation remedy was available to the prisoner in the state courts, where he would have had a meaningful opportunity to be heard. The Court therefore declined to find the defendants liable under § 1983.

The reasoning in *Parratt* was couched in tort rhetoric. The Court began by observing that a predeprivation hearing was not feasible where only negligence and a random, unauthorized act were charged. For this reason, stated the Court, the defendants could only reasonably be expected to provide a post-deprivation hearing. In the view of the Court, the availability of this post-deprivation hearing satisfied requirements of procedural due process. However, the Court's use of tort rhetoric may have led it to ignore the possibility that the plaintiff's property loss could have been avoided, or at least that the risk of such a loss could have been reduced, through the establishment of prison procedures for handling incoming inmate packages.

Parratt reflected the Court's apparent preference for sending many proposed § 1983 procedural due process cases to state court, so that state tort principles would be applied in a post-deprivation hearing. The Court appears to have believed that cases involving prisoners who challenge the loss of personal property do not belong in federal court, where they require the expenditure of scarce judicial resources. Further, the Court apparently believed that such cases are essentially tort actions because they involve negligence; thus, state courts, not federal courts, should decide them — and on state law grounds, not federal grounds.

Tort rhetoric also influenced the Court in *Daniels v. Williams*, a 1986 due process case in which a prisoner claimed that he was deprived of his "liberty to be free from bodily injury" when he slipped on a pillow that had been left on some prison steps. The Court, partially overruling *Parratt*, held that mere negligence by a state official is not enough to deprive a person of his liberty of property under the fourteenth amendment. The Court did not make clear the minimum state of mind required of a defendant before due process guarantees apply. It reasoned that the due process clause was meant to protect against governmental abuses of power and that, consequently, more than negligence is required before the Court will find that a state has deprived a person of life, liberty, or property without due process of law.

Even though the Court used constitutional rhetoric to assert that the due process clause was meant to prevent abuses of power, it made the question of the state officials' state of mind determinative of the threshhold inquiry in due process cases: was there a deprivation of a life, liberty or property interest? In *Daniels*, the Court's response was negative because the plaintiff alleged only negligence; accordingly, the Court did not need to reach the question of the availability of state post-deprivation remedies. In this way, the Court used state of mind requirements derived from tort law to cut back the scope of due process and thereby similarly to cut back the scope of § 1983.

* * *

[II] C. POST-STRUCTURALISM I: DERRIDA

Post-structualism is built on the work of Nietzche and Saussure, though it in many ways specifically uses the structuralist form of analysis to reject structuralism itself. Specifically relevant to my analysis of the Supreme Court's § 1983 jurisprudence are Jacques Derrida and Michel Foucault.

In his philosophy, Jacques Derrida broadly attacks Western philosophy for mistakenly assuming that speech — the "word" — captures reality better than written language because it is immediate and does not have to be interpreted, while writing requires interpretation of texts. He argues that this emphasis on speech in Western philosophy is a manifestation of the "metaphysics of presence": the idea of "seeing for oneself" is somehow more reliable than reading. Derrida analyzes the implications of this hierarchy and explores the possibility of basing a theory of language not on speech but on "generalized writing."

Derrida's focus on inverting this textual hierarchy is called deconstruction. Derrida's deconstructionist approach is based in part on the fundamental instability and indeterminacy of language emphasized by Nietzsche and on what Saussure calls the arbitrary relationship between the signifier and the signified. If signifiers and signified are only arbitrarily related, then the text has an existence separate from its author. Thus, the *presence* of the author cannot guarantee that the text reflects a *definitive* meaning. There can be no definitive meaning; there are only meanings. In a famous passage, Derrida puts it this way:

> [R]eading . . . cannot legitimately transgress the text toward something other than it, toward a referent (a reality that is metaphysical, historical, psychobiographical, etc.) or toward a signified outside the text whose content could take place, could have taken place outside of language, that is to say, in the sense that we give here to that word, outside of writing in general. . . . *There is nothing outside of the text.*

A central strategy of deconstructive criticism is to discover and invert the "margins" of the text being criticized. Derrida is willing to make use of anything marginal — slightly inconsistent rhetoric, less than perfect word selection, or contradictory information that the author has attempted to hide in a footnote. He will then, against the author's intention, develop these margins to show the text's contradictory meanings and the ways in which any argument has the seeds of its opposing argument.

This deconstruction of margins helps us to understand the relative ease of the previously described shift in emphasis from constitutional rhetoric to tort rhetoric in the Supreme Court's § 1983 case law. Section 1983 contains constitutional rhetoric in the phrases "under color of [law]" and "to the deprivation of any rights, privileges, or immunities secured by the Constitution." This constitutional rhetoric appears to occupy a central position in the title of § 1983: "An Act to enforce the Provisions of the Fourteenth Amendment to the Constitution of the United States, and for other Purposes."

Section 1983 also contains tort rhetoric in the phrases "subjects, or causes to be subjected," and "shall be liable to the party injured in an action at law." From a deconstructive perspective, this tort rhetoric has the potential to undermine the constitutional rhetoric. I have demonstrated how tort rhetoric has increasingly moved toward the center of the Court's § 1983 discourse, while constitutional rhetoric has lost its central position. This shift in the kind of rhetoric used, and thus in § 1983 discourse, disguises a move away from a pro-plaintiff, pro-civil rights stance toward a pro-defendant, anti-civil rights stance.

[II] D. POST-STRUCTURALISM II: FOUCAULT

Michel Foucault both criticizes and transcends Derrida's focus on separate and independent texts through an emphasis on discourse. He defines discourse to include the contexts in which texts are written, the relations among texts and what is excluded from texts due to the limitations of a particular discourse. Strongly influenced by Nietzsche, Foucault concludes that knowledge cannot be separated from power. For Foucault, there are different kinds of knowledge; each kind of knowledge — scientific, philosophical, medical, and so on — has its own discourse, within which certain ideas can or cannot be formulated. Those who claim the right to discourse must always struggle to center their discourse, marginalizing others whose discourse threatens their own. Foucault maintains that at any point in history there exists a set of power relationships that establish the conditions of discourse.

Foucault thus believes that prevailing discourse reveals the nature of social power. Discourse, however, is not simply current wisdom; it also disguises and actually constricts the objects it discusses. For example, study of the history of madness demonstrates that its discourse is designed to allow those in power to control the mind. Similarly, study of the history of sexuality shows that it, too, has a discourse which, contrary to popular opinion, is not liberating but actually makes us more compulsive. Indeed, Foucault asserts that in allowing the disclosure of sexual desires and practices to others, the discourse of sexuality actually creates the potential for greater control by those in power. Foucault raises significant questions regarding the legitimacy of discourse: who owns it and how is it controlled?

Inasmuch as we are unable to transcend our own discourse, it is very difficult for us to escape and criticize it. Foucault nevertheless undertakes to provide histories of various discourses in an attempt to free language from the "myth of signification." He attempts to show that every rule or norm is arbitrary by studying texts whose discursive mode departs from the discursive mode of their predecessors.

Foucault uses this theory of discourse to attack the status quo and to promote radical breaks in history. His strategy is wedded to an activist ideal of change, but there is nothing coherent about it beyond that. Indeed, there appears to be no prescriptive content to Foucault's utopianism. It is nihilistic.

Yet it is not necessary to accept Foucault's nihilism to recognize the power of his approach to the nature of discourse. As applied to the move from constitutional rhetoric to tort rhetoric in the Supreme Court's § 1983 jurisprudence, Foucault's approach suggests at the very least that an event of deep significance has occurred. It is to the implications of this event that I now turn.

III. The Implications of Tort Rhetoric

As I suggested earlier, the shift from constitutional rhetoric to tort rhetoric was foreshadowed by the Court's repeated use of the term "constitutional tort" in § 1983 cases. This term gives priority to "tort" while according secondary significance to "constitutional." And indeed, what was once marginal is now the central object of discussion. The Supreme Court has accomplished a considerable inversion of § 1983 discourse by manipulating the language it uses to discuss § 1983. I now analyze some implications of this move.

A. The Implications of Tort Rhetoric: Doctrine

The shift from constitutional rhetoric to tort rhetoric operates at several different levels. The first and most obvious level is that of doctrine: tort rhetoric encourages the explicit use of tort doctrines to determine the scope of § 1983. A prime example, noted earlier, is the use of tort absolute immunity doctrines to insulate legislators, judges, and prosecutors from the threat of § 1983 litigation. The rule that presumed damages are not available in § 1983 suits, which had its beginning in *Carey v. Piphus* and culminated in *Memphis Community Schools v. Stachura*, is another example. Still another example is the Court's use of proximate cause in *Martinez v. California*, in which the majority found the harm to the § 1983 plaintiff to be too remote from the defendants' conduct to be actionable.

To the extent the Court emphasizes tort rhetoric in § 1983 litigation, it tends to model § 1983 doctrines on tort concepts of fault. Recall that even in *Monroe v. Pape*, the Court asserted that § 1983 was to be interpreted against a background of tort liability that makes a person responsible for the natural consequences of his or her conduct.

A fault model, built on notions of individual responsibility, has proved especially difficult to apply in cases involving local government liability. On the one hand, the Court in *Monell* ruled that an official policy or custom causing the deprivation of rights must exist before local governments will be held liable, a requirement that parallels the notion of individual responsibility in a fault model. Yet in *Owen v. City of Independence*, in justifying its holding that local governments are not protected by qualified immunity, the Court explained that equitable loss spreading, a no fault concept, is an important consideration in interpreting § 1983. This tension between fault and no fault, coupled with the difficulty of ascribing wrongful states of mind to government bodies, illustrates the problems the Court continues to have in defining the proper standards of local government liability. Such problems are especially evident in attribution and failure to train cases. The justices are divided over the appropriate model for § 1983 in these cases, with the majority, influenced by tort rhetoric, insisting upon a fault model.

Tort rhetoric also has had an impact on substantive constitutional law. Because § 1983 provides a remedy for violations of the fourteenth amendment, every decision narrowing the scope of the fourteenth amendment also narrows the scope of § 1983. I have already set forth examples of the effect of tort rhetoric on constitutional interpretation in § 1983 due process cases. The same phenomenon has occurred as well in the Supreme Court's fourth amendment and eighth amendment jurisprudence.

In addition, substantive due process/affirmative duty cases in the federal courts, virtually all of which have been decided against plaintiffs, regularly rely on the tort concept of "special relationship." Tort doctrines, supported by tort rhetoric, therefore play an increasingly prominent role in constitutional adjudication. Many of these fourth, eighth, and fourteenth amendment developments have occurred in the setting of § 1983 litigation.

B. THE IMPLICATIONS OF TORT RHETORIC: COST-BENEFIT ANALYSIS

Tort rhetoric also operates at a somewhat more subtle level than that of explicit doctrine: it facilitates the use of cost-benefit analysis. While it is true that there has been growing interest in, and scholarly support for, a "rights" approach to tort law, one can fairly describe the current judicial perspective on tort law as a "law and economics" approach that emphasizes either efficiency, loss-spreading, or some combination thereof. Courts taking this latter approach only recognize those values that can be actually or theoretically quantified. Consequently, constitutional values are often discounted significantly.

Harlow v. Fitzgerald is the clearest illustration of the Court's use of cost-benefit analysis to determine the scope of § 1983 relief. In *Harlow* the Court's explicit cost-benefit analysis led it to adopt an objective qualified-immunity test that eliminated any subjective inquiry into a defendant's state of mind and instead focused strictly on whether the defendant violated clearly settled constitutional law at the time of the alleged act. Notably, the Court did not address the loss resulting from the possible underdeterrence of constitutional violations. Moreover, in *Anderson v. Creighton*, the Court provided even more protection for § 1983 defendants by directing that the clearly settled constitutional law inquiry for qualified immunity should not be made at too general a level.

C. THE IMPLICATIONS OF TORT RHETORIC: MARGINALIZATION THROUGH CHARACTERIZATION

Tort rhetoric operates at yet a third level: it marginalizes § 1983 by characterizing it as a tort statute. If § 1983 is viewed primarily as a tort statute, then it becomes easier to argue that § 1983 actions belong in state court because they are in reality no different from garden-variety tort actions. In addition, state courts have as much expertise as federal courts in adjudicating tort cases.

The debate about exhaustion of judicial and administrative remedies can perhaps best be understood at this level. Although *Monroe v. Pape* explicitly ruled that § 1983 does not require plaintiffs to exhaust state judicial remedies, it was argued that there ought to be at least a requirement of exhausting administrative remedies in appropriate cases. The Court effectively settled this debate in *Patsy v. Board of Regents*. Stressing the distrust of state adjudication processes that is clearly reflected in § 1983's legislative history, the *Patsy* Court ruled that the section imposes no exhaustion requirement. Nonetheless, in *Parratt v. Taylor* the Court held that adequate state post-deprivation remedies eliminate procedural due process violations in certain circumstances. This holding in fact bars plaintiffs from federal court more effectively than would an exhaustion requirement because under *Parratt* plaintiffs can *never* return to federal court. Thus, the Court, through constitutional interpretation, was able to end-run the clear no-exhaustion legislative history of § 1983 and send certain cases to the state courts.

With its decision in *Younger v. Harris*, the Court was similarly able to ensure that certain § 1983 cases are conclusively sent to state courts. In *Younger*, on grounds of "our Federalism" and comity, the Court held that a § 1983 plaintiff cannot secure federal injunctive relief against pending state court criminal proceedings. Such a plaintiff must remain a state defendant and raise any constitutional arguments in the state proceeding with only the remote possibility of certiorari in the Supreme Court. The Court has applied *Younger* very strictly to § 1983 plaintiffs — exceptions are few and far between — and has extended the decision to cover pending civil proceedings involving important state interests. Several justices have even suggested that *Younger* should apply to § 1983 damages actions when state proceedings are pending.

Furthermore, characterizing § 1983 as a tort statute and thereby sanctioning tort rhetoric makes it easier to apply the tort concepts of absolute and qualified immunity to certain defendants. When a court holds that an individual defendant is protected by immunity, the defendant is exonerated from damages liability even though he or she may have violated the plaintiff's constitutional rights. Viewing the injury to the plaintiff as functionally comparable to a tort injury comports easily with the Court's use of the tort defense of immunity.

Tort rhetoric also supports the Court's pejorative descriptions of § 1983 actions and those who bring them. In *Harlow v. Fitzgerald*, the Court made very clear that it viewed many *Bivens* and § 1983 suits as "insubstantial." Similarly, in *Anderson v. Creighton*, the Court expressed concern with "harassing" litigation and "clever" § 1983 plaintiffs.

It therefore is no coincidence that prisoners have brought many of the recent major § 1983 cases in which the Court either has cut back or at least refused to expand the scope of due process. Prisoners, whose constitutional rights the Court has gradually narrowed, are unappealing persons with whom the Court apparently identifies much § 1983 litigation. To signal its view that many § 1983 suits waste time and resources, the Court has chosen to review § 1983 cases brought by prisoners — in particular, ostensibly trivial cases involving lost hobby-kit materials and injuries resulting from pillows left on prison stairs. From the Court's perspective, the prisoners who brought suit in *Parratt*, *Hudson*, *Daniels*, and *Davidson* used § 1983 as if it were a garden-variety tort statute. The intended message is that little will be lost if the Court narrows the scope of § 1983 and due process.

D. THE IMPLICATIONS OF TORT RHETORIC: FEDERALISM, THE STATE-CITIZEN RELATIONSHIP, AND POLITICAL SOCIETY

I contend in the final sections of this Article that the Court's increased use of tort rhetoric in § 1983 cases also implies that certain restraints should characterize the federal-state relationship, the state-citizen relationship, and the nature of political society.

1. Federalism

Our federal system, which is thought to promote experimentation, efficiency, individual liberty, and democracy, is premised on several beliefs. One belief is that state courts should not be viewed as less competent than federal courts to deal with important constitutional issues. Another is that the federal judiciary should strive to minimize its supervision of state and local government affairs. On those occasions when some involvement by the federal judiciary in state affairs is unavoidable, the federal judiciary must be sensitive to the effects of its involvement on state and local government operations.

Federalism concerns are often raised in § 1983 litigation because it is state and local governments or their employees who are § 1983 defendants. True, the fourteenth amendment was intended to bring about a dramatic shift in federal-state relations whereby the federal government became responsible for protecting individual rights in cases in which the states could not be relied upon to do so. It is also true that the legislative history of § 1983 rather clearly indicates that the 42nd Congress enacted § 1983 because of a profound distrust of state institutions. Nevertheless, the current Supreme Court is very sensitive to federal-state issues in § 1983 litigation and has developed a host of judge-made doctrines that are designed to strengthen the role of states. This is true with regard to § 1983 injunctive-relief actions and § 1983 damages actions. Indeed, many of the Court's decisions appear to treat § 1983 as a symbol of antifederalism.

The use of tort rhetoric encourages this strategy of promoting state power. To the extent the Court views § 1983 primarily as a tort statute, it is able, as noted earlier, to send what might otherwise be § 1983 claims to state court. State courts have the requisite expertise and experience to deal with tort claims and can do so using state law. In addition, concern for the role of states in the federal system played a significant role in the Court's recent decisions interpreting the due process clause. *Parratt v. Taylor*'s post-deprivation remedy approach for certain procedural due process cases, and *Daniels v. Williams*'s insistence that more than negligence is required for due process violations, have the purpose and effect of sending many cases to the state courts.

Similarly, the use of the forum state's personal-injury statutes of limitations in § 1983 actions, together with the applicability of state preclusion rules to § 1983 actions, promotes state interests. And at least four justices prefer to use state law to determine local government liability based on attribution from high-ranking officials.

The current substantive due process case law regarding whether the government has an affirmative duty to provide rescue and other services to citizens demonstrates the importance of federalism issues in § 1983 adjudication. From the beginning, federal courts have emphasized that the decision whether to provide services belongs to state and local governments and not to the federal courts. These courts usually speak of the generally applicable tort rule that there is no affirmative duty in the absence of a special relationship. Consequently, in virtually all of these § 1983 affirmative duty cases, federal courts have declined to find a duty. They have been worried not only about the effect of federal judicial intervention on government finances but also about the displacement of state and local decisionmaking. Significantly, the Supreme Court recently articulated this position in *DeShaney v. Winnebago County Department of Social Services.*

2. The State-Citizen Relationship

The affirmative duty cases and their use of tort rhetoric imply a particular view of the state-citizen relationship. Tort cases are usually bipolar; that is, they involve suits between two private parties in which public law issues ordinarily do not arise. To the extent that tort rhetoric predominates in § 1983 litigation, courts tend to treat § 1983 plaintiffs and defendants as autonomous strangers who have no prior relationship with one another — even though the defendant is a government or government employee. By analogy to the tort doctrine that strangers ordinarily owe no Good Samaritan affirmative duties to one another, tort rhetoric makes it easier for courts to treat the Constitution as a charter of negative liberties, a position the Supreme Court has in fact recently taken.

In contrast, when the Court applies a constitutional analysis independent of analogy to tort law, it becomes easier to ask — regardless of what the answer is — whether in a particular case the constitution imposes an affirmative duty upon the individual or government defendant. Tort rhetoric thus renders it more difficult to confront the constitutional duty issue head on and prompts courts to use tort concepts to determine the outcome.

3. Political Society

The use of tort rhetoric in § 1983 cases also implies a choice among competing visions of political society — the same choice that resonated in the federalist-antifederalist debate of our early national history. A bipolar, individual autonomy approach to § 1983 in which citizens and the state have no necessary relationship with one another implies a pluralist vision of political society. In such a society, interest groups, or factions, fight it out in the political marketplace for temporary supremacy in the same way that products fight for supremacy in the economic marketplace.

In a pluralist society, people are basically selfish and use political processes for their own end. Factions are therefore inevitable. It is true that by analogy to the economic marketplace, some consider pluralist politics to be the best way to promote the public welfare. Nonetheless, legislative outcomes under the pluralist model are the result of bargaining about individual preferences and are primarily a reflection of shifting political alliances.

This view of political society, reflected in the Court's use of tort rhetoric, assumes that the Constitution is a charter of negative liberties that prohibits federal courts from interfering with pluralist politics at the state and local levels. Such a hands-off approach allows individuals and groups to attempt to use political muscle at those levels either to maintain the social and economic status quo or to attempt to change it.

Classical and Madisonian republicanism, on the other hand, both assert that there is a public good apart from the clash of private interests and that individuals belong to a political community. If the public good cannot be achieved through the deliberative processes of government, then courts using constitutional rhetoric could impose obligations on state and local governments to assist their citizens affirmatively.

Thus, the federal judiciary might adopt a § 1983 jurisprudence based on Madisonian republicanism and thereby take a prominent role in promoting the public good. In doing so, courts could also fulfill classical republicanism's dictate that civil society should educate its citizens. Because classical republicanism is concerned with civic virtue and its close relation to private virtue, a reading of the due process clause as imposing affirmative obligations on state and local governments to protect and rescue their citizens could serve as a model for the promotion of civic virtue and political community.

The use of tort rhetoric consequently implies a pluralist model of politics in which the Constitution is a charter of negative liberties and in which the federal judiciary should play a minimal role in protecting fourteenth amendment rights. In contrast, when the Court reasons in a framework of constitutional rhetoric, it becomes free to accept a republican model of political society with a correspondingly less restrained view of the proper federal judicial role in § 1983 and fourteenth amendment interpretation.

* * *

Part XI

Alternative Dispute Resolution and Release-Dismissal Agreements: An Empirical Perspective

A release-dismissal agreement is one in which a criminal defendant releases his right to file a section 1983 action in return for a prosecutor's dismissal of pending criminal charges. Although the potential for prosecutorial overreaching is obvious, the Supreme Court has upheld the general validity of such agreements so long as they are truly voluntary and not an abuse of the criminal process. *Town of Newton v. Rumery*, 480 U.S. 386 (1987).

Professor Kreimer's article maintains, in reliance on empirical studies and interviews with prosecutors and defense attorneys, that the benefits of release-dismissal agreements assumed by the Court in *Rumery* were exaggerated. He argues further that the dangers of these agreements are significant. Thus, his position is that *Rumery*'s approval of them (and ours as well) should be more restrained.

Seth F. Kreimer, *Releases, Redress, and Police Misconduct: Reflections on Agreements to Waive Civil Rights Actions in Exchange for Dismissal of Criminal Charges*, 136 University of Pennsylvania Law Review 851 (1988)

I. Introduction

For several years, the Supreme Court has echoed the emerging literature of Alternative Dispute Resolution ("ADR") in encouraging disposition of legal disputes by means short of full-scale litigation. While this trend has not been without its critics, civil rights cases have been fertile fields for the growth of the Court's enthusiasm for negotiated settlements. In *Marek v. Chesny*, the Court extended the settlement incentives of Federal Rule of Civil Procedure 68 to civil rights attorneys' fees, commenting that "Section 1988 encourages plaintiffs to bring meritorious civil rights suits; Rule 68 simply encourages settlements. There is nothing incompatible in these two objectives." In *Evans v. Jeff D.*, the Court overturned a decision forbidding waivers of attorneys' fees in civil rights cases because "a general proscription against negotiated waiver of attorney's fees . . . would . . . reduc[e] the attractiveness of settlement." Settlements, the Court asserted, "will serve the interests of plaintiffs as well as defendants."

The usual paradigm for ADR involves an attempt to avoid civil litigation between two private parties. Last Term, the Court carried the litigation-avoidance process two steps further in the civil rights area. In *Town of Newton v. Rumery*, a majority of five Justices upheld a bargain struck between a public

---

prosecutor and a private criminal defendant that was designed to keep the defendant's civil rights claims against third parties out of court. The majority approved the exchange of a criminal defendant's covenant not to sue the police on a civil rights claim for the dismissal of pending criminal charges. It did so, however, with some trepidation, since the exchange of monetary consideration for the dismissal of criminal charges looks suspiciously akin to extortion or bribery.

Unlike *Evans* and *Marek*, *Rumery* did not purport to be grounded in statutory intent or court rule. It was, rather, an explicit attempt by the Court to resolve the issue by "reference to traditional common-law principles," the application of which leaves substantial latitude for future case-by-case development. This Article will canvass the considerations that should shape that development and will counsel caution in extending the enthusiasm for nonjudicial composition of civil rights claims in this direction.

* * *

II. "Common Law Principles" and "Public Interests"

"Traditional common law principles" and a pragmatic assessment of the public interest shaped the analysis of release-dismissal agreements in *Town of Newton v. Rumery*. Indeed, for the *Rumery* Court the "common-law principles" and "public interests" were identical; the Court's evaluation rested on the "well-established principle" that "a promise is unenforceable if the interest in its enforcement is outweighed in the circumstances by a public policy harmed by enforcement of the agreement."

Reference to the "common law" as a touchstone of section 1983 jurisprudence is a regular feature of the Court's interpretations of section 1983. It is debatable, however, whether the *Rumery* majority identified the appropriate "well-established" common law principle. The common law fairly bristles with other appropriate starting points for analysis, most of which would point to the per se voidability of release-dismissal bargains. Contracts induced by threats of prosecution are voidable at common law, and duress by imprisonment can prevent the enforcement of releases. At common law, obtaining items of value under color of public office constituted the crime of extortion, and the common law offense of "compounding a crime" punished agreements not to prosecute a crime in exchange for payment. It should be no surprise, therefore, that before *Rumery*, the weight of state and federal precedent had prohibited such agreements.

The *Rumery* majority, however, did not refer to any common-law precedent. Rather, it followed the modern tendency to make the balance the measure of all things. The majority determined to resolve the issue on the basis of a fresh comparison between the weight of the interests favoring and opposing enforcement of releases unencumbered by legal doctrine in cognate areas.

According to the majority, the per se invalidation of release-dismissal agreements that the court of appeals adopted from the prevailing line of federal authority "fail[s] to credit the significant public interests that such agreements further" and exaggerates their dangers. It is well, then, to begin the attempt to give substance to the federal common law of release-dismissal agreements adumbrated in *Rumery* by examining in some detail the public interests served by the agreements and then to turn to the dangers they bring in their train.

The Court undertook the analysis of the costs and benefits of release-dismissal agreements in *Rumery* on the basis of the facts of the case and the published opinions. This background sufficed to evaluate Mr. Rumery's release. A useful expansion of the analysis, however, requires some sense of the real world context of release-dismissal agreements. It is difficult to parse the nature of "legitimate law enforcement interests," to evaluate "adverse effects of the release on relevant public interests," or to assess the potential of release-dismissal agreements for eliminating "frivolous" civil rights cases from the information available in the pages of U.S. Reports.

In order to gain some empirical leverage on these issues, during June and July of 1987, I conducted interviews of prosecutors, police, and defense attorneys in twenty jurisdictions. Table I summarizes the interview results.

Table I

Reported Use of Release-Dismissal Agreements By Prosecutors in Twenty Jurisdictions June-July 1987

Do Not Use (as a Matter of Policy)	Do Not Use (Forbidden by Outside Ruling)	Do Not Use (Custom)
* Arizona State Attorney General Cook County State's Attorney (Chicago, Ill.) Denver, Colo., District Attorney Lake County State's Attorney (Waukeegan, Ill.) State's Attorney, Montgomery County, Md. State's Attorney, 15th Judicial District (Palm Beach County, Fla.) Philadelphia, Pa., District Attorney Seattle, Wash., City Attorney (Criminal Division) Suffolk County District Attorney (Boston, Mass.)	* Denver, Colo., City Attorney Monroe County District Attorney (Rochester, N.Y.)	Maricopa County Prosecutor (Phoenix, Ariz.) San Francisco, Cal., District Attorney

No Formal Policy (Some Use, Some Oppose)	Use Without Forms	Use With Forms
New York County District Attorney (New York, N.Y.)	Prosecuting Attorney 12th Judicial District (Fort Smith, Ark.) King County Prosecutor's Office (Seattle, Wash.) State's Attorney, Dade County, Fla. Pima County Attorney (Tucson, Ariz.)	* Columbus, Ohio, City Attorney * Public Prosecutor Riviera Beach, Fla. + Allegheny County District Attorney (Pittsburgh, Pa.)

* Prosecutor represents civil defendants in suits arising out of arrests
+ Initial prosecution at magistrates court often conducted by police officers

The most striking observation that emerged from the interviews is the widespread prosecutorial hostility toward release-dismissal agreements. Far from being a standard tool for advancing "legitimate prosecutorial interests," the policy-making prosecutors in roughly half of the jurisdictions regard the release-dismissal practice as illegitimate, and they forbid the practice. Two of the seven offices that approve of the practice use it only rarely. Moreover, offices that were forced to abandon the practice by court order or bar association ruling report no difficulty in functioning without it.

Almost equally arresting was the recurrence of the open use of form release-dismissal agreements routinely demanded by offices that would represent defendants in civil rights actions arising from the charges released. Rather than constituting a means by which impartial prosecutors screen out frivolous civil rights actions, these situations appear to represent a method for municipal attorneys to routinely eliminate section 1983 claims against their clients.

The details gathered in these interviews form the framework of facts for the discussion of the costs and benefits of the release-dismissal practice in the remainder of this Article.

III. Benefits of Release-Dismissal Agreements

A. *Benefits for the Accused*

The majority in *Town of Newton v. Rumery* emphasized that "[t]he benefits of the agreement to Rumery are obvious." Mr. Rumery's decision was the "highly rational" and voluntary judgment of a counseled and sophisticated defendant. In the Court's view, section 1983 was adopted to protect the rights and interests of individual citizens in whom "Congress has confided the decision to bring such actions." Mr. Rumery's rights are, in short, his to dispose of as he wishes, and as long as his decisions are voluntary, his decision is owed deference by the Court. Justice Powell's plurality "hesitate[s] to elevate more diffused public interests above Rumery's considered decision that he would benefit personally from the agreement."

Judge Easterbrook interprets *Rumery* to be a case that "start[s] from the premise that people may strike such bargains as they please." Enforcement of the bargains regarding statutory rights, in his view, implements the underlying statute:

> A statutory right affects the initial bargaining position of the parties, so that the contract affords people the benefits of the statute even as it alters the rules. The beneficiary of the statutory right may enjoy it or trade it for something he prefers . . . . To forbid the contractual waiver is to make the class of

> statutory beneficiaries worse off by depriving them of the opportunity to obtain the benefits of the statutory entitlement by using it as a bargaining chip . . . .

With regard to "knowledge" and "voluntariness," however, Mr. Rumery's situation shares little with the circumstances often attending release-dismissal agreements. Mr. Rumery was a sophisticated businessman who had been released on bail, consulted at length with counsel, and evaluated the release-dismissal proposal for an extended period of time. By contrast, in *Hylton v. Phillips*, Hylton was arrested and placed in jail, although no complaint had been filed. "Immediately after locking plaintiff [Hylton] in the jail," the arresting officer conferred with the district attorney who "advised him to try and persuade plaintiff to sign a release in an effort to avoid the possibility of any liability for false imprisonment." The arresting officer "presented the release to plaintiff in jail and told him as soon as it was signed he would be released." In *Jones v. Taber*, "Jones was taken from his cell, stripped, gagged, bound, chained to a wall, hosed with cold water and beaten with a night stick. The incident lasted 3 to 5 hours. He was then placed in a special segregation facility and held there for nineteen days until" he was asked to sign a release. In *Hall v. Ochs*, police officers and the Town of Milton had, since the 1950s, insisted on execution of a form waiving civil actions as a condition precedent to a release from custody after arrest.

Such releases hardly flow from the deliberate and informed decision that undergirded the plurality's conclusion that Mr. Rumery had voluntarily decided that he "would benefit personally from the agreement." Given the coercive impact of custody, there should be little doubt that station house releases are generally impermissible. The concern repeatedly voiced in *Rumery* that releases be the result of "considered" and "voluntary" choice requires at least counsel and the liberty of the criminal defendant.

But even in situations where a counseled criminal defendant's will was not overborne by the impact of custody or incarceration, the argument that release-dismissal agreements should be sanctioned because of their "obvious benefits" to the prospective civil rights plaintiff rests on the assumption that the "benefits" are, in fact, real. In his study of misdemeanor courts in Connecticut, Professor Feeley observed that the benefits of the "deals" offered by prosecutors are often illusory:

> It is the salesman's stock-in-trade to represent a "going rate" as if it were a special sale price offered only once. The gap between theoretical exposure and the standard rate allows defense attorneys and prosecutors to function much the same way, making the defendant think he is getting a special "deal" when in fact he is getting the standard rate. Together prosecutors and defense attorneys operate like discount stores, pointing to a never-used high list price and then marketing the product at a supposedly "special" sale price, thereby appearing to provide substantial savings to those who act quickly.

If prospective civil rights plaintiffs are often induced to exchange waivers of section 1983 actions for dismissals that they would obtain in any event, it is hard to maintain that such dismissals should be allowed because the benefits to those plaintiffs outweigh competing public interests.

As a matter of abstract logic, it is hard to predict what would happen if release-dismissal agreements were forbidden entirely. As a matter of fact, interviews suggest that situations in which the dismissal is the "going rate" for the civil rights plaintiff's actions are not uncommon when release-dismissal agreements are obtained, whether or not defendant's lawyers are aware of the "going rate." The comments of the interview participants are summarized in Table II.

Table II

Use of Release-Dismissal Agreements and Case Disposition

Discontinued Use of Release-Dismissal Agreements	Continued Use of Release-Dismissal Agreements
+ Chicago, Ill.	+ Allegheny County (Pittsburgh, Pa.)
* Denver, Colo. (City Att'y)	+ Columbus, Ohio
* Philadelphia, Pa.	° Dade County (Miami, Fla.)
* Rochester, N.Y.	° Fort Smith, Ark.
° San Francisco, Cal.	* King County (Seattle, Wash.)
	° New York County (New York, N.Y.)
	* Pima County (Tucson, Ariz.)
	° Riviera Beach, Fla.

* No change in disposition if release offer refused or practice abandoned
+ Some cases dropped, some go forward if release offer refused or practice abandoned
° No data

Prosecutors in Tucson and Seattle stated that if a release-dismissal offer was refused, their offices generally would not insist on the release. The New

York Legal Aid Society takes the position that such agreements are never in the interest of their clients. So, too, several "natural experiments" in which the release-dismissal practice was eliminated are reported to result in no adverse impact on the interests of prospective civil rights plaintiffs. In Rochester, both prosecutors and defense attorneys observed that the judicially-ordered elimination of release-dismissal agreements has resulted in no change in the number or character of dismissals. In Denver, a state ethics ruling that eliminated the city attorney's practice of requiring form releases of liability before dropping criminal charges produced no discernible change in the nature or number of cases that were actually dropped, and the District Attorney of Philadelphia reported no increase in the number of cases going to trial as a result of his elimination of the practice. It seems fair to infer that if release-dismissal agreements in fact resulted in dismissals that would not otherwise occur, then their elimination would have reduced the number of dismissals reported.

On the other hand, some respondents in Columbus and Pittsburgh suggested that releases sometimes — though not always — generated dismissals that would otherwise be unavailable. In Chicago, some attorneys believe that the elimination of releases in the shadow of federal litigation worked to the disadvantage of criminal defendants, by forcing the prosecuting attorneys to try cases they otherwise would have dropped with releases. On the other hand, the former Deputy Superintendent for the Chicago Police Department's Bureau of Administrative Services sees the demise of release-dismissal forms as a factor in the reduction of disorderly conduct arrests made simply to remove individuals from the street.

If the reports in Tucson, Seattle, Rochester, Philadelphia, and Denver are representative of prosecutorial practices across the country, the availability of the release-dismissal procedure works to the unequivocal detriment of prospective civil rights plaintiffs. The agreement merely extinguishes causes of action by defendants whose charges would be dismissed or never brought if the practice were unavailable. This effect is hardly an "obvious benefit" that supports the enforcement of release-dismissal bargains.

On the other hand, to the extent that the Columbus, Chicago, and Pittsburgh experiences are typical, the existence of release-dismissal bargains benefits some prospective plaintiffs at the same time that it disadvantages others. In these jurisdictions, release-dismissal agreements allow some criminal defendants to obtain a "discount" on their criminal exposure by invoking possible section 1983 actions. But they also allow prosecutors to bluff other defendants into relinquishing their civil rights claims in exchange for dismissals that would be granted in any event, and release-dismissal agreements encourage police to press charges that otherwise would not be brought so that they may trade dismissal of charges for release of civil rights liability later. Even in these jurisdictions, therefore, the question is not simply whether release-dismissals benefit some prospective plaintiffs, but whether the benefits to those plaintiffs are worth the costs imposed on others.

It nonetheless remains true that to some extent those costs are the result of the choices made by defendants who bear them. The *Rumery* plurality's reference to "Rumery's considered decision that he would benefit personally" might be read as pointing to the importance of giving the choice of evaluating the prosecutor's probable reaction to the person most directly affected. There is a moral value, perhaps, in giving the criminal defendant a choice even if she may choose unwisely, and no one can account the benefits of avoiding the risks of prosecution more accurately than the defendant who avoids them. A presumption in favor of the validity of the release-dismissal agreement as a recognition of the criminal defendant's accurate evaluation of her own interests is in tension, however, with the actual role played by lawyers in the criminal justice system.

Mr. Rumery "was represented by an experienced criminal lawyer," a fact which seemed to weigh heavily in favor of the validity of the release. Release-dismissal bargains are most common, however, in cases involving relatively minor misdemeanors, in which counsel, though constitutionally guaranteed before imprisonment can be imposed, is often unavailable or unutilized. And, as Professor Schulhofer reports, in misdemeanor courts, "even when counsel was present, informal procedures, unofficial norms, and rapid case processing remained the order of the day." Thus, in the situation in which the release-dismissal practice is most prevalent, the confidence that releases will be the result of informed legal judgments is least warranted.

Moreover, when a defendant is represented her attorney will often have both a professional predisposition and a personal interest that encourage the acceptance of the release-dismissal bargain. At the most benign level, Mr. Rumery's attorney testified that he overrode Mr. Rumery's initial inclination to reject the proposed agreement because of what he regarded as Mr. Rumery's insufficient appreciation of the risks of the criminal process. Mr. Rumery's counsel, an "experienced criminal attorney," was intimately familiar with the risks of the criminal process. He was not a civil rights lawyer. He had never filed a complaint in federal court, while he had obtained dismissals and acquittals on a regular basis. It would be unnatural for him not to favor the relief with which he had experience, and was sure he could obtain, rather than speculate outside of the area of his expertise regarding the possible merits of a section 1983 claim. There is an understandable tendency to want to play on one's home court and to succeed as one habitually defines success.

Defense lawyers also have an economic interest in encouraging the execution of release-dismissal agreements, which risks coloring the advice tendered to a client. Many private defense lawyers are paid a flat rate in advance, a system that provides an incentive to avoid protracted litigation whenever possible. Commentary suggests that this system provides a substantial incentive to avoid trials. Moreover, relatively few defense lawyers handle plaintiff's civil rights litigation. They thus have little economic incentive to preserve civil rights claims for they would not handle the claims if they are brought. Public defenders suffer from their own incentives to dispose of cases rapidly and are often entirely barred from private litigation.

Thus, as the matter appears to a defendant's lawyer in the light of self-interest, the release-dismissal bargain is one that gives up a speculative cause of action, about which the lawyer may be relatively ignorant, and from which he cannot profit, in exchange for the inexpensive achievement of short-run client satisfaction. The criminal lawyer is engaged to win a dismissal of charges, and the agreement allows her to accomplish that task without undue expenditure of time or effort.

There is thus substantial room for doubt that approval of release-dismissal agreements facilitates the knowing and intelligent disposition of the criminal defendant's civil rights claims in accordance with her self-interest. The best that can be said is that it benefits some defendants at the same time that it disadvantages others. And those benefits, the *Rumery* court recognized, come at a cost to society.

B. *"Unjust Claims"*

The plurality in *Rumery* suggested that release-dismissal agreements could be defended from an entirely different perspective. As well as claiming that releases benefit individual defendants or provide them with an opportunity to exercise autonomy, the plurality envisioned the releases as a method of screening out section 1983 actions that would otherwise impose unwarranted costs on public defendants.

> Many [section 1983 suits] are marginal and some are frivolous. Yet even when the risk of ultimate liability is negligible, the burden of defending such lawsuits is substantial. . . . To the extent release-dismissal agreements protect public officials from the burdens of defending such unjust claims, they further this important public interest.

In *Rumery*, the plurality read the trial court's findings as giving "little credence" to Mr. Rumery's version of the events leading up to his arrest. Implicitly, the plurality accepted the characterization of Mr. Rumery's particular claim as nonmeritorious. The release, therefore, was simply an expeditious means of arriving at the result that ultimately should have been reached at trial. If one is to generalize from this conclusion, however, there must be some reason to expect that claims barred by release-dismissal agreements are peculiarly likely to be "unjust." Otherwise the release-dismissal practice would be no more effective at reducing the incidence of "unjust" claims than a procedure that invalidated a similar percentage of section 1983 actions at random.

To justify the release-dismissal practice as a means of screening out "unjust claims," therefore, the courts must rely on some prediction that the agreements themselves are particularly likely to be signed in cases in which the civil rights claim is without merit. They could believe that the class of cases where bargains are possible is particularly likely to be frivolous, that the cases in which the releases are actually sought are particularly prone to frivolity, or that the bargains are accepted disproportionately in frivolous cases. None of these beliefs seems to correspond to reality.

The release-dismissal agreements often arise from arrests or criminal charges. But there is no reason to think that section 1983 actions growing out of arrest situations are by definition disproportionately frivolous. Frivolous cases clearly exist in the police area. The federal courts, however, have seen their share of arrests associated with legitimate complaints of constitutional violations, and field studies suggest that a major determinant of the police decision to arrest is simply an attitude of defiance toward police officers. Similarly, there are recurring reports of situations in which police officers who have abused citizens file "cover charges" as a means of justifying the violence they have perpetrated.

If the section 1983 claims likely to be extinguished by release-dismissal agreements are not by their nature disproportionately frivolous, neither can it be said that the releases are selectively invoked by prosecutors in a "frivolous" subset of cases. A majority of the *Rumery* Court apparently believed that prosecutors seek release-dismissal agreements in cases where they accurately judge the civil rights claim to be meritless. The plurality emphasized the "independence of judgment" of the prosecutor, and Justice O'Connor adduced cases where "prosecutors . . . legitimately believe that . . . police properly defused a volatile situation by arresting a minor misdemeanant." The image at the root of the majority's analysis seems to be that of a prosecutor who fairly evaluates the merits of potential civil rights claims, and demands releases only in cases properly deemed frivolous. But this approach probably does not characterize the bulk of release-dismissals.

Two of the offices that admitted using release-dismissal agreements maintain that they seek such bargains only in what they believe to be frivolous civil rights claims. On the other hand, the State's Attorney of Dade County, Florida, does not negotiate for the dropping of a charge without the approval of the lead arresting officer, who often attempts to obtain a release. The State's Attorney only refuses to seek a release in the case of an "innocent victim." Her office pursues releases in cases in which there is probable cause, but not "reasonable probability of proof beyond reasonable doubt," *or* where in the judgment of the prosecutor there is a false civil rights claim. A fourth prosecutor's office, in King County, Washington, which includes Seattle, consults the police before any dismissal, and "tr[ies] to protect" the police if there is not enough evidence to reach court; releases are regarded as inappropriate in "high profile situations" or cases where there is "real police brutality." The Pima County Attorney, in Tucson, Arizona, similarly, seeks a release if the office is approached by a law enforcement agency "because the individual is a troublemaker." The office only seeks releases regarding police conduct that is linked to the validity of the arrest. Excessive force charges are not within the legitimate scope of release agreements.

Two other offices countenance the practice as a means of accommodating police. The criminal division of the Columbus, Ohio, City Attorney's office endeavors to obtain form releases in assault, resisting arrest, and petit theft cases whenever the prosecuting witness, who is the police officer in resisting arrest and assault of officer cases, requests it. In Allegheny County, the jurisdiction that includes Pittsburgh, Pennsylvania, release-dismissal negotiations are entirely delegated to the arresting officer, the police legal advisor, and the city solicitor, who defends the city in civil rights actions. The District Attorney, whose jurisdiction contains 114 municipalities that have their own form releases, acts only as an advisor and acquiesces in the municipal police decision except in cases in which the alleged abuse resulted in serious injury or was so egregious as to warrant criminal investigation. Similarly, before being discontinued in Chicago, Philadelphia, Rochester, and Denver, the prosecutors' offices regularly sought releases in cases in which a civil rights action might be brought against the police.

In most of the situations in which prosecutors reported seeking releases, they did not use the practice to weed out marginal or frivolous civil rights cases. The agreement was often invoked to accommodate and to routinely protect police and municipalities. This experience should not be surprising. While the police and prosecutors experience a mutual "traditional antagonism" due to differing roles and priorities, police and prosecutors feel themselves to be a part of the same enterprise. There is a tendency on the part of prosecutors, therefore, to regard a threatened civil rights complaint as an attack on a member of "their team."

Prosecutors, moreover, depend on police for the investigation that makes individual prosecutions viable. Without the cooperation and good will of the police, a prosecutor cannot succeed. At times, the unavoidable conflicts between the police and prosecutor in other areas can be mitigated by seeking those release-dismissal agreements that do not adversely affect the prosecutor's goals. We can expect that the prosecutor will give such a police request more serious consideration than she will to the speculative merits of a hypothetical civil rights action, which she lacks the resources to investigate in any event.

These tendencies are, of course, accentuated when offenses are in fact prosecuted by the police officers themselves. Thus, in Allegheny County, Pennsylvania, where police officers initially prosecute many misdemeanor complaints, the District Attorney, who believes that the releases are legally unenforceable, defers to the decisions of the police to request releases, except in cases of serious injury. While atypical, police prosecution is not uncommon. In one national survey of 660 misdemeanor Court judges, 12% reported that a prosecuting attorney infrequently or never conducted the trial of misdemeanor defendants.

More prevalent is the situation in which the same office that prosecutes the offenses for which releases are sought will defend the civil rights action if the releases are not obtained. In a 1977 nationwide survey of 1136 prosecutors, 48.4% reported that they had responsibility for representing local governments in damage and injunctive actions. While this civil representation may consist only of counseling county agencies that have limited law enforcement responsibilities, it is a relatively common pattern for prosecution of misdemeanors, including prosecution of resisting arrest and assault cases, to be vested in the city attorney's office, which represents the police department in civil rights cases. Such offices are duty bound to protect the municipalities they serve. To rely on their evaluation as a basis for the belief that release-dismissal agreements achieve just results seems at best dubious.

The problem is exemplified by the history of release-dismissal agreements in the 15th Judicial District in Florida. Until 1975, misdemeanor charges were prosecuted by attorneys employed by the local municipalities who operated from the same office as city attorneys. The municipal prosecutors regularly requested form releases for the benefit of municipal police officers. In 1975, when court reform vested most prosecutorial power in the state attorney with county-wide jurisdiction, that state attorney, who owed no allegiance to particular municipalities, disapproved the release practice. However, in the sole municipality that retains control of misdemeanor prosecutions, release-dismissal bargains continue to be the norm. It is possible that some peculiar "legitimate prosecutorial interest" is operative in Riviera Beach, but not elsewhere in the Palm Beach area. It seems more probable, however, that release-dismissal agreements are retained simply as a means of protecting the municipal prosecutor's client against section 1983 claims that could cost the taxpayers money, both in legal expenses and in verdicts.

This is not to say that it is impossible for fair-minded prosecutors to endeavor to distinguish frivolous from meritorious section 1983 claims against police and to strive to invoke release-dismissal agreements only in the former cases. In most jurisdictions that admitted using the practice, however, this is not the way the practice evolved, and a "realistic appraisal of psychological tendencies and human weakness" counsels against relying on the expectation that it will be so invoked in the future.

Finally, the courts cannot rely on an assumption that defendants will accept release-dismissal agreements primarily to discuss legally meritless cases. Many defendants in the misdemeanor cases in which the release-dismissal practice is most prevalent are uncounseled, many criminal defense counsel are not knowledgeable about civil rights litigation, and criminal defense counsel have a series of professional and personal incentives to accept release-dismissal agreements regardless of the merits of civil rights claims. Moreover, even a perfectly counseled defendant deciding whether to accept a release-dismissal agreement must take into account not only the legal merits of her civil rights claim, but the magnitude of her possible civil rights recovery, the merits of the criminal charge pending against her, the severity of the penalties associated with the criminal charges, and the monetary and psychological costs of a criminal trial. There is little reason to believe that the balance among these factors will result in defendants acceding to release-dismissal requests primarily in cases in which the civil rights claim is meritless. As Justice O'Connor observed, "[t]he risk and expense of a criminal trial can easily intimidate even an innocent person whose civil and constitutional rights have been violated."

C. *"Rough Justice"*

It cannot be said that release-dismissal practices regularly work to the benefit of the criminal defendant. They constitute an unreliable mechanism, both in theory and practice, for screening out civil rights claims in which "the risk of ultimate liability is negligible." Justice O'Connor's concurrence, however, intimates a third "interest" that might militate in their favor. Citing the California Supreme Court's opinion upholding pretrial release-dismissal agreements involving police officers, Justice O'Connor commented that "[s]paring the local community the expense of litigation associated with some minor crimes for which there is little or no public interest in prosecution may be a legitimate objective of a release-dismissal agreement."

As Justice O'Connor articulates it, this interest can be accomplished without release-dismissal agreements. The community can "spare itself" the expense of a criminal trial by simply dropping the charges. Nonetheless, the passage cited by Justice O'Connor goes on to suggest an additional aspect that militates in favor of release-dismissal agreements. While the balance of public concern may tip against prosecution, "'[a]t the same time, it is reasonable to seek to protect the arresting officer . . . from the burden of civil litigation . . . .'" The California Supreme Court concluded that "[i]n requiring a release from the accused . . . the state accomplishes both the imposition of the bargained-for disability and the protection of those it reasonably deems to be innocently involved." The net result, therefore, is the correct one; the release-dismissal agreement achieves a rough substantial justice.

Two rationales may support this claim of "rough justice." First, in situations where the facts seem clear but both the criminal defendant and the arresting officer violate the law — as in a legitimate arrest carried out with excessive force — a prosecutor may believe that "the conduct is about even." According to this reasoning, community interests are best served if both sides simply go home, defusing the situation, rather than pushing it to a legal resolution that would reopen antagonisms.

The second rationale is illustrated by situations in which the prosecutor is confronted with conflicting stories regarding an alleged incident of police misconduct and may be genuinely unsure as to who to believe. If the police officer's story is the truth, the accused "deserves" to be punished, and the officer does not "deserve" civil liability. Conversely, if the arrestee's account is correct, the "right" outcome would require that the citizen be set free and the officer held liable. Given the relevant procedural standards, the conflict in testimony will mean that both the civil and the criminal cases are sufficiently strong to reach trial. In each case, the outcomes will turn on the fact-finders' evaluation of the testimony. Under the second rationale, if the prosecutor relieves the criminal defendant of the necessity of risking trial, the defendant should then be required to reciprocate by signing a release-dismissal agreement.

The first rationale is in essence an objection to the substance of section 1983 actions; it seeks to import a "clean hands" doctrine into civil rights litigation even when the substantive law of section 1983 supplies none. The second is an objection to the procedures by which section 1983 actions proceed and civil sanctions are imposed; it supplants the determination of the judge and jury with the discretion of the prosecutor. Neither rationale merits substantial weight.

Section 1983 provides a cause of action to "any person" deprived of rights, privileges, or immunities. This right is not limited to "innocent" citizens. Although juries may implicitly impose a "clean hands" requirement on civil rights plaintiffs, there has never been any legal warrant for doing so. To allow local prosecutors the discretion to attempt to bar federal civil rights actions when the plaintiff's conduct falls below an idiosyncratic standard of "innocence" both shifts the decisionmaking from civil courts and juries to criminal prosecutors and distorts the substantive standards applied. A guilty criminal suspect is as fully capable of finding herself subjected to violations of her constitutional rights during the course of an arrest as an innocent one, and the purposes of section 1983 include providing a means of redressing such violations. It is not adequate to argue that although the violation has occurred, the victim is also guilty of misconduct as well. When justice requires both a criminal conviction and civil redress, a practice that results in neither is rough indeed. Moreover, the effort to seek criminal convictions as a means of suppressing civil rights claims may well violate the first amendment's guarantee of the right to petition for redress of grievances.

The second rationale is limited to situations where the civil rights claim is the precise converse of the criminal charge. It would not apply in those situations such as a claim of excessive force in which the criminal defendant might admit the validity of the criminal charges but still maintain her constitutional claim. When the elements of the criminal charge and the civil rights claim do not overlap, the prosecutor's lack of assurance regarding the merits of the criminal charge has no bearing on the merits of the civil rights case. No claim of symmetry exists.

Even in cases in which the merits of the civil rights and criminal cases are linked, moreover, one should hesitate before displacing the fact-finding and legal screening functions of federal judges and juries with decisions made by local prosecutors. We are willing to allow prosecutors to drop criminal charges without an adversary hearing or investigation in part because of concern for the presumption of innocence of criminal defendants and in part because of our belief that prosecutors are impartial administrators working in the public interest. To extend comparable solicitude to police defendants in civil rights cases on the basis of the prosecutor's sense of "rough justice" promotes a system that unacceptably skews the enforcement of civil rights toward the section 1983 defendant.

D. *The Problem of the Second Best*

To some degree, the criticism voiced above appears to be at war with itself. If the decision of whether or not to demand releases tends to be infected by the interests of police and municipalities in avoiding legitimate civil rights liability, as suggested by Sections B and C, one might well argue that eliminating release-dismissal agreements will simply result in prosecutors pushing criminal cases to trial to protect police, thus contradicting the analysis of Section A. Defendants, therefore, benefit from release-dismissals by avoiding "liability-motivated" prosecutions.

The prosecutor who seeks to accommodate and protect police interests through release-dismissal agreements but is barred from doing so has the alternative strategy of attempting to obtain a conviction in order to accomplish the same goal. After all, the defendant who pleads guilty or is convicted of the substantive crime is all but estopped from claiming that her initial arrest was without probable cause. The more pervasive the danger that such a strategy will be adopted, the stronger the argument that release-dismissal agreements benefit criminal defendants. Allowing prosecutors to vent their desires to protect the police by directly extinguishing the criminal defendants' civil rights claims, one might claim, is the price of avoiding liability-motivated efforts to convict the defendant on criminal charges.

The argument assumes that the effort to convict will, in fact, protect the municipality and police from civil rights liability. In fact, there will often be reasons to doubt this assumption. First, a criminal prosecution will not always result in a conviction. A criminal acquittal may actually encourage the defendant to retaliate against the police with a civil rights suit. Second, a criminal conviction does not bar civil rights suits unrelated to the merits of the criminal defense. A civil rights suit for excessive force or unlawful search and seizure would not be barred by a disorderly conduct conviction. There will thus be a broad class of cases in which prosecutors will not be able to obtain the equivalent of a release by pressing the charges to trial.

Even when prospective civil rights defendants might benefit from a criminal trial, the benefit is not free. The prosecution of a criminal case will cost even the most police-oriented prosecutor time and money, and criminal lawyers and defendants may well be less willing to acquiesce to a guilty plea than accept a dismissal. Seeking release-dismissal agreements is costless, while seeking convictions must be weighed against the pressures of the prosecutor's docket.

The likelihood of such "liability-motivated" prosecution, moreover, may itself be reduced by eliminating the release-dismissal practice. Legal rules should not be based on the presumption that prosecutors are solely attentive to the interests of police rather than their own legal obligations. While the view that prosecutors can be relied on to evaluate impartially the merits of civil rights claims is unduly optimistic, prosecutors often seek to obey the law. A clear announcement by the Court of that which was articulated sotto voce in *Rumery* — that to "bring frivolous charges, or to dismiss meritorious charges, to protect the interests of other officials" is improper — would fortify the ability of prosecutors to resist the temptation of liability-motivated prosecutions. Eliminating the occasion for explicitly linking criminal prosecutions and civil rights liability in release-dismissal agreements, moreover, would establish patterns of thought and action that facilitate the tendency of prosecutors of good conscience to avoid the linkage elsewhere. If the Court's assumption that prosecutors are incorruptible is extravagant, neither should the law move to the opposite pole of presuming them to be completely compromised.

Some defendants benefit from release-dismissal agreements as a means of avoiding liability-motivated prosecutions. But others suffer the gratuitous loss of civil rights claims, and the institution of release-dismissal agreements tends to suggest that avoiding civil rights claims is a legitimate motive for arrest and prosecution. In accounting costs and benefits, the law should not fixate on the first effect at the expense of the other two.

The imposed elimination of release-dismissal agreements in Rochester and Denver, by all accounts, resulted in no increase in the rate of prosecutions. In Chicago, the elimination was so thoroughly internalized that the policymaking prosecutor now regards the consideration of police liability as entirely inappropriate in the decision to prosecute. While it is possible that liability-motivated prosecutorial decisionmaking continues to exist in these jurisdictions, it has been driven from the center of the stage. Occasional hypocrisy is less destructive of the norms of impartiality than is overt disregard. It would be ironic if a practice that the Court justifies on the basis of its faith in the prosecutor's "independence of judgment" could be defended as the only means of limiting the impact of prosecutorial misconduct.

IV. The Costs of Release-Dismissal Agreements

If the plurality in *Town of Newton v. Rumery* seems to overstate the benefits associated with release-dismissal agreements, it also fails to account adequately for the costs of sanctioning them.

A. *The Right to Petition for Redress of Grievances*

According to the *Rumery* plurality, "the only evidence of prosecutorial misconduct is the agreement itself." The first inquiry under established doctrine should be why such an agreement is itself insufficient to establish a constitutional violation of the first amendment.

During the late nineteenth and early twentieth centuries, a number of populist state legislatures endeavored to prevent out-of-state corporations from removing cases to federal court by conditioning permission to do business within the state on the agreement by the corporation not to invoke federal jurisdiction. After a series of inconsistent attempts to resolve this question, in 1922 a unanimous Court came to the conclusion in *Terral v. Burke Construction Co.* that the effort to extract this waiver of federal jurisdiction was unconstitutional:

> [A] state may not, in imposing conditions upon the privilege of a foreign corporation's doing business in the State, exact from it a waiver of the exercise of its constitutional right to resort to the federal courts, or thereafter withdraw the privilege of doing business because of its exercise of such right . . . . The principle . . . rests on the ground that the Federal Constitution confers upon citizens of one state the right to resort to federal courts in another, that state action, whether legislative or executive, necessarily calculated to curtail the free exercise of the right thus secured is void.

Since *Terral*, the Court has generally recognized the right of access to courts as a component of the first amendment's right to petition for redress of grievances. On its face the release-dismissal agreement seeks to extract "a waiver of the exercise of a . . . constitutional right." *Terral*, therefore, raises doubts that a waiver of first amendment rights is any more legitimate a precondition to the privilege of having a pending prosecution dropped than it would be to condition the privilege of doing business in a state or the privilege of public employment. Indeed, in *Wayte v. United States*, the Court reiterated that "the decision to prosecute may not be 'deliberately based upon an unjustifiable standard such as race, religion, or other arbitrary classification' including the exercise of protected statutory and constitutional rights."

When release-dismissal agreements serve to obtain waivers of civil rights claims in exchange for the dismissal of charges that would be dropped in the normal course of events were waivers unavailable, it is difficult to see how the agreements are constitutional. If a state may not constitutionally make it a criminal offense to bring a civil rights claim, then it is no more entitled to punish the attempt to bring such a claim with a criminal prosecution based on other activities of the section 1983 claimant. The Court's pragmatic acceptance of efforts to induce waivers of constitutional trial rights in connection with its recognition of plea bargaining as an "essential component of the administration of justice" should not be read as approving the use of criminal prosecutions as a lever to extract the waiver of the right to affirmative redress in civil cases. There is reason to believe that a number of release-dismissal transactions involve precisely such unconstitutional threats.

The situation may, however, differ in cases where the dismissal of charges would not come about in the normal course of events without the bargained for agreement. The state does not violate the first amendment by offering to settle a civil rights case for $10,000, although in form this may be seen as an offer to exchange a "waiver of a constitutional right to resort to the courts" for a "privilege." The right of "access to the courts" for "redress of grievances" is a right to seek redress satisfactory to the petitioner and the $10,000 is "redress." Why should it be impermissible to substitute the dismissal of criminal charges for the payment of $10,000?

As a constitutional matter, the issue is opaque. While it is possible to make arguments, the right to petition is so little litigated that reliable guidance is lacking. But, since the issue framed by the Court is one of "federal common law," it is perhaps best to pursue the issue with regard to the narrower class of cases where charges would not be dropped in the absence of a release on that somewhat less exalted plane.

B. *The Role of the Criminal Process*

One substantial factor that impelled the plurality in *Rumery* to approve of release-dismissal agreements was "the burden of defending" "marginal" civil rights actions. If a plaintiff chooses to press a case to trial, a single conflict in testimony may be enough to circumvent the screening mechanisms that might otherwise terminate the process. The possibility of an inaccurate jury verdict makes even a weak case a credible threat.

The threats inherent in the criminal process are more than comparable. Once a prosecutor believes, or acts as if she believes, that there is probable cause, the engine of a criminal prosecution is almost impossible for a defendant to stop short of trial or plea. In most states the criminal defendant has far fewer opportunities for discovery than those available in civil cases, and only a full-fledged legal defense at trial will suffice to avert the possibility of not only financial liability but also loss of liberty. As a practical matter, the legal presumption of innocence is often balanced in the minds of the prosecutor, the court, and the jury by a factual presumption of guilt. Ultimately, a defendant may be acquitted, or an erroneous conviction reversed, but in the interim savage costs can be imposed on a criminal defendant.

We tolerate the prosecutor's essentially unconstrained discretion to impose these pretrial and error costs for two reasons. First, we defer to the importance of the prosecutorial goals. We believe prosecutorial discretion is essential to maintaining the framework of order in society. Second, we have faith in the role constraints of the prosecutor, an officer obligated to act in the interest of criminal justice. The use of release-dismissal agreements, however, undercuts both of these justifications. It encourages the prosecutor to deploy the substantial and unreviewable sanctions at his disposal in the interest of goals other than the enforcement of the criminal statutes, and it undercuts the norms of impartial adherence to the goals of criminal enforcement that would otherwise limit that deployment.

1. "Abuse of the Criminal Process"

Our system of justice has developed distinctive modes of procedure as well as distinctive sanctions appropriate for the adjudication of civil and criminal liabilities. Except insofar as the rules of preclusion allow application of conclusions reached in criminal proceedings to issues in civil cases, the two systems are independent searches for justice. The vice of the release-dismissal agreement is that it uses the balance of procedural advantages and sanctions developed on the criminal side to shape the adjudication of civil liability. Put simply, the prosecutor is given the authority to threaten criminal prosecution in order to deter, convict, and punish criminals, not to protect police and municipalities from adjudications of civil liability. Hence the *Rumery* plurality insisted that "release-dismissal agreements . . . further legitimate prosecutorial interests."

The origins of our legal system recognized this separation between civil and criminal adjudication in at least two areas. First, in the field of legal ethics, it has long been recognized that

> [t]he merest novice in the legal profession should know that civil liabilities may not be enforced by threats of criminal prosecution, any more than they may be enforced by threats of physical violence, and that any conduct which has the appearance of a resort to such course is as bad, in law, as the thing in itself.

According to the Model Code of Professional Responsibility, upon which all opinions of the *Rumery* court relied:

> The civil adjudicative process is primarily designed for the settlement of disputes between parties, while the criminal process is designed for the protection of society as a whole. Threatening to use, or using, the criminal process to coerce adjustment of private civil claims or controversies is a subversion of that process; further, the person against whom the criminal process is so misused may be deterred from asserting his legal rights and thus the usefulness of the civil process in settling private disputes is impaired. As in all cases of abuse of judicial process, the improper use of criminal process tends to diminish public confidence in our legal system.

Second, the common law, incorporated into the federal law by the Hobbs Act, defines the crime of extortion as "an abuse of public justice, which consists in any officer's unlawfully taking, by color of his office, from any man, any money or thing of value that is not due to him," or his office. As the court noted in *United States v. Margiotta*, "it is the utilization of the power of public office to induce consent to the payments that is the gist of the offense of obtaining money 'under color of official right.' The use of public office, with the authority to grant or withhold benefits, takes the place of pressure or threats." The evil of release-dismissal agreements — like the evil of extortion — is the use of public authority granted for one set of ends to achieve advantage in a different arena.

A prosecutor's offer to exchange dismissal of prosecution for release of the city from its obligations on a $10,000 bond would clearly be extortionate. If the consideration is a $10,000 contingent civil rights liability, rather than a bond, on its face, the transaction seems to raise similar problems.

2. The Role of The Prosecutor

Just last Term, seven Justices of the Court joined in the following characterization of the role of the prosecutor:

> Between the private life of the citizen and the public glare of criminal accusation stands the prosecutor. That state official has the power to employ the full machinery of the state in scrutinizing any given individual. Even if a defendant is ultimately acquitted, forced immersion in criminal investigation and adjudication is a wrenching disruption of everyday life. For this reason, we must have assurance that those who would wield this power will be guided solely by their sense of public responsibility for the attainment of justice.

This assurance is provided, in large part, by the norms of fidelity to role that permeate the prosecutor's office. Adversaries, courts, and citizens expect the prosecutor to be a guardian of the interests of justice, not simply the advocate of government positions. In the opinion of a number of prosecutors, this impartial, if not neutral, role is threatened by the release-dismissal practice, which injects the issue of civil liability into the criminal decisions.

The president-elect of the National District Attorneys Association (NDAA) regards the release-dismissal practice as infected by an unethical conflict of interest by its mixing of civil and criminal responsibilities. The outgoing president of the NDAA believes the release-dismissal transaction is an "inappropriate function in plea bargaining." The State's Attorney for Palm Beach, Florida, characterizes the release-dismissal practice as "a distortion of the system," and prosecutors in Boston, Manhattan, and Chicago view the practice as an "unseemly mixing of roles."

The director of the criminal division of the Seattle City Attorney's office observes: "If you are going to drop the case because of the release, the converse is also true; you are prosecuting the case in order to gain an advantage of the civil law suit; that is an abuse of power." Similarly, the Chief Assistant Attorney General of Arizona views the release-dismissal practice as a derogation of the statutory duty and ethical responsibility of the prosecutor.

The threat to the prosecutor's role comes from two dynamics. First, the availability of the release-dismissal practice provides a continuing incentive to modify criminal prosecution decisions in the interests of goals extraneous to the criminal process. In *Young v. United States* ex rel. *Vuitton et Fils, S.A.*, the Court observed that a private prosecutor in a criminal prosecution who represents one of the parties in the underlying case

> may be tempted to bring a tenuously supported prosecution if such a course promises financial or legal rewards for the private client. Conversely, a prosecutor may be tempted to abandon a meritorious prosecution if a settlement providing benefits to the private client is conditioned on a recommendation against criminal charges.

Since such private prosecutors "at a minimum created *opportunities* for conflicts to arise, and created at least the *appearance* of impropriety," the Court found such appointment improper.

When prosecutors use the release-dismissal practice to explicitly trade civil for criminal liability, a similar temptation to inject extraneous considerations into a criminal decision can only be heightened. One need not "assume that prosecutors will seize the opportunity for wrongdoing" or "abandon the independence of judgment required by their public trust" to conclude that the prosecutor who is explicitly authorized to trade civil for criminal liability will be less inclined to resist the blandishments of the arresting officer, the police department, or the city attorney than one who is barred from entering into such trades. So, too, the very availability of the practice will increase the pressures brought to bear. Potential civil defendants will be more willing to seek resolutions that serve their interests if the agreements are permitted simply because they believe that such efforts are regarded as legitimate.

Second, the prosecutor who enters into release-dismissal bargaining runs the risk of losing sight of her appropriate role, not only in this decision, but in others. The norm of impartial prosecution is in part sustained by its consistent application. Once the barriers between the responsibility of the prosecutor and those of the interested civil advocate are weakened in one area by allowing the explicit exchange of civil from criminal liability, they may be undercut in other areas as well. It will be harder for a prosecutor to put the potential interest of a police officer out of her mind in making prosecutorial decisions regarding investigation, charging, pleas, and suppression in a second case once she has bargained them for dismissal in the first. If we take seriously the ideal of the "disinterested prosecutor," we should be hesitant to inject occasions for explicitly incorporating extraneous interests into the criminal processes.

Precisely because individual prosecutorial decisions "are not readily susceptible to the kind of analysis courts are competent to undertake," courts must be alert to structural factors threatening impartiality of criminal prosecutions. Rather than attempting to second-guess the legitimacy of the prosecutor's decisions on a post hoc basis, the Court may more effectively preserve the norms of disinterestedness by eliminating the occasion for partiality. In related areas, the Court has taken notice of the "institutional pressure that . . . might . . . subconsciously motivate [improper] prosecutorial . . . response[s]," and has attempted to assess the "realistic possibility that the [prosecutor's] judgment will be distorted." From this perspective, decisions upholding the release-dismissal practice are not so much an outgrowth of cases that have deferred to prosecutorial discretion as a step toward undermining their ethical presuppositions.

3. The Accuracy of the Criminal Process

In addition to its impact on the nature and legitimacy of the criminal process, the release-dismissal agreement can affect criminal outcomes both by increasing the probability that the innocent will be punished and exacerbating the danger that the guilty will go free.

In the first federal case to discuss release-dismissal agreements at length, Judge Bazelon commented:

> [These agreements] tempt the prosecutor to trump up charges for use in bargaining for suppression of the complaint. The danger of concocted charges is particularly great because complaints against the police usually arise in connection with arrests for extremely vague offenses such as disorderly conduct or resisting arrest.

The release-dismissal practice, therefore, presents the twin risks that innocent citizens will be wrongly accused and that if they refuse to sign the release that they will be wrongly convicted. This concern was echoed in subsequent cases and recurred in interviews with prosecutors who refused to engage in release-dismissal bargaining. Thus, the State's Attorney for Montgomery County, Maryland, stated "We don't do it. . . . Civil liability is irrelevant to criminal charges. [A contrary policy] would risk the prosecution of innocent people for the purpose of protecting police from civil liability."

The *Rumery* majority acknowledged this "temptation," but the plurality adopted the presumption that most prosecutors would not succumb:

> Against this background of discretion, the mere opportunity to act improperly does not compel an assumption that all — or even a significant number of — release-dismissal agreements stem from prosecutors abandoning "the independence of judgment required by [their] public trust." Rather, tradition and experience justify our belief that the great majority of prosecutors will be faithful to their duty.

If the interviews underlying this Article are indicative, a "significant" proportion of the prosecutors who admit to engaging in the release-dismissal practice are motivated by a view that part of their "duty" is the routine protection of police officers from civil rights suits.

This is not to say that such offices would consciously countenance the filing of false "cover" charges to protect police. But even if the prosecutor is steadfast in her adherence to the obligation to acquit the innocent as well as convict the guilty, she is dependent in large part on the information provided by the police to identify guilt and innocence. According to a 1982 National Institute of Justice survey of urban prosecutors, 62% of prosecutors routinely talked to police detectives before filing charges, while only 28% talked to defendants. The temptation to "trump up" charges in the hopes of obtaining a release from civil rights claims is stronger for police than for prosecutors, since the police stand to be found personally liable. Once the charges are filed, a prosecutor with the utmost in good faith will not necessarily — or even probably — resolve conflicting accounts of an incident in favor of an innocent defendant. Thus, Judge Bazelon's concern is not necessarily based on an "assumption of prosecutorial misconduct," but on a lack of assurance of the ability of prosecutors accurately to discern police misconduct. An assumption of prosecutorial incorruptibility is not an adequate guarantee of the accuracy of the criminal process when the temptation falls on the police.

There is, moreover, a cognate threat to the accuracy of the criminal process in the release-dismissal practice. If the practice does not solely extract waivers of civil rights claims from defendants whose charges would be dropped in any event, then individuals who would otherwise be prosecuted are released from criminal liability by reason of the violation of their civil rights. Courts before *Rumery* were skeptical of the release-dismissal agreement because of "its potential for use to defeat the public interest in enforcement of our criminal laws." Prosecutors since *Rumery* have voiced a similar concern that if release-dismissal practices became established, "defendants' attorneys would use it as a lever to scare us off from prosecuting good arrests." Given the present Court's avowed concern with ensuring that the outcome of the criminal process be a function of guilt or innocence of the underlying criminal charges rather than of the merits of collateral issues regarding the constitutionality of the arrest and investigation process, it is disconcerting to observe Justice Powell's plurality crafting a new opportunity for "[t]he criminal to go free because the constable . . . blundered." Indeed, in the release-dismissal case, prosecution is dismissed not because of an adjudicated conclusion that the defendant's rights have been violated, but because of a desire to avoid adjudication of the question.

* * *

V. The Future of Release-Dismissal Agreements

The advantages that the majority in *Town of Newton v. Rumery* assumes will accompany the use of release-dismissal agreements are far from automatic. They are purchased at a substantial cost to first amendment rights, the integrity of the criminal process, and the purposes served by section 1983.

The claim that the release-dismissal agreement offers a net advantage to criminal defendants whose constitutional rights have been violated is empirically questionable. The special situation in *Rumery*, in which the prosecutor had never before asked for a release, and in which it is likely that the dismissal saved Mr. Rumery substantial further costs, is atypical. Elimination of release-dismissal agreements in several jurisdictions has resulted in no greater rate of criminal prosecutions, and the practice, at best, can be said to benefit certain criminal defendants at the expense of others.

In contrast to the conjecture of the *Rumery* Court, the predominant use of release-dismissal agreements appears to be neither screening out legally frivolous civil rights claims nor achieving an undefined but legitimate "law enforcement interest." Rather, the principal function is to protect police and municipalities routinely from liability. It substitutes, at best, the prosecutor's sense of rough justice for the structure of immunities and liabilities that the courts have erected around section 1983.

Many prosecutors who use the practice regard their responsibility not as providing impartial evaluations of the merits of citizens' complaints, but as providing a service to cooperating law enforcement officials. Prosecutors who seek releases tend to do so when the police ask for them; they are often members of the same office that would defend any civil rights cases brought. Indeed, in misdemeanor prosecutions, where release-dismissal agreements are most prevalent, often the police themselves, not prosecutors, make the initial charging and prosecution decisions. The police, therefore, are in a position to extract releases governing their own liability. The image of the popularly elected prosecutor impartially judging the conflicting claims of police and citizens — which lies at the root of the argument in favor of using release-dismissal agreements as a screening device — often bears no resemblance to reality.

Equally important, the release-dismissal practice undercuts the prosecutor's impartiality and compromises the independence of her role in the criminal justice process. Both the tradition of legal ethics and the common law definition of extortion suggest that the use of possible criminal prosecution as leverage to obtain advantage in a civil lawsuit is inappropriate. This concern has been expressed in state case law and by a number of prosecutors, who believe that the prospect of entering release-dismissal negotiations threatens their attempt to separate the criminal gatekeeping functions of their office from public officials' narrower interests in municipal finances. In *Rumery*, the prosecutor maintained, and the Court accepted, that the release was justified by considerations entirely within the scope of his duty to secure the just conviction and punishment of violators of the criminal laws. In contrast, the more customary release-dismissal transaction requires the prosecutor to dilute the impartiality which the Court so carefully preserved in *Vuitton et Fils, S.A.*, by concerning herself with the financial interests and convenience of the municipality and arresting officers.

Finally, an extension of this practice beyond the unusual facts of *Rumery* emperils the important role played by legal remedies in a democratic society. The right to bring a claim before the courts for redress of grievances against officials not only serves the interests of the plaintiff, but also preserves the structure of legitimacy undergirding the rule of law. To allow such claims to be defeated by prosecuting attorneys as a means of "weeding out" frivolous cases is at odds with the intent of Congress, the first amendment, and the structure of limited government — even if the criminal defendant "voluntarily" agrees to such a transaction.

These considerations suggest that the decision in *Rumery*, though perhaps warranted under the special circumstances of the case, cries out for boundaries. Though the Court was understandably reluctant to promulgate a per se prohibition in its first encounter with the potentially diverse problems of release-dismissal agreements, the Court's approval of the *Rumery* agreement is dangerous if left unchecked. Three aspects of the case suggest themselves as vehicles for the development of limiting rules: the merits of Mr. Rumery's substantive case, the relation between the elements of his case and the nature of the prosecution against him, and the nature of the prosecutor's interests in seeking the release.

The majority in *Rumery* emphasized the relative values of the considerations that Mr. Rumery gained and sacrificed in his agreement: "he gained immunity from criminal prosecution in consideration of abandoning a civil suit that he may well have lost." As Justice Powell interprets the case, "Rumery bears the ultimate burden of proof" as to his innocence, and "the District Court's factual findings gave little credence to his testimony."

One could read Justice Powell's opinion as allowing a different outcome if the case for Mr. Rumery's innocence had been stronger. In an echo of the murky law of unconscionability, the federal law of release-dismissal agreements might allow for the voiding of release-dismissal agreements if the agreements are sufficiently one-sided. A showing of a civil rights claim that "may well" not have lost, or a prosecution that would have been dropped even without the release might suffice to induce courts to refrain from enforcing the release. Such an approach would avoid the first amendment problems associated with the release-dismissal practice, as well as ensuring that the bargains in fact redound to the interests of civil rights plaintiffs, and — if the threshold of merit were sufficiently low — perhaps limiting the dangers of suppressing meritorious civil rights complaints.

It would do so, however, at the expense of one of the prime supposed benefits of the release-dismissal practice. A "substantive unconscionability" doctrine would replace the ability of prospective civil rights defendants to rely on releases as a method of avoiding the burdens of defending civil rights claims with the necessity of defending a preliminary hearing into not only the merits of the claims released, but the merits of the underlying criminal charge dismissed. And it would embroil the courts in exactly the necessity for reviewing the exercise of prosecutorial discretion that the majority sought to avoid in *Rumery*. If such a hearing were sufficiently cavalier to retain the benefits of repose, it would sacrifice the advantages of post-hoc judicial review for unconscionability.

These advantages, indeed, are less than overwhelming. The possibility of post-hoc invalidation does not dissipate the "psychological effect" of the releases alluded to in interviews by both prosecutors and plaintiff's counsel. Even if the releases are voidable, once obtained, they may well induce legally naive civil rights plaintiffs to assume erroneously that their claims are meritless. And, to the extent that the very exchange inherent in the release-dismissal practice undercuts the impartiality of prosecutors or the criminal justice policies of states, the fact that the prosecutor pays fair, if unethical, measure for the rights which she purchases is irrelevant. On balance, therefore, a case-by-case evaluation of the fairness of release-dismissal bargains does not seem to be a promising avenue for development.

A second aspect of Mr. Rumery's situation that made enforcement of his release particularly appealing was the fact that the elements of the criminal case dismissed and the elements of the civil rights claim released were in large measure identical. If the criminal case prevailed, the false arrest claim evaporated, and vice versa. This is the situation in which the argument for reciprocity is strongest. Since a successful prosecution would be preclusive, it is the scenario in which the risk is highest that elimination of release-dismissal agreements will result in prosecutions pressed forward simply to ward off civil liability. It is, moreover, a context in which the prosecutor is unlikely to have "trumped up" charges in order to trade for civil rights claims; without the charges, there would be no claims. A bright line rule which limited the enforceability of release-dismissal agreements to the release of false arrest claims, like Mr. Rumery's, might maximize the advantages that can be claimed for release-dismissal agreements without entangling the courts in the necessity of evaluation of the merits of each claim released.

Nothing in the *Rumery* opinions suggests such a rule though it seems to match the practice of several prosecutors. It leaves open, moreover, the possibility of effectively immunizing harassment arrests from judicial review and does nothing to alleviate either the difficulties which arise out of the first amendment or the concerns for the prosecutorial role.

A third, more restrictive, rule is suggested by the prevailing opinions in *Rumery* itself. The majority in *Rumery* found the particular release-dismissal agreement before the Court to be acceptable because "in this case the prosecutor had an independent, legitimate reason to make this agreement directly related to his prosecutorial responsibilities."

The facts of *Rumery* present a somewhat unusual situation. In the plurality's view, the prosecutor was willing to drop the charges against Mr. Rumery only because he wished to spare Ms. Deary, the key witness in the underlying rape prosecution, the necessity of testifying in the less serious case against Mr. Rumery. As Justice O'Connor's crucial concurring opinion put it:

> Mary Deary's emotional distress, her unwillingness to testify against Rumery, presumably in later civil as well as criminal proceedings, and the necessity of her testimony in the pending sexual assault case against David Champy all support the prosecutor's judgment that the charges against Rumery should be dropped if further injury to Ms. Deary, *and therefore the Champy case*, could thereby be avoided.

The prosecutor sought to shield a witness who was essential to prosecuting a case of higher priority than the case against Mr. Rumery. The release agreement, moreover, was the prosecutor's only means of shielding the witness from the necessity of testifying outside of the Champy case. He could obtain the effect desired only if the witness remained shielded and that required the assurance that Mr. Rumery would not press his civil rights action. If Mr. Rumery's threatened section 1983 action materialized, Ms. Deary would be called as a witness in that case as well. Thus, it was only if he could be assured of the elimination of both the civil and criminal actions that the prosecutor could attain the goal justifying dismissal of the criminal case. The release and the dismissal were inextricably linked to one another; they were justified by the same law enforcement considerations, and, conversely, there was no reason to drop the charges without the release.

A final reading of *Rumery* suggests that it is only because of the presence of this peculiar linkage that the practice was upheld at all. Justice Powell's plurality opinion recognizes that to "dismiss meritorious charges[] to protect the interests of other officials" would be unethical and inconsistent with the public interest. The majority upholds the agreement because "in this case, the prosecutor had an independent legitimate reason to make this agreement directly related to his prosecutorial responsibilities. So, too, Justice O'Connor's concurring opinion explains that a "prosecutor is permitted to consider only legitimate criminal justice concerns in striking his bargain — concerns such as rehabilitation, allocation of criminal justice resources, the strength of the evidence against the defendant, and the extent of his cooperation with the authorities." Absent a direct linkage with criminal justice functions comparable to that in *Rumery*, the demand for a release is improper.

This specialized justification for release-dismissal agreements in terms of criminal justice concerns does not seem to characterize those agreements in practice. The reported cases involve attempts to shield arresting officers, their supervisors, or their employers. Moreover, accounts of the practice in reports from the seven jurisdictions surveyed that admittedly use release-dismissal agreements emphasize protecting police from civil rights and other actions, not protecting witnesses from potentially damaging ancillary court appearances, or other "legitimate prosecutorial interests" envisioned by the *Rumery* Court. The chief of the trial division of the Manhattan District Attorney's office characterizes the specialized situation in *Rumery* as being "so rare as to be virtually negligible." Accordingly, if legitimate law enforcement interests must resemble the protection of essential prosecution witnesses from traumatic court appearances, *Rumery* provides a rule that is tantamount to a per se ban on release-dismissal agreements.

Such a result should not trouble us. For the prosecutor in *Rumery* to seek a release as an essential element of his pursuit of a criminal conviction in a rape case is, perhaps, a justifiable exercise of prosecutorial discretion. For a prosecutor to request a release as a means of protecting the police from what she regards as "unwarranted" civil rights litigation is an extortionate attempt to license the exercise of power unimpeded by the rule of law. It is important that a conditional approval of the first atypical practice does not become an unwary acquiescence to the second more prevalent danger.

* * *